Richard
Bexley
~~Gambier, Ohio~~
1100 S. Goodman St.
Rochester, N.Y. 14620
(716) 271-1320

Jewish Literature

JEWISH LITERATURE

FROM

THE EIGHTH TO THE EIGHTEENTH CENTURY:

WITH AN

INTRODUCTION ON TALMUD AND MIDRASH.

M. STEINSCHNEIDER.

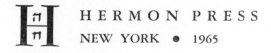

HERMON PRESS
NEW YORK ● 1965

Second, American Edition

PUBLISHED BY HERMON PRESS, NEW YORK

Library of Congress Catalogue Card No.: 65-17981

First Edition: London, 1857

AUTHOR'S PREFACE.

THE German essay, a translation of which is here given, was written for Ersch and Gruber's Encyclopædia during the years 1845—1847; but it was not placed by the editor in the printer's hands till the spring of 1850. The author had in the meantime an opportunity at Hamburg of glancing over the Michael MSS., now in Oxford, which enabled him to introduce a few emendations. Since 1849 he has devoted himself almost entirely to the catalogue of Hebrew books in the Bodleian Library. In 1850, having finished his notes out of the old catalogues and the bibliographers, he made his first acquaintance with the books themselves in Oxford. While thus occupied in England, the essay was printed in Germany without his superintendence, and reached p. 432. (p. 174. of the English translation) without his even seeing the proof-sheets, in consequence of which he was unable to give the authority for his discovery about the translation of Barlaam, introduced in one of these (see Zeitschr. d. d. m. Gesellschaft, v. 89.). He could make but very few corrections in the last sheets, as will be easily conceived; and while his new bibliographical studies and his visit to the Bodleian, that incomparable store of old Hebrew editions and manuscripts, did not induce any alteration in his general views, they enabled him occasionally to make some corrections in the article *Jüdische Typographie* (vol. xxviii.

pp. 1—94. and p. 475.). But there remained a large mass
of minor corrections which the author discovered while ela-
borating the materials for his Catalogue. He found out
even more than was agreeable, namely, that the principal
older authorities, such as Wolfius and De Rossi, and even
Jewish writers like Zacut, were erroneous in very many
cases; and that recent authors, with but few exceptions,
repeated too readily the old reports and misstatements. Of
the reliance to be placed on the Catalogues he had already
a misgiving while writing the essay; and § 31., containing
a short survey of the *Sources and Fate of the History of
Jewish Literature,* has accordingly, in compliance with his
express desire, been omitted from the English translation.
The matter will be more profoundly treated in the Introduction to the Bodleian Catalogue.

Jewish literature is peculiar in all its branches, but especially so is the history of its study. One fact will at once
illustrate this observation, and give the reader a clue for the
critical examination of the present work. When the author
undertook the arduous task of giving a scientific survey of
the development of the entire Jewish literature of the last
1800 years (the older Hebrew literature having been treated
by Christian authors under the separate heads *Hebrew Literature* and *Bible*), his only encouragement to venture on this
but partially trodden path was, that he had agreed to confine
his essay within the narrow limits of two sheets; a condition
tacitly implying another, namely, that only the most superficial outlines were to be given, all the details being left to
the special articles, biographical and miscellaneous, of that
large encyclopædia, which, even should it never be finished,
will always remain a singular monument of the profound
erudition and self-denying labour of the scholars of Germany. This first conception proved impracticable, and there
was not the slightest objection made by the learned editor
and the renowned publishing firm, on whom the expense of

the work devolved, when the essay swelled out to a size seven times greater than was at first intended. Yet the author in no instance trespassed on the ground of the special articles, even in cases where these had been omitted from their proper places in the portion of the Encyclopædia previously printed. How very much remained to be done in this department is now obvious from the extent of the articles on Jewish authors treated under the name Josef in the 31st volume of the second section. (pp. 44—104.) This involved another peculiarity of the greatest importance to the translator. The author, fearful of being too prolix, and feeling the necessity of not suppressing the essential and leading ideas and matters of fact, expressed himself as concisely as he could without becoming obscure; and the German language is so elastic, and allows so much freedom in the formation of new expressions, that a great deal can often be said in a few words. It need hardly be added, that this has materially enhanced the difficulty of translation.

Since the completion of the essay, the author's time has been entirely occupied on the *Catalogue of Hebrew Books in Oxford* (to which the word *Catal.* in this translation refers); the printing of which was only interrupted by repeated visits to the Bodleian Library, a trip to Trieste in 1852, for the purpose of gleaning some bibliographical information from the Saraval collection (now in Breslau)*, and a trip to Amsterdam and Leyden in 1854, where he was charged with publishing a catalogue of about 120 very interesting manuscripts, especially for Karaitic literature (see p. 309. n. 1. of the present work), now in the press. His attention being at this time directed to a vast mass of particulars, was necessarily averted from the general development, but at the same time his researches into these particulars prepared a more solid basis on which to found his opinions, and added flesh to the "dry bones" of names and dates of individual

---

* Cf. Serapeum, 1853, p. 281., and 1854, p. 187.

authors. Having, soon after the appearance of the essay in
the Encyclopædia, resolved on a thorough revision and republication of it in a separate form, the author made short
marginal notes, corrections, and additions for that purpose,
when the special articles in the Catalogue, and principally
the references to the authorities noted in the essay, seemed
to call for them: but he never contemplated an immediate
or early execution of his intention, and in the meanwhile
neglected materials furnished from time to time from various
sources, and especially by the periodical press, and these
materials are to this day not completely at his disposal;
nor could he even find leisure to make full use in this essay
of his own extracts from books and manuscripts, or of his
notes made for the Catalogue of the Oxford manuscripts.

When in 1853 a literal translation of the whole was submitted to him for revision, the author found himself in an
embarrassing dilemma with respect to the alterations to be
made, and especially with respect to the notes, and he will
briefly point out his part in its form and matter as it appears
now before the public.

1. He first read the translation with the view of insuring
a faithful reflex of the German original, the German expressions having been weighed and measured anxiously, and
often rewritten before their final adoption; and he tried to
keep up its general character as a literal translation. Perhaps this was not the best method, certainly not the easiest.
Besides the difficulty arising from involved construction, and
from the conciseness mentioned above, there was but little
assistance to be found in the common dictionaries, even for
the simple conceptions of criticism and philosophy which
form the pillars of sentences, such as *Begriff, umdeuten,
Bearbeitung, Wechselwirkung, Haltpunct, Anhaltspunct,* or
special terms, like *Wettgedicht,* or even the formulæ for cau-
tious restriction, as *wohl, theilweise,* &c. Indeed, between
the anxious fidelity of the author and the necessary care for

his English readers on the part of the translator, the original meaning and the strictness of expression may both have suffered in some places unwittingly, imperfection being an inherent quality of human work. The translator having introduced the common English spelling of Hebrew names, and the author being in constant use of his different spelling in the Catalogue, some inconsistencies have escaped the attention of both, especially with respect to the letter ח being sometimes rendered *ch* instead of *h*.

2. The important alterations of matter made by the author consist principally of hundreds of scarcely perceptible but sometimes very essential emendations in dates, names, &c., as far as his memory or the marginal notes supplied them. Since 1853 he has turned his researches for the Catalogue more carefully to the advantage of the essay, and the result is evident in the notes, and some final corrections at the end of the work. Of some omissions in the text an account has been given above (p. iv.); they bear no proportion to the additions of all kinds, and some parts and longer passages are almost entirely new, for example, parts of §§ 11. 13., pp. 113, 114. 222—236., §§ 23. 29.

Although the essay in its present shape does not come up to his original idea of a German reconstruction, still he has endeavoured to give it a more independent form; and what in the German encyclopædia is supplied by the special articles will be in most cases found in the Catalogues mentioned, and *vice versâ*. It is neither agreeable nor easy to dispose of materials belonging to the same subject for three works printed almost at the same time; and the author could not avoid some repetitions and cross-references in the notes. Some of his friends were of opinion that the notes should be entirely omitted, and that the work should merely introduce the English public to studies almost unknown to them: but the translator thought differently, and as he considered them necessary for those who seek further information, the author has endeavoured to render them complete by revising them according to his system in the German essay, so that this part claims a strict scientific value. The important alterations made in it are obvious, and need no comment. The omissions are more considerable, because of mere references having been substituted where the matter has been treated or the authorities collected somewhere else; but such omissions are indeed additions, and altogether the notes have increased in extent. The numbering has not been altered for many reasons. The notes of Period III. have been omitted, being almost exclusively references to Wolfius and the Oppenheim Catalogue, then the chief authorities: almost all the authors mentioned in this Period are to be found amongst the 3000 and more treated of in the Catalogue.

With respect to Period I., which contains the peculiar collective literature of Talmud and Midrash, the author confesses that he has had of late years less opportunity of referring to it; and as the German essay left the particulars to special articles, whose turn to be printed will not arrive for many years, he meant to treat of these, even in his intended German reconstruction, only as an introductory part, necessary for the understanding of the rest, and with this view he has revised the translation. With respect to the final dismissal of the sheets for press, he must remark that his revision of the MS. was again revised by the translator; that the author read one proof of the print without the assistance of the MS.; and that he sometimes altered the proof-sheet again, and the corrections being very numerous some slight mistakes arose, which have been corrected in the notes and corrigenda, as far as he hasdetected them by occasional reference to the fair sheets.

In this way did the present essay receive its external form. Perhaps some readers might expect a few observations upon its inner nature, the general views of the author, his tendencies, and the like: but this is a theme for an essay in itself longer than the present; it belongs to a critical introduction to Hebrew literature, and nothing on that subject seemed to him less advisable than imperfect remarks, easily to be mistaken, misinterpreted, and distorted. He confesses, however, that he treats of Jewish literature as mere literature, that his method is critical, his exposition historical, and that he has neither in a personal nor in a literary view anything to do with theology in its strict sense; theology itself being partly an object, nowhere the subject of his writings.

The author has thought it useful to add a Hebrew and Arabic Index, which may be also considered as an indirect contribution to the much-neglected Hebrew lexicography, upon which some very interesting remarks have been lately published by his celebrated friend Dr. Zunz, in the *Zeitschrift der deutsch-morgenl. Gesellschaft,* x. 501.

The author has also heard that an English translation of the whole essay has been inserted in an American journal, *The Asmonean,* but he had no opportunity of seeing one sheet of it, nor does he believe that journal much known or read in Europe.

The purpose of the present translation is obvious; it is to render the English people familiar with the literature of a race, the name of whose very language is used by them to denote something hopelessly beyond their comprehension. And strange it is that such a phrase should exist in a country which possesses in Oxford a Hebrew library now undoubtedly the first in the world.

Berlin, December, 1856.

CONTENTS.

PERIOD III.

FROM THE SIXTEENTH TO THE EIGHTEENTH CENTURY INCLUSIVE.

JEWISH LITERATURE.

§ 1.] DIVISION OF THE SUBJECT.

THE *principal Periods* into which we may divide the part of Jewish Literature treated of in this essay, depend upon general characteristics; they can, however, be distinguished only by criteria which form varying limits to special branches of literature. Within these, the arrangement may be regarded from various other points of view in turn, e.g. form, subject, scene, language.[1]

Period I., from the time of Ezra, to that when the influence of Arabian philosophy began to be felt, and Europe first appeared on the scene, is characterised by the Oral Tradition and Midrash.

Period II., till the expulsion of the Jews from Spain, and the invention of printing, exhibits a great development of studies of all kinds in various countries and languages; it may be characterised as a process of new formations first struggling for existence, then in full possession, and finally perfected by cultivation.

Period III., till the time of Mendelssohn and the appearance of German philosophy (as yet unexamined), is, in general, one of decay. From this, a recent *Period*, IV., leads to new formations now in the course of elaboration, and, consequently, does not belong to this treatise.

PERIOD I.

FROM THE TIME OF EZRA, TO THAT WHEN THE INFLUENCE OF ARABIAN PHILOSOPHY BEGAN TO BE FELT, AND EUROPE FIRST APPEARED ON THE SCENE.

FIFTH CENTURY, B.C. — EIGHTH CENTURY, A.D.

§ 2.] *Development.*

JEWISH Literature, in a more restricted sense, begins with the Restoration, and thus comprises the Canonical and Apocryphal Scriptures posterior to the Captivity. These, in fact, bear some analogy to the Talmud and Midrash, which were not reduced to writing until later, although certain fragments of them—and, indeed, entire treatises, now extant only in name—belonged originally to an earlier age. So, e. g., the first germs of Midrash, especially the Legends, are found in the Books of Chronicles[1], and perhaps also in Job. xii. 4. (conf. Gen. vi. 9.).[2] In Haggai (ii. 12.) may be traced the elements of Halacha; in Daniel, and perhaps in Psalm lv. 18., "the prayer three times a-day" is mentioned.[3] The formal contradistinction of Law and Prophecy is followed by the developments of Halacha and Haggada; the language of Ecclesiastes approaches very nearly to that of the Talmud, and many apocryphal books are, in fact, Midrash reduced to writing.[4] Parseeism, the influence of which may be perceived in the Talmud[5], was at work during the Babylonian Captivity, not long after Zoroaster; and it shows itself unmistakeably in the Book of Ezechiel. But every foreign element which was assimilated up to the time of Ezra's Restoration, became a national element for the Jews then organising themselves afresh. As regards the *locality,* we have, during nearly the whole period, with the exception of Esther, no book composed at Babylon; Palestine and Egypt divide the whole literature. The *language* is the *Aramaic,* subsequently to the Greek supremacy alloyed with Greek, and later still with Latin elements and the *Greek.* To the literary monuments of that time belong the genuine coins * and some Greek and Latin inscriptions. With Ezra are connected the most remarkable men of the time; they formed the *Synagoga Magna*,[6] the influence of which extends to the time of the Maccabees. These Soferim (סופרים, *scribes*, afterwards *scripturists*) collected the Pentateuch, or the written Law and the Prophets, and thereby the foundation of the *Masora* was laid.[7] On these, regarded from every point of view, they insisted, as the centre of all thought and religious action; and thus gave a centre to the Jewish mind and a direction to literature, which, predominating in the first period, have remained active till the present time. The general and lasting consequences of this may be collected under the following heads:—

1. The awakening and promotion of mental activity in general, and the establishment of suitable institutions, schools, and lectures. Study appeared as the highest guide for faith and feeling; the teacher took his place at the head of the Honoratiores; and to speak in the words of the Talmud, "The crown of the Thora surpassed that of the Priesthood, and of Royalty."

2. Mental activity submitted itself to Scripture, for the right understanding of which it therefore became necessary to take some careful steps. This would be tinged with more or less of individual character, thus giving rise to the various interpretations of Scripture, from the Targum to the Midrash, since the object was both to investigate the sense of the divine Word without any previous hypothesis, and also to discover the presupposed meeting-points for the whole mental and religious development of the nation.

3. From the state of culture at that time, the institution for the investigation of Scripture amounted to little else than a verbal lecture. This and the before-mentioned causes tended to soften down individual characteristics, and afterwards to produce a collective literature of a peculiar structure.

4. In the investigation of Scripture there are two principal divisions, *Halacha* and *Haggada*, analogous to those of Scripture itself, the Law and the Prophets.[8]

---

* On the subject of Jewish Coins, cf. the article "Jüdische Münzen," in Ersch und Grube's Encycl. vol. xxviii.

The whole of this movement, the literary ramifications of which are not perceived till later, begins from a common germ in the period of the Persian dominion in Palestine (B.C. 458—330). Under Alexander the Great, Greek philosophy was transplanted to the East; thence the Jewish mind awoke first to self-consciousness, and then to divisions, religio-political parties, and schools[9]; and, indeed, besides the writings of the Hagiographa, certain individual writers appear with all their individual features as historical persons, e. g. Sirach, Aristobulus (B.C. 190—70). In the struggle against the Syrians, the connexion of doctrine with national existence became apparent, and Polemics placed itself in the vanguard; but in Palestine the widely spread practice of religious ceremonial took the first place, at the time when the syncretism of Egypt gave rise to the *Alexandrian school.* The Synod[10] established by Simon (B.C. 143) wielded the authority of the Law. Gradually the Hagiographa was collected; and then began the formation of the *Apocrypha.* Against this, however, some opposition arose (Ecclesiastes, xii. 12.), from the fact that the traditional element could not be fixed by writing.[11] This first period, till the composition of the Mishna, although somewhat mythical, is the most interesting, and in many respects the most important. It is, however, the least known, since so many of its elements have reached us only in collections of fragments made in later times[12], and scarcely any step has yet been taken towards a scientific analysis and a historical investigation of them. This is the literature of the Talmud, Midrash, and Targum, the truly national literature of more than a thousand years, to which nothing analogous can be found elsewhere, and which has been rescued from a chaotic state of wildest misconception by Rapoport's sound critical perception, and the surprising results of Zunz's scientific deductions.[13] Our present object is to treat not of separate and particular writings, such as the Greek works of Philo, Josephus, or the poet Ezechiel[14], but of a great collective literature, which comprises the whole mental activity of centuries; so that some general remarks on the very peculiar character of the whole should precede the survey of particular groups.

§ 3.] *Midrash.*

In the literature of the Midrash, taken in its widest sense, the usual expressions, which connect the writer as an individual with the reader, are wanting. With few exceptions the works in this branch of literature are anonymous, some have had fictitious names added afterwards, some few have had them from the first. In their present shape the works are disfigured by literary, manuscript, and typographical errors, either intentional or otherwise; they have been frequently touched up[1], extracted, and compiled from original compilations, or from single older writings now lost; many more from collected discourses and oral traditions sometimes not written down till after the lapse of centuries; from old sayings, facts, and individual occurrences, the authority for which is often not indicated, scarcely to be recognised even by means of combinations and parallel passages, and which are frequently even contradictory. Besides this, there is in the form of the writings a continual interchange of exposition and discussion, narrative and debate, and even of persons introduced with transitions frequently imperceptible, either expressed only by niceties, or not expressed at all; so that an intelligible translation cannot possibly retain the character of the original. Nevertheless, historical criticism has in most works, particularly in the older, an important and tolerably sure footing for details, in certain authorities frequently mentioned by name, the long traditional chain of which is drawn out with a scrupulousness always considered as a particular duty, and in legal matters actually necessary.[2] And these single names, together with other criteria of the contents, the form, and the language, supply a footing for the criticism of the whole works; so that, e. g., it has become possible to determine that in the Midrash Rabbot, the redaction of the second part (Exodus) is about five centuries, and the concluding section of the first part (Vajechi) considerably later than the beginning. Moreover, the transition from this strange state of mere aggregation, to a form of more studied composition, as well as the separation of the parts according to their subject, is a clear indication of a later time, when Arabian science and literature had appeared on the stage, and the creative power of the Midrash gradually vanished.   In the older periods the most varied subjects are blended with each other, from the highest questions of the philosophy of the day, to the most indifferent things of common life.   The latter owe their place among the former to their connexion with persons and things, to their mode of treatment, or even to some external accident.   This remark does not however apply to the entire collection; there are throughout definite sections, and the materials are arranged either according to their subject, or according to their connexion with the Bible.[3]

The relation of the whole of this literature to the Bible is in general the centre for the true apprehension of its peculiarities, and is of the greatest importance for the development of the later periods.   The *Soferim* had made first of all the Law (the Pentateuch), and next the remaining Canonical Scriptures, the centre of their mental activity, and these have continued more or less to hold that position until the present time.   This was especially the case when Judaism was engaged in the contest with the two daughter religions, which alike take their stand upon the Old Testament, but make it subordinate to subsequent revelations.   The most prominent religious divergences among the Jews themselves,— e. g. the Alexandrian school, the Sadducees, the Caraites, the Cabbalists —likewise exhibit a particular treatment of the Bible.   This relation to the Canon forms a characteristic of the Jewish literature as distinguished from all others.   The latter develop themselves freely, and therefore with more marked individuality.   But the period of the Midrash is distinguished from later ages not so much by any greater amount of activity, as by this supremacy of the Bible, so nearly absolute that (as in Christendom about the same time[4]) no other science could attain an independent position.   " Turn it (the Bible) over and over again, for everything is in it," was the saying of an old teacher. [5]

The Institution, which formed the connecting link between intellectual activity and practical life, was that of *public* Discourses, the history of which stands in the closest connexion with the literature originating in it.   Preachings

from the Law for general instruction take their origin from
the earliest times; Ezra and the Soferim established and extended them. Next to them Prophets, trained in schools, acted
in a freer manner, but always with reference to the Law.
Even these preachings must have exhibited various modifications, from mere reading and explanation to homilies. When
the biblical Scriptures, and the written discourses of the older
Prophets, &c. became unintelligible to a people who spoke
hebraized Aramaic, the reading and exposition of Scripture
must have taken the character of a translation or paraphrase;
and thus gradually arose the literature of the *Targumim*, both
the Chaldee and Greek, and also, according to recent researches,
the Syriac.[6] These, like the Midrash, were developed for a long
time only in the mouth of the reader and teacher, before they
were collected and reduced to writing, and in their internal
character do not differ very widely from the Midrash.[7] Even
the Arabic translation of R. Saadja has the character of a
paraphrase; and Mendelssohn's German translation of the
Pentateuch, in legal matters, rests on traditional interpretation. In the time of the second temple this reading and
explanation of Holy Scripture on festivals and days of
assembly partook of the character of divine service, and
finally became an integral part of the worship. In the
place of the earlier Levites and Priests there now came the
Lawyers (Soferim), viz. the director of the school (רבן), gra-
duated Rabbins (רב), or learned men in general, and members
of societies (חברים), who modestly, like the Philosophers,
called themselves scholars of the wise (תלמידי חכמים).[8] Like
the earlier schools of Priests and Prophets, it was necessary
now to establish schools of the learned, in which the principal
point was the study of (מדרש) the Law. Here were found
both prælections for students and the learned, and also popular lectures, sermons, and homilies (דרוש) for the whole
people, who also were in the habit of praying — variously
indeed, according to the customs of time and place in the
synagogue, i. e. house of assembly (בית ועד, בית הכנסת
συναγωγή). But public speaking was not confined merely to
this institution; various occasions of public and private life,
e. g. circumcision, marriage, death[9], were celebrated and con-

secrated by lectures and discussions. All these discourses, for the most part centered in Holy Scripture, opened with a text, or returned to its interpretation as their result. They were on this account called *Midrash* in the widest sense (מדרש, Aramaic infinitive, from דרש, properly the investigation and explanation of Holy Scripture, hence, later, a cycle of such explanations),[10] and *Darush* (דרוש, properly the result of the investigation); the lecturer in general, *Doresh*, *Darshan* (דורש דרשן, properly, one who explains, explainer). The form and subject of these discourses depended upon the occasion. The cycle of Scripture readings was accompanied by a cycle of paraphrases and homilies, and the subjects of the strictly doctrinal discourses were connected with them. On the other hand, the popular discourses were carried on freely through the whole range of Holy Scripture, and it was for the later collector or redactor to determine from what point of view he would arrange his materials. And, since the Bible itself contains many very different elements, the Midrash system, the oral tradition, the explanations constructed on one another, the varied compilations, could not fail to produce a varied web, as described above.

In a scientific treatise on this literature in particular, it is therefore necessary to separate the elements, to establish the particulars according to time, place, and individuality, to pursue the historical development, and to recognise the original oral communications in the later written form, in order to form a complete judgment. But as long as one hesitates to undertake this really difficult task, one will in vain discuss the " Ethics, and Exegesis of the Talmud ;" for a conglomeration of fragments of such a kind will furnish arguments for almost any kind of views. Even the consideration of the scene of this movement is important.[11] It was developed in Palestine, and thence passed to the countries either immediately adjoining or connected with it by the Roman dominion, Egypt, Asia Minor, Greece, Italy, &c. In the third century Babylon, having long recognised the weight of the authorities of Palestine, takes a prominent position.

After these general remarks, we pass on to particulars.

§ 4.] *Halacha.*

In the whole movement of that time, and even within the Midrash itself, a difference was developed at an early period. The foundation of this lies in the very essence of Judaism; it found a footing in the Bible itself, and in later times led to important divergences,—the difference of Halacha and Haggada. The theocratic law of the Jews contains precepts for life, and presupposes certain doctrines as true. In this the difference between Politics, Law, and Religion is only partially developed. The Pentateuch brings the whole of private and public life within the field of its legislation; but this is done in general outlines, the application of which to practical details, together with the administration of the Theocracy, is entrusted to certain bodies; e. g. Priests, Levites, Judges, &c. The great revolutions, which the Jewish polity underwent from the time of its foundation till the second captivity, and the still greater which followed, must have introduced important modifications in the whole life of the people.[1] These required a higher sanction. Moreover, the tendency of particular parties to be influenced by the national and religious characteristics of foreign nations, showed the necessity of a rule for modifications of the Law, and of measures on the part of the religio-political leaders and teachers for the maintenance of Judaism; and thus the contest for the national life was the same as that between the parties for their leaders, and the schools for their fundamental doctrines.

The fundamental idea whence arose the literature of which we are about to speak (the *Pharisaic* or *Rabbinical*, as it is called), was as follows. Moses had received, together with the Pentateuch or *Written Law* (תורה שבכתב), also an *Oral Law* (תורה שבעל פה), which was faithfully transmitted from him, by an unbroken line of leaders and teachers (Joshua, Judges, Kings, &c.), to the members of the Great Synod, and thence to the teachers who immediately succeeded. For this reason it was called *Tradition* (קבלה)[2];

and a single law was termed *the Mosaic rule from Sinai* (הלכה למשנה מסיני). Besides this there are single institutions and laws,—laws preventive and defensive of the wise and pious of all ages, and manners and customs of various origin. Their sanction rests upon the general divine command (Deut. xvii. 11.) of obedience to rulers and teachers, or upon special exegesis, according to rules of interpretation considered as traditional. Generally speaking, that which was acknowledged in practice was brought into connexion with the Bible by a "leaning" (סמך), as it was called, even if it did not originally arise out of the passage of Scripture in question.[3] The principal point for its authentication was the fact of its having been received (or "heard," מפי שמעתא (השמועה) by members of the chain of tradition, or by men of recognised authority, i. e. by learned men of note (pupils of the former), &c. Many things were ascribed to old biblical personages, even without forging or attributing to them books for this particular purpose; in this lies a characteristic difference from the later especially the historical Haggada, and likewise from the newer Kabbala.[4] From the theocracy was derived the fundamental notion, that the exercise of religious duties, as a kind of legal relation to God, should be defined and watched in the most minute particulars with scrupulous exactness, almost in the same way as the legal relations between man and man. Hence arose a juridico-political point of view; hence also the maintenance of ecclesiastical discipline and the censorship of the religious life in reference to jurisdiction and casuistry came into intimate connexion with the legal and criminal administration; and hence, finally, the varied fate of the Jewish autonomy necessarily introduced all kinds of conflicts in religious theory and practice.[5] But by means of the opposition to foreign nationalities and their adherents, as well as by the general ascetic tendency of the time, all life was drawn into the sphere of religious law. The written law contains, according to the tradition, 613 commands (תר'ג מצוות), viz., 248 commands and 365 prohibitions[6]; and according to a later explanation (which is, however, now given up by almost all

Hebrew scholars), the *Soferim* derive their name from
" numbering " * precepts.[7] They certainly occupied themselves both with the preservation of the letter (see below),
and also with the development of the spirit of Scripture, i. e.
especially of the Law (in which they were followed by
later teachers); hence much of the Law is characterised as
Soferical (מדברי סופרים) or *Rabbinical* (מדרבנן). This
whole field of juridico-political religious practice, in a certain
sense a doctrine of human and divine law (" humani et
divini juris "), is termed *Halacha* (הלכה, rule, precept).[8]
If men occupied themselves in it, it also had reference to
actual life. But it was considered important not to deliver
over the old traditions, and that which gradually grew up in
daily life, to the slavery of the letter, as this would have
placed it on the same footing as the written Law (on which
point the contest of Sadducæism arose).[9] A large portion
of matter was therefore propagated orally for centuries ; and,
at most, a few learned men, in order to assist their memory,
noted down what was necessary in *Secret Rolls* (מגלות
סתרים).[10] If then we wish to form a conception of the
literature of the (written) Halacha, which did not begin till
a later period, we must commence with oral tradition. We
here adopt the common division, according to which the
period treated of in this introductory part is arranged in five
subdivisions, viz. : —

1. The Soferim ; 2. the Tannaim ; 3. Amoraim ; 4. Saboraim ; 5. Gaonim (up to the end of this introductory
part).[11]

1. The SOFERIM (סופרים), the members *of the Great
Synod* (אנשי כנסת הגדולה), (who always filled up their
number) from Ezra to Simeon the Just, until the beginning
of the Grecian Sadducees, and down to the Greco-Syrian
persecutions, were, as their name implies, *Scribes*, viz. of
the Law in particular, and therefore acquainted with Scripture, and generally the literary men of the time.[12] To their
great care is due the preservation of the Biblical Scriptures

---

* The Hebrew ספר is also " to number."

in their present character [13] and form; a matter which is
more closely connected than is generally supposed with the
Jewish tradition, and therefore with the legal part of the
Pentateuch, and especially with the Halacha. For this reason,
in the criticism and exegesis of the Pentateuch, the more attention should be paid to the Halacha. From the Soferim
are derived explanations and interpretations (פירושי סופרים),
especially determinations of measure and quantity (שיעורי
סופרים), which in theory form a contrast to the simple
letter of the Law (דברי תורה), but which, in authority, are
equal to it, since, as a traditional view of the Law, they
are esteemed "divinely-legal" (מדאוריתא). They were
therefore not separately fixed [14] and taught, but in a great
measure "ascribed to Scripture," by means of certain signs
(סימנים) or indications (רמזים); and these formed the
foundation of the *Masora*, which, at a latter period, took an
independent position. To this belong, e. g., the writing of
vowel-points, large and small letters, unusual formations of
words (e. g. the well-known נער for נערה,) keri and
ketibh, &c.[15], the object of which is to indicate a Soferistic law, and generally speaking a doctrine. Connected
with this, also, are probably variations, or other marginal glosses in the MSS. of the Law, the existence of
which is perhaps mentioned in the time of the Tannaim,
e. g. in R. Meir's copy of the Pentateuch.[16] In this way
arose the *Soferistic emendations* or modifications (תיקוני
סופרים) of Holy Scripture, a matter which has not yet been
sufficiently treated. The results of these glosses with respect to the interpretation of the Bible, in so far as they
lie at the foundation of those modifications, are perhaps
the *Soferistic reasonings,* as they are called (or subtle-
ties : (דקדוקי סופרים) [17], in contrast to the unwritten
reasonings on the Bible (דקדוקי תורה) of the Soferim.
Besides these, they made prohibitory laws on their own
authority, called Fences (סיג, גדר, later גזרה), &c. ; and this
Soferistic precept (דברי סופרים), "Tradition of the Elders"
(in Greek works, e. g. the New Test.), forms a contrast to
the traditional laws which are deduced from the Bible (עקר
דאורייתא) and similar authority.

2. The TANNAIM. To their time belong the fixing, collecting, and final redaction of the Halacha, which we will
discuss, as to its matter, and as to its history.

(A.) The additions to the Halacha which were gradually
collected in the times of the Soferim, whether indicated
in the MSS. of the Law, or known from practice alone,
were for the most part not taught in the schools. By the
changes of the Persian, Egyptian, Syrian, and the later
Roman dominion, and the consequent divisions among the
people, the changes in national and private life were accele-
rated, and rendered more striking. The endeavours of the
national schools were turned towards bringing out a greater
conformity in practice by a more scrupulous theory; and
thus more credit was given to the notion that everything
which was left undetermined by the Law was to be established, in spite of all controversy and doubt, by the decision
(שיעור) of the wise. In this way it became necessary to
formularise the subject matter of the Halacha. On the other
hand, a connexion between the Bible and that which was
recognised and determined having been established, certain
general rules of interpretation (מדות, properly, measure,
determination, &c.)[18] were necessarily put forth; and these
themselves became an object of theory. Among the points
determined by the Law, those relating to judicial matters required particular attention. These were, however, not carried
out in detail in the Pentateuch in proportion to their
urgency, but were rather given up to the individual who
filled office, and therefore the most exposed to great reforms
during political changes. The theory of judicial matters
was developed in accordance with the natural feeling of
justice by means of single sentences and statements (גזירות,
חרתוכי דינין)[19], which were either of general (הלכות
קבועות), or only of local and provincial application (הלכנת
מדינה); and these last either were deduced from the provincial customs (מנהג מדינה), or were the foundation of them.
The Sadducees had a book of sentences (ספר גזירות, גזירתן)[20]
differing from the Halacha, which book was set aside in the
time of R. Jochanan. The influence exerted by the Roman
dominion on the formation of Jewish Law, and its termi-

nology, is a subject of dispute amongst the learned of modern
times. [20 a] The subject matter of the Halacha was fixed
by compressing simple practical rules into a short and often
enigmatical formula; this was called " a Halacha" (הלכה).
These oldest Halachot* are composed in a scholastic Hebrew
(the common language of the people was at this time
Aramaic), which was subsequently called the " language of
the wise" (לשון חכמים) [21]; and the preservation of a formula once established was a solemn duty among the scholars.
The relative age of these Halachot, i. e. of the formulæ,
is to be discovered from their form and contents, e. g. by
Grecicised or Latinised expressions for certain classes of
ideas; the mention of late events is a sure sign of a recent
date; on the other hand, the contents may be older than the
form in which it is enunciated. But when many teachers
ascribe certain Halachot to the old kings, prophets, &c., this
is generally *not* to be considered as intentionally an historical
or critical testimony, even to their contents.[22] Thus the
expression *Mosaic Halacha* (הלכה למשנה מסיני) is extended to all the old traditional matter of the Halachot, even
when it clearly belongs to the time of the Soferim, and is
actually noticed as such (מדברי סופרים). A great number
of Halachot respecting the Temple certainly belong to eye-
witnesses; and if matters which had fallen into disuse afterwards became a subject of discussion (see below, C.), still
the formulising of simple Halacha generally belongs to the
time when it was practically needed. The recorder and the
original composer of a Halacha are both called in Hebrew,
שונה הלכה; in Chaldee, תנאי; in the dialect of Palestine, תנויא [23]; without reference to his position or learning
in other respects. Both as regards their contents at the time
of their formation, and still more in consequence of a long
oral tradition, the changes in life, and the external impedi-
ments to study, these short Halachot frequently needed a
further elucidation and discussion; so that the oral Halacha,
in this respect, like Holy Scripture, had its exposition, which
might be called (with Krochmal) the *Midrash of the Halacha*
(מדרש הלכה). But the Halacha had itself originally in

* הלכות, Halachot, is the plural of הלכה, Halacha.

part been deduced from the study of the Bible, and in a still greater degree been referred to the Bible by the later discussions. The investigation of the relation between Halacha and the Bible was called *Midrash of the Scriptures* (מדרש הכתובים), and the complete treatment of the Halacha formed the Halacha studies; in Hebrew, *Talmud* (תלמוד); in Chaldee, *Gemara* (גמרא)[24]; which, in opposition to the formularised Halacha of tradition, gave full play to the subjective element. Hence, in later times, the prevalent tendency of particular teachers to follow out either the old traditions or their own opinions becomes especially prominent; as, e. g., R. Elieser boasted that he had never said anything which he had not learned from his teacher. Hence also this element first appears as supplementary (תוספתא) [25]; but, when the old Halachot were finally collected, the element of Talmud could no longer be clearly distinguished.[26] The subject matter of the Halacha, and even that part which was of the highest authority (דין תורה) underwent in the course of time all the various modifications (תקנות) which were established (התקינו) and sanctioned by individuals or schools. On the other hand, older and original regulations (תיקונים, from the verb (תקן) were referred to the oldest authority possible, and consequently often connected with the Bible by means of Midrash. Thus, finally, the contrast between the Bible (מקרא) and Halacha was developed with the most varied traits in respect of origin and authority.

(B.) The *compilation* of the single Halachot took place gradually, and in different ways. It is natural to suppose that, as soon as the number of particular Halachot increased, a rubrication of them should be made for the sake both of method and of memory. The compilation may be reduced to three principal heads, which are still discernible in the later collections. (1.) According to the *contents* and *form* of the Halacha, in respect of similarity either of the object, or the tendency (e. g. alleviation or aggravation), or even only of the external formulæ (similar or dissimilar, universal and particular, numbers[27], &c.), which give an opportunity for an artificial arrangement; this was called a web (מסכת, *Massechet*).[28] These, however, grew again to such a size, that they were

[margin note: f. n. argues against "completion"]

divided into orders (סדרים, *Sedarim*), the reduction of which to the number 6 is ascribed to Hillel. Particular doctors occupied themselves especially with particular divisions, according as their mode of life, their school, or inclination suggested, and they often became great authorities in such matters, e. g. Rabbi Eliezer ben Jacob in the determination of measurements (מדות) respecting the Temple; R. Simon, of Mizpa, in the Ritual of the Day of Atonement, which he, as Krochmal judiciously supposes, perhaps collected for liturgical purposes for the inhabitants of the country, and for exiles (see below § 6. 19.); and Hillel in the genealogy of those who returned from Babylon, a subject of practical importance (see below § 5 b.). (2.) According to the order *of the Bible*, as far as the simple Halacha was connected with it by means of its Midrash; so that here, instead of those independent "webs" of Halacha, we meet with certain collections arranged and named after the sections of the Bible (פרשיות [28 a], *Parashiot*). With these two divisions of Halacha is connected the expression *Mishna* (משנה), which was used for Halacha (how early is unknown), and employed in both senses by the later schools.[29] (3.) According to the *method* by which it was deduced. After the Midrash of the Halacha had itself become an object for theory, and certain rules and methods of interpretation for the deduction of the Halacha from Scripture had been fixed upon (seven of which were ascribed to Hillel, and others known as Rabbi Ismael's), Halachol were finally composed on and according to these "axioms," and called "Measure" (מכילתין, מכילתא, the Chaldee interpretation of מדה), or *Mishna of the Midrash* (משנת המדרש). All these different systems were represented in particular schools, and in the collections which they produced.

In order to form an opinion of the method of the Talmud, it is necessary to give due weight to the *memoria technica* and signs (סימנים) of the narrators and collectors. Even some formulæ used in exegesis, e. g. explanation of letters and numbers (" grammatica," and " geometria "), which in mystic writings and the Kabbala were believed to be real, were originally meant only for memoria technica.[30]

(C.) The *History* of the composition and gradual collection of the Halacha is connected with the history of the people, especially with that of the Schools, their leaders, and the principal judicial colleges. By the establishment of a superior Court of Law, the *Synedrium* (B. C. 142)[33], a certain unity of practice became possible, since the dissentient (זָקֵן מַמְרֵה) was forced to obedience by the strong hand of the Law. Hence throughout those times the names of the presidents only are preserved. During the wars of the last Maccabees and the aggressions of Rome the political power of the Synedrium decayed; the Schools and doctrine which had flourished in Palestine up to that time were suppressed; tradition, if not entirely interrupted, was at least dimmed, and was restored only by Syrians, Babylonians, and proselytes.[34] Thus the old Halacha became more and more the subject of dispute, and took the hue of particular teachers and schools. HILLEL, the Babylonian, is considered as the restorer of the Oral Law at the time of Herod. He effected much the same in the oral that Ezra did in the written Law; he collected and arranged the materials, and applied himself to the diffusion of doctrine. But it was no longer possible to restore the ancient uniformity in practice; for, although SHAMMAI himself, Hillel's colleague, differed from him in only a few points, yet there arose so wide a difference in the theory of the Halacha between their respective schools, that, to use the expression of the Talmud, "The Thora was become as it were two." During the dominion of the Roman governors, through the last struggles of the declining nation (45—70), and under the cruel measures of the conquerors, learning could not fail to decay; yet there arose under GAMALIEL the older (i. e. the first) the flourishing school of Jamnia, — whither migrated R. JOCHANAN BEN SAKKAI, with other learned men. This gave an opening for the further development of various tendencies and schools, and a new impulse to the study of the Halacha. By the destruction of the Temple, and the Captivity, a great part of the collected Law fell, either at once or by degrees, into disuse. Yet theory clung to it only so much the closer; for the Captivity was

C

looked upon as but a transitory state, the end of which, the glorious restoration by the Messiah, was expected every moment, and minutely calculated by various persons with contradictory results. Under the Halacha were gradually comprised more and more things, which could not become of practical importance until the time of the Messiah (הלכתא למשיחא).[35] On the other hand the notion arose, that the obligation of the Law, to fulfil which was impossible, might be satisfied by mere study; " Since the Temple was destroyed, God had only the four ells of Halacha." * Finally the Halacha, although it had become unpractical, was, through its methodology and its exegetical part, too much interwoven with everything else to be ever entirely excluded from study; and this remark is applicable even at the present time. Once more an attempt was made to restore unity of practice among the contradictory schools, by means of external authority. After the death of R. Jochanan ben Sakkai (about A. D. 100), Rabbi GAMALIEL BEN SIMON BEN GAMALIEL collected round himself a new Synedrium at Jamnia, as president of which he was probably the first to bear the title of Prince (נשיא, Nasi). He proposed the statements of the school of Hillel as normal, and tried to put down every contradiction by a power ecclesiastical rather than temporal. But his labours were wrecked by the opposition of his own college, which wished to maintain the right of tradition uncurtailed. The old traditions and their teachers again came forward; and it is possible that a theory of tradition was actually propounded at this time.[36] Men of note exerted themselves independently in the Schools at different places, e.g. R. ELIEZER BEN HYRCAN at Lydda, R. JOSHUA at Pekün, R. JEHUDA of Batyra at Nisibis, &c.; and as after the Captivity Jewish learning generally travelled with the exiled Jews beyond

---

* According to the Talmud, the space occupied by a man is four ells ; the sense, therefore, is, that God resides at those places where men are engaged *in study*. Eisenmenger, in his desire to make the Talmud ridiculous, translates, " only four ells of space *to go*," while הלכה can be taken only mischievously in such an unusual sense for הליכה; and this translation shows even an ignorance of the whole genius of the *language*, which would require an entirely different grammatical construction to express this meaning.

the limits of Galilee and Syria, to Arabia, Asia Minor, and even to Rome [37], so for its maintenance institutions were established, which retained some connexion with each other.[38] Thus the renowned proselyte R. AKIBA [39] laboured during his extensive travels, no less than in his school at Bene Barak. He also extended the rules of interpretation; and to him the first composition of Mishna arrangements is ascribed.[40] As a follower of the Pseudo-Messiah Bar Kochba in the war of Trajan and Hadrian (ending with the conquest of Bethar (Beth Zor) A. D. 122?), he sealed a life of enthusiasm for religion and doctrine with a martyr's death. He thus occasioned the subversion of his numerous school, and directed the oppressive decrees of Rome against these first buds of learning, and especially against the ordination or promotion (סמיכה, laying on of hands) which communicated the dignity of Rabbi to the learned. But before his death he had taken great care to preserve this dignity, which in the course of circumstances underwent various modifications.

Jerusalem was rebuilt as a heathen city, Christianity began to assume a concrete form, and Rabbinism found it more and more necessary to support practice by a theory of principles. The religious polemic against the Samaritans and Christians, political persecutions, scholastic controversies (especially those between Palestine and Babylon), of an intricacy and detail hitherto unattempted, all brought about the transplanting of doctors and schools; e. g. the fall of the school at Jamnia through the instrumentality of SIMON BEN JOCHAI [41], and the removal of the learned to the north of Palestine, where finally, under the mild rule of the Antonines, Tiberias became a city renowned and influential in Jewish lore. The fate of the Synedrium during this war requires a more thorough investigation. Immediately after the Destruction mention is made of one located first at Usha (אושא), and subsequently (about A. D. 160) at Tiberias. R. SIMON BEN GAMALIEL, who fled as a schoolboy from the destruction of Bethar, was considered as the successor of his father in the rank of Nasi; by his side stood R. NATAN, the Babylonian, as "Father of Court" (אב בית דין), and R.

MEIR, the proselyte, as "Wise Man" (חכם). The school
at Jamnia, called "the vineyard," from the lines or ranks
of its members, flourished once more. At this time the
Methods (see above, B.) began to be distinguished in a more
decided manner, and to be represented by individuals;
thus e. g. R. MEIR taught principally simple Halacha; R.
NEHEMIA principally discussion; R. JEHUDA BEN JLAI [42],
and R. SIMON the Midrash of the Halacha, in a form which
became the foundation of the later collections of *Sifra* and
Sifri; R. ISMAEL, and R. ELIESER BEN JOZE the Galilæan
propagated hermeneutical studies. Besides these, there were,
as at an earlier period, some schools named after their
masters [43], and some teachers of Mishna, now again called
"Wise Men" (חכמים), and distinct from the mere Repe-
tentes (מסדרי מתנייתא, תנאים), with whom indeed they
often fell into controversy. At this time R. SIMEON, the
Nasi, impelled probably by the same motives as his father,
endeavoured to collect a Canon from the pile of Halacha;
and this work, begun in the time of Hillel, was completed
by his son and successor [44], R. JEHUDA, called RABBI κατ'
ἐξοχήν (died about A. D. 191); he is therefore usually designated as the composer or redactor of the Mishna. This "redaction" consists, as was shewn above, in a continuous sifting
and arrangement of the Halacha material from oral and
written sources, according to the method of R. Meir, in
which discussion and exegesis were not considered as proper
elements of the Mishna. It is nevertheless a great point of
controversy among the learned of recent times, whether R.
Jehuda was the first actually to reduce the complete Mishna
to writing.[45] At all events the Mishna of R. Jehuda is not
that which has come down to us, since it was retouched by
his pupils. At this point the next period begins.

3. The AMORAÏM (אמוראים). This name was given
in the preceding period to the lecturers, expounders, or
interpreters (מתורגמן), who delivered publicly the words
of the master, or "Wise Man," in the popular dialect,
and enlarged upon them. He thus occupied a rank subordinate to him. After the redaction and general reception of the Mishna, this expression came to signify the

" Wise Men " themselves, to whom nothing more than
a simple report of the received Halacha was permitted.[46]
In this sense the immediate pupils of R. Jehuda form
the transition from the Tannaïm to the Amoraïm; and
among them ABBA ARICHA (ob. A. D. 243), distinguished
by the name RAB,[47] was reckoned by some later
writers as one of the Tannaïm.　He transplanted to
Babylon, then under the newly established dominion of the
Persians (A. D. 226), the last amended recension of the
Mishna; and in connexion with his illustrious colleague,
SAMUEL, he gave the first impulse at that city to a more important and productive study of the Halacha.[48]　The Mishna
of R. Jehuda excluded not only traditions theoretically false,
or critically suspected, but also for the most part discussion
(Talmud) and exegesis (Midrash); although both were at that
time in a flourishing state, and had gained the respect due
to antiquity (the latter even the authority of tradition),
besides being regarded with predilection by some masters.
Indeed, through internal and external causes, the Mishnijjot
(משניות, Chaldee מתניתין also מתניתן, משנתנו　" our
Mishna ") of R. Jehuda came to be looked upon as a canon
to which public lectures were confined, and to which appeal
was made in practice.　It could not, however, fail to happen,
especially in early times, that individual doctors should have
preserved Halachas, either single or collected from periods
still more ancient [49], so that, beside the official collection,
another of an apocryphal character might be formed; and
this in fact was done by the above mentioned ABBA ARICHA,
and his uncle R. CHIJJA, and about a generation later by R.
OSCHAJA, called "the Father of the Mishna."　The Halacha
collected by the latter is called the *external Mishna* (משנה
חיצונה, Chaldee מתניתא בריתא, the last two used also
singly : *Matnito, Boraito*[50]).　Similarly also R. CHIJJA and
R. OSCHAJA collected the discussions and other additions to
the Halacha, which had been omitted in the Mishna, after
the method of R. Nehemia, called *Toséfta* (תוספתא).
Still more pressing was the need for collections, which should
comprise the *Exegesis* and *Methodology* of the Halacha, as
they were treated by the old doctors.　Such are the works

Sifra, Sifri (edited in the School of Rab), and *Mechilta*.[51]
All these and other individual collections are still extant, partly
as separate works, partly in later editions, and partly only
as fragments in other works, particularly in the Talmud; they
are for the most part composed in the dialect of the Mishna.

Materials so rich, handed down from past ages with such
pious care, and the continual additions from living sources,
afforded to the increasing schools in Palestine and Babylon
matter sufficient to raise a superstructure.   The next generation were occupied still more with the critical treatment of
Halacha literature.   But although a part of the discussions
and exegesis was already intruded upon the Mishna, or in
separate collections was so far perfected as to succeed in
establishing a claim to currency for itself, yet, like the old
simple Halacha and the Bible, it again necessarily became
the object of oral interpretation and discussion, and had to
be linked with the Bible; so that the exposition of Scripture became more and more arbitrary, the methodology more
and more complicated, until finally the traditional element
of the Halacha was obscured by speculation (הויות, subjective discussion).[52]   The history of this development, the
separation with respect to countries, schools, and individuals,
awaits, with but little hope, a self-denying, indefatigable, and
unprejudiced inquirer.   The further the study of the Halacha evolved, or rather involved itself, the more pressing became
the need of sifting the new material and arranging it under
the old; and after the old Halacha and its elucidation had
been fixed in writing, and made canonical, the subsequent
discussions followed periodically.   These were, however,
produced by external causes, and carried on in written
redactions, which must always be regarded as the work of
a school at the instigation of one prominent individual.   In
Palestine, such was the case about A.D. 370—380, after its
schools had lost the right of ordination, and had been destroyed by the influence of Christianity, then in full power.
In this way, at Tiberias, sprang up the *Jerusalem* (more
properly *Palestine*) *Talmud* (more properly *Gemara*), which
is falsely attributed to R. JOCHANAN (ob. A.D. 279).[53]   Soon
after this the Patriarchate became extinct, and the import-

ance of Palestine declined; but the lasting connexion of
this country with Babylon [54] familiarised the literati of Babylon with the Mishna and Gemara of Palestine.[55] In Babylon there flourished, under more favourable circumstances,
the schools at Syra, Pum-bedita, Nehardea, Mahusa, Neresh
(נרש ?) under the Heads of Schools (ריש מתיבתא, *Resh
Metibta*), and the Princes of the Exiles, *Resh Geluta,* as
they were called, whose more subtle and refined doctrines
met with scorn and reproach at the hands of some of the doctors of Palestine.[56] The *Babylonian Amoraïm* number from six
to seven generations, according to the heads of the schools :
Rab and Samuel, Huna and Jehuda, Rabbah (רבה) and
Joseph, Abbaje and Rabba (רבא), Ashe and his son Mar
and Rabina. Rab ASHE, head of the school at Syra, was permitted, in a long official life (said to be of sixty years), and
after a long period of external peace, to direct his numerous
scholars in the collection and arrangement of his entire Halacha
writings. He died, however, before the completion of this
revision (A.D. 427). From these circumstances he or his
son (ob. 25th Sept., A.D. 467) is considered as the *last
Talmudical authority* [57] (סוף הוראה). The redaction of the
Babylonian Gemara was effected by R. JOSE, president of the
Academy of Syra (ob. A.D. 475); but the *Babylonian Talmud* appears first as a complete whole in the time of

4. The SABORAÏM. In the latter half of the fifth century,
the persecutions under Jezdegerd, Firuz, and Kobad[58], who,
amongst other things, degraded the office of Resh Geluta to
a venal title of the rich, had caused the decline of the Babylonian schools, and interrupted the chain of ordination
in a most palpable manner. In consequence of this, the
succeeding doctors did not again assume to themselves
any authority in opposition to tradition, and they confined
their teaching and judgment simply to the comparison and
reconciliation of what was in their hands, to explanation and
opinion (סברה); hence they were called Saboraïm [59]
(סבוראים, conf. the form of Amoraïm). By them, however, certain additions, particularly the methodological and
mnemonical signs (סימנים), have been introduced into the
Babylonian Gemara.[60] But the latest Saboraïm must have

had this Gemara (excepting a few later additions and variations) already in the same form as that of the few remaining MSS. and earliest editions.   The Gemara (Talmud in
the narrower sense) being subordinate to the Mishna (according to the Babylonian recension), the word Talmud
received the wider signification, comprising both Mishna and
Gemara.   The Saboraïm consequently stood in the same
relation to the Babylonian Talmud, as the Soferim to Holy
Scripture.   It lay before them as a book ready to hand,
as an object of exposition, investigation, and discussion.
To them, or rather to itself as the last effusion of
tradition (which was considered as uninterrupted), in
the midst of great intellectual pressure and authoritative
belief, is due the esteem in which the Talmud is held as contrasted with later productions (some older parts being similarly
contrasted with the newer); it was not made canonical by
any individual or college, for its own nature would have
rendered this impossible.   So it came to pass, that the Talmud,
including the Mishna, as a living commentary on Scripture,
and like Scripture itself, was made the foundation of all later
developments,— a fact which is the more conceivable because
the Talmud forms almost the only literature for more than
five hundred years; the few Halacha-Midrashim above
mentioned having been partly scattered about the Talmud
itself.   All the other collections of Halachot of that time
have been lost, probably in consequence of the reverence
paid to those which were received.   More detailed information on the contents, form, and fate of the two Talmuds, is
not the purpose of this essay.   Concerning the many hundred *Scholars of the Talmud* (חכמי התלמוד) mentioned in
that work, only what is absolutely necessary can be here
noticed.   By a compilation of their remaining fragments
pictures of them as physical and intellectual persons might
be drawn; and for this purpose the Talmud is our only
resource.   But we cannot here do this even with respect
to the most remarkable of these men.   It was, however,
necessary to give a sketch of the history of the origin
of the Talmud as the foundation of all the later literature of the Halacha and Haggada; for a proper treat-

ment of the Talmud and Midrash gives the true point of
view whence to consider the subsequent cultivation of independent science and its controversies. The following principal circumstances form the transition to the next period.
The *language* of the two Talmuds in the narrower sense
(exclusive of the older fragments), in contradistinction to the
scholastic Hebrew of the Mishna, is principally the east and
west Aramaïc dialect, as was rendered necessary by free
discussions and popular lectures. But in Persia the language of the country, of which some specimens are to be
found in the Talmud [61], gradually became prevalent among
the Jews; and the Talmud then required philosophical explanation and textual care. The study of the Talmud with
its all-comprehensive contents absorbed the whole powers
of the mind, and scarcely even the titles of the original
works of the Saboraïm have come down to us.[62] To their
time perhaps belongs the collection or final redaction executed in Palestine of some of the *lesser treatises* (קטנות
מסכות), as they are called, forming an apocrypha to the Talmud.[63] Generally speaking the period which follows is
obscure and dark, and the uninteresting pages of literary
history are filled with accounts of persecutions traced in
blood. Even the limits of this period are differently given,
the idea of the Saboraïm given above being in fact extended
to the period which follows, viz. to the first among

5. The GAONIM. After the revival of the school at
Tiberias during the wars of Rome and Persia, and the decline
of the office of the Resh Geluta, and after the attempt to
restore Jerusalem (A. D. 610),[64] the mental and ecclesiastical
power of Palestine seemed to be leaving the country. At
this crisis Babylon, from some circumstances and causes
but too little known, raised itself to a primacy in religious
and mental affairs by means of the Heads of the Schools
at Syra and Pum-bedita, of whom CHANAN (A. D. 589) was
the first to bear the title of Gaon (גאון, Excellence).[65] The
supremacy of these Babylonian heads appears to have been
but a consequence of the Arabian dominion established in
Irak; and it is difficult to draw the line between the last
Saboraïm and the first Gaonim, since even the latter pro-

duced no independent Halacha literature, but only continued to promote the study of the Talmud (and almost
the Babylonian exclusively [66]). In their practical views,
they considered that they were not bound by the letter of
the Talmud, and independently of others made institutions
in accordance with the spirit of the age [67]; but the same
had also occasionally been the case with the Saboraïm,
although their times were less adapted to the reception,
propagation, and maintenance of such institutions than those
of the Gaonim, who were assisted by external power and by the
universal respect and esteem paid to their learning. [68] The
literature of the times of the Gaonim does not begin until
the termination of this introductory part (at the middle of
the eighth century). It is not a Gaon nor a Babylonian
who begins the series, but R. SIMEON of Kahira [69], perhaps a resident at that place, and acquainted with the
Palestine Talmud, through the close connexion which had
subsisted from the earliest times between Egypt and Palestine. He composed a compendium of the most important
Halachot from both Talmuds with the title, Great Halachot
(הלכות גדולות), the introduction to which contains the first
known attempt to arrange all laws under the old canonical
number 613, i. e. to determine accurately these 613 precepts
from the Halacha literature then extant. The occasion of his
undertaking this purely theoretical labour is unknown, and
would be worth investigation (conf. inf. § 9.). In language
and style this composition, which was extant in the eleventh
century as a separate work, resembles the older Halacha.
But the work now extant under this title is a fusion of the
old work with different later matters, viz. the decisions (הלכות
פסוקות) discussions and opinions (שאלתות) [71], — distinguish-
able only by their Aramaïc dialect, and often directly
contradictory to the older parts — by Gaon JEHUDAI, the
Blind, who flourished soon after, and by his school, particularly by his follower, R. CHANINAI (or ACHUNAI) [72], who
was probably executed, and likewise by other teachers and
pupils, whose names are unknown, and who are designated
as " the Doctors of that time." [74] Thus the final redaction
of our Halachot Gedolot [75] must be placed at earliest in the
middle of the ninth century. From the school of R. Cha-

ninai, it may be added, the *Midrash Esfa* (מדרש אספה
Numer. xi. 16.)[73] probably emanated, Some passages of the
work of R. Simeon were translated during the period of
the Gaonim, from Aramaïc into Hebrew, in the *Midrash
Hashkem* (מדרש השכם); and it is a pity that this Midrash is only known by a few fragments, so that we are
enabled to speak of its early date, and probably mixed (Ha-
lachic and Ethical) character, only by quotations recently
discovered. On the other hand, as early as the middle of the
eighth century, R. ACHA of Shabcha—who, vexed at seeing
his own pupil preferred at the election of Gaon by the Prince
of the Exiles, went to Palestine, composed a work, which
combined all the different characteristics of the study, viz.
Halacha, Midrash, Talmud, and responsa, arranged according
to the sections of the Pentateuch, and explaining their respective laws and observances, by means of extracts from the
Babylonian Talmud, and original expositions in the favourite
form of question and answer (שאלתות). Our printed *Sheel-
tot* [76] are for the most part only extracts and compendia.

In Palestine, since the completion of the Talmud which
bears its name, there seems to have been nothing important
done for Halacha literature. At all events, the complete
failure of everything that might have been effected shews
to how narrow a sphere it was confined. Some remarkable
decisions, affecting practical cases, may have been recorded
by the learned, and transplanted to Babylon, as can be
gathered from the citation of a work, *Events in Palestine*,
(ספר המעשים לבני ארץ ישראל), by the later Gaonim, and
from some references in the genuine Babylonian fragments
of the above-mentioned Halachot Gedolot. Some apocryphal books of the Talmud (lesser Treatises), composed in
Palestine, belong either to an earlier or to a later date. On
the other hand, in the sixth, seventh, and eighth centuries
we meet with the development of the *Masora* from its earlier
elements to an extensive science, and with the composition
of particular *Targumim*. Palestine, however, together with
the countries closely connected with it, viz. Asia Minor,
Greece, Italy, exerted itself principally in a department of
which we have now to speak.

§ 5.]   *Haggada.*

Action—as required by "the doctrine of Divine Law,"
Halacha—and Thought—either ending in itself, or leading
to action,—sometimes blend, sometimes contrast themselves.
Thought itself, as being without the sphere of duty, is not
an object of law, but is presupposed or considered true
when produced by Revelation and Reason, and kept alive by
the general sense of society.   She is the living internal law,
which produces and upholds the external, but breaks through
it when it becomes rigid ; she is the spirit which creates her
own form and expression, yet disdains to be confined to
words and formulæ ; and these, which in her alone have any
value, she abrogates, or silently transforms.   She is brought
forth and guided by teaching and life, by culture and
custom, but cannot be restrained by merely human authority.   Thus free, in strong contrast to all law, and limited
only in herself, thought has always found her expression in
Judaism ; during the time of the unimpaired unconscious
national life, in the free words of the Prophets [1], which
were often a stumbling block to the men of law and justice ;
during the time of the full self-consciousness developed by
the school of life and scholastic science, in the word of the
" Wise Man " (חכם), who, to use the thoughtful expression
of the Talmud, is the heir of the Prophets [2], standing yet
higher than the Prophets, and whose sayings are the out-
pourings of the Revelation given of old.[3]   So neither the
authority of the written oral law, nor that of its representatives and administrators, nor the sanction of the Traditions was here necessary as in the case of the Halacha
(which was designated as something received externally,
or " heard ") : it was sufficient for thought that it should
be expressed.   Hence every expression of it, so far as it
did not purposely aim at the investigation and establishment
of legal practice, nor fundamentally lay claim to any practical
weight, is designated as merely " said," *Haggada,* in Chaldee
Aggada (הגדה, אגדה) [4] ; a distinction which, however, must
not be so finely spun as to exclude incidental points which

might and actually did lead to a different view, and to
render conceivable the independent cultivation of the two
parts. The Haggada was developed, like the Halacha,
principally by *oral discourses*, i. e. by lectures, homilies,
sermons, and discussions, which were held [5] on specified days
and upon various occasions of life, in assemblies of the people
or of families, by men who were competent to speak, or who
thought themselves so ; so that the Haggada may be considered as the first of Jewish *Homiletics*. But the Halacha
and Haggada were separated only by degrees, as manifest
and recognised divisions and groups of learned men ; in the
treatment and combination of which there was developed an
artificial form of discourse [6], varying according to time and
country, to be specially considered in their *treatment of the
Bible*.

The Haggada afforded by far the wider field for the development of the *Midrash*, under which expression, in its more
restricted sense, only the *Haggada Midrash* (מדרש ההגדה)
is to be understood ; since the study and exposition of the
Bible, gradually extending itself and overcoming the fetters
of the letter with less resistance, became united more and
more to the free expression of thought. But as regards
Halacha in the treatment of the existing law and customs,
this study and exposition sank lower and lower, till it became a mere memoria technica, tracing out connexions and
making notes (רמז) [7], unauthoritative, and consequently un-
important. Holy Scripture was the centre also of the
Haggada ; but the Haggada Midrash had no need to distinguish between the Pentateuch (Law) and the other books
of the Bible [8] ; it was able freely to trace combinations,
and consequently the Midrash was no fetter or strait
jacket to the Haggada, but a large, elegant robe, which
restrained no ordinary motion nor even distorsion, and
which might be drawn on and off unperceived. By adapt-
ing the whole Bible as current and typical to its own purposes, both in its contents and in its form, there was ensured
ample matter for the fancy, sharp and pointed weapons for
the wits, plenty of incitement for the intellect and mind, and
still a continual check reminding them of holy earnestness,
and consecrating their thoughts and words to the highest

ends.   This is not the place to enter upon the special exegetical resources of the Haggada, or on the use or misuse[9] of
them; we here only glance at the principal relations of the
Haggada and Midrash, which will suggest a point of view
for the subdivision of their voluminous literature.

The Haggada mode of treatment was either mainly subjective or mainly objective ; its end was either the simple understanding of words and things, *Peshat* (פשט)[10], or else a homiletical application, reflecting the present condition of things
in the mirror of Prophecy, where the words of the Bible and
subjective thought were evenly balanced, as much being
brought into the Bible as was taken out of it, *Darush*
(דרוש), in a restricted sense; and, finally, there were some
themes confined to a narrower circle of students, *Sod* (סוד,
mystery).[11]   The desire of a simple explanation of words
was but little felt, scientific exegesis was unknown or perhaps
avoided, and the secret science was considered a prerogative
of individuals; but Darush was favoured alike by internal and
external causes, and thus found its way into both Targum
and Halacha.   An independent Haggada, free from all
Midrash, is not extant in the literature which took its rise
in that time ; for anything of that kind was considered unimportant, and consequently would not be preserved except
in connexion with other things.   The Haggada is therefore, as far as we are concerned, identical with Haggada-
Midrash, and must be divided into two principal classes,
viz. *General Haggada,* in which the reference to the Bible
is subordinate to the subject matter ; and *Special Haggada,*
in which the biblical exposition takes the precedence ; so that
the Haggada-Midrash is connected with the Halacha-Midrash,
inasmuch as both had originally been developed from general
Midrash.[13]   The original elements of the Haggada, both
oral and written, must however be distinguished from the
later collections and extracts.

As regards the *written composition* of the Haggada[14], some
considerations arise different from those noticed in the case of
the Halacha.   The former must not and cannot, like the old
rules of the Halacha, be set down in definite unchangeable
formulæ, since it was almost entirely merged in Midrash.

The necessity for preserving the matter once produced, was
not generally a practical one, but was rather the result of the
predilections and studies of individuals; and the expression
took its hue from the particular prism through which the ray
of thought was refracted.   On the other hand, excepting in
the case of the Mysteries, there was less danger in committing
these matters to writing.[15]   Hence men began earlier to com-
mit the Haggada to writing in marginal glosses to the Bible,
and in particular rolls or books, both for their own use, and for
their schools and public lectures. In this manner the greater
collections, now extant, were gradually developed, though
often with important modifications of the originals.   These
must now be treated separately according to their contents
and form.   The Haggada, in contradistinction to the Halacha, proceeds more upon theory than upon practice; the
General Haggada (Haggada-Midrash in its wider sense)
treats of (1.) Ethical, (2.) Metaphysical, or (3.) Historical
truths. (4.) Special Haggada (Haggada-Midrash in its
narrower, Midrash in its narrowest sense) is principally
concerned with biblical exposition, and for that purpose
employs all the various elements of general Haggada.   (5.)
All these tendencies, however, have points of connexion with
Halacha, and (6.) come in as conflicting elements in the
simple explanation of words, the Targumim. Omitting various
kinds of transition, we thus have the six principal groups of
Haggada literature already specified by Zunz, of which three,
belonging to general Haggada, are independent, and meet in
a fourth, the special Haggada, and then become elements in
the literature of the Halacha and Targumim.   The latter, for
reasons given in our preface, are excluded from this sketch.

1. *The Haggada in connexion with Halacha.*   The
original explanation of the Bible, especially of the Pentateuch, was at one time of a Halacha, at another of a Haggada character, according to the contents of the text; and
consequently the single as well as the collective Halacha-
Midrash could not fail to contain important portions of
Haggada, as e.g. the old collections Sifri, Sifra, and Mechilta mentioned above.   But the Halacha, in its narrower
sense, and the discussions belonging to it, e.g. in the

Toséfta, and even in the older Masora [16], had also their points
of contact with ethics, metaphysics, and history. This was
the case both with their contents, which comprised not only
law but the whole of life, and still more with their organ, oral
tradition, which, together with the pith of the tradition, included a mass of accessory matter. In this way there grew
up whole collective works of a common character. But in
the larger collections the contents of particular parts diverged
from the whole so completely, that they owe their place only
to their form or connexion, and consequently require an independent treatment. In the Talmud, a Boraita, *Seder Olam*
(סדר עולם), of R. JOSE BEN CHALAFTA (Sæc. I.) is quoted ;
our Seder Olam, " rabba," resembles the historical Midrash
in its language and contents. [17] Lepsius, in his researches
on Egyptian Chronology, invites the learned to investigate
the manuscripts of this chronology, which give the date of
the exodus differing " only one year " from the true tradition.
The Boraita of the famous Haggadist, R. ELIESER BEN JOSE
OF GALILEE (Sæc. II.), called also 32 Middot (ל"ב מדות),
and treating of hermeneutic rules which partly relate to
Halacha, is of a mixed character. The last chapters of
the Boraita or Mishna, *Description of the Tabernacle*
(מלאכת המשכן) [18], belong to the veritable Halacha. The
peculiar character of the Mishna properly excludes the
Haggada ; still the Haggada is to be found there : 1.
in separate treatises, e. g. Abot (see inf. 2 a.), Middot
(see sup. § 4., 2 B.), neither of which have any Gemara ;
2. in the concluding passages of many treatises, containing
blessings and consolations, the style of which was in imitation of the Prophets [19] ; and, 3. in particular Halachot, which,
being essentially related to the Haggada, combine with it.
Among the Boraitas, fragments of which (in the Talmuds
and other collective works) contain Haggada parts, the
following are the most important : that of *the school of R.
Ismael* (תנא דבר ישמעאל), which seems to be a kind of
Midrash on the Pentateuch ; and *Seder Elijahu* (סדר אליהו),
which is said to contain communications from the Prophet
Elijah to R. ANAN (A. 280), and existed as a separate work
as late as the twelfth century (cf. infra, 2 a.). Many Boraitas

belong especially to ethics.[20]   Again, to the Haggada partly
belong the *Lesser Treatises*, six of which appear as apocryphal books in our editions of the Babylonian Talmud:
seven others have been recently published as belonging to
the Jerusalem Talmud, to which they are partly anterior,
and partly posterior.   There is one among the more recent
of the six (in the ninth century at earliest) particularly
interesting (but much mutilated in the extant edition),
called *The Treatise of the Scribes* (מסכת סופרים), the
substance of which concerns the scribe and reader of
the Law.[21]   Amongst the seven, two, treating of the Samaritans (מסכת כותים) and of proselytes, merit general
attention.   Lastly, the two *Gemaras* or *Talmuds* contain
Haggada parts; the Jerusalem Gemara, it is true, in a much
less degree, since this older Gemara, being a Halacha exposition, keeps closer to the Mishna, while the Palestine
Haggada was developed more independently.   In Babylon,
where the tendency to the Halacha prevailed [22], the Haggada
did not form a separate literature, but rather found a place
in the Gemara, as in the Halacha writings of the Gaonim
mentioned above (§§ 4, 5.), the lost work, *Practice of the
Gaonim* (מעשה הגאונים) [23], and others of the same kind.

Lastly, to this age belongs also the commencement of *individual sciences* [24], which form the transition from Halacha
to special Haggada, particularly to Secret Doctrine; e.g. physical science, medicine, mathematics, and astronomy, which
came into consideration in the laws relating to food, leprosy,
festivals, and other points ceremonial and judicial (in respect to records, &c.), and which are also indispensable in
common life.   The study and knowledge of these were developed first within the nation itself, and still more afterwards
during the Dispersion, under the influence of the prevailing
culture.   From them, in a great degree, proceeded the trans-
formation of Jewish views, that great internal revolution,
which, spreading in different degrees, by means of the various
external connexions of the separate branches of the nation,
either became general or remained merely local.   Proportionately various was the influence of these theoretical sciences
upon national life, which had been fast bound by the Halacha;

and in accordance with their influence on intellect and manners in general, traces of these sciences, each step of which
rendered all previous steps useless, have been preserved in
literature.   From the collection and investigation of these
scattered fragments some interesting contributions to the
history of science may be expected.[25]   We have here to do
with the literary formation of scientific elements; which
in that respect appear to have taken the literary character
of the Halacha and Haggada, at all events with the collectors of the latter, so that themes in medicine, physical
science, astronomy, and mathematics appear as *Boraitas*.[26]
This is particularly the case with *astronomy*, the study of
which was carried to a high pitch among the Jews, so
that it was characterised as the "Jewish Wisdom" (Deut.
iv. 6.): in this the influence of the Chaldeans during the
Babylonian Captivity offers an interesting subject for investigation.[27]   Astronomy has two sides, according to which it
approaches either to the Halacha or the Haggada.   These
were, first, the Kalendar, and especially the determination of
the Jewish cycle of festivals (originally agrarian, and since
the Jewish year was lunar, it required correction for the solar)
by the proper authority, the fixing of proper times for prayer,
&c.[28]; and, secondly, Astrology, which was very prevalent
in the East, together with the studies dependent on it.[29]
In Palestine, as late as the dissolution of the Patriarchate,
or, at all events, till the patriarch HILLEL (A. D. 430), great
grandson of R. Jehuda, the new moon was determined by
testimony, a fact which, however, could not supply the place
of astronomical calculation.   The Jewish computation of
the Passover was continued by the early Christians.[30]
Rapoport [31] believes it probable that R. Joshua (about A. D.
89) was able to calculate approximately the appearance of
Halley's comet.   But the more important astronomical
movement seems to belong to the Babylonian scholars; at
least, SAMUEL, who boasts of extraordinary knowledge in
astronomy (called also "Jarchinai," or learned in the moon,
or, according to others, "of Orchon," a place renowned for
its astronomers), is to be considered as the founder of the
calculation of the Kalendar, by the introduction of the

Julian year. Improbable as it now seems that the older astronomical results and calculations were transmitted only by
word of mouth, it is sufficient to admit that some such matters were inserted by the learned as particular Halachot in
the "Secret Rolls" (cf. supra, § 4. n. 10.). We are not
justified in admitting that a separate *astronomical literature*
was formed before the progress of science had exercised
any general influence; so that the titles of astronomical
works mentioned by later writers are to be regarded with
great caution. These writers can, in fact, be speaking only
of Halachot named after their contents, and the explanations
of them, or of later pseudepigraphic works. To the former belongs the well-known Boraita of *The Mystery of Inter-*
calation (ברייתא דסוד העבור), and perhaps also *The Boraita*
of Samuel (ברייתא דשמואל); to the latter probably *The*
Boraita of R. Ada (ברייתא דרב אדא).[32] The same is the
case with *geometry* and *mathematics* in general, which were
of importance in various Halacha decisions; the Talmudical treatises *Middot, Arachin, Erubin* contain many
of them. A particular collection (Mishna, Boraita, or
Midrash), *The* 49 *Middot* (מ"ט מדות), was ascribed to
R. NATAN; and he was identified with the Babylonian of the
same name, who is known as the collector of Mishnas, and
as the author of many decisions of a mathematical or astronomical character, and who was fond of the combination of
Halacha and Haggada by the symbolism of numbers.[33] In
proportion, however, as the elements of theoretical sciences
and of practical knowledge and experience were more completely beyond the field of the Halacha, they, as the free expression of thought, fell within that of special Haggada, to the
literature of which we now turn.

2. *Of the independent Haggada*, some late productions extend to the age when Arabian science commenced; and
the whole subject may be divided, according to the remarks
made above, into A. *General*, B. *Special* or expository Haggada. The former of these may be again subdivided into
three principal groups:—

a. *Ethical Haggada* (MASHAL). If the Halacha, as a
religio-moral law, supplied only the fundamental idea of

right, the " suum cuique," in the whole doctrine of duty [34],
and thus accurately determined the measure of all external
action, then morality, piety, custom, experience, and prudence must needs find elsewhere a free expression; this
again gradually became typical and prevailing, and thus
not unfrequently repassed into the fixed form of Halacha.
The richer the Jewish life was in transformations, so much
the more complicated must have become the expression of its
ethics in the widest sense, although it may not yet appear in
the form of a complete system.   But since we are here concerned only with the literary phenomenon of the old Jewish
ethics, the expression of it, or the form of language in
which the thoughts are communicated to us, is especially
worth our consideration.   Ethical thought either created for
itself an entirely new form, or else chose one already extant,
whether from an earlier literature, or from society, national
or foreign.   It then appears as simple reflexion and exhortation [35], but for the most part in an æsthetic form; just as the
philosophy of the East, and of an earlier stage of civilisation, is
generally clothed in a semi-poetical garb.[35 a]   This gave rise
to a peculiar kind of didactic poetry, which in all its forms
is expressed by the term *Mashal* (משׁל).[36]   The Mashal is,
according to the Jewish view, " a small light by which the
lost jewels (truth and philosophy in their generality and
abstraction) are rediscovered."

(*a.*) The simplest form of the Mashal is the *Gnome*, a
short doctrine, sentiment, or maxim, which, first spoken by
an individual, becomes the expression of the popular mind
in the shape of a proverb; and if the reference to the fact
or the person giving rise to it still hangs like a clod on
the transplanted flower, it becomes a proverb of example.[37]
All the usual forms of Gnome—parable, similitude, and
contrast of conception and expression, parallelism, rhythm,
&c. — are to be found in the Gnomes of the Haggada [38]; but
intentional rhyme is the product of later artificial poetry.
Together with the generally known features of Gnomonics,
there are certain particulars, of some importance also for the
later periods (infra, § 20.), which must be brought forward
here, regarding the origin, history, meaning, originality,

age, country, and founders of the Gnomes. The Jewish
Gnomes have been formed and become general, either immediately from actual life, or under the influence of earlier
literature. They are either peculiar to the Jews, or taken
from other nations, as must have been more especially the
case in the ultimate fortunes of the Jews; and sometimes
they are expressed in such general terms, that a simultaneous
originality is conceivable. But, as a general rule, even the
most universal utterances of wisdom and prudence, verbally
repeated as the sentiments and maxims of teachers, and becoming popular sayings (משל הדיוט, Mashal of the Idiotæ),
are stamped with a different character [39] in different nations
and regions. This was the case also among the Jews of
various countries, as of Palestine and Babylon.[40] A difference in age [41] can be of importance only in connexion
with the points above mentioned. In this continuous flow
of history it is not possible to draw accurate distinctions
amongst the various fields of literature before us; e. g.
Bible, Talmud, Midrash. Even maxims, sentiments, and
proverbs undergo perpetual changes; yet the introduction of Arabian Gnomes is distinctly visible in the later
literature. As criteria for these categories, we have,
besides their subjects and historical and geographical allusions,
the literary works themselves, the Jewish as well as the early
Christian and Muhammedan, the Old Testament, the Koran,
and the Sunna [42]; and besides these, the language, e. g.
East or West Aramaïc dialect, older or Arabico-Hebraisms.
Proverbs, however, arise in common life out of witticisms,
the application or "moral" of fables, narratives, &c., and
become condensed into mere proverbial sayings, and finally
into simple metaphors or types, which are of special importance for philology.[43] There is some peculiarity in the
influence exercised by the Bible on Jewish Gnomonics,
by means of which they are brought into closer affinity with
the Midrash. The linguistic side of these which we are here
considering, forms one phase of style in Hebrew literature
down to the present time. Amongst the peculiar circumstances of Jewish literature, Holy Scripture influences
both the language and subject-matter; and these two ele-

ments come into mutual action through the medium of the Midrash. Some of the books of the Bible borrow from one another the form of expression as well as the thought. The more these books become separated as canonical, and the more their style becomes the object of careful treatment and exposition, so much the more importance is attached to the preservation of the biblical phrase in the quotation; and after the Hebrew had ceased to be the popular dialect, the Hebrew biblical expressions stood out with all their external distinctness, although translated and paraphrased in Aramaïc. As with the Bible, so it fared with Halacha at a later period, with forms of prayer, and all separate branches of literature. It must, however, be borne in mind, that the Haggada literature, at least the older part of it, and especially the Gnomonics, must not be considered as having been generally produced in a written form.[44] The influence of the Bible on Gnomonics in particular is shown in the following steps: (1.) Biblical precepts were used, unchanged in meaning and expression, as sentiments or favourite sayings of particular persons (e. g. Abot, iv. 19).[45] In this way biblical sayings from the Book of Proverbs, the Psalms, &c., found their way straight into the Koran[46] and the Sunna[47], and at last became common proverbs among the Arabs.[48] (2.) Biblical sentences, unchanged in form, were made by extending or contracting their contents into new expressions of various truths, which had elsewhere been clothed in known proverbs, so that these last were in some sense deduced from the Bible. A wide field was thus opened for the Midrash; and, finally, the words of the Bible were made into proverbs with an entirely different sense.[49] The last result happened also to the Halacha formulæ, which were likewise composed in the form of sententiæ, and consequently became liable to this change of sense.[50] (3.) Lastly, biblical phrases and ideas were used more or less intentionally in newly formed sententiæ[51], and passed into proverbial forms, as they are to be found in the old Halacha (e. g. Peah, ii. 2.). The supremacy of the Bible, considered as sacred both in its subject-matter and in its expression, is the forming and transforming power. Its application depended, in single cases, upon the attention paid by the teacher, speaker, preacher, or collector of fragments, to the way of expressing or clothing his thoughts.[52] The internal character of this Gnomonic literature is marked by a certain chastity, sobriety, and mildness in its satire.[53]

(β.) A less simple form of the Mashal is the more concealed expression in the Riddle and Apologue, Fable and Parable, of which, as it is well known, some specimens occur in the Bible; but although no independent literature of the kind, belonging to this period, is extant, they still form an element of the ethical Haggada, are connected with the Bible by the Midrash, and also stand in close relation to the Gnomonics.[54] The connexion of this with the corresponding literature of the Indians, Persians, Arabians, and Greeks, is as yet too little investigated for us to say anything certain here on the originality and other points touched upon above regarding the Gnomonics. In the Talmud mention is made of *Fables of Foxes* (משלי שועלים) and *Fables of the Dates or of the Washers* (משלי כבסים) [54 a]; and R. MEIR is celebrated as the person in whom the composers of fables became extinct. His cotemporary, BAR KAPPARA, was acquainted with fables and riddles, apparently from Greek sources, and consequently adopts an almost artificial style.[55]

The literature of the ethical Haggada thus consists principally of Gnomology and Morals, the particular parts of which exhibit the gradations of form described above.[56] To this place belong, first, some *apocryphal books*, viz. *Sirach*, which, composed in Hebrew in Palestine, and early translated into Aramaïc, was at a later period enriched with additions at Babylon, and of which particular elements appear in the small work of a later age, *The Alphabet of Ben Sira*, or *Ben Sira's Book* (א"ב דבן סירא ספר בן סירא) [57]; the addition *Of the Wisdom of Zerubabel* in the Pseudo-Ezra; and perhaps also an Aramaïc translation, made from the Greek *Book of Wisdom*. To the earliest ethics, i. e. collections of Halachot with ethical sententiæ, belongs the lost *Megillat Setarim*, or *Megillat Chasidim* (מגלת סתרים מגלת חסידים, Secret Rolls, Book of the Pious), which contained precepts of JOSE BEN

Jehuda (cotemporary of Rabbi), renowned for his piety, his sententious teaching, and his Midrash-like method. The most famous and generally the most important, as well as the oldest, Gnomological work now extant is the Treatise of the Mishna, commonly called *The Sayings of the Fathers*, Capitula Patrum (פרקי אבות מסכת אבות).[58] It consists of five chapters, of which the first four, beginning with the delivering of the Law by Moses to Joshua, &c., contain sayings and sententiæ of sixty-three of the most remarkable Jewish doctors, from Simon the Just to the immediate followers of R. Jehuda Hanasi, and thus through a period of about five centuries. Next follows, as the sixth chapter, a Boraita, called *Chapter on the Acquisition of the Law* (פרק קנין תורה, also ברייתא דאבות).[59] There appear, however, to have existed other Boraitas containing sententiæ of this kind, and likewise called Abot, some of which have found their way into our Mishna. The Gnomology is in general of a double importance : on the one hand, it shows us one of the principal motives for making such collections, giving us historical information on the unbroken chain of authorities in tradition, as characteristics of whom the sententiæ come in[60]; and on the other hand, these sayings became a centre for the Jewish writers on ethics of a later date, who frequently introduced their scientifically developed ethics into these older, and somewhat enigmatical[61], pithy sayings, by means of a commentary, as it was called. These again became, and still are, the subject of many lectures and expositions, translations and editions ; so that they gained a place in the Prayer-Book (for the long afternoon of the Summer Sabbath, originally in the six weeks between Passover and Pentecost). Connected with these is a similar work, *The Abot of R. Natan* (אבות דר' נתן), which, in its present form (in our editions of the Talmud), has, according to *Zunz*, been compiled from three sources—viz. (1.) *The Older Boraita* (or *Mishna*) of R. NATAN; (2.) *Extracts from the Middot* of the same, mentioned above, supposing that this Middot contained ethical arguments, and that it was by the same author, which is now rather doubtful ; and (3.) *Later Additions*, which bring its final redaction into post-Talmudical

times.[61a] One of the lesser treatises noticed above contains a
real and general system of ethics. It consists, in its present
form, of three parts : (1.) *Derech Erez* (מסכת דרך ארץ); (2.)
Derech Erez Minor (ד"א זוטא); (3.) The last chapter, entitled,
Of Peace (פרק השלום). The first, derived from an old nucleus, belongs, from chapter 3. [62], to an earlier date; the
second part, a mirror for the learned, of use even at the
present time, extends to the ninth century. The treatise
Fear of Sin (יראת חטא), of which scarcely any recent
quotations are known, is indeed extant as an appendix
to the Arabic Siddur of Salomo ben Natan of Segelmas (iii. § 19.); but it consists only of the chapters 1—4.
and 9. of our *D. E. Minor*, and is followed immediately by
chapters 5—8. (which in our edition are said to be taken
out of the *Machzor Vitry*); and those last only bear the
name of *Derech Erez Minor*. In the unprinted book *Ha-
Orah of Salomo Isaaki* (§ 206.), the eighth chapter of our
edition is followed by another (not extant in our edition),
where the sentences are exemplified by narrative. Another
manuscript contains, under the title *Hilchot Derech Erez*,
only the first four chapters of the same treatise. The above
circumstances, but recently discovered, may serve to give an
idea of the history of these works in general. Another
offshoot of the ethical Haggada is the work *Tana debe
Eliahu*, or *Seder Eliahu* (סדר אליהו תנא דבי אליהו)[63], which
is divided by a compiled addendum into two parts, distinguished as major and minor (רבה and זוטא). This ethical
Midrash, composed by a Babylonian about A.D. 974, took
its name from the way in which he clothed his subject
(not however maintained strictly throughout),—viz. as instruction given by the Prophet Elias in the school at Jerusalem: it occasionally introduces passages from the Talmud.[64]
In reference to its contents, it is remarkable that the author
carefully inculcates the avoidance of customs not Jewish, as
well as the most exact justice towards those who were not
Jews. There is an apocryphal book of the ethical Haggada,
of a date probably not earlier than the end of the twelfth
century, viz. *Midrash of Contradictions* (מדרש תמורה)[65], in
which the notion that contradictions are necessary in the

world, is treated in the form of a Midrash on Ecclesiast.
iii. 1.   Other small tracts, or rather extracts or compilations, of the Midrash of a later period refer principally to
ethics, although not in a regular form; e. g. a collection
of sentences (3—10.) called *Maase Tora* (מעשה תורה), and
ascribed to RABBENU HAKADOSCH, by which name R.
Jehuda, the author of the Mishna, is commonly called;
and a similar tract, *Chuppat Eliahu* (חופת אליה), continuing
to 11—15.

   b.   *Historical Haggada* (Sagas and Legends).[66]   In
contradistinction to ethical, historical truths occupy only a
subordinate place; but the causes which called forth and
formed the historical Haggada gave it a wide sphere of
action.   We bring those forward which had the greatest influence on the form of these collections, and constitute the
foundation of their division: (1.) The Midrash in general
spun out the historical matter of the Bible like that of
any other work, and interwove it with legends, introducing all the subsequent history of the present and past into
the Bible;[67] the wives and daughter of Muhammed, for instance, are introduced by the Targum into the Pentateuch!
(2.) The *Halacha* offered many meeting-points of history and
legends: on the one hand, there were individual practical
interests, such as the maintaining of *genealogies*, especially
under the conflict of the strong laws of separation, with the
intermixture of races by which the Jews were always
threatened in their Dispersion; or the recollection of the
origin of national or family festivals as connected with their
celebration; or those points in the drawing of documents and
deeds which depend upon chronology and history; — on the
other hand, the whole character and organism of the Halacha
and tradition afforded a vehicle for history and legends.
Even the discussion of the Law often led to a result only
through the mention of some fact; thence we find, as early
as in the Mishna, facts (מעשה) introduced as vouchers for
the Halacha.   Through the importance of personal authority
and through the conscientious strictness requisite for tracing
back a precept to its first originator, and often, indeed,
through a long series of narrators[67a], persons and characters

frequently came into the foreground, and became the objects
of Sagas and Legends. Lastly, the theory of the Halacha
and tradition, — notwithstanding the contradiction which it
met with early at the hands of the Sadducees, the many ob-
scurations which it underwent in the fate of pupils and teachers, and the endless varieties of opinion among the learned,
whose precepts were scarcely even scattered about in collections,—attained to a control over the spiritual descent, as it may
be called, and to the preservation and chronological arrangement of the chain of tradition of the most important teachers.
With this, again, other Haggada elements were readily united,
as was shown above (*a*) in the Mishna Abot. [68] (3.) The form
of narrative, originally a merely semi-poetical clothing for
ethical and Halacha subject-matter, was taken at a later period for more than this.   (4.) With the particular formation
of Haggada literature in general, Saga and Legendary matter
finds its way into collective works. This, however, is brought
about only by external and accidental circumstances, since
the principal tendency of these works is altogether different.
From this point it first attains to an independent literary
structure and form. The latter is in consequence principally
either that of the Midrash, according to the arrangement of
the Bible, or something more independent and chronological,
forming a kind of transition to history, especially the history
of the learned. With respect to the *originality, antiquity,*
and *country* of individual Legends, Sagas, and Stories (actual
fables do not belong here), the same circumstances occur as
in the case of the Gnomonics. But though both of them are
connected with old authorities, still the historical Haggada
in general, as far as its contents are concerned, offers more
criteria for determination of its date even in those places
where it forms a legendary embellishment of the past, at
least in so far as the materials for it have been taken from
the present. The historical Haggada is, indeed, during
several centuries the only source for Jewish history; and yet
it has hitherto been far too much neglected in this respect.
The determination of the originality of certain groups of
Sagas and Legends is more difficult; for while the Gnome
and the Proverb once formed, generally speaking always

preserve their original type, the Saga receives a new birth at the hands of the narrator, or, like an avalanche, increases in its course, and gradually becomes more concrete by the addition of names[69], numbers, &c.; so that its origin is difficult to discover, and an arrangement of it according to even great periods is almost impossible. To the critic of Jewish Sagas, the study of the general history of Sagas is quite as indispensable and important as the consideration of the Jewish is to the student of Sagas in general. The originality of the Jewish Sagas, and their power of accommodating themselves to foreign circumstances, render this a profitable task; and the connexion between the two is by no means confined to the later periods of romance (iii. § 20.), but may be followed up to its first commencement in the East. Both the *Christian* and *Muhammedan*[70] legends have been developed from the Jewish; and one or two valuable attempts have been made at explaining the New Testament and the Koran by means of the latter. If the elements of the Muhammedan are to be found only in the more recent Haggada writings[71] and in the later Rabbies[72], it is still difficult to decide whether the latter authors have not drawn from older Jewish, independently of the foreign, sources. We will not, however, deny the natural tendency of Jewish authors to consider matters as originally Jewish (cf. note 25.), although such a conclusion is supported only by a total ignorance of their real source. A striking instance has been pointed out in a different field of literature; viz. tales, &c., of the celebrated Greek Barlaam and Josaphat (§ 20.), quoted in Hebrew works as sayings of old Rabbies! Moreover, the biblical legends contain traditional elements of historical and philological import, in the garb of the Midrash.[73]

The offshoots of the historical Haggada stretch far into the following period of Judæo-Arabian science, and these take the place of historical science. The first traces of it are to be found in the Bible itself.[74] At this point begin the exposition and extension of history, the clothing of ethical truths in a historical garb; and thence the oral and written Haggada, with their mutual reaction, proceed onwards without any perceptible variety or interruption. Unlike the Halacha, the Midrash does not distinguish between canonical and uncanonical books; and only important epochs of history produce any modification, and that but partial, in its course and contents. For the historical Haggada overshadows the fate of the nation and of individuals with its wide-spread wings, whilst it points out a deeper ethical significance in the wonders of Omnipotence, and daily unfolds higher truths to be learnt from new marvels. The divisions of the historical Haggada would then coincide with those of the Jewish national history, if the literary works of that time were at all more numerous. Before the period of the last general Dispersion, which coincides with the commencement of Christian literature, and with the first attempts at a redaction of the Mishna, the more important facts of history had been illustrated by the Haggada. This had been done, in some degree, in particular writings, either preserved as apocrypha, or known only from fragments, citations, and later editions[75]; such are the *Additions to Esther and Daniel*, the story of *Aristeas* about the composition of the Septuagint, all in the Hebrew, Aramaïc, or Greek language. The historical work of *Flavius Josephus* also draws in many places from the living fountain of the Haggada, and must be estimated from that point of view.[76]

The following are the most important and characteristic works : —

(*a.*) *The Period of the Talmud* (A.D. 140—500). To this belong several historical Midrashim, which are no longer extant in their original form, amongst which some are of a mixed character. The *Easter Haggada* (הגדת פסח), devoted to the ritual of Easter eve (סדר), and called Haggada, *par excellence*, on account of its general use, is partly of a Halacha character. Its origin, together with the ritual itself, probably reaches far into antiquity; and to it passages of Mishna, Tosefta, Mechilta, Sifri, and Talmuds, and, in later times, prayers and hymns, have gradually been added.[77] Originating in the Halacha, but important as a historical source, is the *Megillat Taanit* (מגלת תענית, fast-roll), extant in Aramaïc as early as the beginning of the second century; originally it was a list of historical days of re-

joicing, on which people were not to fast, and with it
Stories and Sagas became connected. The work printed
under this name [78] is, however, a commentary on fragments
of the original work, of a later date indeed, but, according
to Zunz, known as early as the eighth century (?). To the
numerous lost *Books of the Haggada* (ספרי הגדה) [79] belongs
Megillat Juchasin (מגלת יוחסין, genealogical roll), of which
there were probably several after the Babylonian Captivity,
owing to the interests above noticed [80], and perhaps also an
apocryphal *Book of Adam* (ספא דאדם) [81], which, however,
is by no means to be identified with the *Life of Adam*, or
Apocalypse of Moses, or *Lesser Genesis;* a book containing,
indeed, Haggada elements, but bearing evident marks of the
Alexandrian or Christian Pseudepigraphy. [82]

(β.) *The Period of the Gaonim.* The Tannaim and
Amoraim, the heroes and victors in " The War of Doctrine,"
as Jews and Muhammedans called the study of Theology [83],
the martyrs for belief and knowledge, gradually attain to
the position of the old kings and chiefs, in the field of the
Saga, and become at once its subject and object ; whilst their
names, renowned by their doctrine and deeds, are finally
transformed into mythical persons, into categories for ethical
allegory. This allegory freely uses the plentiful subject-
matter for stories found in the Halacha and Haggada literature ; at an early stage it works with self-consciousness,
and not without regard to the literary form, but finally
it degenerates into actual Pseudepigraphy. This last character, however, designates the productions of the later Gaonic
times (A. D. 800—1040), when the historical Haggada, under
the influence of science, which was awakening in Babylon,
was continued in two distinct directions, that of history and
chronology, and that of ethical narrative. Some few books,
however, remained isolated with regard to the estimation in
which they were held and the influence which they exerted,
as the *Book of Serubabel* [84] ; or else belonged to the epi-
goni of an earlier period, as the Aramaïc *Book of An-
tiochus* (מגלת אנטיוכוס) [85], which received some support from
its connexion with the feast of Chanuca (encæniorum). While
we postpone the principal really literary labours of this pe-

riod, which belong to chronology, history, and the biography
of the learned, such as *Seder Olam Sulta, Seder Tannaim,
Josippon,* &c., to the main part of this essay, we will conclude the survey of the historical Haggada with some old
biblical and post-biblical groups of Sagas, whose tendency is
rather to afford information, relaxation, and entertainment.
The time of their composition or redaction for the most part
cannot be accurately determined. The following works
treat of *biblical Sagas,* generally in a semi-poetical Hebrew,
and in a more and more puristic biblical language; e. g. the
History of Abraham (מעשה דאברהם אבינו) [86], written perhaps
partly after the Arabian legends [87], in a later Hebrew, and
not to be confounded with a recent translation from Oriental
sources. The wars of the sons of Jacob are treated of in the
Midrash Wajjisu (מדרש ויסעו) [88], i. e. of Genesis, xxxv. 5., and
the Life of Moses in the *Chronicle of Moses* (דברי הימים של
משה), and the older *Midrash of the Death of Moses* (מדרש פטירת
משה) [89], which resembles special exegesis. Even a tract, inscribed *Midrash of Goliath the Philistine* (מדרש של גלית
הפלשתי), has been found by the author in an old manuscript
of the Bodleian library. The *Histories of Solomon* (משלים של
שלמה) [90] are legends of an Arabian cast. One of the most
favourite themes is the *History of Asmodai* (מעשה אשמדי),
the king of the Dæmons, who deceived Solomon, and sat
on his throne for some time. The foundation of the legend,
which is already traced in the Babylonian Talmud, is the
passage in Ecclesiastes (i. 12.), I, Kohelet, "have been" king,
&c. The learned Silvestre de Sacy, speaking *en passant* of
an imperfect manuscript of this tale (of which a later Hebrew
recension is printed in a collection mentioned below), thinks
that he is " abusing the patience of the reader by dwelling
on such a frivolous subject," which is familiar to him as the
source of the Muhammedan legend in the Koran, where
Asmodai is called " Sachr ; " while Rapoport digs psychological and ethical ideas out of the fanciful Oriental legend,
which he compares, not without reason, to the German
" Faust." It may be remarked, by the way, that even the
mission of Asmodai for the " Shamir " seems to be alluded
to in the Koran (xxi. 82., xxxviii. 36.).

Of *Talmudical Sagas* we mention those which are brought
into connexion with a celebrated Haggadist himself, R.
Joshua ben Levi.   A legend of his being taught in one
of his journeys by the prophet Elias, that the justice of God
is not to be judged by appearances, is now well known
through the Koran (where Moses is substituted for our
Rabbi), and also through many metrical versions.   Another
legend of his entering alive into Paradise, called *History of
R. Joshua ben Levi* (מעשה דר' יהושע בן לוי), has been
spun out and wrought into what may be called the first
" Divina Commedia,"[91] It is to be remarked, that in the most
common Hebrew recension of this legend, the Rabbi is begged
by another Rabbi to look " whether there are Gentiles in
Paradise or Jews in Hell," of which question only the latter
part is answered in the affirmative, and that indirectly.   The
tale was afterwards metamorphosed into an " epistle" of
Rabbi Joshua himself; and some cabalistic author of the
fourteenth century (?) forged an appendix, where all the
wise and pious of Paradise are said to be studying some
remarkable works : amongst them, *R. Simon ben Yochai* is
reading the book Idra (part of the Sohar)!   But our legend
seems to have previously undergone several combinations
with eschatological ideas and fancies, which are to be met
with in different recensions, under the titles of *Treatise of
Paradise* or *Hell* (מסכת גן עדן מסכת גיהנם), and which themselves have been otherwise combined with the tracts on the
Torment of the Grave (חיבוט הקבר), *Creation of the Child*
(יצירת הולד), &c.   The *Hechalot* (see § 13.) are closely and
especially connected with this legend, as well as with the
History of the Ten Martyrs (עשרה הרוגי מלכות מעשה
דהרוגי מלכות), called also *Midrash elle Eskera* (מדרש אלה
אזכרה), a description of the execution of ten renowned Mishna
Doctors of the second century[92], and many others.   The *Midrash of the Ten Commandments*[93] (מדרש עשרת הדברות)
is a collection of stories on the contents of the Decalogue,
the subjects being mostly taken from the Talmud.   One
of the two different recensions, although printed four times
under the title, *History of the Decalogue* (מעשים של עשרת
הדברות), has escaped the notice of even the editor of the

Beth ha-Midrash (1853). We consider neither the histories nor the precepts to be the principal object of the writer, but rather the illustration of the Decalogue; and we would range the work under that class of Homiletics which is closely connected with the liturgy (cf. below, *d.*). It partakes also of a hymnical character, reminding us strongly of various Arabic hymns on the Decalogue, one of which is printed under the name of SAADIA GAON. No less unknown hitherto was a collection of histories, printed also four times with the Midrash of the Decalogue, under the title : *Collection of Histories, Midrashot and Haggadot* (חיבור המעשיות והמדרשות והגדות). It contains twenty pieces, without any visible connexion, some of which are to be met with in separate manuscripts, and are very old. But our literature is not deficient in larger and better collections; for example, one composed for his father-in-law, by NISSIM THE GAON, as a book of consolation and morals, and, according to Rapoport's probable supposition, either entirely or partly in the Arabic language. [93a]

c. *The Secret Doctrine* is that part of the Haggada which has had the greatest interest for Christian students, on account of its pretended reference to Christianity, and of its supposed identity with the later Kabbala, which also numbered Christians among its disciples. This latter tried to gain the authority of antiquity by means of intentional pseudepigraphy; but, on the other hand, the Jews protested against it at an early period. By the thoroughly critical investigations of Rapoport and Zunz[93b] however, the historical separation of the two has been established on a sure footing, which cannot be injured by superficial investigations or by arguments apparently critical, whose evidences are taken from delusive and suspected sources, nor by arbitrary selections of individual points, and combinations built thereupon.[94] A solution of the important questions which here meet us, can be obtained only from a more accurate and thorough acquaintance with Oriental philosophy, especially that of ancient Persia and of Syrian Arabia in the middle ages. But until this be effected, the external means of

E

criticism (especially for the fixing of dates) must guide and
determine our judgment.

If religious and moral truths have generally expressed
themselves with precision in law and custom, and the national consciousness has found a home in history and sagas,
reference being made in writing and speaking to the original source of all things; then the highest metaphysical
questions on the essence of God and his relation to the world,
must needs have occupied the minds of individual thinkers
even at an early period, and the apparent contradiction between the prophetical images of visions and wonders, and the
great idea of the " I am that I am," must have driven men
to reflexion.   An impulse in this direction might be traced
in the fact of the intellectual centre of the nation having
been carried away to Chaldæa[95], a country by its position
well suited to the observation of the heavens, and one which
had at an early period emerged from unthinking Paganism
to the more developed form of Dualism (Lam. 3, 38.).   Thus
on the old ethical and political prophecies there was grafted a
metaphysical offshoot, fantastical in its expression, and having
a tendency to become systematised, just as the introduction
of a syncretic philosophy into the images of Scripture was
produced only by the confluence of the minds of the East and
West in the Western-Asiatic Hellenism and Alexandrianism.
The whole field of Jewish wisdom (חכמה) in the highest
sense[96] was collected, under the influence and form of the Midrash, into two principal groups, comprising the two spheres of
being, heaven and earth.   Under the names, *The Doctrine
of the Divine Throne* (מעשה מרכבה) and *The Doctrine of
Creation* (מעשה בראשית)[97], it proceeds to treat, in the Midrash manner, of the vision of Ezechiel (also Is. vi., Jacob's
dream, and Moses's vision), and the history of the creation
(Gen. i. 1.); of the doctrines of the essence, attributes,
influences, (names,[98]) and manifestations of God, of the
heavenly courts, stars, and angels[99], and also of the first and
continuous growth and nature of creatures.   For this reason it was properly called by Maimonides, "metaphysics and
physics."   To this part of our subject belong some matters
connected with the above, taken from the Parsee doctrine

of dæmons, astrology, chiromancy and sympathetic healing, treated of in certain Boraitas as before mentioned; and also some treatises on the hidden *grounds* and tendencies of the precepts, which, belonging rather to special exposition, were designated *Mysteries of the Law* (סתרי, רזי תורה)[100], and were at variance with blind faith.　The union of all these subjects in a systematic whole marks out the later Kabbala.

The exposition of the vision of Ezechiel is older than the *Chronicles*, and that of the chapter on the creation older than *Sirach*, who cautions the reader against it; the influence of the Alexandrine school is visible in the book of *Wisdom* and Philo affords philosophical elements for the later Kabbala.[101] This Midrash, from its nature, could only be the work of individuals.　Its consequences, dangerous to strict monotheism, and its practical effect upon the Halacha of the time, demanded and obtained the strictest forethought and consideration among the Jewish wise men in Babylon and Palestine, of whose labours on this subject only a few traces are extant. On this alone rests our designation, *Secret Doctrine*.[102]　It is not impossible, although improbable, that individual litterati had written something of this kind on *Secret Rolls*, but in the period of the Talmud and earlier Gaonim there seems to have been no *literature*, certainly none in the popular dialect (the Aramaïc).[103]　The first really literary productions appear so late, that we prefer to treat them in connexion with the following period (§ 13.).

B.　*The special* or *expository Haggada* (Midrash strictly so called)[103a] is in some sense the old Jewish Exegesis and Homiletics, and aims at an explanation of the text, without excluding the tendencies and methods of the general Haggada, or even those of the Halacha.　On the contrary, it sometimes applies and makes use of them in constructing a whole, of which the text forms the centre.　The works are collected from fragments, and in their complete form constitute a kind of commentary on particular books of Holy Scripture, and are named after them, as Bereshit (Genesis) Rabba, Midrash of the Psalms, &c.　So far, however, as they for the most represent the usual cycle of Sabbath and Festival Lectures (Sermons and Homilies), their particular sections are divided and called after the divisions of the Pentateuch (*Parshiot*), or those of the prophets (*Haftarot*), and after the five *Megillot* received into the ritual; consequently Midrashim on particular books of the Pentateuch, written at different periods, would in an uncritical age be treated as a whole, e. g. *Midrash Rabbot*. The exposition extended itself to everything that could be brought into connexion with the text, and thereby introduced, by an almost imperceptible combination of ideas, the most distant objects. The materials swelled like an avalanche; the later Midrash having reference to the older, and the collectors being not very particular in the selection of their matter. They expounded the whole contents of Scripture, even the names[104], and not unfrequently the exposition itself[105], laying particular stress sometimes on the contents sometimes on the expression, any external features of which served as a connecting link for the interpretation. Of these we will mention only the best known: the Masoretic definitions, alphabetical changes, abbreviations, numerical value of the letters (*Geometria, Grammataia, Notarikon, Temura*), and even the similarity of words in foreign languages. [106]   As regards the form and arrangement of particular lectures and collections, we may perceive some progress in the care and art bestowed on them; although, from the influences described above, it could never have attained to any high degree of excellence.

Further investigations are still requisite for the *special history* of this Midrash, the principal literary works of which have been subjected by Rapoport and Zunz to a general critical examination. The oldest traces of such an exposition may be found in the *Bible* and *Apocrypha*.[107]   At the time of the redaction of the Mishna there were certain *Books of Haggada* which were studied, although not without some fear of the misuse of free thought if it were allowed to become paramount; but these are known to us principally by fragments and quotations from existing works.

The special Haggada consists (1.) of great and important Midrashim on the entire Pentateuch, or on particular books of it, and also on the prophets and the Hagiographa; (2.) of lesser and later offshoots of the Haggada on the particular sections of Scriptures. To the first belong the ten Mid-

rashim known˜by the name *Midrash Rabba* (*Rabbot*) on the
Pentateuch, and the five Megillot, of which the earliest (Genesis) was completed as early as the sixth, and the latest
(Numbers) in the twelfth century. A complete cycle of
lectures corresponding to the Pericopes of remarkable days
is formed by the old *Pesikta*[108], begun about A. D. 700, the
text of which as restored from fragments in an edition of the
Pesikta Rabbati about two centuries later (composed A. D.
845), and from other quotations, is calculated to give an idea
of the history of the Midrash; to which we may add that
Zunz's investigations are fully borne out by researches in
MS. works. In the *Midrash Tanchuma*, or *Tanchuma-Jelamdenu*, the history of which as exhibited by its text is no
less peculiar, we have the oldest expository Haggada, originally comprising the whole Pentateuch. It was collected
probably in South Italy, in the second half of the 9th century.
Among the non-pentateuchal Midrashim, *the Midrash of the
Psalms* (called also *Shocher Tob*) belongs to the same country,
and as regards the older half (1—118.), to a still earlier date.

The *Boraita* of R. ELIESER (BEN HYRCAN)[109], composed in
Palestine, Syria, or Asia Minor, shows a peculiar character
with respect to its arrangement and contents. It is an incomplete Pentateuch Midrash, with an intentionally false
name ; it contains some lengthy disquisitions on the objects
of worship, of the ethical and historical Haggada, and of secret
doctrine, and in its artificial arrangement answers to the
benedictions of the prayer *Shemone esra* (see inf. § 6.).

Of the second class of special Haggada, the relation of which
to the liturgy (cf. above, p. 49.) we hope to see illustrated
by the master Zunz himself, we may mention, out of the eight
works noticed by Zunz, the *Midrash Vajosha*, or מדרש על
שירת הים (on Exod. xiv. 30. sq.), which contains the first form
of the old Armillus (Romulus) legend after the analogy of
the Arabian Deggiâl (دجّال), and a small *Midrash Esther*.

These various Haggada works, of which we have taken
a rapid sketch, constitute the creative period, and consequently that most fruitful in literature. Even the collective
works of the time show, at least in the treatment of their
materials, a certain generative power and independence. It

is not impossible to follow the whole length of the stream in its manifold intersections, as an unbroken natural channel, up to the living source. Gradually the course of the stream comes to a stand still, its bed is lost in the sand, while canals and artificial reservoirs carry off the water. In the place of the productive energy of the Haggada and Midrash, the 11th century presents to us nothing but servile extracts, compilations, and comprehensive collections made from all sources. But these latter belong to the succeeding period; for the new elements which indicate the termination of one period are in fact the beginning of another, just as the extinction of the Midrash itself is perceived by means of the new elements by which the epochs are marked out. They were however, from a general want of criticism, placed in the series of the old Midrashim. Moreover, the less independent, the more faithful, and the more unmeaning the compilation, the less accurately can its date be determined. These compilations, and especially the larger and more comprehensive of them, contain elements of works either lost or but little known to us, and consequently afford materials, in many respects important, for the criticism of the Midrash. We will mention here only the best-known work; *Midrash Jalkut*, by R. Simon Kara (see § 9.).

This brief development might justify the assertion made above, that a more intimate acquaintance with the Midrash literature, in which nearly all the mental energy of a people, equal at least in this respect to its contemporaries, is concentrated and reflected throughout more than 1000 years, is worth, and actually needs, a lengthened and unprejudiced examination of details. Few, however, seem inclined to undertake this labour.

§ 6.] *Liturgy.*[1]

Since we have found in the literature of the Halacha and Haggada an expression for all the intellectual interests of life, we shall not expect prayer to have been an isolated development. And, in fact, the whole liturgical literature of the Jews stands in the closest connexion with the development of the Midrash, and particularly with the earlier period of its foundation, in which the Jewish prayers assumed their peculiar character.[2] For the usual Jewish prayer-book consists of elements belonging to a period of 1000 years, and offers to criticism a field of greater difficulties than the Midrash, from the absence of all external criteria; while the accounts preserved in the Midrash, of prayers being composed by certain Rabbies, must be received with caution, as the prayers now in use with the same beginnings have in many cases been enlarged. Moreover those Rabbies must not be considered as their authors, but merely as having handed them down.[3] Other prayers, not received into the liturgy, have still to be collected from the Midrash literature[4], and are of importance for our historical development.

The Bible recognises but one kind of public worship incumbent as a matter of duty, viz. the sacrificial worship at Jerusalem, with which certain confessions of sins and ritual formularies are connected; and in general it leaves prayer to the requirements of individuals. Of independent forms of prayer there is no mention anywhere made; still some of the psalms and prayers anterior to the captivity may have been composed for worship or introduced into it, and finally have become disseminated among the people. If other individual prayers were composed and written at that time, they belong to history, not to the law. To the interruption of the sacrificial worship, to the revolution in the popular dialect, to the more extended development of the religious consciousness by the later conflicts, to the influence of the schools and the Halacha, which made everything the object of law, is to be ascribed the general fixing and formularising of prayer; so that the commencement of a liturgy falls at earliest in the time of the great synod, when, together with the restoration of the sacrificial worship, prayer accompanied with teaching from the Bible took an independent position.

t what time men began to pray at stated hours, and consequently to have a fixed ritual, when and how congregations first met for prayers and public worship elsewhere than at the Temple, and when the relation between *reciter of prayers* Cantor (חזן, שליח צבור) and congregation (קהל) was developed,

are questions not yet satisfactorily determined; nor has it
even been asked, whether the ancient prayers were propagated
orally, or written down by their composers ! On the whole it
is certain, (1.) that prayer is connected with the development
of the Midrash, in so far as in the case of the history of Midrash,
additions, extensions, and embellishments gradually grew up
around the old nucleus of prayers, whether originally composed
for general use, or first introduced into public worship at a
later time; until, finally, the Midrash itself encroached upon
prayer : (2.) that a considerable portion of the oldest prayers
grouped itself about passages from the Bible, and thus approached very near to the Haggada, so that in general, to use
the expression of a Talmud Doctor[5], a form of prayer enjoined
as a duty at particular times can no longer be regarded
as confined to the narrow limits of mere feeling: (3.) that
the Halacha and Haggada lectures gave occasion to prayer
meetings, and conversely.   The prayers when once fixed and
circulated came into a certain analogy with the Bible ; they
were cited, instead of the passages of the Bible on which they
were founded[6], they were used as texts for the construction of
Midrash[7], and their form of expression involuntarily returned
to the memory.[8]   We learned above (§ 5. 2 b.) to recognise
Easter Haggada as something between liturgy and Midrash.
At a later time the Halacha found its way into the daily
ritual.

  The *language* of the older prayers, particularly the ritual,
is Hebrew; a few only are Aramaïc, as the *Kaddish*
(קדיש), originally a form for concluding Haggada lectures.[9]
Their *style* likewise has its history.   The oldest are little
else than compilations of Biblical sentences, together with
actual pieces of the Bible ; and throughout the whole period
they maintain a Biblical Hebraism.   The language is simple
and clear, without any artificial form, without any congeries
of synonymes, and their tone is consequently hearty and
elevating.   At a later period they first adopt a kind of
artificial form in composition, with inflexional rhymes and
alphabetical acrostics ; as is the case in the Books of Lamentations, Psalms, and in the Targum Esther.[10]   On the
other hand, actual rhyme and acrostics of names belong to
the following period.

The liturgical literature is divided in its progress into two classes, not entirely distinct: (1.) The general *prayers for Divine service* or worship in a restricted sense, which are obligatory on each individual, and are not connected with any definite occasions; as are (2.) the *Benedictions* (ברכות) at meals, on the performance of certain cere-monies, at lectures, &c., which we will not particularise further, as they do not exercise any actual influence on the later literature. The former class comprises daily and fes-tival prayers (in which are reckoned those for all remarkable days, such as fasts, &c.). The daily prayer was developed out of the two oldest principal groups of the liturgy, which, on account of the general character of their contents, are entirely adapted to public worship. The first was called by its initial word, the *Shema* (שמע), afterwards also *Reading of the Shema* (קריאת שמע), and was originally a mere collection of pieces of the Bible, in which the acknowledgment of the unity of God, and the memory of his government of Israel, are expressed. It was probably introduced in or after the period of the Syrian war, as a morning and evening prayer, and was enlarged with suitable additions. The other group, the *Tefilla* (תפלה) [11], the actual supplication, contained a form of hymnical Introit and Exit, with the addition of the sacerdotal blessing (דוכן, originally, *pulpit* of the priest). The nucleus gradually grew into twelve sayings (ברכות), and thence the whole took the name *Prayer of the Eighteen (say-ings)*, (תפלת שמונה עשרה); and this name was preserved for the corresponding prayers of the Sabbath and festivals, which contained, instead of the twelve supplications, a proper hymn of, triplets referring to the offering proper to the festival.[11 a] And since on these days an additional offering, *Musaf* (מוסף), was made, there were formed similarly for this an *eighteen prayers*, which was called Musaf. After the complete cessation of the sacrificial worship, prayers received a greater extension; the Halacha exalted prayer to a vicarious duty, and thus involved its formularisation almost as a necessary conse-quence. In the synagogues and schools teaching and prayer went on; and the president of the academy was generally also director of public worship (ריש סדרא, later ראש הסדר).[12]

The agrarian signification of the principal feasts was, in prayer and preaching, gradually pushed more and more into the background by its religio-historical signification (e. g. the offering of the firstlings at the Pentecost, by the commemoration of the giving of the Law). Amongst them the day of Commemoration (subsequently the New Year's day, and day of Judgment), and especially the day of Atonement and Fast day, must at an early period, on account of their original meaning and importance, have had a longer liturgy, in which preaching and prayer had a part, following immediately upon the extraordinary sacrificial worship. We have mentioned Krochmal's opinion above (§ 4.), that at an early period a description of the Temple ritual on the day of Atonement was composed for liturgical purposes.[13] By degrees the lecture of the doctor, also on the subject of the Temple ritual, naturally passed into the hands of the reciter of prayers, since they were often both the same person. In earlier times the reciter of prayers spoke in public worship as the *plenipotentiary of the congregation* (שליח צבור, later קרובא, as in Aramaïc), and the congregation joined only in the " Amen " and short responses. This, with the old variations, now extant, and also the argumentum a silentio, that in the Talmud nothing upon liturgical writings occurs, makes it more than probable, that the older prayers were not circulated among the people in writing.[14] By their spreading from the centre of authority, by the gradual interpolations of individual doctors and reciters, by the tendency to arrange and settle things constantly evinced by the Halacha (as the object of which certain prayers were now considered), by the continually increasing care in retaining that which was once produced, by the growing respect for learned writers and the need of a uniform public worship, and by a combination of all these causes, the dissemination of written prayers must have gradually advanced. Among the authorities in the period of the Talmud who were active in composing or fixing the liturgy, we may mention GAMALIEL II. and R. JOCHANAN in Palestine, RAB and SAMUEL in Babylon.

From the time of the Saboraim and the first Gaonim, the history of the liturgy is obscure; but it is improbable that there was any great activity on the subject.[15]   Prayer took a new form from the liturgical poetry of the next period.

§ 7.] *The earliest Jewish Literature of Arabia.*

With the extension of power which Judaism received in the first century after Christ in Arabia (in its widest sense), and with the religious controversies which necessarily occurred, it was impossible for the Jews of Arabia to be destitute of all science, as their heathen countrymen were at the time of *Ignorance* (Djahelijje).   The inhabitants particularly of the small kingdoms to the north (Hira, Ghassan, Hidjaz, Nabatæa, and Idumæa) were too near to Palestine not to take part in its civilisation and literature.   The "Religion of Abraham" of the Arabian Jews is a Muhammedan invention easily explained; and the legends of the two learned Jews of the lineage of Karisa, in Medina, who prophesied of Muhammed and converted the Tobba[1], can at best be treated only as a sign of the existence of Jewish learning in Arabia, with which the journey of R. Akiba thither, and the mention of a learned Jew Malluch in the Talmud[2], coincide.   At the same time, single Beduin families might have remained untainted with Rabbinism.

The *Judæo-Arabic literature*[3], the importance of which will be demonstrated in the following period, shows early traces of being the (genuine) national literature of the country; for contemporarily with *Amriolkais*, the Singer of a Moallaka (i. e. a golden song), the Jew SAMUEL BEN ADIJJÂ whose friendship for him was proverbial, and others but recently made known by Hammer, composed their poems.   The important Rabbinical elements of the *Koran* indicate a certain cooperation on the part of learned Jews and Jewish renegades.   As such the following may be mentioned: ABDALLAH BEN ES SELÂM, FINHAS (BEN AZURA), and according to some (but with less probability), WERKA BEN NAUFIL and the monk BAHIRA, or BOHEIRA.   As a main authority for the *Sunna*, we have KAAB OL AKBAR; and one of the oldest Islamite sects, the Sabaites, who deified the Khalif Ali, derives its origin from the Jewish renegade ABDALLAH BEN SABA.   We soon see the Jews also take an

active part in those sciences which necessarily established
themselves in the first warlike centuries of Islamism, e. g.
ABU HAFSA JEZID, a physician in Yemen, who professed
Islamism to Omar (A. D. 650); and MÂSERGEWEIH of Bosra
(A. D. 683), who translated the Syriac medical Pandects of
the presbyter Aaron into Arabic.

But up to this point the participation in the Arabian literature is rather isolated, without direct influence on the
whole, and having some other analogy with the literatures of
the other lands of the Dispersion. The wide-spread dominion
of the Arabian power and science first brought about a
general development of Jewish literature; and with this we
enter upon the next Period.

PERIOD II.

FROM THE BEGINNING OF ARABIAN SCIENCE TO THE EXILE OF THE JEWS FROM SPAIN.

FROM THE EIGHTH TO THE FIFTEENTH CENTURY.

§ 8.] *Introduction and General View.*

THE beginning of the Second Period is not without analogy
to the First. The First Period, that of the Midrash, lay
in the obscure age of the great synod, and its literary productions refer to the Bible and the Apocryphas. The introduction of Greek and Roman culture called forth religious
parties, and required a more distinct formation in faith and
society; and finally, the Midrash, in all its breadth and depth,
was developed from the complete canon of Scripture. In
like manner, at the time of the middle Gaonim (8th century),
were formed the first seeds of the new Arabian science, preserved to us almost like scattered plants on the broad ground
of the Midrash. The new wisdom gradually becoming
universal, met and arrested the living creative power of the
Midrash, made the Midrash itself the object of scientific
inquiry, and gave a definite form to scientific and religious

systems and schools. This second period is distinguished from the first by very important characteristics. The development took place at once with the Dispersion, under the influence of different nationalities and languages, and of two complete religious systems springing from Judaism. It proceeded more from literature than life, and, being founded on the foregoing period, was in general richer and more diversified. Moreover, the individuality of the author becomes now better ascertained; and the particular writings receive the stamp of an intellectual purpose, acting with due attention to the outward form, as may be perceived in the division, &c., and in the titles[1] of the books. Finally, oral tradition gave way to written literature. We find that this period also began with the formation of an actual sect, the *Karaites* (about 750); and immediately afterwards[2] the *Arabian language* became the usual organ for the new objects and forms of thoughts. Reference to geographical position, and its historical influence on particular intellectual tendencies is also more apparent.

The most general type is afforded by the distinction between the countries under *Christian* or *Muhammedan*[3] dominion. From Babylon and Irak, where the Gaonim and Khalifs held the ecclesiastical and civil power, the Arabian science and language together with the study of the Halacha flowed with the Arabs over Northern Africa and Spain, and reached Southern Italy and the South of France (Provence). Both of these countries afterwards occupied an influential position. We name this school after its chief representative (Spain) the *Sefaradic* (from ספרד, with the Rabbies, Spain). Palestine was now suffering from the inroads and wars of the wild hordes of the East, and had lost its literary importance, being unable to raise itself from Masora and Midrash to more independent study. But from that country when the Talmud was in full vigour, the Halacha and Haggada had spread over Asia Minor, Greece, Northern Italy, France, and Germany; and towards the end of the 9th century a closer connexion between Germany, Northern Italy, and France was promoted by means of an important learned family, whom the king of France brought from Lucca to

Mayence.[4] The scientific activity of the Jews under the
Arabian dominion had thrown into the background the
separate study of the Halacha, which however was indispensable to religious life ; and thus they became dependent
for it upon the Babylonian Gaonim. But this came to an end
when in the 10th century the Jewish literature of Europe
finally took the foremost place.[5]   An effect described
below more in detail was produced by Italy, through the
means of certain influential personages, upon various kinds of
literature.   Amongst other things the transplanting of three
distinguished learned men from Bari to Kahira, Kairovân,
and Cordova (948—960), gradually emancipated men's minds
from the Halacha authority of the Gaonim, which in 1037
completely fell to the ground with the Babylonian academies.[6]
Spain now independent (united with Mauritania) had not
long been adorned with the noblest specimens of Judæo-
Arabian literature, when the fanaticism of the Almohaden
threatened to crush it (about 1150) ; but this fanaticism,
in conjunction with the movement of the Crusades, only
caused them to be transplanted to the north-east (Provence).[7]

The 12th century forms a new era in this period.   In it
began, not only the important development of Talmudical
learning among the glossatores of Northern France and
Germany, but also the influential activity of the *translators*
from the Arabic in Provence.   By them Arabian science
was made accessible to the Jews of France and Italy.   In its
more consistent formation, however, it became a stumbling-
block by the religious system of Maimonides.   And thence
arose, in the 13th century, the sharp polemical dispute
about philosophising, which ended (1306) in the prohibition of the early study of philosophy.   The intellectual
tendencies of this century generally, even in the West, had
approached one another more nearly. *Toledo* had become the
Jerusalem to which the combatants of the pen had drawn
together to obtain Arabian learning for the benefit of the
Christian faith ; and Jews or Jewish apostates were here the
usual channels through which they obtained it.[8] But the
more the Arabs were driven back by the power of Christian

Spain, so much the more did the treasure which the Jews
had to offer become an object of desire. Thus we find in the
13th century Christian princes, for example, the Emperor
Frederic II. (1232), King *Alphonso* the Wise (1256—1277),
Charles of Anjou (1279), and *Robert* of Anjou (1319),
mentioned as protectors and favourers of Jewish litterati.[9]
This however did not happen without exciting bitterness on
the part of fanaticism and envy [10]; which vented itself in the
numerous writings of this century hostile to the Jews, and
occasioned persecutions of the Jews, and the burning of
Jewish books. *Manfred* is said to have translated a pseudo-
Aristotelian work, as it seems from the Hebrew. The intellectual intercourse between Jews and Christians, in the
countries where the language of literature (the Latin) was
more accessible to the Jews, from its affinity with the
vernacular, was far greater than the deficient state of inquiry into that very interesting subject might lead us to suppose; and it has even recently been ascribed to subordinate
causes. At the same time, through the western syncretism
in Provence and Southern Italy, where the Arabian-Spanish
and the Judæo-Christian lines of thought met, the new
Kabbala with its *pseudepigraphic* literature was developed,
in opposition to the rational school, out of the old secret
teaching. In the 14th and 15th centuries this literature
took possession of the leading minds, not only of the darker
North where the light of Arabian science had not penetrated,
where no sunshine of culture and humanity had warmed the
soil, and where systematic superstition reigned both in the
schools and in society, but also of the more cultivated South.
This may be ascribed to the fact that science, having passed
out of the fruitful stage of struggle into that of peaceful possession and cultivation, had lost in depth what it had gained
in breadth; Christian scholasticism being, by its nature,
able to react upon the Jewish only polemically, and indeed herself soon becoming a disciple of the Jewish Kabbala.
Jewish literature, in general, not excepting even the subject
of theology, took a prominent part in the different Romance
languages, and in the learned Latin, in the way either of
original composition or of translation and editorial labours.

From the 13th century, the Italian school approaches nearer
to the Spanish, and at last absorbs the best strength of the
Spanish exile.   These are the outlines of the intellectual
movement, which future investigation must illustrate.

We must now consider briefly what disciplines were
brought into shape during this period, pointing out their
connexion with the literature of the first period. This
must be done in order that the *encyclopædic division*, here
to be developed, may be followed by a closer observation
of what was doing in the particular departments.

In the First Period nearly the whole literature was ranged
under the great banner of the Midrash, and we distinguish
as principal groups, Halacha, Haggada, Targum, and Prayer.
Of independent science in the stricter sense, there was
none.   This first found entrance among the Jews through
the Arabs;   although certain Jews, as for example Mâ-
SERGEWEIH (683), MASHALLAH (754—813), SAHL ET
THABERI (800—830), with his son the renegade, and
others, cooperated by their translation of Greek works
(apparently from the Syriac).   In what manner the Jews
were influenced by the Greek literature, transplanted to
the Arabian soil in the 8th century by means of the
Syrians, can only be guessed by bold conclusions from a
later age, on account of the want of certain criteria, and of
literary documents of the time.[11]   In this inquiry regard
must be paid to the development of Arabian science, as yet
but imperfectly determined.   The dates which have been
hitherto ascertained, point to the oldest *Karaitic* literature as
the key for the solution of this most difficult question (see
below, § 12.), and it may prove that *religious polemics* are
to be considered as one of the most important elements in
it.   At any rate, the scientific literature known to us
begins with Arabic writings, partly polemical and religio-
philosophical, and with translations from the Bible by SAADJA
Gaon (about 892), and his Karaitic contemporaries, some of
whom were older than himself.   The principle of the literal
interpretation of the Bible adopted by the Karaites, who
rejected the Halacha and Haggada-Midrash, necessitated
the use of objective *Exegesis*, and the *grammatical studies*

inseparable from it. It must also have imprinted the character of the old Targum upon the translations necessitated
by the altered circumstances of language, and, by bringing
forward religious principles, have led to a regularly constructed system of doctrine (*dogmatism*). In consequence
of this, as well as of the progress of science generally, it
followed that the Haggada, which had never been much
studied in Babylon, fell still more into the background.
The Halacha, which on the completion of the Gemara was
no longer developed by the Halachaic Midrash directly
from Scripture, began to take a formal shape; while, on the
one hand, the substance, and especially the practical results,
were systematically put together, so, on the other, the Methodology of Talmudical deduction was discussed. With
this were connected inquiries concerning the history of the
Talmud and of the Talmudists, and the commencement of
Chronology and of the *history of literature*. Finally it became
necessary to explain the Talmud itself according to both its
substance and language.

As soon as the homiletical element of the Haggada was
fettered by writing and rule, it became necessary that another
element should be introduced into the synagogue. This was
prayer in the form of the new poetry (*Pijjut*) with *rhyme* and
metre, with which, as cultivation in thought and language advanced, it became usual to clothe all kinds of literature, after
the example of the Arabs. Still later, poetry ceased to be
didactic, and its form was considered as a worthy object
of study. Besides these peculiarly Jewish departments of
literature, considerable progress was made, as regards both
matter and form, in *Mathematics* and *Astronomy, Medicine*
and *Physics*.

The *language* of the Jewish literature of this period varies
with the department of literature and the geographical
locality. It is at first the *Aramaïc* or Aramaïc-Hebrew of
the Talmud, even as late as Anan the Karaite[12]; and it
generally remains the same among the Jews in Christian
countries. Among those under the dominion of the Arabs
the prevailing language after the 9th century is the *Arabic*,
in which even liturgical writings, prayers, and poems are

extant. But few traces of *Persian* literature [13] remain to us.
In the countries of the *Romance* languages a few Jews in
later times took part in literature. Among the grammarians
and poets, and even among some old French Bible expositors
(as Joseph Kara), the Hebrew retrograded towards purism;
but a corresponding attempt on the part of Maimonides to
restore the language of the Mishna in the Halacha produced
no result. The preponderance of legal studies in Germany
and France made the mixed Talmudic idiom predominant,
while their Pijjutim still displayed that imperfect state of
language out of which the Sefaradim had early risen to a
more correct form. The *translation* of Arabic writings laid
the foundation for a *scientific* prose (תכונה, properly astronomy.), the Arabisms of which were gradually softened
or entirely naturalised. The Kabbalistic pseudepigraphy,
veiling itself under the old Aramaïc idiom, and in part translating from the Hebrew, is itself also in some degree puristic, but it fell into strange mistakes, and even grammatical
blunders; on the other hand, it extended the capability of
the language for new ideas. Finally foreign elements pressed
in from all sides, and became in a measure assimilated. [14]

Besides their own literature of translations, &c., we are
also indebted to the Jews for the preservation of various
works in *foreign languages* written in Hebrew characters,
amongst which the Arabic, from its affinity, takes of course
the first place. The neglect of several valuable contributions to the general history of literature has arisen only from
ignorance of the letters in which they were written; through
this they have been misinterpreted, and foreign authors
have been converted by bibliographers into Jews. Many
works of the celebrated *Averroes* (§ 12.) in the genuine
Arabic are preserved only in Hebrew MSS.; an Arabic
lexicon in Hebrew characters, and older than the year 1380, is
extant in the Escurial; but no one, as far as we know, even
noticed it, at a period when every corner of the libraries was
thoroughly examined by Arabic scholars. A *Polish* translation of the Psalms, written as early as 1510, is to be found at
Parma; and at a later period even a *Turkish* work on Muhammedan sects was written in Hebrew characters, and has

been recently discovered at Leyden by the author of the present treatise.

The *external* history of literature (that of manuscripts, transcribers, and libraries) begins properly in this period, but it has unfortunately as yet been but little cultivated.[15]

A little more attention has been paid to the literature of *gravestones*, interesting in many respects; and Zunz, the originator of so many researches, has also written an essay, exhausting whatever of these monuments was spared by the barbarism of the middle ages. We are, however, from time to time edified with discoveries of old inscriptions which are only monuments — of ignorance.

We now proceed to the particular departments of literature.

§ 9.]   *Halacha.*

We have above (§ 4, 5.) pursued the Halachaic literature as far as the works of R. ACHAI, JEHUIDAI GAON, and SIMEON KAHIRA, which form the transition to independent systematic works of this period, and are perhaps in some measure affected by its influences. We have seen that the Gemara of Jerusalem, and the line of thought connected with it, maintained their authority principally in Italy, while the Gemara of Babylon was carried by the reputation of the Gaonim into the countries subject to Arabia, and over Northern Africa, as far as Spain. There however, by the transplanting of learned men from Southern Italy to Kahira, Kairowan, and Cordova, attention was again directed to the older and simpler Gemara of Jerusalem. But this occurred too late for them ever to be placed on an equal footing; and since the Babylonian, which was besides in many respects preferable, lay at the foundation of the established practice, the other could never boast of any great literary attention; and subsequently a whole Order (Seder) of it was lost. The activity of the later *Gaonim* (800—1037) was thus exercised principally upon the Babylonian Talmud, which they expounded, as regards both substance and language[1], in continuous commentaries or lexica rerum. Besides this they delivered Judgments or Responsa (mostly *legal* judgments), even for Spain and

France, of which several collections are still extant, one by
JOSEPH TOB-ELEM.[2]   They also composed Monographies
upon practical subjects, partly in *Arabic*, and partly in
Hebrew *memorial verses* (§ 18.).   ZEMACH (872—890),
SAADJA, SHERIRA, HAI (who died 1037), and his father-
in-law SAMUEL BEN CHOFNI, composed writings of this
kind.   After the Gaonim the same subject was treated in
the first half of the 11th century by CHEFEZ, author of a
Book of Precepts (ספר המצוות),[3] and NISSIM BEN JACOB
and CHANANEL in Kairowan, both pupils and the latter
son of Chuschiel of Bari, who combined the learning and
methods of Babylon and Italy, and exercised an important
influence on the system of the Halacha.[4]   NISSIM, who succeeded his father as religious head, and was the means of
carrying on the correspondence between Hai Gaon and
Samuel Hannagid in Spain, composed a double " Key "
(מפתח) to the Talmud in Arabic, which was intended to
make up for its deficiency in arrangement, and its entire
want of notices of parallel passages, &c.   He gives as an
introduction, a historical account of tradition and of the
Talmud, and is the first in those countries to take into
consideration the Talmud of Jerusalem.[5]   His successor
CHANANEL (who died 1050 ?)[6], in his Hebrew commentaries
on the Talmud, selected those parts which had not fallen into
disuse, and gave the result of the whole at the end of his disquisition.   He thus furnished an example to ISAAC ALFASI
(1013–1103) of Fez, a Rabbi in Lucena (a community which
was celebrated for learning, until 1148[7]), whose " Halachot,"
a compendium of the Talmud with its final results,[8] obtained
great authority as the first code of laws, and found its way
as far as France.[9]   It however soon met with a bold critic in
Provence, the young SERACHJA HALEVI of Lunel, who had
observed the connexion of general logic with the methodology
of the Talmud, but who was opposed by MEIR of Carcassone
(1220), and NACHMANIDES.   Commentaries were written by
JONATHAN KOHEN of Lunel (cir. 1200), ISAIAH DE TRANI,
jun., JONAH GERONDI, AARON HALEVI of Barcelona (who
died 1293, and whose nephew AARON BEN PINCHAS made a
compendium of some sections)[10], NISSIM BEN REUBEN GE-

RONDI (about 1350), JOSEPH CHABIB (about 1400), and many
authors in the East. Meanwhile, in *Spain* an independent
study of the Halacha flourished in the school of R. MOSES,
who had been removed from Bari to Cordova, and, by means
of the minister Chasdai ben Isaac, had been raised to the
office of teacher, in which he was succeeded by his son R.
CHANOCH.   JOSEPH IBN ABITUR (Abi Thaur ben Santas?),
a pupil of R. Moses', seems to have written an Arabic compendium of the Talmud (or of the Mishna), for the Khalif
Alhakim.[11]   Soon afterwards R. SAMUEL called HANNAGID
(the Prince), composed an *introduction to the Talmud* [12], in
which the Haggada is already distinguished in principle from
the Halacha, and the talmudical form of discussion is explained.   By the time therefore that the Halacha had lost
its chief fosterers in the East, it was already in full bloom in
the West ; and through the variation of practice in different
countries, it gained in breadth, and its method became more
copious.   For even in Western Germany (Worms, Mayence,
Regensburg), and in France (especially in the South), there
had been since the 11th century an unbroken line of distinguished teachers of the law, commencing in Germany with
the descendants of R. MOSES of Lucca, the real founders of
the German-French Halacha, which reached to England and
the Slavonic east then known as " Kanaan " and "Russia."
In France we must mention first Rabbenu GERSON " the
ancient," called " the light of the Exile," the founder of
monogamy and other " institutions, " who was already,
through his teacher R. Leontin, acquainted with the views
of the Gaonim[13], and had composed a commentary on the
Talmud, &c.   His brother MACHIR (1030) attempted an
alphabetical dictionary of the Talmud, as the Gaon Zemach
had formerly done, and probably also HAI GAON, almost at
the same time.   Amongst other pupils of R. Gerson was
R. MOSES of Narbonne, called " Ha-Darschan," because he
distinguished himself particularly in collecting and explaining the Midrashim.[14]   Yet in the German-French treatment
of the various subjects contained in the Talmud and Midrash,
the Halacha and Haggada are less clearly distinguished.
Soon after R. Moses, we find R. SIMEON HA-DARSCHAN,

author of the famous and comprehensive collections on the
Midrash, called *Jalkut;* and R. TOBIA, son of the famous
R. Eliezer "the Great" (which means the old) of Mayence,
who travelled to the East, and was the author of a
" Midrash," different in its character from those of earlier
times.[15]   NATHAN BEN JECHIEL of Rome (who died 1106),
the famous author of the Rabbinical dictionary called *Aruch*,
was a pupil of R. Moses Ha-Darschan.   From the works of
the latter[16], R. SALOMO ISAKI (called Rashi, erroneously
Jarchi) of Troyes gained much information; his model *Commentaries* on the greater part of the Talmud superseded those
of R. Gerson, and called forth similar works among his chief
pupils and kinsmen.

A new epoch commences with the rise of MAIMONIDES,
who, after his complete Arabian commentary of the Mishna[17],
and partial explanation of the Gemara of Babylon and that
of Jerusalem, accomplished (about 1180) in a remarkable
manner the gigantic plan of what may be called a "second
Mishna."   His *Mishne Torah* is a compendium embracing
the whole extent of the Halacha, even of that part which
was no longer of any practical use.   In its principal features
it follows the Halachot of Isaac Alfasi; but it is remarkable
for its scientific form and plan, and leaves nothing to be desired but special references for the conclusions drawn from the
two Talmuds[18], a deficiency which he had intended to supply.
This work, written in Egypt, was soon disseminated among
the schools of Maimonides in the East.   Parts of it were
translated, contrary to the author's intention, into Arabic;
and the Hebrew text was explained in Arabic by SALOMO B.
JESHUA KOHEN, by an anonymous writer of the 15th century, and by SAID BEN DAÛD (Saadja b. David) EL-ADENI
(1473—1479).   It was carefully glossed by the learned, but
mystic and not very scientific, ABRAHAM BEN DAVID junior
of Posquieres (who died 1198), son-in-law of the famous
ABRAHAM BEN ISAAC (see below), and pupil of MESHUL-
LAM BEN JACOB (who died 1170); and it was defended
against MEIR ABULAFIA HALEVI (before 1200) by AARON
son of Meshullam.[19]   Afterwards, it was widely disseminated, and obtained a high reputation; learned men wrote

commentaries on it, and even in modern times the hy-
percriticism of the Halacha has been exercised upon it.
As an introduction, Maimonides wrote in Arabic his *Sefer
Hammizwot*, an enumeration of the 613 laws (see above, § 4.),
prefixing 14 canons on the principles of numbering them, di-
rected principally against the Halachot Gedolot and the
"Asharot" (§ 19.). This work was in part disputed by
NACHMANIDES (about 1250), in his glosses, but was never-
theless used as a foundation for their works by R. AARON
HALEVI of Barcelona (who died 1293, and was said to be the
author of the *Sefer Hachinnuch*), and by many others both
French and Germans.[20]

Up to this time, in France and Germany (for example, in
Mayence, Regensburg, Speier, and Worms), and partly also
in Italy, the explanation of the Talmud had been the chief
occupation of the learned; and in the twelfth and thirteenth
centuries, distinguished teachers, the first of whom were of
the family of Rashi, collected glosses and disquisitions, called
Tosafot (תוספות), or Additions.[21] The greater part of
these are printed in our editions of the Talmud, together
with the practical conclusions *Piske Tosafot* (פסקי תוספות), or
Decisions of the Additions[22], collected from them by a
German in the fourteenth century. At the time of the
burning of the Talmud in France (1244—1248) the Tosafot
were written on the margin of the extracts of Alfasi, as
was done by MOSES BEN JOMTOB of Evreux.[23] The persecution of the Jews at that time reached also teachers of
note, such as MEIR BEN BARUCH ROTHENBURG, who died
in 1293—1303, and whose pupil ASHER BEN JECHIEL
was obliged to remove from Germany to Toledo. The latter
wrote, besides other things, a work like the Halachot of Alfasi,
from which his son JACOB BEN ASHER (cir. 1339) extracted a
shorter compendium. At a later time, Jacob wrote an independent book of the law in four parts, *Arba Turim*, which
takes in only the part of the Halacha still in practice, and
forms the foundation of the normal code of Joseph Karo
(§ 25.).

With the fourteenth century the study of the Halacha
declined, particularly in France and Germany, and the dis-

tinction between the older or " former " (ראשונים), as the
great authorities, and the " latter" (אחרונים) began; so that
the older were called the " ancient " (קדמונים).   The sad
condition of the Jews, which could be alleviated only by
bribery, rendered learning, often indeed the mere degree
and title of Rabbi (" Morenu" and the like)[21], an object of
desire to the poor, and brought even the learned into a
lamentable dependence upon the Mæcenates (Nedibim); dis-
cord was excited by the disputes of the schools; and the
reciprocal anathemas of the Rabbies formed an echo to the
scandal of the Antipopes.   But even learned schools and
writings soon became scarce ; and not until the end of the
middle ages did a new life begin to be developed in Hungary
and Austria, although even there it manifested no real progress.
Study indeed increased to a gigantic extent; but being left
to itself, and guided by no general scientific knowledge, it
unavoidably degenerated into a method repulsive to the few
who were really profound scholars, or whose minds were
less distorted.   The transition from the short explanation of
words and things of the older commentators of the Talmud,
— through the discussions and disputations of the Tosaphot
(in the narrower sense),— to the exercises of wit of the
" Nürembergers " (Blauser) *[25] and " Regensburgers " (so
called from the principal schools), and the pettifoggings of
modern times, has not yet been specially investigated.
There are many analogies in Christian Jurisprudence and
Muhammedan Theology to this kind of casuistry and discussion [26] (Pilpul), which gradually devotes more attention
to the mode of treatment than to the subject itself.   For it is
the nature of a practical science—and the Halacha must be
regarded throughout as a theory of law,—that over-theorising
causes it to degenerate from a practical aim to a mere play
of intellect.   During this unhappy time rules derived from
idle speculation were enforced as rules of life belonging to the
religious law, more strictly than at any former period; and subsequently the authors of the Tosaphot and their successors,
together with the great Spanish and Provençal legal authorities (particularly the authors of Compendiums, Judgments,

* The word is derived from the German " bloss," by which the query was
introduced.

&c.), were comprised under the expression " Decernents " (Poskim, פוסקים).[27] Finally, the Spaniards became the pupils of the French and Germans who immigrated to their country.

The Halachaic writings are distinguished in a variety of ways with reference to their subject, form, and inscription (title).[28] They are: I. *Commentaries* (קונטרים, פירוש) on the Babylonian Talmud, for the most part only on the more important parts (1000 — 1300). — II. *Glosses*, Appendices (Tosaphot), Remarks (שטות, נימוקים) on the Talmud and on the commentators (1130—-1340), which correspond with the Novellæ (חידושים, חידושי הלכות) of the Spanish and Italian schools (1150—1350); e. g. those of CHANANEL, JOSEPH IBN MEGAS, ABRAHAM BEN DAVID, JONAH GE-RONDI, NACHMANIDES, SALOMO IBN ADERET, JOMTOB BEN ABRAHAM, NISSIM GERONDI, JES. DE TRANI, and others.— III. *Collections* (ליקוטים), Compilations (קובץ), Compendiums (קיצורים), principally for practical use (in the 12th, and still more in the 13th and 14th centuries).—IV. *Decisions* (פסקים) and Judgments (תשובות), Rules emanating from them (דינים), and Ordinances (תקנות).[29] — V. More independent or more *systematic works,* in which the foremost rank, with regard to form and plan, is due to the Spanish school. (a.) Those upon the entire Halacha: as the *Sefer Hammiz-wot,* collected from expositions by MOSES BEN JAACOB of Coucy (about 1236)[30], to the practical abridgment of which, the *Amude Hagola* by ISAAC BEN JOSEPH of Corbeil (1277)[31], supplements and glosses were made by PEREZ, MOSES of Zurich, and ISAAC (Eisak) STEIN (ob. 1495); and the edition of the Halachot of Alfasi, by MORDECAI, at Nüremberg (1300), reedited by SAMUEL (of) SCHLETZSTADT (in the 14th century). (b.) Editions of separate branches of the subject, judicial or ritual: as those by JEHUDA BEN BARSILLAI at Marseilles (fl. 1130)[32]; especially the rules respecting food, for the most part in " Portæ " (שערים), as those of ISAAC (of) DUREN (about 1320), and of PSEUDO-JONA in the 15th century. (c.) Collections or Miscellanies, generally with symbolical titles; the principal authors of which were SOLOMON ISAKI, ABRAHAM BEN ISAAC at Narbonne (who died 1158?)[33], ISAAC BEN ABBA MARI at Marseilles (1179 1189), ELIEZER BEN SAMUEL of

Metz, Eliezer ben Nathan at Mayence (fl. 1140) [33 a], Baruch ben Isaac in Germany (fl. 1200), Isaiah di Trani the Elder in Italy, Eliezer ben Joel Halevi (fl. 1210), Eleazar of Worms (1240), Meir Abulafia ben Todros at Toledo (ob. 1244), Gerson ben Solomon of Beziers[34], Zedekiah ben Abraham (1244) and Jehuda Anaw (cir. 1320) at Rome[35], Isaac ben Moses at Vienna (cir. 1250), Solomon Ibn Aderet and his glossator Aaron Halevi at Barcelona, the unknown author of the *Kolbo* (referred to by Aaron Kohen of Lunel), Menahem (Vidal) ben Solomon Meiri at Perpignan (cir. 1300), author of an introduction of historical interest [36], Jerucham ben Meshullam in Provence (1334), Menahem Ibn Serach ben Aaron, who wrote particularly for those who held office at court, and who might, through ignorance, transgress the law, Isserlein in Germany (1450), and others.

As authors of *Judgments* (called also שאלות ותשובות, that is, *Enquiries and Decisions,* because the enquiries are also put down), particularly of those which are preserved and best known, we must mention Rashi, and his grandson Tam (Jacob of Rameru), Joseph Ibn Megas (died 1141), and Maimonides, son of his pupil (died 1204), Abraham ben David of Posquieres, Nachmanides (1266), Meir ben Baruch Rothenburg (1280), Menahem Recanati (in Italy, 1290—1330), Solomon Ibn Aderet at Barcelona, Asher ben Jechiel, and his sons Jacob and Jehuda [37] at Toledo, Nissim ben Reuben Gerondi (of Gerona, 1350, at Barcelona), the families Scheshet (1374) and Duran in Algiers, Jacob Levi (ob. 1427), Jacob Weil (1460—1470) in Germany, Joseph Kolon (ob. 1480 in Pavia), Moses Minz, Jehuda Minz (ob. 1508), and others. These writings are of great importance for history, for the history of literature, for antiquities, and particularly for legal history.[38] With the expository works are connected the *Dictionaries* of Machir in France (1030), and of Nathan ben Jechiel at Rome (ob. 1106)[39], from whose Aruch extracts were made, and supplements added, in the 14th century, by Menahem ben Eljakim, who translated the difficult words into German, by Samuel ben Jacob

(before 1189 ?), and by ABRAHAM ZACUT (15th century).[40]
TANCHUM of Jerusalem (cir. 1250) wrote an Arabic dictio-
nary of the Mishna as an appendix to the great work of
Maimonides.

To the Halachaic *Methodology*[41] belong, amongst other
works, an Arabic Monography by SAADJA GAON; MAI-
MONIDES' Introduction to the Mishna; JOSEPH IBN AK-
NIN'S Arabic work upon the measures, the reckoning of
time, and the coins of the Talmud, probably forming a part
of a methodological introduction; the *Sefer Kerithot,* by
SAMSON BEN ISAAC of Chinon (cir. 1300); the Methodology of ISAAC KANPANTON in Castille (ob. 1463, at the
age of 103); the *Halichot Olam* of JESHUA BEN JOSEPH
HALEVI (1467, at Toledo); a MS. treatise by MOSES IBN
BEN DANAN JOSEPH of Coimbra, pupil of Isaac Aboab; and
other writings, which form the transition to the following
branch of literature.

§ 10.] *Histories of Learned Men. — Chronicles.*

During the First Period, that of the historical Haggada
(§ 5 b.), national pride was able to point to the nation as a
whole, and to connect its present condition, or the history of
recent events, with former times. But now that, through the
Dispersion, a national history properly so called had ceased to
exist, this feeling was necessarily confined to a pride in the
intellectual powers of individuals. Although, in the controversies with religions descended from Judaism, the Jews not
only refused to admit this circumstance as an argument against
themselves [1], but even appealed to the remains of their own
temporal power [2] (of which views the book of *Eldad* may be
regarded as an example [2a]), still they took advantage of it
against the Karaites, who were despisers of tradition, and in-
tellectually inferior to themselves. In later times also this
national tendency is displayed in the apologetic historical
writings of Cardoso, Barrios, &c., even by their titles, *Excelen-
cias de los Hebræos,* and the like.[3] In this the example of the
Arabs could have but little influence; as their historical literature must have remained, for the most part, unknown to the

Jews, and there could have been no opportunity for imitation.   Serious scientific study must have been opposed to the
writing of dry chronicles, or of legends leading to pseudepigraphy, such as are to be found among the Arabs.[4]   But
although the *history of learned men* was in both nations developed under like influences[5], still, owing to the peculiar
character of Jewish literature, and want of knowledge respecting the writers and their works, the soil to be cultivated
was far more sterile.

We have seen above how the form and method of the
Halacha naturally led, on the one hand, to its great teachers
being made the heroes of traditions and tales, and, on the
other, to their chronological and didactic connexion becoming the subject of methodical inquiry.   Indeed we found,
even in the Talmud, besides a mass of traditions referring to
Talmudical times, a kind of chronological exposition of tradition in the Mishna treatise called *Abot.*   Throughout the
Talmud and Midrashim, — where hundreds of names are
quoted concerning whose authority, and connexion with time,
society, and doctrine, we can obtain information only by a
critical combination of scattered passages and fragments, —
there must have been an increasing necessity for chronicles
of learned men, combined with methodological discussions, as
an assistance in the Halacha.   In fact, we possess such a
treatise upon the Tannaim and Amoraim (סדר תנאים ואמוראים),
from the year 885 or 887[6], besides fragments of a lost work
by NATHAN BEN ISAAC HABABLI (956)[7]; and, as a principal
source of information, the famous answer of SHERIRA GAON
(980) to a question of Jacob ben Nissim at Kairowan, about
the composition of the Mishna[8], and a fragment of a treatise
by the same.   Perhaps also polemical animosity to the
Karaites may from time to time have had some effect[9], as
appears clearly in a part of the book of Cusari, by JEHUDA
HALEVI (1140), and in the well-known *Book of Tradition*
(especially following Sherira) of ABRAHAM BEN DAVID
(erroneously called Ben Dior) HALEVI, or the Elder, in
Spain (1061)[10], which forms the principal foundation of the
historical part of the astronomy of ISAAC BEN JOSEPH IS-
RAELI (1310).   A brother of R. Meir of Speier (1210)[11]

composed an alphabetical biographical dictionary of the teachers of the Talmud.   Of the Halachaic methodological writings and introductions, besides MAIMONIDES' introduction to the commentary on the Mishna (§ 10. at the end), that of MENAHEM MEIRI to his commentary on the Tractatus Abot (§ 9.) and that of MENAHEM IBN SERACH (§ 9.) deserve to be mentioned.   Besides these, there are also some notices belonging to this subject in the preface to *Schaare Zion*, by ISAAC DE LATAS (1372)[12]; and a catalogue written in the fourteenth century by [AARON BEN ABRAHAM] a grandson of R. Samuel Schletzstadt, and lately published[13], gives some extracts from it.   In this case also we see the scientific and critical tendency proceeding from *Babylon*, and extending as far as *Spain*.

Other glimpses occur in single historical writings, among which are to be distinguished the extracts from, and supplements to, the Seder Olam (§ 5. 2 b.), called *Seder Olam Sutta* (סדר עילם זוטא)[14], a chronology from Adam to the fifth century of the. Christian æra, the object of which is to prove, by means of records, that the Babylonian patriarchal families are lineal descendants of the house of David.   The arrangement of the prophets and learned men in appropriate dynasties, reminds us of the plan of similar works among the Arabs; the attempt to bring Babylon into the foreground is still observable in the *Answer* of Sherira[15] mentioned above.   To similar genealogical interests[16], in later times, we owe the preservation of many registers of descent, and accounts of families, not however altogether free from deliberate inventions and falsifications : for even in the Seder Olam Sutta one piece of a genealogy, in opposition to the older historical Midrash, is borrowed from the Book of Chronicles ; and subsequently the Karaites borrowed their genealogical table from Anan upwards, from our Seder Olam Sutta.   As an offshoot from the fully developed Midrash of Arabian and Latin literature, there appeared in Northern Italy[17] (in the tenth century) the Hebrew edition of the Latin Hegesippus by the so-called Pseudo-Josephus, "Josippon," or JOSEPHUS GORIONIDES, who, as late as the eighteenth century, was supposed by the genealogist Jechiel to be the real Flavius Josephus. It was partly translated into Arabic by Zacharia ben Said el-Jemeni. [18] The opposition of the later intentional pseudepigraphy to the older historical Midrash is most apparent, on account of its strict biblical style and artificial plan intermixed with Arabian elements, in the *Sefer Hajashar* (ספר הישר), which was apparently written in Spain in the twelfth century, as a reading-book, and purported to be the book of that name mentioned in the Bible (Jos. x. 13., 2 Sam. i. 18.). This has been again confounded with a similar fabrication, by the famous London printer *Ilive* (1751), said to have been brought over by Alcuin; a literary forgery, which was aggravated by a pirated reprint at Bristol, in 1829. [19]

The joys and sorrows of the nation and of individuals, particularly of the pious, expressed themselves in literature in various ways. Plain records after the manner of chronicles or elegiac effusions (*memorial books*, as they were termed), catalogues of martyrs (ס זכרונות פנקם) for the celebration of the dead (הזכרת נשמות)[20], and the like, were written: for example, by Eliezer ben Nathan in Mayence (fl. 1130—1150), Ephraim ben Jacob of Bonn, and others, upon the massacres of the crusaders[21]; by Schemtob Palquera (cir. 1250) and Chisdai Crescas, upon the persecution in the year 1392 [21a]; and by a contemporary of Jacob Levi (about 1449), upon the times of the Hussites.[22] Consolatory epistles and dissertations in times of general persecution were written by R. Maimon, his son Maimonides, and Joseph Ibn Aknin (12th cent.). Many elegies were written for *Divine Service,* or were used afterwards for that purpose (§ 19.). Besides this, much material, valuable for history and biography, is contained in the ethical *Testaments* (§ 12.), in occasional *poems* of all kinds, partially collected in Diwans (§ 20.), and in the Halachaic *judgments* (§ 9.), and generally in *titles, prefaces, dedications,* and *signatures* (for genealogy), and catalogues of writings by authors themselves, for example, by Ibn Caspi.[23] As a recent discovery of our own it may be mentioned here, that Mazliach Ibn ol-Bazak, judge of Sicily, on coming from Babylonia to Spain, presented to Samuel Nagid a very interesting treatise, describing the manners of Hai Gaon (ob. about 1037), quotations from which, by authors of the twelfth century, excite our regret for the loss of the whole. [23 a] The two chapters of the Arabic Poetics of MOSES IBN ESRA (1130 — 40) are most interesting, and have been only recently made use of by Munk and the author. They treat, historically and critically, of the older linguists and poets of Spain (cf. § 20.), and seem to have been the source from which JEHUDA CHARISI (cf. § 20.) drew the substance of his more æsthetic chapters on the same subject. They were not improbably used also by ABRAHAM BEN DAVID (cf. § 20.). The work was certainly known, although perhaps through a Hebrew translation, to ABRAHAM SACUT, of whom, with some others belonging to the end of this period, we shall speak in the following period (§ 29.), because they form a connecting link between the two. The same Moses Ibn Esra also wrote a treatise on celebrated men of another class, probably famous for their study and promotion of "literæ humaniores," and "noblesse," of which the author has but recently discovered a quotation, and the Arabic title (מקאלה פי פצאיל אהל אלאדאב ואלאחסאב), furnished by Ibn Esra himself in the work above mentioned.

The *chronological system* [24] which had been developed in the earliest times from the necessities of civil and religious life was now gradually changed, on account of the extension of writing, and the alteration in external circumstances, — not however without injury to our computation of time. The Seleucidic or "Greek" æra (חשבון היוים), called also *Æra Contractuum* (מנין שטרות, לשטרות), or the cessation of prophecy [24a], was adopted as the general date for MSS. even by the *Karaites*. This however involved the difference of one year, which depended upon older Jewish dates (the departure from Egypt), and was retained in the different countries and schools, as may be gathered from the books of the Maccabees. [25]   The reckoning from the destruction (לחרבן) of Jerusalem (3828 of the world, A. D. 68) was less often used. [26]   We meet first with the æra of the creation (לבריאה, לבריאת עולם) in the work of SABBATAI DONOLO (in Italy, 950) and in the book *Tana debe Elijahu*. [27]   The date of the world in Sherira's Decisions (986) was introduced by European transcribers.   The use of this æra by

the old Gematria (גמטריא) [28] is found first in Charisi (1204). [29]
When it became more general after the year of the world
4000, the 4000 years were gradually omitted, as had been
the case already after the year 2000 of the Seleucidic æra. [30]
This system of mentioning only the hundreds and lower
numbers was called " the small æra " (לפרט קטן, abbreviated
לפ"ק), in contradistinction to the full numbering (פרט גדול),
so that at the beginning of the sixth 1000 years, there
are still instances of the use of the small number, as 1002
(= 5002), &c. [31]   Amongst the Jews under the dominion of
the Arabs we sometimes find the *Muhammedan computation*
of time (חשבון הישמעאלים) [32], and also the Spanish æra,
"*Alzafar*," i. e. the Christian. [33]   The dating from the birth
of Christ is found in Hebrew writing only as an exception. [34]
Moreover researches concerning chronology are connected
with astronomy (§ 21.).

Information important for *universal history and ethnogra-*
phy is furnished by the Jewish *Travels, Letters*, &c., which
are generally distinguished by an ingenuous observation,
and a description of the writer's own experiences, or of traditions, views, ideas, and manners found in the countries visited.
They do not however generally contain much original matter, being often older accounts newly embellished.   The
greater number of Jewish authors may be classed as
travellers. [35]   The instruction in reading and writing, which
had prevailed amongst the Jews from very early times, made
even the least learned capable of keeping a journal of travels,
&c.   Moreover, to the Jews of old no less than of the
present time, the hard lot of necessity has been the hurricane
on which the seed of knowledge was borne over all countries;
while, on the other hand, learning, as a garment of honour,
has protected and enveloped the wandering beggar.   The
Dispersion, and trade, as well as meetings for the preservation of their educational institutions, promoted travelling
for both business and pleasure.   The astonishingly rapid
and wide extension of Jewish literature can be explained
only by these circumstances.   One principal object of the
pilgrims was their ancient father-land, and the graves of
their pious, learned, or brave forefathers.   Accounts of

these had come from various sources; they had been multiplied after the Oriental manner, by their pious or superstitious descendants [36], they had become more attractive as
places of pilgrimage, and had also arrested the attention of
literature.   On this account, these and many other Jewish
sources of information are important to the *Geography and
History of Palestine*.[37]   Another and particular inducement
to travelling and epistolary correspondence lay in the sympathy of the Israelites with one another throughout the
whole world.   On this subject Gentiles have always exhibited ignorance, partiality, and want of sympathy, by
filling up their own deficiency in knowledge and experience
with the most absurd, and often the most deplorable opinions
and prejudices [38] drawn from questionable sources.   The
country inhabited by the ten tribes, who did not return
to Palestine, forms a particular subject of discussion, in-
volving also the consideration of the nations and lands in
which the Jews lived.   Thus, *Ethnography* was represented
by polemics [39], by the mutual relations of the literature of
different countries and of particular branches, and lastly by
cosmography written after the Arabian style, with a purely
scientific view.

The most prominent authors of *Travels* are [40], — ISAAC, a
member of the embassy of Charlemagne to the Khalif
Harun er-Raschid (802), perhaps the first who effected a
communication between France and the Babylonian Gaonim; ELDAD HADANI (cir. 900) [41]; JACOB גרגירין, whose
accounts of the East and the Sultan of Singiar (?) are inserted by the Karaite JEHUDA HEDESSI (see § 15.) in a
work containing some historical and cosmographical information; the celebrated BENJAMIN OF TUDELA (1160
sq.), of whom very different estimates have been formed,
and whose travels have been recently, for the first time,
critically edited [42]; PETACHJA of Regensburg (1170—80);
SAMUEL BEN SAMSON of France (1210), apparently the
precursor of more than 300 French and English Rabbies who
travelled to Palestine (1211); MENACHEM BEN PEREZ of
Hebron (A. D. 1219), a somewhat fabulous account of whom
has been recently discovered by the author in the Bodleian

Library; the poet Jehuda Charisi (1216—18) (see § 20.);
Jacob of France (1257); Elia of Ferrara in Palestine
(1438); an anonymous writer of Maghreb (cir.1473); and
Obadiah di Bertinoro (ob. between 1500 and 1510), a
fragment of whose epistle has been recently found by the
author in the Collectanea of Jochanan Allemanno. The following works also belong here: — The correspondence of
Chisdai ben Isaac with the king of the Chozars (959)[43];
the Cosmography of Gerson ben Solomon Catalano of
Arles (13th cent.), perhaps grandson of Nachmanides; the
important work of Esthori (not Isaac) Parchi (1322),
recently reprinted, but miserably incorrect; the Hebrew
translation of the *Image du Monde* (1245); and a part of the
pretended letters of Prete (or Petro) Joan to Pope
Eugene or Frederic IV. (1442—1460.)[44]   At the end of
the fifteenth century Portuguese Jews occupy no unimportant place in the history of geography.[45]

§ 11.] *Conflict between Science and Haggada.*

In the earlier periods we found, in contradistinction to the
Halacha, the *Haggada* usually developed in the form of Midrash; and, by way of a simpler study of the Bible, the Masora, with its censorship of the text; and, finally, the textual
expositions of the Chaldee, Greek, and probably also Persian Targumim (Paraphrases). The Haggada comprised the
objects of the most various sciences; not however in a scientific
form. The philology of the Bible was founded upon a view
of the Hebrew tongue derived from actual life and tradition,
and not upon any elaborate theory. We must now consider
its ramifications corresponding to those of the Halacha in this
period. At an early stage of the conflict between the social
system then in process of formation, and the restrictions of
the Law, the authority of faith was obliged (especially on account of the communication with foreign nations and religions,
and with the corresponding parties and sects in Judaism
itself), to seek for support and guidance in the definitions of
pure thought. But in the collision between Judaism and
the religious and philosophical opinions of heathens and Christians,[1] the *Alexandrine School* alone grew into a syncretical

system. The scattered precepts of the national Haggada did not, like the Divine jurisprudence of the Halacha, take the form of a distinct theory, but were moulded by their connexion with the Bible into the Midrash; and since Judaism must stand or fall with the authority of Scripture, all parties within its circle, even the Sadducees, appealed directly to the letter of the Law. So long, moreover, as the doctrine and law of Judaism had to fight against the derivative religion of Christianity (a religion which in general confirms, but in special matters abrogates, Judaism) with weapons furnished by the Midrash, such subjects as the motives of the laws, the exposition of the text, and the truth and meaning of legends, did not lead to a system built upon mere laws of thought. Men guarded themselves rather against error by secret oral teaching, without devoting much attention to the Haggada. When through the agency of Arabian science Muhammedanism began to discuss the highest religious questions in a rationalistic manner, and even Judaism thence became conscious of a severance between faith and knowledge, the essence of the Midrash (the natural justification of doctrine and law by their connexion with the all-comprising Bible) was for the first time set free; and its contents, disengaged from the tangled web of the Haggada, were formed on a scientific foundation. The Midrash and Haggada were radiations of the national spirit through the prevalent oral tradition. With the Graeco-Arabian civilisation individual minds came forward; and at this period there arose for the first time writers, composers, and separate sciences, properly so called. This opposition between the national and individual elements could not fail to give rise to a conflict, which beginning in Arabia was renewed wherever they came into contact. A clear insight into the essence of this struggle was not indeed attained until the most important separate parts of Jewish literature had been affected by it.

From the contest about the validity of the Halacha, on which depended the whole form of Jewish society, the sect of the Karaites arose (A. D. 750); but, with the practical value of tradition, tradition itself, as well as the importance of its supporters the Rabbies, was called in question. A strong feeling thus arose for going back to the Bible, and making a verbal and real *exegesis*, independent of Midrash, on the foundation of *grammar* and the *philosophy* of religion. But it was necessary at the same time also to establish the philosophy of religion upon its own basis by a new interpretation, irrespective of the general value of the Haggada, which was now nearly closed.

In the last instance there arose the question which runs through the whole history of religion, concerning the relation between Reason and Revelation; only that here the exposition of the Bible and the Haggada gave the first impulse. In this case, as in most others, it is difficult to distinguish the first germs of the movement; we know, however, that this contest of thought with the simple Haggada had begun during the last days of the Midrash. SAADJA, for instance (ob. A. D. 941), contends for the use of Reason.[2] At the time of SAMUEL BEN CHOFNI, when the reading of Arabic works had become general, various views respecting the value of the Haggada were brought forward[3] by HAI the Gaon, CHANANEL, and their pupils; but, on account of the decline of Oriental civilisation, they did not exercise any important influence.

In *Spain*, in the twelfth century (probably through the oppression of the Almohadi), some Jewish philosophers, especially editors of Arabian works, appear either actually to have apostatised, or at least to have become estranged, from Judaism: as the neophyte PETRUS ALFONSI (see § 20.); JOHANNES HISPALENSIS, or ABENDEHUT, perhaps the same as (Ibn) DAVID; and ANDREAS, whom Roger Bacon states to be the real author of what Michael Scotus published as his own works. The translations by Johannes Hispalensis, of Arabian works, amongst others that of ALBENZU-BRUN (see § 12.), and the celebrated work *De Causis*, the Arabic text of which, although still extant, escaped the notice of Jourdain, were interdicted as "Aristotelian" by the University of Paris (A. D. 1209).[4] We find other men of this class amongst the Arabs; as for instance, the persecuted poet IBN SAHL (see § 20.). Others, once renowned amongst the Jews, figure as illustrious *Arabians* amongst Christian scholastic authors on account of their Arabic writings[5];

c. g. IBN GABIROL himself, whom even Leo Hebræus
(§ 23.) seems to know only from Christian authorities,
although he calls him " our Albenzubrun." About the end
of this century the Aristotelian philosophy had struck so
deep a root in Judaism, that Averroes found his immediate
pupils only amongst Jews (see § 12.).[6] Lastly, the Karaites
tried, but in vain, to take a more important position in the
Peninsula (§ 14.).

In strong contrast to this stands the simple faith of the
Northern *Franco-German* (Halachaic) school, ignorant of
the Arabic language, isolated, and consequently free from
the conflict of opposing elements, which first made their appearance, through MAIMONIDES. (ob. in Egypt A. D. 1204),
in Provence. He first combined considerable Halachaic
power with a philosophical basis. His work on the Law,
written in Hebrew (§ 9.), begins upon a religio-philosophical
foundation[7]; his commentary on the Mishna, written at an
earlier period in Arabic, contains the famous *Thirteen
Articles of Belief* and a fragment on psychology; and his
philosophical *Exegesis*, especially the *More Hanebuchim*
(*Doctor perplexorum*), intended for his pupil JOSEPH IBN
AKNIN at Haleb and the initiated, and translated into Hebrew
in his lifetime, carries out to its consequences the principle
taken up long before by SAADJA and many Karaites[8], that
the Bible must be explained metaphorically by established
fundamental truths in accordance with rational conclusions.
He also employed the same course of procedure to some
extent in the Haggada. This spiritualism, to which the
French Jews appeared in the light of anthropomorphisers[9],
necessarily became involved in all kinds of disputes. Thus,
for example, the doctrine and exegesis of Maimonides' school
in general, misused by the *Mystics* (§ 13.) and deformed by
exaggerated rumours[10], gave great offence to the pious people
of France and Provence[11], as will be shown more in detail
hereafter.

Provence, from its peculiar position, was a meeting-point
for Arabian science and civilisation and French Talmudical
lore.[12] There dwelt the last collector of the Haggada (§ 9.);
there (as in Italy, since the end of the thirteenth century)

laboured many translators from the Arabic[13], beginning
with JEHUDA IBN TIBBON, the "Father of the Translators" (A. D. 1160), who in conjunction with JOSEPH IBN
KIMCHI translated the Ethics of Bechaji (Bachia) for
Meshullam ben Jacob at Lünel (ob. A.D. 1170), teacher of
Abraham ben David (§ 9.), and later (A. D. 1167—1186)
also the writings of Jehuda Halewi, of Gabirol (for Asher,
son of Meshullam), of Ibn Gannâh, and of Saadja. In like
manner his son, SAMUEL IBN TIBBON, and at the same
time the poet JEHUDA AL CHARISI (beginning of the
thirteenth century), translated the *Moreh* and other writings
of Maimonides. To this great and illustrious family of
translators belonged among others JACOB ANATOLI, pupil
of his father-in-law Samuel Ibn Tibbon; and probably
also of the Christian Michael Scotus (A. D. 1217), who
worked, like the last, at Naples (A.D. 1232), under a commission from Frederick II. When the controversy about
philosophy broke out, he translated, at the request of his
friends at Narbonne and Beziers, the middle Commentary of
Averroes (Ibn Roshd) on Aristotle's logical writings.[14] He
also delivered a course of philosophical homilies on the Pentateuch, entitled *Molmad*, which were much approved in
Provence, and consequently became the object of various
attacks. His father-in-law Samuel Ibn Tibbon published a
Commentary on Kohelet (as yet known only by catalogues
and some quotations), to which he added, as an appendix, a
translation of Averroes' treatises on the Intellect; and he
also wrote a philosophical work on the Creation, &c. It
seems that the contest, which had begun in the life of Maimonides, came to its height through these and similar works,
in consequence of their being accessible to a large class of
readers, and having been written for them by the authors
whose translations had introduced the Arabic writings of
Maimonides into Provence and France. The differences of
opinion were thus developed from single dogmata to the
principles of religious philosophy.

In this attempt to give a short survey of a struggle the
results of which have influenced Judaism to the present time,
we can neither enter into the questions themselves, nor trace

the systems and opinions represented even by the individuals who took a prominent part in it. We must however, according to the general purpose of this essay, draw the attention of our readers to the literary documents in which the debate found its expression, although the subject deserves a separate treatise. On the other hand, the documents bearing upon the controversy are far from complete or sufficient. Some of them, belonging to about A. D. 1232, are collected and inserted in the Responsa of Maimonides by an anonymous writer, whose understanding was unequal to his task, or was dimmed by partiality. A considerable number of *poems*, mostly satirical or laudatory, might be collected; but they are rather unintelligible from our ignorance of the facts alluded to in enigmatical phrases. We shall mention in their proper place other works but recently published; a collection of valuable supplements, belonging to successive periods, and deserving a more thorough investigation, has been lately discovered by the author among the manuscripts in the Bodleian Library. Some of the following statements are extracted from it.

The first seeds of dissension were certainly sown by the introductory part of the great Hebrew Codex of Maimonides (§ 9.) called the book *Madda*. Soon after this work became known in Provence, the learned Talmudist ABRAHAM BEN DAVID (ob. A. D. 1198), in his glosses to it, defended the simple believers in the Talmudical creed against the rigorous spiritualism of Maimonides (§ 9.). His style is short and abrupt, and his views are, after all, not far removed from those whose exclusive authority he condemns.

MEIR ABULAFIA (Halevi) of Toledo, a man of more general knowledge, but no philosopher, went a step further. As soon as the book was published in his country he took offence at Maimonides' Eschatology, perceiving how it bore upon the general theory of miracles, &c. He wrote a letter to JONATHAN KOHEN, the celebrated head of the learned at Lünel, imploring him, as it seems, to defend the orthodox belief with the authority of his learning. But he received a sarcastic reply from AARON BEN MESHULLAM of Lünel, who objected that he did not properly understand the system of Maimonides, and that for a long time previously Rabbis of high authority, such as Saadja and Hai, had not considered a literal belief in the Haggada sentences of the Talmud necessary. Meir replied briefly, and addressed a circular to all the learned men of Provence (perhaps also of Northern France), appealing to them to decide between the opponents. He seems to have met with more sympathy from the French Rabbies; and the learned SAMSON BEN ABRAHAM of Sens combated the theory of Aaron ben Meshullam with arguments drawn merely from the Talmud. He always remained an opponent of Maimonides (see below).

At the commencement of the thirteenth century the theory of Maimonides began to be better understood through the translation of his Moreh, and the more popular works mentioned above. Hence a serious conflict arose; both parties being engaged in a struggle for life or death during the space of about thirty years. This time the head of the assailing party was SOLOMON BEN ABRAHAM of Montpellier [15]; one of the Northern French School, who had earned a great reputation as a Talmudist. It may be considered as certain that he first directed the attention of the French Rabbies to the obnoxious works of Maimonides; and that he was assisted by his pupils DAVID BEN SAUL and the famous JONA BEN ABRAHAM GERONDI. [16] The latter was sent to France to canvass for his teacher, who had met with great opposition in his own neighbourhood, principally at Beziers. Solomon and Saul, in an unpublished letter said to have been written to Nachmanides (although at the very beginning it appears to address Rabbi SAMUEL BEN ISAAC as an old friend of Solomon), profess the highest respect for Maimonides himself and his Talmudical views and decisions, and accuse their opponents, especially an old man called "the bearded" (בעל הזקן, perhaps David Kimchi (?), see below), who travelled about on behalf of the other party, of having forged the letter of Solomon to the French Rabbies, whom they affirm to have been impelled by their own zeal against the book Moreh, &c. The answer to this letter is quite favourable to Solomon, but written in a pacific spirit. It further cannot be denied, that the most zealous of the orthodox party had anathematised

the study of the accused works, and that their opponents in
Provence, even in Montpellier and in Spain, had replied with
a counter anathema; a copy of which still exists, dated A. D.
1332, at Saragossa, where BECHAI BEN MOSES was the leader.
The latter also endeavoured to propagate their opinions in
France and Spain.   Their spokesman and delegate was the
celebrated grammarian and interpreter of the Bible, DAVID
KIMCHI, then advanced in years, who during his journey
entered into a controversy with the revered physician JE-
HUDA AL-FACHAR of Toledo, a man of spirit and independence, who, notwithstanding his respect for Maimonides,
defended Solomon and his pupil's opinion.   The younger
SAMUEL BEN ABRAHAM SAFORTA (or Sporta) [17] addressed
to the French Rabbies a respectful but zealous epistle,
still unpublished, proving by learned arguments and quotations that the Haggada passages of the Talmud are not
obligatory in their literal sense, defending the opinions of
Maimonides, and urging those who condemned them to show
reason for so doing.

The position of NACHMANIDES (Moses ben Nachman of
Girona) in this struggle is not yet accurately ascertained; and
the passages throwing any light upon it appear to have been
in some degree altered by the editors.   His mystic system
(cf. § 13.) was strongly contrasted with the sober philosophy
of Maimonides; and it seems therefore that he as well as
many others defended the high personal authority only,
not the system, of the great Talmudical teacher, whose
memory was not to be insulted by the interdiction of his
works.   It appears that Nachmanides disapproved no less of
the anathema against Solomon ben Abraham, whose cause
he pleaded in a letter to Meir Abulafia.   This letter has
been in part published; but was erroneously interpreted by
the editor, as having been written on behalf of Maimonides.   MEIR ABULAFIA himself, already advanced in age,
and surrounded by people of different opinions, now declined
to take any prominent part.   He is alluded to by ABRAHAM
IBN CHISDAI, in a letter to Jehuda Alfachar, as having
lowered himself by mixing with people of inferior rank.

Veneration for Maimonides seems to have been the turning

point; and before several of the letters were written, the orthodox and fanatical party, deserted by the more moderate, inconsiderately took a further and fatal step; one which has been subsequently repeated, even up to the present time. They submitted the Jewish Creed to the judgment of Christians; they denounced the pupils of Maimonides as heretics; and they brought the accused books to the stake. By this however they did not benefit themselves; some of them, perhaps Solomon himself, having been, as it seems, convicted of libel, were punished, according to the barbarous laws of the time, with the loss of their tongues, and finally expiated their crime with their lives (before A. D. 1235). This excited the zeal of the Christian clergy, who made it a pretext for a war of extermination against Jewish literature in general. According to a recently published letter of the physician HILLEL BEN SAMUEL, whom we shall have occasion to mention hereafter, it was only forty days after the auto da fe of Maimonides' works, that the Talmud and other books, commentaries, &c., to the number of about 12,000 volumes, were publicly burnt at Paris. Thus the ashes of both were mingled, and on the same occasion the blood of more than 3000 Jews was shed in France. According to Zunz however the latter event took place on the 17th of June, 1244, after the bull " Impia " of Innocent IV. dated 9th March, 1244, partly at the instance of the convert DUNIN (Jona), or Nicolaus, whose disputation will be mentioned below (§ 13.). Hillel, who at a subsequent period attended during three years the lectures of Jona at Barcelona, tells us that this man was the chief leader and cause of the catastrophe, but that he repented publicly, and vowed a pilgrimage to the grave of the offended Maimonides. He delayed the performance of this vow; but having eventually set out, he was detained on his passage through Toledo, by the wish of some who asked him to deliver his lectures. There he died, but the piety of Hillel towards so pious and learned a man forbids him to describe his end. Its suddenness was attributed to his sin, for others who kept their vow better were spared. By this statement the identity of the leader Jona (who had a cousin Jona ben Josef) with the renowned moralist

(§ 12. B.) Jona Gerondi (ob. A. D. 1263), first conjectured by Rapoport, is placed beyond doubt. A controversy such as this could not but lead to personal attacks and defamations of various kinds. Solomon the son of Nachmanides had married the daughter of Jona, and according to Abraham Sacut they were themselves first cousins (sons of two sisters); at all events they seem to have been kindred. When therefore some ten learned men of Beziers tried to cast a stain on the extraction of Jona and his family at Girona and Barcelona, by insinuating that a marriage, which took place some 130 years before, was illegal, Nachmanides was provoked to take energetic measures against the calumniators. He demanded an anathema, and directed a circular to all the synagogues of Provence; and perhaps this odious affair was not without its influence upon his emigration into Palestine. Nevertheless about the year 1373 the same calumnies again produced a sharp controversy, part of which is still extant in MS., although Solomon Aderet and his son Astruc did not attach sufficient importance to the attack to prevent their uniting themselves with the calumniated family.

In the *East* also, at an earlier period (1190), SAMUEL HALEVI, head of the school at Bagdad, attacked Maimonides' doctrine of the resurrection[18], and called forth a refutation of it. He was perhaps protected by an anathema of the Prince of the Exiles, DAVID BEN HODAJA, at New Nineveh, against the adherents of Maimonides and the opposition Prince of the Exiles, SAMUEL (?). DANIEL THE BABYLONIAN, a pupil of Samuel Halevi, soon after the death of Maimonides, animadverted upon his great Talmudical work and the *Books of Precepts*, partly in Hebrew and partly in Arabic, in the form of queries to ABRAHAM, the son and follower of Maimonides at Kahira. He answered, with an allusion to the little foxes and the dead lion, censuring the new and arbitrary method of certain people, but admitting some errors which Maimonides himself had corrected in his own copy. This Daniel, and the above-mentioned SAMSON of SENS[19], who removed to St. Jean d'Acre, carried on the controversy, principally on the subject of Demonology, &c. For this reason, Maimonides' pupil, JOSEPH IBN AKNIN[20], mentioned above, de-

manded an anathema from Abraham. He, however, as a
party concerned, satisfied himself with a controversial work
against all previous attacks (1235), while the Prince of the
Exiles, David, fulfilled the wish. When afterwards some
German and French, of whom Solomon Petit (?) mentioned
by Hillel seems to have been one, tried to force their way into
the East (1286-90), a new interdict of the head of the school at
Damascus, Isai ben Chiskia, to whom others at Acre, &c.,
joined themselves, put an end to the conspiracies.[21] Copies
were sent to Barcelona, &c., and called forth an apology for
the Moreh, perhaps by Schemtob Palquera.

In the meantime Arabian science gradually found more
adherents in Provence and Italy, while the translators, many
of whom lived in Christian Spain, facilitated the study. On
the other hand, the French school forced its way into the
North of Spain and Castile, which had been freed from
the Arabs; and even thus early a mystical school, as yet
orthodox, began to be formed (see § 13.). The contention
broke out again about the year 1300; and a new element
is observable in it, viz. the employment of *Astrology* [22],
which, like all superstitious usages of the kind, had been
opposed by Maimonides himself with a rigour remarkable
for that time. But the example of Abraham Ibn Esra,
and other influences (see § 21.), made even his school
infidel in that respect. To this period probably belongs
the defence of Aristotle's doctrine of providence, partly
accepted by Maimonides, the author of which is a certain
Kalonymos.[23] Generally speaking, the subject of controversy was no longer the person Maimonides, but rather
the philosophical exposition of Scripture, which, having
been laid down in writings like those mentioned above [23a],
made its way in lectures and *sermons* (see § 12.) as an explanation of Scripture and Haggada. Amongst the authors
most violently attacked appear Levi ben Abraham, a
poor travelling teacher of philosophy and astrology; the
renowned astronomer (§ 21.) Jakob ben Machir (called
Prophiat); and Tibbon of Montpellier (ob. cir. 1309),
whose allegorical and astrological explanations of the Bible
are quoted without mention of his name. In this new field
the contest was carried on with more distinct consciousness

of the relation between Philosophy and Revelation. As a party-leader against philosophy, and yet also an opponent of astrology, we find at this time at Montpellier ABBA-MARI BEN MOSES, called ASTRUC of Lünel [24], author of a collection of controversial writings (*Minchat Kenaot*), who declared only three articles of belief (unity and incorporeality, creation *ex nihilo*, and Providence) to be essential. Amongst his principal opponents, besides those mentioned above, was JEDAJA PENINI, author of an interesting apologetic epistle to Solomon Aderet. Many Provençals likewise took a position different from that of Astruc.[25] This man tried to obtain from the celebrated Rabbi at Barcelona, SOLOMON IBN ADERET, pupil of Jona Gerondi and Nachmanides, an interdict against too early a study of philosophy. Ibn Aderet struggled long, in the expectation that those who were of the same opinion as himself in Provence would take the lead; but he finally determined — at the same time that the Council at Vienne interdicted Ibn Roshd's writings — to forbid the study of "philosophical works" (excepting medicine) before the age of twenty-five for the next fifty years.[26] Among others, ASHER BEN JECHIEL, then chief Rabbi at Toledo, also joined in this determination.[27] On the other hand, a rival interdict was brought forward by the opposition, which was followed by a host of dissertations and epistles, *pro* and *contra*; amongst which is one of MENAHEM MEIRI, answered by Don DURAN, younger brother of Abba-Mari, in a long unpublished dissertation. While however at Montpellier each interdict strove for the sanction of the law, the government (1306) drove all Jews out of France; and the pastoral persecution in Navarre, which followed soon after (1320), laid waste the North of Spain. This was fatal to the position previously held by the North of France in Jewish literature, while that of Provence was gradually transferred to Italy. Political events, the newly formed Kabbala, the revival of classical literature in Italy, the decline of Jewish civilisation in Christian Spain, and the greater interest in Christian literature occasioned by the polemics of both parties, turned the thoughts of individual minds in different directions. Still not only are the traces of those two characters preserved: SEFARADI (Spanish-Portuguese, Arabian, scientific) and ASHKENASI (German-French, [Zarfati], Romanesque, &c.), but the controversy about philosophy is connected, in the offshoots of this period, e. g. in the Kabbalist SHEMTOB IBN SHEMTOB (ob. A. D. 1430) and his opponent MOSES ALASHKAR (about the end of the fifteenth century), and even down to the present time, with Maimonides and his opponents.[28]   A curious instance may be drawn from a manuscript of the Oppenheim Collection at Oxford.[29]   We now pass on to the individual branches of this literature.

§ 12.] *Theology and Philosophy.*

In respect of the origin, tendency, and form of the theologico-philosophical literature, there are but slight foundations for a division of the subject during the period anterior to the twelfth century; up to which time only names, titles, or fragments, or at most incomplete translations from the Arabic, have come down to us. The first systematic philosophy of religion in the East appears to have followed, as regards at least its method, the Arabian scholastics (*Mutakallimun*), and in particular the Mu'tazelites.   This is demonstrable in the case of the Karaites and the oldest known rabbinical religio-philosopher SAADJA[1], and also the older Spaniards JOSEPH IBN ZADDIK and ABRAHAM BEN DAVID (see below).   At a later period the peripatetic school of Farabi and others obtained the preponderance in Spain through the agency of Maimonides.   Soon afterwards the Jews began to follow the opinions of Averroes (Ibn Roshd); whose system (*Averroism*) and works became the centre of a great movement in scholastic philosophy and theology, and were carefully preserved and propagated by the Jews, as is now generally acknowledged. But this and other points, such as the comparison of Averroes with contemporary Jewish writers, Joseph Ibn Aknin and Maimonides for instance, deserve further investigation.   Opposed to this was a kind of orthodox sentimental theology, e. g. that of JEHUDA HALEVI (A. D. 1140), and subsequently the *Kabbala;* both of which, in the controversy with " the Philosophers [2]," availed themselves of the ambiguous polemics of the Arabian Ghazali.

According to the arrangement of Aristotle generally adopted[3], the rational sciences are preceded by the " Organon" or Logic (חכמת הדבור) علم ابنطق or הגיון, which expression occurring once in the Talmud, and signifying something wrong, has been made a topic for controversy between the different parties mentioned, § 11.). They are, moreover, divided into 1. Prefatory or Mathematical (§ 21.), 2. Physical (§ 22.), and 3. Metaphysical or Theological (אלהיות). The works of the last class are : —

I. Editions (Translations, Explanations, Commentaries, Super-Commentaries, and Refutations) of Arabian writers : the principal of whom are Farabi (870—950); Avicenna (Ibn Sina) (980—1037); Ghazali (ob. 1111 or 1126), of especial influence in ethics; Ibn Sâig, or Ibn Bâge (ob. 1138); Ibn Tofeil (about 1150); Averroes (Ibn Roshd) (ob. 1198); and others from whom a knowledge of the Greek philosophy, especially that of Aristotle and his Greek expositors, and Plato, &c., was derived; e. g. the translator Honein (809—873), and his son Isaac (ob. A. D. 910—911). Later also the writings of *Christian Scholastics* were edited; amongst them those of the translator Constantinus Afer, Michael Scotus, Vincent Bellovacensis, Ægidius, Albertus Magnus, Petrus Hispanus (whose compendium of logic has been translated several times), Occam, Robert of Lincoln [3a], Thomas Aquinas, Thomas Bricot, and even some things of Augustine, Allessandro Piccolomini (1550), and others. In these works of course various kinds of alterations of the texts were made on account of religious differences; on the whole, however, the translators from Arabic, Latin, &c., proceeded with some knowledge of the subject and scientific enthusiasm, if not always with careful philological fidelity. They were very skilful in using and enlarging the powers of the Hebrew language for new conceptions, although at first they fell into a somewhat hard and obscure style.[4] Many works otherwise unknown, and many interesting data, have been preserved in this way[5]; but it is to be regretted that scarcely any of them have been printed, and that none of the numerous MSS. in the public libraries of Europe have been used for the history of mediæ-

val philosophy. We will here mention only two examples.
The errors about Michael Scotus' translation of the Liber
Animalium, committed by Buhle and Schneider, might easily
have been avoided if the Hebrew translation in the Oppenheim Collection had been known. Supposing the Hebrew
title to be correct, this MS. contains the Commentary of
Averroes; to which neither Jourdain, nor Renau in his great
work on Averroes, makes any allusion. Another Hebrew
MS., now at Oxford, contains a work by Robert of Lincoln,
De Anima (unknown to Tanner), in which Albertus Magnus
is quoted. A complete answer to those who imagine all
Jews in the Middle Ages, except the Arabians, to have been
trades-people and privileged usurers, is found in the prefatory
remarks of Jehuda ben Moses of Rome (beginning of fourteenth century); who professes to have translated various
short dissertations by several celebrated Christian authors, in
order to show his brethren that "the Christian nation is not
destitute of all true science," as some of them believed. The
Jews have never been entirely excluded from the scientific pursuits of their contemporaries, except by force ; the
general ignorance respecting that part of the literature of the
Middle Ages is shown by the fact, that a Hebrew translation
of a work by Thomas Aquinas has been recently introduced
to the public as a great curiosity, and ascribed to a special
motive of no value.

The most important *Translators* and *Commentators* of
Arabian works (by Arabs or Jews) are,—the family Tibbon
(mentioned at § 11.) of Grenada at Lünel; viz. in a direct
line, Judah ben Saul (1160), Samuel (1200), and Moses
(1244—1274); and as collateral branches, Jacob Anatoli
(1232) and Jacob ben Machir (1289—1303); moreover,
Jehuda ben Cardinal (1211?), Jehuda Charisi (ob.
before 1235), Abraham ben Samuel Ibn Chisdai at Barcelona (1230), Solomon ben Joseph Ibn Ajub of Grenada
at Beziers (1240—1265), the physician Solomon ben Joseph
Ibn Jaakub at Saragossa (1298), Jehuda ben Solomon
Cohen of Toledo in Tuscany (1247), Shemtob ben Isaac
of Tortosa (1264), Shemtob Palquera (1264—1280), Serachja ben Isaac ben Shealtiel Halevi at Rome (1284

—1294); SERACHJA HALEVI, called SALADIN (1412);.
ISAAC ALBALAG (1307), who savoured of heresy[6]; KALO-
NYMOS BEN KALONYMOS of Arles (nat. 1287), at Avignon
(1311—1317), Rome (1320), and in Spain, who also trans-
lated into Latin[7], and was versed in many languages; ISAAC
BEN JOSEPH IBN POLKAR (Alfasi?) in Spain (about 1300);
CHAJIM BEN JOSEPH IBN BIBAS (1320); LEVI BEN
GERSON, or Gersonides, at Perpignan (1320—4), whose
attacks on Ibn Roshd were afterwards refuted by SABBATAI
COHEN BEN MALKIEL of Crete (1473) and ELIA BEN
MEDIGO (1491); SAMUEL BEN JEHUDA of Marseilles (1321
—1326), JOSEPH CASPI (1330), KALONYMOS BEN DAVID
THEODORUS (at Narbonne?), THEODORUS THEODOROSI of
Arles in Trinquetaille (1337), ISAAC BEN NATHAN of
Cordova (Xativa?) (1348), MOSES NARBONI, called Ma-
estro Vidal בילשׁום (1344 — 1362), JEHUDA BEN SOLOMON
NATHAN in Provence (1354), MOSES BEN SOLOMON of
שׁלון in the South of France (not Xilon) (before 1390),
SALOMON IBN LABI, MANOAH SHUALI, and others.[8]
All these were acquainted with Arabic, though in their
works they availed themselves of their Hebrew, and after
the thirteenth century also of their Latin, predecessors.
Others took as the foundation of their editions the Hebrew
translations and the Christian Scholastics above mentioned:
JEHUDA BEN MOSES BEN DANIEL ROMANO (nat. 1292)[9],
SAMUEL BENVENISTE (at Saragossa?) translator of the
book De Consolatione Philosophiæ by Boethius (about
1320?), JECHISKIJA BEN CHALAFTA in Provence (1320)[10],
ABRAHAM BEN MESHULLAM ABIGDOR (1367) at Mont-
pellier[11], and JEHUDA BEN SAMUEL SHALOM (about 1400).
The Ethics of Aristotle was translated from the Latin of
Boethius (who lived in the thirteenth century)* by Don
MEIR ALGUADES (1405), physician to King Henry III. of
Castile; and this translation was commentated by JOSEPH
BEN SHEMTOB at Segovia (1455). MICHAEL COHEN in
Crete (1448 — 1451), the physician MENAHEM ZEBI BEN
NATANEL of France in Sinigaglia (1474), ELI BEN JOSEPH

---

* Boethius, the translator of the Ethics, is not the older author of that
name, as has been proved by *Jourdain*.

Habillo (Xabillo) of Monçon on the borders of Aragon, (1470), Baruch Ibn Taish ben Isaac (1485), David ben Samuel Ibn Shoshan (of uncertain date), Abraham ben Shemtob Bibago in Aragon (1489) and his opponent Isaac Arama, Abraham ben Joseph Ibn Nachmias (1491), Isaac Abravanel (see below), Elia Misrachi at Constantinople (1490), Elia ben Joseph de Nola (1538), and Moses Almosnino at Salonichi, form, with contemporary translators into Latin, the transition to the next period (§ 23.).

Between these and the following class we may place those who composed larger systematical or encyclopædical works from foreign sources, either directly or indirectly; as Samuel Ibn Tibbon, whose *Opinions of Philosophers* is scarcely yet known, and will be described in the catalogue of the MSS. of Leyden; Gerson ben Solomon (§ 10.); and Mose di Gaggio di Rieti, whose Italian work in the same library has been described as a system of ethics by all bibliographers, not excepting Dukes.

II. The more *independent writings* are partly,—

A. *Dogmatic Theology*, or *Philosophy of Religion*: investigations respecting the rational grounds, the importance, and duration of the law (a kind of philosophy of the Halacha); the authority of the Bible and tradition; the essence, object, and necessity of revelation and prophecy in relation to the mental and moral nature of man; the essence and attributes of God, and his relation to the world; the principal doctrines of the Jewish faith, such as Monotheism, Creation, Eschatology, &c.; e. g. the works of the Spaniards Solomon Ibn Gabirol, i. e. Avicebron (eleventh century), whose system is original; Moses Ibn Ezra (1138)[12]; and Joseph Ibn Zaddik of Cordova (ob. A. D. 1149), whose dogmatical work *Mikrokosmos*, on the system previously adopted by the celebrated Arabic Society, *The Brethren of Purity* (اخوان الصفا), did not much please Maimonides; the reasons for this opinion, however, owing to a mistake in the translation, have been hitherto misunderstood by every one, not excepting the editor (A. D. 1854). The dogmatic treatise by Abraham ben David (the historian, § 10.) has been described by Guggenheimer, and edited with a German translation only within the last few years ; the refutation of Ibn Gabirol is perhaps the most interesting part of it. About the same time JOSEPH IBN AKNIN (ob. at Aleppo, A. D. 1226) wrote at Maghreb (as has been proved elsewhere by the author) the greater part of his profound and learned works, founded on the Aristotelism of Alfarabi, &c. Later he became a pupil of Maimonides, whose works (e. g. the Thirteen Articles of Belief, and especially the Moreh) form a kind of epoch, and constitute the centre of religio-philosophical activity down to the present time. Of the many commentators of the Moreh [13], we will mention the translator himself SAMUEL IBN TIBBON and his corrector SHEMTOB PALQUERA (1280), JOSEPH IBN CASPI (1330), MOSES NARBONI (1362), PROPHIAT DURAN (Ephodæus) (1394), SHEMTOB BEN JOSEPH BEN SHEMTOB (1488) grandson of the opponent above mentioned (§ 11. fin.), ASHER BEN ABRAHAM BONAN CRESCAS, DON ISAAC ABRAVANEL, and DAVID IBN JAHJA. There soon appear also *Kabbalistic* interpreters, as ABRAHAM ABULAFIA (1280)[14], and German commentators, as MENAHEM, brother of Abigdor Kara (about 1439).[14a] By the way, it is an interesting fact, that some general philosophical passages of the Moreh, as well as of the great Halacha work of Maimonides (the latter translated into Arabic, against the intention of the author), found commentators even amongst the professors of Islamism, probably in the thirteenth century, and were disseminated amongst Christian scholars in the same century by means of Latin translations. Other writers on the philosophy of religion are: MOSES (Levi) ABULAFIA (ob. 1255), author of an essay on the Primum Movens ; JEHUDA IBN SEBARA, probably at Montpellier (subsequently to 1293), author of a tract upon the resurrection ; CHAJIM BEN ISRAEL (1272—1277)[15] ; LEVI BEN ABRAHAM BEN CHAJIM, the leader of the liberal party in Provence (§ 11.) ; DAVID BEN JOMTOB IBN BILLA (Bilia, Villa?) (1320), who wrote on the Thirteen Articles of Belief [16] ; CHANOCH BEN SOLOMON AL-CONSTANTINI (about 1350), who stood in bad repute with the orthodox ; MOSES NATHAN BEN JEHUDA (1354); the original JEHUDA BEN JOSEPH CORSANI,

imprisoned in Fez (1365)[17]; ELNATHAN BEN MOSES KILKES
(1368), who engaged in a dispute with the Karaites, but
was no critic; and the celebrated LEVI BEN GERSON (1329),
who had the audacity to confess the eternity of matter, so
that his philosophical work, *The Wars of God*, was ironically
called *The Wars with* (against) *God*.   CHISDAI CRESCAS
(1377), and his pupil JOSEPH ALBO (1425), attacked Maimonides' Articles of Belief, and reduced them to three,—The
Existence of God, Revelation, and Retribution; the former writer was opposed by SIMON DURAN in Algiers (ob.
1444).   HILLEL BEN SAMUEL at Rome (thirteenth century) wrote a Psychology and Eschatology in the sense of
the philosophers — although in respect of Halacha strictly
orthodox, — and boasts (bk. i. chap. 3.) of being acknowledged by Christian scholars, who adopted his views in their
writings.   A work on Eschatology, attributed to MACHIR,
but really written by Moses de Leon (A. D. 1290), expresses
a diametrically opposite opinion.   It is found only in a miscellaneous collection, printed under various titles, and variously edited and translated.   We may here remark, that the
different views of Jewish theologians about the future state
of the Gentiles are given in an interesting essay by Zunz.
JOSEPH BEN SHEMTOB (A. D. 1442) tried to reconcile the
substance of the orthodox creed, and even the mysteries of
the Law, with the formal principle of Aristotle, that the
highest good is speculative and not practical; a striking
proof of the influence exercised by ancient study and learning upon later times, until external oppression had given rise
to ignorant bigotry.   The same author propounds the question how far the study of pagan philosophy is lawful for
Jews, and decides in favour of its lawfulness; but he advises
restrictions as to the age of the students (conf. § 11.).   He
intended to publish a selection of such passages of Aristotle
as are opposed to the Jewish creed, together with a refutation.
ABRAHAM BIBAGO (1489), ABRAHAM SHALOM BEN ISAAC
CATALANO (ob. 1492), and JOSEPH IBN JAHJA (ob. 1539)
complete the period; to which also belong JOSEPH KILTI the
Greek, author of a Logic (1450—1500)[18], and many others.
    B. *Ethics* (חכמת המוסר) never attained to any independent

scientific treatment.   External duties and jurisprudence continued to form an integral part of the Halacha, and grew
more severe and ascetic in practice [19]; while the theory was
elucidated by the above-mentioned SOLOMON BEN GABIROL
in a celebrated Arabic treatise, which might perhaps be
also called a practical Psychology. It gives a systematical
survey of the different virtues in connexion with the human
senses, short remarks upon each, and a collection of sentences taken from the Bible, from the old philosophers, and
from anonymous authors, interwoven, according to the taste
of those times (§ 20.), with quotations from Arabic poems
(omitted in the Hebrew translation, but extant in the Arabic
MS. in the Bodleian Library).   Among the latter we may
perhaps reckon a work mentioned under the name of *Kuti*,
hitherto unknown, but apparently written by a Jew named
CHEFEZ AL-KUTI, who was probably the composer of an
Arabic paraphrase of the Psalms in rhyme cited by Moses
Ibn Esra, by whom he is called once *Al-kuti*, and once *Alfuti*,
a variation easily explained by the Arabic characters.   The
aim of BECHAJI BEN JOSEPH at Saragossa (circa 1050—
1100), in his Arabic work *The Duties of the Heart,* was to
construct a system (הכמת המצפון ‏علم ‏الباطن ?) [20] out of the
ethical Haggada (§ 5. 2 a.), which system was probably
overthrown by the important discussion on the fundamental doctrines of the Philosophy of Religion.   Ethics there
fore appear either as a new treatment of the *Aristotelian*, the
abridgment of which by Averroes was first translated from
the Arabic about the year 1321, by SAMUEL BEN JEHUDA
of Marseilles, and thence again abridged by JOSEPH IBN
CASPI (1330), or else as an exposition of the Haggada, and
especially of the Talmudical treatise *Abot.*[21] This treatise
was explained not only by those authors who included it
in their commentaries upon larger portions of the Talmud,
but more especially by those who selected it for the sake
of its subject matter, and the various directions which it
gave suitable to different countries, general views, special
philosophical systems, &c.   Some of the later writers lose
themselves in digressions and introductory disquisitions;
for instance, MAIMONIDES wrote, as an introduction to his

Commentary, the celebrated "eight chapters" on psychology,
MENAHEM MEIRI a historical and methodological essay
(§ 19.), and SIMON DURAN a philosophical or dogmatical
work, much larger than the Commentary itself.   Amongst
those which are still extant one is ancient, and one commonly
occurs under the name of RASHI (SALOMO ISAKI); they
have been variously altered and ascribed to different authors.
Others were made by JONAH GERONDI, ISAAC BEN SO-
LOMON ISRAELI (cir. 1300), and others.   Moreover, we find
ethics as a component part of Halacha and exegetical works,
and in certain lesser writings, in the form of *parænetic epistles*
(אגרת המוסר), among the Sefardim ; e. g. those by ABRAHAM
BEN CHIJJA (1130), JEHUDA IBN TIBBON (1170), MAIMON-
IDES (1200), NACHMANIDES (1260?), SHEMTOB PALQUERA
(1260), JOSEPH IBN CASPI (1330), and SOLOMON AL-AMMI
in Portugal (1415) [22], partly addressed to the sons of the
authors, and consequently appearing as *testaments* (צואה),
which, especially in Germany, form a part of popular literature.[23]   Finally, ethics were introduced into poetry, rhetoric
(§ 20.), and homiletics, affording but few names and titles for
particular mention : such as in Germany ELIEZER BEN ISAAC
of Worms (1050); JEHUDA BEN SAMUEL, "the pious" (Chasid), of Regensburg (cir. 1200), who was acquainted with
Ibn Ezra, and with the translation of Bechaji's Ethics, and
probably also with Maimonides, and to whose school belongs
the renowned *Book of the Pious* (ס' חסידים), which Wulferus
compares with the Ethics of Marcus Aurelius and Seneca ;
his pupil ELIEZER BEN JEHUDA of Worms, JONA GERONDI
the Spaniard, and MENAHEM MEIRI of Perpignan (before
1287), all of whom wrote essays on penitence; BECHAI BEN
ASHER, who composed an alphabetical work on ethics and
asceticism (1290)[24]; SERACHJA HAJEVANI (the Greek),
author of the book on ethics (before 1387) ascribed to R.
Tam from an interchange of similar titles (ס' הישר)[25];
JECHIEL BEN JEKUTIEL BEN BENJAMIN ANAW at Rome
(cir. 1287) [26]; R. MATATIA (1430); the anonymous author
of the figurative *Orchot Zaddikim;* and ISAAC BEN ELI-
EZER at Worms (cir. 1460—1480): the last two wrote originally in German. The compilation of JEHUDA CALAZ,

edited by his grandson (1537), is not popular in Germany.
The *Menorat Hammaor* of ISAAC ABOAB of Castile (ob.
1493, in Portugal) is one of the principal works of the next
period.   With these are in some degree connected the
Spanish *Flores de Derecho*, compiled by order of Alfonso (son
of Alfonso the Wise) by JACOB DE LAS LEYES, or his
attendant MOSES ZARFATI, and the *Libro de Dichos de
Sabios é Philosophos*, a compilation from the Old and New
Testaments and ecclesiastical authors, &c., by JACOB CA-
DIQUE (i. e. Zaddik) of Ucles (middle of the fourteenth
century).

C. *Exegesis and Homiletics.* The former, the development of which can be treated only in connexion with Hebrew
philology (§ 17.), will be mentioned here merely as a field of
literature, in which, especially since the time of Maimonides,
the Philosophy of Religion principally flourished ; thus, one
ALEXANDRI (?), in the tenth century, wrote a long commentary on the chapter on the creation [27], and his contemporary
the physician ISAAC ISRAELI [28] a similar treatise on Gen. i.
20.   The biblical commentaries of IBN EZRA (ob. 1168),
TANCHUM of Jerusalem (cir. 1250, in Arabic), LEVI BEN
GERSON (1327—38), IBN CASPI, IMMANUEL of Rome and
his Roman contemporaries (cir. 1300) [29], IBN BILLA (1320),
SHEMARJAH of Negropont or Crete (Ikriti) patronised by of
Robert of Anjou (1328), ISAAC ABOAB, ABRAVANEL (ob.
1506), and others ; many of the innumerable super-commentaries on Ibn Ezra [30], e. g. by JEDAJA PENINI (cir. 1300),
MOSES BEN JEHUDA of the Roman family of NEARIM (cir.
1300), SOLOMON BEN CHANOCH AL-CONSTANTINI (1325),
JOSEPH IBN CASPI who introduced the form of double commentaries, separating the " Mysteries" from the rest (1300—
30), JOSEPH BEN ELIEZER TOB-ELEM (Bon-fils, cir. 1335);
that in Arabic by SOLOMON IBN JAISH at Seville (ob. 1345),
translated into Hebrew by JACOB BEN SOLOMON ALFANDARI
for the well-known super-commentator IBN ZARZA, and those
by SOLOMON FRANCO (attacked by ABRAHAM BEN EL TABIB,
but used by EZRA BEN SOLOMON ASTRUC IBN GATIGNO
(1372) [31]), SHEMTOB BEN ISAAC SHAFRUT (1385), perhaps
also PROPHIAT DURAN (Ephodæus), and others, are as im-

portant for philosophy as the many Kabbalistic Commentaries for the discipline of that school.

To this class likewise belong the Sermons (דרושים, דרשות)[32],
for the most part on the various sections of the Bible, especially the Pentateuch, which explain Scripture and the Haggada in a philosophical manner ; and works in which biblical
commentary and theology are interwoven : e. g. by JACOB
ANATOLI (§ 11.), NISSIM, JOSHUA IBN SHOEIB (1300 30),
JACOB BEN CHANANEL SIKELI in the East (cir. 1400)[33],
JOEL IBN SHOEIB at Tudela (1469), JOSEPH BEN SHEMTOB
and his son SHEMTOB BEN JOSEPH (1489), the Spanish
exiles ISAAC ARAMA and ISAAC KARO, and others. The
Arabic homilies, favourites even with the Karaites in Egypt,
and attributed to DAVID grandson of Maimonides, stand
at the limit of this period (1503).[34] The theory of Homiletics is treated by JOSEPH BEN SHEMTOB (cir. 1440), and
Rhetoric in general by JEHUDA BEN JECHIEL, called
MESSER LEON of Naples, at Mantua (cir. 1454), with references to Cicero and Quinctilian. Finally, we may mention
philosophical expositions of Midrash and Haggada, by MOSES
IBN TIBBON and JEDAJA PENINI, &c. ; MAIMONIDES intended to write a work of this kind, but it became merged
in the Moreh.

D. The *Terminology* of Philosophy, in its widest sense,
was treated by MAIMONIDES, who wrote on Logic in
Arabic (ante 1160); by the author of the רוח תן[35]; by
MENAHEM BONAFOUX PERPIGNANO, in the form of a lexicon; by the author of the ספר הדרבן[36]; and in glossaries
appended by SAMUEL IBN TIBBON (who used the celebrated
كتاب العين of Al-Chalil), in his translation of the Moreh
of Maimonides, and in the preface to his large work on *the
Views of the Philosophers.* We know of no special work
on Methodology, &c. ; but some essays are to be found
inserted in several works, e. g. by JOSEPH IBN AKNIN
(before 1180), PROPHIAT DURAN (1403), &c.

§ 13.] *Mysteries and Kabbala.*[1]

We have above (§ 5 c.) given the essence of the olden
Mysteries, and traced the commencement of a special litera-

ture in that period (cir. 800), when the two principal subjects,
the History of Creation and Theophany (Theomorphy),
began to be transformed into Physics and Metaphysics by
the introduction of Science, and when the Haggada passed
from oral tradition to writing, accessible as yet only to the
initiated. The Mysteries were transformed into Kabbala
first in Europe, and subsequently in the East. The principal
difficulties in the historical development of this comprehensive and important field of literature consist in the frequent
occurrence of Pseudepigraphy, and the prejudice and superficial views to which it has given rise. Another difficulty
is the obscurity, intentional or otherwise, of the language;
and, lastly, another is to be found in our scanty information
respecting the Oriental Mysticism, with which the Jewish
is connected. We must here confine ourselves to what is
necessary for establishing our views on the historical development of this literature.

The following points must be carefully attended to,
if we would avoid falling into errors, and into anachronisms especially : — 1. The date of a written composition
must be clearly distinguished from that of the origin of
the doctrine, which has often been orally preserved. We
can only form a definite judgment on the writings in
their present shape ; and in so doing more weight is
given to language and style, quotations and reminiscences
from writings whose dates are known, and the like, than
to the indications to be gathered from the contents; but,
nevertheless, whole groups of investigations and leading
ideas, as the doctrines of Spheres, the Trinity, &c., form
important landmarks. — 2. Titles and quotations from
writings which cannot be found have often only a negative
value, on account of the frequent Pseudepigraphy and direct
forgeries. The Pseudepigraphy may be explained by the
author's fear of giving his own name, or by the desire for
the sanction of antiquity for new ideas, to which the usual
explanation of Scripture (Midrash) afforded but slight foundation. This abuse, however, which reached its height at
a later period, appears to have been influenced by non-
Jewish apocryphal writings, e. g. those of Christian Gnostics,
and especially those of Muhammedans, whose doctrine of pro-

phets and legends, though partly constructed by Jewish and
Christian renegades, doubtless called into existence a prophetic literature of this kind.[2]   At all events, we must first
investigate whether the few quotations, &c., which occur in
older writers are not merely Hebrew translations of Arabic
titles[3]; and, if they refer to Jewish works, whether these
works are not entirely different from later forgeries bearing
the same titles; as for instance, the book *Tagin* (תגין), on
the ornamental crowns, &c., in the rolls of the Pentateuch,
&c. (§ 16.) — 3. We must not start with the premiss, that the
Mysteries were a definitely developed philosophical system,
and that the principal doctrinal statements in them were,
unless obviously the reverse, older than Christianity.   In
certain individual cases the Kabbala has been united with
a philosophical system; but in general it rather designates a
kind of Haggada or Exegesis, forming a kind of Midrash
applied to the Mysteries and common philosophy.[4]   Particular connexions between such systems and other philo-
sophies or religions, Parseeism for instance, are of no use as
criteria for the age of the writings[5], since many older Gnostic,
Philonic, and Persian doctrines were not intruded upon the
Jewish literature until a later time.[6]   Some valuable suggestions have lately been made by S. Sachs, who traces the
two opposite philosophical systems, " Transcendentalism "
and " Immanence " (combined in the Kabbala with Emana-
tion), in the Jewish philosophers of the Peripatetic school,
and in the peculiar philosophy of IBN GABIROL and ABRA-
HAM IBN EZRA, from whose influence he derives the Kabbalistic system of Nachmanides.   But the subject requires
further investigation before we can estimate the value of
any general remarks.   The *practical Kabbala,* on the other
hand, belongs to astrology, magic, &c.; which certainly
made their first appearance in the shape of a left-handed
science in Jewish literature through the instrumentality of
Arabia[7], and which together with the prevalent superstitions
did not find their way till a much later period into the Syncretism of the Kabbala (§ 12.).

   The *Secret Science* is in fact nothing else than Metaphysics in the garb of the Midrash and Haggada; an
intentional obscurity in which, down to a late period, the

teachers of liberal philosophy were in the habit of enveloping
them, lest they should offend the multitude.[8] It treated principally of the old subjects, Creation and the Celestial Hier-
archy. Philosophy and Secret Science fought respectively
in the ranks of Spiritual Theology and Oriental Sensualism.
On the one hand, the Aristotelians sought to bring their clear
system of νοῦς (שכל), and the spheres enlivened by Intelligences (גלגלים, פלכים, فلوك), into harmony with the Bible
and Haggada, by means of allegorical interpretation; and
on the other, the Secret Doctrine lost itself among fantastic
images and exaggerations, and took possession of everything
that is inexplicable in the world of nature and spirit.[9] An
instance of this is to be found in the descriptions (if we may
use such a term) of the "body" of God, called *Shiur Koma*
(שיעור קומה), satirised in verse by SALMON BEN JERUCHAM
(tenth century). Hence with this school even the plainer
miraculous legends of the Haggada gave an agreeable opportunity for further embellishments. The ordinary Midrash
deduces a manifold signification from the mere letter of the
Bible, considered as divine, and also uses a play upon letters
by way of memoria technica (v. sup. § 5.); but here we meet
with a mystical treatment of letters in general, with reference
to their sound, form, and numerical value.[10] The Book
Jezira (ס' יצירה, i. e. Book of the Creation, or אותיות דאברהם
אבינו *Letters of Abraham the Patriarch*), which opens the
literature of the Secret Doctrine, enunciates as a fundamental idea, that the ten digits (ספירות) and twenty-two letters
(the thirty-two *paths of wisdom,* ל"ב נתיבות פליאות הכמה) are
to be considered as the foundation of everything.[11] The
following writers gave a philosophical explanation of this
work: SAADJA (ob. 941), ISAAC ISRAELI (ob. 940—953),
and JACOB BEN NISSIM (?) at Kairowan, all in Arabic [12];
SABBATAI DONOLO in Italy (born about 913), JEHUDA BEN
BARSILLAI in Provence (cir. 1130), and JEHUDA HALEVI
in Spain (1140). The third and fourth chapters of the *Boraita* of R. ELIEZER (§ 5 B.), the greater and lesser *Hechalot*
(היכלות), said to be written by R. ISMAEL (cf. § 5. p. 48.),
the old book *Raziel* (רזיאל), attributed to Solomon, extant
only in detached portions, the Midrash *Konen* (מ' כונן)[13], and
likewise the lost *Hajashar* (erroneously ascribed to R. Akiba),

and *Juchasin*, are the principal works on the old Secret Doctrine.[14]   One of them, the *Alphabet* of R. AKIBA (א"ב דר'
עקיבה), older than the tenth century, lays great stress upon
the letters, and gives a preference to the knowledge (בינה)
over the practice of the Law, thus opening the door to a controversy between a new kind of Gnosis and the Halacha.

The Secret Doctrine, originally unfettered as a part of
the Haggada, was first stamped as *Kabbala* (קבלה) or *Tradition* [15]; this occurred in Europe, and at the point of contact
of the two principal intellectual tendencies frequently mentioned above, in Italy and Provence, a fact, which is characteristic of its development and of its subsequent position
with respect to Halacha.   The oldest traces of this movement
point to Apulia and Northern Italy (Lucca); although no
historical value is due to the names and conflicting traditions
to be found in later authors, and still less to the legends and
fables, according to which, for instance, Eleasar of Worms
makes a journey through the air into Spain, to teach Nachmanides, &c.   From Northern Italy we have the name of one
KASHISHA[16], a descendant of the Gaonim, as the author of
a Kabbalistic work written for his pupil JEHUDA OF COR-
BEIL, of whom ELEASAR OF WORMS is said to have been a
pupil.   The latter however traces back his Secret Doctrine
through various stages up to one ABU HARUN, who migrated
from Lucca, and was son of the Babylonian Prince Samuel.
His pupil MOSES [17] and his family are said to have brought it
back to Germany, and finally handed it down through ELEA-
SAR OF SPIRES, his son SAMUEL, and his grandson JEHUDA
the Pious (cir. 1200), who like Nachmanides is called "Father
of Wisdom," to his great-grandson DAVID.   Perhaps from
this quarter issued also the Kabbala of Provence and Spain,
although it claims origin immediately from the Prophet Elias
(see below).   Mention is also made in connexion with it of
a Doctor NEHORAI of Jerusalem.

At this point, the Doctrine of Mysteries enters upon a
new course.   The Haggada had, as early as the First Period,
exhausted itself in the Midrash; this again on the one
hand had undergone a poetical metamorphosis in the Franco-
German Pijjutim (§ 19.), and on the other evaporated into the

Arabising Philosophy.   In the North, social and political
circumstances, and the spirit of the surrounding nations,
fostered a tendency towards feeling and superstition, which
are always associated with the embodiment of the spirit
in the traditional letter.   In the South, Magic, Chiromancy,
Demonology, &c., were added as a kind of philosophical sequel
to the highest sciences; and the Oriental Mysticism of the
Sufi found a resting-place in the old remains of Judæo-
Christian gnosis.   The Crusades and other political revolutions brought all intellectual tendencies together.   Thus was
developed a fresh Jewish Theosophy[18], in which first the
letter, and afterwards also the practice of the Law (Halacha)
were degraded to a mere husk of the Mystery (סוד) contained
in it.[19]   This again was carried back to antiquity by means
of Pseudepigraphy, by the imitation of the external forms
and expressions of the old Midrash, and finally by the after-
thought of pretended Inspiration and forgery.   But the intermixture of well-known foreign elements made it evident
that the so-called " Kabbala" was the reverse of that which
its name (Tradition) designated.   In such a wide choice of
thoughts and means for exegesis a large field was open to the
subjective element; and hence " the number of the systems
and expositions was nearly as great as that of the writers." [20]

R. ISAAC THE BLIND, called the " Father of the Kabbala,"
son of the celebrated Abraham ben David of Posquieres (§ 9.),
is perhaps to be considered as the founder of the new mystic
literature.[21]   To him Landauer [22] ascribes the book *Bahir*
(הבהיר 'ס), or *Midrash Nechunja Ben ha-Kana*[23] (at all
events belonging to this age), in which the ten *Sefirot*
(numbers) of the Book Jezira were brought into connexion
with the attributes (מדות) and fingers, or members, of God.
A foundation was thus laid for the doctrine of the Sefirot,
which was finally merged in the Aristotelian spheres, and
introduced by way of interpretation into the Book Jezira.
His pupil EZRA (ob. 1238 ?) is said to have been the teacher
of Nachmanides (in Spain); but, although much has been
written upon the subject, it is not yet clear whether he is not
the same person as AZRIEL (ben Solomon, or ben Menahem ?)
mentioned as a pupil of Nachmanides.[24]   According to Moses

ben Solomon ben Simon of Burgos, a not very trustworthy author of the thirteenth century of whom we shall speak hereafter, a work called *Masoret*, by a R. ELCHANAN, is one of the sources whence Nachmanides drew his system. About the same time lived JOSEPH BEN SAMUEL, a fragment of whose Exposition of Genesis is inserted by Jacob ben Sheshet. R. ELEASAR OF WORMS (1220) in Germany was author of many Kabbalistic works; among others of a Commentary on the Book Jezira and on the Prayer-book, and also of the סודי רזיא, a compendium of which is called the *Greater Rasiel.*[25] To his numerous pupils belong, among others, ABRAHAM BEN ALEXANDER (or Achselrad) of Cologne, and the author of the *pseudo-Saadianic* Commentary on Jezira[26]; a certain MENAHEM however seems to have been a pupil of Nachmanides.

To the thirteenth century, especially the latter half of it, belong some important men, whose writings still require thorough investigation for the history of the Kabbala; and also a mass of pseudepigraphical writings[27] which became more numerous in the fourteenth century, and were ascribed to Patriarchs, as Adam, Enoch, Abraham; to Prophets, as Moses, Elias, Jeremiah, &c.; to Doctors of Talmud, as Akiba, Ismael ben Elisha, Nechunja ben Hakana, Simeon the Just[27a], Simeon Hapekuli, especially Simeon ben Jochai; to Gaonim, as Saadja, Sherira, Hai[28], and the fictitious Chammai[28a] and Dositai; and also to later learned men, as Ibn Ezra[29], and even Maimonides.[30] Lastly, appeal was made to forged or fictitious names and titles, as by the notorious Spaniard MOSES BOTAREL, who wrote a Commentary on the Book Jezira, nominally for a Christian named Maestro Juan.[31] The persons first mentioned, principally Spaniards, are divided by Landauer[32] into four schools,—I. *The Orthodox School* of IBN ADERET[33], which cultivated the doctrine of the Sefirot according to the Book Bahir, and the Commentary on the Pentateuch by NACHMANIDES (finished A. D. 1267 in the East). The following are representatives of this school: TODROS HALEVI ABULAFIA at Toledo (ob. 1283 at Seville), erroneously called "Tedacus" by Reuchlin; the notorious SHEMTOB BEN ABRAHAM IBN GAON (Jaen?), who calls himself a pupil of Aderet; ISAAC BEN TODROS (1325 at Safet)[33a], and his colleague ISAAC OF AKKO (i. e. St. Jean d'Acre) (see § 17.); BECHAJI BEN ASHER at Saragossa (1291); perhaps also some less known, of whom we shall speak hereafter; and, according to Landauer, Menahem de Recanati in Italy [34]; but we must place this author later (see below). Among those more independent of Nachmanides were PEREZ, the supposed author of the famous *Maarechet ha Elahut*[35], the pseudo CHAMMAI GAON, and others. — II. *The Aristotelian Kabbalistic School* (called by Landauer "Kabbalistic Philosophical") of the ambiguous ISAAC IBN LATHÎF (1280, not 1244), who expounded the mystic doctrine philosophically, and consequently incurred censure and persecution. — III. *The Philosophical Kabbalistic* School of JOSEPH IBN CHIQUITILLA (Gekatilia, erroneously also Karnitol), and his teacher ABRAHAM ABULAFIA, who viewed the Kabbala as the foundation of Philosophy, but nevertheless gave greater prominence to the literal Kabbala than to the Sefirot. Hence was developed — IV. *The Zoharic* School, which forms a new and important phase.

The famous or infamous mystical Midrash on the Pentateuch ascribed to SIMEON BEN JOCHAI, entitled *Zohar* (זוהר, splendour)[36], certainly dates no earlier than the thirteenth century, when there was an intimate connexion between Judaism and Christianity, and when false prophets and soothsayers appeared everywhere.[37] Its advocates themselves acknowledge that it was unknown even to the great Kabbalistic authors before that time. This work develops the sexual distinctions in respect to the Deity given in the Book Bahir[38]; and also the older Sefirot doctrine, by means of a literal Kabbala, into a Trinitarian doctrine [39], nevertheless openly attacking Christianity [40] as well as Talmud and Halacha.[41] Anti-Kabbalists and critics have hitherto considered MOSES BEN SHEMTOB DE LEON of Guadalaxara (1287—93) as the author of it; and the researches commenced by Jellinek seem to confirm the opinion that this author, who is known to have been guilty of plagiarism, was concerned in the forgery, if indeed he was not the principal actor in it. From want of good critical grounds, although not without some

appearance of probability, Landauer came to a different conclusion.   In the course of the discussion, however, some
interesting particulars have come to light respecting an
author of that time, previously but little known, ABRAHAM
ABULAFIA BEN SAMUEL (nat. 1240 at Tudela)[42], a celebrated fanatic, who has since become the subject of special
researches.   He had been taught the Book Jezira [43] by
twelve expositors, and himself composed a pseudonymic
commentary on it (1289). He understood Arabic (Greek?)
and Latin, had studied Plato[44], gave himself out as a
prophet and " Messias " or considered himself such[45], went
by Barcelona to Capua, and is said to have tried to convert
the Pope (Martin IV.) at Rome (August 1281)[46]; but he
was persecuted for his opinions, and forced to seek an
asylum at Cumino in Malta.[47] He was the author of more
than twenty Kabbalistic (and grammatical) works; part of
which he calls " prophetic," frequently adopting the ana-
grammatic name RAZIEL.   Amongst others, there is a
Commentary on the Moreh (1280, 1291), and a book called
Zacharia or האות (the sign or wonder), composed A. D. 1288
at Cumino. In this he affirms that Jesus was a prophet,
but not yet acknowledged; reminding us of a similar opinion
expressed 150 years before by the Karaite author Jehuda
Hedessi (§ 14.).   Whether some of the substance now
forming the great body of the Zohar was taken from his
writings is a question which cannot be answered until both
have been more thoroughly investigated.   The Zohar, which
like many works of that time was intended to be written
in pure Aramaïc, fell back to some extent upon Hebrew.
It has been since edited in Aramaïc [48]; but the language
is inelegant, and neither pure nor correct.   This fact,
proved by Luzzatto, may be considered as a complete
answer even to those who explain, by means of a miracle,
all the objections to the antiquity of the Zohar raised
on the score of improbability.   They can hardly assert
that Simon ben Jochai wrote a book in a style and
language used by no one except the followers of the
forgery, amongst whom all grammatical knowledge of
Hebrew and Aramaïc was extinct (comp. § 16.).   Our

various editions contain different original elements and additions, and without the assistance of manuscripts a critical history is out of the question.[49]

In Spain, where the forgery did not impose upon every one, we have the only certain and almost coeval witness against it, in an account given by the above-mentioned Isaac Akko, and the book never attained to great authority or popularity in that country. Landauer goes so far as to suppose that it was never brought there at all.[50] But the author has recently found it quoted as a work of Simon ben Jochai, in a book by Moses de Leon, and in another remarkable passage of Joseph Ibn Wakkar, of whom we shall have occasion to speak hereafter. This author, in mentioning the books which are to be relied upon, recommends of the "latter" only Moses Nachmanides and Todros Abulafia; "but," he adds, "the book Zohar is full of errors, and one must take care not to be misled by them." This is an impartial and indirect testimony that the Zohar was recognised scarcely fifty years after its appearing as one of the "latter" works, and not attributed to Simon ben Jochai. Through what circumstances it so soon found its way into Italy is not explained, if we reject Landauer's conjectures. His adoption of the older statement about the date of Menahem de Recanati cannot in any case be admitted; for the latter wrote his Commentary on the Pentateuch (which is, in fact, little else than a commentary on the Zohar), not in 1290, but about 1330[51], when Immanuel ben Solomon of Rome makes mention of that book. From Italy a knowledge of it spread among the Jews to the north and east, and subsequently also amongst the Christians. There also the first opponents of its genuineness arose at the end of this period; during which individuals of the Spanish Philosophical School, and even Germans, as LIPPMAN OF MÜHLHAUSEN (cir. 1400), himself an author of Kabbalistic works, took up the cudgels against some doctrines of the Kabbala as un-Jewish.[52]

Amongst the Spaniards of the latter half of the 13th century there are several authors whose works and even whose names are scarcely yet known, although they are honourably mentioned by writers who flourished shortly afterwards.

I

Many of them were, or represented themselves to be, pupils of Nachmanides; and they were perhaps the real authors of some anonymous and pseudonymous works of that period. Some of them quote, as ancient, writers and works which either never existed, or had been forged by themselves. Further information is therefore necessary for the history of this interesting period, into the literature of which we have as yet been able to obtain but little insight. We may mention, as examples, DAVID COHEN, quoted under the anagram מרדכאי (Mardochai); ABNER, supposed to be the apostate of Burgos, and subsequently celebrated as ALFONSO OF VALLADOLID (conf. § 13.); JACOB BEN SHESHET of Girona, who wrote a work against Samuel Ibn Tibbon, and an epistle, more zealous than argumentative, against the philosophers; JACOB KOHEN BEN JACOB the Spaniard (Sefardi) of Soria, probably the same as JACOB CHIQUI-TILLA who died at Segovia; and his younger (?) brother, ISAAC KOHEN, both of whom were at one time in Provence. The latter wrote, amongst other things, an essay containing explanations of the book *Malbush* (מלבוש). He certainly belongs to the class of suspected authors, and whether himself misled or not, his statements are calculated to mislead others. He mentions a Kabbalistic essay by a fictitious author, MAZLIACH BEN PELATJA of Jerusalem, brought to Arles by one Gerson of Damascus; and he quotes JOSEPH BEN ABITUR and ISAAC IBN GAJJAT as Kabbalists, &c. With these brothers we must class their pupil MOSES (BEN SOLOMON) BEN SIMON of Burgos, who quotes JEHUDA BEN JAKAR and ISAAC HALABAN, &c.

In the 14th century JOSEPH IBN WAKKAR BEN ABRA-HAM made an attempt to reconcile the Kabbala with philosophy. He was the author of a short unpublished essay on the principal doctrines of the Kabbala, which is perhaps the best introductory compendium of the subject. He already complains of differences respecting the classification and exposition of the names of the ten Sefirot—much to the disgust of Shemtob ben Shemtob, the defender of the traditional Kabbala,—and, as mentioned above, cautions his readers against the use of the book Zohar. At the same time the philosopher JEHUDA BEN MOSES of Rome identified the *Ideas* of Plato with the Sefirot of the Kabbalists; and not long afterwards the Kabbala obtained so firm a footing, that philosophers attempted to explain it by means of philosophical exegesis; e. g. MOSES NARBONI, &c.

The Kabbalistic literature of the 14th and 15th centuries, principally anonymous or pseudonymous, and as yet but little investigated, consists chiefly of editions of older works: biblical commentaries, e. g. by BECHAI BEN ASHER (end of 13th cent.), and JOSHUA IBN SHOEIB (cir. 1330); and super-commentaries on Nachmanides, e. g. by ISAK BEN SAMUEL ex Acco, and by JACOB BEN ASHER, who substituted for the speculative passages of Nachmanides the trifling but popular explanations of Gematria, &c.; and also on Ibn Ezra, e. g. by SAMUEL MOTOT (1412). Commentaries on the book JE-ZIRA were composed by JEHUDA BEN NISSIM IBN MALKA (in Arabic) (1365), JOSEPH SAR SHALOM[53], Pseudo ABRA-HAM BEN DAVID (1390) [54], BOTAREL (1409), SAMUEL MOTOT (1412), and others. The Liturgy (§ 19.) also became the object of Kabbalistic exposition as early as the beginning of the 13th century; we will here mention only a few authors of monographies of that kind: ELEASAR OF WORMS and EZRA mentioned above, MENAHEM RECANATI, ISAAC BEN TODROS, SAMUEL MOTOT, and MEIR IBN GABBAI. We conclude this paragraph with the names of some authors in Germany and France: DAVID BEN ABRA-HAM HALABAN (cir. 1300); HISKIA BEN ABRAHAM, author of the *Malkiel;* SAMUEL BEN SIMEON (1400); ABIGDOR and his brother MENAHEM KARA at Prague (1439); ME-SHULLAM BEN MOSES; SOLOMON, father of Joseph Kolon in France (cir. 1450).[55] JOHANAN ALLEMANNO, JEHUDA CHAJJAT in Italy, and others, form the transition to the next period.

§ 14.] *Karaitic Literature.*

In opposition to the adherents of the Halacha and Hag-gada, or *Rabbinism* (Talmudism) as it is called, there stands at this period a party which is distinguished from the Sad-

ducees of Period I. by a theory carried out in an elaborate
literature. This party thus forms an actual sect, the essence
(*Karaism*) and development of which however will be here
treated of only from a literary point of view.[1] From the
fact of their principal residence being in the Crimea, recent
events have drawn public attention to them; but the
accounts which have been lately given of them are mere repetitions of older works. It seems that no advantage has
been taken of this opportunity of enlarging our very small
store of Karaitic literature; and there is but little hope that
amongst the warlike trophies of Sebastopol any Hebrew
parchments will be found.

The retiring character of Karaism prevented its ever attain-
ing a position of such immediate importance in the general
history of literature as Rabbinism, nevertheless it assisted
materially at the period of its origin (750—900) in the reformation of Rabbinical literature; so that perhaps this obscure and incomplete section of the history of the latter is
itself to be cleared up and completed by the fragments of
the former. The subsequent separate formation of the Karaitic literature has, however, some peculiar attractions for
the student.

Whatever we may think of the connexion of Karaism
with similar Jewish tendencies of an earlier date, the Karaitic literature and sect begin apparently with ANAN BEN
DAVID (cir. 760); for the long genealogies of precedent
Karaitic heads of schools are taken from a Midrash.[2] But
the later Rabbinites also were claimed by the younger Karaites as belonging to them, because they are quoted as authorities by the founders of the sect; e. g. the proselyte DAVID
BEN MERVAN AL-MUKAMMEZ, author of a dogmatic work,
the information on Jewish (Christian and Muhammedan) sects
contained in which appears to form the foundation of the
accounts given by the Arabians Makrisi and Shahristani[3];
JEHUDA IBN KOREISH; IBN EZRA, and others; also a
funereal inscription for the converter of the king of the
Chasars, ISAAC SANJARI, was forged, and a great number of
rabbinical works were counterfeited.[4] On the other hand,
there are certain peculiarities in this literature with respect to

the arguments and method ; for instance, a freer exegesis, in opposition to the Halacha, which is however by no means a safe criterion for the Karaism of the author.[5]

Karaism soon became connected with the earliest sect (in the narrowest sense) of the Muhammedans which arose at that time, viz. the *Mu'tazile*, and with the *Mutakallimun* (متكلمون, Hebrew מדברים) in general, who, starting from the Word (كلام) of God, the Logos [5a], tried to bring philosophy, the atomistic not the peripatetic, into harmony with revelation[6]; entering next upon the fundamental doctrines of religion (اصول الدين, שרשים, עקרים), and thence receiving the name (اصوليون, שרשיים) " Radicals," or more properly, " Doctrinaries." [7]　On this account the Karaites were the first to reckon the number of the (10) *Articles of Belief*[8], and are proportionately rich in dogmatic literature. Muhammedanism also in general influenced their dogmatic theology[9], and even their religious practice[10], thus giving occasion to the conversion of many Karaites to Islamism[11]; and this again provoked a reactionary controversy (§ 15.).

The opposition of Karaism was directed against the Halacha- and Haggada-Midrash[11a], and consequently promoted a simpler exegesis and grammatical study among the Rabbinites themselves.　But whilst the philosophy of the latter expounds even the Haggada-Midrash in a philosophical manner, the Karaitic was obliged to throw itself solely and wholly upon the Bible, and finally could not help having recourse to the intermediate elements of the sagas and legends of the Rabbins, with some modifications received from Muhammedanism.[12]　In religious practice there appears in the place of the despised tradition of the Halacha a not dissimilar but often false tradition (העתקה) or inheritance (סבל הירושה)[13], and a closer reference to dogmatics and philosophy; e. g. in the rules for slaughter[14], and also in the Liturgy.[15]　Levi ben Jefet tells us that ABU SOLEIMAN DAVID BEN HASSIN introduced into his Liturgy so much of exegesis, demonstrations, and polemics, that the Hymns can scarcely be recognised as such.　At the same time their religious poetry loses the Midrash materials of

the Pijjutim (§ 20.); and finally the fantastic and mystic
tendency of the secret doctrine and Kabbala could not fail
to dissolve entirely in the firm grasp of rational knowledge.

Karaism, when fully elaborated, was thus opposed to Rabbinism as a theory and dialectical exercise keeping itself
aloof from the natural development of the nation, having
been called into existence by external circumstances, and continuing to propagate itself by its own resources. Happier
in attack than in defence, wherever the direct words of the
Bible did not afford a firm footing for the new intellectual
movement, Karaism could not fail to be aware of a contradiction and harshness in the Law; to their own interpretation of
which, however, they inflexibly adhered.[16] But from its very
origin Karaism was broken up into sects or schools, some of
which professedly separated themselves on account of peculiar
and unrecognised customs, while others maintained their connexion with the prevailing tendencies of the time merely by
means of doctrinal statements.[17] Writings are expressly
ascribed to the individual founders; e. g. the Pseudomessias Abu Isa Abdallah (Obadja), Ishak ben Jaakub
el Isfahani (754—775), Ismail el Okbari in Irak (833
—842): and with some degree of probability also to others;
e. g. the camelherd and Pseudomessias Judsgân (يرذنان)[18];
Abu Amran (not "Omran") Musa (Moses) el Saaf-
rani (زعغراني)[19] Al-Tiflisi, contemporary of Okbari, and
probably identical with Moses ben Amram Ha-parsi, or
Jehuda (Al-Jehudi?) Haparsi[20]; and Mesue (Moses) of
Balbek, at Bassra (afterwards baptised). All their writings
must be considered as lost. But the whole Karaitic literature
is so little known and so inaccessible, that any attempt at
its internal history appears, to the writer of this work at
least, too bold an undertaking[21], particularly since the chronology brought forward by some of their own more recent
authors is both arbitrary and contradictory. The foundation
of it seems to be an incidental passage of Elia ben Abraham Misrachi, who, in his work upon the differences between Karaites and Rabbinites, enumerates, although not in
chronological order, about forty names, which he pretends to

have met with; the list however is neither correct nor free from repetitions. It is again given by JOSEPH BAGI BEN MOSES, who is the authority for a passage in Warner's Collectanea at Leyden; and hence Wolf has inserted the names in the third volume of his Bibliotheca. Another list of teachers, purporting to be chronologically arranged, was borrowed by MARDOCHAI BEN NISAN from MOSES BASHIATSHI (ob. 1572), and is the foundation of again another list by SIMCHA ISAAC, which is arranged geographically. But even the latter is not much more trustworthy than the former, the part which traces the names up to Anan being, as already observed (p. 116.) an evident forgery. We must therefore content ourselves with some general remarks.

The writings of the Karaites now known to us are principally[22] religious, and in the form of dogmatic treatises, biblical exegesis, books of the Laws (ס' המצוות), religious poetry, and a few grammatical works. Some works on medicine and other subjects (§ 22.) have been partly preserved by the Arabians. Anan and some of his followers, e. g. BENJAMIN BEN MOSES NEHAWENDI[23], in editing their law works, wrote in the Halacha idiom of the time; for, on account of the tendency to dogmatic polemics having become prevalent, the Hebrew and Aramaïc had fallen into the background, being ill adapted to the new conceptions, and unwieldy in poetry, as we find in the rhyming prose of SALMAN BEN JERUCHAM and JEHUDA HEDESSI. Moreover, since the Karaites lived for the most part in countries where Arabic was spoken, Arabic became their principal dialect; and, as they thus had less occasion for translations than the Rabbinites (§§ 8. 11.), the development of the Hebrew fell into arrear, and a more Arabising type was stamped upon it. Subsequently (in the 14th century) their writers learnt of the Rabbinical school, and transplanted a still greater number of Talmudical expressions into their works.[24] The form and disposition of their works are strictly scientific, even to pedantry. Their relation to the *Masora* also is worth notice.[25] The most important writers, especially those whose works are still extant, are the polemical contemporaries of Saadja, CHIWI AL BALKI or BELKI, and BEN SUTA (?); SALMAN

BEN JERUCHAM; MENAHEM; JOSEPH BEN JACOB (Abu J.)
EL KIRKISSANI EL BASSIR (البصير, Hebrew הרואה) [26], called
also after his work HAMAOR (السراج ?) (910—930); JOSEPH
BEN ABRAHAM (Ibn Zadakah ?) COHEN HAROËH, and his
pupil JESHUA (Abu Ali Isa) BEN JEHUDA; JAPHET (ABU
ALI HASSAN EL BASRI) HALEVI (953), and his son LEVI
(ABU SAÏD).   Munk identifies Jeshua ben Jehuda with
ABU 'L FARADJ FORKAN BEN ASAD, the author of an Arabic
translation or exposition of the Pentateuch; but, amongst
several authors named Jeshua who occur in the confused lists
mentioned above, there is a JESHUA AARON or ABU 'L
FARADJ HARUN, from whom Mose Bashiatshi quotes some
Arabic passages belonging to an exposition of the Pentateuch.
The Arabic name Forkan being only a translation of the
Hebrew Jeshua, it is not quite so evident as Munk supposes
that Jeshua ben Jehudah is the Abu 'l Faradj whose pupil
IBN AL-TARRAS introduced his work into Spain (see below).
Moses Ibn Ezra seems to imply that Abu'l Faradj of Jerusalem changed his faith, which however might be interpreted
that he went from the Rabbinites to the Karaites.   We may
mention also ABU SARI SAHAL BEN MAZLIACH; JACOB
BEN REUBEN (1098—1099) [27]; and JEHUDA HA-ABEL
HEDESSI (of Edessa) at Constantinople (1149), whose polemical work on the commandments in Hebrew rhyming
prose is a great authority for the earlier history of Karaism.
    About this time (1150) Karaism had made an ineffec-
tual attempt to extend itself in Spain, where IBN EZRA [28],
JEHUDA HALEVI (1140), and ABRAHAM BEN DAVID
(1161) [29], at the same time as MAIMONIDES and his son
ABRAHAM [30] in Egypt, encountered it with the weapons of
the Peripatetic school.   AARON (the elder) BEN JOSEPH,
a physician at Constantinople (1294) well acquainted with
Rabbinical works, tried to oppose it in a way different from the
old dogmatics of the Kelam; he however proved unequal
to the task. [31]   On the other hand, AARON BEN ELIA the
Nicomedian, with the most comprehensive learning [32], wrote
in opposition to the principal works of Maimonides on philosophy and law a Karaite dogmatical system, *Ez Chajjim*
(1346), a Codex of Law (1354), and a Commentary on the

Pentateuch (1362).   But little is yet known of his contemporary and compatriot the Rabbinite ELNATAN KILKES, and
his polemics against Karaism.   Once more at the end of this
period the Karaites at Constantinople fell into a controversy
with Rabbinism.[33]   The attacks of ELIA MISRACHI were
refuted by ELIA BASHIATSHI (ob. 1490).   The mediæval
Karaitic literature of the East, so far as it is known to us,
ends with his pupil and brother-in-law KALEB AFENDOPOLO,
the polyhistor[34]; the physician and biblical commentator
ABRAHAM BEN JEHUDA BEN ABRAHAM at Constantinople,
whom the bibliographer erroneously refers to the year 1527,
when his grandson JEHUDA BEN ELIA TISHBI finished a
copy of his work; the poet JEHUDA GIBBOR (1502), and
a few others.   The MS. remains of this period are to be
found in the Crimea[35], at Kahira, and also in the library at
Leyden.

  Subsequently a literary movement of no great importance
appears at Constantinople, in the Crimea, and in Galizia, the
principal representatives of which are: the dogmatist MOSES
POZZI MAROLI; the writer on Law JEHUDA POKI, grandson of Elia Bashiatshi; the great-grandson of the latter,
MOSES BASHIATSHI BEN ELIA BEN MOSES, who is said to
have composed two hundred and forty-five works before he
was sixteen years old, but who on account of persecutions
retired into the East, and there met with an early death in
his eighteenth year (1572); ELIA RABBENU BEN JEHUDA
TISHBI, who wrote his Expositions of the Introductions to
Joseph ben Aaron's Commentary on the Pentateuch, under
the title *Peer* (crown), in the year 1579, and who by an incon-
ceivable mistake of some bibliographers has been supposed to
be the son or grandson of Abraham ben Jehuda, mentioned
above; SERACH BEN NATHAN TROKI, the friend of del Medigo (cir. 1620); the traveller SAMUEL BEN DAVID (1641)[36];
MORDECAI BEN NISAN, the correspondent of Trigland
(1698), to whom has been ascribed an unpublished essay,
which seems to belong really to a Rabbinical Kabbalistic
author; the polemical writer SOLOMON BEN AARON TROKI
(1710); and SIMCHA ISAAC BEN MOSES (1757), author of an
alphabetical catalogue of Karaitic works (ארח צדיקים, Vienna,
1830).

The following persons wrote on *Grammar:* (Abu) JUSSUF
HASAKEN (Haroeh?)[37]; SAHL BEN MAZLIACH [38]; AARON
BEN JOSEPH, who borrows from the celebrated Rabbinites
Jehuda Chajjug, Jonah Ibn Gannach, and Moses Cohen
Chiquitilla[39]; and subsequently SOLOMON TROKI and
MORDECAI BEN NISSAN. The oldest of these authors are
only known by quotations, but a more accurate insight into
their grammatical views would be interesting.

15.] *Polemics.*[1]

The various tendencies of Jewish theology and philosophy,
hitherto treated of, manifest an influence from foreign schools
and religious sects, and an internal contest which a contact
of this kind always calls forth. In closest connexion with
this stands the polemical tendency of the whole of Judaism
against what was external to itself. The treatment of this
part of Jewish Literature must therefore be kept free from
external references and prejudices, calculated to influence the
discussion of it; such, for instance, as would arise if any
one were to view all Jewish dogmatism and exegesis only
with reference to Christianity, and to set down as "polemical"[2] every divergence, however natural, or to consider
every occasional expression about persons or things not
Jewish only as a hidden attack, instead of as a contribution
to the history and characteristics of this nation and religion.[3]
It must moreover not be overlooked, that renegades, proselytes, and neophytes are the principal representatives of
the ever-changing polemical literature; that many works
are known only from the quotations of opponents[4]; and that
many are mere fictions[5], or rest upon misrepresentations.[5a]

Besides this, scientific criticism meets with both external
and internal difficulties; such as the peculiar, frequently ill-
defined, and uncertain designation of nations and religions
in the Hebrew language[6], the suppression and mutilation
of manuscripts and printed works from fear or necessity
(§ 23.), and the connexion of entire polemical literatures,
requiring a knowledge as comprehensive as it should be
sound. Finally, the polemics are important, inasmuch as

the external fate of the Jews was made dependent upon their religion.

The *First Period* (that of the Talmud and Midrash), in accordance with its general character, presents no particular work to be noticed here (except the apologies of JOSEPHUS and PHILO, which are quite peculiar); although, from the very origin of Christianity to the present time, there could have been no lack of attempts at conversion both by books and oral teaching[6a]; and also many fathers of the Church and later theologians had Jews for their instructors. The necessity to take notice of Christians might indeed be perceptible in the Halacha, in so far as Christianity, fed in a great measure from Paganism, might be regarded in the same light as Paganism, or the Sadducees, Kuthæans (Samaritans), or other sects. What particular legal definitions in the Talmud are to be referred to this head requires further investigation, since the name *Nazarites* (נוצרים), subsequently in use, does not occur in our editions printed under censorship[7]; and other names, subsequently given to Christians, admit of various explanations.[8] Even the dates respecting Jesus and his disciples, which are in general very scanty, have not been critically established.[9] On the other hand, unquestionable remains of particular conversations between learned Christians and Jews, and also of others with heathen philosophers[10], traces of *Institutes* for disputations[11], and some allusions to Christianity and the relation of the then Christian Church to the Jewish are preserved in the Talmud and Midrash.[12] The accounts of disputations, such as that of RABBI JULIUS of Pavia with Magister Petrus (790)[13], are older than the Jewish literature of Europe. Even Muhammed, with his learned weapons the Koran and Sunne, wages war against Judaism as well as Christianity; and these works contain fragments of similar disputations, which, throughout the whole of this age, have the character of simple Midrash.

In the *Second Period* (that of Exegesis and Philosophy) we first meet with really *controversial* writings; while in general *Dogmatics* and *Exegesis*, in their scientific foundation, become unavoidably involved in polemics on every side. Exegesis is

concerned principally with the "Messianic passages" of the
Bible; amongst which Isaiah, lii. 13., stands foremost: so that
we find monographies in explanation of these passages; for
instance, by NACHMANIDES, SOLOMON ASTRUC of Barcelona,
DAVID DE ROCCA, SAADJA IBN DANAN, and ISAAC ELIA
COHEN.   Philosophy of Religion, on the other hand, treats
of the three principal groups : — 1. The unchangeableness
and rational foundation of the Law and Tradition, against the
Karæans : 2. The theory of Revelation and doctrine of the
prophets in connexion with the criticism of human (natural)
knowledge in general, against Muhammed and the Sufi, and
subsequently against the Kabbala[14], and in connexion with
Eschatology and the doctrines of the Messiah, against Millennianism and Pseudomessias[15]: 3. The doctrine of the Deity,
Monotheism and Spiritualism, against Christianity and the
Kabbala.   Lastly, the despised and scorned *Ecclesia pressa*
retaliated and indemnified itself by means of sarcastic and
sometimes poetical sallies (§ 20.), against its apostate opponents, and also by means of pictures of manners and compari-
sons which deserve to be noticed.[16]   The *Gospels*, and in a less
degree the other books of the New Testament, were treated
critically.   Among the libels on the life of Jesus, the famous
Toldot, or *Maase Jeshu* (composed before 1241), was disseminated in many recensions and under various titles (e. g. מעשה
תולי, תולע), even amongst the Karaites, and was interdicted
by Benedict XIII. (1405); it was never used by Jewish controversialists, and was even rejected by them as a spurious
and mischievous work.[16 a]   In matters of this kind, forgeries
easily recognised by the learned, but often a stumbling-block
to the class of readers for whom they are intended, will never
fail to recur.   Thus, while some recent Christian writers
about the life of Jesus were ignorant of the real Jewish
authorities, the author of a German book published in 1853,
whose aim seems to be to give a popular account of their views,
pretends to have drawn his information from a manuscript
work by a converted Jew of the 11th century, the description
of which is alone sufficient to convince every one who knows
anything about Jewish literature, that it is a mere fiction.
Apologies in answer to accusations hostile to the Jews (§ 2a.)

are brought forward in this period in rare and occasional remarks, such as those on the pretended effusion of blood at the festival of Easter (1260).[16b] Under this head we may also mention the scornful and often ignorant abuse of passages of the Talmud (resembling the strictures made by Eisenmenger and others at a later period) which were apparently favoured by the mystic explanations of the Kabbala; such passages were philosophically explained by MOSES IBN TIBBON, SHEMTOB SHAFRUT, and others.   It is remarkable, that even Christian ideas appear to have been impressed upon Judaism by means of controversy; for example, that of the Messias ben Joseph.[16c] On the other hand, Jewish converts did not scruple to interpolate the Hebrew originals.   A survey, however, of the tendencies of any age, when derived from controversial writings alone, is seldom impartial.[17] We divide the controversies into those: A. Against *Christianity;* B. Against *Muhammedanism.*

A. We know of no entire Jewish work written in the East against Christianity, although SAADJA (as early as 913[18]) devotes to it one chapter of his Dogmatics, and the Karaite JEHUDA HEDESSI (of Edessa? 1148-9, at Constantinople) two of his Polemics against Rabbinism[19], appealing to many older Karaites.   Perhaps the works of DAVID MUKAMEZ and SAMUEL BEN CHOFNI contained also some remarks upon Christianity.   On the other hand, anti-Jewish works in Arabic by Christians are still extant; e. g. by Abraham ben Aun (fl. 854); Isa ben Zeraah at Bagdad, addressed to the Jewish mathematician Bashar (997); Sabar Jesu (cir. 1000); Daniel Ibn al-Chattab (end of 12th century); Jesu-Jabas Bar Malkon, archbishop of Nisibis (1190); the apostate Abd al-Massih at Kahira (1241); and Tekriti. We have also the disputation of the monk Tabarani, and some anonymous writings[20]; and some Syriac works by Theodorus, Abukara, and others.[21]

Concerning the intercourse between Jewish and Christian authorities in Babylon, we are able to quote an authentic anecdote, related by Mazliach in his description of the life of HAI GAON (comp. § 10. p. 78.).   When this Rabbi discussed in his academical lectures a difficult passage of the Psalms of

David, and no satisfactory explanation was given, Hai ordered
inquiry to be made of the "Katholicos" regarding what he
had learned about it. Upon Mazliach expressing his astonish-
ment at such a thing, Hai demonstrated that, according to
the Talmud, we must seek information from everybody.

In Europe Moses, christened (1106) PETRUS ALPHONSI,
wrote *Dialogues* against the Jews.[22] But the earliest strictly
polemical work known is the Book Cusari of JEHUDA
HALEVI (1140), which, however, is directed against the
Muhammedans, Aristotelians, and Karaites, and is defensive
rather than offensive.[23]   The oppression of the Arabians
after the battle of Tolosa (1212), and the diversion of the
fanaticism of the Crusaders towards the west, form here an
epoch.   Direct refutations begin at the end of the 12th
and the commencement of the 13th century, when the
General of the Dominicans, Raymund of Pennaforte, introduced Oriental studies for the conversion of the Saracens
and Jews.[24]   About the same time the persecution of heretics led to the establishment of the Inquisition ; in France
Jewish writings (1244—1254), in Germany Jews themselves
were given up, and regents and popes instituted actual disputations (ויכוחים)[25], the history of which would be worth a
monography.

The most important authors of independent and recognised
works belonging to this part of the subject, the majority of
which were scientific treatises of the Spanish school, and narratives of disputations[26], are: JOSEPH KIMCHI (cir. 1160);
JACOB BEN REUBEN (1170), whose work however seems to
have undergone some alterations, and needs a more special
disquisition [26a]; JECHIEL BEN JOSEPH, who, together with
JUDA BEN DAVID, SAMUEL BEN SOLOMON, and MOSES OF
COUCY, held a public disputation with the neophyte Nicolaus
at Paris (1240)[27]; MEIR BEN SIMON disputed with the Archbishop of Narbonne (1245), and NACHAMIDES with FRÀ
PAOLO, in the presence of Raymond Martin (author of the
Pugio Fidei) (1263); MORDECAI BEN JEHOSEPHA probably
wrote against the same Paul (1270—1280)[27a]; MOSES NAR-
BONI (fl. 1344—1362) translated a controversial work by
Ghazali from the Arabic, and defended freewill against a
fatalistic essay by ALPHONSO OF VALLADOLID, formerly

called ABNER OF BURGOS (conf. § 13. p. 114.). The latter,
whose anti-Jewish work is the source of Alphonso de Spina,
is perhaps the same as ALFONTIUS BONIHOMINIS, who is
said to have translated from the Arabic (1339) the letter of
the pretended neophyte SAMUEL MAROKKI [28] against the
Jewish faith (see below, B.), a forgery which was refuted by
various authors. Polemics against Alphonso were written
by ISAAC IBN POLGAR (before 1339), JOSEPH SHALOM,
and ISAAC NATHAN (1437), author of the *Concordantia*.
Other authors are CHAJJIM GALLIPAPO, a liberal author
(after 1348), who relates the accusations against and persecutions of the Jews; MOSES COHEN TORDESILLA (?)
(1379) [28 a], who wrote against a neophyte of Avila; JONAH
RAFA (Rofe?), who composed (1380) a keen satire against
the Christian (Catholic) festivities at the Carnival and Easter,
in the form of a parody of the Easter Haggada (§ 5. b. *a*);
DAVID DE ROCCA MARTICA (?) on Original Sin (1370—
92?); ABRAHAM ROMAN, against the Bishop Cyrillis Lu-
caris (before 1410); and SHEMTOB SHAFRUT (1385), who
translated [29] the Gospels into Hebrew: an apostate monk
NESTOR may also be placed among these authors. PRO-
PHIAT DURAN had, in 1397, composed a polemical work,
and subsequently the well-known satirical epistle *Alticabo-
tica* (commencing אל תהי כאבותיך,) against the neophyte
Bonet Bongoron.[30] The latter part of the 14th century,
and the beginning of the 15th, seem to have been the
most productive period in polemics; the complicated reasons for which circumstance are to be found partly in the
history of the Jews, and partly in general circumstances.
The above-mentioned work of Prophiat was popular, and
is the unacknowledged source whence Simon Duran drew
much of his materials (see below). It was dedicated to the
celebrated teacher CHISDAI CRESCAS (conf. § 12.), who
himself wrote a short essay in Spanish, attacking the principal articles of the Christian faith on mere philosophical
principles. A copy of the Hebrew translation of this work
by Joseph ben Shemtob has been recently discovered by the
author in the University Library at Leyden. About this
time several learned Jews relinquished their faith; a later
writer, Joseph ben Shemtob, believes that these persons,

being led by their rationalistic views to despair of future happiness, were induced to seek at least earthly prosperity and ease by embracing Christianity. Amongst them were SOLOMON LEVI, afterwards PAULUS DE BURGOS, and JOSHUA LORKI, afterwards HIERONYMUS DE SANTA FIDE. There is still extant a correspondence in Hebrew between them, in which the latter, still retaining the faith of his fathers, though already beginning to waver, asks the former his reasons for deserting it. Under the auspices of Peter de Luna, Pope Benedict XIII., Hieronymus held in 1413 a disputation at Tortosa (not Girona), celebrated for both its length and the numbers who attended it. Shortly afterwards he published his main objections to Judaism in two small books, and thus provoked a literature extending to the end of the 15th century. His opponents were JOSEPH ALBO, MOSES BOTAREL, ISAAC NATHAN, SOLOMON DURAN (1437), VIDAL BEN DON BENVENISTE BEN LABI, and others, and also ISAAC ABRAVANEL. One of the most important essays upon the scientific and fundamental criticism of Christianity and Muhammedanism is to be found in some chapters, printed separately, of a theological work by SIMON DURAN (1423), parts of which were introduced by transcribers into the writings of ABRAHAM FARISSOL (1472). It has been asserted, as we have already observed, that he mainly followed Prophiat Duran; but why the name of the latter was not mentioned is not certain, unless it may be, that the liberality of his opinions caused him to be disliked.

A discussion and detailed refutation of Christian doctrines and attacks are to be found in many chapters of dogmatical works, such as those of MAIMONIDES, LEVI BEN ABRAHAM (1299), ALBO (1425), and others. This is still more the case in exegetical works; since the Christian evidences, after the example of the New Testament, were principally exegetical. This tendency also consequently found its way into the German-French school; on which account the Vulgate met with especial attention (§ 17.).[30a] Scattered passages are to be found in the biblical commentaries of RASHI, JOSEPH KARA, IBN EZRA, KIMCHI, NACHMANIDES, LEVI BEN GERSON, BECHAI BEN ASHER (1291); JACOB BEN

ASHER, ABRAVANEL, ARAMA, &c.[31] Collections of such passages, or oral biblical expositions partly arising out of disputations, form the greater portion of the productions of the German-French school, which bear the title Nizzachon (נצחון).[32] The most famous of them was that by JOMTOB LIPPMANN MÜHLHAUSEN (1400); to which may be added the collections from JOSEPH and DAVID KIMCHI's writings.[33] Finally also the prayers and hymns contain allusions to the fortunes of the people of Israel[34]; which however generally end in lamentations and petitions on account of persecutions, or in praises of their preeminence and the glory of their future redemption. Minds hostile to Judaism have always dwelt upon this fact; and, in spite of all history and criticism, have discovered in it a hatred of Christianity, as in the prayer *Alenu*, composed by Rab at Babylon.[35]

 B. The polemics against Muhammedanism[36] differ from those against Christianity in some important points. The former, from its strict monotheism, its numerous ceremonial laws, and the Oriental character of the nations which represent it, approaches more nearly to Judaism. The political and social position of the Jews among the Arabians, the share which they took in their civilisation and science, and the ignorance of the Arabians respecting Jewish literature, and even the Bible[37], were in general less favourable to polemics. The literature of Islam (Koran and Sunne) begins indeed with disputations[38] and attacks on Judaism; among which, the accusation of tampering with the Bible plays a principal part.[39] But unlike Christianity, Islam withdrew its records and disputations from the mockery of the Jews, who from the first considered them only as imitations and distortions of their own[40], and were occasionally even forbidden the use of Arabic literature.[41] Thus Maimonides, who generally prefers the monotheism of Islam to Christianity, which he regards as mere Pagan polytheism, forbids the teaching of the Jewish law and the Bible to the believers in the Prophet, because they deny the authenticity of the Jewish text; while he allows it to Christians, who might be convinced of their misinterpretations. The Muhammedan attempts at making converts were fewer and of a more political character than the Christian, so that their controversial writings were for the most part connected with legal definitions on the political existence of Tributaries (اهل الذمة), and on the toleration of synagogues and churches.[42]   One might be inclined to suppose that the contact of Islam with Christianity, during the Crusades, first provoked the persecution of the fanatical Almohades, and called forth various polemical writings against the Jews and answers to them. [43]   Although DAVID MOKAMMEZ (in the 9th century) and the Karaite JOSEPH BEN ABRAHAM (920) give some information about the Muhammedan sects, and SAADJA (913) and the Karaite JAPHET (953) occasionally touch upon Islam in a controversial manner; still the first important notices of Muhammedanism appear in JEHUDA HALEVI (1140) and MAIMONIDES, whom the Moslems, probably by way of retaliation, charge with double apostasy.   SAMUEL BEN JEHUDA (Jahja) IBN ABBAS, who had migrated to the East with his father on account of the Almohades, and there (1163) went over to Islam [44], wrote an interesting refutation of Jehuda Halevi, from which apparently ALPHONSO (see above, p. 127.) forged his famous letter of SAMUEL OF MAROCCO.[45]   Subsequently we find in the East many Arabic works, directed against Christians and Jews alike, by Ahmed ben Idris es Sanhagi (ob. 1285), said to have been a learned Hebraist; Abdallah ben Ahmed el Nesefi (ob. 1300); Ibrahim ben Muhammed, and others unknown.[46]   Only one refutation of the Jews in particular, by Ala-ed-din Ali ben Muhammed el Bagi (ob. 1314), is mentioned under this head by the well-known bibliographer Hadji Chalfa (No. 5421.); but we may add a most interesting Arabic MS. work in the Bodleian, treating of Judaism, Christianity, and Islam, by SAAD BEN MANSSUR IBN KEMUNAT (1280), who pretends to be a Muhammedan, but was certainly a Jew by birth (as will be proved elsewhere).   This work is in some way a statement of the objections made to each of these religions, and the answers preferred by their advocates, and may be characterised as an answer to the celebrated book *De Tribus Impostoribus*, if such a work ever really existed.   It was subsequently answered by Sarigia el Malathi (ob. 1386).   SIMON

DURAN (1423), in his above-mentioned controversial work [47], professes to know of no other special refutation of Islam, except the few paragraphs of the Book *Cusari*, by Jehuda Levi. After the expulsion of the Arabians from Europe there ceased to be any occasion to make mention of Islam in Christian countries. Perhaps, on account of his connexion with the Turks, R. JACOB LEVI (ob. 1636 in Zante) translated a Latin version of the Koran, together with an introduction, into Hebrew.[48] Lastly, an Arabic controversial work by the Samaritan Elmakin Abul Hassan of Tyre makes mention of the Karaites.[49]

§ 16.] *Hebrew Philology.*[1]

The literal text of the Hebrew Scriptures became the object of great activity in hermeneutical and exegetical studies, such as in translations, grammars, lexicography, and notes both critical and explanatory accompanying the text ; though at the same time there was but little scope for historical elucidation [2], owing to the high authority of the biblical records. After the Hebrew had ceased to be a vernacular language it was still employed in learned works, poetry, and rhetoric; and in this use philology exercised a powerful influence upon it. At the same time the languages of other countries were advanced by the employment of them for biblical expositions. It is important also to observe the connexion, often hostile, of the philological study of the Bible with that of the Halacha and Haggada.[3]

The " Translation," or rather rendering of certain difficult passages and words, first into *Aramaïc* (Chaldaic and Syriac), and later (cir. 280—200 B. C.) into *Greek* and *Persian*, combined with public explanations and instructions for youth, is at least as old as the Midrash. These must have been collected and compiled, like the Midrash itself, from oral tradition, and from marginal notes on manuscripts of the Bible, &c.[4] Subsequently, as the oldest interpretation (*Targum*), they were the representatives of the simple verbal exposition (*Peshat*), in contradistinction to the varied interpretations given by the Midrash and Haggada. On this ground, SAADJA, the first well-known Arabian translator and interpreter of the whole (or nearly the whole) of the Bible [5], frequently appeals to the Targum [6], and KOREISH (cir. 900) strongly recommends the Chaldee. But Saadja's translation, made after the manner of the Targum, keeps clear of anthropomorphism, changes names into those better known in Arabic [7], uses Hebraisms in his Arabic, and in the notes supplementary to the translation [8] makes a beginning of a philological and philosophical exegesis. This important translation was used by all the Jews who spoke Arabic, and was not easily superseded by another even among the Samaritans; the subsequent Arabic exegesis and lexicography of particular passages was subsidiary to it. The necessity of similar aids was felt also in other countries, particularly in the case of women and children. [9] Hence arose *Glossaries* accompanying the Bible [9a], and running translations, particularly of the Pentateuch; among which one in *Persian* is said to have been composed many centuries before Mahomet [10], and another in *Russian* (*Slavic*) in the year 1094 (?). [11] Those in *Modern Persian, French, Italian, Spanish* (which last is falsely attributed to DAVID KIMCHI [11a]), *Modern Greek*, and perhaps also that in the *Tatar* language (of the Karaites), date from the middle ages. [12] The Hebrew translations of the Chaldee portions of the Bible in some respects belong to this part of our subject. Centuries before Leusden they were inserted in the Commentaries of LEVI BEN GERSON and that of the Karaite ABRAHAM BEN JEHUDA, whose work is extant in the Library of Leyden.

The *grammatical* (i. e. linguistical) treatment of the Hebrew text is later than the time when Hebrew and Chaldee flourished in the numerous schools of learned men in Palestine and Babylon, and later than the exclusive supremacy of the Midrash. [13] It began with grammatical *terminology*, which, although afterwards adopted by the schools, is not to be found in the Talmud and older Midrash, even for the common distinctions of language. [14] The first things which required attention were the preservation and committal to writing of the traditional and practical knowledge of the Bible. The text consisting of consonants alone, had indeed the advantage of being anxiously guarded even by the earliest copyists (*Soferim*, § 4. n. 12.) and readers (קראים *Karaïm*) of the Bible, many centuries before the rise of grammatical study.   Hence, exclusive of the variation between the " Eastern and Western lands " (Babylon and Palestine), but few have their origin in older times.[15]   But there was no particular literature on this subject.   The rules which were then applied to the copying and reading of the Bible belonged to the *Halacha* (see §§ 4. and 9.); as traditional were also called *Masora* (העתקה קסורת, קסורה)[16] ; and their history is identical with that of the Halacha in general.   They were originally very short sentences, and were subsequently extended to their present length in the *Masora Magna;* and even now a part of them is to be found in those sections of Halachaic works which treat of the synagogue rolls of the Pentateuch, &c. (see below). We may here mention the titles of some books, quoted by old authorities, which perhaps belong to the earliest works containing Masoretic (and grammatical?) rules.   *The Book of the Crowns* (סי התגין), or ornamental letters, is older than Saadja Gaon (beginning of 10th century), and perhaps still extant ; but it must not be confounded with the spurious and anonymous Kabbalistic work *Tagin* . (see § 13. p. 106.).   *The Book of the Sounds* (المصوّنات, Hebrew הקולות) is attributed by Abu'l Wâlid to the Soferim.   The Book אכלה ואכלה, probably so called because it begins with these two words (like one of the first sections in the Masora Magna, which may indeed be taken from the former), is highly commended by Joseph Ibn Aknin (about 1180), and Elia Levita (1538) considers this " small " work to be the only one extant on Masora ; no manuscript, however, bearing this title seems to be known at present.

The division of the verses and a kind of intonation and gesticulation[17] are also as old as the exposition of the Bible ; and even in early times there existed a variation in the *number of the verses,* corresponding to the difference in the course of readings between Palestine and Babylon.[18] But this period of old tradition did not require the assistance of any written signs ; and certainly the formation of the

K 3

system of the *accents* (נגינות, כעמים), originally intended as aids for pronunciation, and afterwards for syntax, belongs to the second period. Besides the various Aramaïc names of the signs in the later schools[19], we find in authorities of some antiquity[20] mention made of the different accents and vowel points of *Tiberias*, of *Babylon* (Assyria), and of *Palestine*.[21] The Haggada of the Talmudic and Gaonic age mentions neither the sounds nor the signs of the vowels (נקודות, i. e. points, תנועה=حَرَكَة *motio*[22], which, as well as the accents, were never marked in the liturgical rolls of the Pentateuch) as separate elements of the language[23]; while they form abundant matter for the later Kabbalistic Midrash, and are even made the subject of philosophical allegory.[24]   But the greatest grammarians and exegetes (until the 11th century) exhibit variations in their vocalisation[25], division of verses, and accentuation.[26] All this indicates the formation of a simple system of accents and vowel points suggested by the method of writing and reading practised (Halacha) at the time of the first Gaonim, in Palestine, particularly in *Tiberias*, always famous as a place where the old "natural" language was preserved, and where several authors of works belonging to this section are said to have lived; for instance, JAHJA [JEHUDA] BEN [ABU?] ZACHARIA AL-KÂTIB (i. e. the scribe).[27]   The invention or introduction of pointing (ניקוד, comprising also accents) was followed by the use of points by transcribers of the Bible, and afterwards by grammatically instructed *punctuators*.[28] When and how the old Masora, i. e. the determination of the original text, became independent of Halachaic literature (see § 5. n. 21.), was assimilated with the rules of accents and vowels, was treated in anonymous monographies and memorial verses, and finally was changed again into glosses on the margin of the text, has not yet been sufficiently investigated.   From the want of historical criticism, the expression *Masora* seems to have been extended over the whole of this literature perhaps as long since as the 11th century; and modern students and writers on the subject have designated all monographies or chapters of grammatical works upon accents and vowels as *Masoretic*.[29]   Some minor variations

with regard to punctuation were collected by BEN ASHER
(said to have been of Tiberias) and BEN NAPHTALI, whose
place, date, and names are doubtful, but who were certainly
not later than Saadja Gaon.　According to Luzzatto[30] they
were Bible punctuators who arranged on certain principles
the results of codices then extant.[31-32]　The codex said to
have been corrected by Ben-Asher, which is Maimonides'
standard, was still in existence at the end of the 15th century, according to a note of Saadja ben David.

According to the unanimous judgement of those who
have inquired into the subject, grammar properly so
called, that is etymology and syntax as an independent
literature, took its origin in, and was imitated from, the
Arabian; so that the oldest remains which have been preserved are written in Arabic.[33]　On the other hand, lexicons,
or collections (אגרון)[34] of Hebrew words, intended as subsidiary to and explanatory of grammar, or subordinate to
it, were preceded by similar lexicons of the Talmud (for
example, that of Zemach, see § 91.), which were indeed
explanatory rather than etymological.　The oldest work of
the kind is a small one, which has lately been edited four
times; namely, an explanation of 70—90 Hapaxlegomena of
the Bible (for the most part explained from the Talmudical
Hebrew) by SAADJA; who also wrote [35] a comprehensive
alphabetical dictionary, forming perhaps only a part of his
grammar written in Arabic; this, however, being only a
collection of words, contained nothing Arabic.　He even
took the trouble to calculate and count all the forms which
might be derived from one root, and found them to be 1169.
The undeniable influence of Karaism upon this developement
of philology has been already described above.[36]

The general contrast of the tendencies of Palestine, early
Italy, Germany, and France, on the one hand, and of Babylon, Africa, Spain, and later Italy, on the other, is here particularly prominent.　The grammatical writings and lexicons
of the latter were, until the 12th century, almost entirely
Arabic.　The most important authors are SAADJA (ob.
941-2), " the chief of the speakers " in every kind of study;
an anonymous writer of Jerusalem, author of the work

المشتمدة, who admitted the biliteral roots; ADONIM BEN
TEMÎM the Babylonian (at the end of the 10th century)[37];
SAMUEL BEN HOFNI (?), and his son-in-law HAI GAON
(ob. 1038), apparently the author of a lexicon[38]; in Africa,
JEHUDA IBN KOREISH (not Karish) of Tahart (cir. 900),
who established the principle of the comparison of language[39]; and DUNASH IBN LIBRAT, in Hebrew ADO-
NIM[40] HALEVI of Fez, author of a Hebrew work against
Saadja, afterwards refuted by Ibn Ezra, and of a partly
metrical criticism of a dictionary written in Hebrew by
MENAHEM IBN SARUK of Tortosa, at Cordova, the fallen
favourite of the minister Chisdai (cir. 950). This dictionary
contains an introductory grammar, and even Hebrew *voces
memoriales*, but adopts no fixed terminology. He admits
only of biliteral roots[41]; while the uncertain author of a
commentary on the book Jezira (conf. § 13.) recognises
even roots of one letter. The Hebrew writings of both
Dunash and Menahem were already known throughout
Italy and France, when JEHUDA BEN DAVID, called ABU
ZAKARIA JAHJA CHAJJUG of Fez, "the father of the
grammarians," led by the analogy of the Arabic, first
carried out in Spain the principle that the roots in weak
branches have three letters; he also established seven vowels.
He was favoured by SAMUEL the Prince (ob. 1055), the
pretended author of twenty-two grammatical writings, but
was vigorously opposed in particular cases by the physician
JONAH or ABULWALID MERWAN IBN GANNAH (disciple of
ISAAC CHIQUITILLA). Jonah was intimately acquainted
with the Arabian grammarians, and was celebrated as the
founder of the complete grammar and lexicography, soon
also as the "great teacher;"[42] but he was even at that time
regarded with enmity by those who distrusted a method of
criticism opposed to the ancient Midrash treatment of the
language, and substituting for it the simple meaning of the
words.[43] ABU IBRAHIM ISAAC IBN JASOS IBN SAKTAR,
whom Moses Ibn Ezra quotes, together with Abu'l Walid, as
"the Sheikhs" of the Hebrew, is the same as the physician
ISAAC IBN CASTAR, whose linguistic works were known to Ibn
Abi Oseibia. The author has but recently ascertained this

identity, and thereby established the year of his death, 1057,
as given in the MS. of Oseibia.　SOLOMON IBN GABIROL
of Cordova, who was born at Malaga, educated at Saragossa, and died at Valencia, wrote a Hebrew didactic poem
on the letters of the alphabet; since which time the Hebrew
language, already much cultivated and improved, begins to
supplant the Arabic in this department of literature.　The
taste of the French and Italians for translations cooperated
in this change.　For them MOSES HAKOHEN IBN CHIQUI-
TILLA of Cordova, and ABRAHAM IBN EZRA at Rome (1140
—1167), translated the writings of Chajjug, and SOLOMON
PARCHON of Calatayud at Salerno (1161) did the same
for the lexicon of Abu'l Walid; this last was also translated,
together with the grammar, by JEHUDA IBN TIBBON (1171)
for Provence.[43a]　JEHUDA IBN BALAAM of Toledo wrote a
lexicon called *Homonymik* (تَجْنِيس), some small treatises
upon particles, &c. (חרوف المعنى, אותיות העניינים), *verba de-
nominativa*, and one on accents in reading, which are still
extant; in them he compares Hebrew with both Arabic
and Persian.[44]　We know scarcely anything but the name of
ABRAHAM IBN KAMBEL (KAMNIAL?).　After ABRAHAM
IBN EZRA (1093—1168), who, like Jehuda Halevi, reduces
the Hebrew vowels to the three used in Arabic, we find
the following Hebrew writers upon grammar and lexicography: JOSEPH KIMCHI (fl. 1160—1170), perhaps JEHUDA
CHARISI (see § 18.); ISAAC BEN ELASAR HALEVI[45] and EL-
KANA in Spain; and JACOB BEN ELASAR (not Eliezer)[46],
apparently a contemporary of MOSES and DAVID KIMCHI.
The last of them, a schoolmaster in Provence, by his method
threw all the earlier works on the subject into the background
(particularly those in Arabic which had not been translated),
and caused them to be forgotten [46a]; so that the attention of
inquirers has not until lately been again directed to those more
critical and ingenious founders of the study of the Hebrew
language.　His reputation also warded off the attacks of his
critics; for example, those of SAMUEL BENVENISTE (cir.
1300), and that of the philosophical EPHODÆUS (אפד'ץ),
more properly ISAAC BEN MOSES, called PROPHIAT DURAN
(1403)[47], who was the first to recognise in his grammar the

true application of the form Niphal, but his arguments were controverted by Elisa ben Abraham[48], as were also the critical remarks of Elia Levita upon Kimchi, by a Pole named Sabbatai (of Przemislaw § 27.). A few grammatical works, mostly belonging to the 13th century and to authors of Provence, are preserved in anonymous MSS ; e. g. צח שפתים, שכל, טוב פתח דברי, לקח טוב, &c. In the East, at the same time, Tanchum of Jerusalem, the biblical interpreter, quotes his own grammatical work, probably in Arabic, which has not hitherto been noticed by the writers on this author.

The study of the Hebrew language began with that of the Bible ; but at the same time many independent works were composed, requiring skilful *transcribers.* In Spain there apparently were, up to the 12th century, very many Bible scribes who were at the same time general writers, Masorets and philologists; the technical names for grammar and philology, and for their representatives generally (דקדוק מדקדק), were taken from exactness, subtilty, and correctness, thus signifying properly *Criticism* and *Critics.*[49] Hence the Spanish copies of the Bible were famed for the correctness of their punctuation, and were used even by the Germans and French.[50] As in the East the *Codex of Ben Asher* (conf. supra, p. 135.), so in Spain and Provence the *Codex Hilali* (commonly derived from a man's name, Hillel) was considered of high authority. Meir Abulafia and Menahem Meiri endeavoured to gather correct data for a normal codex.

From Spain the study of the Hebrew language spread to France and Germany, and (perhaps also from Northern Africa) to Italy[51] ; but only by means of Hebrew works, from Seruk and Dunash (950) to Parchon (1060), which alone were intelligible there. The researches which had been carried on between those periods were introduced into these countries by Ibn Ezra and Kimchi. However, this science continued to be employed principally upon the ritual and in exegesis. Hence grammar was used only by exegetes; and most of the independent writings belonging to this period, except the standard codices of the Bible, are to be referred, for the most part, to the province of the Masora and the Halacha. They are:

(*a*) *Technical rules* for the writing and reading of the rolls of the Pentateuch, punctuated Bibles with the Masora, &c., partly in *rhyme*, and commonly entitled ניקוד (*punctuation*), or *directions for readers*, and the like ; the authors of which are therefore generally designated *punctuators* (נקדנים), or *correct writers* (דייקנים).[52] We possess writings of this kind by CHAJ-JUG [52a], JEHUDA IBN BALAAM, and JOSEPH KIMCHI.[53] (*b*) *Grammatical Treatises.* (*c*) A few *Dictionaries* (מחברות).[53a] The most important authors of the first class are JACOB BEN MEIR, called Tam (ob. 1171), author of a *Kassidet* upon accents in forty-five strophes; SAMUEL NAKDAN ; JOSEPH BEN KALONYMOS, the Nakdan (1230—50), author of a long acrostic poem upon the accents, with a commentary (discovered in MS. by the author); MOSES CHASAN of London (perhaps BEN JOSEPH KATTÂB [54]), author of some printed rules upon points and accents, and acquainted with Chajjug, Ibn Ezra, and Parchon ; SAMSON (circa 1240); and, moreover, JEKUTIEL BEN JEHUDA HAKOHEN (SALMAN) of Prague (1250—1300). In the middle of the 14th century the Nakdanim disappear, and the later scribes content themselves with the extant rules of their predecessors.[55] Grammatical writings, on the other hand, were composed by ABRAHAM HA-BABLI, who was probably older than Abraham Ibn Ezra, and whose country is unknown (a small but interesting essay of his, containing some striking grammatical and etymological remarks, has been discovered in the Bodleian Library, and will be published by the author); the above mentioned TAM, who took the part of Menahem Seruk against Dunash Ibn Librat [56]; MOSES BEN ISAAC HANNESIA of England (in the 13th century); and JOSEPH CHASAN of Troyes. There are also several anonymous writings, amongst which is דקדוקי רשי, an explanation of the grammatical parts of Rashi's commentary on the Pentateuch (cir. 1400). Finally, dictionaries were composed; for example, by MENAHEM BEN SOLOMON (1143), perhaps in Italy, who was unacquainted with Chajjug[57] ; SAMSON of Germany (circa 1200), who, although acquainted with Parchon, admits biliteral and uniliteral roots ; MOSES HANNESIA, who endeavours to surpass Parchon in arrangement and completeness ;

and JOSEPH BEN DAVID JEWANI, " the Greek," who dedicates his work to Elia ben Chananel, and must therefore
have lived about 1350; he introduces in his grammatical
compendium some mystical observations respecting the form
of the letters.   Also the fragment of a German-Hebrew
dictionary seems to have been preserved [58], while the above-
named lexicons and some commentaries (§ 17.) give explanations in the language of the country.

Kimchi's very accessible editions of the earlier independent
works on the subject left but little to be done by the intel-
lects of Spain, France, and Germany, which either became
relaxed or were occupied elsewhere.   The few grammarians who have yet to be named lived in Provence and Italy,
where the revival of classical philology prepared a new phase
for the study of Hebrew.   MEIR BEN DAVID (probably
about 1300) criticised, and JOSEPH IBN CASPE commentated Abu'l Walid.   Ibn Caspe, who grounded his compen-
diaria on logic [58a], wrote a lexicon, as did also IMMANUEL
of Rome, arranging it in a peculiar manner [59]; ABRAHAM
BEDARSHI in Provence (1280), and SOLOMON URBINO in
Italy (1480) wrote upon synonyms.   A Hebrew-Arabic-
Romaic alphabetical glossary (מקרי דרדקי) appeared in Italy
about 1488, but its Hebrew-Arabic part is certainly older.[59a]
ISAAC NATHAN (1437) composed a concordance after the
example of Father Arlot (1290).   Works upon grammar
were written by SOLOMON JARCHI (i. e. of Lünel) [60] who
states the seven conjugations of verbs now generally given
in grammars; AARON ALRABBI of Catania; JOSEPH SAREK
BEN JEHUDA (or Sarko) (1429) [61] ; MENAHEM BEN MOSES
TEMAR (1449, not 1524); MESSER LEON JEHUDA BEN
JECHIEL, Rabbi in Mantua (1454) [62] ; DAVID IBN JAHJA ;
MOSES BEN CHABIB of Lisbon, in Naples (1486); and
others, who form the transition to the following period (§ 23.);
such as ELIA LEVITA, ABRAHAM DE BALMEZ of Lecci,
and KALONYMOS BEN DAVID (1523), who completed Abra-
ham's work, and whose grammar is written in Hebrew and
Latin.   The Karaites have been already noticed above (§ 14.).
As writers upon the Masora we must also mention MEIR
ABU'LAFIA BEN TODROS (ob. 1244); MENAHEM MEIRI

(1306); and Joseph Sason (ob. 1336 ?).[63] The well-known
verses upon the number of the single letters in the Bible are
erroneously ascribed to the Gaon Saadja; the real author
was probably Saadja ben Joseph Bechor-Shor (about
1200), in France.

§ 17.] *Exegesis.*[1]

The form of commentary is of frequent occurrence in Jewish
literature; but this fact must not be regarded as indicating
a want of independence of mind, when compared with the
middle ages in general.[2]   The exception in this case rather
forms the rule; the many changes occasioned by external
circumstances, which may be traced through a long period,
in the cultivation of Jewish literature, required and obtained
sanction by being connected, in the way of explanation, with
the old sacred records.   This homiletical character, essential
to the old Midrash, passes during the second period from an
oral to a written form.   As during the first, the law (Halacha), ethics, secret doctrine, sagas, and the undigested
matter of the Haggada, generally centred in the exposition
of Scripture (Midrash), and took the form of special expository Haggada; similarly, during the second, philosophy,
Kabbala, and polemics form the subject of explanation in
Maimonides' Moreh[3], the Sohar, and the Nizzachons; and
these again gave rise to supercommentaries.   But in the old
Midrash, as well as elsewhere, the consciousness of a simple
meaning of the text was never entirely lost; it was kept
alive by means of the polemics of the Sadducees, Christians,
and Mohammedans, in opposition to the Jewish tradition
and interpretation of Scripture, although both parties were
really equally fettered in their views.[4]   In this contest Karaism boasted of its superiority to Rabbinism in objective exegesis; although, as regards its own philosophical, dogmatic,
or other premises, it is not less constrained.[5]   It is difficult
for us to decide how far the origin and first struggles of this
sect were the cause or the effect of their more independent
treatment of Scripture by means of grammar, etymology, and
Arabian and Syrian science.[6] This treatment, however, rendered the contradiction between exegesis and the Halacha-

and Haggada-Midrash only the more apparent, and the only
resource was to acknowledge, beside the simple sense of the
text, the Halachaic in its practical application[7], and either to
restrict the Haggadaic to ethics and homiletics, or to explain
it in a philosophical manner (§ 11.).   Thus finally we have
four principal tendencies in exegesis, afterwards designated
by the acrostic *Pardes* (פרדס)[8], viz. the simple *philological*
explanation of words (פשט), the *allegorical* (רמז), the *ethico-
homiletical* (דרוש), and the *mystic* (סוד); amongst which the
Halachaic, as the one not generally attacked, had no particular designation.[9]   This division, as might be supposed,
cannot be strictly carried out, and various transitions and
combinations are discoverable, as in the case of the Midrash
of the first period.   We have already mentioned the *allego-
rico-philosophical*, the *ethico-homiletic*, the *Kabbalistic* and the
Karaitic exegesis, in their proper divisions of literature; and,
as far as exegesis is concerned with polemics, we might have
also added a *polemical* (conf. § 15.).   There now remains
little besides the *grammatico-critical*, which also originated
in the East, and which in Europe took its peculiar forms
from the several countries so frequently mentioned above.

The grammarians and lexicographers of the Arabian
school, from SAADJA to KIMCHI (900—1250), were not
merely exegetical expounders of words (אנשי הפתרון
פותרים)[10], but many of them were likewise authors of
actual commentaries (Arab. تفسير شرح, Heb. פירוש, ביאור,
of which the *nomen agentis* is מבארים, מפרשים); so that it is
often doubtful which kind of work is alluded to in the citations of them by later writers.   Pure exegesis was emancipated
from the philosophical influence of the Orientals (§ 12. n. 27.)
first in Spain.   From the time of Saadja some attention was
occasionally paid to historical criticism[11]; but the growing
respect for the Masora deprived conjectural criticism of the
little ground it had previously gained.   Even ABRAHAM IBN
EZRA, whose doubts respecting the authenticity of the Pentateuch (noticed by Spinoza) have become celebrated, condemns
in strong language the arbitrary emendations of JONAH IBN
GANNACH.   The oldest commentary on the Pentateuch still
extant is that of JEHUDA IBN BALAM (about 1070—90) in

Arabic; two books of which have been discovered by the author in the Bodleian Library. Its great peculiarity consists both in explaining the text grammatico-philosophically, and almost Halachaically, and also in criticising the Arabic translation of Saadja, even as regards the Arabic lexicography.

In Germany and France the literal exegesis of the Bible was connected principally with the practical requirements of oral teaching, biblical lectures chiefly on the Pentateuch, and polemics. The Haggada (Midrash) was not idealised by philosophy, but taken in a simple and literal sense, and thus it could not fail to come into collision with simple biblical exegesis. When, therefore, the philology of the Hebrew writers MENAHEM BEN SERUK and DUNASH IBN LIBRAT found its way into the above-named countries, the Darshanim (דרשנים), who explained by means of the Haggada, were opposed by the literal exegetes (פשטנים) [12], as authors of commentaries (נימוקים, פירושים), following the developement of the Halachaic exegesis (§ 9.). The Bible, like the Talmud, was at first treated objectively, and mostly explained orally in a natural way. The simple view which had been preserved by the Targums and even by the Midrash and tradition, was continued by common sense; to which, even now, appeal is made for conjectural criticism.[13] This (and doubtless also the gradual influence of the Spaniards) not only led the lexicographers by means of compilation and comparison to the results of modern philology [14], but also induced individual exegetes to make critical notes, and finally brought about a systematic limitation in the use of the Midrash.[15] The Aramaïc Targum being no longer of any use for general exposition, the language of the country was adopted both for the explanation of particular words, and for connected translations (§ 16.).

Beside the Darshanim of the 11th century, JEHUDA DARSHAN, SIMEON KARA, and TOBIA BEN ELIEZER (of Mayence) in Palestine (§ 21.), and later probably in Provence MACHIR BEN ABBA-MARI BEN MACHIR BEN TODROS, who collected from all the earlier and later Midrash his *Jalkut* upon the prophets and the three hagiographa (Psalms, Job,

Proverbs), and whose writings have been preserved, we may consider the lost works of JOSEPH TOB ELAM (Bon-fils) at Limoges, MEIR BEN ISAAC, MENAHEM BEN CHELBO[15a], and many others, as forming a transition from the Midrash to exegesis. The latter received a peculiar character from the famous SOLOMON BEN ISAAC, called RASHI (רש״י), of Troyes (ob. 1105); but his works, which arose partly out of lectures, have not yet been critically examined. The important and independent exegete JOSEPH KARA (cir. 1100), nephew of Menahem ben Chelbo, mentioned above [16], edited and completed Rashi's commentary, particularly the part on the Pentateuch; and some transcriber (המעתיק) of the great school of the latter made additions (*Tosaphot*) to his own copy [17] after the manner of the Halacha (§ 9.), from which the commentaries entitled Tosaphot in the 13th century arose.

In the 12th century there may be mentioned SAMUEL BEN MEIR (1085—1153), a sober exegete who appeals to the "intelligentes" [18]; MESHULLAM THE GREAT (i. e. elder); SAADJA, author of the commentary on Daniel attributed to the Gaon; the lexicographer MENAHEM BEN SOLOMON (1130 — perhaps in Italy), who was acquainted with Chananel's commentary, and corresponded with Solomon ben Abraham, nephew of Nathan ben Jechiel at Rome; besides many Halacha Tosaphists: also JESAJA DE TRANI the elder in Italy; JACOB HA-NASIR at Lünel (§ 13. n. 21.); JOSEPH BECHOR SHOR (cir. 1170) in France [19]; JACOB TAM of Orleans (killed in London 1190); SHEMAJA of Soissons; and MENAHEM BEN SIMON at Posquières, pupil of Joseph Kimchi (1191), and therefore more approaching to the Spanish line.[20] But although towards the end of the 12th century the writings of PARCHON and IBN EZRA were well known, still about the same time the Kabbalistic tendency of Northern Italy and Provence became apparent in the exposition of the meaning of letters and numbers, and the Halacha discussion (*Pilpul*) of the Tosaphot was transferred to exegesis, especially to that upon the legal Pentateuch. A great number of *supercommentaries* were written here on *Rashi* [21], as in the Arabian school on Ibn Ezra (§ 12.); afterwards mere compilations, until in the 14th and 15th centuries

biblical studies were obliged to give way entirely to the
Halachaic and Kabbalistic trifling.[21a]   But few names of importance are therefore connected with the German-French
exegesis of this period, and these have been for the most part
already classed as Kabbalists (§ 13.)   We may here however
mention [22] ELIA SAMUEL BEN ELIEZER; MOSES COUCY
(1235—1245), author of some short expositions (פשטים);
EPHRAIM BEN SAMSON, who had a profound respect for Maimonides, although he did not imitate him; NATHAN OFFI-
CIAL; JOSEPH CHASAN at Troyes; the anonymous authors of
the *Nizzachons* (§ 15.); HISKIA BEN MANOAH of France,
author of a commentary [23] compiled from twenty others, among
them that of D. Kimchi; ELIESER of טוך (1270)[24]; MEIR
ROTHENBURG [25]; and ISAAC HALEVI BEN JEHUDA, author
of a compilation rich in authorities.   Of the 14th and 15th
centuries, JEHUDA BEN ELIEZER in France (1313); a considerable number of anonymous Midrashim and Scholia
(גליון?); ASHER BEN JECHIEL and his son JACOB (1340)
at Toledo, who introduced German exegesis into Spain [25a],
and from whose commentary on the Pentateuch the bad
taste of succeeding centuries has extracted nothing but some
worthless verbal trifling, often quoted and held up to ridicule
by Christian critics, the entire work having been published
only in the last century; JACOB DE ILLESCAS; JACOB OF
VIENNA; LIPPMANN MÜHLHAUSEN (1400), acquainted
with Latin (see § 15.); SAMUEL of Spiers; SOLOMON
RUNKEL at Mayence and Spiers (ob. ante 1426); ABIGDOR
KARA at Prague (ob. 1439); the Kabbalist MENAHEM
ZIUNI of Spiers; ISRAEL ISSERLEIN of Marpurg in
Neustadt (ob. post 1452); JOHANAN LURIA at Worms;
JOSEPH KOLON at Pavia (1466); and others.

    We conclude with the names of some important exegetes,
especially of Provence and Italy, whose writings, hitherto
known principally from catalogues of MSS., have not yet
found a definite place in any arrangement: JEHUDA BEN
SAADJA, a Spaniard (13th century?), who explained the
book of Job philosophically, and wrote in Arabic at Toledo
some smaller essays, which he subsequently translated into
Hebrew at the request of the physician Israel Kohen [26]; RA-

PHAEL ZARPHATI (cir. 1280)[27]; NATHAN BEN SAMUEL
TIBBON (Rofe) (1307), whose short exposition of the Pentateuch is ethical, philosophical, and allegorical[28]; BENJA-
MIN הב׳׳א (perhaps an abbreviation) BEN JEHUDAH of Rome
(still living in 1312), who represents the sound and simple
exegesis of the Spanish school, and whose commentaries,
abounding with quotations from Jonah Ibn Djannah, Ibn
Gikatilia, Ibn Balam, Ibn Ezra, Joseph Kimchi and David
Kimchi, are of considerable interest for the history of exegesis; JOSEPH IBN NAHMIAS (1330); SOLOMON (ASTRUC)
of Barcelona, author of a homiletical exposition of the Pentateuch; ISAAC BEN JACOB DE LATAS (Lattes), who
wrote a philosophical and Halachaic commentary on the
Pentateuch (1372); DON ABRAHAM BEN ISAAC LEVI (ob.
1393), erroneously called Tamach, who explained the Canticles literally and allegorically[29]; MOSES GABBAI and his
son-in-law AARON BEN GERSON ALRABI (1430) of Catania,
whose rare supercommentary on *Rashi* contains passages of
extravagant hypercriticism[30]; ABRAHAM BEN JEHUDA CHA-
DIDA (?), according to De Rossi a Spaniard of the 15th
century; JEHUDA IBN SHOSHAN BEN ISAAC at Magnesia
(about 1500); and the Portuguese writers JOSEPH CHAJÛN
and DAVID IBN JAHJA BEN SOLOMON at Lisbon (cir.
1492), whose Mæcenas, SHALOM BEN ABRAHAM, figures
among bibliographers as author of their commentaries, and
is confounded with his namesake of the 16th century.

§ 18.] *Poetry, Rhetoric, Stylistic.*[1]

The history of the later Hebrew poetry is most peculiar.
It is but recently that it has been made the subject of
inquiry, and it has been regarded in the most various ways.
Seldom has poetry been developed to the same extent in
any language whose existence was dependent on literature
alone, thus bringing it into such close connexion with
philology, grammar, and exegesis.[2] The Hebrew language,
even after it was excluded from common life by the various
local dialects (Aramaïc, Greek, and Persian), had always
been preserved in public worship; and the older literary
remains (e. g. the Psalms) were used for poetical purposes,

and in particular for prayer.[3] Hence, without any foreign influence, a kind of oral, and by degrees also a written poetry might continue to exist, which, as an instinctive application and imitation of biblical passages, would take an intermediate position between popular and elaborate poetry (or rhetoric). An instance of this may be found in the additions to the prayers, belonging doubtless to the First Period (§ 6.). The gap between these and the really elaborate poetry (i. e. works which purposely aim at an artificial form) written in Babylon, Africa, Spain, Palestine, and Italy, and even in Germany and France (from the 9th century),—this general gap in Jewish literature, extending to the time of the Saburæans and the first Gaonim, can here be filled up only by a few prayers and fragments in the general collection of prayers, or citations of beginnings (the rest of the prayer being possibly of a later date) in the Midrashim and apocryphal books of the Talmud.[4] Their external (linguistic) form however, as well as their contents, give no certain grounds for the determination of dates, unless the general development of the Jewish literature (Haggada and philology) be followed as a guide.[5] It has hitherto been usual in these researches, partly owing to external circumstances, either to confine the attention to " religious," or more properly " liturgical " or " synagogal " poetry [6], and, starting from the old prayers, to exhibit the later artificial forms, even rhyme and metre, as possibly an original development [7]; or else to admit the influence of foreign national and literary characteristics, and to decide in favour of the preponderance of the Persian [8], Arabian, or Syrian in the various corresponding periods. The person whose position in time and place is made the central point of these different views, and even the interpretation of whose name is a matter of doubt, is R. ELASAR (ben?) KALIR of " קרית ספר," author of the rhyming acrostic prayers, which are artificial in every respect, except that they are not metrical.[9]

We here comprise under the term *Poetry* (and *Rhetoric*) all literary records in which an artificial form of language is adopted intentionally and according to certain rules, independent of the æsthetical standard which we have received

from classical literature, and which is not applicable to the
Bible and Haggada.[10]   Among the Jews, as among the
Arabians, this artificial form of language constitutes the
essence of poetry and rhetoric ; and we must therefore take
it in connexion with the history of divine worship as a
starting point.   The assumption of the existence of a liturgical poetry in Palestine [11], such as that of Kalir, at the time
of the Talmud, needs no refutation.   Even the Syrian
psalmody, which, through the Gnostic and anti-Gnostic poems
of Bardesanes and Ephrem Syrus, had been reduced to rhyme
and metre (in the 4th century), can have had no influence
on Jewish orthodoxy.[12]   It must be admited, for reasons
given above (§ 6. n. 15.), that the time of the Saburæans,
so wanting in independence, produced no essentially new
form of poetry ; the later introduction of rhyme and metre,
and of the artificial use of the Midrash, will be satisfactorily
proved below.

In the second half of the 8th century are to be found
the first definite traces of new additions to the liturgy, a
sanction for which could have been given only by the earlier
Gaonim.[13]   But the assertion, that the artificial form of
poetry began in this department, and thence passed to others,
is by no means established ; inasmuch as it is doubtful
whether some instances adduced in support of it, such as the
enumeration of the 613 precepts or *Azharot* (§ 19.), were
originally intended for the liturgy.[14]   Some prayers artificially arranged in strophes, but without rhyme [15], are indeed
older than the 10th century [16]; but we meet with others
long after the general adoption of rhyme.[17]   In order to
establish the earlier existence of a liturgical poetry, appeal
has moreover been made to the expressions *Pojetes, Pajtono,
Pajtan, Pajtani* (פייטס, ποιητής, and Aramaïcised פיטנא, פיטן,
פייטני), which, in some later Midrashim, were confined to
the authors of hymns.   But such a limitation of these expressions, and of the Hebrew form *Pajjât* (פייט), with the
corresponding denominative *Piel*, פייט (like קיים), *nomen
actionis et acti*, פיוט, *Pijjut*, plur. פיוטים, to liturgical
poetry (also comprised under the general name of חזון or
חזנות, derived from חזן, *cantor*), belongs to a later age.[18]

The oldest traces of rhyme and metre in Asia and Europe
are to be found almost as much in didactic as in liturgical works.[19] It is thus not impossible that the example of
the rhyming prose, in the didactic memorial verses of the
Arabians in the Arabic or Persian language[20], may have exercised a general influence on the Hebrew style even before the
Arabic had been adopted as a literary language amongst the
Jews.   Subsequently, the older poetical forms having been
found insufficient, others were introduced ; and it was not
until Hebrew philology had made some progress in Spain,
that the biblical style, and even biblical purism, came into
general use.   In the meantime the ungrammatical French-
German school, becoming more deeply involved in Midrash
and Halacha, brought all their elements of language to bear
upon an almost exclusively liturgical poetry ; to the tyranny
of which over both language and thought, the more cultivated
philological sense was always opposed.[21]   A stricter theory
of the artificial style, a system of poetry or prosody, could
be developed only in the grammatical and scientific school of
the Jews under the influence of the Arabians[22]; who, in
their philological and exegetical researches, appeal to the
usages of the " poets " and stylists[23], in the same way as the
German lawgivers and exegetes do to the comprehension
and exposition of the hymnologists[24], amongst whom KALIR
was reckoned as a doctor of Mishna (Tannai).

Before passing on to the particular kinds of poetico-rheto-
rical literature, we will touch upon the most important of its
general *forms*[25], with their subdivisions ; a subject which,
however, could be properly treated only in a special work.
It may be here remarked that some of these forms, such
as an alphabetical arrangement, are almost peculiar to the
Jews, while others, such as the use of rhyme and strophe, are
to be found in their poetry long before they were introduced
into the modern languages of Europe.

1. The *Acrostic*, or arrangement of words, lines, and
strophes according to initial letters, which may be divided
into two classes. (A.) With respect to *alphabetical* order
(hence אלפבטין, subsequently פביטין, with the Arabising
omission of the אל [25a]), something analogous to which occurs

already in the Psalms, &c. (§ 6. n. 10.): thus some fragments
of prayers so arranged may possibly belong to the first
Period, although we have no definite evidence before the
second [26]; for instance, some *Selichot* contained in Saadja's
liturgy.   It should be observed that the order of the alphabet itself underwent various changes, called by early writers
גמטריא (conf. § 4. p. 16.).   Subsequently this conceit was
carried so far, that religious and moral meditations were composed, often consisting of 1000 words with the same initial
letter, generally א [27]; for example, those by SHEMTOB PAL-
QUERA ; ABRAHAM BEDARSHI, and his son JADAJA PENINI
(13th century) in Provence ; JOSEPH BEN SHESHET IBN
LATIMI at Lerida (1308); SHEMTOB BEN ARDOT (Ardotiel,
not Andrutil) (post 1330) [28]; ELIA HA-LEVI at Constantinople (cir. 1500—20); DAVID VITAL of Patras (1532—46),
and his imitator MOSES BEN ISAAC of Bisenz in Moravia, at
Cracow [29], who composed his prayer of 2150 words at Leipnik in 1591 ; SAADJA LONGO at Saloniki (MS. in the Bodleian); the Karaite JOSEPH BEN MARDOCHAI TROKI (cir.
1600); MOSES ZAKUT (ob. 1698) [29 a]; SAMUEL MODON
(1725); and even as late as 1820 by ISRAEL (NACHMAN) BEN
JOSEPH DROBICZER.   Shorter imitations are to be met
with in prefaces and epilogues by ISAAC BEN JONATHAN
of Posen (1595); JOMTOB, probably at Prague (1598);
ISAAC BEN SOLOMON LEVI at Saloniki (1600); in a letter
of SOLOMON ZARFATI in Turkey (16th century); in an
imitation of the arrangement of the 119th Psalm, where each
letter contains eight sentences (thence called תמניא אפי), by
SIMON HABILLO, as late as the 17th century; and in the
Seder Aboda of JOSE BEN JOSE and SAADJA GAON (see § 19.),
where each letter contains ten sentences.—(B.) Acrostics of
names, words, and *sense,* to be found first in introductions in
rhyme prefixed to treatises, in letters, &c., at Babylon, Italy,
and Spain, from the 10th century downwards, and even in
the beginnings of chapters of an astronomical work by JAKOB
BEN SAMSON (1123—42) [30]; also in the prayers of JANNAI,
KALIR, SAADJA GAON, and their successors, many of whom
thus immortalised the names of themselves and others.   This
practice continued until it was censured by subsequent

writers, such as Isaac Arama towards the end of the 15th century; and even at a much later time Moses ben Israel Landsberg finds fault with its being still used in epistles. There are also acrostics consisting of whole words, passages of the Bible, and the like.

2. *Rhyme* (הרוז, Arab. قَافِيَة, properly a string of pearls, a row of lines [31]) appears as an artificial form perhaps first in memorial verses on the Masora, and on the 613 precepts (§ 19.), and about the same time in the hymns of JANNAI and KALIR, in some Selichot of SAADJA's *Agenda* [32], and in Italy and Spain during the 10th century in SABBATTAI DONOLO, and MENAHEM SARUK.[33] The German-French school, however, cultivated it less artificially than the Spanish.[34] The latter followed Arabian models, and considered the identity of the consonants preceding the vowel in the final syllables of a rhyme as essential: sometimes several syllables were made to rhyme (שיר מיוחם), but a repetition of the whole word was admissible only at the end of the strophe. This repetition occurs most frequently when the burden of the poem is taken from the Bible. They also cultivated *homonymous* poems (שיר נצמד, Arab. تَجْنِيس [35]) of a peculiar kind, and composed, after the manner of the older Arabians, poems often of many hundred lines with the same rhyme throughout [35a]; a performance which is much facilitated by the Semitic inflexion and iambic accentuation. This was done by the Karaite JEHUDA GIBBOR in a hymn of no less than 1260 lines; and similarly by JEHUDA HEDESSI, all the strophes of whose huge Karaitic dogmatical poem end with the suffix of the second person. To this class belong also the poems called by the Arabic name קצידה *Kassida* (قَطِيدَة). On the other hand, JOSE BEN JOSE, in his order of *Tekiot*, and Kalir and his followers, made the same word recur frequently and often without intermission.[36] The metaphor of pearls and necklaces, alluded to above, is also carried out in some other kinds of poetry distinguished by special names. The Hebrew ענק denotes alike the grammatical verses of GABIROL, and the homonymes of MOSES IBN EZRA and CHARISI. The Arabic term مُوَشَّع (מושח) *Muwasseh* is applied to poems where the rhymes recur every

seventh line like pearls in an elaborately arranged neck-
lace.

This mixed form is said to have been invented by the
Arabs in Spain in the 10th century; not, however, according
to Almakkari, by Ahmed Ibn Abd Rebbihi (ob. 940), who
borrowed it from Mokaddem ben Moârife al-Kabari; and
amongst twenty-nine writers reckoned excellent in this kind
of poetry we find ABRAHAM IBN SAHL of Valencia, probably
the well-known Jew (§ 20.). It was originally used in
encomiastic and descriptive poetry instead of the older and
more simple Kassida; but although the term occurs almost
exclusively in the titles of some of the profane poems of
MOSES IBN EZRA, and JEHUDA HA-LEVI, the form itself is
already applied to religious poetry by ISAAC IBN GAJJATH
(ob. 1089). Also alternative rhymes, unknown in European
languages before the 12th century, may be found in Jewish
hymns of at least two centuries earlier.

The influence of the love of rhyme and metre extended
even to the titles of books. *The Echo* (הד) was a favourite
conceit of the later Italians[37]; and internal rhymes, asso-
nances, and puns of all kinds embellish the rhyming prose
even to excess. Poems arranged in figures after the Arabian
taste also occur.[37a] To this class probably belongs the *Cake
Work* of JECHIEL BEN ASHER. The theory of such figures,
labyrinths, &c., is treated by MOSES ABUDIENTE.

3. *Metre* (מקצב=وزن, משקל=تقطيع, *scansio*; מדה, מדות,
measure)[38] consists of two elements: (*a.*) the syllable with
the simple sound, תנועה (vowel), corresponding to the Arabic
سبب; (*b.*) the syllable with the preceding *shewa mobile*
(wanting in Arabic), יתד (peg), وتد. From the various arrangements of these all particular metres are formed.[39] Their
canonical number, as among the Arabians, is nineteen, but
JACOB ROMAN extends it to fifty-two. The oldest known
example of metre, which as well as its name is imitated
from the Arabic, is to be found in DUNASH IBN LIBRAT[40],
who must bear the reproach of having introduced a foreign
element into the holy language; an enormity which had not
been committed even by Saadja Gaon (ob. 942). But the
Spanish school of the 10th century at first only imitated

a few of the Arabian metres; and, in consequence of their adhering to the uniformity of the rhyme, Moses Ibn Ezra compares them to the old Arabic poets before Muhammed. Some of the poetry of the old Spaniards he says, especially the religious, was not metrical at all; their Hebrew style was natural and simple, not embellished by any artificial means and inventions; they neither cultivated the "literæ humaniores," nor did they even adhere strictly to grammar. Subsequently most of them introduced mathematics and Astronomy into their hymns, thus "imposing upon the Hebrew language that which it is not suited to bear;" so that devotion degenerated into speculation and disputation. After the Berberic invasion (about 1070), which drove many Jews into poverty and exile, and impeded the progress of learning, especially at Cordova, a new generation arose under the auspices of SAMUEL NAGID, who in his work אבן תלים composed metrical prayers with music, which, according to Ibn Ezra, no one did before or after him. According to Zunz he perhaps introduced metre into the synagogue, although it is not often met with in the religious poetry even of the Spaniards. Metre found its way from Spain into Provence and Italy before the 12th century. In the North of France JACOB TAM (ob. 1170) was the first to adopt it." [40a] In contradistinction to the essentially metrical poems (שיר שקול, rarely נשרל or שיר, lay, شعر, also מחובר, *ligatum*), we find the rhetorical speeches in rhyming prose (מליצה, הליצה, سجع) [41], which substitutes for metre the melody of words and artifices of all kinds. The metrical poem consists of verses or lines in rhyme (בית, house, بيت) [42], which again are composed of two halves (مصراع), viz. דלת (door), and סוגר (shutter).

4. The *Rhythm* and *Melody* of Hebrew poetry (conceivable either with or without any particular metre, and in the closest connexion with the use of *Music*) belong to the most interesting, but, in consequence of the uncertain terminology, to the most obscure parts of the history of Jewish literature and culture. [43] The Prophets often denounced song and melody at feasts, while the author of the Chronicles frequently speaks of the music [44] which accompanied

public worship in the Temple, and the headings of the
Psalms indicate elements of melody in the old Hebrew
poetry.[45]   These parts of the Bible gave rise to the sentences in the Talmud and Midrash relating to song and
music (זמר שיר), censuring or approving, according as they
are used in a frivolous or pious manner.   In Bagdad, once
the seat of the Gaonim, the traveller PETACHJA of Regensburg (in the 12th century) heard some traditional psalmody
with instrumental accompaniment.[46]   The lively mode of
expression prevalent in the East, and generally in the in-
fancy of a nation, which readily combines with a kind of
cantillation and gesticulation, together with the practical
use of verse as an assistance to the memory[46a], had established a peculiar mode of reciting biblical passages and
the lectures of the Mishna at an early period (§ 4.); so
that for both these purposes the *Accents* (§ 16.) were invented.   A treatise of the Mishna was printed with accents
as late as 1553.[47]   In what connexion the arrangement of
the older prayers and the later poems stand to this recitative, and what influence Arabian music may have had
upon it, are not known.   Down to the 12th century SAADJA
is the only writer, known to the author, of whom any
fragment on the theory of music is extant[48]; in fact, the
theory and expression of music (חכמת המוסיקא), or sequence
of sound (ח' הנגון), belongs, like all similar sciences, originally to the Arabian school.   Among the Arabs (and
also among the Christian scholastics connected with them)
music belongs to the sciences, or " seven free arts," and
poetry (ابوطيّا, אבוטידא, מלאכת השיר) is only a frivolous
art[49], the best part of which, according to the well-known
Aristotelian expression, is deception.[50]   According to JE-
HUDA HALEVI (1140)[51], the enthusiast for everything
national, who is said to have given up poetry before his
death, the old Hebrew poetry, constructed upon melody
alone, was injured by the rhyme and metre of the Arabians;
his contemporary ABRAHAM IBN EZRA states the connexion
between melody and metre.[52]   According to unexception-
able testimony[53], Hebrew liturgical poetry was already
about this time sung and even composed to profane Arabian

and Romanic (עלגים, كَجَم) airs [54]; so that the traditional melodies (לחן [الحن] נועם נוגין) of some of these (as in the present
Jewish song-books) are still named after the corresponding
foreign or Hebrew model airs.   Even ISRAEL NAG'ARA
(1587) composed his songs to Arabic and Turkish melodies,
for the purpose of superseding the original words; and as
late as the 17th century a Sabbath hymn by MENAHEM ZION,
to the melody of the German lay " Steyermark," was inserted in the Kabbalistic Sabbath ritual.[55]   JACOB LEVI of
Mayence (ob. 1427) is reckoned the founder of German
synagogue music, which was previously based upon no
regular system; and, according to Zunz, some melodies,
especially those for penitential days, may be nearly as old
as the corresponding hymns.   On the other hand, pious men
declaimed against the precentors (חזנים, משוררים), who used to
obtrude their own music (חזנות, נגון) at the expense of true
devotion.[56]   As early as the 12th and 13th centuries they were
attacked by satirical poets, such as JOSEPH IBN SABARA and
IMMANUEL of Rome, who quote authorities for the physical
connexion between an agreeable voice and an empty skull.
The modern performances, especially those of the Polish
singers, so much admired by persons who once or twice a
year feel themselves brought back by them to the devotional
feelings of their youth, deadened either by neglect or by a
mechanical attendance on public worship, are characterised
by a kind of recitative, having so little reference to musical
time, that it spoils the ancient melodies.   These singers,
moreover, are so wanting in attention to the original simplicity of the music, that their ornamentation far surpasses
the bravuras of Italian opera-singers and the execution of
modern pianists, to say nothing of the total disparity between
them and their assistants.   The return of so many synagogues to a purer musical taste could not be accomplished
without at first borrowing the style of Christian composers,
and even introducing some of their melodies, and then gradually substituting for them original compositions of Jews (although not those highly esteemed in the opera and concert-room,
which obtain but little favour in the synagogue), or by restoring
the sacred songs to their ancient purity.   The recitation of

the Sefardim kept closer to its original simplicity, and therefore underwent fewer changes ; but it is deficient in the
peculiarity and vigorous effect of the other.   This is owing
to the circumstance, that the nature of their public service
was more rigid and unvarying (§ 19.), and retained some of
the old hymnology, by which even their own compositions
were much influenced.

With metre and melody is connected the construction of
the *Strophe*, which is more simple or complicated, according
to the various classes and schools.   The ancient prayers
of the East, without metre or rhyme, are generally distinguished by the acrostic (§ 1.), and imitate the biblical strophe
constructed on *parallelisms* (ازدواج), or are still more artificial.[56a]   The older pieces of rhyme of every kind, and the
unmetrical German-French prayers, are divided into members
by rhyme, biblical *refrain*, and the like.[57]   The Spaniards
imitated the Arabic forms (*Ghasel*, &c.); subsequently the
Provençal and Italian literature obtained some influence,
and IMMANUEL of Rome (as early as cir. 1300) contracted
the 14-lined Arabic Ghasel to a sonnet of 10 lines.[57a]   The
real *Terzine, Sestine,* and the *Ottava rima* (whose origin
Hammer claims for the Arabic زجل) were perfected in
Italy.[58]   The strophe of two lines (مثنوي) occurs in some old
hymns, but the term שינה appears not to have been used
amongst the Spaniards.   The strophe of three lines (שלישיה)
is common, as well as that of four lines of different lengths.
Real strophes of more lines are less usual in the old hymns
of either school.   But few profane poems of the Spaniards
bear the original Persian name דוביח (دوبيت, i. e. double-
Beit), essentially the same as the Arabic رباعي, *Quatrain*,
consisting of strophes of four lines with the same rhyme.
The progression or chain of rhyme, like the triplet, is an old
form.[59]

Finally, a *Mosaic* of biblical phrases and whole passages
(اقتباس and تضمين)[60], an important and peculiar element in
Hebrew poetry, became a special art, influencing the whole
style, particularly that of satires and parodies (§ 20.) and the
construction of the strophe [61], and assisting in the formation
of the refrain or repetition of a word (קיקלור קוקלור, perhaps

"circular," or some other derivative from κύκλος)[62], the response or repetition of a sentence (פזמון[63], originally any composition in rhyme, probably also סיידי, from ἀείδω, or generally the verse termination גמרא), the biblical acrostic (صحیاب, also מסתאגיב)[64], and the like.

Other foreign terms, occurring only in religious poetry, and hitherto not sufficiently explained, appear to the author to indicate the form[65], viz. the Chaldee רהים or רהוטה[66], the Arabic מהרך (moved ?)[67], רתבה, or מרתבה (שיר) חמעלות?)[68], and the Romanic עסתריוטא.[69]

§ 19.] *Liturgical Poetry (Pijjutim).*

The Halacha itself had never been entirely fixed, or come to a visible conclusion ; it was thus unable to give a general type for the Liturgy, which was indeed but partially under its influence.[1] When, therefore, the new style of literature and poetry led to an extension of the old and widely diffused prayers, it necessarily followed that the daily service, and still more that for the festivals, should be variously modified in different countries. On this account, R. AMRAM GAON (870—888)[2], having received a request from Spain, sent thither his *Order of Prayer* (סדר, order, or סדור, also יסוד, institution[3]), which, however, was not adopted in that country to the same extent as it was later in Germany. The name *Siddur* was afterwards given to the simple collection of the daily prayers, and the oldest of those for festivals, which differ but very slightly in the German and Spanish rituals. By degrees liturgical poetry, adapted to every special time and occasion, was produced ; the various kinds being designated sometimes by appropriate technical terms, often ambiguous and not sufficiently known, and sometimes by names taken from the titles given to particular collections[4] by writers and printers according to the purposes for which they were intended. We shall endeavour to comprise all in the following short and very general enumeration : —

1. *Machsor* (מחזור, cycle, in the more restricted sense) contains only the poetry for festivals ; *Pijjutim* proper.

2. *Kerobot* (קרובות, or with a French plural form קרוביץ[5]), which is sometimes taken as synonymous with the former, or

with *Jozerot* (יוצרות, from being inserted in the morning prayer *Jozer*), including not only the poetry for festivals, but also that for extraordinary Sabbaths and the like.

3. *Penitential Prayers* (סליחות, *Selihot,* plural of סליחה, forgiveness, and thus סלח *Sallâh* and סלחן *Salhan* the author of such a prayer)[6], originating in the rite of the great penitential Day of Atonement, and extended first to a time of preparation preceding that day, then, in the course of centuries, to other fasts and days of a similar character, and finally, in the following period, to a special morning service for every day except Sabbaths and festivals.[7]

4. *Elegies* (קינות *Kinot,* תמרור, مرثیة [8]), properly for the fast day of the 9th Ab.

5. *Hosiannas* (הושענות), particularly for the 7th of the feast of Sukkot.

6. *Petitions* (בקשות) and exhortations, or religious and moral meditations for private use.[9]

Particular pieces of the Pijjutim are named, for the most part, from the first words of the prayer in which they are inserted[10]; thus the song for the end of the Sabbath is called *Habdala* (הבדלה).[10a] The *Introduction*, or *Captatio benevolentiæ* of the singer, who is the composer, called also רשות (*asking permission*)[10b], and the close (חתימה = خروج, and סלוק)[10c], form the limits of the larger groups. Some are named after the purpose for which they are intended; as, for example, the *Celebration of the Dead* (השכבה, אשכבתא).[10d] Under the name *Zemirot* (זמירות, *songs*) were afterwards (§ 28.) understood particularly those which are used on Friday evening. Others are named after the argument; for instance, *The Death of Moses* (פטירת משה), used on the feast Simchat Torah; *The Decalogue* (עשרת הדברות), for Pentecost, &c. The different subjects are generally taken from history and dogmatic theology, the Haggada, and the Halacha, and are clothed in allegory[10e]; their poetical value is various.

Concerning the earliest poets and hymns, which, according to Zunz, may belong to Palestine and Syria, nothing has been satisfactorily ascertained. JOSE BEN JOSE, who is certainly earlier than Saadja, and probably also than Kalir,

was twenty years ago thought by Zunz himself to be a Provençal of a much later date. This is a striking instance of
the uncertainty of such inquiries.

In the *Arabian* school, which originated in Babylon, the
Haggada never occupied a very important place ; and the
same scientific inquiries which were fatal to it raised the
Halacha to the rank of a science.[10f] This school, therefore, takes the materials for poetry alike from the Halacha and from science, both of which must be investigated
for the present history. In elegiac descriptions of the past
greatness of the nation, in searching the depths of their own
hearts, in a joyful communion with the original source of all,
they rise to true poetry, subjecting the materials furnished
by the Bible, Talmud, and profane science, to thought and
feeling, and making new creations from them. From the
first we find a representative description of the former service
of the Temple of God on the Day of Atonement, *Seder
Aboda* (סדר עבודה)[11], forming an important part of the
liturgy and private devotions for that day (מעומד, מעומד)[12] ;
it was already, in the 8th century, combined with Kerobot
and Selichot and cultivated in Italy and Spain in the 10th
century. The oldest Seder Aboda is perhaps the אתה כוננתה
of the Spanish ritual, which Saadja, in his Liturgy, ascribes
to " the learned of Israel " (גמיע עלמא ישראל). Opening a
historical introduction with the creation, and proceeding to
the Aboda, which is supposed to have taken place on the
Day of Atonement, it seems to be the prototype of the more
artificial hymn of JOSE BEN JOSE, discovered by the author
in the Agenda of SAADJA GAON, who himself imitates the
form of Jose in his hymn, giving ten lines to each letter of
the alphabet (§ 18. p. 150.). Both of these will soon be
published (by the author) from a MS. in the Bodleian.
Various other Halachaic subjects, upon which instruction
was to be given (called, therefore, אזהרות, *Azharot*, Admonitions) on the Saturday before the festivals[13], were, for the
advantage of the great body of the people put into rhyme,
perhaps after the example of the Arabs (§ 20.), and were
afterwards incorporated in the liturgy.[14] This was the
case with an enumeration of the 613 precepts (§ 4.), which

were, even among the Karaites, considered as being included in the Ten Commandments.   The name of Azharot
is now usually applied to the 613 precepts for the Day of
Pentecost, the Day of the Giving of the Law; and the
earliest author of Azharot is considered to be SAADJA GAON
(ob. 942.) [15], to whom some authors ascribe the derivation
of the precepts from, or their subordination to, the Ten Commandments.   In fact, the Agenda of Saadja contains a very
elaborate hymn on that subject, being part of a *Keroba* to
the Musaf prayer of Pentecost, and bearing the title אזהרות.
There is also prefixed to it a particular enumeration of the
613 precepts in a more simple form, the same rhymes being
continued for four successive lines, and the alternate lines
commencing alphabetically; in a preliminary note Saadja
remarks, that he made this to take the place of an incorrect
enumeration, from which people used to recite on that day.
Both pieces will be found in the *Seder Aboda* mentioned
above.   In contradistinction to these, there are penitential
prayers and petitions (confessions of sin, exhortations, and
the like, for the ten days of penitence), which, according to
the old Arabian custom, begin with the praise of God; after
this follows the hymn itself, with historical descriptions of
the subject of the festival.   By degrees, dogmatic theology
and the Halacha were versified and introduced into the
liturgy; for instance, the celebrated *Keter Malchut* of SA-
LOMO IBN GABIROL, now to be found in the evening service of the Day of Atonement, is, in fact, a versification of
Aristotle's book *De mundo*.   Finally, the different occasions
of life, such as birth, marriage, and death, were made the
subjects of synagogue poetry.   Notwithstanding this, neither
the *Babylonian* ritual, until the end of the Gaonim (1037),
nor the Spanish and Portuguese (*Sefaradic*), overburdened
their liturgy (*Agenda*), although the latter was not quite free
from French influence; a few only of the numerous poems
composed for the service being really recited in it, according
to the several localities and various circumstances.   For many
distinguished teachers opposed any change in the original
prayers, the accumulation of prayers in general, and the obscurity of some of them to the unlearned; and philosophers

objected to the continual anthropomorphism and metaphors, in fact, to poetry in general, in the same way as formerly the teachers had resisted the precentors.[16]　The various views and judgments on the Pijjutim in general were carefully collected some years ago; and we may here add two remarkable criticisms mentioned elsewhere in this essay: viz., that of MOSES IBN EZRA (§ 18. p. 153.), and that of the Karaite LEVI BEN JEFET (§ 14. p. 117.).　The authors of liturgical poems of the Spanish school, especially those whose productions became a part of public worship, were few, but they were very prolific; according to Zunz, the five most popular of them composed about 1000 liturgical pieces, besides other poetry.　In fact, most of these poets (from about the end of the 10th century to the 13th)[17] were also authors of non-liturgical poetry, to be treated of in § 20., or else were men of general learning, and are thus mentioned in different parts of this essay; for instance, JOSEPH IBN SANTAS or ABI THAUR (end of 10th century), ISAAC IBN GAJJAT (not Giat, the Hebrew translation is מושיע) (ob. 1089), BECHAJI (about 1100), MAIMONIDES, NACHMANIDES, and others.

In contradistinction to this school there was developed at the same time the *German-French* poetry, the derivation of which from an older Italian rests on a doubtful conjecture. Their poetry, like all the other literature of the Jews of Germany and of Northern France, was confined almost entirely to the Haggada and Halacha; their productions, through which the expressions *Pijjut* and *Pajtan* became restricted to *liturgical* poetry [18], being mere versifications of the Haggada and Halacha, and consisting of short phrases put together like mosaic work, so complex and obscure that it is almost impossible to translate them.　This soon rendered an explanation necessary in order to point out the references to the Talmud and Midrash, which were here considered of at least equal authority with the Bible.[19]　The language comprising the whole range of the Hebrew-Aramaïc of the Haggada and Halacha, was but little understood in these countries (§ 15.), and increased the difficulty; and poems written entirely in Aramaïc [20] were here more fre-

quent than in the other school, where some in Arabic are to
be found. They were originally recited by precentors, who
were rivals of the Darshanim, and with whose occasional pieces,
and introductory *captatio benevolentiæ* (§ 18.), the general
liturgy was continually deluged. For only in the house of
God was the Jew of those countries at home.[21] The Haggada had now come to a close, and various collections of it
had been made; but its philosophical explanation is as rarely
to be met with in these countries as most other scientific
disquisitions. Thus the hymnical recension of the Haggada,
being invested with the charm of novelty, fully occupied the
intellectual activity of the time, until it was supplanted by
the new and more fashionable Kabbala; while the older
elements of the mystic doctrine formed the subject of the
Pijjutim themselves. The often-repeated observation of Rapoport [22] strikingly characterises both schools: " The Sefaradic Pijjutim are interpreters between the soul and her
Creator, the German (and French) between the Israelitish
nation and their God." Zunz also remarks, " The poetry
of the one is the Pijjut, the Pijjut of the other is poetry."
The justly celebrated ELEAZAR BIRIBI KALIR (or perhaps
his older contemporary JANNAI) may be regarded as a
prototype of these Pajtanim: perhaps, like the Italian SAB-
BATAI DONOLO, he obtained the art of rhyme through the
Arabs, but his subject-matter and ritual are principally derived from Palestine; for instance, from the Pesikta (composed about 845). These sources were not so accessible to
his successors in Germany and France; and thus as early as
in the 11th century Kalir's date and native country were
unknown, his poetry does not appear in Saadja's *Siddur*, and
he is mentioned only incidentally [23] by the same author in
an Arabic commentary on the book *Jezira*. Kalir, probably
himself a precentor, by versifying the prayers for the whole
year (called *Machsor*, i.e. *cyclus*), did in the form of poetry
what the author of the Pesikta had done in the form of
Haggada (§ 5. B.). His prayers were introduced first into
Italy [23a], and afterwards into France, Germany, and perhaps
also Greece, and were imitated even by the highest authorities; and so this poetical Haggada and Halacha came into
contact with the homiletical.

The school of Kalir, in the narrowest sense, is the flower of the Pajtanic age (ending cir. 1100). Among its members are reckoned the most celebrated composers of prayers for festivals; such as MESHULAM BEN KALONYMOS of Lucca, and his son KALONYMOS at Mayence; MOSES [24] and CHANANEL, sons of the latter; SOLOMON BEN JEHUDA, " the Babylonian," from whom some Selichot are denominated שלמוניות [25]; the renowned R. GERSON (§ 9.); the prolific SIMON BEN ISAAC BEN ABUN; ELIA BEN MENAHEM of Mans, called HA-SAKEN (the elder); BENJAMIN BEN SERACH, perhaps the most prolific writer of this school (1058); JOSEPH TOB-ELEM at Limoges; MEIR BEN ISAAC the precentor (about 1100), author of pieces in Aramaïc; JOSEPH BEN SOLOMON of Carcassonne; ELIEZER BEN SAMUEL (1096); KALONYMOS BEN MOSES, and his brother JEKUTIEL; BENJAMIN BEN SAMUEL; ISAAC HALEVI at Worms, and his pupil SOLOMON ISAKI; ELIA BEN MORDECAI; and others. In the 12th century there was a great increase in the number of writers [26], although not in the number or variety of works : the form and language were improved at the expense of the matter and vigour ; secret doctrine and philosophy obtained an entrance, and changed the type of the versified Haggada ; and the casuistry and dialectics of the *Tosaphot* attracted to themselves all thinking men. Thus the Pajtanic school fell into decay, numbering but a few stragglers in the 13th and 14th centuries ; at which period the German-French literature in general yielded to the universal barbarism of the age. The authors are in the main the same as those mentioned above (§ 9.); most of the teachers and writers on Halacha being at once precentors, copyists, preachers, or Rabbies.

In the 12th century the two main divisions described above had been in some degree blended, especially in Provence and Italy ; and, even earlier, different liturgies had borrowed single pieces from each other : but at this time a type of Pijjutim and liturgy, approaching more nearly to the Spanish, was formed on the points of contact of the different schools. To this class (omitting in general the poets who will be mentioned in § 20.) belong : in Provence [27], JEHUDA

BEN BARZILLAI BARCELLONI (fl. 1130), probably at Mar-
seilles; ISAAC HALEVI and his sons the famous SERACHJA
LEVI (ob. 1186) and BERECHIA; JOSEPH KIMCHI and his
son MOSES; JEHUDA BEN NATANEL and his sons SAMUEL
and ISAAC (1218); MESHULLAM BEN SOLOMON; JEHUDA
HARARI of Montpellier; DON KALONYMOS; MOSES BEN
JEHUDA; PINCHAS BEN JOSEPH HALEVI; SOLOMON BEN
MAIMON; SOLOMON BEN ISAAC NASI; ABRAHAM BEN
CHAJIM; ISAAC KIMCHI (1290); JOSEPH IBN CASPI;
ABRAHAM IBN KASLAR, probably the physician (1323);
ISRAEL KASLAR, physician at Avignon (1327); JACOB DE
LÜNEL, perhaps the physician at Carcassonne; ISAAC DE
LATAS (1372); JACOB SOLOMON (1443); MOSES BEN
ABRAHAM (1466) at Avignon [27a]; and others: in Italy [28]
ELIA BEN SAMUEL (ob. 1298); several of the name of
JOAB; BENJAMIN; and others later.

The *Collections* of Pijjutim are of different kinds [28a]: —
1. *Liturgies,* or compilations of prayers according to the use
(מנהג, ritual) of different countries or cities, the peculiarities
of which depend upon particular hymns, not always written by
persons of the country where they were used. But of these
rituals some have never been published, others are very rare,
and very few have been accurately described. The final
redaction of some of them was not made until the time
when they were printed in the following period (§ 28.);
and thus it is necessary to examine minutely the MSS.
themselves for the history and mutual influence of the various
rituals. In this interesting subject so little has been done,
that we must confine ourselves to a dry enumeration: the principal countries and towns connected with it are, Germany,
and afterwards Poland; France (צרפת); Spain and Portugal
(ספרד, קאטלאני); Italy (לועזים), identical with Rome; the
Levant (Romagna) or Greece (גריגוש, הוניא) [29]; and some
towns in Provence and France, such as Avignon [30], Montpellier, Carpentras (Cavaillon, Lille). The rituals of the
states and cities of Barbary are of Spanish origin; for example, those of Algiers (אלגייר = الجزيرة); Tripoli, or Mostaa-
reb (מסתרב); Oran [31]; Marocco; Tlemsan; — Fas, whence
a MS. has been recently purchased for the library of Leyden.

Scarcely anything is known about the rituals of Asia and
Egypt, where, however, poetry in general was but little cultivated (§ 20.); a collection of hymns, from Aleppo as it
appears, in the Bodleian Library, has been recently recognised as such by the author.　2. A few collections of writings
by particular authors are known; for instance, by SIMON
DURAN and REUBEN BEN ISAAC (1400).[32]

The treatment of the prayers and benedictions (§ 6.) with
reference to the public service and private devotion [33] varied
according to the different laws of rituals, and gradually
formed a *use* (מנהג) or *ritual*.　This subject was not only
treated in the general Halachaic compendiums (§ 9.), and
occasionally in commentaries and glosses; but it also called
forth particular branches of literature, according either as
the ritual directions were appended to the prayers, thus
forming a *liturgy* (מחזור, סדור) proper, or as the prayers,
either by name or in full, were inserted in the ritual directions (*Agenda*).　In the German-French school, which is
the richest and also the most minute in these writings, the
latter are often called *Minhagim* or *Minhagot* (מנהגים or
מנהגות).[34]　The oldest *Siddurim*, like that of AMRAM GA-
ON, a recension of which has been discovered by Luzzatto,
were frequently composed from the results of inquiries addressed to famous authorities at a distance [35], and contained
also compositions by these same persons, with explanations
of the subject-matter and language.　Afterwards other additions were made, such as calendars, small ethical tracts,
&c., often written on the margins of the prayers and agen-
das, so as to form a perfect " Vade-mecum."　The earliest
works of this kind are apparently all lost, with the exception
of one of the oldest, the Arabic *Siddur* of SAADJA GAON (ob.
942) discovered a few years ago in the Bodleian Library by
the author.　The frequent quotations made from it by Zunz
(according to some extracts furnished to him) show the
importance of this Siddur, of which we shall here give a
short description, illustrating the class, though the almost
pedantic arrangement and division are peculiar to the individual work.　The subject is divided into two parts; the first
treats of the duty and necessity of prayer, with reference

to the institutions during the time of the Temple, entering into an investigation of the whole subject; of this, however, only the end is preserved in the MS.   The second
part, inscribed *Book of Prayers, Praises, and Benedictions*
(ואלתסאביח ואלברך כתיאב אלצלואת), is introduced by
some general remarks upon the changes which took place in divine service, in the way of omission, addition, and abbreviation,
through the exile of the nation.   It then proposes to give a
simple " Canon" of the standard parts of the service, adding
only the alterations made by some later authorities which
were not contradictory to the original purpose of the service,
premising that they have no foundation in tradition; and it
adds the rules for some ceremonies connected with the service
and the cycle of the year.   This part is divided into two
sections; the first containing the service for every day, and
the second that for special seasons, viz. for Sabbaths, festivals, and feasts.   Most of the prayers are given entire in the
original Hebrew; and it is important to remark, that the
author repeatedly mentions that he excludes all חזנות, by
which term he can only mean the " solos" of the precentors,
so that all that are in the book must be considered as prayers
for the whole congregation.   For the private or " volun-
tary" prayer on week-days, or Sabbaths and feasts, he gives
his two celebrated invocations (دعا); an Arabic translation
of which has been made by ZEMACH BEN JOSHUA, whom
some bibliographers have therefore regarded as the author
of the whole work.   In this way Saadja preserved many of
the old prayers, with remarkable variations (for instance,
in the Shemona-esre), some hymns by JOSE BEN JOSE, and
some by anonymous authors, and others by himself, some
of which are nowhere else to be found; and it is only to
be regretted that it is in some instances doubtful whether
Saadja is the collector or the author of them.   We now proceed to name the authors of similar works: — the Gaonim:
KOHEN ZEDEK [36]; HAI (ob. 1037); NISSIM and CHANANEL
at Kairowan;   and ISAAC IBN GAJJAT at Lucena (ob.
1089) [37]: — in France and Germany: JOSEPH TOB ELEM
(1050);   MEIR BEN ISAAC the precentor; SOLOMON the
Babylonian [38]; RASHI; SIMCHA of Vitry (1100); TAM [39];

ELCHANAN [39a]; ISAAC of אורביל, מנויל (cir. 1250—1260); SAMUEL BEN SOLOMON (or R. PEREZ?) [40]; MEIR ROTHENBURG (1270); CHAJIM PALTIEL (cir. 1280); and ABRAHAM KLAUSNER (1380—1400):—in Austria, EISAK TYRNAU (cir. 1440):—in Italy, ZIDKIA ANAW, and his epitomiser (1314) [40a]:—in Provence, perhaps SERACHJA HALEVI, and ASHER BEN MESHULLAM (cir. 1170) at Lünel [41]:—and in Spain, ASHER BEN JECHIEL [41a]; and ISRAEL ISRAELI (1330) at Toledo, whose Arabic explanatory work was translated by SHEMTOB BEN ARDUTIL. The critical and explanatory liturgy of DAVID BEN JOSEPH ABUDIRAHIM at Seville (1340) is the best known. The comprehensive work of SOLOMON BEN NATHAN of Segelmessa (12th century) in Arabic deserves notice.[42] The work of JACOB LEVI (ob. 1427 in Mayence) is one of the most celebrated.—The Karaites also had writings of this kind; for instance, that of Muallim (magister) FADHEL (cir. 1290?), who wished to meet the reproach of the Rabbinites that the Karaitic liturgy was left to the arbitrary will of the individual.[42a] Within this literature the *Easter Haggada* (§ 6. and § 26.), interpreted Kabbalistically by JOSEPH CHIQUITILLA, forms a branch of its own.

These works form the transition to the special commentaries on single pieces and on whole collections, which were soon found necessary for Kalir's productions. The Halachaic Pijjutim also, and those of the old Spaniards which presented difficulties either scientific or philological; for instance, the *Seder Aboda* by JOSEPH IBN ABITUR (in the 10th century) [43], the *Azharot* of SALOMON IBN GABIROL, and various poems by JEHUDA IBN GAJJAT (ob. 1089) [44], were commentated in Provence by ANATOLI, MOSES TIBBON, ISAAC BEN TODROS, and others, and by the Spaniard SIMON DURAN at Algiers (1417). The German-French school seems to have here shown the greatest activity. Single explanations of Pijjutim are already quoted as bearing the names of MENAHEM BEN CHELBO (cir. 1050) [45], RASHI, and others; but it is uncertain from what kind of writings they are taken. Actual commentaries were certainly written by EPHRAIM BEN JACOB of Bonn (1171—98) [46]. JACOB NASIR at Lünel (§ 13.),

SHEMAJA of Soissons [47], and AARON BEN CHAJJIM KOHEN (1227), may be considered as the forerunners of the Kabbalistic method of explanation, which was applied also to the prayers (see § 13. p. 115). Later Pijjutim were sometimes written with Halachaic and grammatical explanations by the authors; for instance, the *Azharot* of MENAHEM BEN MOSES TAMÂR (1449). The Karaites also have commentaries of this kind; for instance, those of MOSES BEN ELIA PASHA (? פשׁאַ) and JOSEPH BEN SAMUEL (unfinished)[48], and a *Siddur* by ABU SOLEIMAN DAVID BEN HOSSIN (see p. 117.), mentioned by Levi ben Jefet. Their present order of prayer[49] is ascribed to AARON BEN JOSEPH (about 1290). Even before this, perhaps at the time when Karaism attempted to force its way into Spain [50], they had introduced into the service several Rabbinical poems from that country. It was completed by means of some later Karaitic poems in the biblical style, and according to Spanish forms.

All kinds of translations of the prayers also take their origin in this period, although it is difficult to fix the exact time of the commencement of each (see § 28.). In the Bodleian Library are preserved some Arabic translations of penitential prayers which are scarcely later than the 14th century; the translation of Saadja's prayers (see p. 166.) is probably older.

Thus the liturgy forms a mirror for both internal and external experiences, a focus whence intellectual movements radiated in all directions. It was more especially the German and French Jews who sang their manifold sufferings and persecutions in the House of God, thereby elevating the melancholy sound of their harp to be a significant but mysterious echo of the story of the human race.

§ 20.]   *Non-Liturgical Poetry.*

We may here confine our attention almost entirely to the Arabian school and its offshoots in Provence and Italy, since the religious severity of the Karaites restricted their poetry, nearly without exception, to the liturgy and to theological controversy. We have described the various forms of poetry

in general above (§ 18.). With respect to matter, the secular
poetry, like the religious, is characterised by seriousness and
morality : wit, irony, and satire appear to have been exercised
only in the continual allusions to the classical literature,
—the Bible, the Talmud, prayers[1], &c. ; a circumstance
which considerably increases the difficulty of perfectly understanding it, and of imitating it in other languages.   The
poetry of the Arabs, which was the model for the Jews,
drew from the many springs of life; but that of the Hebrews,
which depended entirely on Scripture, could draw only from
the hallowed waters of the Temple.   Herein, to speak in the
language of writers of this time, the neglected " Sarah "
celebrates a triumph over the upstart (Prov. xxx. 23.)
Egyptian maid, whose overbearing tones were for a long
while alone heard, until the rightful champions of the
former arose, and zeal for the holy language appropriated
the sweetest sounds of the Arabs to her cause.

If the Arabic poets among the Jews had not alluded to
and sometimes attacked Judaism, they might have been
passed over here without notice, and their writings and
names left to be preserved in the history of Arabian literature[2]; although certain Arabic Pijjutim, for instance those
of MARZUK (Saadja), were received into the liturgy.[3]
CHEFEZ AL-KUTI (or al-Futi ?) seems to have versified the
Psalms in Arabic; quotations from this work have been
found by the author in Moses Ibn Ezra's Poetics : he is probably older than Gabirol (§ 12. B. p.101.). Even MAIMONIDES,
who denies that there is any real advantage to be gained
by the reading of Arabian songs[4] and traditions, possibly
composed poems which found a place in Arabian anthologies[5]; and the famous Hebrew poet MOSES IBN EZRA
(1138) exhibits a perfect knowledge of Arabic poetry and
Poetics. JEHUDA IBN KOREISH, ABULWALID, GABIROL,
and TANCHUM of Jerusalem quote Arabic poems; which
quotations were sometimes omitted by the translators of their
Arabic writings.[6] SAMUEL NAGID addressed King Habus of
Granada in a poem of seven Beit, each of which was in a
different language; and in several Muwassheh (p. 151.) of
JEHUDA LEVI the point of the whole consists in an Arabic

distich. The oldest authority for the tradition of the *Cid*
(ob. 1099) is his " Officer," the apostate IBN ALFANGE. To
the highly prized Arabic poets of Spain belong ABRAHAM IBN
OL FAKKHAR (ob. 1239?); ABRAHAM IBN SAHL (1200—
1250) (conf. p. 152); IBN EL MUDAWWER; and the poetess
KASMUNE.[7] JOSEPH IBN CHASAN (חזן), whose date is
uncertain, transformed every chapter of the Hebrew work
of Isaac Ibn Crispin (see below, p. 174.) into an Arabic Kassida: it may be added, that of the Hebrew itself was an
imitation of Arabic poetry. KOREISH wrote some Arabic
rhyming prose, and the Hebrew Diwans of MOSES IBN
EZRA and JEHUDA HALEVI were commentated in Arabic.

The origin of the Hebrew poetry, together with that of
science and the Magreb[8], in Spain, may be traced to the
patronage of the minister CHISDAI BEN ISAAC (cir. 950); it
came to its greatest perfection under the prince SAMUEL
(ob. 1055?); and as early as the 12th century it had been so
far exhausted by its most original and able representatives,
that even Provence and her rival Italy tried to surpass the
classical times in artifice rather than in real art; poems
written as trials of skill, after the manner of the Arabs and
Provencals[9], were admired; stereotyped poetical phrases became universal; there was scarcely any writer who did not
try his hand at poetry; and Moses Ibn Ezra devoted a
special chapter of his Poetics to verses made in dreams.[9a]
The rhyming prose, at this time as at all others, from the
earliest to the most recent, maintained its place in the
writings which concerned daily life. The poetry of the Jews
of the middle ages in the East, judging by the description
of the Provençal Charisi (1218), deserved the fate of bad
poetry, " to die before its authors;"[9b] he praises only those
who came from the Magreb, such as JEHUDA ABBAS,
JOSEPH IBN AKNIN, and MOSES BEN SHESHET.

We find the poetical form in works on the most various
subjects, for instance, memorial verses for the Masora, grammars, &c. (§ 18.). To this class belong SAADJA'S and HAI
GAON'S rhymes on jurisprudence, and some short astronomical
rules by Saadja (§ 21.). CHARISI versified Maimonides' chapter
on diet in the *Jad*[10]; PALQUERA (cir. 1250) the Talmudic

treatise *Chullin*; MORDECAI BEN HILLEL at Regensburg
(cir. 1300) the laws of slaying; and PROPHIAT DURAN a
chapter on astronomy. MATATIA KARTIN (1363?) wrote a
commentary in rhyme on the Moreh; SOLOMON IBN AJUB
of Grenada, at Beziers (1262), imitated the ارجوزة or صذظوصة
of Ibn Sina [11]; IBN EZRA, BON-SENIOR IBN JACHJA, and
others, wrote verses upon the game of chess[11a]; an anonymous author (probably not Jedaja Penini) alludes in a poem
on the same subject to the game of cards; SERACH (SARIK)
BARFAT (1364), probably in Africa, versified the Book of
Job, the edition of which by ELIA LEVITA (1544) has
been erroneously attributed to this writer [12]; the Karaites,
SALOMON BEN JERUCHAM, MENAHEM BEN MICHAEL (in
the 10th century), and JEHUDA HEDESSI (1149), wrote
polemics in rhyme against Rabbinism, and MATATJA BEN
MOSES (1300—1360) against Christianity and Islamism;
DUNASH IBN LABRAT wrote in verse a grammatical polemic,
which was answered in the same manner by MENAHEM
SARUK or his pupils in Spain, in the 10th century; ISAAC
IBN POLGAR exchanged epigrams with the neophyte ABNER,
and PROPHIAT DURAN and SOLOMON BONFED replied in
satirical epistles; besides which, there was the polemical
poetry of the 13th century, mentioned above (§ 11.). In
Germany also we meet with the satirical poem of GUMPLIN
against the Jews on the Rhine.[12a]

Epigrams form the transition from scientific rhymes to
occasional poetry in general, a comprehensive class in which
the Jewish literature can rival any other; they are often
to be found among dedications, introductions, epigraphs, heads
of chapters, and summaries of treatises and books; for instance, by JEHUDA IBN TIBBON, JECHIEL BEN JEKUTIEL,
and others. In their references to individual and national
life they afford rich materials for history and biography. We
will mention here only one of the oldest panegyric poems
(recently published), addressed to Samuel Nagid by JOSEPH
IBN CHISDAI (after 1027), whom Hammer in his history of
Arabic literature confounds with a later physician of the
same family, who was a renegade. The well-known observation that every good poem must be an occasional one is

remarkably confirmed in Hebrew poetry. Particular attention is due to epitaphs[13], many of which were written by persons for themselves. To this class belong also larger historical
poems not intended for the liturgy (as was perhaps that of
Saadja [cir. 1000])[14]; for instance, that of Palquera (cir.
1250), which appears to have been unfortunately lost, and
others.

Gnomonics[14a], which were much used in this period,
and which became almost a separate art, are closely connected with the epigram. Amongst the Arabs the weaving
together of wise proverbs is considered an indispensable condition of good poetry, and we find the poets of the Muallakât
first becoming famous by their gnomes.[15] There were also
poets who devoted themselves specially to writing proverbs.[16]
Semitic poetry, however, in general is not so much a continuous evolution of thought and sentiment, as (to use the well-
known metaphor) a chain of costly pearls strung together,
which may be separated and taken independently, or ranged
in a different order (as *Anthology*).[17] The older proverbs of
the Arabs originated in their own poetical life. The Koran,
the Sunna, and perhaps also the Arabic writings of Jews
and Christians, introduced Jewish and Christian elements
among them.[18] Translations of the Greek philosophers enriched them with ideas, which, from their simplicity, clearness,
and pointedness of thought, may be recognised as classical,
even in their Arabic form. The poet paints the thought of
the philosopher, the philosopher analyses the picture of the
poet; and hence arise the stereotyped forms of quotation, "as
says the proverb, the poet, the wise man (החכם, which,
however, sometimes refers to King Solomon's books, especially the Proverbs), or the philosopher," and the like.
The simple proverb is often succeeded by a metrical version
of it.[19] All these remarks are applicable to Jewish literature enriched from Arabic sources. Arabic proverbs are
already quoted in the *Alphabet* of Ibn Sira[20], by Jehuda
Ibn Tibbon[21], by Palquera (1290)[22] and Gavison (ob.
1605) in Arabic, by Albo[23] (1425), and others; Maimonides[24] also appeals to the old proverbial poets. In the
translations from the Koran, Sunna, &c., either the proverbs

which occurred gave place to others to the same effect
from the Bible or Talmud, or else the form of quotation was
changed.   In this manner (besides the quotations from the
Koran to be found in linguistical works by SAADJA, HAI
ABULWALID, and in the Poetics of MOSES IBN EZRA,)
KALONYMOS [24a] quotes the " Prophet," and IBN CHISDAI [25]
keeps the first Sure of the Koran as a pattern prayer, although
in some places he substitutes poems of Jehuda Levi.   With
the proverb and the gnome, moreover, are closely connected
figures, phrases, parables, and other kinds of poetry.   To
the gnomic literature, properly so called [26], belong preemi-
nently the larger ethical collections of proverbs, even when
the particular sentences are woven into one continuous work.
Nothing in the Arabic language belonging to this period is
known, except the *Selection of Pearls* by GABIROL (1040),
which, as well as the *Sententious Ethics* of GABIROL, was
translated by JEHUDA IBN TIBBON (1167) for Asher ben
Meshullam (conf. § 11.); a metrical version of the former
was given by JOSEPH KIMCHI, and Tibbon's prose translation of it was enriched by the French Jews of the 14th
century with appendices (Tosaphot) and commentaries in
rhyme; it was afterwards frequently expounded, was translated into various languages, and has ever since remained
a standard book in this class of literature.[27]   Hebrew works
of the same kind were written by SAMUEL NAGID, whose *Ben
Mishle* and *Ben Kohelet* seem to have been exhortations to
his son Joseph; MOSES IBN EZRA (cir. 1138), in continuous
homonymes; the composer of the מזמר השכל, attributed
to HAI GAON[28]; JOSEPH EZOBI (cir. 1270) in Provence;
his imitator, contemporary, and countryman LEVI BEN
ABRAHAM BEN CHAJJIM[28a], author of a long poem with the
same rhyme throughout; BENJAMIN ANAV BEN ABRAHAM
at Rome (about 1300); and JOHANAN LORIA in Germany
(cir. 1500).   Single chapters full of proverbs are also to be
found in the comprehensive works of CHARISI, IMMANUEL,
&c.   With these must be classed the works on ethics composed in rhetorical or rhyming prose (conf. § 12.); for example,
that of PALQUERA; the famous *Examen Mundi* (בחינת עולם)
by JEDAJA PENINI (cir. 1305), so often commentated and

translated; the satirical *Lapis Lydius* (אבן בוחן) by KALO-
NYMOS in Castile (1323); and similar works by MATATJA
(1430–50) in Germany, and others.[29]   The moral sentences
of the Greek wise men, and the *Sayings of Alexander* [29a],
by HONEIN BEN ISHAK (not CHANANJA BEN JIZCHAK),
were translated from the Arabic by CHARISI (before 1235)
for some learned men at Lünel, and became a great mine
of Arabic-Jewish sayings.   The famous *Disciplina Clericalis*
by the neophyte PETER ALPHONSI (baptized 1106) consists
chiefly of Arabic and Jewish gnomes.   A part of this work
still exists in the Hebrew translation, and is known as the
Book of Enoch (Idris).[30]   Here, as also in the case of the
Mashal (§ 5. 2*a*.), in the didactic semi-poetry of Fables,
Parables, Apologues, and Riddles, and in the popular Tales
and Novels, the Jews have cooperated in propagating the
literature transplanted by the Arabs from India and Persia
into Europe, and have at the same time interwoven their own
particular traditions (§ 5. 2*b*.)[31], thus making many hitherto
unnoticed contributions to the old romantic literature.   JA-
COB IBN SHEARA (at the end of the 9th century?) is said
to have assisted in the first translation of Bidpai's Indian
Fables of the Jackal, *Kalila and Dimna*, into Arabic for
King "Alzafac"(?).   These were afterwards translated into
Hebrew, and thence into Latin, by the neophyte JOHN OF
CAPUA (1262 — 1278); both these versions being accom-
panied with illustrations.[32]   A Rabbi JOEL is mentioned as
the Hebrew translator of these and of the *Mishle Sandabar*.[33]
KALONYMOS translated in one week (1316) the work on the
Nobility of Man, one of the fifty treatises by " the Brothers
of Purity," a celebrated society of a kind of freemasons in
Egypt, whose works were studied by the Jews in Spain at
the beginning of the twelfth century.[33a]   In the *Prince and
Derwish* of ABRAHAM IBN CHISDAI (cir. 1235) the author
has first brought to light a translation of the celebrated
Greek tale of *Barlaam and Josaphat* made from a hitherto
undiscovered Arabic source.   The poetic encyclopædia of
PALQUERA (1264) recalls to mind a similar work of Ghazali.[34]   The half-poetical, half-philosophical works of Ibn
Batrik, translated into Hebrew by CHARISI, might assist

in the solution of many questions concerning pseudo-Aristotelian and Kabbalistic writings.[34a] MOSES NARBONI (1349)
at Barcelona wrote a commentary upon Ibn Topheil's philosophical romance *Hai ben Joksan.* BERACHJA HANAKDAN
in Burgundy (cir. 1260) edited freely and completed the
store of fables then in existence. The Hebrew translation
of those of Æsop[35] is apparently not taken from Arabic
sources. Peculiar interest attaches to ISAAC IBN SAHULA
(1281), apparently of Guadalaxara, who enters the lists on
behalf of Jewish originality against Arabianism, but nevertheless at last yields to the latter. The morals of the fables
bear the stamp of the Kabbalistic tendencies of his time,
visible also in contemporaneous Christian works; they are
also illustrated with drawings.[35a] The book מושו by ISAAC
CRISPIN (12th century?) mentioned above (p. 169.) seems
to contain imitations rather than direct translations of Arabic
tales, poems, &c. A satirical novel by JOSEPH IBN SABARA
(or SEBARA, end of 12th century), which has escaped most
bibliographers, is an ingenious mixture of narration, sayings,
and poetry in the Arabian style, and contains the history of
Tobias.

Particular notice is due to Parodies, Travesties, and
Humorous Writings, the literary element of which was the
imitation of the expression of the older classics, while their
application to life was especially connected with the feast
of Purim; their prototype is perhaps to be found in the
parodies of Hariri.[36] Not only were passages from the Bible
itself detached from the context, and applied to frivolous
and obscene objects, but even the Halacha, Pijjutim, &c.,
were parodied and travestied, without its being felt to be
any insult to these much reverenced writings. We have
pieces and works of this kind by KALONYMOS and his friend
EMMANUEL at Rome (cir. 1320); even earlier, ABRAHAM
BEDARSHI, in a serious panegyric, had parodied the Easter
Haggada, and the same thing was done during the following
century in a polemical work (§ 15. p. 127.). The oldest
parody is probably that of the Aphorisms of Hippocrates, if
we are not wrong in considering the above-mentioned
JOSEPH IBN SABARA as the author of it.

The Arabic form of the *Makamas* (מחברות) [37] was certainly used by Joseph Ibn Aknin at Ceuta (before 1185) [38],
probably by Salomon Ibn צקבל, a relation of Joseph Ibn
Sahl, and perhaps by Isaac ben Israel, the head of a
school at Babylon (cir. 1218). [39]   Charisi himself had translated the famous Makamas of Hariri into Hebrew, and after
his journey to the East (1216—18) he drew up a rival work
in Hebrew, which included some older pieces.   He was followed by Emmanuel of Rome, who (cir.1332) added a kind
of *Divina Commedia*, after the style of Dante. [40]   His satires
and parodies, which unite religious zeal and scientific earnestness with frivolity of expression, and the novels which he has
inserted, rank him with Boccaccio; but Emmanuel and his
book were soon forbidden, owing to the stricter views on the
subject which were gaining ground.   A great *Paradiso* in
terza rima, with literary and historical notes, was written by
Moses Rieti (born 1416) [41], who excludes Emmanuel from
the regions of the blest, and who is also said to have repented of his own poetry as a waste of time.   This would
show that he possessed more judgment than those who have
published this unattractive work as the production of the
" Hebrew Dante."

Finally we possess some collections (*Diwans*), made either
by the authors themselves or by others after them, and
some greater poetical works, known only from quotations and
catalogues, by Moses Ibn Ezra (ob. after 1138), and Jehuda
Halevi (ob. before 1160), which two, with Gabirol, form
the triple star of Jewish poetry in Spain; by Jacob ben
Eleazar, who wished to imitate if not to surpass the
Arabs [42]; and by Abraham Bedarshi (1289), and Solomon
Bonfed in Provence (1400); besides various anthologies,
for the most part only in manuscript.   Jehuda Halevi
ben Isaac ben Sabbatai composed (1214) a *Contest of
Wealth with Wisdom*, and (1217-8) a *Gift from Jehuda the
Woman-hater*, a satirical romance, dedicated perhaps to
Abraham el-Fakkhâr, in which the father of the hero, in fact,
the author himself, bears the name of " Tachkemoni," thus
occasioning a confusion with the book *Tachkemoni* by the
poet Charisi, written about the same time.   To the latter of

these works he added an appendix, containing an ingenious parody excommunicating some of his adversaries at Saragossa, found in MS. by the author in the Bodleian Library. NEHEMIAH BEN MENAHEM KALOMITI (1418) wrote *The War of Truth* [43a], and MESSER DAVID BEN JEHUDA LEON *The Praise (and Blame ?) of Women*.[43b]

Non-liturgical poems and rhyming prose epistles are to be found also in Aramaïc; for instance, those by the contemporaries of BEDARSHI in Provence [44], and by SOLOMON DURAN at Algiers (before 1444); on the other hand, in Germany all knowledge of Aramaïc had been lost in the 14th century.[45]

From the extensive use that was made of the poetical form, and the estimation in which it was held, there arose some persons who made a profession of it; such as the teacher JEHUDA SICILIANO at Rome (cir. 1300), perhaps the author of a lexicon of rhymes still extant in MS.[46] In order to facilitate the art, lexicons of rhymes, homonymes, and synonymes, were probably written by CHARISI [47]; and, with special reference to etymology and grammar, by JOSEPH IBN CHAJJIM (cir. 1292) [48] and SOLOMON DA PIERA (1412).[49] The more ancient grammar received its superstructure from poetry (§ 16.), and at the same time extended its theories to both prosody and poetics. On this subject we have some chapters by JEHUDA HALEVI (1140); ABRAHAM IBN EZRA (1145); PARCHON (1159); the author of the שקל הקודש [50]; DAVID IBN JAHJA; ELIA LEVITA; ABRAHAM DE BALMES (ob. 1523); and later writers (§ 28.). Special treatises were composed by MOSES IBN EZRA, DAVID IBN BILLA (1320)[51], ABSALOM BEN MOSES MISRACHI [52], MOSES IBN CHABIB of Lisbon at Bitonto (1486), with an introductory grammatical chapter, and by a certain ISAIAH of unknown date: also Excursuses, by ABRAHAM IBN EZRA (on Eccles. v.); by ABRAVANEL (ob. 1505), in his commentaries on Ex. xv. and Isa. v.; and others.[53] Almost all these writers must be considered as followers of the Arabising poetry of Spain; but the Italian writers show the influence of classic literature, for example, JEHUDA BEN JECHIEL, called Messer Leon, who took Cicero and Quintilian as his models. The interesting

N

work of Moses Ibn Ezra, so often alluded to, will shortly
be published by the author of the present treatise, from a
unique MS. in the Bodleian Library.   Besides the historical
part (§ 10.), it contains, in twenty short chapters, an ingenious exposition of the beauties and ornaments of poetry, illustrated by numerous examples from the Arabic and Hebrew.

The Hebrew poetry of the Jews, according to Detitzsch [54],
everywhere preceded the national poetry of the particular
country; but the Jews also took a part in the latter.   Don
Santo (or Santob, perhaps Shemtob), famous as an adviser
of the King of Spain, was one of the most celebrated trou-
badours of his age (1360); Juan Alphonso de Baena
(1449—54) was a collector of poetry, and himself a poet;
Moses Chassan (Açan) de Zaragua wrote a poem on
chess, beginning with the Creation and containing moral
applications, in the Catalonian dialect, which was translated
anonymously into Castilian (1350); his namesake, Don
Moses, physician to Don Enrique (1368—79?), is one of
the poets mentioned in Baena's collection; Valentin Bar-
ruchius (perhaps in the 12th century) wrote the history of
Count Lyonnais (Palanus) in pure Latin.   The *Disciplina
Clericalis* of Peter Alphonsi (1106) is, according to Ticknor, the first European collection of tales (or *Makama*) composed in the Oriental style; and he considers this popular
work, which has been translated into various languages, as
a prototype of the *Conde Lucanor* by Don John Manuel.
The Jew Süsskind of Trimberg, in the 13th century [55], was
a Swabian minstrel.   Some German legends, for example
The Court of Arthur, (1279) attracted the attention of the
Jews [56], to whom we are indebted for the preservation of a
German edition of this work in ottava rima, written in Hebrew characters.   To the middle ages belong some genuine
popular works, partly ethical (§ 12.), partly translations (§ 16.)
and versifications of the Bible; for instance, the *History of
David*, by a lady of Regensburg, Litte [57], in the German
dialect generally used at the time, interspersed with a few Hebraisms. In consequence of the isolated position of the Jews,
and their dislike of change, their language became more
and more different from the vernacular; this was especially
the case with German, so that at a later period (see § 28.)

the language used by them was called "Jewish-German," and was considered as a kind of slang. This fact is not un-important in the history of literature.

§ 21.] *Mathematical Sciences.*

We are here principally concerned with the Arabian school and its off-shoots, on which, at the commencement of this Period, the knowledge inherited from earlier times exerted a perceptible influence; while the Arabian Jews played an important part in the cultivation of this branch of Arabian science. The encyclopædic method[1] which was then in vogue, comprised Mathematics (חכמה למודית, or, in the plural, Arab. علم التعليم), as a science preparatory (ח' השימוש, علوم الرياضة) to philosophy, and divided it into various disci-plinæ (generally seven), e. g., Mathematics in the strict sense (ח' המנין והשיעורים חכמה חמדות, הספירות), including Arith-metic (ח' החשבון), Algebra (ח' התשבורת, conf. Arab. علم الجبر), and Geometry (ח' המדידה), besides Astronomy and Music (§ 18. 4.). Astronomy (חכמת הכוכבים later תכונה), is divided, according to ABRAHAM BEN CHIJJA (1134)[2], into 1. Astronomy proper (ח' החזיון, the science of observa-tion), treating (*a*) of the form and position of the heavenly bodies (astrography, spherical and empirical astronomy), and (*b*) of their measurements and motions (theoretical astro-nomy), with scientific demonstrations; and 2. the art of Astrology (מלאכת הנסיון, art of experience), depending upon traditions and opinions of secondary value. One portion of astronomy is astronomical geography.[3]

1. *Astronomy.* The labours of the Jews in this department have not yet undergone a proper special investigation. On this head much ignorance is displayed by Christian writers, and even Delambre and Ideler are not better informed than others.[3a] The subject is rendered more difficult by the fact, that the oldest works are scarcely known except by quotations, and that the later Jewish astronomers were occupied in endea-vouring to trace the views they had formed from their own in-vestigations, or had adopted from others, in the old practical

rules, or in the precepts scattered about the Talmud and
Midrash, and generally referred to ancient authorities. The
entanglement of the subject, and the complicated hypotheses
adopted from time to time, as knowledge advanced, add considerably to the difficulties in the history of Jewish astronomy.
It will be necessary to examine the connexion between this
department of literature and the Halacha, Haggada, and Polemics, with reference to Chronology, and between it and
Philosophy and the Kabbala with reference to Astrology.

The points of contact of the Halacha with astronomy
have been mentioned above (§ 5. A.). We must here pre-
mise a few remarks upon the nature of the *Kalendar*. It
depends upon a regular compensation of the luni-solar cycle
by means of *Intercalation* ; hence חכמת העבור, *Science of
Intercalation.*[3b] The old Arabians intercalated a month in
every third year[4]; but there are various opinions respecting
the principle on which this was done.[4a] The Karaites were
inconsistent in admitting the regular system of intercalation
with a cycle of nineteen years[5], and yet rejecting the Rabbinical method of reckoning the new moon, in favour of the
older way of determining it by the testimony of witnesses.
They also, contrary to the rule of the Rabbinites, admitted the evidence of Muhammedans on the point.[6] It may
be mentioned, that at an early period, ABU AMRAN EL-
TIFLISI[7] adopted the astronomical solar kalendar, so as to
avoid the Rabbinical postponement of feast days. In order
to defend themselves against the attacks of the Karaites, Muhammedans, and Christians, on the mode of calculating the
kalendar[8], — especially the determination of the feast of
Easter, — SAADJA, CHANANEL, MESHULLAM BEN KALO-
NYMOS at Lucca, or in Germany[9], ABRAHAM BEN CHIJJA,
JEHUDA HALEVI (1140), and later writers, tried to claim
for the astronomical calculation of the moon a high respect on
account of its antiquity. Some authors went so far as to
assert that the Greek astronomers were pupils of the Jews[10],
others even interpolated the Talmud.[11]

Among the most interesting remains of Hebrew literature
of the first period, there are, besides the *Boraita* of SAMUEL,
known only from quotations[12], three astronomical, but unfor-

tunately much interpolated and corrupted, sections of the *Pirke derabbi* ELIEZER [13], in which the year is made to consist of $365\frac{1}{4}$ days, the month of 30 days $10\frac{1}{2}$ hours, the cycle (מחזור קטן) of 4, the period (מחזור גדול) of 28 ($= 7 \times 4$) years, the lunar month of 29 days, $12\frac{1}{2}$ hours, the lunar cycle of 3 [14], the period of 21 ($= 7 \times 3$) years; so that three solar and 4 lunar periods ($3 \times 28 = 4 \times 21 = 84$ years), form the hour of a divine day of 1000 years. [15]   All this is made to correspond to the seven planets according to their cosmical order or regency in the hours of the day, and with reference to passages in the Book of Job.   This work also mentions a cycle of 19 years with 7 leap-years, although not in the usual order, and the creation of the stars (first novilunium?) placed at the evening of Wednesday [16]; it is said that there are in heaven 366 "windows" for the days of the solar year, and the like.   The *Boraita* of R. ADA is probably nothing else than another name for the kalendar rules (*Te-kufa derab* ADA)[17], adopted with the solar year of the Arabian Albatani (880).   Connected with this are the remarkable astronomical and astrological works of the physician SABBATAI DONOLO BEN ABRAHAM of אורם in Italy (946).[18] According to his own not very lucid account, his countrymen rejected entirely, through ignorance, the old and obscure Jewish writings on astronomy, as they believed that this science was to be found only among other nations.[19] He consequently studied Indian, Babylonian, Arabian, and Greek astronomy, but found that they coincided with the Jewish.   After a long and fruitless search for a teacher among the Christians, he at last found the Babylonian בג'דש, and set about explaining these works, with the help of figures.[20]   His comparison of the sun to a "roasting egg" is worth notice.

In the mean time Jewish astronomy in the East had taken part in the new studies of the Arabians, e. g., MASHALLAH (754—813) [20a]; SAHL, called Rabban (not "Zein") el Thaberi (800), whose translation of the Almagest is the only one containing the chapter on refraction; SIND BEN ALI (829—833), one of the principal contributors to the Maamunic tables; and JACOB IBN SHEARA (? in the 9th century), who is said to have met with some mathematical works in India, and

caused them to be translated into Arabic.[21]   To this age also
probably belongs the Babylonian ANDRUZGER BEN SADI
FARUCH.[21a]   Subsequently there occur BASHAR BEN
PINHAS IBN SHOEIB (997), IBN SIMUJEH (1087), and
others; and in Africa ABU SAHL BEN TEMIM (or ISAAC
ISRAELI? about or before 955), who composed an astronomical work by order of Ismaïl ben Kaim al-Mansuri.

The nature of the *Kalendar* (עבור, hence subsequently
the titles עבדומת, also תקופות ומולדות, i. e. " Quarter-day
and New-Moon"), from its connexion with the cycle of
Holy-days, naturally formed a constituent part of the liturgical writings mentioned above (§ 19.)[22]; as appears later
in the Arabic writer SOLOMON BEN NATAN of Segelmas[23];
SIMCHA of Vitry in France; ABUDIRAHIM in Spain; in the
Karaitic work *Tikkun*[24], and in some general Halachaic
works mentioned below. Supplements were, however, added
to Solomon ben Natan's short rules by SAADJA BEN JEHUDA
BEN EBJATAR in Egypt (1203), who also wrote a commentary on the verses of JOSE ALNAHARWANAI, hitherto unknown. To NACHSHON the Gaon (877—885) is commonly
attributed the perpetual kalendar, founded upon a period of
19 years; which was proved to be not quite correct by the
learned Spaniards of the 10th and 11th centuries[25], but
was, nevertheless, made the foundation of kalendar tables
(לוחות, from לוח, a table), by some later writers, as JACOB
BEN ASHER at Toledo[26], and has retained a place in some
works nearly to the present time.

Scientific astronomy could not fail to come into collision
with the Biblical expositions of the Haggada, and also with
Dogmatics.[27]   The researches concerning the creation of the
world, the spheres, and their spiritual movers (the *physical*
astronomy of the time), form a leading subject with Philosophers and Dogmatists, e. g. MEIR ALDABI (1360),
and Kabbalists, such as JOSEPH CHIQUITILLA and Pseudo-
ABRAHAM BEN DAVID.   Hence many works have been
reckoned as astronomical which, according to our notions, belong to Philosophy[28]; and some really astronomical works
were originally parts of philosophical encyclopædias, such as
those by LEVI BEN ABRAHAM and LEVI BEN GERSON.   It

is sufficient here to have pointed out this coincidence, and to have made a reference to philosophical literature (§ 12.).

In Spain the Jewish astronomy began simultaneously with the Arabian[29], and we find there a celebrated astrologer as early as 810 (see below, 2.). HASSAN, judge at Cordova (972), perhaps first established the solar year of Albatani (*Tekufa* of R. ADA) as the basis of the Jewish kalendar[30]; and great pains were taken by the physician ISAAC BEN RAKUFIEL, partly at the instigation of less learned Rabbies, to explain the old Talmudical kalendar rules and the astronomical passages in the Bible and Midrash, according to the recent results of science; by ISAAC BEN BARUCH ALBALIA (EL-KALAJA ?) of Cordova (1035—1094), teacher of mathematics at Granada, and astronomer to the Arabian prince Samuel; and by others. ABRAHAM BEN CHIJJA of Spain, at Marseilles (?), first (1134) attempted to treat of the whole of astronomy in Hebrew[31]; ABRAHAM IBN EZRA (1093 —1168) carried out the astrological part at some length; and both wrote special treatises on Intercalation.[32] JEHUDA HALEVI (1140) devoted a part of his polemical work to astronomy; his younger contemporary and opponent, the apostate SAMUEL IBN ABBAS (§ 15.), renowned as an astronomer among the Arabians, likewise wrote on the nature of the Kalendar and Chronology.[33] Among the most prominent authors of the Halacha, we may mention SERACHJA HALEVI of Lünel (§ 9.). The following also composed some valuable works: MAIMONIDES, who treated of the Jewish kalendar rules in an Arabic commentary to the treatise *Rosh Hashana*, also in a special work (1158), and again in a section of his Codex of Law (the last-named work was commentated by many later authors, as, OBADJA BEN DAVID in Egypt (1325), an anonymous Arabic writer (1387), and LEVI BEN CHABIB (cir. 1520) (§ 30.); ABRAHAM BEN DAVID (cir. 1160); and others, whose works are lost.[34]

Nearly all the independent works hitherto named were written in Arabic, and made use of the Arabic-Greek literature[34a]; even MAIMONIDES and his pupil IBN AKNIN (1185—1190) emended the works of Ibn Aflah, Heitem, and Ibn Hud.[35] But in the 13th century first began the epoch

of the Hebrew translations and editions of Arabic, Latin, or
Spanish[36] works, comprising those of the Greek astronomers
and mathematicians, Ptolemæus, Euclid and his continuer
Hypsicles, Archimedes and his commentator Eutocius of
Ascalon, Autolycos, Menelaus, Nicomachus[37], and Theo-
dosius, after the editions of the Syrians and Arabians;
Honein and his son Ishak[38], Costa ben Luca (864 — 923),
Thabet (836—901), Abu Djaafar Jussuf, and others: moreover, the Astronomical works of Abu Maasher (813?), El
Kindi (813—873), Fergani (844), Batani (fl. 880), Ku-
shiar ben Lebbân Ibn Shahdi (11th century) in the East;
Ibn Heitham (ob. 1038), Ibn Afla of Seville and Al-Zarkala
(cir. 1080) at Toledo; Petrongi or Batrugi (1145–54?),
and Averroes (ob. 1198): the Astrological writings of Chalid
ben Jezid (ob. 704)[39], Alcabitius (القبيصي, al-Kabissi, 10th
cent.)[39a], Meriti (ob. 1007), and Abûlhassin Ali Ibn Radshal [40]: and the Arithmetical works of Abu Kâmil (Shad-
sha ben Eslem?), and Abu Ahmed ben (Abd) el Khassad
(אלחצד?).[40a]   The Jewish editors, some of whom made use
of Latin translations, are, JACOB ANATOLI, who improved
Johann Hispalensis' translation of the Alfergani by comparing it with the original, and added a chapter [41] on which
Christmann lays much stress; JEHUDA BEN MOSES (erroneously called ben Joseph) COHEN (1256); ISAAC (in
Spanish "Zag") IBN SID (1252—1266) CHASAN, precentor at Toledo[42]; SAMUEL EL LEVI ABULAFIA; and
ABRAHAM of Toledo (1278—9); all commissioned by Alphonso X.: JEHUDA BEN SOLOMON COHEN of Toledo,
in Tuscany (1247)[43]; MOSES IBN TIBBON in Provence
(1274); NATHAN HAMATI at Rome (1273—1283) KALO-
NYMOS BEN KALONYMOS at Avignon (1314); SOLOMON
IBN PATIR COHEN of Burgos (1322); SHALOM BEN
JOSEPH ענבי; WILHELM RAIMUND DE MONCADA, who
went over to Christianity; ISAAC ABULCHEIR BEN SAMUEL
(later than 1340)[44]; JACOB BEN ELIAH; the Karaite
MOSES BEN JEHUDA GOLI; SOLOMON BEN ABRAHAM
ABIGDOR (1399), who translated Sacrobosco's (ob. 1256)
compendium *De Sphæra*[45], and some time before, at the
age of 15, the Medical Astrology of Arnoldus de Villanova
(ob. 1312); JACOB BEN JEHUDA KABRUT at Barcelona

(1382); BARUCH BEN SOLOMON BEN JOAB (?) (1451); and others.

Alphonso X. had a great predilection for Jews and Arabians, for which he was reproved by the Pope. He commissioned several Jews, with the assistance of his secretaries, to translate the most important works of some older Arabic authors. This has been transformed into an " Astronomical Congress " by an uncritical author; and, notwithstanding the anachronisms which it involves, the mistake has passed current with all modern writers, not excepting Humboldt.

As authors of independent astronomical works, the following may be mentioned: — JACOB BEN SAMSON, probably in France (1123 — 70), whose work, אלרושי, known only from a fragment in the Bodleian Library, treats of the Jewish Kalendar; SOLOMON BEN MOSES MELGUEIL (1250); LEVI BEN ABRAHAM BEN CHAJJIM in Provence, whose voluminous work seems to be a *réchauffé* of Abraham Ibn Ezra, and forms part of a philosophical encyclopædia; JACOB BEN MACHIR IBN TIBBON, known by the name of Prophiat, professor at Montpellier; ISAAC ISRAELI BEN JOSEPH (1310 — 30), author of the important work, *Jesod Olam*, written for R. Asher at Toledo; SHESHET BEN ISAAC GERONDI at Barcelona (1320); LEVI BEN GERSON (1328 — 40), whose *New System of Astronomy*, forming part of his philosophical work (§ 12.), is said by Munk to be worth examination; EMANUEL BEN JACOB at Tarrascona (about 1346), author of the popular work, *The Six Wings;* JOSEPH IBN NAHMIAS at Toledo (1300 — 30), who wrote in Arabic; ISAAC (ben Solomon ben Zadik) IBN ALCHADIB (אלחדב, the humpbacked) in Castile (1370 — 80)[46]; PROPHIAT DURAN in Provence (1392); and many others. In the *Jesod Olam*, Isaac Israeli quotes from the Almagest a third irregularity of the moon, which has been also mentioned by the Arabic author Abu'l Wefa, and hence mistaken by Sedillot for the variation of Tycho Brahe : this confusion has been cleared up by Munk.[46a] In Germany, only MEIR SPIRA and his son ISAAC need be mentioned.[47]

Most of the above-mentioned writers are known from catalogues only; and for a true estimation of their relative value, the labours of both the astronomer and bibliographer are required. In the absence of the former, the author adds such few general remarks as he is able.

The foundation of the *Kalendar*, depending upon the motions of the sun and moon, was one of the main objects of the study of astronomy among the Jews. And this again, so far as local circumstances are concerned, is closely connected with other branches of astronomy and mathematical geography. Ptolemy's *Almagest* (אלמגיסטי, also תבורגדון, μεγάλη σύνταξις) was the text-book, and most of his figures, for instance the comparison of the spheres to the skins of an onion[47a], remained canonical among the Arabians and Jews. The same was the case with his numbers, notwithstanding the advance of science; for example, that there are 1022 fixed stars, or with the planets 1029[48]; that the sun is $166\frac{3}{8}$, or, in round numbers, 170 times larger than the earth, and 5000 or 6800 times larger than the moon[49]; that the earth is about 24,000 miles in circumference[50], and that Saturn revolves round the earth once in 59 years.[51] According to Ibn Ezra and others, the year is 365 d. 5 h. 19 m. 15 s. in length; according to Levi ben Gerson the sun moves differently from the zodiac, and advances one degree in $42\frac{2}{3}$ years; the obliquity of the ecliptic, stated by Albatani, Ibn Ezra, and Levi ben Gerson as 23° 33′, is reduced by Prophatius (Jacob ben Machir) to 23° 32′; Jacob Poel (p. 188.) calculated that the sun arrives in 31 Egyptian years 15 d. 23 h. 34 m. 21 s. to the same height, and thus formed his thirty-one tables for the conjunction and opposition of the sun and moon. The endless discussions about the number of spheres and their intelligences are now obsolete, but they were intimately connected with the theory of the movement of epicycles, &c. The efforts made by the Arabs, Thabet Ibn Corra, Abu Bekr (Ibn Bage), and his follower Batrugi, to remove this most obvious difficulty in the Ptolemaic system, were shared and carried on by Jews. The numbers, however, in the printed works and MSS. are very often mutilated, and perhaps sometimes intentionally altered.[52] The sphericity of the earth, the antipodes[53], and the regions in which the day and night were each of six months [53a], were known. Whether the five planets and the fixed stars received their light from the sun, was not decided in the 12th century; and some works were considered necessary to demonstrate the point even in the case of the moon, while Joseph Ibn Chiquitilla (§ 14.) maintained that the moon was self-luminous.[54]   The Jewish astronomers frequently had their own nomenclature for the stars, and made some accurate observations; thus Saadja (928—941) tells of a lunar eclipse at Bagdad, which did not coincide with the new moon.[55]

Amongst writers on the theory, improvement, and invention of astronomical instruments, the astrolabe, quadrant, sphere, sun-dial, &c., we find ABRAHAM IBN EZRA, who also is said to have suggested the division of the celestial globe by the equator, besides various things which other astronomers appropriated to themselves[55a]; SAMUEL HALEVI (1280 — 1284); JACOB BEN MACHIR (1300), who invented as a substitute for the astrolabe a kind of quadrant, known in a Latin translation of Armengaud Blasius of Montpellier (1299) as "that of Prophatius;" EMANUEL BEN JACOB; ISAAC ALCHADIB; JEHUDA IBN VERGA of Seville (probably after 1450); MORDECAI COMTINO (1460 —85); JOSEPH TAYTAZAK; JEHUDA FARISSOL at Mantua (1499); CHAJJIM VITAL [56], and JOSEPH PARSI [57], who are uncertain; perhaps the astronomer R. JOSEPH, who was a member of the commission which reported on Columbus's project (1480), and recommended the use of an astrolabe at sea to John of Portugal[58]; LEON DE BAÑOLAS, inventor of an instrument for observation[58a], who is no other than LEVI BEN GERSON (1328—70), and who wrote a Hebrew poem on this invention; and BONET DE LATTES (1506), celebrated by Reuchlin as a physician, who dedicated his invention of an astronomical ring to Pope Leo X.

The Jews were in many ways active, both independently and in conjunction with others, in the preparation and production of the most celebrated astronomical tables, לוחות הרתכונה, زيج)[58b], e. g. those of Maamun, of Alphonso, and the Persian tables.[59] Among the learned men, whom the skilful patron and biographer of celebrated Jews, Ahmed Ibn Szâïd, collected about himself for the preparation of the Toledo tables

(1080), were twelve Jews.[59a]   But almost all these works have been hitherto known from uncertain sources; and so, in order not to mislead the reader, we will here give only a few names of authors, translators, and commentators, without entering into details:—ABRAHAM BEN CHIJJA, who edited the tables of Ptolemy ; IBN EZRA (1160), whose translation of Albatani's commentary on the Chowaresmic Tables of Muhammed ben Musa in question and answer, contains an introduction of historical interest[60] ; JACOB BEN MACHIR (1300) whose tables are still extant in Hebrew MSS. and in a Latin translation, where they are described as the " Almanack of Prophatius;" LEVI BEN GERSON (cir. 1320); EMANUEL BEN JACOB, who defended Albatani's system[61], and, in accordance with it, calculated tables of the variation in length of days and nights (1365 ?); his opponent ISAAC ALHADIB[61a], JOSEPH BEN ELIEZER of Saragossa (1335)[62] ; JACOB BEN DAVID BEN JOMTOB POEL (1361), called San Bonet Bon-Giorno (or in a Latin translation in MS., Jacob Bonædiei), who calculated his tables (p. 186.) for the latitude of Perpignan[62a] ; ISAAC BEN AARON (1368); SOLOMON BEN ELIA SHARBIT-HASAHAB at Saloniki (1490 ?)[63] ; ABRAHAM ZACUT, whose tables are printed in Latin and Spanish (the latter in Hebrew characters); and JEHUDA ISRAELI (1339 ?).[64]   The greatest confusion pervades the accounts of the *Tables of Alphonso*.[65]   Even writers of our own time speak of Ali Ibn Ragel (Wagel?) and Alchabitius (10th century), as Rabbies at the head of the commission for drawing them up; while Ricius, who derives his information from Abraham Zacut (see however pp. 189-90.) thinks that none but Jews were entrusted with that work; ISAAC IBN SID (Çid, 1252) was certainly the chief commissioner or final redactor. Some doubt attaches to the supposition of Ricius, that these tables, bearing date 1252, were really a revision, ordered in 1256, in consequence of the translation of a catalogue of stars by JEHUDA BEN MOSES KOHEN from the Arabic of Abul Hasin (not Avicena).[66]   The *Tables of Peter III.* (1278) have been hitherto entirely unnoticed.[67]   According to Gans[68], JACOB אלקרשי (1260) translated the tables of Alphonso into Hebrew; and MOSES BEN ABRAHAM of Nismes (" Kirjat-jearim"), at Avignon [69], translated the commentary of John Nicholas (? de Saxonia), of Paris; his pupil FARISSOL MOSES BOTAREL, however, complains of the obscurity of the translation (1465). The *Tables of John Bianchino* were perhaps translated by MORDECAI FINZI at Mantua (1440—6).[70] In a prefatory chapter, belonging to an anonymous work, but probably written by Finzi, the astronomical tables are divided into simple and compound. To the former belong those of ABRAHAM BEN CHIJJA, after Ptolemy; those of EMANUEL BEN JACOB, after Albatani; those of ISAAC ISRAELI, after the Toledan; those of Alphonso; and the Persian; all extant in Hebrew. To the second class belong the Parisian; those of JOHN BIANCHINO; the *Six Wings* of EMANUEL BEN JACOB; the work *Orach Selula* by ISAAC IBN ALHADIB; and the *Tables of the Almanack*, which expression is either general or refers perhaps to the tables of Prophatius mentioned above; or to those of JACOB POEL. The same author edited also a complete kalendar for the use of the Synagogues, which, as he mentions, is usually called נייר הכנסת (Synagogue-sheet). Tables of this kind are still to be found in the form of sheet-kalendars for walls, while the usual house-kalendars seem not to have been introduced before the 17th century.

In the 15th century the following belong to the more important astronomical writers, besides others already mentioned above: ELIA MISRACHI, pupil of MORDECAI COMTINO (p. 187.)[70a], the Karaite ELIA BASHIATSHI, and KALEB AFENDOPOLO[71], all at Constantinople; ABRAHAM ZACUTO BEN SAMUEL, professor of astronomy at Saragossa, and, subsequently to 1492, astronomer and chronographist to Immanuel of Portugal, some Arabic tracts by whom were extant late in the 16th century; his pupil AUGUSTINUS RICIUS (1521), who wrote a Latin essay on the movement of the eighth sphere, i. e. the fixed stars, and another, said to be lost, in which he proposed to demonstrate the Jewish origin of astronomy; and others. To judge by the quotations in the printed work, Ricius derived some of his information from sources unknown to us; but his statements, faithfully repeated

by many later authorities, without any allusion to the probability of his being a Jew, are not free from suspicion. There
are some other writers who carried on the mediæval astronomy
down to the 16th century, and the time when the Copernican
system was introduced; for example, the translators and
commentators of the writings of George Purbach or Peur-
bach (nat. 1423, ob. 1465), and his pupil Regiomontanus
(Johan Müller, ob. 1476), viz. MOSES ALMOSNINO (ob.
1574—8) in the East, who also, like MATATJA DELACRUT
at Bologna (1550), wrote a commentary on the sphere of
Sacrobosco[72]; the celebrated Talmudist MOSES ISSERLS
(ob. 1573); and MANOAH HENDEL (ob. 1612) in Poland.
Particular works of Regiomontanus were probably translated into Hebrew as early as 1466.[73]

   2. *Astrology*, as a science, as the Arabians considered it[74],
and according to the Arabian Encyclopædia a part of Physics,
is founded on the supposed influence of the stars (גזירת משפטר,
הכוכבים, احكم النجوم; hence also חכמת המשפט, *Astrologia
Judiciaria*) upon the fate and freedom[75] of men and the formation of the sublunary world. Even its keenest philosophical opponents, such as Maimonides, who boasts that he
had perused all works on astrology — " that error, called a
science" — written in, or translated into Arabic[76], and who
attributes the general authority of astrology to the simple
belief in every thing written, and especially in that which
claims or pretends to antiquity[77], protests only against
the doctrine of chance, and opposes to the influence of
the stars the mediation of the intelligences which guide
the spheres. Nevertheless, some important doctors, e. g.
ABRAHAM BEN CHIJJA[78], IBN EZRA, and others, have
admitted that astrology might have a practical influence.
Other pious men, even adherents of the Kabbala, resting on
the Bible and the leading views of the Talmud, struggled
vainly against it; although the general mass naturally paid
homage to the notions prevailing in the surrounding media
of Muhammedanism and Christianity.[78a] Thus arose usages
which, like most Jewish customs, gradually partook of a religious character; and which even promoted astronomical investigation, although they were not approved by the learned

themselves.[79] Intelligent Astrologers tried to harmonise their
views with the genuine Jewish doctrine of foreknowledge
and freewill[80]; the hope of a Messiah, strengthened by external circumstances and Millennianism, availed itself of the
assistance of astrology[81]; exegesis (especially that of the
14th century[82]) where the Kabbala already occupied an
authoritative position, admitted astrological elements in philosophical writings; and thus astrology first ceased in the
15th century to be an independent science. But the study
of this branch is indispensable, on account of the astronomical
and mathematical materials to be found in it. The Jewish
astronomers in the service of courts were obliged to adapt
themselves to the fashion of the time, and to the commands
of persons who considered the practical object of astronomy
to consist in prognostications, drawing of horoscopes, &c.
Thus we find the following mentioned as astrologers: ABU
DAÛD at Bagdad (about 912); BURHÂN EL FULUK (which
means *Demonstration of the Sphere*), perhaps the Arabic
name for SOLOMON, at Nineveh (1160–80); and others,
although it is uncertain whether they left any written books
behind them, such as the *Prophecy* of DAVID BEN JACOB MEIR
(1464) in Italy. The number of strictly astronomical works
is very small, even if we include the Arabic translations
(sup. p. 184.); for example, those of Alkabiszi, 10th century,
and Ibn al-Radjal, and Abu Djaafar's commentary on Ptolemy's *Pantiloquium*.[83] The following wrote in Arabic:
MASHALLAH (754—813) EL-ANDRUSGER[84] in the East;
and SAHL or SOHEIL BEN BISHR (810) in Spain, whom the
author has recently discovered to be identical with "Zahel
Bembiç Ismaelita," a name under which two astrological
works have been printed in Latin, although one of them is attributed in other editions to Mashallah. The following wrote
in Hebrew: ABRAHAM BEN CHIJJA; ABRAHAM IBN EZRA,
whose works were translated into Latin by Henricus Bates
(1281), and Petrus d'Abano of Padua, about the same time,
and whose influence in Italy was so great, that we do not
hesitate to recognize him in the "Abraham" who represents
mathematics in a fresco of the seven arts in an Italian church;
LEVI BEN ABRAHAM IBN CHAJJIM; the otherwise unknown

Nehemia ben Samuel (1399?)[85]; Joseph ben Isaac Ashalmer (?)[86]; and the apostate Martin of Toledo (in the 15th century?).[87] Of the various branches of Physics and Medicine connected with astrology, mention will be made below (§ 22.).

Pure Mathematics (arithmetic, algebra, geometry) were already used in the first Period in various Halacha works[88], and in the second were applied, in the French-German school, to the explanation of the Talmud, &c.[89] The knowledge of them was limited[90], but the self-taught progress only so much the more surprising. The Arabian school investigated the mathematical parts of the Halacha, such as measures, weights, coins (the reduction of which to the standard current in various countries was necessary), in general introductions or monographies; for instance, Joseph Ibn Aknin (ob. 1226); and Isaac Alchadib.[91] On the other hand, Mathematics were treated as an introduction to astronomy, e. g. by Isaac Israeli.

Many monographies may be attributed to the above-mentioned astronomers, such as Abraham Ibn Ezra, who used the Arabic numerals, and, besides various other mathematical formulæ, is said to have invented that called "the stratagem," on the occasion of a storm, when, it being decided that some of the crew should be thrown overboard, he so arranged that the lot should fall only on infidels[92]; Abraham ben Chijja; Levi ben Gerson; and others. Beside the editors of Euclid, Hypsicles, &c. (v. p. 184.), we may here mention Abu Sahal ben Temim (955, or Isaac Israeli?), who wrote on " Indian Calculations," the so-called *Gobar*, and was acquainted with the calculation of Knuckles[93]; Jehuda ben Solomon Cohen of Toledo (1247), who, at the age of 18 years, puzzled the "philosopher" of Frederick II.[94]; Elia Alfagi; Elia Misrachi; Isaac ben Moses Eli (?), of Oriola in Aragon, whose date is uncertain; and others.[95]

We may measure people's acquaintance with Mathematics by their view of the relation between the diameter and circumference of a circle; the number $3\frac{1}{7}$ is stated as given already in the 49 Middot of R. Natan, mentioned above (p. 35.). Most works, even the commentaries on the

Talmud, &c., are, whenever necessary, accompanied by diagrams, many however of which have been lost.*

§ 22.] *Medicine and Natural History.*

The labours of the Jews in the department of Medicine belong to that part of the history of literature and civilisation which is generally supposed to be known, but is seldom specially investigated. Sprengel[1] mentions three Jews among the Arabians, but omits Maimonides, as well as all those who wrote in Hebrew. Amoreux[2], whose information was limited[3], mentions the Jewish physicians only to accuse them of avarice[4], although his evidence applies but to Arabians and Christians.[5] The laborious Wüstenfeld[6] has incidentally collected much information about Arabic works, and translations from the Arabic.[7] The various aspects in which this subject may be viewed greatly enhance the difficulty of dealing with it. We can here only touch generally on some important materials for the History of Medical Science ; and, confining our attention to authors and books, we must omit all mention of hundreds of men known from their practice of the art.

For the present Period these consist chiefly of the very numerous but imperfectly known MSS.[8],—of which the Hebrew belong to Spain, Provence, and Italy,—for the circulation of which there was but little demand owing to the subsequent progress in science ; the few which have been printed, are rare and bad Latin translations of Arabic works. A classification of them is the more difficult because a great number of Hebrew MSS. bear the general title ספר רפואה (medical work), מלאכת היד and Arab. גאראחות (surgery). The difficulty of determining the authorship is greatly enhanced by the various translations, editions, and copies, by the mutilation of names in various languages, &c. Many on practical medicine, moreover, have been preserved in the literature of other languages, although their authors were not known to have been Jews; as in the case of some Arabic treatises, especially by Karaites.[9] The other parts of Jewish

* On Music, vide suprà, § 18.

literature give but little assistance on this subject, on account of its slight connexion with them[10], although medicine, as a part of physical science, was frequently treated from a purely theoretical point of view.[11]   On the other hand many practical physicians are known as writers only, or principally, from works unconnected with their art, and therefore do not come under our notice at present.[12]   Moreover, the Jewish ceremonial required, in general, an acquaintance with medicine[13]; and Jews distinguished themselves, not merely as general practitioners ("Maestri") and physicians in ordinary, but also as members of the public institutions and schools of Christians and Arabians, e. g. at Bagdad[14], Kahira, Salerno.[15]   They also took part in the establishment of the School at Montpellier[16], a fact which was not without its effect on the dissemination of their writings.[16a]

The medical literature of the Jews comprises all the departments of this science cultivated in the countries where they were living, not excepting the Veterinary Art.   They wrote independent works, that is to say, so far as their age produced such; they compiled, commentated, and translated the most celebrated works into and from all languages, and were brought, as teachers and writers, into close connexion with Arabians and Christians.   With reference to the form and language, we must further remark that Jews composed also medical rhymes (ארגוזה)[17] in Arabic[18], and imitated them in Hebrew.   In Persian the author of this treatise is acquainted only with the Compendium of ABI SAAD[19], of which the old Catalogue of the Leyden MSS. gives an incorrect account, confounding different works; in Greek he knows only the fragment of a certain BENJAMIN.[20]

We may perhaps consider those who wrote in Arabic as the most independent writers of the time; although the Arabian medical literature begins with translators from the Syriac and Greek: such as MASERDJEWEIH (not "Ibn Gialgial")[21], whose treatise on the small-pox is not without some peculiarities; SAHL (§ 21. p. 181.), who probably translated from the Syriac[22]; and his apostate son ABU'L HASSAN ALI (1035 — 1055), who was tutor to the celebrated Razi and Ainzarbi.   Amongst the best known are

the physicians in Africa and Spain who wrote in Arabic, such
as, at Kairowan, ISAAC (BEN SOLEIMAN) EL-ISRAÏLI [23],
known under the name " Ysaacus" (840 — 950), skilful in
dietetics and uroscopy, the best of whose works were published in a compendium by Abdallatif, appropriated by Constantinus Afer [24], and variously edited by Jews after the
Arabic and Latin; at Kahira, HIBETALLAH IBN GEMI, in
Hebrew NATHANEL, physician in ordinary to Saladin, whose
ارشاد is considered as one of his best writings; his pupil
the Karaite ABULFADHL DAUD; IBN MUBAREK (nat. 1161),
teacher at the Nosocomium Nasiricum, where, among others,
the celebrated Ibn Abi Oseibia was one of his auditors; and
many other Karaites [25], among whom perhaps was ABUL
MENNI BEN ABI NASSAR BEN HAFIDH EL-ATTHÂR (i. e.
the apothecary), a much esteemed pharmacologist (1259—
1260). [26]   At Kahira (Fostat) MAIMONIDES composed some
general works, for example, compendia of sixteen works by
Galen, then in common use (perhaps the same sixteen which
Joseph Ibn Aknin recommends) combined with five others;
and also his Aphorisms (*Pirke Moshe*) extracted from all
Galen's works, with the addition of his own valuable critical
remarks, one of which, respecting an observation made by
Galen in his book *De Usu Partium*, against the prophet
Moses, has become a locus classicus, and has been curiously
interpolated by the Latin translator, who joins Christ to
Moses; these Aphorisms, which according to Mercurial
deserve to be ranked with those of Hippocrates, must not
be confounded with Maimonides' commentary on the Aphorisms of Hippocrates.   Besides these larger works, we have
some smaller essays, written partly by order of the princes
in whose service he was, Saladin and both his successors,
Malek al-Aziz (1193–8) and Malek al-Afdhal.   Among
these we may mention an essay upon simple antidotes to
poison, written at the desire of the Vezir Alfadhel (and
thence called *Alfadhelijja*) on the occasion of a man having
been bitten by a viper, and dying from being unacquainted
with any simple remedy (1198); and also the celebrated
dietetical epistle to Malek al-Afdhal,   nt in Arabic MS.,
and incorrectly printed in Hebrew and Latin, of which a

corrupt German translation [27] has recently been published. In Irak and Syria we may mention the two apostates, ABUL-BERAKAT HIBETALLAH, called "Auhad ez Zemân" (the only man of his time) (1161—1170), SAMUEL IBN ABBAS of Maghreb (1163); and finally at Haleb JOSEPH IBN AKNIN (ob. 1226), the pupil of Maimonides and friend of the celebrated el Kifti (not Kofti).

In Spain also the series begins with a translator the fellow-labourer of the monk Nicolaus, who was called to Cordova to assist in the translation of Dioscorides, CHASDAI BEN ISAAC SHAFRUT or BASHRUT (959)[28], who also first made treacle (called *Alfaruk*), at Cordova[29]; AMRAN BEN ISHAK of Toledo (997) is only known on the doubtful authority of Leo Africanus. We may mention, besides the grammarian JONA (cir. 1040), JOSEPH BEN ISHAK IBN BEKLARISH (or MIKLARISH) (1126); ABU GIAFAR JUSSUF BEN AHMED IBN CHISDAI (1128), the friend of Ibn ess Izaigh, who travelled to Africa; SAMUEL ABENHUCAR (IBN WAKKAR ?), physician in ordinary to Alphonso (1295—1311)[30]; HARUN BEN ISHAK, at Cordova[31]; ISHAK BEN HARUN SOLEIMAN, at Guadalaxara (1425 ?)[31a]; JEHUDA BEN ABRAHAM of Toledo[32]; JOSHUA BEN JOSEPH IBN BIBAS LORKI contemporary of, and perhaps the same as, the apostate Hieronymus de Sta. Fide (cir. 1410); and IBN KHANI, who translated the work of a Spanish Christian on tobacco, and who completes the series.

It is worth remarking, that original Medical works in Hebrew occur even prior to the period of translations (§ 8.), for example, one by the astronomer mentioned above, SABBATAI DONOLO in Italy. [33]   The cosmographico-medical work of one ASAF, interesting from his historical introduction, known in France as early as the 11th century, and used by Christian and Arabic authors[34], may, however, with much probability, be referred to the Arabic pseudepigraphical literature.   In the middle of the 13th century we first meet with translators, commentators, and editors, from the Arabic (Jews, Muhammedans, and a few Christians), and from the Latin, Spanish, and Italian (principally Christians). The Greeks who were the authorities of the age, Hippocrates,

Galen, Dioscorides, &c., influenced also the Jewish medical literature, and at the same time were themselves represented as pupils of the old Jews.[35] The Arabians, whose writings were edited either directly or indirectly are, Honein (Johannitius) (809—873), and his son Ishak (ob. 910—911); Mesue the Elder (Janus Damascenus) (ob. 857), and Mesue the Younger (1015); Serapion (cir. 900), and Ibn Serapion (post 1068)[35a]; Razi (Rhazes) (ob. 923—932); Ali Ibn al-Abbas (ob. 994 ?); Ibn al-Gezzar (920—1004); Ibn Sina (Avicenna) (980—1037); Ibn Wafid (Aben Guefit) (997—1068); Ali Ibn Rodhwan (ob. 1061—1068); Ibn Gezla (ob. 1100)[35b]; Abulkasem el Zahrawi (ob. 1106); Abu 'l Salt Omaya (ob. 1137); Ibn Zuhr (Avenzoar) (ob. 1162)[36]; and Ibn Roshd (Averroes) (ob. 1198). CHARISI'S Hebrew translation of a work by Galen on early burial, which according to Maimonides was translated into Arabic by Batrik, and was not genuine, is worth noticing.[37]

The principal Jewish editors and commentators of these and the Judæo-Arabic works were nearly all Italians and Provençals, namely SOLOMON BEN JOSEPH IBN AJUB of Grenada, at Beziers (1259—65); MOSES IBN TIBBON (1260); SHEMTOB BEN ISAAC of Tortosa (1264); MESHULLAM BEN JONA; FARADJ BEN SALEM (Farragut) of Girgenti commissioned by Charles d'Anjou (1279); NATHAN HAMATI (or GAD) BEN ELIEZER, probably of Provence, at Rome (1279—1283); his son SOLOMON (1299), to whom we are indebted for the Hebrew translation of Galen's Commentary on Hippocrates' work *De Aëre, Aquis, et Locis*, recently discovered by the author in the Bodleian Library, which proves to be the original of the printed Latin translation of MOSES ALATINO (16th century), the Arabic being probably lost; SERACHJA BEN ISAAC BEN SHEALTIEL of Barcelona (1284), at Rome; JEDAJA PENINI, at Beziers (1298); KALONYMOS of Arles (1307); SOLOMON, at Beziers or Montpellier (1298); SOLOMON BEN ABRAHAM IBN DAUD; MOSES RIETI (at Rome, 1388-1457 ?), author of a commentary upon the Aphorisms of Hippocrates; and others.

The works (mostly Latin) of the following authors, translators, and commentators: — Constantinus Afer (1050), whose *Liber de Gradibus* has not yet been recognised in the well known anonymous 'ס המעלות; Nicolaus Præpositus of Salerno (1100—1150); Jordanus Rufus, surgeon to the emperor Frederick[38]; Gerhard of Cremona (1175); Geraut (Gerbert) de Sola; Bruno de Lungoburgo (1252); Roger of Parma; William of Piacenza (of Saliceto) (1275); Petrus Hispanus, son of the physician Julian (John XXI.); John de St. Amand (de Monte); Nicolaus Alexandrinus (post 1287); Lanfranc (1296); Bernard de Gordon (1300—1304); Ermengaud Blasius of Montpellier (1306)[39]; Arnaldus (Bachuone) de Villanova (ob. 1312), celebrated as an astrologer[40]; Gentilis and Francisco da Foligno, and John Cenobarba (1348)[41]; Guy de Chauliac (1363)[42]; Saladin (Asculanus) de Montpellier; Peter de Tusignano[43]; Antonio Cermisone (Parmesane?) (ob. 1441); John of Tornamira (1401); Pictioncelli (?); Roger Brocarde[44]; and the work *Circa Instans* (secundum Platearium)[45]—were edited in Hebrew by HILLEL BEN SAMUEL at Rome (13th century)[46]; ESTHORI BEN MOSES HAPPARCHI at Montpellier (1306); CRESCAS VIDAL DE KISLAR (Israel ben Joseph) (1327); DAVID CASLARI BEN ABRAHAM (perhaps the same as Bongodas at Perpignan, 1337?); JEHUDA BEN SOLOMON (BONGODAS) NATHAN (1352-9); MOSES BEN SAMUEL, known as a Christian by the name of Juan d'Avignon, at Seville (1360); ABRAHAM BEN MESHULLAM ABIGDOR at Montpellier (1379); JEKUTIEL BEN SOLOMON at Narbonne (1387); LEON JOSEPH (?) at Carcassonne (1394); THEODOROS BEN MOSES (1394); JEHUDA BEN SAMUEL SHALOM (cir. 1400); ISAAC BEN ABRAHAM KABRUT (1403); TANCHUM BEN MOSES (1406); JACOB KARPHANTON; SOLOMON BEN MOSES SHALOM (1441—1486)[47]; MENAHEM; and others[48];—and also by the following, whose dates are mostly uncertain: GABRIEL (BEN JEHUDA?)[49]; JACOB HALEVI (1300?)[50]; MORDECAI BEN SOLOMON; MOSES BEN MAZLIACH[51]; SOLOMON BEN ABIN[52]; and others. Perhaps also Magister MAYNUS (?), who translated from Hebrew into Latin (1304), was a Jew by birth.

There are besides a great number of medical works with polyglot glossaries or indices of medicines (frequently mentioned in catalogues as separate works) which are useful for comparative materia medica and lexicography.[53]   Of these we will here mention only the most common glossary, originally composed by NATHAN HAMATI, and appended to his translation of the *Medical Canon;* in several editions it bears the title of *Synonymes,* which seems to be a general denomination for the whole class.   There are also copies of Arabic works in Hebrew characters, such as the Canon of Avicenna, &c.

As authors of original works the following may be named: SHESHET HA-NASSI (cir. 1170—1216), on purgatives[54]; ISAAC LATTAS BEN JEHUDA in Provence (1300)[54a], ABRAHAM DE KASLAR (BEN DAVID) in Catalonia (1349), on fevers and pestilence; BONGODAS (JEHUDA) COHEN (1353), on midwifery[55]; THEODOROS of Cavaillon, on botany[56]; NATHAN BEN JOEL PALQUERA, who wrote a large work founded upon older authorities, from Aristotle and Galen to Maimonides[57]; MOSES NARBONI[58], mentioned above (§ 12.) as a philosopher, who occurs frequently in his own and other medical writings under the name Vidal בלשום, hitherto neither identified nor interpreted, but perhaps to be explained by means of the Provencal dialect; Magister SALVI VIDA DE MURIAN(?) (1384); DON MEIR ALGUADEZ, physician in ordinary to Henry III. of Castile (1405)[59]; JEHUDA BEN JACOB, who wrote on dietetics[60]; JACOB BEN DAVID PROVENÇAL of Marseilles, at Naples (1490), said to be the author of a letter, recently published, from a Paris MS. on the study of science generally, and particularly of medicine, which in its present form is certainly not free from interpolation, especially as regards some pretended quotations from older authorities; DAVID BEN JEHUDA (MESSER LEON) (1490)[61]; and other Italian physicians towards the end of this period.   As regards authorship, date, and names, the following are still more doubtful: JOCHANAN JARCHUNI; JOSEPH BEN ISAAC ISRAELI, erroneously said to be a son of the celebrated Isaac Israeli mentioned above; ABRAHAM BEN JEHUDA, and some anonymous authors of compendia on urine[62]; ABRAHAM BEN SOLOMON CHEN, on fever (1349?)[63]; GALAF (CALEO=KALONYMOS?), author (?) of an Antidota-

rium[64]; ELIA BEN JEHUDA of Marigni at Tivoli, author of
a dialogue on the diseases of women [65]; JOSEPH ALGUADEZ,
whose Spanish work *Secreta Medica* was translated by the
historian JOSEPH COHEN at Genoa (1546) [66]; and SAMUEL
אשפיריל of Cordova, author of a Spanish Surgery written for
David of Jaen. [67]

With medical studies *Natural History* (חכמת הטבע,
علم الطبيعية) is closely connected. Although, according to the
scientific classification [68] of the time, the former is only a
branch of the latter, the principal end and object of the study
of nature was medicine, and the only attempt then made at
Physics, in the narrower sense, consisted in philosophical definitions of conceptions according to the system of Aristotle.
Under this head may be reckoned the old works of the
physician ISAAC BEN MUKATIL [69], entitled " Physics;"
those of the translator DAVID [70]; and those quoted by the
Frenchman Eliezer of טוך.[71] Natural history is consequently
represented by the authors already (§ 12.) noticed as philosophical. Here belong only a few individual works, such as
the cosmography of GERSON BEN SOLOMON (cir. 1290), who,
besides preserving some old traditions and tales, has brought
forward much that is interesting, from his own views and
experience. Some particular points of natural history are
also scattered about in works and commentaries of the most
various kinds.[72] We will mention only one favourite sub-
jeèt, treated also in separate works, viz. jewels and their
healing (partly sympathetic) powers. Although Jewish authors connect this mode of treatment with the passage of the
Pentateuch where the jewels of the Urim and Thummim are
mentioned (Ex. xxvii. 30.) its origin seems to be foreign,
probably Arabic. At all events, the special essays now
known are almost exclusively translations into Hebrew; that
quoted in an anonymous Glossary of the Bible of the 13th
century is perhaps by BERECHJA NAKDAN. The library of
the Escurial possesses a Spanish work upon 360 stones or
minerals, corresponding to the stars in the 48 constellations,
translated, at the desire of King Alfonso (1250), by JEHUDA
BEN MOSES COHEN from the Arabic of Abolays (?), who
had translated it from the Chaldee (?). There is also another

Lapidarium from the Arabic of Muhammed Aben-Quich, perhaps translated by the same person; but although De Castro gives a sufficient description of this and the former works, the names of the authors have been corrupted, and as far as we know are not yet deciphered.   The Leyden Library posesses a small Hebrew essay on jewels in MS., translated, under the title of *The Book of Riches* (ס' העושר), by JACOB BEN REUBEN (of uncertain date, and not to be confounded with the Karaite of that name (§ 14.), whose Commentary bears the same title); in the preface the discovery of the powers of jewels is attributed to a fabulous king, perhaps alluding to Alexander the Great.   We possess also a similar Hebrew Lapidarium attributed to Aristotle. It is still uncertain, from which of these the above-named Gerson ben Solomon, and perhaps Bechai ben Asher, made extracts.   A small essay treating of the 12 principal jewels, according to the 12 tribes of Israel and the signs of the Zodiac, is quoted by Abraham Jagel (about 1600); perhaps it is the work of MESHULLAM of Volterra, who is known from quotations by Abraham Portaleone (§ 29.).

Magic, connected with astrology, and extending its influence almost to the present time [72 a], is the opposite to natural science.   So little has yet been established respecting its origin and diffusion, that we can venture only to mention a few names illustrating the part taken in it by the Jews and by Jewish literature.[73]   The connexion of this art with the Secret Science (Theosophy) and practical Kabbala (§ 13.) is too recent to lead to any decisive conclusion. The principal representatives of Jewish literature—philosophers, simple believers in the Bible, and doctors of the law—express themselves strongly against the magic forbidden in the Bible and all such things; and SOLOMON DURAN (1437) answers the attacks of Hieronymus de Sta. Fide (§ 15.), by saying that necromancy was a subject of public teaching at Salamanca.   The common people still had recourse to it, according to the prevailing tendency of mind.   To such influences we may ascribe the notes scattered about old MSS., sometimes written by their possessors; but there could be no real literature in a subject so ill adapted to writing.

It thus happens that whatever appears in a scientific form belongs to the Arabian period; and the few works worth mention bear marks of foreign origin.

The principal sources for the historical and critical treatment of the secret arts of the pagans by Jewish writers on the philosophy of religion and commentators of the Bible, are the extremely interesting writings of IBN WAHSHIJJA (903), which have been drawn from Nabatæan (Syriac) authorities. They were studied by JEHUDA HA-LEVI (1140) and MAIMONIDES (§ 21.), whence some valuable information respecting the old Sabæans has been derived by recent authors who had access to the Arabic sources.[74] The work מלאכת מושכלת, ascribed to Apollonius of Tyana, was translated by SOLOMON BEN NATHAN in Provence (cir. 1400).[75] Besides the translations of Arabian astrologers mentioned above (§ 21.), we meet with some works in the original language written in Hebrew characters, for instance those of the Christian Abdallah ben Masrur (9th century)[76], Joan Gil de Burgos[77], &c.

Of the various branches of astrological medicine and physics there are some germs as early as in the Talmud and Midrash; they found even some support in the biblical dogmatism and philosophy of the time, as e. g. the *Oneirocriticism* (פתרון חלומות)[78], which the Arabians and Jews ascribe to JOSEPH and DANIEL. A work on this subject was supposed to have been written by HAI GAON (ob. 1038)[79]; and another on the philosophers' stone (אבן הפילוסופים), was ascribed to SAADJA, who combated the popular astronomical superstitions.[80] On *Augury* (דעת העתדות), we have the *Books of Fate* (גורלות), some of which were ascribed to Achitophel (2 Sam. xv. 12.); others are by IBN EZRA[81] and JEHUDA CHARISI. Meteorogical remarks and rules for agriculture are to be found in the old kalendars and rituals, &c. (§ 19.). *Geomancy* (حكمת החול, علم الرمل), traced by the Arabians to Enoch (Hermes), Daniel and others, furnishes no names of Jewish authors belonging to this period[82]; the same is the case with *Physiognomy* (חכמת הפרצופים) علم القيافة[83] or the more biblical (הכרת פנים); but a complete essay on physiognomy in connexion with the form of the letters of the alphabet is inserted in the book *Zohar* (Section Jethro).   On *Chiromancy* (חכמת הין, also ראיית הידים) there is a tract printed under the title תולדות אדם, alluding to the biblical passage (Gen. v. 1.) from which some Jewish Midrash authors deduce physiognomy ; later editions give, we do not know upon what authority, ELIA GALLINÆ BEN MOSES as the name of the author, who, if we are not mistaken, quotes an Arabic authority.   The pseudo-Aristotelian physiognomy and similar subjects are parts of the *Secretum Secretorum*, translated into Hebrew from the Arabic of JAHJA IBN BATRIK (cir. 800), by JEHUDA CHARISI.[84]   Under the head *Soothsaying* may be reckoned a work on the prognostications to be gathered from convulsive motions in the limbs of the human body (פרכוס, רפפות), which is not rare in MSS., and has been printed and recently reprinted under the name of HAI ; but it is certainly a translation or imitation of similar Arabic works recently described by Prof. Feischer.

PERIOD III.

§ 23.]   *Transition.*

THE grounds for our division into periods belong partly to the general history of civilisation and of the world, and partly to the particular history of the Jews ; but, as transitions of this kind are never sudden, and some authors seem to belong exclusively to neither period, it will be necessary to introduce their names in this as well as in the preceding.

In the middle ages, the Arabic and Latin languages were almost the only organs of Muhammedan and Christian authors, and the two principal groups of Jewish writers arrange themselves accordingly ; but, in this Third Period, nearly all the languages of Europe, with their important varieties and written characters, came into use among the

Jews, the Hebrew still remaining the only one generally understood. The invention of printing was soon hailed by the Jews as an important means of communication — and thoughts, now so easily reproduced a thousand times, actually flew over the limits of countries and continents, although their wings were certainly bound or clipped by the hostile and often laughably ignorant censures of the clergy, and even of the better-informed Italians. A kind of internal censorship was also imposed by the custom, subsequently pushed too far, of requiring approbations from the rabbies and learned men as a recommendation, and also as a security against piracy, on pain of excommunication. This custom has afforded some rich materials for the history of literature and civilisation. We cannot here follow out in detail all the effects produced on Jewish literature by the invention of printing, such as correctness of text, &c. The expulsion of the Jews from the Peninsula, their migration to the Slavic nations of the East, and the increasing external communication among Jews, changed the scene, and brought fresh influences to bear on the character of their literature; but at the same time some particular works became rare, others were entirely lost. Spain vanishes entirely; France (including Provence, but not the German Alsace) retreats far into the background; and we lose all sight of Northern Africa, now under the Muhammedan dominion. The foreground is occupied by the æstheticism of Italy (including Corfu, Candia, and in some measure Greece), the mysticism which it shared with Palestine, and the controversy, philology, and antiquarian research common to it and to Holland; as well as by the casuistry of the Halacha, which was transplanted from Germany to Poland, and thence returned with over-ripe fruits. This continued until the influence of the school of Mendelssohn made Germany the centre of the philosophical and historico-critical movements of the present times, some rays of which were first reflected from Poland and Italy. From the rise of this school a new period of Jewish literature will be dated.

The connexion of the Jewish development with the general change from mediæval to modern science is difficult and obscure, and will become clear only after the issue of the struggle now going on within it, if indeed any issue can be expected without a general revolution of the world, such as took place at the former epochs. We ourselves stand too completely within the circle of modern times, and are in other respects not yet sufficiently free from the influences of the middle ages, to be able to describe all the characteristics and features of the movements in Jewish literature which have followed the course of European civilisation. The difficulty is increased by the encyclopædic framework of the huge and undigested mass, in which the literary form threatens to disconnect itself entirely from the contents; while sometimes the subject-matter, sometimes the plan of the earlier collective and normal works, has the greatest weight; and in which the great variety of language renders a considerable part of the literature unintelligible. The prevailing languages, besides the Hebrew, are Latin, Spanish, Portuguese, Italian, German, Dutch, and, in some instances, Persian, Turkish, Modern Greek, and Polish (§ 27.). Nearly all knowledge of the Arabic in Europe had at this period died out; and JOSEPH DEL MEDIGO (before 1629) declared that the study of Arabic science was superfluous, since the Greek sources themselves had become accessible. The fact of the attention of the learned having been turned from Arabic science and scholasticism to the pure fountain-head, classical and Hebrew literature, demands a special investigation of the 15th and 16th centuries, during the whole of which time the movement in philosophy, astronomy, medicine, &c., continued. The Jews took part in this in various ways, and under circumstances no less various.

In the middle ages the Jews, by their external position and the close connexion of the Arabic language with the Hebrew, gave independent assistance in the cultivation of Arabian science. In Christian (Romanic) countries the Latin continued to be used for literary purposes even after the rise of its affiliated languages, whose scanty scientific literature was confined to a few learned Jews and apostates from Judaism, secured for the most part from the persecutions of the times by the temporal and spiritual rulers, and

employed as oral or literary interpreters for the translation
of Arabic works.   The controversial use of these languages
by Christian theologians, and Jewish apostates, such as
PETRUS ALPHONSI (1106), ALPHONSO DE BURGOS and
others, was little to the purpose.   " Greek philosophy" was
from very early times considered as synonymous with atheism
and paganism, although individual followers of Arabico-
Greek science drew nice distinctions, or altogether denied the
imputation.   The Græco-Roman mythology could not fail,
even in its most beautiful poetic and classic formations, to
offend Jewish spiritualism (§ 28.) by its idolatry.   The dark
and fanciful pantheon of the Kabbala alone was always
open for the reception of new forms.   Thus the new classical
studies could exercise an important influence on the general
movement of Jewish literature only when science was freed
from theology, and Judaism and the Jews from spiritual
and temporal oppression ; individuals and classes of writers
soon participated in the new movement.

The Arabian love of books had had some influence among
the Jews in Spain and Provence ; but at the beginning of the
14th century the Italian bibliomania spread generally ; even
at the present day the greatest proportion of Hebrew MSS.
are to be found in Italy.   Some learned Italians of the 15th
century are distinguished for their knowledge of Christian literature ; and the influence of classical Latin is visible in the
writings of JEHUDA BEN JECHIEL (1460) (§ 20.).   JEHUDA
ABRAVANEL, called MESSER LEONE HEBREO, author of
the *Dialoghi d'Amore* (1502) is called " the Flower of Italian
Philosophy " by his father the celebrated DON ISAAC ABRA-
VANEL, who himself had transferred the last spark of Arabian
scholasticism to Italy (where the Zohar was attacked by
ELIA DEL MEDIGO, and philosophy by JOSEPH JAABEZ), in
the same way as ISAAC ARAMA carried it to Saloniki, and
MOSES ALASHKAR to Egypt.   In opposition to these men,
Leo Hebræus represented the Neo-Platonic School of Pico
della Mirandola in its connexion with the Jewish Kabbala.
By him and his cotemporaries, e. g. ABRAHAM FARISSOL,
notice was first taken of the new maritime discoveries, which
in fact laid the foundation of a realistic science.   ASARJA

DE ROSSI at Mantua (1514—1577) not only made himself
master of the learning of his time, but raised himself—the
only man who did so before the last century—to a height
of criticism and historical research which soon excited the
envy of fanatics and plagiarists. He has not, however, in
modern times, received the credit due to him; and his
Christian namesake, G. B. De Rossi, has been obliged to
defend his praise of a Jew in a work the substance of which
is borrowed from Asarja.

In the last struggles of the Arabists it was Jews, principally Italian physicians and public teachers, who translated
philosophical, medical, and astronomical works into Latin
from the Hebrew (the Arabic being generally lost, inaccessible, or not understood), such as ELIA CRETENSIS (del
Medigo), public teacher of philosophy at Padua (1493), who
translated for Pico della Mirandola (1485, 1486); ABRA-
HAM DE BALMES (de Palmis), professor at Lecci (ob. 1523);
CALO CALONYMUS (KALONYMOS BEN DAVID) of Naples,
at Venice (1527); JACOB MANTINO of Tortosa, at Rome
and Venice (1534-50); MOSES ALATINO, at Spoleto; and
MOSES FINZI (1558). Ritter, the Historian of Philosophy,
denies that the Jews had either knowledge of Latin, or
" true love of their work;" although he has no foundation
for the opinion beyond the general inveterate prejudice
against them. On the other hand, Renan does them more
than strict justice in attributing to them the translations
of Averroes which appeared under the name of Burana;
but he could not resist a sneering allusion at " some money "
as a probable stimulus to the labour. Besides these, various
others wrote in Latin, as BONET DE LATTES (§ 21.) on
astronomy; and OBADJA SEFORNO, who dedicated to the
king of France the Latin translation of his Philosophy of
Religion (1548); others wrote in Italian, as DE POMIS.

But Jewish Literature was not merely passive, it had also
an active influence on the study of the Bible, and the Hebrew
language, which was cultivated as well as the classics, and
upon which the reformers of the Church grounded their
labours. The Kabbala influenced the Neo-Platonists, the
Christian Mystics, and even the medical reform of Paracel-

sus, and the philosophy of Spinoza.   The Bible and Kabbala — the latter having been afterwards studied also by
theologians — were the principal parts of " Rabbinical literature," and Hebrew literature generally, in which Christian
students interested themselves.   For centuries, the Biblical
scholars and students of modern Hebrew literature, from
Reuchlin to the Professors Delitzsch and Ewald, were, like
Jerome, directly or indirectly pupils of Jews (§ 28.).   But
theologians expressed their gratitude principally in attempts
at conversion, or applied for instruction rather to those who
understood Judaism in a Christian sense, and made it an
object of attack.   Baptized Jews taught Hebrew to the
founders of classical studies, as Poggius ; not to mention
the revivers of Hebrew studies, Reuchlin, Seb. Münster,
and others.   A former controversialist against Christianity
taught Agricola (1443 - 1485); and MATTHEW ADRIAN
was (about 1513) the teacher of W. Capito (ob. 1541),
and perhaps also (A.D. 1518) of Trotzendorf (ob. 1556).
In later times CHRISTIAN DE POMIS was tutor of Wülfer
(ob. 1714); EZRA EDZARD of Franke, the German founder
of the Mission; and BAPTIST JONA of Safet (ob. 1668) was
the guide of Bartolocci.   Among the Jews of important
literary celebrity who were faithful to their creed, JOCHANAN
ALLEMANO was teacher and friend of Pico della Mirandola
(ob. 1494).   Widmanstadt (1532), the pupil of Reuchlin
and friend of Ægidius de Viterbo, speaks with respect of
his teachers, DAVID IBN JAHJA BEN JOSEPH of Lisbon, at
Naples (born A.D. 1465, ob. at Imola 1543), and BARUCH
of Beneventum.   Through the instrumentality of Ægidius,
who was the pupil of the well-known ELIA LEVITA, the
above-mentioned Baruch first introduced the book Zohar
among Christians; and Reuchlin himself was pupil of JACOB
JECHIEL LOANZ, physician in ordinary to the emperor at
Linz (1472), and of OBADJA SFORNO at Rome (1498).   To
JACOB BEN ISAAC ROMANO, teacher of Harlai de Sanci at
Constantinople (ob. 1650 at Jerusalem), Buxtorf is indebted
for the valuable supplement to his *Bibliotheca Rabbinica*.
Hottinger, whose *Promptuarium* owes much to MANASSE
BEN ISRAEL'S materials for a Bibliotheca Rabbinica, was

induced to study Oriental literature by the linguist SAADJA BEN LEVI ASANKOT (1644). Unger's correspondence with JACOB ABOAB at Venice (1727), ISAAC CANTARINI at Padua, and others, assisted Wolf in his *Bibliotheca Hebraïca* &c. Scaliger, a pupil of PHILIP FERDINAND, confesses that Jews were the only teachers of Hebrew; and Ockley asserts that no one can understand the New Testament so well as a Jew. Even public educational establishments were obliged to seek Jewish teachers, the number of whom is considerable, e. g. the physician PAUL RICCI at Pavia (1529), *protégé* of Erasmus; PAUL CANOSSA of Venice at Paris (1530); PETER FLÜGEL at Strasburg (ob. 1564); PHILIPP D'AQUINO at Paris (since 1610); and many others. In the Vatican, Jewish converts, for example, IO. PAUL EUSTATHIUS, probably the same as ELIA DE NOLA BEN MENAHEM (1552), and others, were employed as copyists; but they were not always well selected, as is shown by their mistakes, some of which are pointed out by Assemani. The series of anti-Jewish works for the purpose of conversion was considered as the special task of the converts to Christianity. A flood of these writings inundated Germany, where more stringent laws respecting Jews were enacted than in any other country, and where, had it not been for Reuchlin's strong opposition, and the keen satires of the *Epistolæ obscurorum virorum*, the avaricious PFEFFERCORN and his associates at Cologne (1509) would have gained as complete a victory in the internecine war against Hebrew literature, as their companions did in Italy, where the burning of the Talmud at the instigation of neophytes (1553 -4) was felt for centuries.

With what intentions and success other attempts to acquire a knowledge of Hebrew literature were made, we may gather from the instance of Thomas Murner, commissioned by the Minorite Friars, to which order he belonged, to translate more than twenty tracts from the Hebrew, of which only the Passover-Haggada (§ 5.) and the Benedictions appeared (1511 – 12). Soon afterwards the convert BÖSCHENSTAIN concluded a few specimens of the Jewish Prayer-Book with the following characteristic remark: "From these every one may perceive that the Hebrews also desire the grace and mercy of God, and hope for future blessedness;" and Aug. Sebastianus at Marburg, who filled up a few remaining pages of his Hebrew grammar with passages from the litany and the Sephardic Selichot (1537), went so far as to say, that these prayers, if recited in a right spirit, might be used even by a Christian. But these were isolated opinions; and Arias Montanus in return for his great undertaking, the Antwerp Polyglot (1569–71), was rewarded by the Pope with exile, "because he had introduced too many Rabbinical explanations." Even the series of better translations (chiefly in Latin) of later Hebrew works, beginning with Buxtorf (1603 sqq.), who may be called the Christian Ibn Tibbon (§ 12.), were in general undertaken less for the sake of instruction than for polemical and other purposes unconnected with the literature itself; and an imperfect knowledge of the idiom, together with a very partial acquaintance with the various branches of the literature, occasioned even in the best translations made by Christian writers, from Seb. Munster (1525 sqq.), celebrated for his perversions, to Bialloblotzki (for the Oriental Translation Fund, 1835), grosser errors than would have been possible in any other literature.

Besides this one-sided tendency, there was also the fact that most information respecting Jewish literature was drawn from sources obscured by the fanaticism, hatred, ignorance, and fraud of such persons as GALATIN (1518), MARGARITHA (1530), J. C. OTTO, NAPHTALI MARGALIOT who disbelieved all religion (1605), BRENZ (1614), GERSON (ob. 1627), and their followers, whose tendency has been justly appreciated even by Christian students like Wülfer (1681) and Muhl (1701). By degrees, and especially when Biblical study was considered to have become independent of Jewish literature, the latter was entirely left in the hands of the missionaries to the Jews; and thus a singular "ghetto" in science was established, almost more inextricable than that which restricts their political and social condition. But to the attacks either written or oral, multiplied by peculiar literary circumstances, answers were not wanting in this period; and

with this class of writings we open our concise survey of the
particular branches, premising, however, that no new kind of
literature appears within the limits of this period, and that
our details, though revised afresh, will still need correction by
means of a laborious study and investigation of particulars,
and we therefore claim indulgence from those who understand
the subject.

§ 24.] *Polemical and Apologetic Writings.*

The known authors are mostly of Spanish descent, some of
them being persons who had feigned themselves Christians in
order to escape from the Spanish Inquisition in Holland and
Italy, where from 1584 a compulsory conversion of the Jews
was carried on. Hence the writings are, for the most part, in
Spanish and Italian; but few are in Latin or German (Jewish
German), because in Germany so many obstacles were thrown
in the way of printing Hebrew works of this kind that it
was seldom attempted. The circle of ideas having been
already exhausted, little novelty in dogmatic matter was
possible; and therefore most persons confined themselves
merely to the publication of older writings. The use of
European languages, however, gave an opportunity of direct-
ing this literature more pointedly against the Christian
aggressors; while the older literature had aimed rather at
furnishing the Jews with weapons for their own defence,
and for the preservation of the faith of their fathers. At
the same time the reproaches cast upon the Jews, to justify
their unhappy fate, are retorted upon their oppressors. Thus
we find, closely connected with the polemical literature,
either lamentable but heart-stirring descriptions of persecutions combined with the hope of the promised Advent, such
as SAMUEL USQUE's *Consolacion a las tribulacoens* (1553);
or apologies for Judaism and tradition, some treating historically of the departed glory and splendour of the Jewish
power and wisdom, and some deserving more attention
and better treatment from science and true Christianity,
for example, DAVID DE POMIS *De Medico Hebræo* (1588);
EMANUEL ABOAB's Spanish *Nomologia* (1629); SIMON LUZ-

ZATTO's *Discorso* (1638); MANASSEH BEN ISRAEL's (1650) tracts, some in Spanish and some in English, e. g. the *Vindiciæ Judæorum*, recently again translated, and his *Esperanza de Israel*, upon the Ten Tribes; ISAAC CARDOSO's *Excellencias de los Hebreos* (1679); DANIEL DE BARRIOS's Spanish works (1683); DAVID D'ASCOLI's (1559) *Apologia* against the badge ordered by Paul IV., punished by a long imprisonment; and THOMAS DE PINEDO's (1678) learned Latin edition of Stephen Byzantinus, in which he recognises the merit of Christianity in the struggle against Paganism. We may also refer to similar tendencies JOSEPH SEMAH ARIAS's Spanish translation of Flavius Josephus's work *Contra Apionem* (1687), and some Hebrew works by LEWA BEN BEZALEL, a Rabbi of Prague (1599—1600).

The following are authors of important and interesting polemical writings: MORDECHAI DATO (1575-89); ISAAC ONKENEIRA, the pretended editor of a disputation by JOSEPH NASI (Miquez) the Duke of Naxos (1577), a brother of the later DAVID NASI, who is said to have been the author of a work in which not only the Thirteen Articles of the Jewish, but also conclusions adverse to the Nine Articles of the Christian faith, given by the author in a notice of a parody on the Hebrew hymn יגדל, are drawn from passages of the New Testament; and ISAAC BEN ABRAHAM TROKI the Karaite (ob. 1594), whose famous *Chizzuk Emuna*, completed by his pupil JOSEPH BEN MARDOCHAI TROKI, is preserved in its original form only in MS., the corrupt edition being taken from a copy altered by a Rabbinical author (cir. 1605). This work is interesting for its quotations from some little-known Christian and polemical works in the Polish language; it has been made use of by critical writers upon the New Testament from Voltaire to Strauss, and a refutation of it was undertaken by Duke Louis of Orleans (ob. 1752) who was dissatisfied with Gousset's refutation. Some translations made by Jews are still unpublished, e. g., in Spanish by ISAAC ATHIA (1621); in German by the baptized Jew MICHAEL GELLING in Hamburg (1631-3); in Italian by MARCO (Mardochai) LUZZATTO (ob. 1799 at the age of 80), who translated also (1753) into Hebrew the Spanish *Forta-*

lozza of ABRAHAM THE PROSELYTE (Peregrine) (cir. 1600);
SALMAN ZEBI OFFENHAUSEN, author of the *Jewish Theriak*
against Brenz (1615); JACOB BEN AMRAM, who wrote in
Latin (1634); JACOB LOMBROSO, the defender of Judaism
against Hugo Grotius (1640); JEHUDA DI MODENA, who
boasts in his unpublished polemic (1613) that he has not
allowed any anti-Judaic work in Latin, Italian, or Spanish
to escape his notice; ISAAC LUPERCIO, who defended Judaism against a monk of Seville (1658); SAUL LEVI MOR-
TERA (ob. 1660), the opponent of Sixtus; ISAAC ABENDANA,
who carried on a controversy with Hulsius (1669); ISAAC
ABOAB (ob. 1687), whose Spanish work is the foundation of
the *Israel vengé* of HENRIQUEZ (1770); MOSES GERMANUS
(Spaeth), who after having changed his religion several times
ended as a Jew, and who had a controversy with Wachter
(1699); the learned JEHUDA BRIEL (1702), and DAVID NIETO
in London (1705), the former of whom wrote in Hebrew
and Italian, the latter in Spanish, against the Inquisition and
the Archbishop of Cangranor; and others. The continued
auto-da-fés of the Spanish Inquisition, many of whose victims were relations of the Jews who had fled to Holland,
provoked JACOB BELMONTE to write some Spanish polemical
poems (17th century); perhaps also the *Silva contro la
Idolatria* of MOSES BELMONTE owes its origin to the same
influence. MENDELSSOHN'S answer to Lavater belongs
more to the present times, the peculiar polemics of which
have the common characteristic of freedom of thought.

§ 25.] *Halacha.*

The most important representatives of this, in the 16th
and 17th centuries, were the Rabbies and heads of schools of
the Spanish and Portuguese congregations in Turkey and
the Venetian islands. From the beginning of the 16th century downwards the schools of the Slavic countries (Bohemia
and Poland) began to be held in high esteem, to over-
spread Germany, and to extend their influence as far as
Italy, where, since the burning of the Talmud (1543),
study in general had declined (§ 23.). Holland and after-

wards England must here, to a certain extent, be considered as colonies, since, in general, the wide diffusion of
both the earlier and later literature allows of no such sharp
and fundamental division of schools as existed in earlier
times. The old beaten paths were still trodden; and there
are only two separate classes to be distinguished:—1st, that
of *Armour-bearers* (נושא כלים) to the ancients (*Rishonim*,
ראשונים), i. e. as commentators and the like; 2nd, that of
independent *Decidentes* (מורה הוראה), as advocates and judges
in the casuistic doctrine of the Law of God. The former
had, again, two principal fields of operation, namely, the discussion of the Talmud and Halachaic Midrash, and the
Compendia of the Poskim (§ 9.); the latter deliberated upon
actual or fictitious questions arising out of judgments. Among
the former, who had the predominance, the abbreviation
גפ"ת, i. e. גמרא, פוסקים, תוספות (Gemara, Poskim, Tosaphot), signified the entire Halachaic discussions with their
various denominations, such as, ביאורים *Expositions*, חירושים
Novellæ, תירוצים *Solutions of difficulties.* Jacob Pollak,
i. e. the Pole (ob. 1530), is regarded as the founder of the
Chillukim (חילוקים), a kind of school disputations or dissertations upon a given theme, still in use in Poland, Hungary,
&c.; this led to the last and greatest degeneration of Halachaic spirit, חריפות. Amongst those who opposed this abuse
we may mention the celebrated David Oppenheimer, a
Rabbi of Prague (ob. 12th Sept. 1736), whose pamphlet,
written in the form of a Responsum (printed before 1707), is
almost unknown, being omitted even in the printed catalogue
of his library, where there are many copies of it.

Various literary and other circumstances caused the Halachaic literature to increase in an incredible manner; and
although the greater part of it may not be of general interest,
yet it furnishes indispensable materials for the complete
history of Judaism, and will reward the patient inquirer
with fruitful results. On the other hand, the practical
requirements of the Halacha occasioned many valuable
monographies: for instance, those upon Jewish names,
by Abraham Motal (ob. 1658), Simha ben Gerson Cohen at Belgrade (1657), Samuel ben David

HALEVI in Germany (1668), and others. The study of
older writings caused the issue of many new editions, and
the adoption (particularly in the 16th century) of references
to passages (מראה מקום), so much neglected by the ancients,
of various kinds of indices and keys (מפתחות), and of other
practical aids to the use and study of the Halachaic and
Haggadistic literature (§ 26.): for example, the cross references (*Masora*) of the Talmud (1523), enlarged by JOSHUA
BOAS; the list of the passages of the Bible explained or
quoted in the Talmud (הגדות התלמוד, 1511), enlarged by
JOSHUA BOAS (1546), SIMON BEN ISAAC (Aschenburg?)
(1571–2), AARON PESARO (1583–4), and AARON BEN
SAMUEL (1690); a supplement to the Jerusalem Talmud,
which was published by JACOB SASPOSTAS at Amsterdam
(1650); a similar index to Jacob ben Asher's *Turim*, by
SABBATAI HASSAN (1652); the *Key* (ס' הזכרון), by ISMAEL
COHEN in Egypt (1543); an alphabetical index of subjects
by CHIJJA COHEN DI LARA (1753); &c.

The commentators, who generally borrowed from their
predecessors, became very prolix, and often lost sight of
their primary object, turning aside to something else, and
thus approaching more nearly to the Tosaphot (§ 9.); we
find even in this period supplements to the old Tosaphot, for
instance one by ISSACHAR BEN ISRAEL (1614). There are,
however, praiseworthy exceptions. We may mention some
of the most widely known, in the order of their subjects.
The Mishna was explained by OBADJA BERTINORO (ob.
1500— 1510) in the East, and a glossary was added by
LIPPMANN HELLER in Prague (1600), JACOB CHAGIS
(ob. 1689), EMANUEL RICCHI (1714–31), DAVID CHAJJIM
CORINALDI (1738–9), and DAVID PARDO BEN JACOB(1752):
a Spanish translation of it was made by JACOB ABENDANA
(ob. 1696 in London); and a Latin one by his brother ISAAC
ABENDANA, which was used by Surenhusius. AARON IBN
CHAJJIM of Fez (1609) wrote a commentary on Sifra;
DAVID PARDO on Sifri; and MOSES FRANKFURT (1712) on
the Mechilta. The Babylonian Gemara had been already, for
some time, treated in so-called novels (§ 9.); and ingenious
explanations of this kind, either shorter or longer, in the

form of glosses, were written by MEIR LUBLIN (ob. 1616);
SOLOMON LURIA (1581–1587); SAMUEL EDELES (Eidels)
(1612 sqq.), who also, in a separate work, gave a glossary of
passages of the Haggada; MEIR SCHIFF at Fulda (1734);
JACOB JOSHUA LEMBERG; and others; critical notes were
also given by the learned ELIA WILNA (ob. 1797). The
Jerusalem Gemara was expounded by DAVID FRAENKEL
at Dessau (1743); and BEZALEL ASHKENASI in Egypt
(1530) made a collection from the old Tosaphot. The Halachot of Isaac Alfasi were edited and expounded by JOSHUA
BOAS in Italy (1554), and MENACEM DAVID BEN ISAAC
TIKTIN (1597); and the code of Maimonides by JOSEPH
KARO (1574) and EPHRAIM BEN NAPHTALI SHOR who
completed his work 1615; by ABRAHAM DE BOTON (1609);
JEHUDA ROSANES (ob. 1727); JEHUDA AJJASCH (1747);
ISAAC NUÑEZ BELMONTE (1771), &c., whose chief object
was to exercise their ingenuity in bringing the conclusions
of the great teacher into harmony with the older authorities,
especially in Germany (Poland), where the "difficult passages of Maimonides" became almost a stereotyped expression; and a key to it was written by SAMUEL ATHIA of
Tunis (16th century). The four Turim of Jacob ben Asher
were commented by JOSEPH KARO, ABRAHAM BEN ABIG-
DOR a Rabbi at Prague (1540); JOSHUA FALK COHEN
(beginning of the 17th century); JOEL SIRKS (1631–70);
and JOSEPH ISCAPHA (אישקאפה, 1658).

An epoch is made in the history of the Halacha by a work
said, in a legend, to have been miraculously composed, viz.
the *Schulchan Aruch* by JOSEPH KARO at Safat (written
1554–7, published 1565), who arranged the practical part
of his subject in four divisions, according to the example of
Jacob ben Asher, and adopted the brief style of a law book,
imitating Maimonides in the exclusion of all discussion. Additions concerning the different usages of their respective
countries, consisting, for the most part, in elaborate and
ascetic observances, were written nearly at the same time
by MOSES ISSERLS (1570–7) for Poland, and by JACOB
CASTRO (ob. 1610) for Egypt. These contained the general
conclusion and result of the practical observances of the

exiles, arranged according to the parts and chapters of the
Tur and the Schulchan Aruch, for the benefit of succeeding
writers (*Aharonim*, אחרונים), who directed their attention to
practical results. The subjects of the 3rd and 4th parts (respecting women and jurisprudence) found less application in
practice, and were therefore less studied. The best-known
commentators and editors of Karo's Schulchan Aruch (who
generally completed the text from Books of Sentences) are,
JOSHUA FALK COHEN (1614); ZEBI HIRSH BEN JOSEPH
COHEN (1646); DAVID BEN SAMUEL LEVI OSTROW
(1648); SABBATI COHEN (ob. before 1663 in Leipnik);
ABRAHAM ABBELE COHEN GUMBINNER (ob. 1682);
MOSES BEN ISAAC JEHUDA LIMA of Slonim (1670); HIL-
LEL BEN NAPHTALI (ob. 1690 at Zolkiew); HEZEKIAH DE
SILVA (1692); MOSES CHABIB of Constantinople (ob. 1696);
MOSES JEKUTIEL KOFMAN COHEN BEN ABIGDOR (1700);
ISAIAH BEN ABRAHAM (1708); JEHUDA ASHKENASI
(1742); JONATHAN EIBENSCHÜTZ (ob. 1757) who was
very discursive; and CHAJJIM COHEN of Aleppo (ob. cir.
1662) who expounded in a Kabbalistic sense. A list of
authorities, with an explanation of difficult words, was given
by MOSES ZEBI RIBKAS (1662); alphabetical indices or
keys were added by BENJAMIN BEN JECHIEL LEVI at
Lublin (1617), and the same was done to the 4th part
only by SAMUEL BEN ALEXANDER (1691). Of various
other forms in which the subject of this work was treated,
we may mention the Rhymes by ISAAC CHAJUT at Cracow
(1591); ISAAC BEN NOAH of Meseritz (1599); a certain
JECHIEL (1616); and others; also the forms of Problems or
Riddles already employed by JACOB LANDAU (end of the
15th century), and later by ISAAC BEN JOSHUA BEN
ABRAHAM (1606), and some quite recent authors. A popular
Hebrew Compendium was composed by JOSEPH PARDO of
London (edited by his son DAVID PARDO, 1686), and another
in Spanish by a certain MEIR, probably in Turkey (about
1568); the last-named writer admonished his brethren not to
print his work in Roman characters, as an anonymous author
had done in the case of a compendium of Jacob ben Asher's
four Turim, for the use of the Crypto-Christians in Flan-

ders (?); it was, nevertheless, reprinted in that way by
MOSES ALTARAS (1609). Finally JOSHUA BEN BOAZ IBN
BARUCH (1554), in his various Indices mentioned above,
also furnished the Talmud with references to Maimonides,
Moses Coucy, Jacob ben Asher, and Joseph Karo's law
works, thus establishing a connexion between discussions
and decisions. More important and independent collections,
however, were made upon the Tur and the Shulchan Aruch,
for example, at an earlier period, by JACOB LANDAU in Italy
(1487), and afterwards by MORDECHAI JAFE at Prague
(1594–1599), whose commentator is ELIA SPIRA of Prague
in Poland (1689–1712); the most learned of all was written
by CHAJJIM BENVENISTE in the East (1658 sqq.).

The older form of works on the 613 Commandments had
already issued in the rhymed and mostly liturgical *Azharot*
(§ 19. and § 28.), which now became again little else than
memorial verses. Such were composed by DAVID VITAL
of Patras (1536), and JEKUTIEL BEN SOLOMON LEVI
(1696). The few dissertations on that subject were either
mere balances between the conflicting opinions of earlier
writers, like that by MOSES BEN ABRAHAM MAT of Przemislaw (1581); or Compendia, like that of J. Corbeil's
Amude Gola by JEKUTIEL (SALMAN) BEN MOSES (1579),
and that of Moses Coucy's work, probably made by Mün-
sterus with the assistance of a Jew. There exist some
more independent works by ELEAZER ASKERI in the East
(1588) and JEHUDA BEN THILLEL of Schwersenz (1693),
translated into Latin by Schultenius. The trifling spirit of
the time is also here exemplified in the deduction of the 613
commands from the 613 letters of the Decalogue, alluded
to by David Vital, and treated especially by JACOB BEN
JEKUTIEL in Germany (1627).

Finally, to this class belong, besides many miscellanies
which can scarcely be brought under definite heads, the
Sentences (שאלות ותשובות), generally arranged according
to the codex (or indexed), of which almost every Rabbi or
teacher of importance made a collection, generally also
publishing it " In majorem Dei gloriam." Amongst the
hundreds of authors, we will mention only the following

(omitting, indeed, the greater number of those who have been already mentioned in this section): MOSES ALASHKAR in Egypt; BENJAMIN (SEEB) BEN MATATJA (1534); JACOB BERAB (ob. 1546); his opponent LEVI IBN CHABIB; MEIR KATZENELLENBOGEN at Padua (ob. 1565); DAVID IBN SIMRA (ABI SAMIRA); JOSEPH IBN LEBB (till 1579); SAMUEL DI MEDINA (ob. 1589); ISAAC ADARBI (1585); SAMUEL COHEN in Saloniki; MOSES DE TRANI; and MOSES GALANTE (1608); all in the East; LÖWE BEN BEZALEL (the "high Rabbi Löwe," ob. 1609) and EPHRAIM LENT-SCHÜTZ (ob. 1619) at Prague; CHAJJIM SABBATAI (ob. 1647); SERACHJA GOTA (Gutta? ob. 1648); ABRAHAM BRODA in the East (1696); ABRAHAM CHAJJIM SHOR in Poland (1628); SIMON LUZZATTO at Venice (1630–60); GERSON ASHKENASI at Metz; AARON BEN SAMUEL KAIDENOWER at Frankfurt on Main (ob. 1676); CHAJJIM JAIR BACHRACH (ob. 1702); DAVID OPPENHEIMER at Prague (1690–1737); MOSES CHAGIS of Jerusalem at Altona (1704—1738); ELIA ALFANDARI at Constantinople (1719); ELIA COHEN at Smyrna; ZEBI HIRSH ASHKENASI at Hamburg (1711); SAMSON MARPURGO at Ancona (ob. 1740); MEIR EISENSTADT (ob. 1744), JOSEPH STEIN-HARD (1747–1774), and ARJE LÖB BEN ASHER, at Cracow and Metz (1739 sqq.).

Methodological Works were written by SOLOMON FINZI (not Panzi) of Rovigo (before 1622); JOSEPH IBN VERGA (1554); JOSEPH KARA; IMMANUEL SEFARDI; DAVID BEN SIMRA; SAMUEL ALVALENSI (not Albalnasi); IBN MUSA; (the writings of the last four were edited by ABRA-HAM IBN AKRA, 1599—1601); AARON IBN CHAJJIM of Fez (1609); ELIEZER RIETI at Conian (1612); SOLOMON ALGASI (1639—1663); JACOB CHAGIS (1647); SOLOMON DA OLIVEYRA (1688); MOSES BEN DANIEL of Rohatin (not Rathen) (1693); MOSES CHAGIS (1704) and DAVID MELDOLA at Amsterdam (1754), both of whom treated of the ethical and disciplinary part; CHIJJA COHEN DE LARA at Amsterdam (1753); MOSES CHAJJIM LUZ-ZATTO, who tried to reduce the method of the Talmud to logical principles, an attempt which, at any rate, was more

honest and meritorious than the pretended mathematical
formulæ of Dr. Hirschfeld's " Halachische Exegese ;" Luzzatto's friend JEKUTIEL WILNA, who also intended to write
a Methodological work for the use of young persons; and
MALACHI COHEN (1767), whose learned work has recently
been republished with the notes of JESAIA BERLIN.

§ 26.]   *Homiletics, Ethics, Religious Philosophy, and
Kabbala.*

The civil and social life of the Jew, even in its smallest
manifestation of the moral and religious sense, was closely
and rigidly bound by the Law ; the *Pilpul* was subtle and
complicated for the understanding, and the *Pesak Din* was
a dry exercise of memory ; but all these circumstances, together with the necessity of the unlearned for education and
improvement in religion and morals, combined to direct attention to the old institution of public lectures, which, as early
as the 15th century, had inherited an immense treasure of
literature, of great authority for the connexion of different
parts, and presenting every variety of form:—Bible, Talmud, and Midrash, seen through the medium of the earlier
expositors, and frequently interwoven or simply connected
with the Halacha.   The Rabbi, or the travelling preacher
(דרשן, *Darshan*),—particularly known in Germany as Moral
Teacher (מוכיח), and Expounder of Sagas (מגיד, *Maggid*),—
collected his *discourses* (דרשות, דרושים) into a cycle according
to the Perikope text, in the same manner as he arranged his
decisions according to the *Shulchan Aruch.*   Others, often
without any apparent reason, imitated this fashionable and
convenient form of literature.   The lectures, properly so
called, were generally delivered in the language of the
country (although the exiled Spaniards and Portuguese
carried their own to the East and the North), with oratorical
method and art, for which theoretical and practical rules
were framed ; and they were published either in their original
language or in a Hebrew translation for the use of the whole
Israelitish nation.   But in Germany, after the 16th century,
the language, hitherto pure, was corrupted into the so-called

Jewish German.   In the absence of institutions for improvement and instruction (except the Halacha) this system of
lectures also either fell into decay, or went astray among
the mazes of the Halacha described above, or else lost itself
in the trifling fancies of the Kabbalistical interpretations,
against which the censure of well-meaning learned men, as,
for example, that of Del Medigo and others, and the efforts of
M. Ch. Luzzatto to introduce general principles for Rhetoric
and Homiletics (1742), availed as little as the mockery of
the enemies of the Jews, until the period of the Mendels-
sohnian revolution.

The general tendency of Halacha and Haggada to produce
something new, and the desire to furnish the young and unlearned with the appearance of learning, gave rise to the novels
(חידושים) on the Pentateuch, a fashionable literature of the
18th century; e. g. one in question and answer by JOSHUA
(FALK) LISSER at Hamburgh, printed at least seven times,
(1699—1738); and several collections gathered principally
from the lectures of celebrated Rabbies, such as ISRAEL
BEN ISAAC LEVI, ABRAHAM BRODA BEN SAUL, &c.,
published under various titles (חידושי הגאונים, אסיפת חכמים,
דברי חכמים).   They were the sources from which the young
student at the academy (ישיבה), drew his "specimen erudi-
tionis" called *Pshetel* or *Pshetchen* (a diminutive of פשט),
or *Gleicher* (a German Hebraism), being too often just the
contrary of what the name implies.

Homiletics, properly so called, in its literary formation,
is distinguished from exegesis (§ 28.) not so much by
practical tendency, as by the above-mentioned artificial
arrangement, especially by its making the treatment of
the Haggada and Midrash a particular, if not the principal, point; and it is thus connected with the adding of
references, the collections, and the real and verbal explanations of all the Haggadistical authorities (§ 5.), by references
to the Bible and to the various methods of treatment used by
the writers of the middle ages (Philosophers and Kabbalists);
all these have again many points of contact with the Halacha,
and, moreover, afford some useful information for modern
criticism and history.   To this class belong, for instance, the

famous abridgement of the Haggada from both the Gemaras
by JACOB IBN CHABIB, called *En Jacob*, and in later editions (1566 sqq.) *En Israel*, and another similar work published anonymously in 1511, and confounded by bibliographers
with the former.   Jacob Ibn Chabib intended to give in
this anthology not only the Talmudical text, but also extracts
from the most celebrated expositors (Rashi, Tosaphot, Nachmanides, Ibn Aderet, Jomtob ben Abraham, and Nissim
Gerondi), and occasionally explanations of his own.   This
he did in the parts which he himself published; but after his
death, which occurred before the publication of the larger
portion (the seven last Orders of the Talmud), his son LEVI
IBN CHABIB completed the work in a very imperfect manner as respects the explanations.   The work consequently
became the subject of various others; some authors wrote
commentaries comprising a selection from the text, and
also the explanations given, which were printed with the
work itself, for instance JOSIA PINTO at Damascus (1643);
others made books of reference to his explanations, e. g.
ZACHARIA PORTO (1675), whose list was augmented by
the printer S. PROOPS (1725).   Some editors omitted all
the explanations (even the prefaces of the author and his
son, which are only to be found complete in the first and
most rare edition), and gave the mere text, or a short
exposition extracted from various authors; others wrote independent commentaries upon the text (some of which are
named by Azulai sub voce); finally, to the passages collected by J. Chabib under 12 heads, JEHUDA DI MODENA
(1625) added others with his own explanations.   Valuable
independent commentaries, or novels, upon the Haggada
(חידושי הגדות) were written by SAMUEL EDELS (1627) and
many others; and on the Jerusalem Gemara by SAMUEL
JAFE at Constantinople (1590), and JOSHUA BENVENISTE
(cir. 1648).   The Easter Haggada offers (as in the former
period § 19. p. 167.) various points of connexion with the
subsequent expositions.   Indices of the passages of the Bible
quoted in the Babylon and Jerusalem Talmuds were composed by several authors mentioned above (§ 25.); Alphabetical References to the Sagas connected with Biblical

personages, by JEHUDA BEN BENDET (1688), and SIMON
BEN JEHUDA PEISER of Lissa (1728); Alphabetical Lexica
of subjects, and Concordances of the Talmud, Midrash, &c.,
by MOSES PIGO (1554); NAPHTALI ALTSCHÜLER (1602);
ELIEZER RIETI (1612); MOSES RAPHAEL D'AGUILAR
(cir. 1660); ABRAHAM BEN JEHUDAH PRZEMISLAW of
Olianow (1691); DAVID BEN HIRZ POSNER of Krotoschin
(1691); SIMON AKIBA BÄR, and SELIGMAN LEVI of
Zeckendorf (1702); SAMSON MODON (cir. 1725); DAVID
NIETO (1727); and ISAAC LAMPRONTI (ob. 1756) who shows .
the most astonishing industry. The works of the latter were
bought by the Library of Paris; but the publication of the
last volumes, at the expense of the government, announced
when this essay was first written, is still one of the many
pia desideria in Jewish literature. For the *Kabbala* in particular we have the *New Jalkut* (1648), the author of which
seems to be ISRAEL a Rabbi of Belcziz and Lublin; the
completion of it by NATHAN BEN JACOB BONN at Frankfurt; and the *Jalkut Reubeni* of REUBEN HOSHKE (1681).
Moreover commentaries were written on the Midrashim,
and particularly on the Midrash Rabboth (§ 5. n. 2.) by
AARON BEN ASHER at Haleb; MEIR BENVENISTI at
Saloniki (1560); NAPHTALI (HIRZ) BEN MENAHEM KRA-
KAU (1569); ISSACHAR BEN NAPHTALI COHEN in Palestine
(1584); SAMUEL JAFE (cir. 1597); JEHUDA BEN MOSES
GADILIA (GEDALJA) (1594); and ELIEZER ARCHA at Hebron
(1630); a commentary on the Jalkut was written by ABRA-
HAM GADILIA (1630—1640), and a key was composed by
ABRAHAM FONSECA at Hamburgh (1627), &c. In Germany
some older ethical and historical Midrashim were also trans-
lated: for instance, the book *Hajashar* (§ 10.) by JACOB BEN
JIRMIJA HALEVI (1674), and the *Midrash of the Death of
Moses* by AARON BEN SAMUEL (1693). With the older
Talmudic-Aramaïc Dictionaries (§ 9.), and also with Hebrew
lexicography, are connected the explanatory works in various
languages by ELIA LEVITA (1527); MENAHEM LONSANO
in the East (1618); DAVID DE POMIS (1587); DAVID
COHEN DE LARA at Hamburgh (1638); BENJAMIN MUSA-
PHIA (1655); and ELIA WILNA (ob. 1797).

Ethics, moreover, are connected with the explanation of older writings (§ 12. C.), such as the Talmudic Treatise *Abot*, expounded by SAMUEL UCEDA (not Oseida) at Safet (1579); Bechai's *Duties of the Heart*, translated into Spanish by ZADDIK BEN JOSEPH FORMON (16th century, printed in Roman characters by DAVID PARDO at Amsterdam, 1610), and into Jewish German by REBECCA TIKTINER (Prague, 1609); and JEDAJA PENINI's rhetorical *Bechinat Olam* explained by SAMSON MARPURGO (1704); the Letters of Seneca were translated, but not published, by JEHUDA BRIEL (1712), and others. Besides these there were special moral writings for both the learned and unlearned, treating of the vanity of terrestrial things, exhorting to a moral and pious life, inculcating the most important moral and ceremonial precepts, introducing Haggadistical elements, and sometimes taking a rhetorical and poetical form (§ 29.). They are often composed in the language of the country, particularly in Jewish German, or translated into it; and, as popular books, they bear the stamp of various stages of cultivation. Thus we find ethical admonitions in the form of tablets to be fixed on the wall, e. g. by JIFTACH of Worms (cir. 1660), and ELCHANAN BEN ISSACHAR COHEN of Prostitz, who recommends his *Zier-Spiegel* (Looking-glass) published in Hebrew and German (1693) to be used even on the Sabbath. Indeed, long before Knigge, JOSEPH DACOSTA in his *Tractado de Cortesia* (1726) taught, amongst other things, the proper manner of behaviour at balls. These books were intended for the young; and there were also others, for example, one in Portuguese by SAMUEL DA LEON (1712), and a Catechism by ABRAHAM JAGEL (1595, translated into German in 1678); the Spanish *Fundamento Solido* of JEHUDA LEON PEREZ at Amsterdam (1729) seems to be something similar. Among the oldest and most widely known writings of this kind are, the Hebrew *Menorat Hamaor* by ISAAC ABOAB (first printed in 1514), translated into Spanish, and afterwards into German by MOSES FRANKFURT at Amsterdam (1722), and lately into pure German by Fürstenthal; and the *Sur Mera* against gambling by JEHUDA DE MODENA (1596), which has been translated into almost every language.   The following, moreover, deserve especial mention: GEDALJA IBN JAHJA, who wrote in a rhetorical style on the seven principal virtues of the Jews (cir. 1543); MOSES DE TRANI (1553); MOSES ALMOSNINO (in Spanish, 1567); the Kabbalist ELIA DE VIDAS (1575); his epitomisers, JACOB BEN MARDOCHAI POGETTO (1580), and JECHIEL MELLI (1623), both in Italy; his German translator, NATHAN HEKSHER (1750); ISAAC BEN MOSES ELLES at Cracow (1583); CHAJJIM BEN BEZALEL of Friedburg (ob. 1588); ABRAHAM ZAHALON (1595); ISAAC OBADJA BEN JACOB in Italy (1597); MOSES HENOCH, author of the *Brant-Spiegel* (1602); the authors of the anonymous *Rosengarten* (1609), and *Sitten-Spiegel* (1610); BENJAMIN BEN AARON SALNIK of Grodno (1577), erroneously called BENJAMIN ARDONO, who re-edited the *Weiberbuch* (1552); SHMELKA BEN CHAJJIM of Prague, who did the same (1629); ISAAC BEN ELJAKIM POSEN (1620); the author of the *Sepher Sichronot,* ISAAC JESHURUN, or according to others SAMUEL ABOAB (1631–51); JACOB ZAHALON (1665); ABRAHAM ISRAEL PEREIRA, who wrote in Spanish (1666–1671); JEHUDA BEN JOSEPH PUCHAWITZ at Pinsk (1681–1700); JOSEPH BEN ELIMELECH at Torbin (1690), who introduces poetry; ZEBI HIRSH KAIDENOVER, author of the favourite קב הישר (Hebrew and German, 1705); HÄHDEL KIRCHHAHN, author of the שמחת הנפש (1707); SOLOMON BEN SIMON WETZLAR, who wrote in German; ELIA COHEN at Smyrna (1712); ISAAC PINTO, the opponent of Voltaire (1762–1774), and many others.

Of those who founded their ethics on Scripture (§ 27.), we shall here mention only the celebrated favourite of the women, JACOB BEN ISAAC RABBINO, author of the *Zeena-u-Reena,* a title originating in a mistake about the motto. It would lead us too far from our present purpose to enter further into particulars respecting individual works; we shall therefore briefly remark, that in all times and places we find a struggle going on against abuses of every kind.   We take the following instances at random out of a great mass:— the remarks upon study by MOSES BEN ABRAHAM MAT (1584 91); the interesting essays on education by SAMUEL

BEN JACOB (16th century), and MOSES BEN AARON MO-
RAWCZIK at Lublin (1635); and the denunciation of luxury
in women by ISAAC ZOREF of Nikolsburg (1715).

Thus the pen and the press were engaged, with uninterrupted activity, in a variety of ways in the cause of religion.
But the intellectual movement necessary for this activity was
neither new nor original, nor was it free from external dis-
turbance.   The struggle of faith and authority with science
and philosophy, to which the most important changes in
Jewish literature belong, had already, some centuries before,
apparently ended in the dogmatic system founded upon
Aristotle, and in the fantastic eclecticism of the Kabbala;
and the broad battle-field had now become fertile soil.   By
means of some exploded applications of scholastic gymnastics
OBADJA SEFORNO (1537) easily demonstrated his 15 orthodox theses, speciously and with fatiguing uniformity, using
sometimes single axioms of the "inconsistent" Stagirite
himself as expounded by the Arabs, and at others pretended arguments from the Bible; and AARON BERACHJA
tells us, in a manuscript work, that it is said in some
Philosophical Writings that Aristotle denied prophecy, because, if any such existed, it would certainly have been
granted to himself.   The great changes subsequent to the
Middle Ages were much influenced by Judaism, but did
not produce a corresponding effect in return.   The Spanish
exiles, finding Greece and the East recently subjugated by
the Turks, who had not yet appropriated the Arabian
learning, gave themselves up entirely to the influence of
Oriental mysticism.   Neo-Platonism, the first-fruits of the
Classical studies which passed from Constantinople into Italy,
could thrive only on the soil of the Jewish Kabbala.   There
was not any new philosophy properly so called; the Jew
Spinoza was an immediate follower of Cartesius.   The
Christian Reformation in Germany was analogous to the
Karaitic movement in Judaism, and was founded upon a
knowledge of the Bible, that which related to the Old Testament being derived from the Jews (§ 23.).   The darkness
of the Middle Ages arrayed its latest, and sometimes vic-
torious, champions against the new and threatening light;

and superstition of all kinds found advocates.   Paracelsus
and his followers tried to popularise the mystic doctrine, in
the same way as others did the sciences in general.   The
same took place also among the Jews.

At the beginning of the 16th century the later Kabbala
had already found its way into the East and Poland.   JE-
HUDA CHAJJAT (1496); JOSEPH JAABEZ, the opponent of
philosophy; DAVID IBN JAHJA, the teacher of Widmanstadt (§ 23.); JOSEPH IAYTAZAC; DAVID IBN ABI SIMRA
in Egypt; ABRAHAM IBN SABA of Lisbon, perhaps at
Adrianople, in the beginning of the 16th century; ISAAC
GIACON; his pupil ABRAHAM LEVI BEN ELIEZER, called
"the old" (הזקן), and erroneously said to have been a
pupil of Isaac Loria, in Turkey, who, in a manuscript
work, opposes the students of ancient wisdom according
to private judgment (סברא) unassisted by a teacher, and
was the author of a remarkable treatise against the invo-
cation of angels, which deserves to be published; MEIR
IBN GABBAI (1523–1539) in Italy and Constantinople; the
fanatical proselyte SOLOMON MOLCHO at Mantua (1529);
SOLOMON ALKABIZ at Safet (fl. 1529-53); MATATIA DE-
LACRUT in Poland and Italy (cir. 1530); and the renowned
MOSES CORDOVERO in Palestine (ob. 1570), who is said to
have had a revelation from the prophet Elias, at the end
of that century; are the names of the authors of the most
important monographies and commentaries of this class. The
opposition of ELIA DEL MEDIGO and others had had no
effect.   ISAAC DE LATTES in Italy collected Sentences for
the printing of the Zohar (1558); against which the voices of
the Rabbies had been raised in consequence, it was said, of
the previous burning of the Talmud; and EMANUEL BEN
JEKUTIEL BENEVENTO at Mantua employed his money
and philological learning in the publication of Kabbalistical writings (1558–1560).   A new phase of the Kabbala
was formed by the school of the famous oral teacher ISAAC
LORIA ASHKENASI at Safet (1534–1572): amongst his
followers we may particularise, as an author (see below),
CHAJJIM VITAL CALABRESE (ob. 1620 in Damascus), and
as apostles, ISRAEL SERUK who travelled in Europe, and

his son-in-law SOLOMON BEN CHAJJIM MEINSTREL of
Lautenburg at Safet.   In a very short time the master and
some of his pupils were made the subjects of miraculous
legends; and a new flood of supposititious writings and
interpolations threatened to overwhelm the history and
criticism of this literature.   The restored Kabbala was not
a systematic theosophy, but was a bold and conscious in-
trusion of the Kabbalistic doctrine, now called the *Theoretical Kabbala* (קבלה עיונית), upon practical and religious
life, thus forming the *Practical Kabbala* (קבלה מעשית).
Against the latter it was now necessary for the orthodox
Halacha to defend its authority amongst the masses, in the
same way that philosophy had formerly withstood the Kabbala in general in the narrow circle of independent thinkers,
until the aberrations of astrology, &c., had laid claim to the
highest authority in religion.   Now, however, the popularised
Kabbala (a Hebrew translation of the book Zohar is at least
as old as 1506) made its way into all branches of life and
literature.   The secret meaning ascribed to the letters of the
Bible, to the signs (vowels, accents, even ornaments), and
to their Masoretical rules, and the higher intention (כוונה)
attributed to the prayers and ceremonies, reached their
greatest pitch; and to the exercise of this knowledge was
ascribed a powerful influence in the affairs of the present and
future worlds.   It was no wonder that at last this Kabbala
regarded the Zohar in the same light as the Bible and Shulchan Aruch, and that it led to a degradation of Judaism;
for instance, to the extravagances of the Sabbatians and of
the Chassidim, amongst whom appeared the last effort of
mysticism, the apotheosis of their master.   A compendium
of Kabbala, perhaps by a pupil of M. Ch. Luzzatto, extant
in MS., and written in the form of question and answer,
defends these doctrines against attacks from different quar-
ters; and amongst the objections answered are those of philosophers believing only in scientific demonstrations, who
called the Kabbala Anthropomorphism; of others who said
that it led to apostasy, by suggesting an analogy between
the Ten Sefirot and the Christian doctrine of the Trinity
(an observation as old as the 10th century); of others who

merely preferred the simple Jewish faith without speculation or philosophy ; of others who objected to learning from
writings without teachers ; and of others who said that life
was scarcely long enough for the study of the Talmud alone,
and that the Kabbala was too dark and deep to be fathomed.

The strictly Kabbalistic literature of this period consists
principally in commentaries on the Bible, and the books
Jezira and Zohar (the last being also furnished with indices
and keys of all kinds); and in super-commentaries on Nachmanides, Bechai ben Asher, Recanati, Gikatilla, and other
older writers, and also on LORIA's pretended traditions, and
the writings of MOSES CORDUERO and CHAJJIM VITAL.
Besides this, the Kabbala gave a colouring to homiletical,
ethical, and other writings.

It may be considered certain that ISAAC LORIA neither wrote
himself, nor, as an oral teacher or leader, at all encouraged
his pupils to write down his ideas, if such a word is applicable to his fancies.   If he has any literary merit, it consists in
his having written some notes of critical value on the margins
of older printed books and MSS., e. g. those published upon
the Zohar, some of which, however, even the editor and corrector, Moses Zacut, did not believe to be by him.   CHAJJIM
VITAL, whom later Kabbalists pronounce to be the only
authentic interpreter of Loria's ideas, thought it necessary to
apologise for writing down the mysteries of his teacher by
the altered circumstances of literature.   His example gave
a great impulse to his fertile followers; and not long afterwards AARON BERECHJA of Modena declared (in a manuscript work, 1629) that he had somewhere read, that it is the
duty of every student to write down the principles of the
Kabbala.   With respect to the authenticity and arrangement of these writings, nearly all of which bear the name
of Chajjim, and are extant in hundreds of MSS. (the very
few that are printed having appeared together with other
older Kabbalistic works at Korez, 1784–5), we find an *Apparatus criticus* of no less than four recensions; and Chajjim himself began his comprehensive work with such care,
that he distinguished what he found taught in Loria's name
from what he considered as authentic tradition.   But his

own acount of the different ways in which he arranged
and rearranged his materials, and the accounts of those who
again prepared his writings for the press (viz. his son SA-
MUEL VITAL at Damascus; the polygrapher JACOB ZEMACH,
a Portuguese physician in Palestine, 1619-52; and his German pupil MEIR POPPERS at Jerusalem, ob. 1662), and lastly
a comparison of the different forms in which the same formulæ
and plays upon letters appear and reappear, must make every
honest student despair of ever producing light and order out
of this vast mass of confusion; and we might sum up our
judgement, like an ingenious bibliographer, in the words,
" The dream of Pharaoh is one."

The most remarkable authors are: NAPHTALI (HIRZ)
TREVES BEN ELIEZER (cir. 1530); ABRAHAM GALANTE
(1568), and MOSES GALANTE (ob. 1618), at Safet; SIMON
BEN SAMUEL (1560); ELIA DE VIDAS in Palestine (1575);
MORDECHAI DATO in Italy (1570–1600); SAMUEL AREPOL
(1576-1586); SAMUEL UCEDA of Safet (1579); ISRAEL
BEN MOSES at Lublin (1592), whose work was translated
by Voisin; ELIA LOANZ (1606–1620); MENAHEM-ASARJA
FANO at Mantua (ob. 1620); ISSACHAR (BAER) BEN MOSES
PETACHJA at Krzeminez (1609-1611), who tried in various
ways to make the Zohar accessible; ELEAZAR PERLS ALT-
SCHÜLER at Prague, who collected older books and MSS.
(1609–1616); SABBATAI (SHEFTEL) HORWITZ (1612–17);
his renowned kinsman ISAIAH HORWITZ at Frankfurt,
Prague, and Safet (1622, seq.), author of the ethical של"ה
(*Shene luhot habrit*) of which compendiums were made by
JECHIEL EPSTEIN in Prossnitz (1683) and SAMUEL DAVID
OTTOLENGO in Italy (1705); ABRAHAM JAFE KALMANKAS
(1652); CHAJJIM COHEN of Aleppo, who was censured for
introducing the Kabbala into the *Schulchan Aruch* (§ 25.);
two Germans of the name of NATHAN SPIRO, the one (ob.
1603) at Cracow, the other (of Jerusalem, ob. 1662) at
Rheggio; ABRAHAM ASULAI (ob. 1644); NAPHTALI HIRZ
BEN EICHANAN JACOB in Frankfurt on the Main (1648),
a suspected author; ABRAHAM CHASKUNI and ABRAHAM
COHEN HERERA (IRIRA) in Holland (1659); REUBEN
HOSHKE (ob. 1673), author of the *Jalkut Reubeni*, an imita-

tion of the old Jalkut (§ 9.); DAVID DI LIDA (of Lithu-
ania) at Amsterdam (ob. before 1710); MOSES ZAKUTO
at Mantua (ob. 1697); the voluminous writer SAMSON
OSTROPOL (1655 seq.); ABRAHAM ROVIGO (1701–1710);
ALEXANDER SÜSSKIND at Metz, who wrote for Professor
Ouseel in Leyden (1708); NEHEMIAH CHAJJUN (1713–
1716), against whom a vehement controversy was carried on
from London to Mantua, among others by JOSEPH ERGAS,
DAVID NIETO, MOSES CHAGIS, JEHUDA BRIEL (ob. 1722),
and EMANUEL RICCHI (ob. 1743); and lastly the remarkable fanatic and poet MOSES CHAJJIM LUZZATTO (1727),
who, according to the opinion of Professor S. D. Luzzatto,
attempted to effect a reformation of mysticism.

Besides the Kabbala, Religious Philosophy employed
itself principally in the explanation of the older recognised and more important writings: for instance, the *Cusari* of Jehuda Halevi was explained by JEHUDA MOS-
CATO (1573) and ISRAEL SAMOZC (ob. 1772) at Brody,
and translated into Spanish by JACOB ABENDANA (ob.
1663) at Amsterdam; the *Moreh* of Maimonides by JO-
SEPH BEN ISAAC HALEVI (1611–1614), MORDECHAI
JAFE, and others; the *Ikarim* of Albo by GEDALJA LIP-
SHATZ (1618), &c. A compendium of the *Summa* of
Thomas Aquinas was written by JACOB ZAHALON (ob.
1693), but never printed. Besides the treatises, excursuses, digressions, &c., included in the commentaries on
the Bible, sermons, and popular dogmatical (ethical) writings, there are also monographies of all kinds in various
languages, mostly by Spanish, Dutch, and Italian authors,
which are bright points in this melancholy period: for
instance, the works of OBADJA SFORNO (ob. 1550); ASARJA
DE ROSSI (§ 23.); JEHUDA (LEO) DE MODENA (1571–1648);
MORDECHAI JAFE in Germany (1600); the wandering physician JOSEPH DEL MEDIGO (ob. 1655); MANOAH HEN-
DEL in Poland (ob. 1612); ISAAC JESHURUN at Hamburg
(1663); MANASSEH BEN ISRAEL (1632–1651); LEO DEL
BENE (1646); SIMON (SIMCHA) LUZZATTO, who in his
Socrate, dedicated to the Venetian Senate, proves the insuf-
ficiency of natural knowledge (1651); NAPHTALI HIRSH

GOSLAR at Halberstadt, who a century later opposed philosophy, particularly the *prima materia*, partly in rhyming
prose; DAVID NIETO (ob. 1728 in London), author of the
Second Cusari against the Karaites and the followers of
Cartesius and Copernicus; and many others, whose writings
were not confined to the circle of Jewish readers.

§ 27.] *The Bible and Hebrew Language.*

The Exegesis of this period, which branched out into
Homiletics (§ 26.), gathered into itself all the earlier studies
to such an extent as to cause them to degenerate. The
Spanish School, like the German (which continued to regard
the Haggada and Midrash as authorities in exegesis), became much involved in trite philosophical distinctions and
pretended Kabbalistic mysteries; and this was the cause of
the frequent explanation of the Commentary of Rashi (a
Judæo-German extract of which was made by JEHUDA BEN
NAPHTALI, 1560); and even of the super-commentaries, e. g.
that of ELIA MISRACHI (1527). In this manner so rich a
treasure of thought, and such a variety of methods of exegesis were brought in, that even literary artifices and tricks
were at last considered admissible; e. g. the explanation of
passages of the Bible in different ways (אופנים): in 26 by
MOSES MARGALIOT (1589); in 50 by MOSES BEN JESAIA
COHEN (1721); in 70 by REUBEN DAVID TEBEL (1626);
in 210 by JEDIDJA GOTTLIEB BEN ABRAHAM of Lemberg
(1671); in 252 out of 1000 by NATHAN SPIRA (ob. 1633);
and in 345 by ELIA BEN ABRAHAM ÖTTINGEN (1642).
Of the fashionable " Novels " we have already spoken above
(§ 26. p. 221.).

The most important Biblical commentators are: the two
JAABEZ (1492—1583); JOHANAN ALLEMANNO in Italy
(cir. 1500); MEIR ARAMA (1505-12); JOSEPH TAYTAZAC
at Saloniki (cir. 1520); JOSEPH IBN JAHJA BEN DAVID
in Italy (1527-1528); ISAAC BEN SOLOMON COHEN at
Constantinople (1549); SOLOMON ATHIA (1549), who in
the preface to his commentary mentions the learned men of
his acquaintance; the family SFORNO in Italy; SOLOMON
IBN MELECH of Fez, at Constantinople (1554), who was

celebrated as a learned compiler of the older grammatical Exegetes, and whose works were translated into Latin (completed by JACOB ABENDANA, 1661); MOSES BEN EISAK ENGERLEIN at Cracow (1561); MOSES ALSHECH (more properly ALSHEIKH) at Safet (1563), celebrated rather than studied, on account of his philosophical prolixity; VIDAL ZARFATI at Fez (1560); MOSES NADJARA (NAGARA) (1571), whose exposition was rather of a Haggada-Halacha character; BARUCH IBN JAISH BEN ISAAC at Constantinople; ELISHA GALLIKO (1576); ELIEZER ASHKENASI BEN ELIA, latterly in Poland (1576–1584); ABRAHAM MENAHEM COHEN PORTA at Cremona (1582); SAMUEL VALERIO in the Morea (1586); ABRAHAM BEN JEHUDA CHASAN at Lublin; SOLOMON DURAN BEN ZEMACH in Africa (1593); BARUCH IBN BARUCH at Venice (1598–99); SOLOMON BEN ISAAC HALEVI (1600); ABRAHAM GAVISON, an Arabic scholar (ob. 1605); MOSES ALBELA (before 1600); SAMUEL LANIADO at Haleb; his son ABRAHAM at Venice (1603—1619); EPHRAIM LENTSHÜTZ (or Lenczic) at Bamberg and Prague (1608); MORDECHAI COHEN at Safet (1610); AARON BEN DAVID COHEN at Ragusa; CHAJJIM FINZI at Urbino (1631); the physician JACOB LOMBROSO, who gave a grammatical explanation and translated the difficult words into Spanish (1639); ABRAHAM HEILBRON at Lublin (1639); SAMUEL COHEN of Pisa (1650), whose works were of a philosophical character; MOSES DE MERCADO (ob. 1652 at Amsterdam); SOLOMON MARINO BEN ISAAC (1652); SEEB ABRAHAM of Brzesc (1685); MOSES CHEFEZ, called GENTILE of Trieste, at Venice (ob. 1711 at the age of 48, not 103 years), author of a philosophical exposition of the Pentateuch, of great prolixity, and exhibiting much research in recent Christian literature; SELIG BEN ISAAC MARGALIOT (1712); DAVID CHASAN BEN CHAJJIM at Amsterdam (1724); CHAJJIM (not Abraham Chajjim) COHEN of Poland (?) at Hebron (1750); and the physician AARON EMRICH, super-commentator of Ibn Ezra (1765). Commentaries and glossaries to the various Targums were written by MARDOCHAI LORIA (1580); JACOB (KOPPEL) BEN SAMUEL (1584); the hymnologist MOSES COHEN of Corfu (cir. 1588), not published;

David ben Jacob Sczebrin at Prague (1609); Chajjim-
Pheibel (not Abraham) ben David at Hanau (1614);
Eljakim Rothenburg (1618); and Mardochai ben
Naphtali of Cracow, who died while his work was printing at Amsterdam (1671–7); all these authors and their
works, although useful for a knowledge of the Chaldee
version, have been neglected by Christian, and even by
recent Jewish, authors on the subject. We may here mention also the Hebrew translation of the 2 Targum Esther
by David ben Elia (Constantinople, 1732). The period
of the *Biurists,* or latest exegete, begins with Mendelssohn's edition of the Bible; they wrote under the influence
of Christian biblical studies, which had made some progress
in the meantime.

With the various editions of the Bible are connected
critical annotations, based upon the comparison of MSS.,
and on grammatical and Masoretic studies, and monographies
on the Masora; such as those by Elia Levita, the founder
of the true view of the origin of punctuation; Jacob ben
Chajjim of Tunis, corrector of the first Bible printed
with perfect Masora (1525), afterwards baptized (ob. before
1538); Menahem Rabba ben Moses at Padua (1582);
Joseph ben Shneor Cohen at Constantinople (1598);
Joseph ben Samuel Ibn Rei (? רײ), who adds some ethical applications (1607); and the sound grammarian Menahem Lonsano of Jerusalem (1618). Sixty ponderous
old works, and many MSS. of the Bible, among which
was that of Toledo of the year 1277 (now Cod. Rossi 782),
were the sources from which Solomon Norzi at Mantua
(1626) drew his celebrated remarks, forming the foundation
of Hahn's Bible. The expositions of Elia Levita were
completed by Samuel (Shmelka) ben Chajjim of Prague
(1610), and others, who however gradually introduced critical, Kabbalistic, and other unsuitable explanations. Among
the latter we may mention: Jacob ben Isaac, Rabbi at
Zansmer (1616); his son Jehuda (1650); Meir Angel at
Safet (1622); Jedidja Gottlieb ben Abraham at Cracow (1644); David (Teble) ben Benjamin of Posen at
Hamburg (1663); Aaron ben Samuel, who published a

specimen (1690); JOSEPH BEN MOSES FRANKFURT (1725);
DAVID VITERBI at Mantua (1748); ANSCHEL WORMS
(1760); and his adversary JOSEPH BEN DAVID ESCHWE;
in a Kabbalistic sense, JACOB (KOPPEL) BEN AARON of
Saslaw (1686–7), an extract from whose work was made by
JEKUTIEL LASI BEN NACHUM (1718); and in an ethical
sense, ELIEZER BEN JEHUDA Rabbi of Pinczow (1723).

Translations of Biblical writings, especially of the Pericopes, are met with at an earlier period (§ 16.). The need
of educational works for youth, and of books for females and
persons ignorant of Hebrew, was on the increase; and consequently the translations which were at hand were published
in Hebrew or other characters (e. g. in the different Con-
stantinopolitan Polyglots of 1546 and 1547), emendated
and extended or rewritten; they were intended by the
booksellers or publishers for the use of Christians also.
MOSES BEN ELIA POBIAN (1576) translated the Bible into
Modern Greek; the Karaites of the Crimea have a Tartar
Bible and Liturgy; Turkish translations are extant in MS.,
as well as a Polish translation of the Psalter by MOSES
BEN MORDECHAI (1510); and a learned society at Ferrara
published a Spanish translation of the Bible by ABRAHAM
USQUE (1553), parts of which were re-edited or translated
anew by MANASSEH BEN ISRAEL (1627), JACOB LOMBROSO
at Venice (1639), JACOB JEHUDA LEON at Amsterdam
(1671), MENDEZ DE CASTRO (1672), and JOSEPH FRANCO
SERRANO (1695). Rhymed paraphrases were published by
DAVID IBN ATTHAR MELO (1626); JUAN (not Moses)
DELGADO PINTO, who dedicated his poetry to Cardinal
Richelieu (1627); and DANIEL ISRAEL LOPEZ LAGUNA
at Jamaica (1720 not 1742). Homilies and reflections or
paraphrases in prose were given by ISAAC ABOAB (1681),
MOSES DIAZ BEN ISAAC (1705), and ISAAC ACOSTA
(1722), all three at Amsterdam. The Glossary, חשק שלמה,
was edited by GEDALJA CORDUERO (1588); the Targum
of the Canticles was translated probably by MOSES LANIADO
(1619). DE POMIS (1571) and others (e. g. ISAAC MORO-
SINI, 1586, and EPHRAIM BEN JOHANAN, 1589, both in
MS.) translated some parts of the Bible into Italian, but

the complete translation, planned by JEHUDA (LEO) DE MODENA, dwindled under the scissors of Catholic censure into a translation of the difficult expressions and passages, and an alphabetical glossary (1612). A similar cause may have hindered the publication of a perpetual glossary to the Bible by JEDIDJA of Rimini (1597), and also the Hebrew translation of some Apocryphal books by the same JEHUDA DE MODENA.

In Germany Luther's translation of the Bible was not without its influence on this literature; and Luther himself complains that an edition of the Prophets (according to Wolf the same as that of Worms, 1527) was made with the assistance of Jews, although it was in fact substantially the same as his own. The Jewish-German had become so indispensable that it was used by baptized missionaries, such as MICHAEL ADAM, whose translation of the Pentateuch and Megillot (Constance, 1544), made with the assistance of Paul Fagius, and published together with extracts from Hebrew commentators, was erroneously ascribed to ELIA LEVITA; this work produced a lasting effect upon the Jews (see below).

Indeed it seems strange that not only Biblical translations, but generally speaking the most valuable and popular (§ 28.) productions in the German language (all printed in Hebrew characters), originated away from Germany, or at least only on its frontiers, in Italy, Switzerland, and (later in the 16th century), in Poland; as if the German Jew felt the want of his native language the more in places where it was not spoken by his Christian countrymen. How the Jews viewed this circumstance may be illustrated by a striking instance. CHAJJIM BEN MENAHEM of Glogau, the author of a short manual for the use of females (shortly before 1717), in explaining the orthography of some names of towns in Poland and Germany, says, that in Germany the " Ishmaelites (meaning Christians) speak like the Israelites," as if German were the Jews' own language. But at the same time (1710) PHÖBUS of Metz, in a similar publication, expresses the opinion, that the neglect of Hebrew philology among the German Jews, in contradistinction to the Spaniards, is to be attributed to the different amount of pains

bestowed by them respectively upon their vernacular languages.   In fact among the various political and social circumstances which explain the singular course of the Jewish-
German language, we may reckon the impulse and example
given to the many German Jews in Northern Italy by their
Spanish and Italian brethren.

To return to our special subject, the Bible, we find far
fewer strict translations than paraphrases, rearrangements,
and versifications, the last perhaps originating in the preceding period.   But the whole subject has never been treated
by itself; and even the notices collected by Wolf have
not sufficiently attracted the attention either of the Ger-
manists (§ 28.), or of biblical scholars (e. g. Gesenius, in
his essay on translations of the Bible, De Wette, and others),
although Wagenseil confessed that he had learned the sense
of some passages of the Bible from Jewish expositions rather
than from any other source.   In fact a due appreciation and
proper classification of the various branches of this literature,
a part of which, perhaps, yet remains to be discovered, would
require a more careful investigation than the author of this
essay has hitherto been able to apply to it.   Only a superficial survey will therefore be attempted, omitting the
anonymous publications, many of which may be much older
than the editions as yet known.

A translation of the Psalms, published in 1545 under the
name of ELIA LEVITA, and afterwards often anonymously
reprinted (and also inserted in prayer-books), was revised by
ELJAKIM BEN JACOB, corrector of the press at Amsterdam (1703), and republished with an interlinear text, by
MICHAEL COHEN BEN ABRAHAM of Fürth (1723).   A
Jewish translation of the whole Bible was not completed
much before the end of the 17th century; but then two rival
editions appeared almost simultaneously. The first translator
was JEKUTIEL BLITZ (1676-8), corrector of the press for Uri
Phöbus; whose translation was revised by MEIR STERN;
and another revision (especially with respect to passages
considered as anti-Christian) was published by JOSEL WIT-
ZENHAUSEN, a compositor at Athia's printing-office, with
the assistance of the bibliographer SABBATAI BASS.   After

this meritorious undertaking, although another translation was published by ELIEZER SÖSSMAN in conjunction with his brother-in-law the historian MENAHEM BEN SOLOMON LEVI (1725-9), no real progress was made, until MENDELSSOHN by his translations gave an entirely new direction to Jewish literature.   Another kind of literature was originated by JEHUDA BEN MOSES NAPHTALI or LÖB BRZESC at Cremona; he revised (1560) Michael Adam's translation of the Pentateuch, and added extracts from Rashi, in German, which ISAAC BEN SAMSON COHEN, at Prague (1608-10), enriched from the Midrash, &c.   This was the origin of the *Teutsch Chummasch* or German Pentateuch, which in various slightly altered forms became, and in some parts of Poland and Russia continues to be, a favourite book with women; it was so popular that Isaac's grandson could not procure a perfect copy of the earlier editions when he undertook the third in 1687.   But it was soon rivalled by a similar edition of the Pentateuch by JACOB BEN ISAAC at Janow, known as the *Zeena-u-Reena* (by mistake, see § 26. p. 225.), the earlier editions of which were so rapidly exhausted, that we know only that of Basel of 1622, which seems to be at least the third.   The same author wrote a similar work on the Prophets entitled *Maggid* (מגיד, 1623-7), published probably after his death; and also an exposition of the Pentateuch (1622), compiled from various sources.   Of those who paraphrased various books of the Bible, inserting ethical applications or legends in the historical parts, generally from the Haggada in Midrash and Talmud, or translating from the Targum, we shall only mention the following, who were almost all Poles and Bohemians: ISAAC SULKES (1579), MORDECHAI BEN JACOB (1582-97); NAPHTALI ALTSCHÜLER (1595); MOSES SAERTELS BEN ISSACHAR (1604-5); JECHIEL (MICHAEL) EPSTEIN (1707); JOSEPH BEN ABRAHAM ISSACHAR, and SIMON FRANKFURTER, at Amsterdam (1711); and AARON BEN MORDECHAI (1718). The historical part of the Bible and also of the Apocrypha (the latter after Luther's translation) was published by CHAJJIM BEN NATHAN (1625-30 ?). The versifications of Biblical and especially the historical books, whose prototype is the

Samuel-Buch (probably 1543, or still older), in "8 Gesetz," i. e. *Ottava rima,* bear considerable resemblance to the last-mentioned class, although their style and form present some interesting peculiarities; they form the transition to the popular songs (§ 28.).   But few authors of this class of po-etry are at present known, e. g.: AARON (BEN ISRAEL?); JACOB BEN SAMUEL of Brzese (1583), who versified the Targum of Megillot; MOSES STENDEL, whose Psalms were copied and published by RÖSEL R. FISCHELS (1586); ABRAHAM BEN MOSES at Prague (1602); DAVID BEN MENAHEM COHEN at Amsterdam (1644); and JACOB BEN ISAAC LEVI (1692?).   Some Apocryphal books were trans-lated into German, as the book Ecclesiasticus from the Dutch by JOSEPH VON MAARSSEN at Amsterdam (1712); and the New Testament was translated or transcribed by one Jewish convert, and published by another, as early as 1540, some parts having previously appeared in Hebrew.

The following lexicographical works are less etymological than explanatory of the Hebrew: Italian and Latin, by POMIS (1587); Portuguese, by SOLOMON DE OLIVEYRA (1682); Jewish-German, by ANSCHEL at Cracow (1534), and JEHUDA (ARJE) BEN ZEBI of Krotoshin, at Carpentras (1719–1721), who wrote also on synonymes and *nomina propria;* a He-brew-Arabic nomenclature was composed by MANASSEH BEN ISRAEL; a Hebrew-German vocabulary, and a Chaldee lexicon, especially on the Targumim, by ELIA LEVITA; and a practical Hebrew-German-Italian-Latin vocabulary by NATHAN BEN MOSES HANOVER of Russia (1660).   As an etymological curiosity, we may mention the attempt made, long before Dupuis and Kanne, by DAVID PROVENÇALE at Mantua (cir. 1570) to deduce all languages from the Hebrew.

Hebrew Grammar reached a new stage of its progress in Elia Levita's (nat. 1472 near Nuremberg, ob. 1549) clear conciseness, which resembled that of David Kimchi (§ 16.). Both were leaders of the Christian grammarians who, down to the middle of the 17th century, did little else than trans-late or rearrange materials furnished by Jews.   Their authority was, however, so great as to throw independent

investigators into the shade.   When we remember that the
Jews were destitute of the encouragement derived from
the hope of distinction ; of all practical interest in other
Oriental languages, except the Chaldee (a knowledge of
which enabled JOSEPH ZARFATI, son of the physician
of Pope Julius II., to become interpreter between the first
Syrian scholars in Europe and Theseus Ambrosius, the
first teacher of Syriac, 1539); that they had no need for the
philological study of a language still in use, and that faith
in the authority of antiquity, and the supremacy of the
Midrash, the Kabbala, and Halacha, were opposed to grammatical studies; we must with Luzzatto think highly of even
the small performances of this period.   Of the important
grammatical and critical commentaries of BEN MELECH,
LONSANO, NORZI, and LOMBROSO, we have spoken above.
Beside the authors of compendia and tables for teaching,
we may name as grammarians, the brothers PROVENÇALE
(1535 seq.) at Mantua; EMANUEL of Benevento (1557);
ISAAC UZIEL at Amsterdam (ob. 1620), whose grammar was
provided with a Hebrew and Spanish index of technical
expressions by his pupil ISAAC NEHEMIA (1627); ABRA-
HAM BEN RAPHAEL at Prague (1623); SABBATAI of Prze-
misl, who defended Kimchi against Levita (1622); ISAAC
BEN SAMUEL LEVI of Posen (1627), who, even before
Alting, based the theory of language on phonetic laws;
SPINOZA (1677) whose views are not without peculiarity;
MOSES ABUDIENTE (1633); MOSES RAPHAEL D'AGUILAR
(1661), and SOLOMON DE OLIVEYRA (1689), at Amsterdam,
who wrote in Portuguese, the latter also on Chaldee; JE-
HUDA LÖB NEUMARK (1693), who wrote on accents;
ALEXANDER SÜSSKIND at Köthen (1718), author of a work
on the same subject in the Jewish-German language (probably after Wasmuth); and JEHUDA (ARJE) BEN ZEBI, who
drew up some rules in rhyme (1719).   Among the primers of
minor importance, we will mention that of PHÖBUS of Metz
(1710), on account of his general remarks, and his desire
to awaken a taste for grammar although his own knowledge
was inconsiderable.   One of the most important writers
was SOLOMON COHEN (of) Hanau (1708–1762), who, like

Kimchi and Levita, was a travelling teacher of children, and gained some credit for his knowledge of the doctrine of accents. The unusually severe criticism with which he attacked the ancients, especially in his earlier writings, gave rise to some ill-will, and met with opposition from REUBEN LEVI (1744), and AARON MOSES of Lemberg (1765); and his strictures on the prayers were attacked by MORDECHAI DÜSSELDORF (1738), and JACOB EMDEN (1769); he, however, fought his way, and met with an imitator and a plagiarist in the converted Jews, CHRISTIAN DAVID BERNARD (1722), and Professor SONNENFELS at Vienna (1757). MENDELSSOHN'S school introduced the grammatical and critical researches of learned Christians among his countrymen and co-religionists, and thereby laid the foundation of the general philology which subsequently flourished again.

§ 28.]   *Poetry and Liturgy.*

The elegant literature of this Period was developed in a different way from that of the first (§ 18.). The use of the older Hebrew artificial forms, generally imitated from the Arabic, was, unfortunately for philology, much too frequent to allow the various classical modes and their modern imitations to be followed out with anything like the same readiness and success. The poetry of the Christians, in its new mythical garb, did not exercise any considerable influence. The isolated position of the nation, the Halacha, and the Kabbala had deprived poetry in general of all freedom of spirit. Moreover, in the voluminous productions of the former period, the Liturgy had already reached its culminating point. But to the Jews the house of prayer had become, in some degree, a home, a school, a forum, a club; and although the letter of the appointed rule of prayer (*Siddur*), and the Pijjut of the Machsor as a " Usus " (מנהג), had been subjected to the decisions of the Halacha, and the free liturgical literature of the preceding period (§ 20.) had terminated in the Schulchan Aruch, still mysticism, especially that of the East and South, which in

general began to chafe against the fetters of the Law and
to introduce the mysteries of Theosophy into the prayers
and hymns (שיר הייחוד, זמירות), suggested new ideas to the
imagination and extended the sphere of the Liturgy; e. g.
by *vigils* (חצות, משמורות), especially those of the feasts
of Pentecost and Hosianna (תיקון ליל שבועות, תיקון ליל ה'/ר,
and other תיקונים), ascribed to Moses Cordovero and
Isaac Loria. In the 16th century there were formed,
particularly in Italy, pious societies for a daily matins
(שומרים לבוקר), which laid the foundation for the literature
of מעמדות or אשמורת הבוקר, compiled from the Bible and
the prayers. The multiplication of the prayers (מזמורים,
תפלות, בקשות, תחנות) used on all occasions, such as birth,
marriage, journeys, death, &c., was quite in accordance
with the spirit of the age; and above all, the circumstances
of the times led to the composition of historical *lays* of
lamentation and repentance (קינות, סליחות) written in blood
and tears. Some imitations of old forms, not intended for
recitation nor for insertion in the liturgy, were made, on
account of the interest which attached to the subjects of the
original compositions: e. g. *Asharot* and *Keter Malchut* (after
Gabirol) were imitated by David Ibn Simra and Joshua
Benbeveniste (cir. 1634-62); and psalms were written by
Abraham ha-Jachini in the East (1655), M. Ch. Luzzatto, both considered as heterodox authors, and by others.
But although the creative genius was extinct, much laborious work remained to be done. It now became necessary to
fix the old and new rites of the many wandering congregations by means of printed forms, a matter which occupied
editors, commentators, and poets. There are collections
for different countries, cities, societies, &c., belonging to
this Period: e. g. for Poland (1522), Mantua (1612), containing compositions by Chananja E. Rieti; Italy (1627) by
Joseph Jedidja Karmi and others in the 17th century;
Jerusalem by Joseph ben Mordechai Cohen and Michael ben Moses Cohen (1707-1708); Corfu (1718); and
Ceylon and Cochin-China (1757), in which there is something by the Babylonian physician Obadja Cohen ben
Usiel. Mystical collections were made by the Russian

NATHAN BEN MOSES HANOVER at Jassy (1662), and
MOSES CHAGIS (1703); there were also various Sabbataic
and Chasidaic collections. The Chinese Siddur, however,
is said to consist almost entirely of passages from the Psalms.
We will mention a few more hymnologists, composers of
prayers, and authors of special collections (for the most part
Kabbalistic), as, MOSES HAMMON, physician in ordinary at
Constantinople (about 1524); AARON THE BLIND of Safet
(1561); SOLOMON LORIA (ob. 1573), who wrote a commentary on his own songs; MORDECHAI DATO in Italy
(1575–1600); MOSES ABBAS, physician at Magnesia (cir.
1580); MOSES COHEN of Corfu (1580–1600); ISRAEL
NADJARA, the most talented man of this period (1587–99)
in Palestine, whose hymns form the main part of a collection
by JOSEPH SHALOM GALLIAGO at Amsterdam (1628-30);
his imitator JOSEPH GANSO at Brussa (cir. 1630); AKIBA
FRANKFURT BEN JACOB (ob. 1597); ELIA LOANS Rabbi
of Worms (1599); EPHRAIM BEN JOSEPH CHELM at Cracow (1605); CHANANJA ASAEL RIETI (1615); AARON
BERECHJA DE MODENA (1624); MOSES JEHUDA ABBAS
in Egypt, and ABRAHAM SAMUEL in the East (1650);
MOSES ZACUTO (1645–97), at Venice and Mantua; and
MOSES PISA, at Amsterdam (1750). Among the various
commentators on the old and new hymns and prayers of
different rites and collections we may mention, JOHANAN
TREVES at Bologna (1540); ABRAHAM (BEN ABIGDOR?)
of Prague (1550); BENJAMIN BEN MEIR at Saloniki
(1553-5); NAPHTALI TREVES (1560); MORDECHAI BEN
JEHUDA (1567); MOSES PESANTE (1567); ZEBI SUNDELS
and MORDECHAI BEN ABRAHAM COHEN (1571-1578);
MOSES SHEDEL (1585); MOSES BEN MACHIR (1594);
JOSEPH BEN ABRAHAM COHEN (1598); ISAAC BEN JE-
HUDA LEVI (1600); ABRAHAM BEN JEHUDA LEVI (1605);
and ISRAEL KIMCHI at Smyrna (1737). Translations of
prayers, published subsequently to the commencement of
this period, served to render the Hebrew text intelligible,
and realised the old maxim of praying in a language understood by the people; instruction in Hebrew prayers was extended also to female children.   German as well as Hebrew

R 2

hymns for the synagogue probably existed as early as the
Middle Ages. The attempt made by Aaron ben Samuel
of Hengershausen (1709) to bring the German element into
common use at the expense of the Hebrew, was frustrated
by the interdict of the Rabbies whom he attacked; but the
German made only so much the more progress in everything
except obligatory prayers. The High-German translation
of the Bible by Mendelssohn became a standard in language for the liturgy (e. g. Isaac Euchel and D. Fried-
länder's translation of the Prayer-Book), which was however combined with new elements; but it would exceed
the limits of our essay to discuss this subject.

The form of poetry and rhyming prose was gradually employed for all possible subjects. Biblical books were versified, e. g. Esther by Moses Cohen of Corfu (end of the
16th century), and Saadja ben Levi Asankot at Amsterdam (1647); the Psalms and Lamentations by Moses
Abraham Cohen of Zante (1719), and as early as the 16th
century by Chananja Ibn Jakar (unpublished); Ruth by
Moses de Milhau (1786); the Halacha after the Talmud
by Abraham Samuel of Venice (1719); the Schulchan
Aruch by various authors (§ 25. p. 217.); Grammar by
Elia Levita, M. Provençale, and others (§ 27.); the
Kalendar by Joseph ben Shemtob ben Joshua (1489)
and David Vital; a poem on chess was composed by
Solomon ben Massal-tob at Constantinople (1518–40);
and even sermons were, after the fashion of the Pijjutim,
introduced with a רשות (§ 19.).

Larger ethical and didactic or collective poems (Diwans),
often with commentaries by the authors themselves, are extant, by Samuel Archevolti (1551); Jacob ben Joab
ben Elia Fano (1554); Jehuda Sarko (1560) and
Saadja Longo, both in Turkey and poets of the first rank;
Menahem Lonsano (cir. 1572); Isaac Onkeneira
(1577), whose subject is the dispute of the letters of the alphabet at the time of the Creation; Meir Angel at Belgrade
(cir. 1620); Moses Abudiente (1633); Leo de Modena
(ob. 1648); Solomon Oliveyra (1665), and Samuel de
Caceres at Amsterdam; Jacob Frances (Francese)

(ob. 1667), of whose works a poem against the Kabbala is the only one printed (1704); his brother EMANUEL; LEO DEL BENE (ob. 1677); DANIEL BELILLOS (not Belilios) (1683); ISAAC CANTARINI at Padua (1718); SAMSON MODON (1725); JACOB LONDON of Lissa (1737), at Amsterdam and in Italy, who besides a commentary on his subject-matter added references to the Biblical words and passages used; MORDECHAI SAMOSC BEN MEIR (1745); and JEHUDA HURWITZ BEN MORDECHAI (1765) whose cotemporary ISAAC BELINFANTE at Amsterdam wrote after the model of WESSELY.

The Gnomics of this period were little else than versified compilations from the Bible, Abot (by SABBATAI MARINI ob. 1748), Talmud, &c.; such as those by SAUL BEN SIMEON (1557), and SAADJA BEN LEVI ASANKOT, author of a Hebrew translation of the Arabic proverbs of Ali and others, extant in the Bodleian, but never published. Riddles are to be found in the writings of ISAAC ONKENEIRA (1577); AKIBA FRANKFURT, mentioned above; and more recent authors. On the other hand there is a copious literature of occasional poetry and epigrams, composed at births, marriages, deaths, consecrations of synagogues, and dedications of Thora-rolls, &c., by learned and literary societies, especially in Italy and Holland (in the 17th century), beside those occurring in dedications, approvals, prefaces, &c. Wit and satire found a place in productions of this kind; but the broader expressions of humour and parody were more strictly than ever confined to the occasion of the privileged national festivals Purim and Chanuka, by the stiff and rigid morality of the time.*   Carnival squibs, such as the anonymous (and perhaps older) מגלת סתרים (1507–18), and other trifles, were written by JEHUDA BEN JACOB of Chenciny (1650); DAVID RAPHAEL POLIDO (1703); and others. Songs or Pijjutim, either translations or original compositions in the Jewish-German, Italian, Spanish, and Latin languages, and even mystic

---

* The author will enlarge upon this subject, and give more particulars of the curious literature belonging to it, elsewhere.

poems, were made on the occasion of feasts. A kind of
sacred drama (e. g. the plays of *Ahasuerus, Goliath, Joseph,*
&c.) was tolerated, and the first who took offence at a parody
on the Talmud (which De Rossi did not recognise as such
in his codex 1199.) was a Karaite. A similar parody was
applied to Chanuka by JOSHUA (ABRAHAM) CALLIMANNI
(1617) at the age of 13. ELIA LOANZ (1600) sang of the
battle between water and wine; SAMUEL SANWIL BEN
AARON SOFER (1693), the praise of tobacco; and an anonymous writer, the battle between Chanuka and the other
festivals, in Jewish-German.

The influence of classical and modern literature on Jewish
poetry is most prominent in Italy, and subsequently also in
Holland. The earliest specimen of the non-Semitic drama
(on the theory of which there exists an unpublished work
by JEHUDA DEI SOMMI in Italian) is the Spanish *Esther,*
probably by SOLOMON USQUE, the translator of Petrarch
(1567) at Ferrara; JOSEPH PENCO at Amsterdam (1673)
was hailed in Latin epigrams by his contemporaries, as the
first author of a Hebrew allegorical " Commedia;" CHAJJIM
SABBATAI MARINI (ob. 1748) translated Ovid after Anguil-
lara; and Dr. ISAAC LUZZATTO translated a canzonetta of
Metastasio at his desire (1779). MOSES ZACUTO and JE-
HUDA OLMO (1720) followed the older imitators of the
" Divina Commedia." In Germany the period, not yet
closed, of poetical translations, with their curious offshoots,
could not have commenced before the revival of the study of
German. A characteristic feature of them is the combination of languages in alternate strophes (cf. § 20.) and in
poems (even liturgical) written throughout in two languages
(Hebrew and Italian, Spanish, or German), for instance the
celebrated epitaph by JEHUDA DE MODENA, and an epi-
thalamium by MOSES CATALANO; this extension of the old
art of Homonyms (§ 20.) did not escape censure. According
to Delitzsch we find reference also to musical performance in
RAPHAEL MELDOLA's songs (1742). SOLOMON DE ROSSI
published Hebrew songs (1623) in from 3 to 8 parts.

Finally, we must bestow a few words upon a kind of
poetry, which, although included in the great class of " oc-

casional poetry" noticed above, deserves particular mention on account of its special object and recent origin. We might call it "loyal" or "patriotic" poetry, its object being the celebration of days and events connected with the history and politics of the countries where it was written and their rulers, and, since the end of the last century, the progress of the emancipation of the Jews themselves. The language is either the Hebrew or the vernacular, or both together. The oldest Hebrew specimen known to the author of this essay is a Hebrew and German song on the birth of Leopold I. (1676) by NOAH ABRAHAM ASHER SELIG BEN CHISKIJJA. A song on the victory of Frederic II., 28th December 1745, by the Rabbi of Berlin, DAVID FRAENKEL, was recited with music in the synagogue, and translated into German by AARON BEN SOLOMON GUMPERZ, then a student " der Philosophie und Mathematik beflissen," and afterwards mentioned as DR. GUMPERZ by Maupertuis; this translation was altered into miserable Jewish-German by MENDEL SCHWAB. Whether the German *Freuden-Lied* on the wedding of Joseph I. of Austria, which is directed to be sung to the air " Baba-Buch" (see below), is of Jewish origin or only transcribed we cannot decide; but we suppose the latter to be the case with two elegies on the death of King Ferdinand (1654), and a song on the coronation of Leopold I. (1658), although the melody of the last is said to be that of a Jewish song. MANASSEH BEN ISRAEL in 1642 addressed a Portuguese and Latin " congratulation to Prince Frederick Henry, when he visited the synagogue; and in 1655 he published a panegyric on Queen Christina of Sweden, whose Hebrew books it was proposed that he should catalogue and complete. JOSEPH PENCO DE LA VEGA celebrated the king of Poland (1683), and William of England (1690), in Spanish. All these are isolated cases, and occasioned by the special relation in which the poet stood to these royal personages; but ever since the time of Mendelssohn the Jews have tried to show (and sometimes to make a show of) their loyalty in answer to the accusations of their enemies, as well as their real gratitude to their benefactors, such as Joseph I. of Austria, the French Assembly, and others.

In external form elegant literature remained nearly as described above until it entirely degenerated. The "mosaic style" (§ 20.) and . its play upon words — used, for example, in the absurd but witty publications of JOSEPH CONCIO (or CONZIO) at Asti (1627) — sunk, especially in Italy, into spiritless affectation and quaintness. Nevertheless we must admire the marvellous dexterity shown in all kinds of linguistic productions, such as those of SAADJA LONGO and his contemporaries in Turkey (1550, &c.), which will never be equalled in any other language; although it must be admitted that there is seldom any object in these exhibitions of art, beyond a display of poetical and rhetorical skill. We have a specimen of these conceits in BENJAMIN MUSSAPHIA'S (1638) *History of the Creation,* in which he exhausted the words of the Bible without a single repetition. At the beginning of the present century this singular production was used as a book of instruction in the Hebrew language, and glossaries both German and Turkish, the latter by a Karaite, were added to it. A new period in this branch of literature commences with the mystic M. CH. LUZZATTO in Italy, and N. H. WESSELY the friend of Mendelssohn.

Hebrew poetry and rhetoric were occasionally treated by PORTALEONE (1550); ASARJA DE ROSSI (1573); SIMON (SIMCHA) CALLIMANI (1751); the grammarian ELIA LEVITA; EMANUEL BENEVENT (1557); ARCHEVOLTI (1602); JOSHUA BENVENISTE (1635) MS. ; ABUDIENTE (1663); AGUILAR (1661); JACOB ROMANO (cir. 1630 at Constantinople), who is said to have treated of 1348 (? ?) Hebrew forms of poetry in a monography ; EMANUEL FRANCESE (1677), whose essay is not published ; and RAPHAEL RABBENIO, who wrote some Italian controversial works against *Clericus* (1709–1710). Lexicons of rhymes were written by SOLOMON DE OLIVEYRA (1618) at Amsterdam, and GERSON CHEFEZ at Venice (ob. 1700 at the age of 17): the latter was edited with additions by S. CALLIMANI. Forms and instructions for business and other letters were brought out by ARCHEVOLTI (1553) in the anonymous יפה נוף (16th century); by JEHUDA DE MODENA (not printed); JOSEPH RAKOVER BEN DAVID (1689); and others. The usual acrostics and references to

the Pericopes were treated by the anonymous authors of
אגרות שלומים (1534), and מגלת ספר, and by their shameless
plagiarists. A book of instruction in German, printed in
the modern Hebrew cursive characters cut expressly for
the purpose, was published by JOSEPH VAN MAARSSEN at
Amsterdam (1713–15).

The Chaldee language was studied by few except the
Kabbalists. That the Jews often took part in the poetry
of the countries where they lived is proved even by the
incomplete accounts we possess. A remarkable instance of
this is to be found in the cultivation of German in Poland,
Italy, and other countries; and of Spanish in Holland,
where for instance JACOB BELMONTE versified the book of
Job, and wrote against the Inquisition; and in Italy,
where Dr. JACOB UZIEL published a heroic poem called
David (1624). Among the best Italian authors are two
women, one of whom, DEBORA ASCARELLI, translated the
religious poetry of M. RIETI (1602). Latin also was not
utterly neglected. Some Spanish, Provençal, Slavic, Persian, perhaps also Tatar poetry, presents considerable peculiarity in the intermixture of Hebrew words and Biblical
passages, which, in the Jewish-German of the period, was
carried to such a pitch as nearly to destroy its Germanic
element. The first High-German poet is EPHRAIM KUH
(nat. 1731 at Breslau, ob. 1790), known from Auerbach's
romance; and, as early as 1771, the *Poems of a Polish Jew*
were published by ISSACHAR FALKENSOHN at Mietau. The
Jewish-German literature has also its popular poetry, which,
though devoid of originality to its very titlepages, formed
a not unpleasing mosaic of older Jewish and Arabic elements in combination with Romance and German.* To this
class belong the *Kleine Brant-Spiegel*, 50 (or rather 49) proverbs taken from Charisi (§ 20.), and increased, partly from
older sources, to the canonical number 70 by JEHUDA BEN
SAMUEL REGENSBURG, called Löb שיבריל of Lundenburg
(1566); *Paradise and Hell* from Emanuel's Divan (ch. 50.)

* The author of the present essay has made but few additions to this part
of the subject, as it is principally interesting to the German reader, and he
intends to treat of it more fully elsewhere.

by Moses Eisenstadt ; Berachja's *Fables of the Fox*, translated by Jacob Koppelmann ben Samuel of Brzesc (1583-4), which, together with Sahola's fables, forms the *Cow-book* of Abraham ben Matatja (1555), known only from quotations of bibliographers; and many ethical works (see § 26.), e. g. the *Eben Bochan* of Kalonymos (p. 174.) by Moses Eisenstadt (1705). The principal books of amusement consist of legends and stories (סיפור, מעשה) collected from the classes above mentioned, among which the well-known *Maase-buch* (1602 ?), partly transcribed in the original language and partly translated into High-German by B. Chr. Helvicus (1611), was taken chiefly from the Haggada ; the *Seven Wise Masters of Rome*, or *The life of Erastus son of Diocletian*, was taken from a German edition of the *Mishle Sendabar ;* and the German edition of Jacob von Maarssen was probably made from the Dutch. In Jewish-German we meet with other favourite popular books and legends, such as the *Baba-buch* of Elia Levita (1507); the *Arthus* (*Arthurs*) *Hof* of Josel Witzenhausen (1683, different from the older work mentioned p. 178.); *Siegmund und Magelone, Floris und Blanchefleur, Kaiser Octavianus Ritter von der Steuermark, Prætiosa, Fortunatus, Eulen-Spiegel, Lalleburger,* &c. ; and even a part of Boccaccio was translated from the Dutch by Joseph van Maarssen (1710). To this class belong also the versifications of Biblical books (§ 27.), and a mass of songs partly historical (§ 29.), the very existence of which has escaped the attention of bibliographers, even of the Germans, to whom they are of great interest not only in themselves, but also for their inscriptions, indicating the proper melody by the names of popular German songs, several of which are otherwise unknown. The author has been able to collect a list of more than a hundred pieces belonging to this class, almost all extant in the Oppenheim collection of the Bodleian library.

§ 29.] *History, Geography, Antiquities, and Miscellanies.*

Chronicles (comprising also the general events of the world), comprehensive historical works, and essays on the biography of

learned men, were composed at the end of the preceding period
by JOSEPH BEN ZADDIK at Arvalo (1467); SAADJA BEN
MEIMUN IBN DANAN in Spain (1485); and ABRAHAM
ZACUT BEN SAMUEL (1505), whose work was published
with arbitrary omissions and additions by SAMUEL SHULLAM
at Constantinople (1566), and again with notes by MOSES IS-
SERLS (ob. 1573). The Spaniard JEHUDA IBN VERGA wrote
a history of the persecutions of the Jews, which was completed by his relative SOLOMON and his son JOSEPH (1554),
and was subsequently translated into Jewish-German (1591),
and into Spanish (1640) by MEIR DE LEON. Of ELIA
KAPSOLI'S various historical compilations and interesting
narratives, continued to his own times (1523), there exists a
MS. copy in Italy; and an imperfect one has been lately
purchased by the British Museum. JOSEPH COHEN wrote
a history of France and Turkey (1554) containing an account of the rebellion of Fiesco at Genoa, where the author
lived, inserted with a German translation in the Anthology
of Zedner, who points out the strange blunders of Biallo-
blotzky the English translator of the whole work for the Oriental Translation Fund. He also gave an account of the
persecutions of the Jews (1575), which was continued by an
anonymous writer down to the year 1605, and has been lately
published with the valuable notes of Professor S. D. Luzzatto.
AS. DE ROSSI (1575) investigated ancient history and chronology. GEDALJA IBN JAHJA'S *Chain of Tradition* (1587)
was called by Del Medigo a *Chain of Lies*. A Compendium
of Chronology (down to 1587) was mostly taken from Zacut
by SOLOMON ALGASI, and a larger Chronicle was composed
by DAVID GANS (ob. 1613), according to Zunz the first German Jew who took a lively interest in history, geography, and
astronomy. MANASSEH BEN ISRAEL compiled a *Bibliotheca
Rabbinica* (see p. 235. and p. 247.). On the Jewish learning
of the East and South in the 16th and 17th centuries, the chronological work of DAVID CONFORTE (1677–1683) is a valuable authority. A profound critical work on the learned men
of the Talmud, made use of and plagiarised by many recent
authors, was published by JECHIEL HEILPRIN, Rabbi at
Minsk (ob. after the year 1728), who also took up and com-

pleted, but with less ability and knowledge, the Bibliographical List of Sabbatai Bass (Bassist, subcantor of Prague, 1680). The Jewish poets in the Spanish language were celebrated by D. L. de Barrios (1683). To point out Bartolocci's hostility to the Jews, and to correct his errors, Sabbatai Ambrun determined to prepare a new *Bibliotheca Hebraïca* (1712). Menahem ben Solomon Levi of Amsterdam wrote a German continuation of Josippon, compiled from second-hand sources (some of which were Christian) with more fidelity than judgment (1741); a Dutch translation with notes by G. J. Polak (partly corrected by the author of this Essay) has just appeared. A Biographical and Bibliographical Lexicon, collected in many and distant journeys, was written by Ch. D. J. Asulai of Jerusalem at Leghorn (1777–1796). Joseph del Medigo shows his critical taste in his Literary Letters to the Karaite Serach (ante 1629).

Ancient history was the subject of a Jewish-German work by Alexander ben Moses Ethausen (1719). Of the rhyming versions of the books of the Bible, we have spoken above (§ 28.); connected with them are the above-mentioned (§ 24.) Apologies of Usque (1553), Aboab (1629), Cardoso (1679), Barrios (1683), and Luzzatto (1638); the translations of Flavius Josephus's *Contra Apionem* by Samuel Shullam (1566), of Pseudo-Josephus (1607), and other Haggada works (§ 26.); and the edition of the History of Bostanai, with other accounts of the Ten Tribes, by Isaac Akrish (about 1577).

There are special historical works on particular cities and events; various memorabilia were preserved by Josel of Rossheim (down to 1547); and a history of the sultans Soleiman and Selim (1520-74), by Moses Almosnino, is quoted in a MS. in the Bodleian Library. An account of the Austrian persecution of the Jews in 1420-21 was translated from the German [printed 1609], by Jechiel ben Jedidja about 1582, and again translated into German in 1725. The earthquake at Mantua (1570) was described by As. de Rossi; the accusation of murder at Ragusa, brought especially against Isaac Jesurun (Oct. 1622), is recounted by

AARON BEN DAVID COHEN RAGUSANO.   A history of the
rebellion at Constantinople (1622) by an eyewitness, extant
in a MS. in the Bodleian, has not been recognised as such by
Uri.   The Legends of Worms were edited from the notes
of the sexton JIFTACH JOSHUA BEN NAPHTALI (1623), by
his son ELIEZER LIEBERMANN, together with an elegy on
the burning of that town by the French (1689), by ISAAC
(SAEKEL) BEN LIEBERMANN LEVI.   An anonymous author
gives an interesting account of the calamities brought on
Jerusalem by a rebellious pasha in 1625 (a remarkable
parallel to the present events at Hebron), through which the
Portuguese congregation of that town was almost ruined.
ABRAHAM CATALANO describes the epidemic at Padua
(1631) in an unpublished work.   An interesting sketch of
the Jews at Mantua during the Italian war was published
by ABRAHAM ALLUF MASERAN (1634).   The cruelties of
the Cossacks and Tatars under the leader Chmelnicki
(" Chmel's calamities "), beginning at the town of Nemirow,
were described by many authors both in prose and verse;
some of these elegies and penitential hymns afterwards
became a part of the liturgy of the Polish fast day of the
20. Siwan (the anniversary of the persecution A. D. 1171).
Amongst those who have given more graphic descriptions of
this event we may mention : SABBATAI COHEN ; MEIR BEN
SAMUEL SZEBRZIN ; his semi-plagiator JOSHUA BEN DAVID
of Lemberg ; SAMUEL PHŒBUS BEN NATAN, who gives a
list of more than 140 towns involved in it, with the number
of Jewish inhabitants in each, the total number of heads of
families murdered being 600,000 ; and NATAN BEN MOSES
HANOVER (1653), whose pamphlet was translated into
German by MOSES BEN ABRAHAM (1686).   Amongst the
poets we may name : EPHRAIM BEN JOSEPH of Chelm ;
GABRIEL BEN JOSHUA ; JACOB MARGALIOT ; JACOB BEN
NAPHTALI of Gnesen ; JOSEPH BEN ELIEZER LIPMANN,
who also sang of the persecution of Kremsir in A. D. 1673 ;
LIPMANN HELLER ; MORDECHAI BEN NAPHTALI of Kremsir ; MOSES COHEN NEROL ; SABBATAI HURWITZ ; and
others.   The siege of Prague by the Swedes (1648), was
described by JEHUDA (LÖB) BEN JOSHUA and in the

Schwedisch Lied. Among the histories we may perhaps also reckon the publications of MANASSEH BEN ISRAEL in behalf of the establishment of the Jews by Cromwell (1650). MEIR BEN PEREZ SCHMELKES, a youth of Prague, who, with several others, was killed on the way to Nicolsburg by the Christians, left a diary, kept during the siege of Vienna by the Turks (1683), which was published by one of those who assisted at his burial. ISAAC CANTARINI describes, in his distorted manner, the persecution at Padua (1684); and the fate of that same congregation was also the subject of a MS. work by his nephew MOSES CHAJJIM CANTARINI. An unprovoked persecution at Posen (1696) is the subject of a German narrative published in 1725, and also of a song by ISAAC BEN MENAHEM. At the beginning of the 18th century two women of Prague published a legend about the first settlement of the Jews in that town, which seems to have been the foundation of a recent publication on the subject in the collection *Sippurim;* and in 1718 the printer CHAJJIM BEN JACOB, of Erbich, brought out a more authentic account of the first settlement of the Spanish Jews in Holland. JOSEPH VAN MAARSSEN was, probably, the German translator (1707) of a Dutch account of a tumult at Amsterdam (1696). An anonymous German writer described the procession of the Jews at Prague at the birth of Leopold (1716). SOLOMON BEN JEHUDA LEVI of Dessau gave an account of accusations brought against the Jews at Hamburg (1730). JESAIA SEGRE, at Reggio (1734), related the Italian war partly in ottave rime; JOEL (LAMEL) BEN SELKE LEVI described the siege of Glogau (1741); ISRAEL FRAENKEL, at Nicolsburg, wrote on the persecution of the Jews in Moravia (1742); JACOB BERAB, at Tiberias, described a catastrophe which befel the Jews of that place at the hands of the sheikh (1742); and JACOB EMDEN, at Altona, published a compilation of documents, &c., referring to the history of various sects (about 1752). It would lead us too far if we were to pursue the reasons why the reformation of Mendelssohn and his school did so little to promote Jewish history, compared with the other branches of science.

Historical poetry adopts sometimes the liturgical name and form of *Selicha, Kina,* &c. (§ 20. 28.), without being always intended for public or private worship. Some poems are accompanied with a German translation, or were composed originally in German (*Klaglied,* &c.). The following chronological enumeration of subjects and authors (omitting the few already mentioned), although incomplete, will give an idea of their variety and interest, since every one of them supplies some particulars concerning historical events. JACOB BEN JOAB ELIA FANO describes the massacre at Ancona (1556); and MENAHEM CHAJJUT the fire at Posen, and the death of a young scholar (1590). Special *Selichot* were composed by MOSES MARGALIOT, and, according to Zunz, by SAMUEL EDELS, on the Polish martyrs (1596–1603); by EPHRAIM LENCZICZ on the *Passover Calamity* at Prague (1611); by LIPMANN HELLER on the conquest of Prague (10th November, 1620); and by MESHULLAM SULLAM (or SALEM ?), who, at the order of the Deputies, wrote a *Kina* on the burning of the synagogue at Mantua (1610). The plundering of the Jews at Frankfurt on Main, and the scandalous conduct of Vincenz Fettmilch (1614–16) are described in the *Vinc-Lied* of ELCHANAN HELEN. Several martyrs and victims of cruelty and extortion in Poland (1631, 1636, 1666, 1676, 1690–91) were celebrated by NATAN SPIRA BEN SOLOMON, ZEBI BEN MARDOCHAI, two anonymous authors, ZEEB (WOLF) BEN JOSEPH, and SAMUEL AUERBACH. The expulsion of the Jews from Vienna (1670) was sung by the precentor JACOB. The conflagrations at Nachod (1663), Prague (1669), Frankfurt on Main (1711), and Altona (1711), were recorded by ZEBI BEN JOSEPH, JECHIEL BEN ABRAHAM SALMAN, DAVID BEN SCHEMAJA SAUGERS, SAMUEL SCHOTTEN, Rabbi of Frankfurt on Main (in a Selicha), by an anonymous author, and by SAMUEL HEKSCHER; the epidemic of Nicolsburg, and the persecutions connected with it (1680), by JACOB BEN SOLOMON SINGER HURWITZ; and that of Prague (1713) by ISSACHAR BEN ISSACHAR GERSONI, and MOSES EISENSTADT, who particularises the sufferers and the medicines employed. To these we may add an ano-

nymous prose account in German, of a great calamity
at Ungarischbrod (in Moravia), where the Turks killed,
amongst others, the Rabbi Nathan ben Moses of Ostroh
(1683). The *Prostitzer Kedoshim*, celebrated by CHAJJIM
BEN SHALOM (about 1684 ?), are two thieves who preferred
hanging to apostasy. AARON BEN JOSEPH, a captive of
Buda (1686), sings the fate of his Jewish fellow-captives
and the generosity of their liberator, Sender Tausk of Prague
(1688). The youth Simle Abeles, who was converted to
Christianity, and whose grave is still shown to the visitors
at the Teinkirche at Prague, is also the subject of two
Klaglieder on the sufferings of his congregation (1694).
The cruelties perpetrated at Kaidan and Zausmer (1698)
formed the subject of special Selichot, with a commentary by
the author, JOSEPH BEN URI SHRAGA of Kobrzin. Lastly,
MORDECHAI ZAHALON wrote a poem on the inundation of
Ferrara (1707), &c.

Legends and martyrologies, partly taken from older
sources, and generally published anonymously, were put into
circulation, e. g. those on R. Amnon, Meir ben Isaac (before
1696), Eleazar of Worms, Solomon Molco (1532), Adam
Baal-Shem (1564-76), Isaac Loria, Sabbatai Zebi, Shechna
at Cracow (1682 ?), Joseph della Reina, and a German elegy
on the death of Lipmann, precentor at Prague (before 1674).
There were also some miraculous and superstitious accounts, for instance, those on exorcisms at Nicolsburg (1696)
and Korez (17th century?); and others pretending to be
true, such as the *History of Shusan* (Susa), or of R. Cha-
nina Albeldi and his ten brothers, who bound themselves
to the Devil! These form the transition to real fables and
poetical inventions (§ 28.). Autobiographies were written
by JEHUDA DE MODENA (ob. 1648) and his grandson ISAAC
LEVI (born 1621); ABRAHAM CONQUE, at the beginning of
the 18th century, related the events of his two missions;
others gave interesting particulars in their wills, e. g.
PINCHAS KATZENELLENBOGEN (cir. 1760), whose curious
account of the celebrated Saul Wahl (said to have been King
of Poland for one day) has been lately published. Other
historical materials are inserted in prefaces and epilogues,

especially by the Spanish exiles, as ABRAVANEL, JOSEPH
IBN JAHJA, JEHUDA CHAJJAT, and later by SOLOMON
IBN ATHIA (1549) (v. sup.).   In memory of general and
particular events, feast and fast days were instituted, and
memorial rolls (מבלה) written, e. g. by MEIR BEN JECHIEL
BRODA at Cracow, called MEIR KADOSH (1632), and by
LIPMANN HELLER (1645); and Selichot by ABRAHAM
AUERBACH (1673) and others already mentioned.   To this
head belong the funeral orations (הספד); and some important contests between the Rabbies and the congregations :
as that of LEVI at Ferrara; of BERAB with IBN CHABIB;
ALASHKAR with KAPSOLI; MISRACHI and NEHEMIA CHAJ-
JUN with their different adversaries (1714); JONATHAN
EBEYNSCHUTZ with JACOB EMDEN; the history of a di-
vorce by MOSES PROVENCALE; that of the taxers at Padua
(1711) by ISAAC CANTARINI, &c., which are to be found
in the Sentences (§ 25.).   Also the statutes (תקנות, תיקונים)
of various congregations, e. g. of Mantua (1620, 1711–17),
Prague (1654 and 1702), Moravia (1655–1722), Amsterdam
(1711, &c.), Fürth (1728), and others; and memorial books,
as that of Worms by JEHUDA KIRCHHEIM (1625), have
been partly printed, although the greater number remain
in MS. and await the labours of the learned historian.

The literature of geography and ethnography increased
in proportion to the means of communication, and to the
interest taken in travels, which received a new impulse
in the 15th and 16th centuries.   The principal subjects of
writers on travel, at this time mostly Kabbalists, were
Palestine and its tombs, the journey thither, &c., on which
we have works, treatises, letters, and the like by BA-
RUCH (1522); an anonymous writer (1537); GERSON BEN
ASHER SCARMELA (1561); ELIA DI PESARO (1563); URI
BEN SIMEON (1564), who made drawings of the tombs;
SOLOMON SCHLIMEL BEN CHAJJIM (1606—1609); and
GERSON BEN ELIEZER (1635), whose Jewish-German work
was publicly burnt in Warsaw by the Jesuits.   More-
over, MORDECHAI BEN JESAIA LITTES (1649) and MOSES
BEN ISRAEL NAPHTHALI of Prague (1650) wrote in Jewish-
German.   SAMUEL PHÖBUS BEN NATAN describes the

towns in Russia and Poland, with the number of their
Jewish inhabitants murdered by Chmelnicki's gang (sup.
p. 253.).   GEDALJA of Semiecz (1716) and JOSEPH SOFER
(1765, in Jewish-German 1767) described the sufferings
of the Jews of Palestine.   We have besides the travels
of DAVID RUBENI, the pretended Prince of the Jews
in Abyssinia, to whom the celebrated proselyte Solomon
Molcho attached himself (1526) ; and those of PEDRO
TEXEIRA (ob. at Verona in the 17th century), who made a
journey to India and Persia.   The latter also wrote a history of the Persian kings, taken from Persian authorities.
MOSES PEREIRA DE PAIVA gave some account of the
Jews in Cochin-China (1687, translated into Jewish-German 1688).   The pretended discovery of the Ten Tribes in
Abyssinia or Arabia gives ample matter for the discussions
of travellers and their interpreters.   On this subject we
have the writings of ISAAC AKRISCH (cir. 1577); ABRA-
HAM IBN MEGAS, Soleiman's regimental surgeon at Haleb
(1585); and AARON HALEVI (ANTONIO MONTEZINOS), who
escaped from the Inquisition, and whose supposed discovery
of the Ten Tribes in South America (1642), supported by
MANASSEH BEN ISRAEL's interpretations, provoked much
controversy.   MOSES BEN ABRAHAM, a proselyte and printer
at Halle, collected all the earlier information on the subject
in Jewish-German (1712).   There is also a doubtful letter of
R. SAMUEL and ASHER of Susa, who are said, on the testimony of JACOB BEN ELIEZER ASHKENASI, to have arrived
in 1579 at Safet; and another letter written to the Beni
Musa in the year 1647 (?).   A topography of Palestine was
written in Latin by JACOB ZADDIK BEN ABRAHAM (1631);
and a geography of the same country (in Hebrew), by
CHAJJIM PHEIBEL BEN ISRAEL of Tarnigrod (1772).
MOSES ALMOSNINO's description of Constantinople (1567)
was translated by JACOB CANSINO (1638) into Spanish;
JONADAB (1575) described Africa ; MENAHEM ZION
(EMANUEL) PORTO of Trieste (1640) wrote a *Breve Insti-
tuzione della Geografia;* MEIR NEUMARK (1703) translated
some geographical works into Jewish-German ; MOSES
CHAGIS tried to prove that the wall shown at Jerusalem as

that of the old temple is genuine (1738); ISAAC COHEN
DE LARA, bookseller at Amsterdam, published a Spanish
Guida da Passageros, together with a calendar for thirty
years; and BENJAMIN CRONEBERG described *geographische
und historische Merkwürdigkeiten* (1752).   There are maps
extant, e. g. by JACOB ZADDIK and ABRAHAM BEN JACOB
the proselyte, the latter (1695) with Hebrew letters.   The
Jewish-German Hand-book for Travellers by the bibliographer SABBATAI BASS (1680) contains posting routes.
Plates, plans, &c., are to be found in editions of the Easter
Haggada.   N. H. WESSELY (1782) laid great stress on the
importance of geographical instruction in Jewish schools;
and B. LINDAU (1789) devoted a chapter of his elementary
work, published at the end of this period, to geography.

The investigation of Jewish antiquities is immediately
connected with the most varied Halacha subjects.   We will
mention the works and treatises referring to the ancient
worship of the Temple, vestments of the priests, music,
&c.; these works are in some degree connected with the
treatise Middol (§ 5.), and are generally accompanied with
illustrations: viz. those by As. DE ROSSI (1575); L.
HELLER (1602); ABRAHAM PORTALEONE BEN DAVID
(1612), who is the most important writer on this subject;
JACOB JEH. LEON, who wrote some essays in Spanish, and
was called *Templo,* because he made a model of the old
Temple (1646), which he exhibited amongst others to the
king of England (1675); NATHAN SPIRA BEN REUBEN
(1655); ELIEZER RICHETTI (1676); MOSES CHEFEZ GEN-
TILE (1696); ALEXANDER ETHAUSEN, in the supplement
to his Jewish-German history (1719); EMANUEL (CHAI)
RICCHI (1737); and JACOB ABOAB, the learned correspondent of Unger (§ 24.), who collected stones and aromatics
for a work on the breast-plate of the High Priest and the
frankincense of the Temple.

Among the Miscellanies on various subjects, or suggested by passing events, may be mentioned, a Hebrew
translation of the prophecies &c. of Nostradamus by MOSES
BOTAREL BEN LEON at Constantinople (cir. 1561); the
Mnemotechnics of an anonymous writer according to the

system of Pierre François d'Orvieto; and a similar work accompanied with a historical introduction on Jewish Mnemotechnics by JEH. ARJE DE MODENA (1612), who, like Gesvaldo a little earlier (1592), treated also of Amnemoneutics.* Secret or cipher writing was cultivated by MENAHEM PORTO (1556); ABRAHAM COLORNI, ambassador of the Duke of Ferrara at Prague, who dedicated his *Scotographia* (1593) to the Emperor Rudolph II.; and by JACOB BEN ELJAKIM in his mathematical work (1613). MEIR MAGIN of France at Rome wrote to Sixtus V. (1588) on the use of silk ; JOSEPH PENCO DE LA VEGA illustrated the business of the stock-exchange from a moral point of view (1688); and JEHUDA BOLAT attempted to make an encyclopædical enumeration of all the sciences (1530). The pseudonymous treatise of JEHUDA DE MODENA against tradition and the Rabbinical system, which has been lately published by S. J. Reggio, is unique and full of 19th century ideas.

§ 30.] *Mathematics and Physical Science.*

1. Mathematics had in the preceding period been developed to a considerable extent as an independent science, and in its newer theories came so little into collision with the peculiar tendencies of the Jewish literature, that had the times been more favourable to, or even tolerant of, a taste for theoretical and scientific subjects, independent original works would doubtless have been written, or those of foreigners translated, besides the writings which were intended to throw light on the mathematical parts of the Halacha and other antiquities (§ 29.): e. g. that by MOSES ISSERL at Cracow (1570); MORDECHAI JAFE at Prague (1595); JACOB KOPPELMANN of Brzesc (1598); and JEHUDA BEN CHANOCH BEN ABRAHAM at Pfersee (1708). The successors of the commentators, &c., in the former period (§ 21.),—to whom in some degree belongs MOSES PROVENCALE, who was led by a passage in

---

* These and some other writings of the Jews on that subject are not mentioned in the article *Gedächtnisskunst* in the Encyclopædia of Ersch, sect. i. vol. iv. p. 411. An analysis of Jeh. de Modena has been given, with supplementary notes by the author of this essay, in the Journal "Oesterreichische Blätter," 1845, p. 709. etc.

the Moreh to compose a treatise on a theorem of Euclid, translated into Italian by JOSEPH SHALIT (1550) and into Latin by Baronius (1586), and erroneously ascribed by the latter to MOSES NARBONI,— are followed by JOSEPH DEL MEDIGO, an independent mathematician and rival of a learned Muhammedan at Kahira (1606); he wrote a book on mechanics for JACOB ALEXANDRI a Karaite of that place, and author of an able supplement to Euclid; he also makes a quotation in his astronomical *Paradoxa* from the catoptrics of Ptolemy.   Multiplication tables (cir. 1610) and arithmetical puzzles were framed in Germany by JACOB BEN ELJAKIM (1613), for primary instruction and an exercise of subtlety; and arithmetics were written by the Italians EMANUEL PORTO (1627) in Hebrew, and ISEPPO (Joseph) LUZZATTO (1670) in Italian.   Subsequently similar works appeared in Jewish-German by an anonymous writer at Amsterdam (1699), MOSES HEIDA (1711), and MOSES EISENSTADT BEN CHAJJIM (1712); and in Hebrew and German by MOSES SERACH EIDLITZ (1775).   ASHER ANSHEL BEN WOLF of Worms (1721), SAMSON GÜNZBURG, and ELIAS BEN MOSES GERSON of Pinczow (ante 1765) wrote on geometry.   BARUCH SKLOW (cir. 1777) translated Euclid; and ISRAEL LYONS (ob. in England 1775) wrote on the differential calculus.

Although Astronomy had lost its practical interest through the general method of determining the Kalendar which was by this time in common use, still the reverence for ancient independent works and treatises on the Law, the complete revolution which had taken place in Astronomy, its influence on dogmatic theology, and the facilities which it afforded for constructing the Kalendar, all conduced to the production of exegetical, historical, polemical, and practical treatises upon this science.   Thus we find perpetually commentaries on Maimonides' Laws of the Kalendar (§ 21.) e. g. by MARDOCHAI JAFE (1594), J. L. HELLER (1632), ARJE (LÖB) at Lublin (1667), JONATHAN BEN JOSEPH (1720), and others; also, on the Astronomy of Abraham ben Chijja, by the same MORDECHAI JAFE and JONATHAN (1746); and on the *Six Wings* of Emanuel ben Jacob, by

Isaac ben Jechiel Ashkenasi (1558), extant in a MS. at Leyden. Various works were explained, and extracts made from them, by Chajjim Lisker (in the middle of the 17th century), probably of Brzesc. The theory of the Kalendar (עברונות) was discussed by Issachar Ibn Susan at Safet (1539–1575); and Solomon Oliveyra invented some Spanish and Hebrew tables (1666, &c.). Of the Kalendars calculated for a longer or shorter period, furnished more or less with general rules, and in various languages, and sometimes referring to the Christian and Muhammedan Kalendars, we will mention the Threefold Kalendar in rhyme by Joseph ben Shemtob (1489, printed 1521), with a commentary by Daniel Perachia at Saloniki (1568), who added the astronomical tables of Abraham Zacut, not however to be found in all the copies of that rare edition; that of Abraham Zahalon (1595); the Italian Kalendar by David Alvalensi (cir. 1660); the Spanish by Abraham Vesigno for 1626–1666; different Hebrew Kalendars by Moses ben Samuel Zuriel for 1654–1674, by Chijja Gabriel of Safet for 1675–1710, and by Isaac de Lara for 1704–1734; an anonymous one for 1713–1827; one in Hebrew and Spanish by David Nieto for 1718–1800; and the *Lunario perpetuo* by Aaron Franco Pinhero (1657). Astronomy in general, or in its more important branches, was treated by David Gans at Prague (ob. 1613), who corresponded on scientific subjects with King Rudolph's astronomer Kepler (subsequently to 1599 at Prague), with Tycho Brahe, for whom he translated a part of the Alphonsinian Tables, and who was also in communication with Johann Müller. Gans, although acquainted with the system of Copernicus, followed the Ptolemaic, considering the former to be the Pythagorean: he also ventured to assert that the Prophet Daniel made a mistake in computation. Menahem (Emanuel) Zion Porto wrote a *Porta Astrorum* (1636), and a treatise dedicated to Ferdinand III. on the astronomical miracles of Joshua and Hezekiah (1643). Solomon Esobi (Azubius the teacher of Plantavitius?) composed (1633) for Schickhard, at the instance of Pereira, an introduction to some as-

tronomical tables, three centuries older (§ 21. n. 61.).   MEIR
NEUMARK translated from the German (1703); TOBIA CO-
HEN (1708) argued against the Copernican system ; and even
DAVID NIETO in London (1714) wrote against the Coperni-
cans, the Cartesians, and the Karaites, with a zeal which
sometimes led him into error.   RAPHAEL LEVI HANOVER
(1734) showed considerable diligence and knowledge of
his subject ; and the same may be said to a certain extent
also of ISRAEL SAMOSC (ob. 1772), the teacher of Mendelssohn, and BARUCH SKLOW, the first editor of the
astronomy of ISAAC ISRAELI, which he illustrated with
diagrams (1777).   ISRAEL LYONS was appointed by the
English Admiralty to accompany Capt. Phipps (afterwards
Lord Mulgrave) on the Arctic expedition (1773), and was
intrusted with the charge of the ship's reckoning.

On Astrology there are but few independent works belonging to this period ; of these we may mention *The Book
of Lots*, by ELIEZER " the astronomer " (1559), and various
productions by the Portuguese Comes palatinus JACOB
ROSALES at Hamburg (1624 seq.).   JOSEPH DEL MEDIGO'S
treatise on practical Kabbala has never been printed.

2. The Medical literature of this period, which is very
poor in Hebrew works, is opened, notwithstanding the papal
restrictions on their art, by some Italian physicians, and by
others who derived their origin from Spain and Portugal.
Among these AMATUS LUSITANUS (1547) first observed the
valve of the unformed veins, and must have been very near
discovering the circulation of the blood ; ABRAHAM PORTA-
LEONE (1564) claims for the Jews the first medical use of
gold.   Two medical treatises by ABRAHAM NAHMIAS at
Constantinople were translated into Latin (1591, 1604); and
ELIA MONTALTO, physician in ordinary to the French
royal family, is said to have been the author of two Latin
works (1614) on the same subject; RODRIGUEZ DE CASTRO,
at Hamburg, wrote on the duties of a physician (1596),
and on the Plague ; this subject was treated also by DE
POMIS (1577), MOSES STAFFELSTEINER (1596), ABRA-
HAM FONSECA (1712), and in a compilation from foreign
authorities by DAVID LANDSHUT.   ZACUTUS LUSITANUS

made a critical comparison between Greek and Arabian
medicine (1629-1642).   Joseph del Medigo translated
(1629) the Aphorisms of Hippocrates from the Latin, and
wrote various treatises on physic; another Hebrew translation of the same Aphorisms, published in his own name
by Gaiotius (Rome, 1647), was certainly not made without
the assistance of a Jew, if indeed the editor had any share at
all in the translation.   Ezekiel da Costa (1642) wrote
on the diseases named after beasts; Chajjim Buchner
composed a work on diet (1669), published with a Latin
translation by Wagenseil. Jacob Zahalon (1683) describes,
in his Comprehensive Pathology, amongst other things the
state of Rome during the plague (1651); the introduction
treats the subject theologically, and the 13th section is devoted to the infirmities of the soul.   In the 18th century
we have scientific dissertations written for the degree of
M.D., which was now more frequently conferred.   Besides
these there were the Kabbalistic mystical works of the
Polish miracle-workers (called Baalshem, בעלשם, i. e. the
possessor of the name of God), whom Tobias Cohen (1708),
physician to the imperial family at Constantinople, opposed in his learned encyclopædic work, undertaken as a
vindication of Jewish science against the calumnies of the
intolerant professors at Frankfurt, and carried out with remarkable learning, and the experience of an extensive practice.   He was also the first to treat, in the Hebrew language,
of the " Plica polonica," from personal observation. Amongst
the writers of this century we may mention Joseph Stella
(כוכב) ben Abraham of Ferrara, in Vienna (1714); Silva
at Paris, who, according to Voltaire's judgment, did better
service by his practice than even by his highly prized work on
blood-letting (1727). Pereira, at the royal library at Paris,
made the first researches on the cure of the deaf and dumb,
in a treatise read before the Royal Academy (11th June,
1749, earlier than De l'Epée).   De Castro Sarmento,
Fellow of the Royal Society of London, wrote on the
use of Peruvian bark, on small-pox, and on Brazil dia-
monds (1755-1762); Israel Lyons wrote on the English
Flora; and Jacob Marx, at Hanover, who promoted

the use of acorn-coffee, answered the exaggerated attacks
of Herz and others on the early interment of the Jews
(1765–1784). Several well-known physicians were brought
up at Berlin, such as LEON ELIA HERSCHEL (nat. 1741,
ob. 1772); MORDECHAI GUMPEL (called Prof. LEVISON),
for some time professor at Upsala (ob. 1797 at Hamburg), an opponent of Mendelssohn; the famous icthyo-
logist BLOCH (ob. 1799 at Karlsbad); and Professor HERZ
(ob. 1803). These close the Third Period, and commence
a series of Jewish writers on medicine and natural history
who have not yet been brought under review.

NOTES.

PERIOD I.

§ 1. Page 1.

[1] We have scarcely any compendious account of Jewish literature not written in the Hebrew language. The Spanish might be collected out of De Castro's " Bibliotheca Española," if this work could be relied upon. Of the printed Jewish-German literature, the author of this essay has given an alphabetical list of 385 books or works (after a MS. catalogue of the Oppenheim collection now in the Bodleian, and Wolfius) in the German journal *Serapeum*, 1848–1849. But this is now superseded by the *Catalogue* of the Hebrew books in the Bodleian by the present author. A monograph on the Jewish literature in the Arabic language, and the translations from that and other languages in the Middle Ages (comp. §§ 11, 12. 21, 22.), was promised by the author ten years ago, when he began collecting materials for that purpose ; but the specimens of his researches given in the *Catalogue* mentioned above will be sufficient excuse for still delaying the completion of this extensive undertaking.

§ 2. Page 2.

[1] Zunz, Gottesd. Vortr. (see note 13.), pp. 22. 31..

[2] Rapoport, Österr. Blätt. f. Lit. u. Kunst, 1845, p. 580.

[3] Zunz, G. V. p. 33.; conf. Geiger, Der hamburg. Tempelstreit, p. 17.; M. Sachs, Die relig. Poesie der Juden in Spanien, p. 167.

[4] Zunz, G. V. pp. 44. 98. 120. 170.

[5] Jellinek (Franck, Die Kabbala, Germ. Transl. by Jellinek), p. 292.; Schlesinger, Einl. zur Uebers. des Buches Ikkarim, p. 21. If, with certain modern authorities, we ascribe to Zoroaster a higher antiquity, the Parseeism which influenced the Jews is not much older.

[6] Krochmal, Kerem Chemed, v. 63.; Frankel's Zeitschr. ii. 301. On the canonical number 70–72 see Steinschneider's essay in the Zeitschr. der d. m. Gesellsch. iv. 147.

[7] See Rapoport in Frank. Zeitschr. i. 355., and also below, § 16.

[8] Concerning the early separation of these see Zunz, G. V. p. 44.

[9] The *Samaritans* are excluded from this account of Jewish literature.

[10] Zunz, G. V. p. 36.

[11] Krochmal, loc. cit. in note 6.

[12] The Mishna Abot (see p. 40.) contains opinions by men of the Great Synod, &c. See Rapoport, Ker. Chem. vii. 167.; conf. Zunz, l. c.

[13] ZUNZ (Die Gottesd. Vortrage &c. Brl. 1832) is the main authority for §§ 3. 5, 6. The popularising "Aphorisms" in Fürst's Litteraturblatt, 1841, are suited to no class of readers.

[14] Among whom JASON, FUSCUS, and THEODORET (Wolf. Bibl. Hebr. iii. 667 c.) are to be reckoned. See Delitzsch, Zur Gesch. d. hebr. Poesie, pp. 28. 134. That PHOCYLIDES was a Jew has been recently demonstrated by Bernays.

§ 3.   Page 5.

[1] The Midrashim *Tanchuma Jelamdenu, Esther Rabba, Midr. Tillim,* for example, have two kinds of redactions. A part of the *Tana debe Elijahu* is introduced into the middle of *Wajikra Rabba,* and a fragment of the *Pesikta Rabbati* is subjoined. The genuine *Pesikta,* a name claimed also by two later works, has been lately reconstructed from fragments discovered some years ago in different recensions. Even the *Halachot gedoloth* and *pesukoth* were long known simultaneously in their separate and their combined forms. The frequent titles רבא (great) and זוטא (small) are important; and perhaps, as with persons (§ 19.), may denote *old* and *young.*

[2] See the author's remarks in the Serapeum, 1845, p. 294. sq.

[3] Id. p. 289.; Frankel, Zeitschr. ii. p. 385.

[4] Zunz, G. V. pp. 41. 322.; comp. Formstecher, Die Religion des Geistes, p. 262.

[5] Ben Bag Bag (Abot, 5. 22.). "As early as the times of Aristeas, Hillel, Jonathan, Philo, and the Apostles, Biblical interpretation was a wide-spread study and an honourable occupation." Zunz, G. V. p. 323.

[6] Respecting the Jewish origin of the *Peshito* see Frankel, Vorstudien zur Septuag. p. 184. (and pp. 170, 171. 197. 210, 211. 217. 223. in the notes upon the influence of the Talmudical exegesis, upon which subject Frankel has since published a monography). Rapoport, Frankel's Zeitschr. i. 358., where more valid grounds than those refuted by Rödiger (Encykl. sect. 3. vol. 18. p. 292.) are brought forward.

[7] Luzzatto, Geig. Zeitschr. iv. 412., v. 124.; Rapop. Ker. Chem. v. 178. sq. 224. sq., vi. 172.; Frankel, Zeitschr. iii. 111.; A. Levy, Geig. Zeitschr. v. 175. sq.; Lit. bl. vii. 337. sq.   See also below, § 16. note 3. 7.

[8] Zunz, p. 38. The opposite to these were the Idiotæ (עם הארץ Pagani), by which term men of the wildest immorality, guilty of murder and the like, are generally to be understood in the Talmud (in opposition to Jost, Gesch. iii. 110., Anhang, p. 150.); conf. Rossi, Della Vana Aspettazione degli Ebrei del loro Rè Messia (Parma, 1773), p. 209. The distinction of "clergy" and "laymen" is but an invention of modern Idiotæ.

[9] Respecting funeral discourses see in particular Dukes, Rabb. Blumenlese, p. 247. sq.

[10] Zunz, G. V. 323. 331. 337.; Geiger, Zeitschr. v. 67. Cf. Wiener Jahrbücher, vol. c. p. 93., and on the Pesikta below, § 5. note 108.

[11] Zunz, G. V. p. 308.

§ 4. Page 9.

[1] The modern works and treatises on this subject, viz. by BRÜCK, CHORIN, CREIZENACH, FASSEL, Frankel, Geiger, Holdheim, S. SACHS (Frank. Zeitschr. iii. 133. sq.), and others, form a literature of themselves, a sketch of which would exceed the limits of this article ; conf. ZUNZ, Kurze Antworten auf Cultusfragen (Berl. 1844), p. 15.

[2] It is important to observe that the same expression is also applied to the prophetical books (Zunz, G. V. 44., contra Brück, Rabb. Cerem. p. xi.). On the later signification of *Kabbala*, see § 13. note 15.

[3] The notion that Jewish practice has grown up principally from this kind of interpretation of Scripture (cf. Maimonides, Introd. to the Mishna-Comm.) has been of late successfully combated.

[4] Zunz, G. V. pp. 42. 421., § 13.

[5] So, for example, even after the termination of penal jurisdiction, up to recent times, the Jewish "Court" (בית דין) could enact the most severe disciplinary punishment (מכת מרדות) for transgression of the ceremonial law. This is still the case in Turkey, &c. The expression דין, judgment, remained in the ritual decisions of later times. To the writers on Jewish law and rabbinical authority mentioned by Zunz (Kurze Antw. § 9.) we may add the names of FRANKEL, FASSEL (cf. Lit. bl. viii. 203.), SAALCHÜTZ, BODENHEIM, STEIN, and others.

[6] Creizenach, Tharjag (conf. Geiger, Zeitschr., ii. 548.) ; Brück, Das Mosaische Judenthum, and l. c. p. 1. On the part of the older Karaites, the treatise of Hedessi, § 242., must be mentioned.

[7] Zunz, p. 43., cf. Jalkut, § 1000.

[8] The Chaldee Paraphrase has הלכה for the Hebrew משפט (Ezech. xxi. 9.) ; for which the Chaldee סוגיא (rad. סנא) was then adopted ; corresponding to the Arabic السُّمَّة (Nathan, s. v. in Dukes, Glossar. zur Blumenl., conf. Zunz, G. V., pp. 42, 43.) ; and thus it originally meant the simple thesis, doctrine, in contradistinction to מדרש, study, investigation (see also Targum Koh. 12. 12.) ; then also the result of investigation, final judgment (Gerson in Buxtorf, Lex. s. v.), as a rule for practice (מעשה), and finally everything relating to practice, in contradistinction to Haggada. Respecting Eisenmenger's mistake, see the foot note, suprà, p. 18. Besides Zunz's enumeration of authorities, see also Succa, 28., and especially Sanhedrin, 101., conf. Jalkut, Proverbs, § 953. The remarks of Graetz (Gesch. p. 489.) against Zunz are, like some others (cf. n. 53. and § 5. n. 17.), founded on a distortion of his views. I wish here to remark, once for all, upon the extreme uncertainty of this and all other technical terms used in this article, in consequence of which the determination and development of the various periods of literature are rendered extremely difficult, and have frequently occasioned various mistakes and anachronisms.

⁹ The Midrash, after its manner, interprets the end of Ecclesiastes as a warning against apocryphal books, as Krochmal (Ker. Chem. v. 80.) acutely remarks. A similar case is found in the Muhammedan literature, vid. Hadschi Chalfa, ed. Flügel, i. p. 97.; conf. Mills, Hist. du Mahommétisme, p. 37. The Gauls also were prohibited from committing their traditionary songs to writing. Cæsar (De Bel. Gal. vi. 4.) recognises in this a precaution against levity in learning them. Thamus (see Plato, Phædrus) makes a similar remark on the disadvantage of writing. See Grimm's preface to the Kindermährchen (Göttingen, 1843), p. xvii. note.

¹⁰ These must have existed long before the date assumed by Brück, p. xxv. See also § 5., and cf. ראב״יה (Mehlsack), Lit. bl. xii. 143.

¹¹ The main authority for this part of the essay is an unfinished work by Krochmal, prepared for the press by Dr. Zunz, with the assistance of the author, in which the first attempt is made to arrange in a historico-philosophical manner the origin and development of the Halacha. That work has been since published, (Lemberg, 1851,) but is printed very incorrectly. The corresponding chapter is the 13th, p. 161. sq.

¹² Even later great litterati retain that name (Kelim, 13. 6.); afterwards it was used for transcribers and notaries, teachers of children and prelectors (conf. קרא, § 16. rem. 15.). Hupfeld (De Rei Gramm. p. 2.) takes it as a denominative participle of ספר, and says of Gesenius's satisfactory derivation, "Nihil cogitari potest absurdius."

¹³ For the transcription from the old Hebrew into the square character, the testimony of Eliezer ben Jacob (Sebachim, 62.), an authority in matters of tradition, is of some importance. (Cf. the dissertation of M. A. Levy on the inscriptions on the vessels discovered by Layard, in the Zeitschrift der d. m. Gesellschaft, ix. 476.) Azaria de Rossi (see § 23.) is to be considered as a leader in these investigations.

¹⁴ See Erubin, 14. b. The expression הלכות סופרים, therefore, does not occur, as Krochmal remarks, p. 167.

¹⁵ Krochmal, l. c. p. 169., gives authorities. That the beginning of the Masora reaches so far back is probable, although the expression Soferim may be referred to the younger transcribers (note 12.). It is worth mentioning that Joseph Ibn Wakkar (see the article in Ersch, sect. ii. vol. 31. p. 96. note 3. c.) designates the variations of Keri and Ketib " variæ lectiones " (נוסחאות). Respecting the changes of punctuation for euphony, after the manner of the Targum, see Luzzatto, Proleg. ad una Gram. Ragion. &c. p. 21. and below, § 16.

¹⁶ Hither, according to Krochmal, p. 167., is probably to be referred the warning of R. Ismael, Erubin, 13. (contrà Jost, iv. Anh. p. 225.). On תיקוני סופרים, Buxtorf, in his Lex. Chald. p. 2631., says, " Explicationem prolixiorem, imo tractatum justum, res ista requirit."

¹⁷ See the commentary to Succa, 28 a. Ibn Ezra, Zachot. According to Kircheim (Lit. bl. v. 674.), perhaps grammatical rules; on the other hand, see below, § 16. rem. 49. This subject still requires further light to be thrown on it. See Krochmal, p. 173.

¹⁸ By a similar metonymy מדה signifies a certain ethical deport-

ment, a virtue, מדות (in the plural), the attributes of God, character, ethics. See below § 12. B. and § 13.

[19] Synh. 7. b. Krochmal, p. 175. Parallel instances of the derivation of such expressions for judgment, &c., from roots which signify to cut, to cut off, &c., have been collected by the author from the new Hebrew and Arabic in his notes to Maimonides, Maamar Hajichud, p. 9. note 8.

[20] Megil. Taanit. ; cap. 4. conf., on the subject of " Judges of Sentences" (דייני גזירות), Ketub. cap. 13.

[20a] Frankel, Die Lehre vom Beweis nach jud. Rechte, p. 60.

[21] On the language of the Mishna there have appeared, besides the essays of HARTMANN, REGGIO, and LUZZATTO (mentioned in Luzzatto, Proleg. p. 66.), special tracts by GEIGER and DUKES ; conf. also the author's Die Fremdsprachl. Elem. in Neuheb., &c. (Prague, 1845), p. 24., and Lit. bl. vii. 325.

[22] See below, note 29.

[23] " Repeater." The Hebrew form is the common active participle ; the Chaldee a frequentative, and consequently equivalent to " Repetent" (note 29.) ; conf. sup. note 8.

[24] Krochmal, p. 176., still takes גמרא for השלמה, " completion," comprehension of tradition, and discussion for the purpose of practical results ; but see Zunz, pp. 43. 324. sq. On תלמוד, as a method of teaching, see note 55., גמרא, to learn (from others), in contradistinction to סבר, to discuss. Sabb. 63 a. (Dukes, Blumenlese, p. 195.).

[25] Sabb. 8. 1. Schekal, 3, 2. Krochmal, p. 184.

[26] The expression נשקע, " sunk," was used with respect to elements interwoven in this way, e. g. the Mosaic Halachot in the Mishna ; Krochmal, l. c.

[27] Krochmal, p. 193. Conf. Ker. Chem. v. 183., on the composition of the " Testimonies," and ib. vi. 98. ; also below, § 5., end of note 1.

[28] Krochmal, p. 187. Conf. also Lit. bl. vii. 325. rem. 6., and the احباب of the Koran.

[28a] Moed. Katan, 9.

[29] משנה means repetition, Greek δευτέρωσις (conf. משנה תורה Deuteronomy) ; hence, Second Thora, or oral law in general = תורה שבעל פה (which expression is used already by Shammai, Labb. 31. b., see Wolf, ii. p. 663.), so that Mishna at first would signify the whole Halacha, and have been later applied to single Halachot ; the expression שונה הלכות, however, would be the denominative of משנה. But if we start from the supposition that the Halacha must have been handed down orally, and diligently repeated, then משנה might mean originally a repeated Halacha. Ibn Balam (ad V. Mos. v. 4.) derives משנה from שנן (!). The following is worth notice : the Chaldaic plur. מתניתין corresponds to both משניות and משנה, whilst מתניתא in singular is = ברייתא (see below, note 49.) ; and the frequentative תנאי appears in the same sense as the simple participle שונה. Conf. also on מכלתין and מכלתא, Zunz, p. 47. note, and Krochmal, p. 195. Brück (p. xxii.) makes the Synedrion of Hyrcanus introduce

a new book of the Law, the Mishna, and appeals to the fact that Nehemiah is called Mishna. See, however, above, note 22.

30 Conf. As. de Rossi, Meor Enajim, cap. 15., and Steinschneider, Fremdsprachl. Elemente, p. 9. note 17. The author has collected some information on Jewish Mnemotechnics in the Oesterr. Blätt. 1845, Nr. 91.; see also below, note 58., § 5. note 106. Some more general remarks "Ueber die sogenannte Hamiltonische Methode der Juden" are given by Dukes, Lit. bl. xi. 382.

31 ⎱ There are no notes corresponding to these numbers, the series
32 ⎰ in the text jumping from 30 to 33.

33 See the journal (published by Jost) Israel. Annalen, i. 108. 131.; the Hebrew periodical Jerusalem, ii. 56.; we need some special investigations on the subject of the composition of the Synedrium. Cf. Frankel, Der Beweis, &c. p. 68.; also on the influence exercised by the Maccabees on the Hebrew style.

34 See Jost, iii. Anh. p. 148. note 9., p. 150. note 13.; Brück, p. xxiii.; cf. Zunz, p. 45. 331.; Jerusalem, ii. p. 62. sq.; Kerem Chemed, vi. 143.; Frankel's Zeitschrift, iii. 211.

35 Jost, iv. 318.; Formstecher, p. 311.; Geig. Zeitschr. ii. 417.; M. Sachs, Rel. Poesie, p. 144.; Frankel, Der Beweis, &c. p. 94., and on the practical influence, p. 53.

36 Edujot, i. 3.; conf. Ker. Chem. v. 172. 181.; Frankel's Zeitschr. ii. 171.; Rapop. Gon. ad Quæst. 9. a.; Lit. bl. vii. 622. Respecting the names of the schools conf. also Wolf, ii. 914., iv. 446.; Lit. bl. viii. 100.

37 See Ker. Chem. vi. 138.

38 Ib. v. 217. ⸮ 25.

39 On what follows next see Rapoport's letter to Slonymski, trans lated into German by Delitzsch in Lit. bl. i. 195.

40 See the quotations in Zunz, p. 46.; Brück, p. xxvii.

41 Rapoport, Kerem Chemed, vii. 175.

42 See the Biography by Schwarzauer, Lit. bl. iv. 630, sq.

43 Zunz, p. 49.

44 Rapoport, Ker. Chem. v. 153. sq., and Erech Millin. Cf. החלוץ, ii. 123.

45 On the opinions of Geiger, Luzzatto, Rapoport, and Reggio, see Geig. Zeitschr. iv. 412., v. 68.; Bodek, Jerusal. ii. 53. On the pretended object see S. Sachs in Frankel's Zeitschr. iii. 205. On the sections, Brück, Pharis. Sit. p. 10. (after Geig. Zeitschr. ii. 56.). See also § 5. n. 19.

46 Some antiquated notions are quoted by Jost, iv. Anh. p. 242. A more correct view is to be found in Zunz, G. V. p. 336.; cf. Zion, ii. 58.; Lit. bl. v. No. 18.; Frankel's Zeitschr. iii. 174.

47 רב is Babylonian, רבי Palæstinian. Fürst, Lit. bl. viii. 18. n. 76., explains אריכא, "of Areka?"

48 Rapoport, Ker. Chem., vi. 143, sq., vii. 158. sq. (against Fürst's Gesch. der Babyl. Lit., Lit. bl. viii. 107.) in the preface to the Responsa Gäonim, ed. D. Cassel (Berlin 1847) fol. 10., coinciding with Geiger, vi. 17.; cf. also the articles ארץ שראל in Rapop. Erech. Millin.

49 Conf. Brück, p. xxxi.

[50] Always in the sing., see above n. 29. Wolf (ii. p. 662.) reads מתניתא, which however should be written מתניאתא as in Scherira בריאתא. The usual spelling Borait*o* has been adopted, although it ought to be vocalised either Borait*o* (Chald.) or B*a*raita (Heb.). On the obsolete מחוצה see החלוץ, i. 64. Hedessi, § 224.

[51] Conf. suprà p. 16. and Landauer, Lit. bl. i. 743., ii. 34. An obscure hypothesis, Lit. bl. viii. 410. See Ker. Chem. ix. 23.

[52] Rapoport, Ker. Chem. vi. 169.; Lit. bl. viii. 506.

[53] Id. vii. 169.; and the article Jochanan in Ersch and Gruber's Encycl. by Zunz, whom Graetz, however, attacks, Gesch. p. 482. (p. 290.), with his usual sophistry. (Cf. § 17.) On the interpolations from later sources conf. also Lit. bl. viii. 330.

[54] Jost, iv.; Anh. p. 253. n. 39.

[55] Rapop. in Zunz, G. V. p. 53. sq. ; and in Ker. Chem. vii. 164., cf. vi. 232. 248.; Lit. bl. iv. 753., vii. 325.; Brück, p. xxxii.; Chajes in Bikkure haittim, 5606, p. 14. Frankel also (Vorstud. p. 29.) admits that the Babylonian Talmud injures the more correct ideas contained in the Jerusalem Talmud by many unwarranted additions and inexact statements, and has given examples in different places of his new Monatschrift.

[56] The expression תלמוד was thence used in the signification of method of teaching, see Rapoport, Ker. Chem. vi. 127.

[57] See Rapoport, l. c. p. 100.; Zion. i. 108. 126.

[58] Zunz, p. 53. n. 2.; Brück, ii. p. 9. Conf. Ker. Chem. vi. 254.; Frankel's Zeitschr. ii. 326.

[59] Jost, v. 225. 319.; Ker. Chem. iv. 187. On the other hand, Geiger, Zeitschr. vi. 103.

[60] See passages quoted in Zion, ii. 83. sq.; Ker. Chem. vi. 250., conf. Beer in Frankel's Zeitschr. iii. 473. note ; Rapoport, Erech Millin, p. 10., conf. suprà n. 30. and § 5. n. 106. Jost (Lit. bl. vi. 818.) considers מטריקון to have been secret writings at the time of the Christian persecutions; see K—m, Lit. bl. vii. 326., and the article " Abbreviaturen," printed as a specimen of the intended Jüd. Realencykl. by Cassel and Steinschneider, 1844. According to Jost, iv. p. 35., mention is made of sympathetic ink in the Talmud, Jer. Sabb. cap. 2. On the later interpolations in the Talmud see also Rapoport in Zunz, G. V. 141 b.; Chajes, Mebo ha-Talmud, p. 256.; Oppenheim, Lit. bl. x. 312.

[61] See the author's Fremdsprachl. Elem. p. 20. sq.; Frankel's Zeitschr. iii. 179.; JELLINEK in Debarim Attikim, ii., and Nachtrag zu Sefat Chachamim, Leipsig, 1847. On the Persian literature of the Jews see § 8. n. 13.

[62] שמושא רבא, see M. Konitz, 2, 3. § 15.; Conforte, ed. Cassel, 3 a., conf. Jost, v. 319. Sabbatai, sub voce, ascribes it however to the Gaonim, conf. § 5. note 23. Perhaps it is the foundation of the small treatises Tefillin, Sefer Tora, Soferim, and Zizzit ? cf. the fragment of Jehuda ben Barsillai at the end of Asheri, Tr. Tefillin. (cf. Zion, i. 97.)

[63] See Zunz, p. 89. sq. 310.; Brück, p. 11.; Zion, i. 136., ii. 85. 165. 181.; Rapoport, Ker. Chem. vi. 247.; Frankel's Zeitschr. i. 357. n. 2.

[64] Jost, v. 229.; Anh. p. 341.   The Semicha has however not been restored, see Zunz, p. 309. n. 6.   The Gaonim composed few works, because the oral tradition was still continued and preferred to written documents.   Meiri, Introd. to Abot. (Revue Orientale, ii. 34.)

[65] Conforte, 3 a.   Against Rapoport's artificial derivation of the title (Ker. Chem. vii. 268.) see Jellinek, Lit. bl. vi. 172.   The time of its origin requires to be defined more accurately.   R. Jose (early in the sixth century) is already called Gaon, while Maimonides (Introd. to the Mishna Comm.) speaks of Gaonim in Spain and France.   He designates their writings as Responsa (תשובות), Comm. on the Talmud, and Decisos (הלכות פסוקות).

[66] Rapoport, Ker. Chem. vi. 230. sq.

[67] Brück, p. 13.

[68] Conf. Rapoport, Nissim. n. 16., and epistle to the assembly of Rabbies at Frankfort-on-Main, 1845.

[69] Rapoport's treatise, Ker. Chem. vi. 233., gives some new and interesting dates.   Conf. Geig. v. 441.; see also Zunz, p. 57.; conf. Zion, ii. 159.; Allg. Zeit. d. Jud. 1840, No. 30.; Brück, p. 15. sq., is also here one-sided.   It is, however, remarkable that an anonymous Arabic work on the killing of cattle (composed in the twelfth century) always mentions Jehudai Gaon before Simon Kahira, whose Aramaic statements are said (f. 95.) to be given word for word in the Hebrew מדרש השכם (see above, p. 27.; cf. Zunz, p. 281.): moreover, the same work calls Simon simply קאירא (sic only f. 80., in the subsequent places always קיארא), "the author of the הלכות גדולות;" while Jehudai Gaon is mentioned without the title of his work, and in only two places (f. 80. and 94.) the quotation is literally "the היל ראו הלכות, attributed (אלמנסובה) to Jehudai Gaon."   Jeshua, the Karaite (10th century), quotes both these Hebrew titles without naming the authors.

[70] [Note to "Halacha," p. 26. of text, line 13. from bottom.]   See also Dernburg in Geiger, Zeitschr. v. 399. (and note 69.).   On the different redaction of JOSEPH TOB-ELEM see Rapoport, Introd. to the Resp. Gaeon. § 5., and Luzzatto, Biblioth. f. 53.

[71] Ker. Chem. vi. p. 242. § 20.; cf. Hedessi, Alphab. 131. 151., and הלכתא פסיקתא, Aboda sara Ta.

[72] Rapoport's Emendation (l. c. p. 240. 244.) is confirmed by the new edition of the letter of Scherira (Chofes Matmonim, p. 82, 83.).

[73] [Page 27. line 2. of text.]   Conf. Zunz, p. 279.; conf. Zeitschr. der d. m. Gesellsch. iv. 148.

[74] רבנן דהשתא, Rapoport, p. 246.

[75] Printed at Venice, 1545.

[76] The best edition is Dihrenf. 1786, with the excellent notes of J. Jesaia Berlin.   Zunz, p. 56.; Brück, p. 16.

[77] [Note to "Gedolot," p. 27. of text, line 10. from bottom.]   Zunz, p. 309.; Rep. Ker. Chem. vi. 235. 246., and § 5. n. 23.

§ 5.   Page 28.

[On the whole Section conf. RAPOPORT in the article אגדה of his Erech Millin (published since this es ay), and Abraham SCHIK's Introd. to En. Jakob.

[1] Zunz, p. 322.; conf. Frankel's Zeitschr. ii. 383.; M. Sachs, Rel.
Poës. p. 147.

[2] See the author's "Miscell." in Zeitschr. der d. m. Gesellsch. vi.
539. n. 6.

[3] Conf. M. Sachs, l. c. p. 150.   From the Judæo-Muhammedan
legend of the Covenant of God with all souls, arose the Muhammedan
dogma of the Covenant of the Prophets.

[4] Zunz, cap. 4., conf. pp. 43. 324.; Zion, ii. 107. sq.

[5] Zunz, p. 354.; Frankel's Zeitschr. ii. 385.; Sachs, p. 174.

[6] Zunz, p. 354., conf. 195. 324. 344.

[7] On the later meaning of רמז, see § 17. n. 8.

[8] Sachs' remark, l. c. p. 162., must be restricted to this.

[9] Zunz, p. 325. sq., conf. sup. § 4. n. 30.

[10] פשט = بسط, explanare, hence originally synonymous with דרש
(Geig. Zeitschr. v. 289.); while a later period distinguishes between
Pashtanim and Darshanim (§ 17.).   In the Arabizing style of the
philosophers, פשוט is = بسيط, the simple in a metaphorical and hermeneutical sense.   See also inf. n. 102.

[11] Zunz, p. 59.   On the later exegetical meaning see below, n. 102.

[12] Id. pp. 60. 325. 341.

[13] The limits here traced out are of course not to be taken in too
exact a sense.

[14] Zunz, p. 358.; conf. Rapop., Ker. Chem. iii. p. 48.

[15] Zunz, pp. 172. 324.

[16] Id. pp. 84. 86.

[17] Zunz, p. 85.; Discrepant MSS., Oppenh. 627.   The way in
which Graetz has distorted Zunz's views is shown by the author in
Catal. p. 1435.; conf. § 10. n. 14.

[18] Zunz, p. 86.

[19] On this Geiger and Brück founded an alteration in the division
of the Mishna.   See § 4. n. 44.

[20] Zunz, p. 110., also see inf. 2 a.

[21] Id. p. 95. (and sup. § 4. n. 61.), and inf. § 16. n. 17.

[22] Id. 377 e.; conf. § 19. n. 10. sq.

[23] Conf. sup. § 4. nn. 60. 75.

[24] Conf. Zunz, p. 93.

[25] Jewish authors meet with neglect and contempt from foreigners.
According to Jehuda Halevi (Cusari, ii. § 64., iv. § 31.), medical
notices are found in the Talmud, which were unknown to Aristotle,
Galen, &c.   An author of the tenth century (Lit. bl. vi. 564.) speaks
of a medical work by R. GAMALIEL HA-NASI, "who is called Galen
by the Greeks," which was translated from the Hebrew into Arabic (conf.
§ 21. n. 10.).   The assertion that the learned Greeks were pupils of
the Jews is found as early as in the works of Aristobulus (Formstecher,
Die Relig. des Geistes, p. 317.), Josephus, and Eusebius (D. Cassel on
Cusari, ii. § 66. p. 172.); and afterwards it became a prevalent opinion.
The instances given by Buxtorf on Cusari, i. § 63. (whose principal
authority is Moscato on the same), might be multiplied; e. g. Palquera, Komm. Moreh, p. 7.; Joseph Ibn Caspe (Cod. Uri, 365.
f. 172 b.; see the author's article in Ersch, s. ii. vol. xxxi. p. 72. n. 74.

where he remarks that Roger Bacon already protested against the Christian authorities who took the same views) ; Aaron ben Elia, the Karaite,
Ez. Chajjim, p. 4. ; and others, especially with respect to Medicine : see
also Assaf's Introduction [see § 22. n. 34.] ; and Jonathan ben Joseph,
who, in the commentary on צורת הארץ, speaks of Aristobulus as the
person who communicated Solomon's Philosophy.   On the other hand,
the Kabbalistic opposition to the Peripatetic philosophy gave another
direction to that supposition.   Moses de Leon (משכן העדות, MS., chap.
5. ; cf. נפש החכמה at the end of chap. 2.), the book Zohar, and M.
Recanati (in Az. de Rossi, ii. chap. 2., about the end), pretend that the
old Greek philosophers were more in conformity with the Rabbies, and
that Aristotle took a different turn.   Abraham Levi ben Eliezer
(ס' יהיחוד MS.), however, returns to the old fiction, which makes
Aristotle a pupil of Simon the Just, and attributes to him " secret
writings " containing his true opinions.   The same author believes that
the " Philosophers " took some doctrines from the " truly wise "
(חכמי האמת = Kabbalists), although they did not interpret them in a
literal sense, "which occurred also to some Jews." Joseph ben Shemtob
(see that art. in Ersch, Enc. s. ii. vol. xxxi. p. 92.), an orthodox philosopher, contents himself with the conditional statement, that "if" Aristotle
had met with the Jewish wise men, he would certainly have adopted
their creed.   Moscato also doubts the genuineness of the epistle of
Aristotle in which he confesses his return from philosophy to positive
belief (on that epistle conf. *Catal.* p. 743. op. 6.).   On a passage of
Moses Isserls see *Catal.* p. 1832.   The Jews, moreover, were not alone
in these opinions ; and perhaps they did not even invent them.   The
Arabian " Brothers of purity " (see §12. n. 1.) derive science from
the Jews (Nauwerck, Notiz., &c. p. 41., and in Hebr. iii. cap. 7.) ;
and a passage of Averroes to that effect has become a locus classicus.
In Christian Europe also it was usual to derive arts and sciences from
Biblical personages (Roger Bacon, l. c., and Sprengel, Gesch. d. Med.
ii. 25.).   Cf. also on " Greek wisdom " below, note 96.

     [26] Conf. Rapop. Bikk. haitt. 5588, p. 14.   On Jewish medicine,
especially of this period, the following authorities are quoted by several
authors ; but only a few of them which were accessible to the author : —
J. P. Speeth, De Ortu et Progressu Medicinæ per Judæos (8., Hamburg, at the end of the seventeenth century ; see Wolf, iii. p. 742.) ;
some materials have been collected, but principally in the later periods,
and those in a hostile spirit, by Schudt in his Jud. Merckw. (4. F. a. M.
1714–17) ; Ginzburger, Medicina ex Talmudicis illustr. (Götting. 1743) ; J. H. Lautenschläger, De Medicis veterum Hebræorum
(Schleitz. 1786) ; Meyer Levin, Anal. Hist. ad Medic. Ebræor. (Hal.
1798) ; D. Carcassonne, Essai hist. sur la Médic. des Hébr. anciens
et modernes (Par. 1816, Montpel. 1818) ; Lilienthal, Die jüdischen
Aerzte, eine Inaugural Dissert. (Münch. 1838) ; Israels, Tent. Hist.
Med. ex Talm. De Gynæol. &c. (Lugd. 1845) ; Cohn, De Med.
Talmud. (Vratisl. 1846) ; G. Brecher's long-promised comprehensive
work of the medical parts of the Talmud and Midrash — of which
Das Transcendentale, &c. (Wien, 1850), is a preliminary part.   The
work מאה דפים on this subject is known only from the Add. to
Buxt. Bibl. (according to Jacob Romano ?), and Sabbat. (conf. Israels,

l. l. pp. 8. 29.; the book on the Hundred Maladies of the Indian Tanfestal in A. Sprenger, De Orig. Med. Arab. [Lugd. 1840], p. 14.; Miah Kitab of Abu Sahl in Amoreux, Essai, &c. p. 147.; and Wustenfeld, Gesch. der Arab., Aerzte, § 118. 1.). On CARMOLY's work see § 22. Whether SPRENGEL's long-promised work on Hebrew medicine has ever been published, is not known to the writer. The earliest record of Jewish medicine is the ספר רפואות (cf. טבלא של רפואות [tabula] Talmud Jer. Pesachim, chap. 9.) of King Solomon, said to have been set aside by King Hezekiah, and to refer to Sabaism (contrà, Dukes, Blumenl. p. 29.), see the author's Fremdsprachl. Elemente, p. 10. n. 20.; conf. Moreh, iii. c. 37. p. 259., ed. Scheyer; Joseph Ibn Aknin's Comm. on Cantic. (Ersch, s. ii. vol. xxxi. p. 53. n. 65.); Allemanno, שער החשק, p. 17. (conf. Carm. p. 5.); S. Sachs, התחיה, p. 32., cf. Jalkut Reubeni, f. 25 a.). Of the Physicians in the Talmud, ABBAJA, SAMUEL at Babylon (see n. 32.), and THEODOS in Palestine (contrà, Carmoly, see Geig. Zeitschr. v. 462.; conf. Zion, iii. p. 16.); and besides these, MOSCHION (perhaps A.D. 117—138) is worth mentioning, as a translator of Jewish writings into Latin. See Bergsohn, Lit. bl. iv. 86. sq., and the Magazine for the History of Medicine, Janus, 1853, p. 657.

27 Conf. Franck, Kabbala, Germ. transl. by Jellinek, p. 58., with Sachs, Rel. Poes. p. 230., Reifmann, Pesher dabar, ii. 9. sq. (uncritically used, Lit. bl. viii. 40.).

28 Beer, Lit. bl. viii. 311. Sure, 73. v. 20. of the Koran, seems to be a treatise against the three watches of the night (אשמורות) : see the author's Fremdsprachl. Elemente, p. 18. n. 38 b., and § 21. n. 4.

29 The author's treatise, Orientalische Ansichten über Sonnen-und-mondfinst. in the Magaz. f. die Lit. d. Auslands, 1845, no. 80.

30 On the contrary opinion see Israeli, Jesod Olam, iv. cap. 6. ed. Goldberg; conf. SLONIMSKI, Ker. Chem. v. 104. (Jesod ha-Ibbur, p. 33); RAPOPORT, Ker. Chem. vi. 186., vii. 255. 264. sq.; conf. Jost, iv. 197. Anh. p. 253., and inf. § 21. nn. 9. 17. On the Christian calculation of Easter, see the author's refutation of Ideler in היונה, p. 29.; see § 21. n. 15.

31 RAPOPORT's letter to Slonimski (quoted § 4. n. 38). There are other astronomers in the Talmud, e. g. R. CHIJJA, SIMON, ZEIRA the father of Simlai, JOHANAN, NACHMAN, RABA, and others (see following note).

31a Not " Hajarchi," " the lunatic," as IDELER (Handb. d. Chron. i. 574.) erroneously calls him. The derivation " of Orchon " is proposed by Lebrecht in the Allg. Zeit. des Judenth. 1849, p. 657 ; cf. Lit. bl. 1850, p. 398. where Fürst claims the priority over Böhmer.

32 Slonimski (היונה p. 4. n. 4.) explains סוד העבור as congregation held for intercalation; but see n. 102. Cod. Vat. 285. 11. (conf. Wolf, i. 2130.) begins with a sentence of Samuel's (see n. 26.) on blood-letting, which even Assemani has grossly misunderstood. In a Machsor MS. of 1426 a short piece inscribed ענין הקזה (of blood-letting) begins in the same manner. The same is probably the case with the Cod. Vat. 387. (Boraita of Samuel), see inf. § 21. n. 12.

33 Conf. sup. § 4. 28. Different views upon this subject are quoted by the author, Catal. p. 2032. (conf. n. 61.). The Orientals are generally

fond of combinations of numbers; see Hammer, Wien. Jahrb. vol. cxiii. p. 11.

[34] The precept of the N. T., "Render unto God the things that are God's," &c., is properly a Halacha precept of this description.

[35] Hammer (Wien. Jahrb. cxiii. 1. sq.) goes too far, if he removes all imperatives from Gnomonics to Ethics; in the Ethical Haggada no such distinction can in general be carried out.

[35a] See the author's article on the history of Hebrew Poetry in Frankl. Zeitsch. iii. 405.; conf. Delitzsch, zur Gesch. d. Heb. Poes. p. 135. Lit. bl. viii. 394.

[36] Chald. מתלא, Arab. مثل, &c., see DUKES, Rabbinische Blumenlese, Leipz. 1844, p. 6. (His Zur kabb. Spruchkunde, Wien, 1851, is an appendix to it); Hammer, l. c. pp. 3. 18. 46.; conf. Delitzsch, l. c. p. 32., where the Indian (?) Juda and his son Samuel are noticed, see n. 54.

[37] Höfer, Blätt. f. lit. Unt. 1844, p. 387; conf. Dukes, l. c., pp. 5. 12.

[38] Dukes, p. 48.; also his Introd. to Proverbs (in Cahen's Hebr. and French Bible, Paris, 1847), p. 25.

[39] Conf. Dukes, p. 10. In the Palestine Talmud there is an entire Greek proverb untranslated, of course in Hebrew letters, see Lit. bl. viii. 330.

[40] Proverbs of "Corporations" (Dukes, p. 11., conf. p. 41.) are, however, not a scientific category.

[41] Dukes, p. 18.; Hammer, pp. 3. 5. 46,

[42] GEIGER ("Was hat Muhammed," &c., p. 92.) has pointed out some sentiments from the Talmud in the Koran, but not all; see for instance the author's "Miscelle" in Zeitsch. d. m. Gesell. vi. 538. n. 5., where a varia lectio in the Koran is decided by reference to the Rabbinical source. In the Sunne, see nos. 215. 491. 593. 651. (in Hammer's collection in Fundgr. des Orients) &c.; conf. also Herbelot, art. Hadith. On the N. T., Menschen has already collected the most important points; see also Zipser's "Krit. Untersuchung" (Lit. bl. viii. 733. sq.). Parallels from various literatures in Dukes, Introd. p. 48. n. 18.

[43] Examples in Dukes, pp. 13. 16, sq., and in the author's "Manna," Berlin, 1847, p. 94. sq.; conf. also inf. § 20. n. 18.

[44] Only writings arranged in parallelism, like Sirach, use Biblical phraseology (conf. Dukes, pp. 43. 35.). The funeral orations also in the Talmud adopt parallelisms and Biblical phrases; against Dukes p. 253., see p. 256. n. 4.

[45] Dukes, p. 44.

[46] Conf. Weil, Muhammed, pp. xix. 47. 408., and his Einl. in d. Koran, p. 4.

[47] Hammer, l. c. p. 7.; e. g. Prov. i. 1. in Hammer, p. 47. conf. Fundgr. No. 33. The prayer (ib. 110. 673.) consists also of Biblical passages.

[48] Freytag, Prov. Arab. iii. no. 3265. (Decalogue!) 1904. 2314. 2810. 2815. 1886. 2909. as also 522. 1160., the only sources for which known to Hammer (p. 41.) are the Gospels! Parallels in other languages are to be found in Dukes, Introd. to the Proverb. Salom. pp. 17. 22.; Lit. bl. viii. 518. n. 10.

49 Dukes, zur Kenntn. der rel. Poesie, p. 114. sq., Blumenl. pp. 7. 44. conf. p. 10. Hammer (p. 46.) compares the اقتباس, but to this artificial form, as also to تصمين, Hebrew parallels are first found in later productions ; see § 18. n. 60. On the Biblical phraseology in the Talmud conf. J. Weisse, Introd. to Jedaja Penini, p. xix.

50 Dukes, p. 49.

51 Id. p. 17.

52 According to this, Sachs' views (Rel. Poes. p. 333.) must be modified.

53 Conf. Dukes, p. 16. Trivial and obscene proverbs (as e. g. Freytag, 111. 354.) are not found here.

54 References in Zunz, p. 100.; Dukes, Annalen, i. 100. sq. (Blumenl. pp. 7. 11.), whence LANDSBERGER, Fabulæ aliquot Aram., Pref. p. 9. sq. The fables edited by Landsberger (מלתיה דסופוס) are considered by Jellinck (Leipz. Repert. 1846, part. 32. p. 211.) to have been translated in Syria from the Greek at the latest (?) in the sixth century, and perhaps used by the composer of the Arab. Lokman. But the recent composition of the latter leaves a large margin ; and the Jewish origin of the Aramaïc fables has not yet been proved from the fact that they occur in an Oriental MS. in Hebrew characters. Landsberger's further communications (Lit. bl. 1849) contain some erroneous statements (Ib. p. 70.).

54 a Stein (Kohelet, pp. vi. xii.) suggests "stories [told] to the washers" (conf. Synh. 38. b.); on the improbable emendation משלי כוכבים "Proverbs of the stars," see Lit. bl. xi. 613). Of the works בן תגלה and בן לענה see Wolf, i. p. 932.; Delitzsch, p. 32. (sup. n. 38.); Lit. bl. iv. 250., conf. § 20. n. 32.

55 Rapop. Lit. bl. i. 37. sq. The explanation given by Reifmann (Pesher dabar) is absurd.

56 On what follows see also Dukes, Blumenl. p. 23. sq.

57 The author has refuted Dukes' supposition of a third Ben Sira in the "Spruchbuch für Jüd. Schulen," (Berlin, 1847) p. 102. See also Azaria de Rossi, chap. ii., at the beginning, and § 20. n. 20.

58 Zunz, p. 106.; Auerbach in Busch's Jahrbuch f. Israel, i. 159. sq.; Rapop. Ker. Chem. vii. 166. Also see inf. n. 68. and Lit. bl. x. 414. 428. Frankel, in his Monatschrift, has also tried to carry out under a new and pompous title (Der Lapidarstyl, &c.) the old idea (see Samuel ben Meir, Ker. Chem. viii. 49.) of a reference in these sentences to the history of their authors.

59 A want of information in this respect occasioned the errors committed by Uri in Cod. Bodl. Hebr. 238., conf. inf. § 19. n. 42.

60 But in no wise mystical, still less "with the stamp of mystification . . . ," as Stern (Perlen des Orients, &c. Wien, 1840, p. iii.) designates the sayings which he leaves untranslated.

61 Conf. Lit. bl. vii. 823.; according to Geiger, Zeitschr. vi. 20. sq., it was composed from later Midrashim in Palestine ; but even in that case there is no reason for identifying its author with that of the Middot. Conf. also *Catal.* l. c. in. n. 33.

62 Conf. Allg. Zeit. d. Jud. 1842, p. 447. and *Catal.* p. 251. n. 1636–7, and p. 1874. op. 23.

[63] Ven. 1598. Prag. sine an. (soon after 1676), with a commentary.

[64] Zunz, p. 248. In the Talmud and older Midrash some precepts are ascribed to the prophet Elias (סבא, the old), so that there existed some older collections on this subject; conf. the *Seder Eliahu* above, p. 32. A "Rabbi" Elias appears only in the Midrash Chasith. On Fürst's preposterous hypothesis, that the author is Elia ha-Saken, quoted in Jellinek's not less preposterous combinations (Beiträge, ii. 79.), see *Catal.* p. 749.

[65] See *Catal.* p. 596. n. 3793., where the ed. 1802 in פרדס of Sal. Isaki is to be added.

[66] Zunz, chap. viii. The author's article Zur Sagen-und Legenden-kunde, in Frankel's Zeitschr. ii. 380. sq., iii. 281. sq.

[67] Fremdsprachl. Elem. p. 26. and Emendations ad loc.

[67a] E. g. Baba Kama, 80. b. (Lit. bl. viii. 812.).

[68] See also the author's article on the Talmudical indices rerum, &c. (Serapeum, 1845), p. 295. and sup. p. 17. Among similar influences there was developed the Arabian history of the learned; see inf. § 10. n. 5.; conf. also Rapoport, Pref. to the Resp. of the Gaonim, f. 10 a.

[69] And indeed so early that it is taken as tradition; see Treuenfels, Lit. bl. vii. 62. and inf. nn. 73. 104. With respect to numbers, the author has collected some striking examples in his treatise on the numbers 70–73 (see above, § 2. n. 6.). The number 24000 in Maimonides's אגרת השמד (p. 12. in the German of Geiger) might be also brought under this category. On Ibn Ezra's and Maimonides's views on such pseudepigraphical works see infrà, § 20. n. 4.

[70] The author's article, "Ueber das Verhältniss der Muhammedan-ischen Legende zur Rabbinischen," in the Magaz. f. d. Lit. des Aus-landes, 1845. See p. 286. sq. (used in his usual manner by Fürst, Lit. bl. xii. 290, 291.) and the author's translation of the section upon the Jews by HAMZA EL ISFAHANI, with annotations in Frank. Zeitschr. ii. p. 321. sq., 447. sq., and the illustration of a passage in the Koran by the author in Zeitschr. der d. m. Gesellsch. iv. 148.; and on the Samaritan see the author's "Manna," p. 114.

[71] Zunz, pp. 155. 282 d. 149 b.

[72] E. g. Saadja. See Dukes, Beiträge, p. 91.; Geig. Zeitschr. v. 311. Conf. on the saga of the "Bürgschaft" the author's remarks in the Magaz. f. Lit. d. Ausl. 1845, p. 208.

[73] So e. g. on the tables of nations, see Dukes, Beitr. p. 48. sq. 56. sq.; and, with respect to the example of the Berber, the add. to the German note in the *Catal.* pp. 1806. 1912. &c.

[74] References are given by Zunz, p. 119. sq.

[75] Zunz, p. 121. On the "Roll of Susa," מגלת שושן (Susanna or Judith), see Ker. Chem. vi. 256.; Lit. bl. iii. 814.

[76] Zunz, p. 120. Formstecher, Relig. des Geistes, p. 285.; conf. Jost, Gesch. ii. Anh. p. 58. sq.

[77] Zunz, p. 137. REIFMANN, Zion, ii. 61. sq. (from whom the references made by Mecklenburg in Edelmann's ed., Königsberg, 1845, are to be derived. See Lit. bl. vi. 659.). LANDSHUTH, Maggid. Mereshith, a historical commentary on the whole Agenda, with a German essay by the author, has been recently published.

[78] See Bloch in Geiger, Zeitschr. iv. 221.

[79] Zunz, pp. 129. 278. ; conf. Geig., Zeitschr. v. 441.

[80] Id. p. 128. ; Perhaps 1 Timothy, iv. (conf. iv. 7, sq.) is directed against writings of this kind.

[81] In the authorities for this Zunz (p. 128.) sees, with great probability, only a metaphorical expression ; conf. also Dukes, zur Rabb. Spruchkunde, p. 67 ; on the correction of S. Sachs see § 22. n. 76.

[82] TREUENFELS (Lit. bl. vii. 9. ; conf. 81. 83., and the late opinions about this book ; the same author in Lit. bl. xii. 270.) hastily concludes from Hieronymus, "apud Hebræos," that this book was originally written in Hebrew (conf. also § 13. 4. 2, 3.).

[83] Hammer on Flügel's ed. of the Faithful Companion, &c., by Thaalebi, p. i. (by Muhammed himself), in Wien Jahrb. cx. 16., Talmud, Synhedr. 42.

[84] Zunz, p. 140. ; according to an anonymous author in Zion, ii. 157., of Christian origin. Isaac Troki also (Chissuk Emuna, i. 43.) ascribes the historical Apocryphal books to Christian authors.

[85] On the Hebrew and German translations and their ed., see *Catalogue*, p. 206. It has been printed in 1851 by Filipowski in Aramaïc, together with [Gabirol's] Choice of Pearls.

[86] See *Catal.* p. 609., where Bartol. i. 639. and the French free paraphrase in Carmoly's Revue Orient. i. 181. are wanting.

[87] E. g. that Nimrod will cause the sun to rise in the west (which, according to the Muhammedan legend, belongs to the signs of the last day) ; the quarrel between Gabriel and Michael, and other things of the same kind. (Cf. *Catal.* p. 609., by which Jellinek and Beer, in Monatschr. iv. 59. are to be corrected.)

[88] *Catal.* p. 586. no. 3740., where Asulai sub. וישעו, is omitted. A copy of the Oppenh. MS., and a different recension in a collection of sagas in another old Bodl. MS., were sent by the author from Oxford in July, 1855, to Jellinek, for his 3rd vol. of Bet ha-midrasch.

[89] See *Catal.* no. 3449. sq., 3996. sq. On the מעשה דיוסף בן פרת, see Wolf, i. no. 951. p. 555. ; cf. Lit. bl. ii. 432. (neglected ib. viii. 12.). The צוואת נפתלי בן יעקב (id.) belongs probably to Germany ; conf. § 12. n. 41.

[90] Manna, p. 101. Sabbat. bl. 1846, p. 61. ; and generally *on all these works* see the author's *Catal.* sub vocibus.

[91] On this and the following "Paradise and Hell" literature, which is not yet exhausted, see some additions in the author's catalogue, sub Mose de Leon, p. 1849. ; and his further communications to Jellinek (see note 88.).

[92] See *Catal.* p. 585.

[93] On the two recensions, the difference between which was unknown even to Zunz and the editor of the Bet ha-midrasch, see *Catal.* p. 588. no. 3751. sq. A work of the same name by Asher ben Meshullam, with an introduction by (his brother?) Jacob (see Reifmann, Lit. bl. v. 481. ; conf. Ker. Chem. vi. 181.), probably the Asher of Lünel, about A. D. 1180 ; perhaps a Commentary of the Pijjut of Simon ben Isaac? See § 19. n. 20.

[93 a] See the author's Schene Hammeoroth, præf. add. to p. 11. n. 11., and Ker. Chem. vi. 181.

[93 b] L. c. cap. ix. p. 157. sq., cap. xxi. p. 402. sq. On LANDAUER's Remains in Lit. bl. vi. vii., see inf. § 13.

[94] FRANCK, La Kabbale, &c., Germ. transl. by JELLINEK (Leipz. 1844); (conf. La Cabbale, &c., Compte-rendu par Louis Dubeux, Paris, 1844, and § 14.); GRÄTZ, Gnosticismus und Jüdenthum (Krotoschin, 1845.) Formstecher (pp. 102. 265. sq.) takes the Kabbala as the particular, and the Talmud as the general term.

[95] The exiles, on their return thence, brought with them the names of the months and angels. See Formstecher, pp. 124. 279.; Franck, p. 261.

[96] M. Sachs, Ker. Chem. vii. 273., who is neglected by Landau in Frankel's Monatschr. i. 175., where JOHANAN BEN ZAKKAI is supposed to be the first who founded real schools for secret doctrine with reference to Pesach. 74., Chag. 13. On the forbidden חכמה יונית, see Reggio and Gfrörer in Geig., Zeitschr. ii. 347., Jost, iii. 146.; Brück, Zerem. xxiii. n. 83.; Formstecher, p. 317.; Kircheim, Zion, ii. 83.; Hirschfeld, Halach. Exegese, § 40.; Jellinek, in the notes to Franck, pp. 206. 209. Gräz, Lit. bl. vi. 796.; Dukes, Sprache der Mishna, p. 6.; Szanto, Busch's Jahrb. vi. 244.; conf. sup. n. 25. and § 28. n. 13.; and the old explanations of הגיון, given by Joseph Ibn Aknin and others (see Ersch, s. ii. vol. xxxi. p. 51. n. 31.; cf. § 12. n. 3.); Lembke (Gesch. von Span. i. 245.) laments that heathen writings were forbidden among the Western Goths.

[97] This designation itself does not admit the idea of chapters of a particular science. (Franck, p. 40.)

[98] שֵׁם, 1 Chron. xiii. 6. (according to Zunz, 164. sq.; conf. Fürst, Lehrg. d. aram. Sprache, p. 50.; but might we not read שָׁם?), as in later times اسم (Wetzstein, Lit. bl. ii. 55. n. 2.) is hence probably not an original euphemism. The " Name of the 72 " (Letters) (שם בן ע״ב) is older than Geiger (Melo Chofnajim, p. 49.) thinks; and the number 72 is, like 70, a sacred number among the Jews and Muhammedans. See the author's essay on that subject, mentioned above, § 2. n. 6.

[99] FORMSTECHER, Beitr. zur Angelologie, &c., in Israel. Annalen, i. 361. sq., and his Religion des Geistes, p. 124.; conf. sup. n. 95.

[100] Maimonides, Moreh, i. 33, 34.; conf. נסתרות Jer. Sota, ix. 11. (Jefe Mareh).

[101] On his views, see Franck, pp. 35. 215; see inf. § 13.

[102] סוד in the Talmud does not signify this (metaphysical) mysticism, but everything confined to the narrow circle of the initiated, e. g. סוד העבור (Israeli Jesod Olam, iv. § 14. fol. 29 a.; Ker. Chem. vi. 187.; see sup. nn. 10. 32.). Later נגלה — נסתה, חיצון, פנימי (תוך?) answer to the Arabic باطن and ظاهر (the quotation of Beresh Rabba, cap. 45., in Buxtorf, Lex. Chald. p. 1560., cannot be found); see Maimonides, Moreh, ii. 25. and the emendations and translations in Simeon Duran, (Keshet u-magen, f. 18. l. 3. fr. bot., where lege אהל אלבאטן, according to the Cod. MS. Michael. no. 412.; Joseph Ibn Aknin (in Ersch, s. ii. vol. xxxi. p. 55. n. 79.). Emanuel on Prov. i. 6. (in Dukes, Introd. p. xi.), accordingly distinguishes משל and מליצה. The allegorical or mystical interpretation is called ביאור הסוד. Arab. تأويل

see the author's remark in Frankel's Zeitschr. ii. 112., and inf. § 17.
n. 8. and § 13. n. 19.

[103] See Leon de Modena, Ari Nohem, cap. 22. The passages of the
Talmud connected with metaphysics, magic, &c., have been very carefully collected in BRECHER's Das Transcendentale, &c. See sup. n. 26.

[103 a] Zunz, cap. 10. sq.

[104] Id. 170 a.; Fürst, Zion, iii. p. 3. sq.; Dukes, Beitr. p. 49.;
the author's compilation on Arabian names in Frankel, Zeitschr. ii.
273., and sup. n. 69.

[105] Even the Haggada recognises a kind of (free) tradition (מסורת
הגדה), Zunz, p. 326.

[106] The author's Fremdsprachl. Elem. p. 10.; conf. Lit. bl. viii.
p. 233.; conf. Ker. Chem. vii. 280., and sup. § 4. n. 59.; cf. Jel-
linek (Debar. Attik.) on Levi ben Sisi, and the quotations of Jona Ibn
Gannah in his introduction, repeated by Moses Ibn Ezra and Joseph
Ibn Aknin (Ersch, s. ii. vol. xxxi. p. 56. n. 84.). On *Notarikon* see
sup. § 4. n. 58. So also the Chinese assert of the Book of " Great
Wisdom," that even the particles in it have a meaning. Zeitschr. d. m.
Gesellsch. ii. p. 109.

[107] References in Zunz, p. 171.

[108] According to Zunz, the word פסיקתא means in Chaldee the same
as מדרש in Hebrew (cf. Frankel's Zeitschr, ii. 386.). Almost at the
same time a notice of the old MSS. of Oxford was given by the author
in the Add. to this essay, at the end of vol. xxviii., and in his *Catal.*
p. 631. no. 4002., and privately to Zunz; and by Luzzatto of his
MS. (see Rapoport, Erech Millin, p. 176., cf. p. 170., and Dukes, Lit.
bl. xii. 358., on the MS. de Rossi, 261., inscribed מדרש הפטרה).
The sagacious exposition of Rapoport is not free from an excess of
sagacity; but there are some authors whose errors are more instructive
than the truths of others.

[109] According to Rapoport, Ker. Chem. vii. 17., composed shortly
before A. D. 781. Chap. vii. unquestionably calls eighty-four years the
hour of a divine day, see § 21. n. 15.

[110] [Note to " Vajosha," p. 53. of text, line 9. from bottom.] On
Midrash Vajosha and its two different recensions (formerly unknown),
see the author's *Catal.* p. 585. no. 3734. sq.; cf. Cod. Vatic. 303[20].
(Paris, 206[3]. ?).

In concluding this section, we may remark that a survey of all the
Midrashim according to periods is given by Zunz, p. 304., and a short
conspectus of those printed and mentioned in the author's *Catal.* is
given there, pp. 582–3. We ought to mention here that M. JELLINEK,
a very industrious editor, had also begun the meritorious undertaking of
gathering the smaller Midrashim into a single corpus, when the corresponding part of the author's Catalogue was already printed. But as only a
few articles of the latter were communicated to Jellinek, he was not
sufficiently informed about the bibliographical apparatus necessary for
such an undertaking (e. g. on Eldad he has even neglected a notice of
Dukes in the Litteraturblatt); nor was he able to purchase always the
oldest or best editions when he began printing. We are, nevertheless,
indebted to him for the publication of some inedita. The author here
abstains from entering upon a criticism of his views and hypotheses.

§ 6.   Page 54.

[1] The investigations of this paragraph, which is closely connected with § 19., are founded on RAPOPORT's Biogr. of Kalir (see Geig. Zeitschr. i. 390. sq., 397.) ; ZUNZ, G. V. p. 366. sq., who gives a historical survey of the Liturgy.   Some remarks and deductions by MORTARA are to be found in Israel. Annal. i. 209. sq. ; DUKES, Zur Kenntniss der rel. Poesie, and M. SACHS, Die rel. Poesie, p. 164. ; a continuous historical commentary to the prayer-book, ed. by LANDSHUTH (Königsb. 1846), (conf. Lit. bl. viii. 68. sq.) ; also for some particulars in the most recent controversial writings on public worship, see GEIGER, Der Hamburger Tempelstreit (Breslau, 1842), p. 16. sq.

[2] Conf. the author's article, Frankel, Zeitschr. ii. p. 388.

[3] E. g. Sachs, p. 173.

[4] Dukes, Z. K. 137. ; cf. Zunz, p. 377. note b.

[5] Berach. 29. b., conf. 33. ; Sabb. 113. (conf. Lit. bl. viii. 223.) ; Geig. l. c. p. 21.

[6] E. g. instead of Zech. i. 16., the prayer of Shemona-Ezrah, 14., is quoted with the formula שנאמר in Midrash Ps., see Zunz, p. 267 a. ; and conf. Weisse, Introd. Jedaja Penini, p. 22.

[7] Bor. derabbi Eliezer, sup. 5 B. p. 53., conf. Zunz, pp. 281. 377.

[8] Zunz, p. 315.   On the intentional interweavings in the later artificial style, see Lit. bl. iv. 60. n. 94. ; Manna, p. 97. lin. penult.

[9] The treatise Abot (§ 5. n. 68.) was read on the Sabbath as early as the ninth century (Rapoport, Introd. to Resp. 9 a.).   Since it was and is allowable to pray in any language, there might have existed Persian and Greek prayers, possibly also translations of the typical Hebrew, conf. also Geig. p. 21.

[10] In this Targum (on which see Zunz, pp. 80. 120.) Reifmann (Zion, i. 75.) detected the later alphabetical form (inf. § 18.).

[11] תפלה, the obligatory prayer (Maimonides, Comm. to Berach. iv. 2., ix. 5.), answers to the Arabic صلوة (Sure, ii. 40., ix. 72. ; cf. v. 15. with respect to Jews), which form (Chald. אלותא), like زكوت, (expressing the alms which purify the rest of the property like the תרומה) as well as the thing itself, is to be deduced from Rabbinism, as will be further explained in the author's notes to Simon Duran's Keshet u-magen, f. 19 b.

[11 a] Thence שבעתא, see § 19. n. 10.

[12] See Zunz, Benjamin of Tudela, ed. Asher, ii. p. 116., conf. Frankel's Zeitschr. ii. 356. n. 2., and against Lit. bl. viii. p. 17. n. 72., p. 182. n. 270., see Rapoport's Introd. to Resp. Gacon. 10 b.   On the combination of the judicial office with the functions of public worship (דיין וחזן וכו') see Jer. Jeb. ix. 1., Jefe Mareh.

[13] The passage noticed by Sachs (Rel. Poes. d. Jud. 172., conf. 265.) certainly does not show that people remained in the synagogue the whole day, but only a considerable part of it.   Simeon Duran (Keshet u-magen, 19 b.) deduces the five daily prayers of Muhammedans from the five prayers of the Day of Atonement.   On the seven daily prayers

among the Sabæans (Herbelot, Sabi, iv. 10.), and some Jewish and Muhammedan sects, see the author's Fremdsprachl. Elem. p. 180. and his
essay Die Beschneidung des Araber, &c., (Wien, 1845) p. 27. note
(conf. § 14. n. 10.).   Museilama reduced them to the (Jewish) three ;
see Weil, Khalifen, i. p. 21.

[14] The discussion in the Talmud, on the errors of the reciter, itself
speaks in favour of his having recited by heart.   The Aramaïc קרובא
also is possibly to be derived from " to offer, to bring in ;" conf. Dukes,
Z. K. p. 32.

§ 7.   Page 59.

[1] Jost, ix. ; Index, p. 14.
[2] See the author's Fremdsprachl. Elem. p. 2. and the note, Lit. bl.
vi. 247.
[3] Delitzsch, Hebr. Poes. p. 140.   Respecting the author's special
work on the Arabic Literature of the Jews, to which he refers in the
German essay for special points, see note to § 1.

PERIOD II.

§ 8.   Page 60.

[1] After the example of the Arabians, symbolical, rhyming, and
metrical titles were introduced, which also, for certain kinds of writing,
became typical.   Examples would occupy too much space ; but an instance will be found in D'Israeli's Curiosities of Literature.
[2] Rapop. Introd. to Parchon, p. xiv. ; Ker. Chem. vi. 245.   Compare De Rossi, Annal. Sæc. xvi. n. 57.   With these Judgments the
Muhammedan Fetwas correspond even in form ; compare, for example,
the stereotyped phrase וֹשברך יהא מן שממי, and others of the same kind
in the Zeitschrift der Deutsch. Morgenl. Gesellsch. i. 330.
[3] RAPOPORT was the first to call attention to the consequences of this
opposition, and its effects upon the progress of Jewish literature.   Notwithstanding many important contributions, the whole details of it are not
yet thoroughly understood.   The extensive use of Latin was a principal
hindrance to the understanding of Christian literature in Germany
(Zunz, Z. G. p. 181.).   Conf. § 23. p. 205.   It is questionable whether Hebrew was anywhere spoken by the Jews ; the passage of Mos.
Gikatilia, quoted by Zunz, l. c. p. 187., is rather doubtful.
[4] The Genealogy in Zunz, G. V. p. 365. ; conf. Rapoport, Ker.
Chem. vi. 22. 116., vii. 15. ; Resp. Gaon. 12. b. ; Landauer, Lit. bl.
vii. 45. sq., and recently Luzzatto, Il Giudaismo, i. 30.
[5] To the important subject of the chronology of the learned men of

the 10th century, the present time has contributed some valuable results, but also many superficial and hypercritical suggestions. The authorities are given by S. Cassel in Frankel's Zeitschr. ii. 226. sq., 231. sq. ;
also Lebrecht, ib. p. 422. sq. ; S. Cassel, Histor. Versuche, p. 30. sq.

6 Later, the word *Gaon* is merely a title of honour ; Chisdai Crescas
applies it to his older contemporary Nissim.   Conf. § 4. n. 65.

7 Geiger (Lit. bl. der Israeliten, 1846, p. 134.) names as emigrants
to Provence, Abrah. ben Chijja, Judah ben Barsillai, Tibbon, and
Kimchi ; and to the East, Jehuda Halevi and Ibn Ezra ; although with
regard to some of them he has but slight grounds for doing so.

8 Jourdain, Researches, &c., in the German transl. of Stahr (For-
schungen über Alter und Urspr. d. lat. Uebers. d. Arist. Halle, 1831),
pp. 97. 100. 106. 215. 271. ; conf. Humboldt, Kosmos, ii. 283.

9 Charles employed Faradj ben Selam (see § 21.). Zunz (in Geiger,
Zeitschr. iv. 189. ; conf. Lit. bl. iv. 20.) names also Peter III. (1280) ;
see, however, § 21. n. 68.   The translations into Latin by R. Isaac
(Carmoly, Hist. de Méd. p. 94. ; conf. Anal. i. 63.) belong apparently
to the inventions of Carmoly, since Judah Romano himself translated
mostly from Latin, § 12. n. 9.

10 Innocent III. complained of the preference shown by Alphonso
for Jews and Muhammedans (Jourdain, p. 146.).   Concerning the
envy entertained by Christians towards Kalonymos see Zunz, Geig.
Zeitschr. ii. 317. ; conf. Steinschneider, Lit. bl. iv. 25.

11 From the Midrash itself we can, for the most part, obtain no
definite results on this point.

12 Concerning the decline of it see above, n. 2.   Joseph ibn Megas
still prefers it for Talmudical *discussion*.

13 The Persian translation of the Bible, see § 16. n. 10. ; קצה דניאל
apparently of the 12th century ; see Munk, Not. sur Saadja, &c.,
p. 87. ; compare Herbelot, Odhmat. (iii. 688.).   On a medical work
of Abi Saad see § 22. n. 19.   A Persian elegy (קינה) in Munk, l.
c. p. 68. (conf. Lit. bl. vi. 619.).

14 See the authorities quoted in Steinschneider's Fremdsprachl.
Elem. 1845, p. 27. ; conf. Geig. Melo Chofn, 92.   Goldenthal (Zion,
iii. p. 2.) considers Abrah. ben Chijja as the founder of the Hebrew
scientific style ; but Ibn Ezra (born in 1093) and the Karaite Jehuda
Hedessi about 1140 (§ 14. n. 24.) are his scarcely younger contemporaries.   Dr. Goldenthal has recently published (originally in the Memoir
of the Academy of Vienna) a specimen of a Lexicon of this branch of
literature, professing himself to be the first who had given attention to
the subject ; his assertion (which he proves, p. 423., by a fragmentary
quotation from Lit. bl. iii. 823., without mentioning, however, that
this very quotation belongs to an older essay of some length on the
same subject) has been repeated in nearly all the journals, except the
Litteraturbl. (xi. 419.), whose editor remarks that Goldenthal has omitted to give an account of his predecessors, and names them.

15 We can here name only a treatise by Zunz (zur Gesch. 230. sq. ;
conf. 206. sq.).   Even M. Wiener, who knows the value of his authorities, believes (in Frankel, Monatschr. 1854, p. 118.) the pretended
date, 157, on a tombstone in Cologne, to be a. 397 ! Cf. Zunz, zur
Gesch. 394. 570.

§ 9.   Page 67.

[The further history of the Halacha has, as yet, been scarcely treated at all independently, on which account this section demands the special indulgence of the reader.   Notices in RAPOPORT, Chananel, n. 30.; GEIGER, Zeitschr. i. 22. sq.; and BRÜCK (Pharis. Volkssit. p. 15. sq.), who has much that is one-sided and false.   ZUNZ (zur Gesch. S. 188.) gives a review of the teachers of the Law in Germany and France, conf. p. 192. sq.]

[1] For example Hai in the Comments on Taharot.

[2] See the author's *Catal.* no. 7051. sq.; conf. Maimonides (l. c. § 7. n. 65.).

[3] Several of such by Karaites are older, see § 14.

[4] Rapoport's Biogr. n. 30., conf. Geig. Zeitschr. i. 398. sq. (see n. 6.); conf. Landauer (Lit. bl. vii. 3.), whose chronology must be received with caution, see *Catal.* sub no. 6677.

[5] See *Catal.* s. v.

[6] According to Lebrecht (Frankel, Zeitschr. iii. 422.), he still flourished in 1050.   Rapop. Biograph. n. 30., incorrectly repeated in Geig. Zeitschr. i. 399., conf. Ker. Chem. vii. 185.   Some MS. Commentaries on the Talmud have been falsely attributed to him; they are by a later author, CHANANEL BEN SAMUEL (12th century), see S. D. Luzzatto, Lit. bl. 1850, p. 241.

[7] *Catal.* p. 1837. no. 6494.

[8] Conf. Frankel, Beweis, p. 106.

[9] Zunz, zur Gesch. p. 474.

[10] Geig. Zeitschr. ii. 557.; Mauksch. Lit. bl. v. 155.; Zunz ad Benjam. p. 260., conf. Lit. bl. i. 705.   In the authorities quoted in the German essay, Frankel (Monatschr. iv. 77.) might have found all that is well founded in his invectives against Reifmann, the recent biographer of Serachja, aimed indirectly against D. Cassel's critical recension, and indeed against all history of literature.

[11] See Lebrecht, Frank. Zeitschr. iii. 430.; conf. p. 232.

[12] Geig. Zeitschr. i. 22.

[13] *Catal.* s. v.   The article "Gerson" in the Encycl. of Ersch, by D. Cassel, is now in the press.

[14] Lit. bl. iv. 5.

[15] Zunz, chap. 18., refers to Rapop. Ker. Chem. vii. 4. sq., see Zunz, zur Geschl. pp. 61. 566.

[16] Not as his immediate scholar, as the author of this essay (Lit. bl. iv. 5.) formerly asserted on the authority of Geiger.

[17] See *Catal.* p. 1853.

[18] Dernburg, Geig. Zeitschr. i. 118. 214., conf. the author's treatise in the Serapeum, 1845, pp. 290, 291.; Frankel, Beweis, p. 106. sq.

[19] Dernburg, Geig., and Zunz, Geig. Zeitschr. 212. (conf. v. 458.), ii. 309. 556.   Zunz, zur Gesch. 74.   According to Frankel (Monatschrift, iv. 75.), Abraham ben David is "the most ingenious (scharfsinnigste) critic of the science (*sic*) in general," and not less admirable than Maimonides.   But we must suppose that his conception of "science" is especially derived from that Talmudical dialectic which the same

author has somewhere else called peculiar to Judaism! Jomtob ben
Abraham defended the great teacher of the Law against Abraham ben
David and Shemtob ben Abraham Ibn Gaon (conf. § 13.).

[20] Conf. *Catal.* p. 1968-9.—Concerning the influence on France,
see n. 28.

[21] Zunz, zur Gesch. p. 29. sq., 188.; conf. Beer in Frankel, Zeitschr.
iii. 472. 476.

[22] Zunz, zur Gesch. p. 59.

[23] Id. p. 39., conf. p. 57. With regard to the determination of the
time, conf. Zion, i. 94., and suprà, p. 90.

[24] Zunz, zur Gesch. 184., conf. Lit. bl. i. 108., iii. 686., vii. 521.;
conf. נבון in Zunz, l. c. 518. among the Spaniards; and concerning
other real or honorable *titles*, Rapop. Nissim, note 32. With respect
to Haggadaic authors, conf. Zunz, G. V. 236. note d.

[25] Beer, l. c. 479.

[26] Zunz (zur Gesch. 188.) draws attention to the contemporaneous
dissensiones of the old glossators of the Roman Law, conf. Levi ben
Abraham in החלוץ, ii. 19. For the like casuistry in *Muhammedan*
religious practice, see Wien. Jahrb. lxviii. p. 7, sq.

[27] See the list in Zunz, p. 192.

[28] Zunz, l. c. 160. sq.

[29] Id. p. 182. sq., conf. sup. § 4, 2. A.

[30] See n. 20. A ס׳ המצוות by his somewhat older contemporary,
Samuel of Falaise, see in Zunz, p. 37. Between these, the *Asharot*
(§ 19.) and the ethical writings, stands the work מאמר השכל, v. *Catal.*
no. 3709.

[31] Cod. Rossi, 571. 803.

[32] Proper *Liturgies*, v. § 19.

[33] *Catal.* p. 678.; Mieri, f. 41 b., ed Wien., conf. § 13. n. 21.

[33a] *Catal.* no. 5004. and Add. ad locum.

[34] Zunz, p. 475.

[35] MS. Michael, 653. 673.

[36] Zunz, 477., conf. Lit. bl. i. 704.

[37] Those of the latter are published by D. Cassel (Berl. 1846),
with the life of the author, conf. *Catal.* p. 1291.

[38] Conf. Frankel, der Beweis, &c. p. 11. sq., where a superficial
bibliographical note is given.

[39] See sup. n. 16.

[40] Zunz, p. 120. Rossi (Cod. 140, 2. 180, 2.) calls the author
"Gamah vel Agur." The author of this essay conjectured formerly
that this might be the Arabic (حاصب) and the Hebrew (אגור), both
titles of the work (conf. § 16. nn. 30. 34. and 52.); but neither Rapoport
(Erech Millin, p. x.) nor Dukes, in his notice of Stern (Lit. bl. xii. 357.),
had alluded to it. The former, however, comes to nearly the same
conclusion. Indeed the quotation לשמואל אבן גמיע shows that גמע was
referred to the author by a person who was almost contemporaneous
with him, but who, however, had no other authority than the ambiguous
inscription of the work, where המסנה גמע ופירושו אגור seems to refer
to the first word חבור. Dukes would have done more wisely not to in-
scribe his notice "Samuel Gama." The name Joseph ben Jehuda
Darsham (Lit. bl. ib. p. 359.) has been neglected by Geiger, Parschan-

data, p. 11. A compend. of the עָרוּךְ of the 13th century, Cod. Vat. Hebr. 467. (in Mai. Collect.); conf. MS. Mich. 604.606. Dukes, Sprache der Mischna, p. 17.

[41] Asulai, ii. 66. ed. Wilna ; Lit. bl. ii. 33. sq.

§ 10.　Page 75.

[There is no special dissertation which we can quote for the first part of this Section ; but we recommend the Hebrew and German Anthology " Auswahl historischer Stücke," &c. (by J. ZEDNER, Berlin, 1840).]

[1] Vide Cassel, Hist. Vers. p. 4. This seems to have been done not only with reference to passages in the Bible, as in Gen. xlix. 10. ; conf. De Rossi, Della vana Aspett. p. 70., Bibl. jud. Antichr. no. 47. 79., and the writings in Zunz on Benjamin, p. 212. — Concerning the *Beni Musa*, the author's quotation from Schahrastani's work on the sects (ed. Cureton, p. 168.) has been repeated by the editor of the בית המדרש, ii. p. xxviii. (see following note), conf. Sacy, Christ. Arab. i. p. 360. sq. ; Lit. bl. vi. 140.

[2a] Concerning the three different recensions of Eldad, see *Catal.* p. 923. The falsifications of CARMOLY have recently found an advocate (a writer in Frankel's Monatschr. iv. 106.), who is himself no judge of forgeries by so great a master, and has so little critical acuteness, that he denies that Ibn Caspi wrote an exposition of Ibn Ezra's " Secrets," notwithstanding that the author of this essay has enumerated so many MSS. of it still extant ! See § 12. n. 31.

[3] Vide § 14. n. 6.

[4] For example, Maimonides (upon which see the author's remarks, Frank. Zeitschr. iii. 280., and see § 13. n. 26 a.), Ibn Ezra, Zion, ii. 154. ; conf. Zunz, G. V. 140.

[5] The Arabian history of learned men also took its rise chiefly from the Sunna and from practical interests, as, for example, appears from the writings of the teachers named in Wüstenfeld's *Akad. der Araber.*

[6] Completely and critically edited by LUZZATTO, 1839. Conf. Zunz, G. V. 361. ; Dukes, Beitr. p. 1. Concerning the edition of JOSEPH TOB-ELEM, see Rapop. Resp. Gäon, § 6. On a work under that title by JOSEPH HA-LEVI, according to the very suspicious authority of Carmoly existing in Cod. Paris. a. f. 285., conf. the author's *Catalogue*, p. 1549., and Lit. bl. xii. 455.

[7] Zunz, Notes to Benjamin p. 245.

[8] Concerning the new edition of Goldberg, see Rapop. Resp. Gäon. 10 a. sq. A historical work by JACOB BEN NISSIM was not in existence (see *Catal.* p. 1117.); his son expresses in his " Clavis" his intention to compose a work on the chain of tradition.

[9] It is worthy of remark in relation to this subject, that the *Karaites* completed their genealogy from the *Seder Olam suta* (see n. 16.) ; conf. also Rapop. Resp. Gäon. 10 a.

[10] Zedner, l. c. p. 50. Concerning the last chapter in Josippon, attributed to him by Rapop., see *Catal.* p. 1548.

[11] H. Michael, apud Zunz, zur Gesch. 163., conf. *Catal.* p. 2162. Upon an anonymous author (1290.) see Zunz, p. 166.

¹² Zunz, zur Gesch. 478.

¹³ Published by Ben-Jacob (Leipz. 1846). The name Aaron ben Abraham rests, indeed, upon only the rather doubtful authority of Carmoly.

¹⁴ *Catal.* p. 1435.; and see suprà, § 5. note 17.

¹⁵ See § 4. n. 47.

¹⁶ Zunz, ad Benjamin, p. 6.; conf. Zedner, p. 93. n. 5.; Lit. bl. vi. 739.

¹⁷ *Catal.* p. 1548. Concerning some translations of Josippon, conf. Ewald, Zeitschr. d. Deutsch. Morg. Gesellsch. i. 338., and n. 18.

¹⁸ A mistake of the author in Frankel, Zeitschr. ii. 327., has been corrected (but only half the correction printed) ib. p. 448. Graetz, however (Frankel, Monatschr. iii. 315.), implies that the Arabic version is older than, and even a source for, Josippon. But it should be observed that Graetz had only a short time previously (Novemb. 1853) received notice, in a private communication from the author, of the existence of that Arabic version extant in print and in some MSS., which do not agree together, and which require more profound study and judgment than has been shown by that author in other subjects of this kind; conf. sup. § 5. n. 17., see *Catal.* s. v. Sacharja ben Said.

¹⁹ *Catal.* no. 3581. It is worth mentioning that the Hebrew was originally printed in 1625, contrary to the wish of the Rabbies of Venice, and not until the celebrated JEHUDA DE MODENA had purified the MS. from some passages which he thought too strange, and which he considered to be "lies" (*sic*); vide Ari Nohem, p. 60.

²⁰ Delitzsch, Hebr. Poes. 80. 122.; conf. Wolf, i. p. 165. n. 1051. Conf. the Hebr. journal *Zion*, ii. 104. note

²¹ Adler, Annal. i. 91. sq.; Kirchheim, Lit. bl. vi. 737.; conf. § 29. n. 37.; *Catal.* p. 963. Jellinek, who published in 1854 the account of Eliezer ben Nathan, did not notice the contradiction in Joseph Cohen, who must have confused the two authors named in the text; conf. also Kerem Chemed, ix. 49.

²¹ª *Catal.* p. 1228.

²² Whether the letter printed this year at the end of Ibn Verga, ed. Hanover, from the pretended MS. of Carmoly, is not simply a fabrication of the latter from Gedalja Ibn Jahja, we have no means of deciding; the preliminary remarks by the owner of the MS. contain a curious blunder with respect to Jehuda ben Asher, and a superfluous proof that Chisdai was still alive in 1391. See §§ 12. and 15.

²³ Ersch, Encykl. vol. ii. p. 31. s. v.

²³ª This account is quoted by Moses Ibn Ezra and Joseph Ibn Aknin (see Ersch, Encykl. sect. ii. vol. 31. s v.), and is, perhaps, the מסאלה (leg. רכאלה?) of Mazliah quoted by the author of the twelfth century mentioned § 4. n. 69.; conf. also *Catal.* p. 2041.

²⁴ Israeli, Jesod Olam, iv. § 14.; As. de Rossi, chap. 23. sq.; conf. also Kerem Chemed, v. 198.

²⁴ª Nissim, Lit. bl. viii. 569.; conf. Geiger, Zeitschr. vi. 107.; Abr. ben Chijja, Astron. § 22. at the end. Sup. page 79. read היונים.

²⁵ See the learned treatment of this subject by RAPOPORT, Busch's Jahrbuch, iii. 258. and Erech Millin, p. 73. (conf. Annal. ii. 160. sq.), by which Ideler, Handb. d. Chron. i. 350. 568., is to be corrected. Conf. § 21. n. 26.

[25a] See Afendopolo, Completion of Aderet Elijahu, upon the different Taarich.

[26] According to Jewish chronology, however, Christ died 121 years before the destruction of Jerusalem. See Sim. Duran, Keschet u-magen, f. 11 a.; see below, n. 34. Upon the alterations of the chronology of the LXX. for Christian purposes, see Graetz in Frankel, Monatschr. ii. 432., iii. 121.

[27] Zunz, G. V. 114., and p. 153. the interpolation of Josippon. A simple reckoning by the years of the world is found, however, in Aboda Sara, 9. b. The Arabian accounts of Jewish chronology are worthy of examination; see Abu Maascher, Frankel, Zeitschr. ii. 235.; Herbelot, art. Cainan, ii. 72. of the Germ. transl.

[28] See sup. § 4. n. 58., § 5. n. 106.

[29] Rapop. Ker. Chem. v. 198. The abolition of the Seleucidic æra is ascribed to R. David Ibn Abi Simra, Asulai, i. 7. 19. Concerning the chronological formulæ used in MSS. and in printed works, see ZUNZ, zur Gesch. p. 214. sq., and the art. *Jüdische Typographie* in Ersch, vol. xxviii. p. 27.

[30] Ker. Chem. v. 181.

[31] See Geig. v. 465.; against Carmoly's determination of the date of a Parisian MS. Bible, see § 16 n. 50.

[32] The Jewish authors from Sherira to Conforte (2 b.) state the Hegira to have occurred in the year 4374 of the world, except Chananel, who makes it A. 4381. (See Rapop. Biogr. p. 34.)

[33] Concerning the fact that in 1381 this æra of Augustus was given up by the Christians, and that of the birth of Christ introduced instead, see Abr. Sacut, f. 133 b. ed. Cracow; cf. Zunz, Zeitschr. p. 159.; Geig. Zeitschr. ii 564.; Melo Chofn, 98.; Dukes, Introd. p. 47. n. 44. Concerning the name צפר or אצפר as applied to Edom and to Christians, see the author's Analecta in Frankel, Zeitschr. ii. 327.; and also Herbelot, art. Benu Asfar, i. 623.; Rum. iii. 792.; Rumiah, p. 794. (where also concerning צפו, conf. Zunz zur Gesch. p. 484.). Sacy (Not. et Extr. ix. 437.) derives it from *Flavii;* this derivation has also been recently proved by another Oriental scholar who knew nothing of De Sacy's opinion. See the author's notice in Zeitschr. der Deutsch-morgenl. Zeitschr. iii. 363.

[34] For example, in Meir Katzenellenbogen, quoted by Jost, viii. 196., the common name of the month is more frequently used, e. g., in a Responsum of Leon Jehuda ben Solomon, dated 1 calend. (קליני) August. and 14 Mai. 278 (1518). Soon after the introduction of the æra *nativitatis,* "nascimento" (see note 33.), Prophiat Duran alludes to it in chap. xi. of his polemical work mentioned suprà, p. 127.

[35] Conf. ZUNZ's dissertation *On the Geographical Literature of the Jews* (in the 2nd vol. of Benjamin Tudel. ed. London and Berlin, 1841, p. 230, sq.), p. 310.; and the author's Fremdsprachl. Elem. p. 17. sq.

[36] The belief in נלגול מחילות appears already in Jerusch. Kilajim, ix. 7.; conf. Ketub. 112.; Lit. bl. ii. 422. n. 40., iv. 297.; Zunz, Benj. p. 309.; and see Wolf, i. p. 268.

[37] They should not, however, have been employed as they were by Leon de Laborde, concerning whose plagiarisms from Zunz's treatise see Deutsche Jahrb. 1842, p. 259.; Archives Israel, 1843, p. 56. sq.

On the geography of Palestine from Jewish sources Zunz himself contributed somewhat in his extracts from Esthori ha-Parchi, Benj. p. 393. sq. Some other valuable contributions are given in S. Munk's Palestine, 1841 (a part of *L'Univers*), which is, however, less derived from Jewish sources. Schwarz, in his Hebrew Works (since 1845 also translated into German by his brother), has the advantage of Talmudical knowledge and of a residence in Palestine ; but a little more modesty would better become a person so deficient in general knowledge. The geographical part of Rapoport's Talmudical Lexicon Rerum (Erech Millin, 1852) has been attacked, although not always by those who have studied the subject. The MS. geographical index of the Talmud which was used by S. Cassel (Ersch, vol. xxvii. p. 27. n. 2., it ought to have been quoted also p. 186., was made by B. Porges, director at Prossnitz (see Lit. bl. vi. 130.), who is still employed in extending it to Midrash, &c.

38 Zunz, l. c. p. 312.

39 See § 15. n. 16.

40 The German text had numbers in brackets referring to Zunz's above (n. 35.) mentioned treatise ; but this essay being chronologically arranged and furnished with an index of authors, it was thought superfluous to introduce them here.

41 Vide sup. n. 2.

42 Ed. Asher (Berlin, 1841); see the author's article Lit. bl. ii. 395, sq.; S. Cassel, Hist. Vers. p. 1, sq. The researches published recently by Carmoly are probably a reprint of the Revue orientale, the plagiarisms and forgeries of which are exposed by Geiger, Zeitschr. v. 469. sq.; but the author has not had an opportunity of seeing them.

42 a [P. 82. l. 3., where the reference is omitted.] See *Catal.* p. 1778. sub Moses Aschkenasi of Crete.

43 Concerning Carmoly's forgery of a book, *Actan* (!) of Jacob de Nemez, and the probable introduction of its title into an Oxford MS., see Ersch, vol. xxxi. p. 59. n. 12.

44 See *Catal.* p. 1405. n. 5845. cf. n. 3926.; conf. Humboldt, Kosmos, ii. 292.

45 Maltebrun and Depping in Zunz, p. 265. (whence in Carmoly, Hist. de Méd. p. 124.), conf. § 21. n. 58. We may here mention that Columbus put ashore the baptized Jew Louis de Torres because he possessed some knowledge of Hebrew, Chaldaic, and Arabic ; see Humboldt, Kosmos, ii. 462.

§ 11. Page 82.

1 Whether they were reduced to a regular system is not yet ascertained ; conf. § 15. On the term *Epicurean* as used in the Talmud, see the author's Fremdspr. Elem. p. 22.

2 Frankel's Zeitschr. iii. 404. sq.

3 Geig. Zeitschr. i. 399. v. 85. sq. ; Melo Chofnajim, p. 57. note (conf. also Alfasi in Geig. l. c. v. 112.). The main authorities for the subsequent text, as far as Hebrew writings are concerned, were

originally the essays of RAPOPORT (Kerem Chem. v. 2. sq.) and
GEIGER (Zeitschr. v. 82. sq.), and some independent disquisitions ; the
author has also used for his revision some MSS. previously unknown,
see p. 86.

⁴ Jourdain, l. c. 106. 204., conf. 192. 201. The title " De Physica
perfecta" is a plain misunderstanding. The author has given only a list
of Johannes' works in his *Catalogue*, p. 1702–5., but is now in possession of some supplementary matter.—A. D. 1224, Alnasar also caused all
philosophical books to be burnt (Abulfeda in Sprengel, Gesch. d. Med.
ed. i. vol. ii. 271.).

⁵ On the other hand, however, many Arabians are set down as
Jews, e. g. ALI BEN RADJAL, CHALID BEN JASIKI (Jesid), CHA-
NANJA (Honein) BEN ISHAK (who professes to have translated from
the Hebrew) and his son ISHAK (see § 21. n. 38.), ISHAK BEN AM-
RAN, and JOSUA BEN NUN (by Carmoly), EL-KINDI, ABU NAIM (by
Casiri), the family IBN ZOHR, and others ; as also COSTA BEN LUKA
(mentioned as Lucas ben Costa in Grässe, Allg. Literärgesch. ii. 2.
p. 991.!). The strange name of PHARAO JUDÆUS, translator of the
Gospels (in Hottinger and Le-Long, quoted in Wolfius, i. p. 995.), is
certainly a corruption of the name of a well-known Christian author,
frequently quoted by the same learned men, viz. Abulfaragius Bar-
Hebræus, the son of a Jew. Wolf and others have fallen into mistakes
of this kind, especially through the circumstance of Arabic works being
written by Jewish students in Hebrew letters. In the recent Catalogue
of the Vienna MSS. (no. 149.), this has been noticed as " remarkable "
in an Arabic work of Maimonides ; while it is well known that the
Arabic writings of the Jews were nearly all written in Hebrew characters.

⁶ See Ritter, Götting. Gel. Anzeig. 1847, p. 604. sq.

⁷ The *Sefer hammada ;* a later compendium of which in the
Arabic language, translated by ISAK BEN NATAN, has been edited by
the author, together with three astronomical responsa of ABRAHAM
IBN EZRA, under the title " Schene hammeoroth," &c. (Berl. 1847).

⁸ See the author's remarks in Frankel, Zeitschr. ii. 112. n. 17.;
conf. Aaron ben Elia, Keter Tora (Lit. bl. i. 534.), Hedessi, Alphab.
168. 174., and see § 17. note 9., Geig. Zeitschr. v. 94. 293.

⁹ Maimonides' (?) Letter to his Son, f. 2. b. (Amst.) (Zunz, zur
Gesch. 199.), Abraham ben David in Geig. v. 92. ; conf. Palquera in
Minchot Kenaot, p. 183. ; Ker. Chem. v. 8. 18. Abraham Maimonides
(Epistle, f. 12. 31., ed. Hanov.) thinks that the opponents in Mont-
pellier, as regards their sensualism, differed but little from Christians.
Conf. also the verses of EN-VIDAS MESHULLAM BEN SOLOMON (*Catal.*
p. 1751., ha-Palit, p. 48.), and Cod. München, 239. d.

¹⁰ Conf. Geig. Zeitschr. v. 111. 113., conf. 101. On the symbolical
interpretation of Abraham and Sara Ibn, as form and matter, conf. N.
Roschd's Short Logic (in Hebrew by JACOB BEN MACHIR, called Prophiat Tibbon [as it should be printed p. 92., cf. n. 24.], ob. cir. 1307),
ed. Riva, 48. b., where the latter figure as man and wife ; and cf.
Narboni, Comm. Moreh, ii. 30. (cf. 406.), and i. 72. (Adam and Eve)
and i. 17.; Shemtob Shafrut, Pardes, f. 76. ; cf. also Emanuel's
riddle on the ὕλη (cf. Noblot Chochma, f. 64. b.), David de Rocca,

זכות אדם (see *Catal.* p. 1958.). Jehuda ben Mos. Romano (ad Genes. i.) says, that some recent exegetists, whom he would not mention by name, explain the first chapters of Genesis according to the theory of the eternity of matter (קדמות). The book of Proverbs was also explained in a similar way as early as 1247 by JEHUDA BEN SALOMO COHEN ; but on the other hand JOSEPH CASPI opposes this, although he himself considers the history of Cain and Abel to be a mere allegory, making the pun כי הכל הבל (see Ersch, Encykl. s. v. vol. xxxi. p. 66.). SCHEMARJA of Crete called his work on Matter and Form "The Union of Man and Wife."

[11] How far actual transgression of the Ceremonial Law was associated with it (Geig. Zeitschr. v. 101. 106. 115., conf. ii. 125.) requires farther investigation. Allusions made by Shemtob Palquera (ויכוח), Isaac Sahula, (pref.), and Joseph Caspi (Testam. chap. xi.) may partly allude to *converts*.

[12] See the author's essay, Lit. bl. iv. 24. The position and importance of Provence were first shown by ZUNZ (see the references given in Zunz, zur Gesch. 481. n. f.).

[13] The oldest known by name are ISAAC BEN REUBEN, who translated a Halacha work of HAI GAON in 1078, and MOSES CHIQUITILLA translator of the grammatical writings of Chajug (§ 16.).

[14] From the introduction (in Delitzsch, Catal. p. 306.) the author concludes that the revision was made later at Naples. To Anatoli is referred the citation in Jourdain, p. 175., from which are to be deduced the date of the famous letter of Frederick II. (conf. Humboldt, Kosmos, ii. 448.), and the identity of Michael Scot with Michael in the Malmad MS. (see the author's essay in היונה, p. 31.), as also that of the works there mentioned with the middle commentaries of Averroes.

[15] Zunz, zur Gesch. p. 85.

[16] *Catal.* pp. 1420. 1951.

[17] The letter printed in Ker. Chem. v. 18. contains only extracts ; see *Catal.* s. v.

[18] Geig. v. 89. 97. ; Rapop. Lit. bl. vi. 739. (not mentioned in the reproduction of Fürst, Lit. bl. xi. 446.) ; cf. Cod. Rossi, 166.[6], incorrectly reproduced by Deutsch, *Catal.* p. 82. ; on SAMUEL BEN NISSIM at Haleb, see *Catal.* p. 1313.

[19] Zunz, zur Gesch. 35. On DANIEL BEN SAADJA, the Babylonian (i e. of Bagdad), see the author's Additt. to Uri, n. 225.

[20] *Catal.* p. 1440.

[21] Ker. Chem. iii. 169. On SOLOMON PETIT, see חמדה גנוזה f. 18.

[22] The misconception of Geiger, Zeitschr. v. 108., has been well refuted by S. Sachs, Ker. Chem. viii. 195. On the figure of the lion see Sprengel, Gesch. d. Medic. (1st ed.) ii. 461. ; it is mentioned at the end of chapter vii. of the Hebrew translation of the pseudo-Aristotelian "Secretum Secretorum," and in a medical extract ascribed to Razi, in the Michael MS. 51. f. 148 b. ; hence Jellinek's note to Galen's De Anima, pp. 8. 23., is to be supplied ; cf. § 22. at the end.

[23] Delitzsch (Ez. Chajim, p. 344.) sees in him the beginning of mysticism.

[23a] Geig. l. c. p. 114.

[24] The Jews of Provence, like those of Arabia, have generally a

vernacular, besides their Jewish, name (Zunz, zur Gesch. 462.), from ignorance of which many errors have arisen; cf. e. g. *Catal.* pp. 2112-13.

[25] A list of the men is given by Zunz, zur Gesch. 477. On LEVI BEN ABRAHAM see Geiger in הֶחָלוּץ, ii. 12. (and S. Sachs, l. c. in note 22.), from whom Carmoly has borrowed his notice in the Athénéum Français; whence it has found its way also into the Monatschrift, iv. 122., without any reference to its real origin.

[26] Rapop. Ker. Chem. v. p. 1. Geig. (p. 122.) leaves this term unnoticed.

[27] Geig. pp. 108. 122.

[28] E. g. Rapoport, Ker. Chem. v. 9., vi. 110.; cf. Reggio, Thora and Philos., Chajes (see note to Ez. Chajim of Aaron ben Elia, p. 343.).

§ 12.   Page 94.

[We have not found much new material, or reason for alterations, in the essay of MUNK on Jewish Philosophers (translated from the French, with notes, by B. BEER, 1852), for our general sketch; the undeniable merit of that essay consisting rather in notices of individuals.]

[1] On the Mutakallimun and Karaites see § 14. n. 6.; on Mokammez, ib. n. 3. The doctrine of the Retributio brutorum is to be met with in Saadja (see the author's remark in Lit. bl. 1841, p. 332., see Frank. Zeitschr. iii. 404. n. 6.), and in Joseph the Karaite, perhaps (Abu Jacob) the author of the work אלמנורי (in Joseph Ibn Zaddik, p. 70., see *Catal.* p. 1571.); conf. Schlesinger, Einl. zu Albo, p. xxviii. n. 1. To this head belongs the objection of Maimonides to Saadja's division of the Commandments into rational (שכליות) and positive (שמעיות) (conf. Ez. Chajim of Aaron ben Elia, p. vi. n. 11.). SAADJA and HAI are probably called Mutekellimin in its peculiar sense by Moses Ibn Ezra (see the author's *Catal.* p. 2183.). It is worth noticing that SAADJA's psychological system is not truly Aristotelian; see the *Platonic* division of the faculties pointed out by Munk, Notice, p. 10. (cf. p. 16.; Geiger, Zeitschr. ii. 116.; Goldenthal, Preface to Averroes, p. xvi.; Scheyer, Psychologie, pp. 24. 66.). Also among the Freemasons at Bosra, the *Brothers of Purity* (about A. D. 980; see suprà, p. 98.), whose writings were attributed to the Mu'tazelites (Schmölders' Essai sur les Ecoles phil. chez les Arabes [Par. 1842], p. 200. see § 20. n. 23 a), Jews were probably to be found (Hammer, Wien. Jahrb. ii. c. 67. sq.); conf. also § 5. n. 25. Schmölders (l. c. 106.) asserts that the Jews could not be pupils of the Mutakallimun, since the latter, as simply orthodox (which is however an arbitrary assumption and untrue, see § 17. n. 7.), only endeavoured to combine philosophy with the dogmas of the Koran. But the Jews might have borrowed the scholastic method even from the orthodox.

[2] Gazzali is considered as the representative of scepticism among the Arabians. See Munk's article in the Dictionnaire des Sciences philosophiques.

[3] See Jellinek, Lit. bl. vi. 622., and the author's corrections, Frankel, Zeitschr. iii. 198. sq.; cf. § 18. n. 48. and § 21. n. 1. Conf. Sahula (Mashal hak. 16. b.); Alfonso in De Castro, ii. 625., cf. Nachmanides,

Sermon, p. 20. ed. Jellinek, Joseph ben Eleasar on Ibn Ezra, Exod. xxxiv. 6.—On the expression הגיון in the Talmud, the passages of Joseph Ibn Aknin, Jacob Anatoli (who is referred to by Abraham Abulafia, and also beyond doubt by ABRAHAM SHALOM ben Isaac ben Jehuda in his preface to a translation of the Logic, copied by Mr. Schorr at Odessa), Shemtob Palquera, Hillel ben Samuel, and Joseph Caspi, will be given elsewhere ; cf. also Geiger, Melo Chofn, p. 411. and § 5. note 96. "Sermoniales," in the celebrated letter of Frederick II. (in Jourdain, p. 174.), does not mean physical but logical science. David Mokammez (Lit. bl. viii. 620. 647.) gives the first place to meta-physics, like the old Karaites (Cusari, v. 2.), as Mutekellim (see § 14. n. 7.) ; and Jeh. ben Barzillai (p. 1130.) reckons him among the בעלי המחקר, which is not to be translated "philosophers" (Lit. bl. viii. 616—619.). Gazzali thus arranges the opinions of the philo-sophers — logic, metaphysics, physics,—with the express remark that it is contrary to their own custom. Some other expressions are neither quite clear nor consistently used. Mokammez himself distinguishes between המחקר ח' and כתבי הקודש ח' (ib.). Ibn Ezra (Shne hammeoroth, p. ג.) distinguishes between אנשי המחקר (مبحثون ?) and התושיה א', which latter ascribe a more exalted soul to the moon. Sam. Ibn Tibbon, in his pref. to Deot ha-Phil. (like Isaac Aboab, Menorat, § 236.), identi-fies ח' המחקר with philosophers (conf. pref. to Abot, and Jikkawu hammaj, passim). Palquera and others frequently use חכמי המחקר for thinkers in general ; in Mebakkesh, f. 240., it is applied to Saadja. Aaron ben Elia the Karaite opposes them to the philosophers ; conf. § 14. n. 7., § 16. n. 49. On the seven sciences as connected with Prov. ix. 1. see § 18. n. 49., § 21. n. 1.

[3a] MS. Mich. 176. according to the author's emendation, Register, p. 350., and MS. Reggio, 44., from which the statement p. 96. is taken.

[4] On religious differences see § 20. nn. 24 a. 25.; on the development of language, § 8. n. 14., conf. § 23. n. 9. The author has promised to treat of the character and importance of this literature of translations in his Judæo-Arabic Bibliotheca, the second part of which is to comprise the translators and translations.

[5] Examples, besides those in p. 96., are to be found in the present article, e. g. § 21, 22.

[6] Even Rapoport (Resp. Gäon. 2 b. in fine) ranks him with Zadok and Boethos! And yet his views, denounced by Shemtob (in Geig. Melo Chofn, p. 63.), do not differ from those of Gazzali (conf. S. Duran, Keshet u-magen, 18 b.), whose work was translated by Albalag and completed by ISAAC IBN POLKAR (so that the date, 1307, ascribed to Albalag, is rather to be referred to Polkar). Gazzali probably spoke in the name of the philosophers ; and a similar opinion is to be found in Luther! (see Strauss, Glaubenslehre, ii. 546.). But what is most curious is the fact that a passage of Albalag, to be found in all MSS. hitherto examined, recommends the reader to seek an answer to questions not solved by philosophy in tradition (קבלה !), and even praises three Kabbalists of the end of the thirteenth century! See the author's Catalogue of the Leyden Hebr. MSS., Cod. Warner, 6. But Albalag is not the only author denounced by fanatics and mystics. B. Beer has recently shown that even SAMUEL ZARZA, who is said to have been

burnt, is more orthodox than his mystic calumniators.—With respect to the translators of Arabian philosophy, the author considers every general conclusion respecting the tendency and position of these men within the sphere of Judaism premature. All of them profess to have undertaken their labours for the honour and glory of the true faith; and who would, without sufficient ground, accuse them of hypocrisy and deceit? The question is only what every individual considered to be that faith. Cf. the remarkable attacks of William of Auvergne (ob. 1248) in Jourdain, p. 279.

[8] The author has here omitted SAADJA BEN DAVID of Aden, whom, in the German essay he had conjectured to have written an Arabic commentary on Gazzali's مقاصد اله, in opposition to Nicoll, p. 563., who denied any reference in it to Gazzali, and did not well read the title זכאה אלנפום; a marginal correction reads חיאת instead of זכאה. The truth is that the Oxford MS. is nothing else than the work of Gazzali (*Catal.* p. 1001.), and since the same appears in an autograph of Saadja, it will be hardly possible for an impartial judge to acquit Saadja of plagiarism. About Ssaïd ben Saïd, mentioned in the German note, see the author's *Catalogue*, p. 1114., and infrà, § 21. n. 29. 59 a.

[9] See § 8. n. 9.

[10] MS. Mich. 80. (conf. Zunz, Benj. p. 9. n. 13.), emendated in the author's Index auctorum to the Michael Catalogue, sub voce, p. 334.

[11] MS. Mich. 766. See the author's Index, sub voce, p. 348.

[12] The author has given in his *Catalogue*, p. 1811., the Arabic name of the work translated under the title Arugat ha-Bosem, which Dukes supposed to be genuine. On a work cited by Bechaji see § 14. n. 3.

[13] *Catal.* p. 1897.

[14] See inf. § 13.

[14 a] Zunz, G. V. p. 401., zur Gesch. 165., but confused in the index with an older author (p. 65.). On the dissemination of the Moreh among the Arabians see the author's pref. to Maamar hajichud, p. iv. Thomas Aquinas was probably acquainted with a Latin translation quoted by the commentator MOSES BEN SOLOMON (cf. *Catal.* p. 1896.). From the estimation in which the Moreh is held by Christians and Muhammedans, Joseph Ibn Caspe (about 1320) makes out a reproach against his Jewish contemporaries, who neglected it.

[15] In Zunz, Benj. p. 259., improperly classed with the geographers.

[16] Zunz, Additt. to Delitsch's Catalogue of the MSS. at Leipsic, p. 326.; Dukes, Lit. bl. viii. 116. 456.

[17] According to Carmoly, Annal. i. 156., A. D. 1405! The correct date is given by Biscioni (i. Cod. xxviii. 9.), who nevertheless would identify him with JEHUDA PARSI (see § 14.), mentioned by Ibn Ezra.

[18] Zunz, ad Benjamin, p. 29., not " unknown " (Dukes, Lit. bl. x. 707.).

[19] Id., zur Gesch. p. 123.

[20] Conf. Jellinek's pref. to Ben Jacob's edition (Leipsic, 1846), p. x. and xxi. n. 1. The date 1040 (?) in the Arabic compendium of a recent Karaite (Lit. bl. xii. 738.) is in itself of very little authority until we know the source whence it is derived. MESHULLAM BEN JACOB of Lunel already wrote on Ethics; Zunz, Geig. Zeitschr. ii. 310.

[21] At an early period MESHULLAM BEN KALONYMOS (Zunz, zur Gesch. 124.). The most prominent older commentators are named in the preface and partly quoted in the Commentary of Sam. Uceda; conf. Geiger, Moses ben Maimon. p. 59., and the author's *Catal.* p. 228. sq. One of the oldest commentaries, of which three somewhat discrepant MSS. are extant in the Bodleian Library, has been falsely ascribed to JACOB BEN SAMSON (cf. p. 185.) by Dukes (see the author's *Catal.* p. 2033.).

[22] See the author's bibliographical note in Kerem Chemed, ix. (not yet published), p. 48.

[23] Conf. sup. § 5. n. 89.

[24] See the author's refutation of an unfounded attack in Ersch, Encykl. s. ii. vol. xxxi. p. 52. n. 56.

[25] For " 1387 " read " before 1394." See *Catal.* s. v. Serachja Jewani.

[26] *Catal.* s. v.

[27] Abu Sahal in Dukes, Kuntres, p. 80. ; conf. Ibn Ezra, Introd. to Commentary on Pentateuch (in Kerem Chemed, viii. 67., no reference to this essay is given). SAADJA himself, although he speaks of being brief, has been blamed for his prolixity ; conf. Jacob ben Nissim (?), Lit. bl. vi. 563. The same is the case with MOKAMMEZ (§ 14. n. 3.), KOREISH, JEH. CHAJJUG, GABIROL. Abu Sahal himself (l. c. p. 73.) claims the merit of brevity of expression for the Arabians, later Jewish writers with more justice for the Talmudists.

[28] *Catal.* p. 1116. The author has but recently discovered a quotation from a Pentateuch Commentary by AARON SERJADO (?) a contemporary of Saadja (see *Catal.* p. 2159.) ; he is probably the " Aaron Gaon " quoted by Ibn Ezra. Fürst's great display of erudition with respect to Aaron (Lit. bl. x. 265.) is one of his usual plagiarisms from Zunz ; as also is his notice of CHEFEZ BEN JAZLIACH, to which he refers (l. c. p. 270.). Munk also (Notice sur Aboolwalid, p. 198.) refers first to the Lit. bl., with the remark " on peut aussi consulter une note de M. Zunz," &c.

[29] Zunz in Geig. Zeitschr. iv. 193.

[30] Del Medigo saw 24. ; Vide Geig., Melo Chof. 27. — On an interesting supercomm. of an uncertain author, but probably about 1300., see *Catal.* p. 1696.

[31] See the author's article Gatigno in Ersch, Encykl. s. i. vol. 54. p. 357. ; Kirchheim, who spoke of this author, although not quite correctly, in his notes to Asulai, p. 252., ought to have known that his double Commentary is an imitation of Caspi, who he says (Frankel Monatschr. 1855, p. 107. on a MS. of Carmoly) gave no explanation of the mysteries.

[32] Zunz, G. V. 416. sq. 422. The masc. is more used in the signification of quæstiones مَسَايِل, from דרוש quæstio, investigation ; so e. g. Alfarabi's الْمَسَايِل عيون is translated עין הדרושים (vide Index to Catal. Mich. p. 322.) ; the דרושים of J. Roshd and others are quæstiones (Jourdain, p. 104.) corresponding to שאלות (*Catal.* p. 1972.). On the history of the development of the Derashot, see also Asulai, Waad, 7. 17.

[33] Zunz, G. V. 400., zur Gesch. 516.

[34] Munk, in Isr. Annal. iii. 94.

[35] *Catal.* p. 1181. On a Commentary of SALMAN ZION see Zunz, zur Gesch. p. 166.

[36] Dukes, Lit. bl. vii. 779. The Departicul. למהות (لميه), conf. Lit. bl. iii. 678., was found by the author in MS. translations from the Arabic.

[37] [Note to "Al-Chalil," p. 104. line from the bottom.] See the interesting and useful notices about the كتاب العدين in Jewish authorities collected by the author in the Zeitschr. der deutsch morg. Gesellsch. vi. 414.

§ 13. Page 104.

[1] Our view of the history of Kabbalistic Literature is in general the same as that given in Zunz's short survey (G. V. chap. ix. p. 404. sq.), and in Landauer's Literary Remains. The latter were not left in a form fitted for publication, but were arranged and perhaps altered by another hand; so that they are not altogether free from contradictions (conf. vi. 180. with vii. 125, 126.). His views are the more weighty and instructive, because he originally commenced with opinions of an opposite character (see Annal. iii. 70., Lit. bl. vii. 812.), and changed them only after a study of the rich store of Kabbalistic literature in the Library at Munich. We cannot say the same of his follower JELLINEK. He published in 1844 a German translation of FRANCK's work (mentioned § 5. n. 94.) with notes, in which he endeavoured to remedy and correct the ignorance respecting Hebrew Literature and its history evinced in the French text (see note 4. and the analysis and refutation by CARMOLY, Revue Orientale, i. 430., ii. 159., reprinted in his Itinéraires, 1847, p. 265.). Since 1852, Jellinek has devoted some short tracts specially to the history of the Kabbala and its literature. These were reviewed in a special report by J. M. JOST (entitled *Adolph Jellinek und die Kabbala,* Leipzig, 1852, also printed in the Wiener Vierteljahrschr. 1853, ii. 22., without mention of the separate edition), who concludes with the remark that Jellinek was the man most suited to develop the essence, history, &c., of the Kabbala. The author — considering it his duty to accompany the short references to his authorities with some hints as to how far the student may trust them — must in the present case briefly give his reasons why he differs from the opinion of Jost with respect to the validity of the arguments, and of the method and principles adopted by Jellinek. In his first and most valuable researches about Moses de Leon and the Zohar (vide suprà, p. 111.) the author ought to have begun with an analysis of the collective Zohar, in the same way as Zunz did with the Midrash (conf. Zeitschr. d. m. Gesellsch. vi. 298., and for specialities *Catal.* p. 1847.). As to the short analecta given in the Lit. bl. and published separately under the title *Beiträge zur Geschichte der Kabbala* (i. and ii.), we must defend the author against Jost, who complains of several omissions, as if a systematic history had been intended. But we must decidedly protest against the readiness with which the writer adopts the forgeries and defective criticism of some Hebrew authors as the basis of his opinions, and attributes to some older writers the fragments found in later

authorities ; for instance, identifying, only on account of the name, the
author Chisdai Nasi, whose existence is rather doubtful, with the
minister of the 10th century, and attributing to him a Hebrew work,
while no Hebrew work whatever was written at that time in Spain, to
say nothing of the subject.   But we might justify our judgment simply
by alluding to the points wherein Jellinek himself has more than once
altered his opinion (see instances in *Catal.* pp. 755. 1469. 1853. 1964.).
We will not hold him responsible for the want of MSS. and good
editions, but only for quoting authorities which he has evidently not
consulted (Zunz, Add., quoted in Beitr. ii. 48., cf. p. 64. and the refutation in our *Catal.* pp. 2091. 2093.), and neglecting authorities like
Wolfius (see *Catal.* p. 2058.).   One striking instance will suffice : in
the work, *Auswahl Kabbalisticher Mystik*, 1853, p. 20., he attributes a
Commentary on Exodus to Samuel Chasid, and the passage in the
note is taken, without mentioning it, from the old Oppenheim Catalogue
in 4to fol. 2.; but there we find, not מכבוד, but מכבד , an obvious
misprint for מנכד, i.e. the grandson of Samuel, as he might have
found in the edition of 1828, p. 216.; but why not consult Zunz,
zur Gesch. p. 91., where all the German exegetists are mentioned ?
And on such foundations he builds many of his conjectures, as will be
shown in the following notes.   His notices respecting some authors of
the 13th century might have been more correct if he had consulted
the notes in Carmoly's Itinéraires, Bruxelles, 1847, where there is a
larger store of correct and original information than we usually find
in that author.   With respect to Jellinek's editions and republications
of Hebrew text, see some of the following notes.   Finally, we have to
mention a Hebrew Essay by S. D. Luzzatto, with a French titlepage :
Dialogue sur la Kabbale et le Zohar, et sur l'Antiquité de la Ponctuation,
&c., Paris, 1852, written twenty-five years ago, cf. suprà, p. 112.—The
older Christian authors are given by Wolf, ii. p. 1243., iv. p. 742.
Amongst recent authors we may mention Molitor ; but the present
author does not hesitate to confess that he has not spent much time in
reading large works, whose principal aim is to show, without any solid
support in Hebrew literature, that Christianity was anterior to Christ.
The Trinitarian school (n. 38.) will never lose its attraction for the
Christian student.   The author must conclude with the remark that he
is far from claiming any authority for himself in this department ; he
was prevented by a sudden illness in 1855 from cataloguing, as he
proposed, the Kabbalistic MSS. at Oxford ; and he only wishes to state,
that if ever the special history of the Kabbala is to be made clear and
evident, it can only be so by researches more profound than those hitherto
undertaken.

² The 48 prophets of the Jewish tradition (Seder Olam Rabba, cap.
21.), or 200 or more (Megilla, 14 a.), recur in the Muhammedan
legend.   Further historical vouchers and deductions cannot be given
here.   See also notes 3. and 27.

³ The considerations shortly alluded to in the text ought to be
treated in a special essay, as they have been unnoticed ever since this
essay first appeared ; a striking instance will be given in § 22. n. 34.
We will restrict this note to a short comprehensive remark connected
with that case.   Amongst the typical titles stereotyped in the mystic

literature, those taken from mystery itself are of course most frequently adopted by the Arabs and Jews; and every book or quotation must be carefully inquired into before we identify any two of them. Thus the pseudo-Aristotelian *Secretum Secretorum* (cf. § 22. n. 84.) existed in Arabic certainly as early as the 8th century. At the beginning of the 12th century, perhaps, a work, Secreta Secretorum, is quoted as containing an explanation of the Tetragrammaton (see the quotations in *Catal.* p. 1851., cf. p. 338. רזא דרויץ, a part of the Zohar). Shortly afterwards Ibn Ezra (Exod. iii. 13., short recension), speaking of the name of seventy-two letters, quotes from the הרזים ס'(רזיאל in the retractation to Exod. xiv. 19., cf. Zunz, p. 167., whom our text, p. 107. follows), something about Oneirocriticism (cf. § 22. n. 80.). A book of the same title as the last is mentioned by the Karaite Salmon (about 900–30) (cf. the German text); and this simple notice is made by Jellinek (Bet-hamidrasch, II. p. xxx., where most of his matter is taken from the Catalogue, mentioned in note 6.) the basis of identifications and irreconcilable conclusions (vol. III. p. xxxii.; on the book Raziel, see inf. n. 25.); he neglects even the note of Dukes (Lit. bl. xi. 508.), who gives us to understand that nothing special is mentioned in Salmon; see § 22. n. 34. It is worth noticing that the fragment in Raziel, f. 34., is called in the beginning "a book of the *books* of mysteries" which were given to Noah. There is still extant a הרזים ס' in MSS. (e. g. Opp. 1075. Q.) which Jellinek (Philos. und Kabbala, p. 42.) justly considers to belong to the *practical* Kabbala; but he seems to suppose that no connexion subsists between this one and those mentioned above. Cf. also Zunz, Synag. Poesie, p. 146., and a book רזא רבא mentioned in the Responsum of Hai, concerning which see notes 7. and 21. Some interesting discoveries in Jewish pseudepigraphy might perhaps be found in the Arabic work "Keshef," &c., or in extracts from it (Nicoll, Catal. p. 563.; Assemani, Naniana I. no. xxxviii.; conf. Herbelot, i. 440., ii. 565. 808., iii. 499., iv. 210, 211.; the author's *Catal.* p. 2057.). Allemanno (vide § 22. n. 76.) reckons thirty works of SOLOMON from the works of Abu Aflah and Apollonius, amongst them also the book Raziel.

[4] Many doctrines of the Zohar brought forward by Franck, l. c., as characteristic are only an Aramaïc translation of the Midrash and the Philosophical Writings (see e. g. the author's notes on Maimonides on the Unity, p. 16. n. 25. and p. 24.). Franck must here be certainly accused of ignorance.

[5] Conf. Jost (against Franck), Lit. bl. vi. 811.

[6] Franck (p. 84.) considers the celebrated Book of Avicenna (980– 1036) on Oriental philosophy as lost. This very part of the كِنَاب الِشَّا, also extant entire, is to be found in Hebrew characters in Cod. Uri, 400. [3]; quotations are to be met with, e. g. in Samuel Ibn Tibbon, Chajjim ben Israel, Mos. Narboni, &c.; conf. Ker. Chem. viii. 224., Schlesinger, p. 647., and Renau, Averroes, p. 73. (Roger Bacon). Rapoport admits some influence from the Szufi (conf. Zeitschr. der deutsch. Morgenländ Gesellsch. I. 259.) on HAI GAON (Maim. Treatise on the Unity, p. 22. note).

[7] Hag'i Chalfa (ed. Flügel, iii. p. 584.), No. 7053. (علم السخر),

designates some Arabic works as "after the Hebrew manner." On
the other hand the first of these works is said (sub voce, no. 1890. ii.
p. 62.) to be "after the manner of the Copts and Arabians!" According to Casiri (i. p. 402.), the Arabians had the Kabbala from the
Jews (see § 22. n. 78.). But Casiri (on Cod. 1614. and 1438.) says
also of the Muhammedan Abu Naim, celebrated as learned in tradition
(ob. 1039), "qui ex Rabbin. genere in Persia natus plura ex fabulosis
ridiculisque Hebræorum Tradit. in Muhammetanorum sectam invexit;"
and even of Bochari, "Unde conjici merito (!) licet Albocharæum vel
secta Judæum fuisse vel Rabbinorum ope absurdissima hujusmodi
mendacia confinxisse!" Just as the old Leipsic cataloguer said of Ali
ben Rodhwan (Frank. Zeitschr. iii. 198. n. 6.), "Ali Ismaëlita (gente
puto, nam religione non Mohammedanus sed Judæus fuisse *videtur*)
professione medicus, superbiâ Pharisæus, &c.!" Conf. on Khaled
ben Jesid, inf. § 21. n. 39.; on Alkendi, § 21. n. 74.; on Abdallah ben
Masrur, § 22. n. 716. A work, رمز الحقايق &c., is mentioned by Hag'i
Chalfa, no. 6522. (iii. p. 477.), without explanation; see also § 21.
n. 67., § 22. n. 76. The following are titles of older works on what
was called afterwards practical Kabbala: הישר (perhaps that mentioned
in our text, p. 107.; a MS. under the same title in München is perhaps by
ABRAHAM ABULAFIA), שימושא רבא חרבא דמשה (see *Catal.* p. 2010.),
besides some fragmentary "bits" (? מובתחות, perhaps = مقطعة ?);
see the Responsum which is ascribed to HAI, and printed, as it seems,
with interpolations (*Catal.* p. 602. no. 3843.); cf. also Zunz, Synag.
Poesie, p. 146., and sup. n. 3.

[8] V. Minchat Kenaot, p. 185.; conf. Geig. Mel. Chofn, p. ix. sq.

[9] Landauer, p. 213.; conf. Formstecher, p. 321. Something like
it is to be found in the older mystics, see Sprengel, Gesch. d. Med. ii.
137. Conf. also Zunz, Synag. Poesie, p. 145. On שיעור קומה, explained in a philosophical way, and on its connexion with physiognomy,
we have the interesting opinions of SAADJA, NISSIM, MAIMONIDES
(Geig. Beitr. 1847), HAI (communicated by the author to S. Sachs,
Ha-techia, p. 41.), and others (cf. Dukes, Lit. bl. xi. 509. and *Catal.*
pp. 1027. 1974.).

[10] The Arabians also have all kinds of writings on the form of the
alphabet, &c., a comparison of which would be very useful. See
Herbelot, art. Balathi, i. 564.; Lathaif, iii. 182.; Lauami, p. 179.;
Mamun, p. 287.; Mefatih, p. 361.; Tafhim, iv. 342.

[11] Landauer, Lit. bl. viii. 213., considers this as Pythagorean (?).
Hammer (Wien. Jahrb. C. V. 139.) compares the Sefirot with the
Persian *Sipehr*. For the older meaning of ספירה there is a locus
classicus in Ibn Ezra on Exod. xxx. 16., in the shorter recension compared with the larger. On the title of the book see MS. Mich. 317.
Saadja has merely المنسوب الي, "which was attributed to Abraham." So likewise the dubious commentator soon after Saadja (Lit.
bl. vi. 562.), who distinctly speaks of "arbitrary additions." Saadja's
views on the antiquity of matter, viz. on the philosophical theory of creation, not contained in the work of which we are speaking, are closely
connected with those in his writings against the Karaites (see *Catal.*
s. v.). There is no reason for giving up the views of Zunz (G. V. 164.),

in favour of the uncritical objections recently made. The treatment of the chapter on the creation was called, in the period of the Talmud, הלכות יצירה (v. sup. § 5.); hence our book of Jezira divided into Halachot has received the name given to it by later authors (v. Jost, Lit. bl. vii. 811., similarly in the anonymous translation of the Emunot Wedeoth). It is by no means proved by this (as Jost, l. c., assumes) that mention is made of our book Jezira in the Talmud. These, which are the principal grounds given by Franck (pp. 48. 55. and Jost) for its higher antiquity, rest, however, besides (according to a remark of B. Beer) on an introduction of the words ע׳ פ ס׳ יצירה from a commentator on the Talmud ! Cf. also Reifmann, Pescher Dabar, ii. 64., where an old " printed edition," is mentioned, unknown to the author and perhaps a mistake ? Franck's proof of its " genuineness " (!) has no better foundation. תלי , the dragon, is not Chaldee (p. 58.), but Arabic ; see the author's article " Orient. Ansichten, &c." in the Mag. f. d. Lit. des Ausl. 1845, p. 319. The designation " Friend of God " for Abraham (p. 61.) first becomes typical at a later time (see the author's collection in the Sabbatbl. 1846, p. 79.). On the division of the letters see § 16. n. 27. For a simple symbolism of names in Sar Shalom Gaon, see Rapop. Resp. Gäon. 8, b.

[12] There exist several Hebrew MSS. bearing the name of one of the two authors mentioned in the text, or that of Abu Sahl [or Dunash] ben Tamim (cf. Jellinek, Beth ha-midr. iii. p. xliii.) ; and Munk has tried to prove that the grammarian Dunash (§ 16.) is the author of at least one of these commentaries. The author thus concludes his German note : " There are probably two Hebrew translations, or the commentaries of the two contemporaries and countrymen have been fused into one." The same opinion was soon afterwards brought forward with more confidence by Geiger (Moses ben Maimon, p. 44.), but is considered very " problematical " by Jellinek, Beiträge, i. 6., who (p. 70.) returns to Munk's opinion. The whole transaction is shortly reviewed in Catal. p. 1116. 1244., see also p. 2032., whence it will be clear that we have, in all MSS. hitherto known, only different editions of one original work, and that the authorship of it is dubious. Jellinek, l. c., has given a survey of the commentators of Jezira, perhaps independent of this essay, since he puts (p. 8.) Jehuda ben Barzillai into the eleventh century, and gives (p. 75.) as an addition a remark to be found in the German note 29. The commentary of Jomtob ben Abraham (Beitr. ii. 78.) is a mistake recognisable in the authority Jacob Chabib, where we read ופי׳ ! Jehuda ben Balam, omitted by the author and Jellinek, never wrote a commentary. See Catal. s. v.

[13] The authorities for Hechalot are collected in the Catal. p. 531. and p. 1465. ; the edition of Jellinek (in vol. iii., cf. Philosophie, p. 42) is made from a copy of Goldberg from Cod. Michael, 317. (" 417 " in Catal. p. 532. is a typographical error, of which Jellinek was perhaps not aware, since he identifies no. 3457.). The relation between Hechalot and Henoch is stated there ; and the author has first proved that Eliezer ben Hyrcanos belongs to the heroes of Hechalot and that the eschatological part of his " Testament " is quoted in the older authorities (Catal. p 1849., which part was communicated to Jellinek before he edited vol. iii., but was not mentioned there), to

which may be added the "twenty-four secrets" erroneously ascribed to Nachmanides (MS. Opp. 1665. Q.). On Raziel see *Catal.* p. 640., and conf. nn. 3. and 25. On Midrash Konen see *Catal.* p. 587. On הישר see n. 7.

¹⁴ More particulars in Zunz, G. V. p. 167. sq., and *Catal.* p. 519. From S. Sachs is taken what Fürst gives in the Lit. bl. xi. 525. It is quoted by Salmon, (see Jost, Lit. bl. vi. 814., and again in Dukes, Lit. bl. xi. 508., in Esthori, p. xxiv., in נחל, p. 32.); cf. Jellinek, Bet ham. iii. p. xiv.

¹⁵ The expression קבלה, מקבל signifies, in the Talmud, time of the "Halacha tradition" שמועה (§ 4. n. 2.), subsequently, in the philosophical style of the translators, all positive (also הנחה, מונה) or historical, as distinguished from the *à priori* or purely rational, matter (מצד העיון, מצד השכל), according to which קבלה עיונית "speculative tradition" would be itself contradictory (hence Landauer, Lit. bl. vi. 195., requires much correction; see Zunz, G. V. 402.). Theosophy was first characterised as traditional, although, and even because, it was *not* so, in the twelfth century; and this argument would suffice to show the forgery of some tracts, or at least of their titles (see n. 18.) The expression קבלה מעשית "practical Kabbala," is quite modern, v. sup. n. 7. The expression בעלי הקבלה in Palquera ad Moreh, ii. 6., p. 87. infrà, is instructive.

¹⁶ Rapoport, Nath. n. 57., Additions, pp. 97. 99.; Zunz, G. V. 404 b. Can סבא=קשישא be the same as Elia? (Conf. § 5. n. 64.) The whole of the twelfth century is a mythical period for the history of the rise of the Kabbala; and we have not even yet any sure footing respecting the authorities (cf. inf. nn. 17. 21.). Kashisha is named by Shemtob Ibn Shemtob (cir. 1390–1400), who was a fanatic partisan of mysticism or rather an opponent of criticism, and consequently, if not himself forging, collecting whatever he met with to give authority to the new revelations. It is the business of scientific research not simply to believe his suggestions to be "old traditions" (Jellinck, Auswahl, p. 27., Beitr. ii. 64.; see inf. different notes), but to investigate his authorities. In the present case the author has discovered in a MS. of his own (f. 88.) the same thing as in Shemtob (f. 39 b.), only fuller; the source however is said to be a "tradition of Elazar Worms of the academy of Mata Mehasia," (!) &c. See *Catal.* p. 1321. sub Jehuda Chasid, where other confusions are corrected.

¹⁷ The authority is an extract from Elazar Worms' Comm. on prayers, given by Joseph del Medigo in his ambiguous apology for the Kabbala, f. 14 b. (cf. Shemtob, l. c. f. 40.). According to an emendation of Rapop. (l. c. and Ker. Chem. vi. 23.) we read "*Abu Harun;*" and this being a common Arabic cognomen for Moses (Fremdsprachl. Elem. p. 13. n. 28., and inf. § 14. n. 19.), it might have originally designated the above-mentioned R. Moses. A notice in Landauer's Remains (Lit. bl. vii. 198.) has unfortunately not been published. Botarel (see *Catal.* p. 1781.) mentions one Aaron Praeses, &c., whom Geiger (Melo Chofn, p. 99.) considers to be a mere fiction; Fürst, however, seems to identify him with the opponent of Saadja (Lit. bl. x. 265., see § 12. n. 28.—To David ben Jehuda, amongst others, is ascribed a work, in which Luzzato thinks he finds a know-

ledge of the Zohar (cf. Jellinek, Beitr. ii. Hebr. part, p. viii.); a work of the same title in Cod. Uri, 318., is perhaps that of Moses de Leon. In a mystical exposition of the alphabet (omitted by Uri, n. 340.) the author quotes his Comm. on Jezira, and calls himself in a final rhyme David; it is not quite certain whether he designates "Jehuda Chasid" as his grandfather or father, but he derives his knowledge from Nachmanides! The writer "Tab-jomi" is perhaps Lipmann Mühlhausen. See also *Catal.* p. 868. It seems superfluous to prove again that the fragments, &c., collected by Jellinek (Beiträge, ii.) as those of Hai Gaon and "the Kabbalist-family" (10–11th cent.) are spurious; it will suffice to compare the genuine answer of Hai communicated by the author to S. Sachs (reprinted by Jellinek elsewhere), and even the longer one printed under the dubious name of Hai. Jellinek's combinations about Elia Babli rest on various erroneous suppositions (see *Catal.* p. 949. sub Elia Saken, and § 5. n. 64.; and the author's remarks on a spurious MS. note belonging to the spurious Responsum reprinted by Jell. p. 11. and another in Shemtob, ff. 34. 47. neglected by Jell. Auswahl, p. 8., which will be soon published). On Josia Babli see *Catal.* p. 1949.

[18] Conf. Formstecher, p. 321.

[19] Conf. § 5. n. 102. In Ibn Ezra and Maimonides the allegory (סוד, נסתר) is not yet tradition (קבלה); and both contend against those who seek only for mysteries (Ibn Ezra, Comm. in Pent., introd. n. 4.; Maimon. Introd. to the Articles of Faith, and nn. 3. 8.; Treatise on Resurrection, Introd. fol. 31 b. ed. Frankf.). Abraham Jarchi (on prayer, § 47.) quotes ספרים הפנימים. The Arabian sect of the أما ميَة (Wien. Jahrb. ci. 25.) affords an interesting comparison with a passage in the Zohar (in Franck, p. 48.).

[20] Zunz, G. V. 403., conf. Landauer, p. 343.; Jehuda ben Solomon Cohen (a pupil of Meir Abulafia, who was himself inclined to mysticism) of Toledo, in Tuscany (1247), is also to be noticed as a mediator between philosophy and mystic doctrine (conf. Serapeum, 1852, p. 61.), and Isaac Sahula (§ 20.) as an allegorising poet and commentator on the Canticles (conf. Zeitschr. d. d. m. Gesellsch. vi. 298., *Catal.* p. 1151.).

[21] Abraham ben David defended Anthropomorphism against Maimonides; but the Kabbalists do not refer so much to him as to his son for their special doctrines. Abraham's Talmudical teacher was a pupil of Meshullam ben Jacob at Lünel (cf. § 11.), whose two sons were Jacob the Nasir, and Asher the Ascetic (פרוש). The latter is to be distinguished from Asher ben Abraham ben David, as the name is quoted by the oldest known authority, Todros Abulafia (see sup. p. 110.), mentioned by Zunz in Geig. Zeitschr. ii. 312.; the author has consulted a MS. of אוצר הכבוד, from which the same passage is quoted by Hirz Treves; and the name occurs in the same form in the MSS. of his exposition of the thirteen attributes (which Todros calls "a great book," and is probably alluded to by the general title 'ס היחוד, cf. *Catal.* p. 2167.) in Paris, Turin, Oxford, and two in Munich, 42. and 91. Asher is a brother of Isaac the Blind according to Zunz, l. c., who however remarks, that M. Gabbai calls him Asher ben David ben Abraham ben David (cf. Ghirondi, p. 45. autogr.!), so that he would be a nephew of

Isaac.   According to LANDAUER (Lit. bl. vi. 196.) Asher himself calls
Isaac his uncle.   This must be known in order to understand why
Jellinek (Ker. Chem. viii. 159., cf. Auswahl, p. 14., and inf. n. 28 a.)
gives an extract of Cod. Mun. 91. [92.] under the latter name.—Some
mistakes and conjectures of Jellinek, in his different writings connected
with these authors, &c., are illustrated in *Catal.* p. 602. 629. 678. 1074.
(and cf. nn. 24. 28 a.).   The authorities are all given by Zunz (l. c.,
where read האמונות, f. 36 b., see Zur Gesch. p. 74.).—We attribute,
indeed, little authority to all these legends about the appearance of Elia
the prophet to Abraham ben David or his teacher Jacob Nasir ; but
if BEER (Philos. p. 68.) believes that he can prove by the version of
Isaac Acco (quoted already by Zunz !) *that the beginning of the new
Kabbala is to be placed before* 1140, or even in the *eleventh* century, and
Jellinek derives from the same source (Auswahl, p. 5.) "a genuine
tradition" of the chain—Jacob Nasir, ABRAHAM AB BET DIN (cf.
sup. § 9. n. 33.)—we answer briefly : 1. the oldest authority is not Isaac
Acco but Shemtob Ibn Gaon (quoted by Isaac Acco in the very passage,
but not mentioned by Beer and Jellinek), who distinctly says that Elia
appeared to Abraham ben David, who taught Isaac the Blind.   2. Abraham ben David died in 1198, Jacob Nasir's brother AARON, the
defender of Maimonides (see § 11. p. 87.), died in 1210 (or 1205, if
the conjecture in *Catal.* p. 1690, is correct) ; and how then can Jacob
Nasir be the teacher of Abraham ben David's father-in-law ?—Similar
revelations are subsequently ascribed to Recanati and Chajjim Vital (see
Abraham Jagel, Bet Jaar Libanon MS. sect. ii. cap. 3. f. 6 a).

[22] Lit. bl. vi. 215. (conf. 591.), vii. p. 5.   Jellinek returned to the
same opinion ; see *Catal.* p. 524. 956., adde Jellinek, Philos. p. 42.

[23] Landauer, Lit. bl. vi. 182.—Other titles in Zunz, G. V. 404.
On NECHUNJA and the spurious literature connected with his name,
see *Catal.* p. 2056. (adde Aderet, decision, 220.), and p. 2058. about
CHACHINAI or CHANUNAI and the books פליאה and קנה.

[24] For the complicated inquiries about Ezra and Asriel, the authorities are given in *Catal.* pp. 775. 973. 2092., adde Bet ha-midr.
iii. p. xxxix. — On some authors mentioned p. 110. (and partly p.
114.) see *Catal.* p. 1949. &c., on MENAHEM, see *Catal.* p. 1736.

[25] *Catal.* p. 919.   Jellinek, who (Lit. bl. vii. 255.) had the book
רזיאל printed from an "autograph" (!) seems now to ascribe the
whole to Eleazar (see Bet ha-midr. iii. p. xxxii., conf. n. 3. and § 22.
n. 34.).   The relation of some of it to the works of DONOLO (§ 22.)
has been stated by Luzzatto, Lit. bl. viii. 343. (cf. Il Giudaismo, i. 38.),
and by the author (Serapeum, 1851, p. 61.), not mentioned by S.
Sachs (Monatschr. i. 278. ; see Ker. Chem. viii. 102.) and Jell., Ker.
Chem. l. c. ; see also Donolo, p. v. n. 6., and vi.

[26] Landauer, p. 213., and 3. n. 47.

[27] The false names are founded on the transposition of letters, and
their numerical value (conf. Lit. bl. vi. 181.).   For names framed
on 'אּ, conf. Zunz, G. V. p. 407.   When Maimonides (v. sup. § 10.
n. 4.) attributes to Abraham theological (but still not the book Jezira),
and to Solomon mathematical works (see on Maamar ha-Jichud, p. 23.
and Kidd. hachod. 17., conf. Gans, Nechmad Wenaim, 9 b.), this
does not refer to particular writings ; but later writings were composed
with reference to such passages ; cf. *Catal.* s. v. Solomon ben David.

[27 a] V. Landauer, Lit. bl. vi. 194., conf. Jell., Lit. bl. vii. 198.

[28] *Catal.* p. 1027. On Nahshon and Nitronai, see *Catal.* p. 2020. A work (*Alphabet*) of Nahshon Gaon is quoted by Zidkia ben Abraham in a MS. work.

[28 a] *Catal.* p. 836. and the Catal. of the Hebr. MSS. of Leyden on Cod. Warner. 24.   Jellinek has made different remarks based on the book עיון, but he recognised too late (Bet ha-midr. iii. p. xxxix.) that only two pages of his edition belong to that book, and if he had read the Catalogue of De Rossi, whose MS. he quotes (Ausw. p. 9.), he would have found that the rest of the work was in the book out of which he printed the fragment, &c.   Isaac Cohen says that he found " the book of Chammai " in the possession of only three persons in the whole of Provence.

[29] Perhaps R. EZRA is the author of the Comment. on the book Jezira (Abulafia, Lit. bl. vii. 666., Zarzah, f. 3., cf. Motot, Margal toba, 45 b., and Jochanan Allemanno, 7 a. 51 ! cf. S. Sachs, היונה, p. 42. ; cf. Jellinek, Phil. p. 4. ix., and see sup. nn. 12. and 24.).

[30] References on particulars in Zunz, G. V. 405. sq.   The Arabians also from similar grounds forged mystic works, and ascribed them to men like Farabi, Ibn Sina, Ghazali, &c.   Abelard of Bath (in Jourdain, p. 259.) designates the same custom as one of Christian scholastics ; conf. § 5. n. 25. ; on the book *Semiphoras* ascribed to John of Barro, cf. Graesse.

[31] Is this the reason for his exaggerations and inventions?   See a corrected and completed list of quotations in *Catal.* p. 1781., and a striking instance of how such forgeries afterwards are introduced into valuable authorities, ib. p. 1713.; cf. Pasinus ad Cod. 88.

[32] Lit. bl. vi. 225.

[33] On his mysticism, v. Geig. v. 106., conf. Lit. bl. vii. 700.

[33 a] *Catal.* p. 1536. ; Zunz, Addit. p. 317.

[34] See note 51.

[35] *Catal.* p. 2092-4., where the errors committed by several authors are corrected (cf. n. 3.).

Page 111. [The new statement about JOSEPH CHIQUITILLA is taken from a MS. of Abulafia's work now in the Bodleian library, and quoted in the author's *Catal.* p.1462., as well as Carmoly's statement about his birth in 1248, which was afterwards confirmed by Jellinek, Bet ha-midr. iii. p. xii. and p. 41., where an extract is given from the same MS. (in neither place is Carmoly or the *Catal.* mentioned, although the leaf was communicated to Jellinek some time before).]

[36] On these and similar titles for Kabbalistic writings from the " Glory " of the other world, see the author's work, Die Beschneidung der Araber, u. s. v., p. 22. n., and on Maim. Treatise on the Unity, p. 24.

[37] Vide § 8. n. 10. Nicolaus laments over the Judaizing Christians (Jost, vi. 315.). JEDAJA BEN NAHSHON, who wished to be baptized (Land. 228. ; conf. Zunz, zur Gesch. 469.), speaks of many Judaizing countrymen, who fasted, &c. (Ker. Cnem. iv. 10.), conf. § 15. n. 18., and see § 13. n. 47. In 1295 two ps udo-prophets appeared at Avila and Ayllon (see the authorities in Schud c, iv., Cont. ii. 238-9., Jost, vi. 332. 385. ; Jellinek, Beitr. i. 25., quot s Jost, Allg. (!) Gesch. vii. 313. (??), and instead of Ayllon he gives *Leon,* on which name he built a very

ingenious conjecture ! On a legend of the apparition of the *cross* on the Jews and a pretended work of Moses de Leon (neglected by Jell.) see *Catal.* p. 1851. Jellinek (Bet ha-midr. iii. p. xxxvii.) points out a passage in the Zohar where he finds an allusion to the death of Pope Nicolaus III. in 1280.

[38] Landauer, p. 215. on the Shechina, and Jos. Chiquit. *Catal.* p. 1469.

[39] Zion, i. 155. ; Land. p. 422., conf. 471. 473. (343.) ; Chofes Matmonim, p. 16.

[40] Land. 588. 590. ; Jost. Lit. bl. vi. 811.

[41] Land. p. 571.; Franck (conf. p. 170.) is ignorant of, or does not pay attention to, this important element.

☞ [The author has not been able to follow out the special researches on the Zohar begun by Jellinek ; and in fact the subject requires a large monograph. The edd., commentaries, and authorities are given in his *Catal.* s. v. pp. 538—544. and the various works of Moses de Leon (printed and MS.) critically enumerated, pp. 1847-56.]

[42] We are indebted to LANDAUER (Lit. bl. vi. 89. &c.) for some information about Abulafia and his works, sufficient for the purpose of this essay ; JELLINEK has lately published some tracts and given some more particulars, especially in his " Philosophie und Kabbala" (1854), and has promised (Ker. Chem. viii. 160.) to publish all his works ; most of which exist in the Bodl. libr. and in many other libraries (see Land. pp. 318. 417. ; Jell. pp. vii —x.).

[43] Land. pp. 381. 472. 488. 589. ; conf. Geig. Mel. Chofn. xlviii. n.

[44] Id. p. 488. ; Jell. p. v., where the explanation of the word " Philosopher " proves nothing ; cf. Sam. Ibn Tibbon, Glossary s. v.

[45] On this idea of the Messias, vide Lit. bl. vi. 539. Perhaps he is the ZACHARIA who proclaimed the advent of the Messias in Spain, A. D. 1258 (?) according to Basnage ?

[46] Land. p. 381. sq.

[47] Land. however (p. 489.) confounds the false prophet ABRAHAM BEN NISSIM of Avila, author of the פלאות החכמה, with Abraham Abulafia in Sicily (conf. Zunz, zur Gesch. 516. 625. Jellinek, Beitr. p. 31. neglected this note, but derives the same information from JOEL, Die Religionsphil. des Sohar, 1849, p. 69. ; notwithstanding, he relapses into the same error by enumerating the work as one of Abulafia, see Phil. pp. viii. 46.). ABRAHAM or NATHAN of COLOGNE (conf. Cassel, Rabbinervers. p. 9.) is probably Abraham ben Alexander (sup. n. 26.). This conjecture was made first by the author ; but no evidence has been given anywhere. On the name, and the MSS. neglected by Jellinek, see *Catal.* p. 675. (where Cod. Dubno 10. and Rossi, 1390. to be added) ; the book אחיטוב וצלמון (Land. p. 418.) is the polemic of MATATJA BEN MOSES. Abraham and Nathan are also called pupils of Abulafia (Zunz, l. c.).

[48] The Munich MS. (Land. p. 341.) is important ; another said to be " 491 years old " in Geiger, Zeitschr. iii. 286. n. 39., and a later *Hebrew translation*, will be mentioned in § 26. (cf. also Wolf. iii. p. 1129. n. 2143 b.). ; conf. also on Maimonides' Treatise on the Unity, p. 16. n. 25.—On the comparison as well as the delineation of the celestial spheres as the husks of an onion (Sachs, Rel. Poes. p. 230.), see the quotations in § 21. n. 47 a. On a passage in the Zohar see the author's

explanation in Mag. f. J. Lit. d. Ausl. 1845, p. 319. On another about Antipodes see § 21. n. 21.

49 Land. pp. 195. 326. 590. It is remarkable that Landauer (like Franck, p. 71.) pronounces the " Pastor Fido" (conf. Sachs, Rel. Poes. p. 229.) to be later. On the " *Tikkunim*" cf. Jellinek, Philos. p. xiii.

50 Lit. bl. vi. 325. 710. JOSEPH BEN SHEMTOB, the son of the fanatic Shemtob (n. 15.) in Spain, designates the authorship of Simon ben Jochai as " hearsay " (שמעתי אומרים), see Ersch, vol. xxxi. p. 89.

51 *Catal.* p. 1734. Recanati is still a problem for criticism.

52 Vide § 23., Zunz, G. V. p. 409. and p. 408., note, the passage in the Sentences of ISAAC BEN SHESHT, repeated by Goldberg in Chofes Matm. p. 15., and Jellinek, Beitr. i. 10. The anti-Kabbalistic opinions are collected in JEHUDA DI MODENA : Ari Nohem. On Lipmann's Kabbalistic writings see *Catal.* p. 1413. and Ker. Chem. viii. 206., where some things are incorrect. Also at the end of Cod. Opp. 862. F. there is a note, " I will begin to write the *Alphabet* of R. Lipmann."

53 Zunz, zur Gesch. p. 520.

54 According to others JOSEF ARUCH (see *Catal.* p. 1446. and Jellinek, Bet ha-midr. iii. p. xliii., on whose false statement about *Peliah* and *Kana*, cf. sup. n. 23.

☞ Page 114. [The statements inserted here are taken mostly from the MSS. themselves ; cf. also n. 3. About JACOB of SEGOVIA see also Jellinek, Bet ha-midr. iii. p. xliii., where BARUCH the teacher of Abulafia is perhaps the author of some MSS. in Oxford. Abulafia, however, is not to be considered as a reliable historical authority. On JOSEPH IBN WAKKAR, hitherto little known, see the author's article in Ersch, vol. xxxi.]

55 Zunz, zur Gesch. pp. 165, 166.; conf. Lit. bl. viii. 195.

§ 14. Page 115.

1 The authorities on Karaitic literature will be found in the author's *Catalogue of the Leyden MSS.* prepared for the press, and to be printed shortly after this essay. Two important works on the subject by PINSKER and the Karaite FIRKOWITSCH (the editor of some recent editions) are said to be in the press (Ker. Chem. ix. 51.).

2 Vide sup. § 10. ; Zunz, G. V. 425. ; Rapop. Ker. Chem. v. 203., conf. vi. 250.

3 *Catal.* sub voce.

4 Rapop. Ker. Chem. v. 197. sq. 232. Schaffarik pointed out, in a private communication to the author, the name SANGARI in Slavic authors. On Koreish, vide § 17. n. 5. H. Michael suspected an interpolation in the letter of JOSEPH DEL MEDIGO (§ 29.), and Ibn Ezra (§ 16. n. 1.) is interpolated in MS. Opp. 939. fol. (Lit. bl. xi. 302.).

5 E. g. MENAHEM IBN SERUK (see *Catal.* s. v.), ABRAHAM BEN EZRA, and others. Inversely the Karaites forbade flesh and milk ; see Geig. Zeitschr. ii. 117., Lit. bl. i. 468.

5a The explanations of this and the following expressions, given by various authors of different nations, will be found in the authorities mentioned § 12. notes 1, 2, &c. The older Jewish writers (e. g. Samuel Ibn Tibbon, in the glossary, Jos. Caspi, p. 76. &c.) have the practical object of explaining the subject matter, rather than the etymology; hence, by degrees, they entirely lost the origin of the expression, and were confused by the use of the term חכמת הדבור, for logic (§ 12. n. 3.), and, perhaps, by the uncertainty of the Arabians themselves. Even the learned Joseph ben Shemtob, in his note to the polemical work of Chisdai, chap. iv., in quoting Maimonides' opinion, that the חכמת הדברים was derived from Christian scholars, remarks that the science, called Theology, is the very הדברים ח', " which means a science the doctrine of which is not founded on perception, or on reality, but only on words." The real etymology, however, was known to Samuel Ibn Tibbon (see his note to Moreh, i. 71.) and to Palquera (p. 152.), who observes upon the difference between the above expression and פקיה (not פקיד, see Munk, Saadja, p. 17.), quoted by Renan (Averroes, p. 80.) from Haarbrücker, who quotes a later authority.

⁶ Vide § 12. n. 2. Against Schmölder's views see the author's remarks in Frankel, Zeitschr. ii. 113., iii. 404.; Dernburg, Heidelb. Jahrb. 1845, p. 422.; conf. also Geig. Zeitschr. v. 271.; Schesinger, p. 643. and xxv. On their method conf. Cusari, v. § 2., with Schmöld. p. 223., and suprà, § 12. n. 3. The distinction between the Dogmatists and " Philosophers " was of great importance; and Maimonides reproaches Samuel Levi (see § 11.) with confusing them; the text of Maimonides, however, is imperfect in some editions.

⁷ Hammer, Wien. Jahrb. xcii. 65., ci. 1., cii. 65.; Ez. Chajim, pp. ii. 311. 338.; conf. Lit. bl. i. 698. n. 4. The expression שרשי אמונה and the like abound in Cusari, as ii. § 81. (conf. Sabbatbl. 1846, p. 61.), iii. § 65., iv. § 11., v. § 1, 2. (conf. Ez. Chajim, p. iv. n. 6., and suprà, § 12. n. 3.), § 17. (conf. Ez. Chaj. p. 4. l. 27., p. 5. l. 21., p. 187. l. 11. ab inf., with Cusari, iv. § 11. fol. 19. ed. Brecher; conf. Afendopolo, p. lv.). The principal passage, v. § 15. sq., is, in some editions, corrupted, and the book Cusari itself (comp. 1140. which is thus much earlier than Maimonides, who is considered the first important authority, see Ritter, quoted by Beer, Philos. &c. p. 60.) not yet mentioned anywhere, or made use of, as an authority for the doctrine of the Mutakallim. (iii. § 49.) שושים is even used for tradition against the Karaites (according to which Schlesinger, p. xxix., is to be corrected; conf. also suprà, n. 3.), and Munk's conclusion (Beer, l. c. pp. 14. 98.), that the Karaites " called themselves " Mutakallim, is not warranted even by the perfect text of v. § 15.; and JOSHUA BEN JEHUDA (Cod. Warm. 41. ff. 68. 76.) says distinctly that he is following a method different from that of the מדברים, or אלמתכלמין, without referring especially to Karaites. The designation subsequently became more general; according to Joseph ben Shemtob, Saadja and Bechai " incline " towards the Mutak. (Ersch, ii. vol. 31. p. 85. col. 2.), and DAVID BEN JEHUDA LEON calls Maimonides himself a שרשי (MS. Reggio, 41.). It is natural that the Karaites in general should have remained longer in the older system, and perhaps the opposition of JOSEPH IBN ZADDIK and ABRAHAM BEN DAVID (§ 12.) to the בעלי חכמת הדבר was not without reference to Karaites. These two are also valuable authorities, and older than Maimonides, although their works have not long been published. On the views of the latter and their correspondence with the sect Makariba, or BENJAMIN NEHAWENDI, see Gugenheimer, Lit. bl. xii. 526. The later expression חכמי המחקר (conf.

§ 12. n. 1. 3.) still requires investigation. The comparison of Abul-faradj (in Sacy, Chrest. Arabe, i. p. 326.) is altogether distorted.

[8] Schlesinger, p. 640. xxviii. Can the ten Muhammedan articles of belief (see Reland, de Rel. Muham.) have had any influence? It is curious that even the hymn יגדל, on the 13 articles, was entitled "on the Ten Articles!" (See Munk, Annal. iii. 94.).

[9] See the author's D. Beschn. d. Arab. p. 26.; conf. Dukes, pp. 92. 194. The three or four sources of religious knowledge (not "Rules of Hermeneutics," Lit. bl. vii. 22.) are Muhammedan; conf. Lit. bl. i. 246. 610.; Ez. Chaj. v. n. 10.; also Abulafia (ap. Jellinek, Auswahl, p. 21., who neglected this point); and conf. § 11. n. 8., the author's *Catal.* p. 2163. On the accusation of corrupting the Bible, see the author's essay on Muham. Legends in Mag. f. Lit. d. Ausl. 1845, p. 286. (conf. Strauss, Glaubensl. i. 214.). On the doctrine of prophets see Maimon. Treatise on the Unity, p. 33.

[10] Steinschneider, Beschneidung der Arab. p. 26. (conf. p. 15.; see Lit. bl. vii. p. 18.; conf. § 17. n. 5.); seven daily prayers, v. sup. § 6. n. 18.; Kible (i. e. direction to turn to in prayer), vide Zion, i. 56.; Kalender, see § 21. n. 5. The degrees of relation, Zion, i. 129., Jost, in Busch, Jahrbuch, v. p. 159.; dreams as a sign of full age, Jeh. Hedessi, Lit. bl. vii. 20.; conf. Gulistan, Germ. transl. by G. Wolff, p. 263.; Hammer, Gemäldesaal, i. 347. On the intention in cattle-killing, conf. Zeitschr. der Deutsch. Morgenl. Gesellsch. i. 11.

[11] Munk, Annal. iii. pp. 84. 86.; Frankel, Zeitschr. ii. 109.; conf. Annal. i. 218.

[11a] Hence also, conversely, attacks in the Midr. Jelamdenu (850), Tobia ben Eliezer (cir. 1100), see Zunz, G. V. 236 c. 297 d.; conf. 395 a.; conf. also § 21. n. 9. On Exegesis, see § 17.

[12] Aaron ben Elia, Ez. Chaj. 156. sq. (conf. Lit. bl. iii. 195. n.) 152. l. 5. ab inf. (the fishes in the deluge, conf. Weil, Bibl. Leg. d. Muh. p. 78.) 181, 182.; conf. 148. 16., and the author's note to Maim. Treatise on the Unity, p. 27., to which the author could now add older writers.

[13] Hedessi, 168. 173. 175.; Zion, i. 55. 128.; Ez. Chaj. p. 6.; conf. Kirch. Lit. bl. vii. 20.; also סבל הקבלה, in Hedessi, 169. Of course the Karaites try to establish an essential difference between the Rabbinical and Karaitic tradition, but with less success than they attack the inconsistency of SAADJA, who denies "analogy" to be a principle of law (against the Karaites), and yet admits it in other cases. — BENJAMIN NEHAWENDI introduces a part of the Rabbinical laws in his Codex; cf. Geiger, Zeitschr. v. 277.

[14] Schlesinger, p. 642. n.; on the age of thirteen years, see Ker. Chem. v. 226.

[15] E. g. אשר ברא יסוד המים, Zion i. 57.

[16] Conf. Jost, l. c. p. 142. The same thing which R. Simeon ben G. (Chulin, 4 a.) asserts of the Samaritans is true also of the Karaites, viz. that they perform most scrupulously the religious duties which are recognised among them. On this account the Karaites are preferred to the Philosophers by some people, see Zunz, zur Gesch. 478.; conf. Cusari, iii. § 22. 65.

[17] This circumstance has not yet been noticed; and hence the essence

of those sects, which can be conceived only in connexion with the Muhammedan sects, is generally misunderstood. MUKAMMEZ was probably the authority for Makrisi and Schahristani (vide n. 3.), whose work upon the sects (lately translated into German by Haarbrücker) gives also an account of the Jewish; and according to him the Karaites are the first صِنْشِهَ (i. 96.); see inf. n. 28.; Mukammez's date is not yet ascertained; but probably he was the authority of JOSEPH BEN ABRAHAM the younger, who speaks much of Muhammedan sects: he was probably also used by HEDESSI. The references in Jost, Index, p. 158. (conf. Zunz, G. V. 396. n.); Delitzsch, Michael, Lit. bl. i. 737. sq. 801. sq.; Dukes, Beitr. p. 8. (Lit. bl. vi. 141.), &c.; Jost, Busch, p. 143. sq. (conf. also § 15. n. 6.), must be compared, to avoid over-ingenious explanations, like those given occasionally by Jellinek, see inf. nn. 18. and 28. It is worth mentioning, that Hedessi is the first author who mentions the Assassins (Jost, p. 145.), and Benjamin of Tudela the first European who gives a full account of this remarkable sect (see Asher, ii. p. 158.; cf. p. 63.).

[18] The name يُوذْغَان (sic) is correctly given by Jellinek, Lit. bl. vi. 568., who seems to have forgotten it in Beitr. i. 53., see Catal. p. 2164. On his doctrine compare ABDALLAH BEN SABA (§ 7.), who asserted the return of Ali (Makrisi, in Weil, Khalifen, i. 259.).

[19] Perhaps an adherent of the Muhammedan sect of the same name; on the names of Abu Amran, conf. § 13. n. 17.

[20] Conf. Geig. Zeitschr. v. 278.; conf. § 21. n. 6. On MESUE OKBARI (probably the same as Balbeki), see Catal. p. 2168.

[21] Delitzsch, Ez. Chaj. p. iii. sq., and Jost, p. 154. sq., give the periods, which the author hesitated to affirm in the text; against the former see Jost, Annal. iii. 288. With respect to the authorities for chronology mentioned first in this translation (pp. 118, 119.), we must remark that the date of ELIA BEN ABRAHAM (see Catal. pp. 1334-35.) is uncertain; but probably he was older than Jehuda Hedessi. We must add another unauthentic tradition of JEPHET BEN ZAIR, who, according to Pinsker (Lit. bl. xii. 770.), wrote in 1268; also an anonymous "Book of Tradition," which seems to agree with Moses Bashiatshi (Lit. bl. xii. 741. n. 7., and see the end of this note); and again, another chain of teachers given by DANIEL BEN MOSES in his Arabic compendium of BECHAI BEN JOSEPH (conf. § 12.), as late as 1682 (Lit. bl. xii. 739.). We confess that we expect but little certainty even from a more intimate acquaintance with those hitherto unedited authorities; for the Karaites of the 12th century seem to have already lost their knowledge of the older chronology; one reason for which, probably, was the great gulf of 150 years (1000—1150), during which no remarkable author is mentioned. The only chance of useful information would be from thorough critical researches in the older works themselves; but even here the difficulty is increased by the circumstance that we have, for the most part, only translations and editions, in which later quotations are inserted, or older dates repeated. Confusion has also arisen from certain passages referring to the date of the author (see Lit. bl. l. c., where there appear to be some errors). Another important fact is, that we have scarcely one certain author of any extant work older than Saadja. JOSEPH BEN JACOB

KIRKISANI is placed either in 910, or, more probably, in 930 (cf. *Catal.* p. 2163.). Hence the conclusions drawn by Geiger and Munk, that in Saadja and Jephet some general quotations refer to Karaites, rest on slight foundation (cf. § 16. n. 49.). The date 4610 (850), given for " the chain of tradition" in a MS. of 1692, by Daniel, n. 3. in the Catalogue of Karaitic MSS. (v. inf. n. 35.), is of no authority, since this catalogue is incorrect; it is, however, we understand, to be reprinted by Firkowitsch.

[22] Not " exclusively;" Jost, p. 155. (cf. p. 152.), goes too far in this respect.

[23] Geig. Lit. bl. des Israel, 1846, p. 150.; conf. Sabbatbl. 1846, p. 86.; cf. suprà, n. 13.

[24] Conf. the author's Fremdsprachl. Elem. p. 27. and reference, Lit. bl. iii. 226. 680.; conf. p. 195.

[25] Vide § 16. n. 21. 27. OKBARI (Jost, p. 148.) already declared himself against the Keri and Ketibh and admitted the Samaritan readings; conf. also Hedessi, 48. 173. In general the Karaites follow the Masoretic text (see Munk, Aboulw. p. 39. and the author's remarks to Cod. Warner, 16.); cf. also § 16. nn. 20, 21. 25.

[26] Perhaps " the Blind;" see the author's discussion, Sabbatbl. 1846, p. 65., from which Munk, l. c. p. 10., may be completed. The title of a compendium is מבחצר אלאנואר; hence سراج in the text seems to be a false conjecture. There is another Abu Jaakub or ISAAC BEN BAHLUL (not נהלול); cf. also Lit. bl. xii. 742. n. 7. Perhaps Abu Jaakub quoted by Joseph Ibn Zaddik is a Karaite? (see *Catal.* p. 1543. and Cod. Warn. 41.).

[27] Thus distinct from the Rabbinite polemical writers, § 15. n. 26 a.; see Cod. Warner. 8.

[28] Conf. also Moses Ibn Ezra, Zion, ii. 137., who reproached the Rabbinites with embodying God; the reverse is the case in Shahristani, sup. n. 17.; cf. on the *Makariba* and Abraham ben David Gugenheimer, Lit. bl. xii. 526.

[29] Cf. *Catal.* p. 1851. SOLOMON DURAN copies the same (Milchem. Mizwah, 28 b.) without personal intercourse. According to Carmoly (Annal. i. 156.) DAVID KIMCHI opposed the Karaites in a ספר המעלות; and the inventions of that author have sometimes a real although misrepresented authority. The Responsum of BARUCH BEN SAMUEL of Mainz (1190), quoted by Luzz. (Bibl. p. 64.), is perhaps not genuine.

[30] Zunz, G. V. 401 a., Ker. Chem. ii. 7. Among later writers the Karaites are often called צדוקים *Sadducees*, from whom they are often derived (cf. Meiri ad Abot, f. 3 a., ed. Wien).

[31] Delitzsch, l. c. p. 302. (Schlesinger, p. xlii.; Jost, p. 154.); conf. on his Liturgy, § 19. n. 50.

[32] On his acquaintance with the Talmud and Midrash, vide suprà, n. 12. His *Ez Chajjim* was published in 1841, by Delitzsch and M. Steinschneider, whose name, however, the critic and historiographer Jost, Annalen, iii. 288. 296. 312., has omitted entirely, attributing to Delitzsch even those additions, &c., which Delitzsch, on the title and in the preface, distinctly gives under the name of Steinschneider.

[33] Resp. Elia Misrachi, 58.; Cod. Warner. 30.

[34] *Catal.* s. v.

[35] On the Catal. in Geig. Zeitschr. iii. 442. sq. see n. 21. On the destruction of many Karaite MSS. at Kahira, vide Wolf. iii. p. 205.

[36] The name " JEMSEL " (even in Carmoly, " Itineraires," &c., 1847) appears to the author to have arisen from a misunderstanding of an abbreviation, יעמ׳׳של (conf. Zunz, zur Gesch. 456.).

[37] ניקוד, Hedessi, 165. ; cf. 170.

[38] דקדוק, Id. 167. 173., neglected by Munk, Aboulw. p. 5.

[39] See Cod. Warner, 52. SALMAN BEN JERUCHAM forms words out of two radical letters. HEDESSI, in the grammatical part of his work, enumerates twenty-two genera of Jod (cf. also § 16. nn. 19. 32.). JEPHET complains of the neglect of Hebrew grammar in favour of the Arabic (Munk, l. c. p. 39., gives to this idea an incorrect turn); cf. § 20. n. 1.

§ 15.   Page 122.

[1] Authorities : Alphab. list of authors ; WOLF. ii. p. 1048. sq., iv. p. 483. sq., amplified by DE ROSSI, Bibl. Jud. Antichr. (to which the numbers in the following notes refer) ; an introduction to it (Rossi, Della vana Aspett. p. viii.) is, however, not extant. The views, on writings for the conversion of the Jews, of De Rossi (ib. Proleg. p. iii. sq.), who is no less zealously pious than learned and humane, are interesting. There is a later Hebrew translation (probably unknown to the recent German translator Frankel) by SAMUEL SHULLAM, see p. 252. ; a Spanish one is mentioned suprà, p. 212. Since 1850, GEIGER has published, in " Deutsch Volkskalender," &c., some specimens of Pole-mics in a German translation with valuable literary notes, not, however, affecting the former text of this essay, with the exception of Isaac Troki (§ 27.), about whom the author had, in the meantime, information from the Opp. MS., see *Catal.* s. v.

[2] E. g. סרד קץ הגאולה (Vat. 105. 10.), (R. no. 112.); אותות המשיח (120.). Conf. בשורת משיח בן דוד (19.), ביאת המשיח (20.), and *Catal.* no. 3393.

[3] The Hebrew language does not possess, any more than the Arabic, definite expressions for these still indefinite conceptions : אומה صلה, stands for both. See Scheyer, Moreh, iii. p. 193. n. *e* ; Ez. Chajim, p. 373. note on 3. 1.

[4] E. g. from the work of Abraham ben Aus against the attacks of the Jews on the N. T., vide Cod. Ar. Vat. 120. 135 b. ; conf. no. 54. Mai. apud Collectio, &c. The form of a disputation was a favourite one for polemics.

[5] E. g. no. 37. (conf. p. 41. on no. 60.) 38. 45. 154. Some are simply fictitious inventions of the Christians, e. g. no. 112. On Ga-latin's plagiarisms, and other points for distrust, see Rossi, Della vana Aspett. p. v., and *Catal.* p. 2057. Perhaps also Hebrew writings *con-firming* Christianity (especially by means of Kabbala) were forged ; cf. *Catal.* s. v. Postellus, p. 2111.

[5a] Vide infrà, n. 45., on Samuel Marokki.

[6] Names for Christians, see quotations suprà, § 10. n. 33.; and conf. infrà, nn. 8. and 11.; for Muhammedans, see the author's work, Die Beschneidung der Arab. p. 6. Since the names are, for the most part, taken from the genealogical tables of Esau and Ishmael, or otherwise conveniently from the Bible, it becomes necessary to consult the Midrash and Exegesis in this matter. Zunz has since given a marvellous collection of such names occurring especially in liturgical literature (Synag. Poes. p. 437.). Moreover, it must here be borne in mind, that the schools and tendencies which are attacked are, at one time philosophical, at another dogmatical, at another Halachaic, conf. § 14. n. 17.

[6a] Collection in Wolfius, ii. 994. sq., iv. 457. sq.; conf. v. Raumer, Hohenstaufen, v. p. 235.

[7] E. g. Mishna, Taanit. 27 b. (conf. Maim. Com.); Soferim, 5.; see Duran, Keshet u-magen, 14 a.; conf. also Lit. bl. vii. 619.

[8] On מין, which has been so much talked of, see Lit. bl. iii. 825., v. 204., vii. 620.; Schlesinger, p. 647. sq.; Gräz, Gnosticismus, p. 16. עכ״ום, in the Talmud, is certainly not עובדי כריסטוס וֹמֹרים, but עובדי כוכבים ומזלות. Conf. also " Missions-Wesen und Unwesen, Einblick in das Urchristenthum," Lit. bl. iv. 673. sq.

[9] Vide Wolf. ii. p. 977. sq., on Duran, l. c. 11 a.

[10] Names and passages are collected in Dukes, z. K. p. 17.; conf. Bechorot, 5., vide Isaki on Chulin, 27 b. (ועוד שאלו). On R. JOHANAN BEN ZAKKAI, cf. Landau in Frankel, Monatschr. i. 172; on R. HO-SHIA, Ber. Rab. cap. 11. JOSHUA BEN HANANJA, the " Scholasticus " (cf. the author's essay in Zeitschr. der d. m. Gesellsch. iv. p. 152. n. 52.), may have disputed with Hadrian, Tanchuma, Toldot, 30 a.; Rabb. on Esth. 9. 2.; conf. Micha, 5. 7. (Jalk. § 923., gives Akiba and Chaldee language, although what preceded, from the Debarim Suta [conf. Zunz, G. V. 253.], is Hebrew as usual); conf. Ber. Rabb. cap. 64. fin. (according to which Dukes, l. c., Blumenl. p. 189., is to be corrected and amplified); Chullin, 59. On the disputes with the Samaritans, see Geig. v. 235. On R. Eleazar's saying (Abot, ii. 19.), " Know how to answer the Epicureans " (Atheists, &c.), was afterwards founded the study and refutation of erroneous doctrines.—Lately FRANKEL (Monatschr. iv. 161. sq.) has begun an essay, " zur Gesch. der jüd. Religionsgespräche." Nowhere mention is made of his predecessors; perhaps for the sake of consistency with his opinion given elsewhere (iii. 320.), that in polemics it was not considered necessary to name authorities.

[11] On בי אבידן, conf. Luzzatto, Proleg. p. 18.; Rapop. Erech Millin, pp. 3. and 259.; the latter passage is directed against Lit. bl. vi. 1., where אביוני, translated Ebionites, and נצרני, Nazarenes, was given as an emendation of נצרפי (again proposed in החלוע, ii. 100.); cf. also suprà, n. 6. As a skilful disputer, R. ABBAHU was famous.

[12] E. g. Debar. Suta against the papal prohibition of the Bible, Zunz, G. V. 253. i.

[13] Alcuin, Epist. XV. ad Carol. M. in Zunz, Namen d. Juden, p. 43.; conf. also Agobard, Bishop of Lyons, in Lit. bl. iv. 5. n. 7., and sidor Hispalensis in S. Cassel, Hist. Versuche, p. 4. Dukes' remark (Lit. bl. viii. 83.), that " as early as " the 12th century frequent dis-

putations were held in France, is, even in respect of the traces preserved
in the literature, far from correct.

[14] See the author's collection on Maim. Treatise on the Unity, p. 33.
The dispute is connected with Abraham and Manoah as unlearned pro-
phets; cf. also Isaiah, xxix. 11., quoted e. g. by Paulus Burgensis (in
Wolf. iii. p. 905.).

[15] On the reckoning of the time of the Messiah (principally from
Dan. vii. 25., xii. 12.), ASARJA DE ROSSI gives the first full compilation, used by GEDALJA JAHJA and J. B. DE ROSSI (Della van. Asp.
pp. 100. 103. sq., iii. sq. ; conf. Zunz, Ker. Chem. v. 143., and inf.
§ 23. p. 207.), as also SCHORR, Annal. ii. 23. Other references are
given in the German note ; but the subject wants a special treatment,
which the author intends to give elsewhere.

[16] E. g. Nizzachon on Monasticism (13th century) ; Simon Duran
(Milchem. Miz. 32 a.) on the Italian immodesty, where also Onanism
is mentioned as "*peccato di Ferrara,*" might have deserved at least
as much attention as Eisenmenger and the like.

[16a] Rossi, Della van Esp. p. 189. ; Bibl. Antichr. no. 161. 117 —
121. ; conf. n. 87. p. 62. ; Dizion. Germ. transl. p. 316. ; Catal. MS.
no. 124. ; cf. Delitzsch, Catal. p. 300. The *Mar Mar Jesu* (in
Castro, Bibl. Espagn. i. p. 223., where 1415, not 1405, is the correct
date) is to be emended מאמר ; cf. Dukes, Lit. bl. viii. 85.

[16b] Read 1240. See the author's Epilogue, &c. (§ 5. n. 77.),
p. xxx. n. 23.

[16c] Conf. Rossi, Della vana Asp. p. 206. ; cf. Zipser, Lit. bl. xi.
347. ; cf. Saadja Emunot, viii. 2., and on Ephraim cf. Krochmal,
p. 221., cf. החלוץ, ii. 147., cf. p. 122., neglected by B. Beer (Zeitschr. der d. m. Gesellsch. ix. 792.), who claims for this idea an earlier
origin. Geiger's error, in attributing to Sal. Alammi the idea of original sin, is corrected by Rosenthal in Ker. Chem. ix. 45.

[17] ZUNZ's Treatise (mentioned p. 100.) on the views of the Jews
respecting salvation or beatitude of others than Jews (zur Gesch.
p. 372. sq. ; conf. Geig. Lit. bl. des Isr. p. 80. sq.) is a pattern of
investigations in reference to this. On p. 380. n. 6., conf. Maimonides
in Spinoza, Tract. Theol. cap. 5. (Strauss, Glaubensl. i. 38.) ; on note
f, see Abravanel, Rosh Amana, cap. 12. fol. 13 b., old ed. To p. 383.,
see § 20. n. 40., p. 388. n. to Ptolomæus adde Bath-liusi (§ 12.).

[18] Instead of 913, read 933. Amongst others against the three
times קדוש (which the ZOHAR accepts, see Rossi, d. van. Asp. p. v.),
which is opposed to by ABU SAHL in the Commentary Jezira (Lit. bl.
viii. 83.), and the Karaite JEPHET BEN ALI (953), in his Biblical Commentary. On the Trinitarian ideas of some Kabbalistic authors, blamed
by the orthodox, see § 14., and Jehuda de Modena in Ari Nohem.
DAVID MUKAMMAZ occasionally attacks Christianity with philosophical
arguments in the fragments lately published by Luzzatto (Lit. bl. viii.
622. 632. 643.). Geig. i. 192. assumes, without foundation, that
SAADJA lived principally among Christians.

[19] Alphab. 99, 100., not in print, but still extant in MS. (see *Catal.*
p. 1328.). He there asserts, amongst other things, that Jesus was,
like every pious man, persecuted by the Rabbinites (conf. Warner
in Wolf. iv. p. 1086. ; De Sacy, Chrest., Arab. i. p. 325. n. 60., and

Afendopolo in the Introd. to Psalm cxix., Cod. Warner. 30., quoted by Myses in Jost, Gesch. ix., Index p. 97.; according to which Jost, in Busch's Jahrb. v. p. 195., is to be corrected); he contends against the Christian worship of images, and touches upon the differences of the synoptic genealogies of Christ.

[20] E. g. Cod. Vat. Arab. 159, 3. of the year 1305; Flor. Cod. 70.

[21] The Arabico-polemical literature of the Jews, Christians, and Muhammedans deserves a separate compilation. Above eighty such works are already known to the author, scarcely one of which has been printed. A reference to the MSS. would lead us too far.

[22] Vide inf. § 20. n. 30., and sup. § 4.

[23] Vide Frankel, Zeitschr. ii. 80. His pupil, Solomon Parchon (1160) refers to the polemical object of Exegesis (end of Gram. p. 11 d.).

[24] Carpzov in Schlesinger, p. iv. n.; conf. Jost. vi. 294., where the year 1250 is too late; see De Castro, ii. 601.; Grässe, ii. 2. p. 237., ii. 3. p. 630.

[25] ויכוח is the typical title of the works which hence arose, and thus of polemical literature in general. נצוח, נצחון is the same thing; it corresponds exactly to, and is frequently used by translators for the Arabic جدل‎ (גדליה occurs also as an epithet of the Mutakallimin). The collection of instances would lead us too far; and we must confine ourselves to Cusari, iii. § 70., where we find חכמת הנצחון, conf. v. § 1. Thus נצחון is not "victory" (Zunz, zur Gesch. p. 85.), which would answer to the Arabic زصية‎; this word is also compared in a MS. notice on the cover of the Cod. Arab. 53. 4to. of the Royal Berlin Library.

[26] The characteristics of the different kinds of polemical works are given by Joseph ben Shemtob, Preface to the Comment. on the Letter of Duran; cf. Ersch, ii. vol. xxxi. p. 88., and Catal. p. 2116.

[26 a] Vide inf. n. 29. Joseph Kimchi is doubtful; see n. 33.

[27] Catal. p. 1796. (1280).

[Page 126, line 6. from bot., Raimund is not Martin, as stated hitherto by all authors, but Raimund of Peñaforte; see Catal. p. 2133.]

[27 a] De Rossi, no. 89.; cf. Zunz, zur Gesch. pp. 480. 482.

[Page 126. line 4. from bottom, Moses Narboni's translation of Ghazali is probably a mere fiction of the Vatican Catalogue. See Catal. p. 1969.]

[28] V. inf. n. 45. In Biscioni (p. 112.) Alphons. asserts that he translated the Biblical passages according to Marokki's translation.

[28 a] On the translator Meir ben Jacob, and the time and name of the author, see the author's Register to Catal. Mich. p. 342. He has not yet had the opportunity of further inquisitions.

[29] His translation of Matthæus seems to be that published in the 16th century. The body of his work is only an abridgment of Jacob ben Reuben (n. 26 a); but he added afterwards an abridgment of another polemical work, the title of which is not even indicated, but the author recognised it to be the work of Prophiat Duran. (See Catal. p. 2116., and description of Cod. Warner. 28., and Catal. p. 2164.; Cod. MS. Michael. 231. has not yet been sufficiently investigated.)

[30] On various mistakes, partly arising from different recensions and the omission of a line in Geiger's republication of the epistle, see *Catal.* p. 2116. The plagiarism of Simon Duran has been discovered by Saenger in Frankel, Monatschrift, iii. 320. Frankel, however, in an additional note, doubts whether S. Duran ought not to have been quoted by P. Duran, since they were contemporary. Yet the date (1423) of Simon Duran's work is given in the work itself, and by the author in various of his essays since 1841 !

[30 a] Still we must not conclude from quotations from Jerome that every writer who quotes him knew the Lat. Vulgate and understood it. (Geig. Mel. Chofn. p. 80 !). An interesting remark on the translation of Jerome and his Jewish collaborators is to be found in S. Duran, cap. 12. Moses Ibn Ezra infers that older authors sometimes, but not often, used the " Christian" translation of the Bible (see *Catal.* p. 2183.).

[31] Rossi, p. 91.

[32] Vide n. 25. Zunz, zur Gesch. 85, 86. (conf. Dukes, Lit. bl. viii. 84.), mentions two between 1230 and 1260. The Niz. of Matatja in Rossi, no. 91., rests upon all kinds of misunderstandings, whose origin Dukes (Kobez, p. vi.) might have found in the passage of Is. ben Sheshet quoted in Lit. bl. vi. 149.

[33] The printed הברית ס' is falsely ascribed to Joseph Kimchi. The arguments in the German note have been adopted (though not quoted) and enlarged by Geiger, Proben, i. 63. n. 6. He justly remarks that J. Kimchi, perhaps, never wrote a work Milchamot ; to which we add that Joseph Ibn Sabara, the pupil of Joseph Kimchi, seems to be quoted by Jacob ben Reuben ; see *Catal.* p. 2032. The unsystematic character of the German-French school in collections of this kind needs an acute historical criticism.

[34] Rossi, pp. 59. 107. 116. ; conf. Sachs, Rel. Poes. 227. 244. (Lit. bl. iv. 382.), 266. 231. 301. 337. n. 2. ; Schott, Lit. bl. vii. 499., and Zunz, l. c. in note 6.

[35] See Deutsch Lit. bl. vii. 50.

[36] No previous labours on this subject were or are yet known to the author, who intends to enlarge upon it in his translation of Simon Duran, prepared since 1844.

[37] There was an interdict against reading it ; see Hadschi Chalfa in Hammer, Encykl. Uebers. pp. 137. 150., where " Pentateuch" ('Taurât) is the usual expression for the sacred writings of the Jews.

[38] E. g. with Abdallah ben es Selam and others (conf. Geig., Was hat Muhamm., &c., p. 11., and on p. 82. conf. the more correct translation in S. Duran, l. c. 24 b.). An examination of these passages for the history of Judaism in Arabia, and the origin of Muhammedanism, is still to be desired.

[39] On this point El Armui (ob. 1064), Balathi (ob. 1203), Ibn Teimijje el Harrani (ob. 1328), Ahmed ben Junus el Kindi (1431), Omar ben Hidr e Isfahani (Cod. Leyd. 613.) wrote, as also most of the controversialists occasionally. Ibn Junus (ob. 1242) is said to have explained to the Jews and Christians in Mossul the Thora and the Gospel (the authorities are given by the author in the Magaz. f. Lit. d. Ausl. 1845, p. 286.). The principal passages are 5 Mos. xviii. 18., xxxiii. 2. ; Is. xlix. 1, 2. (v. Cod. Ar. Leyden, 604.) ; Hab. iii. 2.

(Gerock, Christol. of the Koran, p. 102., and Delitzsch, Comm. in Hab. ad loc., cf. Geig., Moses ben Maimon. p. 31.; Jellinek, Beitr. i. 58., without reference to the materials given here) with respect to various Midrashim. Connected with this is the fact that SAADJA wrote his translation of the Bible in Arabic characters, and that certain Judæo-Arabian authors of later times translated the Biblical passages which they quoted into Arabic, so that many Hebrew translators of such writings adduce altered passages of the Bible (see the author's preface to Maim. Treatise on the Unity, p. iv.; conf. sup. n. 28.).

[40] See Sim. Duran, l. c. fol. 25 a.

[41] Dukes, Lit. bl. iv. 810., Beitr. p. 45.; conf. Carmoly, Hist. des Méd. p. 25., and Wüstenf., Gesch. d. Arab. Aerzte, § 177.; conf. Mazeni in Jost, ix., Index, p. 175. The interdict against non-Muhammedan books is still extant in theory. In Spain, however, Arabic writing was, as early as the 10th century, a means of advancement in the world; see the author's preface to the Testament of Juda Ibn Tibbon, pp. iv. xi.

[42] E. g. Ibn Refaah (1300), Ibn Teimijje; Harrani (ob. 1328), El Ahwah (Nicoll. ii. p. 97.), vide also Cod. Ar. Bodl. 97. 3. (Uri), Leyd. 665. 674. Extracts of Arabic writers were given some years ago in the Journal Asiat. A history of the persecutions against the Jews and Christians was written by Sojuthi (ob. 1505). The vituperations of the poetical freethinker Abul Ola (973—1058) spared no religion.

[43] The Saracens are said (according to Matth. Paris, in v. Raumer, Hohenstaufen, v. p. 534, sq.) to have accused Louis IX. of tolerating the murderers of Christ. But according to the Muhammedan Christology, Jesus himself was never nailed to the Cross. A religious disputation was held by ABU KATHIR ڪثير, Saadja's tutor, with the historian Mas'udi in Palestine (Sacy, Christ. Ar. i. p. 357., the name is corrupted in Dukes, Beitr. p. 5.). A Jewish physician in Egypt, EFRANIM (= Ephraim), called ABU KATHIR is named by Ibn Abi Osebia in his MS. history (cf. § 22.); but he is said to have been a pupil of Ali Ibn Rodhwan (who died A. D. 1061-8).

[Page 130. MOKAMMEZ, 9th or 10th century. JOSEPH BEN ABRAHAM was probably later; conf. § 14. p. 120., Saadja, 933. Mokammez, Saadja, and SAMUEL BEN CHOFNI, are mentioned together as polemical writers probably by Bechai, certainly by Moses Ibn Ezra. See *Catal.* p. 2164.]

[44] According to this, Geiger, Lit. bl. d. Isr. p. 134., is to be corrected.

[45] See the author's reference in Frankel, Zeitschr. ii. 109. sq. (and sup. n. 28.), partly repeated, but not mentioned, in Geig., Moses ben Maimon. p. 68. On further frauds or confusions of De Castro, see § 21. n. 42. Whether the pretended disputation of Abu Kaleb with Samuel Marokki (Antonio, Bibl. Hisp. ii. p. 3.; Wolf. iii. p. 1106.) is not the same work under another title is still uncertain. See also *Catal.* p. 1912. and s. v. Samuel Maroccanus.

[46] Cod. Ar. Vind. 279., i. 2., Cod. Berol. 40. fol. probably a fragment by a Jewish renegade. Other controversial works against Christianity may occasionally touch upon Judaism.

[47] Fol. 35 b. Single passages of several authors will be collected in

the work mentioned in n. 36.   Whether the Saraval MS. xxvi. is not
by S. Duran (רשב"ץ instead of רשב"א) we have had no opportunity
of ascertaining.   JOSEPH CASPI perhaps composed an apologetic work,
where also the Islam is reviewed.

    [48] *Catal.* p. 1221., conf. Catal. Mich. p. 335.   [Lately H. RECKEN-
DORF has begun the publication of his own translation of the Koran
(conf. *Proben einer Hebr. Uebers.*, &c., 1855), with notes, with the
practical view of furnishing to the Hebrew reader a book which has
never been published in that language, and promising a large introduction.   Indeed a review of the Koran and Muhammedanism, from
a Jewish point of view, is still a desideratum in literature.   Conf.
Zeitschr. der d. m. Gesellsch. vi. 538.   The author of this essay began
in 1839 a Hebrew translation of the Koran, principally with reference
to the relation of the two languages; it was intended to be an appendix
to an Arabic primer in the Hebrew language.]   Of SAM. IBN JAHJA
(1520—1566) and DAVID IBN SHOSHAN (cir. 1580) at Constantinople,
it was boasted that they were consulted on Muhammedan law by the
Turkish doctors and officials (Conforte, f. 34 a. 39 a.; Zunz, zur
Gesch. 440.).

    [49] Nicoll, Catal. p. 490.

                         § 16.   Page 131.

    [1] Authorities: Ibn Ezra, at the beginning of Meoznajim (cf. § 14.
n. 4.); a chronological list of grammarians from CHISKIJA ROMAN IBN
BAKUDA (1600) in De Castro, i. 74., where there are many mistakes;
conf. Jost, vi. 368. (*Catal.* p. 844. and Add.).   One in Latin of both Jews
and Christians is contained in Cod. Vat. 494. (in Mai).   An alphabetical list in WOLF. iv. p. 231. sq.   In later times: LUZZATTO, Prolegg.
ad una Gramm. rag. della Ling. Ebr. (Pad. 1836); conf. also DELITZSCH,
Jesurun, seu Isag. in Concord. Lips.; RAPOPORT, Introd. to the Lexicon
des Parchon, published by Stern (prob. 1844); EWALD and DUKES,
Beitr. zur Gesch. d. ältest. Ausleg. (Stuttg. and Tüb., 1844), 3 vols.
Concerning the hitherto little regarded German and French grammarians, see ZUNZ, zur Gesch. 60. sq. 107. sq.   Dukes promised some
years ago a history of the study of the Hebrew language; conf. also the
three Commentationes, by HUPFELD: I. et II. De Antiq. apud Jud.
Accent. Scriptt., with addit. to I. et III.; III. De Rei Gramm. apud
Jud. Init. (Halis, 1846); conf. with this the review of Ewald, Gött.
gel. Anz., 1847, p. 722., and Dukes, Lit. bl. viii. 635. sq.   Hupfeld
took no notice of Zunz's very complete treatise upon Nakdanim, and in
general repeats much of what has been said by Dukes.   The partiality
of his attacks prevented him from discovering the errors of De Rossi;
see *Catal.* p. 1304., and vide inf. n. 31.   An essay on the history of
Hebrew grammar, by DERNBURG (in " Orientalia," edited by Tuynboll,
Amst., 1846, ii. 99.) treats of a special grammatical theory; cf. also
GEIGER, Ker. Chem. ix. 61.; and, on the age of the punctuation, the
older essay of LUZZATTO in his Dialogues, &c. (§ 13.), published in
1852, where the matter is treated in general with the same arguments

as in his Prolegg., perspicuously expressed in the form of a Hebrew dialogue.

[2] See at § 17. n. 11.

[3] See n. 35. Ephodi, Lit. bl. iv. 168.; conf. Petah Debarai, pref.; Zunz, zur Gesch. 201. 204.

[4] Frankel in Verhandlungen, d. 1. Vers. d. u. a. Orient. p. 13., and sup. § 3. nn. 6, 7.

[5] The interpolated translation of the historian Honein ben Ishak (ob. 873.; see Krafft, Catalogue of Oriental MSS., p. 531.) is, according to Rödiger (A. d. Zeit. 1844, p. 266.), apparently taken from the Syriac or Greek; on another translator, see p. 134. and note 27.

[6] *Catal.* p. 2182. Concerning the Arabic name for translation, see note 8. Later, " to translate" is called העתיק (نَقْل ; see Maim. Abh. üb. d. Einh. p. 32. n. 15., conf. Dukes, p. 77.); and also הפך, " vertere" (Parchon, pref. p. xx.; and Abraham ben David in his Hebrew translation, p. 65., says that Alfarabi "translated" [הפך] the title of the book Topica, " liber *locorum*;" conf. the Arab. حَلَف); so that this expression in Dukes, p. 197., must not be translated exactly " *rursus* convertisse " (Hupf. ii. 9.); see also n. 44.

[7] Geig. Zeitschr. v. 287. 290.; likewise in the Arabic translation of the Karaites (see Munk, Annal. iii. 86.), and in the Persian (n. 10.), conf. Targum in Rapop. Ker. Chem. vi. 172. (conf. § 3. n. 7.); Midrash in Dukes, p. 49.; conf. Arabian legends in the author's essay in Frankel, Zeitschr. ii. 273., and *Catal.* p. 2182.

[8] Therefore, varying شرح and تفسير. Translation and Comm., see *Catal.* p. 2181. Ewald's category, "expounding translators," suits Saadja and the Persian translators better than Chikitilla, who was rather a translating exegetist.

[9] Zunz, G. V. 414., conf. Munk, l. l. p. 68. n. 1.

[9a] Continuous French glossaries (in Hebrew letters), which deserve notice, as forming a transition from the mere sporadically translating exegesis to the regular translation, go back at least as far as the year 1240; see the reference in Zunz, zur Gesch. 81.; Dukes, Mischle, pp. 41. 50. The last mentions also an "interlinear translation" (?). Perhaps from the continuous glossaries and translations arose the alphabetical, which were again enlarged by new languages; vide inf. 59 [a].

[10] Maimon., in Zunz, G. V. 9.; Delitzsch, Geschichte, 139.; Theodoret in Munk, l. l. p. 63. n. 2. (conf. sup. § 8. n. 13., neglected by Geiger, Moses ben Maimonides, p. 69. n. 50.); cf. also Lit. bl. 1850, p. 509. A modern *Persian* translation of the Pentateuch, &c., in Paris, made probably in 1300, translates directly from passages of the Targum, the place of which in the Liturgy it was apparently meant to supply, and from KIMCHI's explanations; it is generally instructive with regard to the history of the translation of the Bible. From this arose the translation of JACOB TAWUS (TUSI), which followed the text more closely, Const. 1546. (vide *Catal.* s. v.) There are still MSS. in the Krimea (Lit. bl. viii. 24.), and in Cod. Rossi, 1093., Cod. Pers. i. (Zunz, Got. Vortr. 124 a.); on the Persian book Tobias see Wolf. iii. p. 275., and Munk, l. c. on other Apocryphal books.

[11] Delitzsch., Gesch. p. 83.

[11a] *Catal.* p. 195. no. 1320. ; also De Castro, i. pp. 401. 411. 413., where he tries to prove that the Pentateuch was first translated by Jewish converts.

[12] Zunz, zur Gesch. p. 83., G. V. 413. (conf. Lit. bl. vii. 612.) 414. ; (conf. Geig. Lehrb. d. Mishna, p. 15. ; the author's Fremdspr. Elem. p. 23.) ; conf. Wolf. ii. p. 447., iv. p. 173. ; Rossi, art. Moses Arragel, and see § 27. n. 11. sq. ; and in general on the extant translations of Bible, sect. i. of the *Catal.* pp. 165—198. Concerning the so-called *Græca veneta* (from a MS. of the 14th century), see Gesenius in the Encycl. sect. i. vol. 9. p. 31. ; De Wette, Einl. ins A. T. § 56. On *Turkish* translations, see Delitzsch, Turcica, Lit. bl. i. 77. On older translations, cf. § 3.

[13] Jellinek's hypotheses (Leipz. Repert. 1847, p. 339.) are unfounded (see n. 49.) ; and it is also incorrect or inconsistent in Dukes (p. 42.) to claim for the Talmud the merits of Comparative Philology (Sprachvergleichung) ; see on the other hand Id. p. 49., Lit. bl. iv. 167., x. 57. (§ 4. n. 106.) ; conf. also Geig. Zeitschr. v. 273. ; Rapop. on Parchon, p. xiii. We will not enter upon the discussion of the somewhat indistinctly expressed views of S. Sachs (Die Relig. Poesie, p. 161.) on the subject, which are in close connexion with theological controversy.

[14] For example, ממנו, Geig. Zeitschr. v. 416. ; Ker. Chem. ix. 69., against Ewald, p. 124. ; and Kirchheim, Lit. bl. v. 675., who supposes a traditional grammatical theory before the existence of technical words. A monography upon Hebrew grammatical terminology, by N. HIRSCH, already prepared for the press, remains unpublished at Prague, on account of the death of the young author ; conf. also DUKES, Lit. bl. x. 55. sq., and sup. p. 240.

[15] Luzz. p. 24. ; Dialogues, p. 106. ; comp. Zunz, G. V. 96 d. ; for the views of Saadja on the subject, see *Catal.* p. 2162. Lists of imaginary and real variations of quotations in the Talmud and Midrash are given in several periodicals quoted by Landshuth, Maggid. p. ix. ; adde Annal. iii., Lit. bl. v. 284. On the other hand, IBN EZRA (Zachot, towards the end) condemns to the flames the work of a philologer who arbitrarily corrected above a hundred words in the Bible, because this is not permitted even in a profane work ; and this philologer is no other than Abulwalid. This was first shown by Luzz.,.Ker. Chem. iv. 136. On the confusion of Carmoly, Zion, i. 47., and of others about the expression המהביל, which seems to be applied by Ibn Ezra to several persons, see *Catal.* p. 2185. infrà.—Nevertheless, " false statements, which lived in the mouth and in the memory of Punctuators and Masoreths, have long been maintained, with their errors." (Frensdorf, on Mos. Nakdan, p. xiv.).

[16] Vide inf. n. 50. D. Cassel (ad Cusari, p. 181.) shows that in Judah Ibn Tibbon (1167) מסורת signifies " rule ; " conf. בעלי המסורת והקבלות in his contemporary Jos. Kimchi (Lit. bl. viii. 442.) ; conf. Hupfeld, i. p. 3., ii. p. 19., comp. iii. p. 2. ; S. BAER, the author of a meritorious work on the poetical accents (1852), gives (Lit. bl. xii. 21.) a striking instance how the Masora became enlarged, having consisted originally of very short rules (cf. § 4.) ; Jacob Tam (Lit. bl. xi. 378., and ed. Lond. p. 11.) speaks distinctly of later additions, and of errors of the punctuators (cf. n. 25.). But at a later period the whole Masora, and the

signs, were supposed to be of the same antiquity. On the connexion of
Masora and Haggada, see Zunz, G. V. 86. 326. ; and on Kabbalistic
expositions, § 14., and § 27. p. 234.

[17] Dukes, Lit. bl. v. nr. 45. 47. ; conf. Luzz. p. 20., and inf. n. 20.
On a printed Mishna, with accents, unknown to the authors quoted,
see *Catal.* p. 257. no. 1718. Therefore the name of the accent dividing
the verses appears first in a variation of the Tract. Sofer. (Zunz, G. V.
96 a. In the Talmud פְּסוּק הַמְעָמִים is not a sign, as Kirchheim on Chajug
p. 192. supposes. Moses Nakdan also [see Frensdorf, p. xliii.] does
not reckon it). The places where פסוק and העמדה occur are collected
in the author's Fremdsprachl. Elem. p. 12. n. 25. ; cf. also Luzz.,
Dialogues, pp. 83. 85. 88. 93. ; conf. the Syriac accents in Bar Hebreus,
Gramm. Syr. ed. Bertheau, iv. 47. sq., and inf. § 18. n. 51.

[18] Luzz. p. 21., and in Oostersche Wandel. p. 48. ; Rapop., Frankel,
Zeitschr. i. 359. Issachar Ibn Susan (f. 74 b.) derives even the
smaller lections from Ezra.

[19] Kirchheim on Chajug, p. 192. ; DUKES, Kuntris Hammassoret,
Tübingen, 1846, p. 29. (not used by Hupfeld, i. and ii.); Jeh.
HEDESSI's (1149) interesting although obscure communications (Alphab. 163. sq.) have been unnoticed even by those who treated the subject after the publication of this essay ; see n. 32. and § 14. n. 39. ;
conf. also SOLOMON BEN AARON TROKI, l. c. in n. 16. on נועם and ניגון.

[20] Ker. Chem. iv. 203., where also the employment of accents for
gesticulation is apparent ; Hedessi (173.) speaks of a " Masora of Palestine and Babylon and of Ben Asher and Ben Naphtali."

[21] See Zunz, zur Gesch. p. 110., and LUZZATTO's valuable special
researches in Oostersche Wandelungen, published by G. J. Polak (Amsterd. 1846), p. 23. sq., of which the critic of Pinner (Prospectus, &c.)
in the Lit. bl. viii. 24., knew nothing. EWALD has subjected the new
discoveries to his peculiar criticism (Jahrbücher der Bibl. Wissensch.
1849), cf. p. 166. On his hypothesis of the construction of Kamez in
opposition to older testimony, see the author's communication from a
MS. of ABRAHAM BABLI [sup. p. 139., cf. Geiger, Parschandata, p. 36.,
where נקדן is only a general denomination ; but perhaps he is the
ABRAHAM NAKDAN in Zunz, z. G. 117.?] in DAVIDSON, a Treatise on
Bibl. Criticism, i. 47. (cf. p. x.). Hedessi says the same. A leaf of the
interesting old Bible codex is now in the Bodl. library ; and a tracing
of it was communicated by the author to Geiger (l. c. p. 12. ; conf.
also Ker. Chem. ix. 70.).

[22] In the Midrash נקודות still signifies ornamental points of the
consonants (תגין יסרגול, *crowns* ; see Zunz, G. V. 264 b.), which perhaps
were intended to prevent the confusion of similar letters (Lit. bl. vi.
577.) On the older work, תגין, see p. 133., and Dukes, Nahal, p. 24.
(cf. Carmoly, Aktan, p. 6.), the short, but very erudite note of Fürst,
Lit. bl. xi. 149., is but one of his usual plagiarisms, see Zunz, G. V.
405 b. ; (conf. also Jellinek, Auswahl, p. 29. ; see our correction to
p. 20. in § 13. n. 1.). Jehuda Levi (iii. § 31. of the Hebr. transl.)
discerns, ניקוד vocalisation, טעמים accentuation, and מסורה Masora on
consonants, &c.

[23] Zunz, G. V. 264 b. ; Luzz. p. 37., Dial. p. 82. This argument,
which is not regarded by Ewald or Hupfeld, appears to the author

precisely the most decisive in this important and difficult inquiry, because it rests upon an accurate general view of Jewish literature. A
reference to the Dagesh in לֹא תִרְצַח (in the Decalogue), without, however, the mention of the sign, is found in the beginning of the Pesikta
rabbati, chap. 24., where it is explained by לֹא תתרצח. We will not
enlarge here on the interesting arguments and views of different parties,
Kabbalists, Grammarians, Karaites, brought forward with respect to the
antiquity of the punctuation; but it is worth mentioning that HEDESSI
believes it as old as the tables of Moses; and SOLOMON BEN AARON
TROKI is not satisfied with the Rabbinists who attribute it to Ezra.
Hedessi declares a Pentateuch roll of mere consonants to be improper
for the service; yet the expression מתקן הטעמים is also not unknown to
Karaites.

[24] The vowels are considered the souls of the consonants by several
authors after Ibn Ezra, e. g. the book *Bahir*, Ezra (or Azriel), Abr. Abulafia; the *Zohar*, Isaac Acco. Sol. Duran [in Dukes, p. 37.] appeals to
ירושלמי which generally indicates an authority supposed to originate in
Palestine (see Rapop. and Chajes, sup. § 4. n. 54.). Hupf. (i. p. 3.)
appeals, concerning the age of the writings (against Zunz, G. V. 407.),
to a work of Maimonides which never existed, and to Jeh. Moscato,
who wrote almost two centuries later than Hupfeld's voucher, th : famous
MOSES BOTAREL (§ 13., and see inf. n. 50.), who also speaks only of
Kabbalistic writings, and himself wrote a similar explanation of punctuation (MS. Opp. 9669.).

[25] Saadja (in Rapop. n. 37.; Ewald, p. 6.; Dukes, p. 82.), Koreisch (Ew. p. 123.), Dunasch, and Menahem ben Saruk (Dukes, p.
152.; conf. Jeh. Hal. ii. § 78.; Parchon in Geig. v. 409.), Abulwalid,
according to the Palestine readings (Kirchh. Lit. bl. v. 677. n. 12.).
Moses Nakdan and טעמי המקרא (in Frensdorf, p. xxii.). On Masoretic rules, which are not known till after the time of Abulwalid, Parchon, and Kimchi, see Frensdorf, p. xvi. Yet the Karaitic punctuation
in general is the same (§ 14. n. 25.).

[26] Saadja (Luzz. p. 189.; conf. Frankel, Zeitschr. i. 359.; Kirchh.
Lit. bl. v. 694., by which Dukes, p. 85., and Ew. p. xi., are to be corrected), Chiquitilla (Dukes, p. 185). Ibn Ezra indeed keeps, in
theory, to the division of verses; and similarly all Jews and sound
philologists of our time acknowledge, in general, the authority of the
Masoretic text for various reasons, although, in individual cases, they
follow the sense in preference to the accent: examples of this are given
by Luzz. (p. 188., Dial. p. 82., conf. p. 95., and Ker. Chem. vii.
73., and his preface to Isaiah).

[27] As was already witnessed by Hieronymus (in Luzz. p. 38., Hupf.
iii. p. 9., Add. ii. p. 21.); see also the interesting dialectical remarks
of Saadja (*Catal.* p. 2220, against Geiger, v. 273., and Dukes, Lit. bl.
xii. 398.) and his follower (in Dukes, Kuntris, pp. 70. 72.; conf. pp.
9. 34.); cf. also Samuel ben Hofni in Abulwalid (Ew. p. 141.); Men.
ben Saruk (in Dukes, p. 146.), Ibn Balam (in Dukes, p. 197.), Moses
Ibn Ezra (Poetic MS.), who attributes to the air and sea of Tiberias
such an influence on the tongue that even the children of the colonist
participated in its advantages; S. Duran (Kuntris, p. 38.); conf. also
inf. n. 46. In Tiberias lived ELI BEN (ABN ALI?) JEHUDA, the
Nazir (Dukes, p. 133.; conf. Wolf. iii. 764 d. : on Nazir, conf. Dukes,

Blumenl. p. 196.; conf. Busch's Jahrb. iv. 233.; Zunz, zur Gesch.
203.), perhaps identical with the composer of the מאור עינים (in Hedessi, 173.), who belonged to Tiberias, and with Jahja (inf. n. 27.).
Moreover, Ben Asher is said to have been of Tiberias. The name
מעזיה so much talked of by bibliographers (Hupf. i. p. 4.; Add. ii. p.
19.) appears to me to be derived from the proper name ﻣﻌﺰ. What
has been proposed since by various authors (Lit. bl. x. 809., xii.
83. 398. 368., where Dukes ought to have consulted the Arabic
text of Saadja) does not appear to offer any advantage. Luzzatto
(l. l. pp. 13. 26. 37. sq.) believed punctuation to have been introduced
by the Babylonian Saboraim (cii. 500.) under the influence of the
Syrians (whose introduction of vowels even he denies), supporting
his opinion, 1st, upon the agreement of the Karaites (sup. § 14. n.
25.), as if the oral Masora was not sufficient to account for that;
2nd, upon the similarity of the Syriac names of vowels, although the
Arabic are derived from these last, and the fact itself by no means
points to Babylon (comp. Hupfeld, iii. p. 7. sq.); 3rd, because the
different pronunciation of the ר used in Palestine, which is found also
in the book Jezira (conf. the author's Fremdsprachl. Elem. p. 24.), is
not observed; which would indeed only suggest a deviation on the part
of the Babylonians. Recently (in Dialogues, p. 108. note) he admits,
at least, that the punctuation of the European Jews is derived from
Tiberias. On the other hand, Ewald (p. xi. 149.) concludes, from the
variation of the said grammarians, that at their time the theory was
already obscured (against Hupfeld, l. c., Ewald, in the Gött. gel. Anz.,
has brought forward no new argument). In favour of the age and
originality of Hebrew grammatical terminology, Ewald (p. 124.) knows
nothing but the peculiar שׁבא, or שׁוא, in Chajjug (Dukes, pp. 136.
157.; conf. Cusari, ii. § 80.; Luzz. l. l. Hupf. iii. p. 5. n. 11., p.
7., ii. p. 22., by which Kämpf. Lit. bl. ii. 710. is to be corrected).
Upon דגשׁ in Saadja, see Dukes, p. 36.

[28] Vide inf. n. 52.

[29] Catalogues in WOLF (ii. p. 534., iv. p. 226., whence FÜRST,
Concord. p. 1382.); DUKES, Kuntris, p. 14. sq., where also upon the
leader of the school PINHAS, see Luzz. p. 25. Later, a particular ver-
bum denominativum was formed, מָסַר, i. e. to provide Bibles with
Masoretic glosses on the margins (Zunz, zur Gesch. 202., comp. 73 c.).
At last, a Masora upon the Targum was also composed (Luzz. Virgo,
f. j. p. 13.). The so-called "Mas. of the Talmud" is an index of
parallel passages, vide § 25.; on "Masoret Haggada" see sup. n. 16.

[30] P. 22. sq. (conf. MS. Munich. 14.). Hupf. (i. p. 4.) places him
at the beginning of the 10th century, but proves (in the note) "Æta-
tem ejus antemasoreticum esse," &c. Here also appears the ambiguity
of the word Masora.

[31] Hupf. i. p. 17. sq., according to the better recension of a MS. of
Luzzatto, published by Dukes, Kontres, &c.

[32] Id. p. 38.; Jeh. Hedessi (pp. 163. 168.) has, in his work תרין
בתרין, enriched the eighty זוגות of Ben Asher. He counts twelve *reges*,
nine *servi*, and ten *ancipites*, &c.

[33] Ew. p. 124.; Hupf. i. p. 2., iii. pp. 2. 10.; Geig. Zeitschr. v.
274. 416.; Zunz, zur Gesch. 194, 195.; Rapop. Busch's Jahrb. iii

259. The oldest trace is probably the division of the letters in the book Jezira (§ 13.), and the Comment. (conf. Dukes, p. 134.). It is not true, according to Gesen. Thes. Rad. עוּץ (Geig. Zeitschr. v. 314.), that Saadja never appeals to those who wrote before his time (Ew. p. 5.), only he mentions no name; cf. *Catal.* p. 2188.

³⁴ Cf. *Catal.* p. 2199., and on MS. Mich. 59., ib. p. 2162. Perhaps the manner of putting small verses between the letters of the alphabet is very old. Upon the unusual מחריזים, in Menahem (Dukes, Lit. bl. viii. 680., see § 18. n. 31. Upon ﺟﺮ, or אגור, vide sup. § 9. n. 40., and inf. n. 38. Hedessi (p. 170.) has also מדקרקי האגרון. On the lexica of the Karaites, DAVID BEN ABRAHAM, said to be a contemporary of Saadja (Ker. Chem. ix. 51.), and ALI BEN SOLEIMAN (see *Catal.* p. 2199.), we must wait for more special notices.

³⁵ Rapop. on Parchon, p. xiii., has proved that nothing but investigations required the Arabic language (conf. also Chiquitilla in Dukes, p. 181.). Saruk does not know how to explain etymologically the principle of the alphabetical series (מַחְבֶּרֶת); for example, הבית was found under ה.

³⁶ Vide § 14.

³⁷ Munk (Not. sur Aboulw. p. 44.) ascribes to him all the works mentioned in the Commentary on Jezira (see § 13. n. 12.), and even identifies him with ABU IBRAHIM, mentioned in Mos. Ibn Ezra, but who is (according to an old correction of the MS. itself) ABU IBRAHIM IBN BARUN (or BERREIN?), see *Catal.* p. 1335.

³⁸ אלחאוי (Hebr. המאסף), not ﺟﺎﻣﻊ (as first conjectured by the author, see n. 34.), which is a common title of Arabic lexica, and also a name for Ecclesiasticus; see on Maim. Treat. on Unity, p. 15. n. 22. The following are synonymous expressions, ערך (arrangement) and מחברות, with doubtful vocalisation, corresponding with ﺗﺄﻟﻴﻒ (Lit. bl. iv. 35., vi. 171.). The particular alphabets of the lexica are called probably מחברת (Lit. bl. iv. 187., viii. 650., sup. n. 35.; Simson, in Geig. Zeitschr. v. 421., against Rapop. on Parchon, p. x.; Dukes, p. 40.; Zunz, zur Gesch. p. 203.; Hupf. iii. 17. n. 31.; Add. ii. p. 22., none of whom explain the difference of the sing and plur.), or שער, ﺑﺎﺏ (cf. *Catal.* p. 1428. and 2198.). The chapters or articles in the alphabet are called פרק (in Nathan), and ערך. Ibn Balam also quotes a ס׳ דקדוק (perhaps Chajjug?).

³⁹ Karaitic authorities confirm Lebrecht's etymology of Koreisch (*Catal.* p. 1334.); and by this we learn to know the influence of Koreisch's exegesis, § 17. n. 4. " Ibn Koreisch Jehuda " is already quoted in Tobia the Karaite (Cod. Opp. 255. in fol. f. 986.), who seems to mention a work עשרת הדברים; but, unfortunately, the passage is obscure: he speaks in the same place of many Rabbinites having been converted to Karaism; and perhaps this occasioned later Karaites to consider him one of themselves.

⁴⁰ *Catal.* s. v. His criticism on Menahem (ed. Lond. p. 68.) enumerates some roots common to Hebrew and Arabic.

⁴¹ *Catal.* s. v.

⁴² Zunz, zur Gesch. p. 113. Chajjug did not treat of the fixed roots, particles, &c. (Abulw. Lit. bl. viii. 679.).

[43] Ewald (p. 143.) has quite misunderstood the sentence of R. Jochanan mentioned by Jona (Ab. Sar. 58 b., Cholin, 137 b., where, for לעצמה, in Raschi, stands לחוד ; conf. Natan, Aruch, sub voce לשון) ; conf. Parchon (end of the grammar), דרך הפשט לבד ודרך המדרש לבד ; Ibn Ezra (Zachot, verb. neutropass.), לשון מקרא לחוד ולשון תלמוד לחוד ; conf. Tobias in Geig. Zeitschr. v. 416. The sense is, that midrash and simple exegesis exist independently (לחוד, לבד, לעצמו).

[43a] Lebrecht (Lit. bl. iv. 234.) asserts that Chiquitilla also translated writings of Abulwalid, without mentioning his authorities. In his preface (Dukes, p. 181.), which Parchon copies, he says that he is obliged to make use of circumlocution from the want of precise technical expressions. On other translators of Abulwalid's writings, see *Catal.* p. 1418.

[44] *Catal.* s. v.

[45] His רקמה is to be distinguished from Abulwalid's work of the same name, and he himself from the older translator of Jonah ; another ISAAC BEN JEHUDA composed the book האשל about 1250 ; and another ISAAC LEVI, in the 12th century, wrote the book מקור ; see *Catal.* l. c.

[46] Rossi, Dictionary, 287.; Dukes, Lit. bl. iv. 234. Carmoly (Annal. ii. 29.) and Kirchheim (Abulw. p. xii.) make him older than Abulwalid (??) ; perhaps he is identical with the poet, § 20. n. 42. JACOB OF JERUSALEM (בית המקדש, Arab.) is a different person from " the Pilgrim " (חוגג = حاجي) mentioned by Abulwalid (Lit. bl. vii. 663.).

[46a] Upon the extensive circulation of his commentary, even as far as the East, see n. 10.

[47] See Geig. Melo Chofn. p. 63. 101.

[48] *Catal.* s. v.

[49] The history of this technical expression is instructive for the development of terminology generally. It was drawn from the old treasures of the language, and was gradually shaped in the different systems and schools partly by the natural influence of the Arabic, which was in its turn influenced by the Hebrew. In the Talmud, particularly in the Halachaic discussions, דדרק and דקדק (rad. דוק) and their derivatives signify " to be careful in minutiæ, and scrupulous in doing, speaking, and thinking," according to the relative word which is to be supplied (cf. sup. § 4. n. 17.) ; hence *precise* astronomers are called merely מדקדקים ; and in the Hebrew translation of Albatani (M. Michael. 835.), a work upon astronomy is more particularly designated a במלאכתי הדקדוק. In the style of translation of the Tibbonides rad. דק was used principally for " subtle," particularly in conjunction with עיו (نظر), speculation, &c., especially דקדוק and דייקות. With these various shades of meaning is connected the use of דקדוק (not yet used without the correlative לשון) for Grammar (cf. the definition of Jonah, which Ephodæus, MS. chap. viii., says is an explanation of the word, not a real definition). The Hebrew origin is proved by the use of it in an Arabic work by JAPHET the Karaite, but Geig. (Zeitschr. v. 274.) and Munk go too far in concluding that the grammarians quoted by Japhet are Karaites ; see Rap.; Busch. iii. 259.; דקדוק 'ס as the opposite of אגרונות (Lexic.) in Hedessi (Dukes, p. 40., Lit. bl. viii. 636.) ; although, on the other

hand, it seems above (n. 34. and § 12. n. 37.) to include also lexica.
Abulwalid entitles his work on language تَنْقِيح = דקדוק, where grammar and lexicon are taken together, and the study of language is made
a point of. The expressions צחצח in old works, and חכמי הלב or אנשי
לבב (اولو الالباب), are also to be observed.

[50] Saruk in Dukes, 146.; Wolf. i. 339.; Zunz, zur Gesch. 203.
Upon the so-called Codex *Hilali*, see *Catal.* p. 1782. The Parisian
Cod. Suppl. 1. was not written in 1061 (Carmoly), but in 1301 (Geig.
Zeitschr. v. 464.; conf. sup. § 10. n. 31.); the Cod. Ken. 350. of
Vienna is said to have been written in the 10th century, Krafft and
Deutsch, *Catal.* p. 10.

[51] Zunz, zur Gesch. pp. 107. sq. 201. sq.; Rapop. on Parchon (see,
however, sup. n. 41.).

[52] Vide sup. n. 49.; Zunz, zur Gesch. 201. sq. (from which Hupf. ii.
p. 107. must be corrected and completed), דייקן, see also Zion, ii. 105.

[52a] Hupf. (iii. p. 21., ii. p. 19.), without sufficient reason, considers
the printed book to be a later compilation; see *Catal.* s. v.: the same
title is given to the grammar of Saadja.

[53] Lit. bl. viii. 442. ABRAHAM BEN JUDA IBN CHAJJIM probably
wrote upon the technical part of copying the Bible, colours, and the
like (Cod. Rossi, 945.; but the date, 1262, and the country, Spain,
seem uncertain. About that time lived ABRAHAM BEN CHAJJIM, the
father of Levi (§ 11.) in Provence).

[53a] Vide sup. n. 38.

[54] كتاب = סופר? see *Catal.* s. v. Geig. (v. 419.), identifies him
with MOSES BEN ISAAC HANNESIA; but lately (Ker. Chem. ix. 61.) he
supposes the latter to be a native (??) of Provence, in consequence of
DUKES' valuable essay on the latter in Jewish Chronicle, 1849 (vol. v.
n. 37.), p. 295. sq. By the by, Dukes has given (p. 295.) a short
notice about the very few Jewish scholars of England in the Middle
Ages, which might be completed by a few more names, e. g. R. MORIL
(Samuel) of Inghilterra, and some others of לונדריץ, if that is not
rather *Londres* in France; Jacob of Orleans (see sup. p. 144., comp. also
Zunz ad Benjamin, p. 257., z. G. 161. 52., *Catal.* p. 1257. 1319.).

[55] Zunz, p. 204.; conf. p. 118.

[56] *Catal.* p. 1257. His work is now printed (Lond. 1855). The
above-mentioned poem on accents, with the acrostic (JACOB BEN MEIR),
is found also in a MS. (A. D. 1470) amongst several tracts (f. 106 b.)
containing also the poem of JOSEPH BEN KALONYMOS and the דייקות of
SAMUEL, who completes his grammatical observations by others (f. 27.
sq.) arranged according to the order of the Pentateuch, and then (f. 35.
sq.) treats of the accents, &c.; so that it is more than probable that the
grammarian and the Nakdan in Zunz, p. 109., are one and the same
author.

[57] *Catal.* p 1737.

[Page 140. line 1. On JOSEPH BEN DAVID, whose work is extant in
a MS. of the Bodl. libr., DUKES has enlarged in the Lit. bl. x. 707. 727.
755., xi. 173. 183. 215. (cf. also the German note 46 of this §);
but with respect to the date, he is evidently wrong, as he places him
first (p. 707.) in the beginning of the 13th century, and then in the

time of Moses Hannesia; while Joseph quotes Isaac ben Eleazar Levi, (who wrote, not in the " beginning of the 12th century," as is said in Lit. bl. vii. 706., since he quotes Charisi, who lived in 1218), and even Nachmanides (ob. not before 1268), as dead (ל"ז, see Lit. bl. xi. 184.). Hence Joseph cannot have lived before the *end* of the 13th, which agrees with his speaking of the Kabbalists.   To Elia ben Chananel, who Dukes (p. 728.) says is unknown, are dedicated, in 1351–2, some Kabbalistic works of ISAIAH BEN JOSEPH (partly also in Cod. Laud. 220.); this Isaiah (born 1327), " called Rab," was the possessor of the Bodl. Cod. of Joseph's work, and was said by Uri (476.) to be the author.   All this Dukes could have learnt by referring to Cod. Vienna, XCIV. (p. 107. of the Catalogue, a criticism of which was given by Dukes in Lit. bl. 1848).

[58] Vat. 417. 2. (Zunz, G. V. 438 b.; zur Gesch. 120.), as the author concludes from the beginning where the German stands first. See also n. 30. and § 9. n. 39.

[58 a] See Dukes, Lit. bl. viii. 481. sq.

[59] Luzzatto, p. 34.; Dukes, Kobez, p. iv.

[59 a] Vide *Catal.* p. 622. (and upon the origin, sup. n. 9 a.).   The date of the composition כל"ה refers to the French exile of the year 1395, not to 1290, see Mos. Rieti, f. 104. (different in Ibn Verga, chap. 24.)   The title was stereotyped, cf. Portaleone in Zunz, G. V. 442.   A Hebrew Arabic Lexicon was written by SAADJA IBN DANAN, ed. 1473, cf. § 20. n. 50.

[60] Not to be confounded with Raschi, who was not called Jarchi, see Zunz, Israel. Annal. i. nr. 42.

[61] Conf. Dukes, Lit. bl. viii. 441., cf. 516. n. 7.   *Catal.* p. 1524.

[62] *Catal.* s. v.

[63] Zunz, zur Gesch. 410.; Dukes, Kuntris. nr. 12, 13.

§ 17.   Page 141.

[1] Authorities (besides those given § 16. n. 1.): the German-French literature complete in ZUNZ, zur Gesch. pp. 60—107. 194—201.; a catalogue of 148 commentaries on the Pentateuch given by REGGIO, in the Introd. to his Italian version of the Pentateuch (Vienna, 1821, see Annal. iii. 6.); characteristics in DEL MEDIGO (Mel. Chofn. p. 29.); some particulars, rather antiquated however, in LE-LONG-MASCH, Biblioth. Sacra, and DE ROSSI's supplement to it; recently, GEIGER (Beiträge, 1847, and Parschandata, 1855) has given characteristic dissertations of some eminent exegetists of the German-French school (11–12th cent.), not, however, uninfluenced by his subjective tendencies. We ought, perhaps, to mention here a recent work, the *Practische Einleitung in die heil. Schrift und Geschichte der Schriftauslegung*, &c., p. 1. of the Oberrabbiner, L. Löw, at Kanischa (1855), not indeed as one of our authorities, but as a work which has made considerable use of our German essay without mentioning it (*Catal.* p. 2050.).

[2] The author's Fremdsprachl. Elem. p. 7.; conf. Whewell-Littrow, l. c. p. 235.

[3] This was originally meant to be a mere exposition of Scriptural and Haggada passages.   The first part touches upon scarcely anything

but the explanation of Biblical anthropomorphisms. This is probably the reason of the remarkable fact that this comprehensive mind left behind no really exegetical work.

4 See Parchon, Gramm. End. ISAAC TROKI often enters into polemics against Christian exegesis, particularly that of the Gospels.

5 E. g. ANAN's *Ableitung der Beschneidung mit der Schere nach Jos.* v. 2. (Lit. bl. viii. 18.) is certainly not more rational than the Rabbinical derivation of the prohibition of shaving, &c. (conf. also Annal. i. 137.). Geiger (Zeitschr. v. 267. sq. 272. sq.) gives too much prominence to the natural sense of the words in the principles of the Karaites; and Kirchheim (l. c.), who agrees with him as regards the first commencement, is contradicted not only by the instance of Anan, but also by the fact that, of the three points of difference characterising this sect mentioned by AARON BEN ELIA (Lit. bl. i. 534. 609.), the first and third refer to tradition. Saadja gives the four rules of exposition (ib. p. 534.; Frank. Zeitschr. ii. 112.).

6 Conf. § 12. n. 3.

7 See Abulw. § 16. n. 35., and Parchon, Gramm. On the simple meaning, as opposed to Halacha, see § 14. n. 5., SAMUEL BEN MEIR (in Zunz, zur Gesch. 195.), IBN EZRA (in Lippmann, Sefat Jeter, p. 19.; conf. Geig. Zeitschr. i. 311.; Rapop. Ker. Chem. vii. 92. sq.; cf. *Catal.* s. v.). The explanation of anthropomorphisms, a mutual object of reproach, is due to JEHUDA IBN KOREISH (§ 16. n. 39.). We will only add, that they lay a great stress, even in practical deductions, on the connexion (סמיכות) of chapters, &c. (cf. Ibn Ezra, Deuter. xxiv. 16.; cf. Exod. xxi. 8.).—The seventy ways of explanation are a more recent and symbolical number; see the author's essay quoted in § 2. n. 6.

8 ZUNZ, G. V. 409.; conf. 397. On Maimonides on the Unity, 18.; Duran, Keshet umagen, conf. Melo Chofn. p. 64. n. 8.; Abbamari, Minch. Ken. p. 125. l. 3.; Shemtob on the Moreh, ii. 36.; Cusari, iii. § 66.; Immanuel of Rome, on Prov. xxv. 16. (in Dukes, Blumenl. p. 268.); Franck, Kabbala, p. 42.—On the older meaning of רמז, see § 5. nn. 7. 10. 102.

9 Conf. also the interesting classification in Ibn Ezra's Introduction to the Pentateuch, and (Lathif?) Schaar hasch. (in Luzzato, Virgo, f. J. p. vii.); Aaron ben Elia Kar., Introduction to Comment. (Lit. bl. i. 500.), and Del Medigo (see n. 1.).

10 Dunash Ibn Librat seems the first who used the word in that sense; see Zunz, z. G. 197. 568.; cf. § 16. n. 35.

11 Saadja, on the Psalms (Ew. p. 8. [Geig. Zeitschr. v. 308.]; Dukes, p. 184.), and on Proverbs (see *Catal.* s. v.); Isaac (Israeli?), on the Edomite genealogical tables (Lit. bl. i. 303.); explanation of ten punctuated passages in Abot d. R. Nathan and Bamidb. Rab. in Geig. Zeitschr. vi. 23.; conf. As. d. Rossi, Ker. Chem. v. 153.

12 See an anonymous Pashtan of England, in Baruch ben Isaac; conf. Albo, Ikkar, i. 1.; Zunz, zur Gesch. 196.; also in Menahem ben Solomon, who uses פשר and פשט for פתר; conf. פשרונו, in Salmon ben Jerucham (Dukes, Beitr. p. 100.), פֵּשֶׁר, in Sabbatai Donolo (Ker. Chem. vii. p. 65. l. 17.), together with פתרין (id. p. 64. l. 6. ab inf.); conf. Parchon (l c.), Mos. Kimchi, Introd. to Comm. on the

Proverbs (Lit. bl. viii. 26 n. 2.).   Biblical commentaries of the 13th and 14th centuries are called פשטים in Zunz, zur Gesch. pp. 83. 92. 567.

[13] Böttcher, in Verhandlungen, d. i. Vers. d. Orient. p. 56.

[14] MENAHEM BEN SOLOMON (Lit. bl. vii. 440.) is, however, perhaps an Italian.

[15] Zunz, zur Gesch. p. 196. sq.; conf. Geig. Lit. bl. des Israel. p. 70.; Beer, in Frankel's Zeitschr. iii. 477.; Menahem ben Solomon (on metaphorical explanation), in Dukes, Kobez al Jad, p. 36.

[15a] In Dukes' Excerpta (Lit. bl. viii. 346, 347.) he gives the same words in French, as Gerson the elder does in his Commentary on Talmud.

[16] *Catal.* p. 1478.; cf. Geig. Parschand. p. 11.

[17] לבלר (libellarius), or כותב, also expresses such additions and supercommentaries, Zunz, zur Gesch. pp. 196. and 87.

[18] Zunz, 195., and Geig. ll. cc.

[19] *Catal.* s. v., and Geig. Parschand.

[20] Par. Biblioth. Sorb. 85.; Carm. Rev. Or. i. p. 123.; Dukes, Lit. bl. viii. 513. sq.; hence omitted in Zunz, p. 76.

[21] Enumeration in ZUNZ, Biogr. of Rashi in the Zeitschr. f. d. Wiss. d. Jud.; cf. *Catal.* s. v.   The Commentary attributed to "Joel," in the old Catal. MS. Angliæ, repeated by Gagnier (Wolf. iv. n. 797 b.), and in Coxe's Catal. (Cod. Vigorn. 9.), is a curious misconception of the final passage; the work is the Comm. of NACHMANIDES.

[21a] Zunz, p. 199. sq.

[22] Id. p. 76. sq., and *Catal.* sub vocibus.

[23] Zunz, zur Gesch. 94.   He mentions also a work on Physics (§ 22. n. 70.).

[24] Carm. Rev. Or. ii. 399., " Touche;" S. Cassel, Hist. Versuche, i. 29., explains it, " Toucques."

[25] *Catal.* s. v.

[25a] Conf. Geig. Zeitschr. iv. 397.; Zunz, zur Gesch. pp. 103. 200.

[26] MS. Mich. 509. 644.

[27] Zunz, zur Gesch. 465.

[28] Id. Addit. p. 324.; MS. Mich. 399.   מבחר המאמרים, ed. by Piperno (Livorno, 1840); cf. Carm. Hist. p. 91.

[29] *Catal.* p. 693.

[30] *Catal.* p. 717.; cf. Ker. Chem. viii. 84. 205.

§ 18.   Page 146.

[1] The first impulse to inquiry on the history of this branch was given by the religious poetry; hence the first treatise, HEIDENHEIM on the Pijutim and Pajtanim (with additions by M. H. MICHAEL) appeared as an introduction to the Machsor.   RAPOPORT's well-known investigations about Eleazar Kalir form the foundation of more recent critical researches.   A review of the writings connected with this subject, by ZUNZ, DELITZSCH, DUKES, LUZZATTO, STEINSCHNEIDER, KÄMPF, MOHR, M. SACHS (WENRICH's prize essay, which excludes the new Hebrew poetry), and the translations and imitations of KÄMPF, KRAFFT, STEIN, STERN, TENDLAU, ZEDNER (to which was added, in 1847, the author's

Manna and LETTERIS; see Lit. bl. viii. 476.), has been given by the author in the Mag. f. d. Lit. d. Ausl., 1845, p. 429. sq.; MUNK's treatise, extracted from the magazine Le Temps (Delitzch, zur Gesch. p. xii.), is to be found in French and German in Philippson's Schul-und Predigtmagaz. vol. ii. (1835), and contains only some proofs and remarks on the Arabian period. The author has defended Zunz and Rapoport's fundamental views against modern doubts and objections in his Treatise on the History of Hebrew poetry, in Frankel's Zeitschr. iii. 401. sq., where also he rejects the separate treatment of the "religious poetry," and refers to the close connexion of poetic forms with the history of Hebrew philology. The main view of the matter is not altered by the fact that Eleazar Kalir has been proved older than Saadja. Some special authorities will be mentioned below in their respective places, especially on the work of ZUNZ, *Die synagogale Poesie* (1855), see § 19. n. 7. On the collection of poetry published at London in 1850, under the title *Treasures of Oxford*, see Lit. bl. xi. 614. and *Catal.* p. 1006. sq. On DUKES, נחל קדומים, see § 20.

  2 Frankel, Zeitschr. iii. 409.

  3 Rapop., Pref. to Parchon.

  4 See the citations in Zunz, G. V. 377 b. c., and Syn. Poes. 61.; conf. Frankel, iii. 411. n. 14.; Delitzch, zur Gesch. d. hebr. Poesie, p. 131.; Dukes, zur Kenntniss der rel. Poes. p. 6. sq., Lit. bl. iv. 338. (where read "*Anfang*" for "*Um*fang der Kunstform"); Sachs, der rel. Poes. d. Juden in Span. p. 175. sq.; and vide inf. n. 15.

  5 Frankel, iii. 408., which also has weight in the principal part of the subject against Cassel's doubts and opinions (id. p. 194. sq.).

  6 Id. Zeitschr. iii. 406.; Geiger (Zeitschr. iii. 381.) admitted no peculiar Hebrew poetry, and considered the hymns as alone deserving the name. He has however since considerably altered his opinion.

  7 Delitzsch, zur Gesch. pp. 139. 142.; Cassel (p. 192.) becomes almost self-contradictory in reference to the Syrians.

  8 Delitzsch, l. c.

  9 See § 19. n. 21.

  10 Del. pp. 126. 136.; conf. also von Raumer, Gesch. d. Pädag. i. 3., on the æsthetical value of the mediæval Latin religious poetry.

  11 Lit. bl. viii. 72.; conf. Geig. Zeitschr. vi. 17.

  12 Even S. Cassel (p. 192.) affirms (p. 195.) that the earlier Syrian poems are far removed from Judaism. On Syrian metrics see Zingerle (in the Zeitschr. f. d. Kunde d. Morgenl. vii. 1. sq., and Zeitschr. der d. m. Gesellsch. x. 116. sq., on mixed metrum in strophes of several lines), who reckons verses in three lines among the rarer forms (l. c. p. 3.); and see n. 16., also nn. 18. 59. The author's purpose, in the following remarks is to show the weakness of the arguments on which different hypotheses have been built, not to establish or confirm a new one; and he accepts fully the sentence of the great master (Zunz, S. P. p. 85.): "We cannot know which poetry has been the model of the first Pajtanim, of which the time and country are uncertain."

  13 Zunz, G. V. 381.; Luzz. Virgo, &c., p. 10.; Lit. bl. vii. 677.; conf. Sachs, p. 176.

  14 Frankel, Zeitschr. iii. 408. It is of some importance that the 613 precepts in Saadja's liturgy are much less artificial than the real

Azharot (see *Catal.* p. 2206.) and that in JOSE BEN JOSE's Seder Aboda
scarcely any artifice but the old alphabet appears, not even the division of the line into four parts, or the strophic construction, which is
visible in his new-year hymn ; see also n. 17. On the other hand, some
non-liturgical poetry ascribed to the Gaonim seems not to belong to
them ; cf. inf. n. 40.

[15] See the authorities in n. 4. (and conf. Zunz, S. P. 86. 157.), and
the author's remark in Frankel, Zeitschr. iii. 409.

[16] Luzz. Virgo, p. 11., and S. Cassel, l. c., appeal to the influence of
the Syrians (cf. n. 12.), especially Jacob Edessenus (ob. 710. cf.
Wenrich, De Auct. Græc. p. 126.) We refer the reader to the essay on
the rhyme of Syriac poems by Zingerle (Zeitschr. l. c. x. 110—116.),
who states that the Syrians are not *commonly* rhyming people, like
Arabs and Persians, that in the classical time (4—5th cent.) the rhyme
occurs more rarely, and that later rhymes are rather to be ascribed to
the influence of those nations ; and yet he was acquainted with a whole
rhymed poem, the 54 Paræneses of Ephrem Syrus (ob. A. D. 379).

[17] E. g. the רהוטה (n. 66.) of Ibn Ezra, Lit. bl. iv. 338. ; conf. also
Zunz, S. P. pp. 62. 163., and even Selichot without rhyme in the 13th
cent. ; ib. p. 176.

[18] Sachs (p. 174.) and Cassel (p. 224., conf. 226. n.), without foundation, have cited in their own favour the passages in Zunz, G. V. 380.
(conf. Rap., Kalir 20. ; see Frankel, Zeitschr. iii. 409.) ; it seems un-
necessary to repeat the details of our argument ; cf. also Zunz, S. P.
p. 60. ; and on the name פויטן, p. 107. Even Parchon (5 a., A. D. 1161)
has still פייטן, the denom. פייט and וחרוותומשקל פיום as opposed to
the old נגונים, and speaks of פיוטים שקולים of the Arabians; while
Ibn Ezra and Maimonides (even אלפיוטים in Arabian sentences, vide
Lit. bl. iv. 685., and also in Cusari, ii. 78. in the text, cf. n. 51.) seem
to point to the narrower sense. The German Simson (in Geig. v. 429.)
calls Gabirol's upbraiding song פיים, but he probably knew it only from
quotations.

[19] Frankel, iii. 409. ; cf. sup. n. 14., and inf. p. 149. sq.

[20] Vide sup. n. 8. That this was the case in the neo-Persian, used
at first by the Arabians, is a point which cannot be pursued further
here. Conf. also Sachs, p. 302., conf. 270.

[21] See references in Frankel, iii. 462. sq. ; conf. inf. § 19. n. 4. and
n. 19. Hence linguistic phenomena analogous to those censured occur
in Saadja (Lit. bl. vi. 678.), Menahem, Dunash, Abitur, Gabirol, Gajjat
(in Sachs, p. 206.), and even partially in the Arabising translators (Lit.
bl. iii. 815. 823.), and also in the Karaites, as Solomon ben Jerucham and
others (Jost, Busch's Jahrb. v. 155.), according to which, Dukes (Lit.
bl. v. 718.) is to be corrected. The African, S. Duran (in Dukes, Lit.
bl. iv. 687., conf. Zunz zur Gesch. p. 204.), who justifies his poverty
of language by the importance of his matter, forms a remarkable exception.—This important observation has been recently carried out in detail
by ZUNZ, who gives a kind of glossary of these linguistic peculiarities ;
and his general remark (p. 119.) agrees remarkably with that of Moses
Ibn Ezra (Poetic MS. f. 28 a., cf. sup. p. 153.).

[22] Abulwalid learned the poetry of his teacher by heart in his youth
(Lit. bl. xiii. 153—155.), although he regarded poetry as beyond his
peculiar sphere (in Dukes, Mischle, p. xiv.).

[23] Dunash (Lit. bl. iv. 232.) and others (collected by Dukes, Lit. bl. viii. 152. : the mere names are given in Zunz, S. P. 216. ; quotations of verses from different authors, but not in strict chronological order, are collected by Dukes, Nahal, conf. also Samson, sup. n. 18.), and subsequently also philosophers and exegetists, as especially Ibn Arama.   The word שנאמר in Weisse, pref. to Jedaja, p. xlix., is, perhaps, to be translated " as we say "? cf. ונאמר בסדור התפלה in Crescas to Moreh, ii. 4. f. 60 b. ed. Jesnitz, and sup. § 6. n. 6.

[24] References in Frankel, Zeitschr. ii. p. 388. ; conf. Zunz, G. V. 389. 394.   On the later censures, see § 19. nn. 4. 33.

[25] Dukes, *Ueber d. äussern Formen der Piutim*, Lit. bl. iv. 337. ; partly also treated in Zunz, S. P. p. 85. sq., more particularly with reference to his special branch ; and on some termini technici, see Dukes, Lit. bl. xii. 148.

[25a] Sachs, p. 174., analogies in Frankel, ii. p. 303.   It is called in Arabic جناس (Hammer, Encyklopäd. Übers., p. 63.); for details, see Zunz, S. P. 104., and the name גימטריא, p. 105.   On a work of Nahshon named *Seder Alphabet*, see sup. § 13. n.

[26] Rapop. Kalir, note 20.; Zunz, G. V. 370., S. P. p. 86.; Dukes, Lit. bl. iv. 339. 529.   S. Cassel (p. 192.) shows the same in the Syrian, as also Zingerle, l. c. p. 113.   A recent legend derives this artifice from heaven, where Kalir learned it (H. Treves).

[27] References in Dukes, Lit. bl. vii. 780., and in the author's *Catal.* A few more authors could be added to our text, e. g., Aaron Chajjim Volterra (1750), who chose the letter ש.

[28] *Catal.* s. v.

[29] *Catal.* s. v.

[29a] Read 1697. ; see *Catal.* s. v.

[30] Zunz, 380. sq. ; Rapop. Ker. Chem. vi. 19. 538. ; Geig. Zeitschr. v. 268. ; the author's memoir in Frankel, iii. 408. (where nn. 11. and 12. should be transposed, and " 10th " be read for " 9th " century) ; more particulars in Zunz, S. P. p. 106.; Cassel (p. 231., conf. 224.) improperly calls every acrostic poem " Kaliric."   If he misses this among the Arabians, he has also failed to find it among the Syrians (p. 196.).   Cassel seeks the origin of it in rivalry ; Dukes, with an appeal to Gavison (Lit. bl. iv. 436.), in the fear of plagiarisms, on which subject Charisi, Abr. Ibn Chisdai (Busch's Jahrb. v. 385.), and others make complaints (cf. on that subject the remarks of Dukes, Lit. bl. xii. 374., where some particulars are incorrect ; on Joseph ben Jehuda [who is Ibn Aknin] see Ersch. s. v. p. 49.).   The zeal of Sabbatai Donolo for the preservation of his name, and the fate of Zidkija Anaw, Aaron Kohen, and others, are remarkable.   Sabbatai has also the final formula חזק, which Sachs (p. 210.) derives from the call of the congregation to the leader of the prayers ; cf. Zunz, z. G. 306., S. P. 109. 369.   On the use of numerical values (Sachs, l. c.), conf. sup. § 13. n. 27.   On the euphemisms used in acrostics, and their abbreviations, see Zunz, zur G. 316. sq., 369., and S. P. l. c.   We will here mention a passage of the Karaite Jeshua (Cod. Warner. 41 f. 159 b.), who says that a perfect and good poem (פיוט) of alphabetical (על אלף בית) or acrostic (על שם עושהו) form in the Hebrew

language, or any good style (לדבר בלשון מעליא), is not a matter of chance, but requires a knowledge of language, &c.

[31] The feminine form חרוזה appears also in some authors. In the Talmud (Jer. Chag. ii. § 8., Jefe Mareh ; Wajikr. Rab. cap. 16. ; conf. Buxtorf sub voce) חרו or החריז is used for the arrangement of similar biblical passages ; hence Seruk (in Dukes, p. 148.) properly calls the lexicographers מחריזים (sup. § 16. n. 34.). On the form of the Rows of Pearls by which Jewish authors on Cantic. i. 10., explain the word (see Jos. Ibn Aknin in Ersch, s. v. p. 55., and Mos. Ibn Ezra, Poetic MS. f. 14 b. cf. f. 25 a. ; cf. Catal. sub Saadja Gaon, p. 2188.); among the Arabians, see Wenrich, De Poes. Hebr. et Ar. p. 179. (cf. the author's notice, Oesterr. Blätt. 1845, p. 580.) ; Jellinek, Lit. bl. vi. 171. ; Sachs, p. 174. n. 4., and 339. Abravanel (on Exod. xv. in Zedner, Auswahl, p. 70.) explains it לפי שהם שבילים מסודרים ; on the other hand, Kalonymos (wrongly translated in Sachs, p. 174.) calls rhetoric without rhyme מליצה מסודרת, in opposition to מליצת החרוז, rhyming prose. Conf., moreover, שורות יקרות וטורים יקרים, in Abrah. ben Chijja (zur Haar. 1.).

[32] Vide inf. § 19. ; Zunz, S. P. p. 86., "perhaps already in the 8th cent."

[33] E. g. art. גש איתן, and the short introduction to the Lexicon (conf. also Dukes, Kuntris, p. 11.). The paranomastics, &c., and the rhyming final formula in Josippon, are not critically established (conf. Zunz, Zeitschr. p.303., G. V.453.) ; there are rhymes in Koreish's Arabic work.

[34] Delitzch, p. 137. 162. sq. ; Rapop. Ker. Chem. vi. 19. ; Dukes, Lit. bl. 342. 356. sq. The rhymes of Saadia, Donolo (Zunz, G. V. 379.), and even Kalir correspond essentially with the Arabic.

[35] Lebrecht, Lit. bl. i. 122. ; Fleischer, id. vii. 469. ; and the Arabic title of a chapter of Charisi (vide Catal. pp. 1314. 1807.) neglected by Dukes, Lit. bl. xii. 149., and Nahal, p. 22. ; conf. תרין בתרין זונין נצמדים, sup. § 16. n. 32. German imitations from Mos. Ibn Ezra's Tarshish in the author's Manna, p. 110. The remark of Zunz (S. P. 238.), that Abraham Ibn Ezra probably at first but rarely used such rhymes, is, of course, only meant with respect to liturgical poetry.

[35a] See Dukes, Lit. bl. iv. 80. n., xi. 37. n. 14. (ענק חרוז) ; conf. Sachs, p. 220. n. 2. ; Frankel, Zeitschr. iii. 279. ; Zunz, S. P. p. 87. ; Catal. p. 1327. Should the Arabic مردوف (מרדוף) belong here ? see Hammer in Journ. Asiat. 1839, ii. 169. (neither in Freytag's work on Arabic poetry, nor in his Arabic Lexicon, is Merduf or مترجع to be found), and Dukes, Lit. bl. xii. 151.

[36] Vide, e. g., Lit. bl. iv. 451. As early as in the older insertions for the ten days of penitence (Zunz, p. 376. d., S. P. p. 96. ; and see inf. n. 62.) : German imitations in Sachs, p. 209. The Syrians also sometimes repeat the same word (Zingerle, l. c. p. 116.) On "variation," with respect to the Biblical verses, see Zunz, S. P. p. 98. In general, the end of the verse came into close connexion with the beginning (cf. Zunz, l. c. p. 113.) ; and Abraham ben Isaac on Canticles makes the ingenious observation that the end of it, "like all good songs," returns to its beginning.

[Page 151. line 2. from bottom, بوشاع (sic) ; See Hammer, Journ.

Asiat. 1839 (viii.), 158, 159.; Dukes, Lit. bl. xii. 150.; Geiger, Divan, p. 133., from Freytag; Zunz, S. P. 102. Our observation on Ibn Sahl is taken from Casiri.]

37 Abudienti, Gramm. p. 161.; Lit. bl. iv. p. 60. n. 91., pp. 359. 520. 729.; Luzzatto in Busch's Jahrb. vi. 104.; designated as Arabic (עלמשקל הישמעאלים), Lit. bl. viii. 403.

37a Delitzsch, p. 164.

38 DUKES, Lit. bl. iv. 434.; JELLINEK, ib. 142. 615.; KÄMPF, Introd. to the Tachkemoni; ZUNZ, S. P. 215. The termini technici of our text (as also מקצב, קצב, מחצבת, and מחצב) were probably first used in a grammatical sense, which they always maintained. מקצב, in Cusari, ii. 78., p. 187. n. 4., ed. Cassel, is in the Arabic MS. Poc. 284. f. 546. ערוץ=عروض, cf. inf. n. 51. Besides this, the expression and image of the balance (משקל מאזנים) for grammar and logic are typical, and borrowed from the Arabs,—a matter upon which we cannot here enter into details (cf. *Catal.* p. 1000.). On מדה for poetic measure in Charisi, Immanuel, and Kalonymos, see the author's Manna, p. 99. cf. Zunz, S. P. 217.). In Syriac, a poem in strophes is called מדרשא, one which goes on continuously מאמרא (Zingerle, l. c. sup. n. 12.).

39 Ibn Ezra, Zachot, Delitzsch, p. 158.; Dukes, p. 433. sq. The particular metres in Kämpf, l. c.; Sachs (p. 40.) compares the Versus polit. of the later Byzantines. In the East, HAI GAON would be the first known if he were really the author of the moral poem (§ 20. n. 28.), or of the hymn שמע קולי (cf. Landshuth, p. 62.), whose metre the author (*Catal.* p. 2161.) has discovered in pieces ascribed by Luzzato and Dukes to SAADJA, which, therefore, must belong to a more recent author.

40 For "imitated, as well as its name from the Arabic," read, "imitated from the Arabic, as well as its name."

[Page 153. line 18. read: "According to Zunz (S. P. p. 216.), SOLOMON BEN GABIROL (*sic*) perhaps," &c.; and Id. pp. 89. and 219.]

40 a See Jellinek, Lit. bl. v. 167.; cf. Zunz, S. P. p. 248., in general, on the influence of the Spanish school upon the French-German.

41 See Kimchi and Bedarschi in Dukes, Beitr. p. 191., Del. p. 139., on the so-called " sense rhymes;" see the author's Manna, p. 97.

42 As early as in Dunash, Lit. bl. iv. 232.; conf. Del. 158. Dukes (p. 437.) improperly calls בית, "strophe;" and he was not able (Lit. bl. iv. 453.) to find the expression שניה, "couplets," (= مشنوي; conf. Jell. Lit. bl. iv. 91.) amongst the Spaniards. We find titles in rhyming metre in ABRAHAM IBN EZRA (cf. Reifmann, Lit. bl. iv. 606.); while the title of the book, הגיון, of Abraham ben Chijja, as it is given in the MS., does not give any correct metre. In general, the Hebrew titles are shorter, and consequently less fettered by the metre, than the Arabic.

43 Collection of some materials in DUKES, Lit. bl. iv. p. 539. sq. (cf. pp. 687, 688.), v. 709. sq.; conf. also Del. p. 141.; Sachs, p. 343. sq.; Zunz, S. P. 113. 368.

44 Zunz, G. V. 17. 22. 32.

45 Saadja refers Ps. vi. 1. (Ewald, Beitr. p. 8.) to the right الحان melodies, which, however, admits of another explanation (see FLEISCHER,

Lit. bl. iv. 248.; conf. also Pseudo-Saadja on Cantic. in Dukes, Mit-theil. p. 106.); he also treats of them at the end of his Philosophy of Religion, of which, unfortunately, only the somewhat unintelligible Hebrew translation was accessible to the author, so that he has not consulted the Arabic text. Here נגינה seems to signify "chord," and נעימה (conf. نغم), "note" (interval). On גבוה ושפל, conf. Hupf. l. l. i. 16., and הנבהה ואריכות, in S. Duran (Lit. bl. iv. 540.); conf. ܟܠܐ and ܐܪܝܟܬܐ, in Bar Hebræus, Gramm. iv. v. 47. sq., ed. Ber-theau. On the remark on the Music of the Kings, conf. the author's n. 42. on Maim. Treatise on the Unity, p. 20. Of these eight נגינות Petachja (Lit. bl. iv. 541. n. 44.) also speaks; and perhaps Charisi (Lit. bl. iv. 391.) alludes to them in using the expression על השמינית for the 8th century as the commencement of the art of poetry. On Saadja, conf. also Albo, Ikkar, iii. 10. (Schles. p. 661., and Lit. bl. iv. 156.). The Theory of Rhythm and Melody is perhaps connected with the passage in Plato's Repub. (lib. iii. p.398.). In the MS. translation of the compendium of Ibn Roshd, by SAMUEL BEN JUDAH, of Mar-seilles (1321), "περὶ ᾠδῆς τρόπος καὶ μελῶν λοιπόν" is rendered merely סוג מהלחנים. The לחן consists of the three: אשר בו הלחן ניגון, ונעימה מוסכמת, ומאמר; in the original λόγου τε καὶ ἁρμονίας καὶ ῥυθμοῦ, Worte, Tonsetzung und Zeitmass, according to Schleier-macher's German translation: conf. inf. n. 51.

[46] Dukes, p. 541.; conf. n. 45.

[46 a] Lit. bl. iv. 539., v. 710.; conf. sup. § 4. n. 30.

[47] As. De Rossi (Ker. Chem. v. 138.) and Del Medigo (1629—1631) saw the Mishna with accents (see Dukes, Lit. bl. v. 710., and on Chajjug, p. 192.). On the printed text, which the author dis-covered in a vol. of Talmud, see Catal. no. 1718.

[48] See nn. 45. and 55. The translation of the book שיר, i. e. Poetics (of Aristotle), by THEODOROS THODOROSI, has, by many biblio-graphers, been wrongly entitled a work on Music. Passages of Ari-stotle's "Poetics" and Plato's "Timæus," on the relation of poetry to music, are quoted in Arabic by Moses Ibn Ezra (Poetic. MS. f. 72 a.). Alfarabi's work on music was known to the Jews, and is recommended by Joseph Ibn Aknin in his enumeration of works for instruction (Ersch. s. v. p. 52.). Ibn Sahula, in his Comm. on Cantic. i. 1., ap-peals to the "science of music" (ח' הניגון); cf. also the author's com-munication in Zunz, S. P. 220. A passage of Abu el Ssalt (ob. 1134), in his work הספקה, or treatise on music, is quoted by P. Duran (Grammar, MS. chap. vi.); and hence, perhaps, the whole work was supposed to exist in the Oratoire (Wolf. iii. 331 b.). The Cod. Vat. 400, 5. contains questions (a treatise) on mathematics and music, which Zunz (Add. p. 323.) supposes to be translated from Arabic by ABRA-HAM BAR CHIJJA (but see Cod. Rossi, 1170). A passage on music and the different number of chords in the כנור, &c., is to be found in SHEMTOB PALQUERA's Mebakkesh (cf. 39 b.). Immanuel of Rome boasts of his music (Lit. bl. iv. 24.; conf. inf. n. 55.). A Jewish musician was an officer of Alhakem (see Almakarri, ii. 117., quoted by S. Cassel, l. c. p. 231.). On the name and place of the "science (not "sequence," as in the text, p. 154.) of sounds" amongst mathema-

tics, see § 21. n. 1.   In p. 154. lin. 11. from bottom, read "poetic" (*sic*), not "poetry."

[49] See Boethius, Lit. bl. iv. 340.; conf. Adelard of Bath, in Jourdain, p. 249.   Kimchi connects the seven sciences (free arts) with Prov. ix. 1.; vide Dukes, Mishle, p. 30., conf. Zion, i. 47. (Abu Sahal ben Tamim), and vide sup. § 12. n. 3., and inf. p. 351.

[50] The author's Manna, p. 104. احسن الشعر كذبه (Hodschr. [?], in Thaalebi, Synt. Dict., ed. Valeton [1844], p. 36.), is a wrong translation of Aristotle's Ἄριστον τῆς ἐποποιίας τὸ ψεῦδος, to which the Heb. מיטב השיר כזבו approaches nearer. — Opinions of Maim. and Palquera, see in Sachs, p. 341. sq.

[51] Cusari, ii. §§ 78—80. (see the remarks of D. Cassel), and after him Parchon and others.   The whole passage of Cusari, highly interesting with respect to grammar and poetry (see Ker. Chem. ix. 64.), will be given elsewhere in the genuine Arabic, since the Hebrew translation presents much difficulty, e. g. § 70. (where the division of poems is given).   On the terms, conf. Bar Hebrai, Gram. Syr., ed. Bertheau, iv. p. 134., conf. iii. 33.; Maim. Treatise on the Unity, p. 91.; Archevolti, Gramm. cap. 31.   For later parallels see Dukes, Lit. bl. iv. 687.   Albo (ib.) speaks of בקשות שירים, פיוטים, which coincide with the ניגוני מוסיקה; conf. also Duran and Ephodæus (Lit. bl. iv. 540.),   התחלפות יחסי הקול בדקות והעובר.   The expression משורר (Jeh. Ibn Tibbon in Dukes, Mischle, p. xiv., and Lit. bl. viii. 362.; cf. Bedarschi, in Dukes, Beitr. p. 191.) answers to the Arabic שׁעֲרָא, شَعَرَا (Maimon. Mel. Chofn. p. 78., Hebr. text), and cf. כלי החרוזים, in Ibn Ezra, Zachot.

[52] Cf. Zunz, S. P. p. 116.

[53] In Dukes, and Jellinek, Lit. bl. iv. 540. 615. 734., v. 470.; Zunz, l. c. 114.

[54] In Sachs this fact is the more missed, inasmuch as he (p. 180.) calls this far-fetched reason for the origin of the Pijjutim in Dukes "quite comical," while the fact in itself is an important reality.   S. Cassel (p. 192.), on this one point, rejects the mere analogy of the Syriac adduced by Dukes (z. K. p. 7.).

[55] Dukes, Lit. bl. iv. 542.; Sachs, Busch's Jahrb. v. 234., speaking of Nagara (cf. *Catal.* p. 1170.), omits also this circumstance.   So also Tartar melodies are to be found among the Karaites (Annalen, iii. 93.).

[56] Cusari, iii. § 45. (conf. sup. § 6.), Maimon. and others in Dukes, Lit. bl. iv. 687.; Sabbatbl. 1846, p. 92.; Ersch, s. ii. vol. 31. p. 94. n. 7.   Del., p. 56., confuses Jacob Levi (מהר"יל) with ISAAC LORIA ! see also n. 48.

[56 a] Del. p. 127.; Dukes, Lit. bl. iv. 539.; Zunz, S. P. p. 89.

[57] The particular species in Dukes, p. 449. sq., and Zunz, l. c.

[57 a] The author's Manna, p. 111.; we know not whether this observation has been made elsewhere.

[58] Del. and Dukes, pp. 485. 527. (where we find the same ending words).   Cf. Hammer, in Journ. Asiat. 1839 (viii.), 167., to which a mere reference is given ib. 1849 (xiv.), 248., quoted by Dukes, Lit. bl. xi. 288.

[59] Del. p. 163. infra; cf. Sachs, pp. 262. 268.; the author's Dis-

sert. in Frankel, iii. 409.; Zunz, S. P. 86. 105.; cf. 90. 98. 113. 157. 169. 253.

[60] See the author's article in Busch's Jahrb. iv. 228. Munk (l. c. in n. 1. p. 75.) observes that the Arabic poetry does not nearly so often allude to the Koran, which is only natural, since the Bible occupies another place in the history of the Hebrew from that of the Koran in the Arabic; besides that, the Hebrew poets sang in a language which they did not speak, &c.; cf. sup. § 5. n. 49.

[61] Dukes, Lit. bl. iv. 337. 520., vii. 808., where Absalom ben Moses and Ephodi call a poem with Biblical final words, שיר מיוחס; Zunz, l. c. in n. 59.

[62] Lit. bl. iv. 523. 715., v. 27; Zunz, l. c. p. 80.

[63] Dukes, z. K. p. 140., and Jellinek, Lit. bl. iv. 26. 90. 486. 519.; Pseudo-Japhet, 605., v. 719.; Zunz, l. c. pp. 88. (368.) 94. On גמרא, see Dukes, Lit. bl. xii. 687.

[64] JELLINEK, Lit. bl. iv. 64. 91. 141. 521.; Zunz, l. c. 82. 98.

[65] Dukes (iv. 522.) finds himself in a palpable contradiction. JELLINEK has tried to explain some termini.

[66] Dukes, zur Kenntn. p. 38.; Lit. bl. iv. 339. n. 3., p. 489. n. 32., p. 539.; v. 483. רהיטין (sic), 719.; vi. 17. 185.; Zunz, l. c. p. 79. (368.), in Lit. bl. iv. 489., on a non-liturgical poem following the melody [לנועם] of a Selicha; cf. § 19. n. 19.

[67] Lit. bl. iv. 89. 521. 524.; Sachs, p. 247. Zunz, l. c. p. 65., gives no explanation of the word.

[68] Dukes, z. K. p. 38.; Lit. bl. iv. 91. 449. (a couplet without metrum), v. 719.

[69] Lit. bl. iv. 91. 449.

§ 19. Page 157.

[1] Vide sup. § 6.; Zunz, zur Gesch. 164.

[2] Concerning the time, see Rapoport on Parchon, p. xi., by which Sachs, p. 175. n. 1. (Lit. bl. viii. 326.), must be corrected; see also inf. n. 35.

[3] יסוד is a work generally in the German-French school, see Rapop. Saadja, n. 23.; Chan. p. 32., Zunz, zur Gesch. 105. lin. 4.; *Catal.* p. 2171. In the Spanish, חבוד = لِيف تَ, *compositio*, is used.

[4] DUKES, zur Kenntn. p. 33. sq. (cf. inf. n. 32.). The recent work of ZUNZ, *Die Synagogale Poesie der Juden im Mittelalter*, although undertaken before the author of this essay could have even thought of composing his German sketch (see the German note 51. p. 430.), did not appear till April, 1855 (cf. Athenæum, 1855), when the greater part of this translation was already revised and prepared for the press. This book is, indeed, only one part of an extensive work on Selichot (see n. 7.); but the technical section (p. 59. sq.) includes most valuable hints on synagogue-poetry in general. We have endeavoured to take account of these, as far as it was possible without essential alteration of our general plan, in the very short time between the publication of Zunz and the printing of §§ 18—20, and we have added special references to the old notes. We have tried also to give,

z 2

in nn. 5. 7. and 10., the most essential particulars on special classes
and names, &c., which are of great interest to a certain kind of readers;
with more toil, indeed, than might be supposed by those who do not
know the difficulty of the task.

5 See § 6. n. 14., § 18. n. 18.; Zunz, S. P. 63. 65. קרובות designates, in a narrower sense, only the parts inserted in the first three
numbers of the so-called *Prayer of* 18 (*Shemone esra*, § 6.); also
those in the prayer for the fast day of the 19th of Ab, and the half-
feast of Purim, and sometimes those in the second Morning Service
(Musaf). The three pieces have different names, as we shall mention
below; while the cycle of hymns, comprising the " 7-prayer," substituted for the " 18-prayer," on the sabbath, is called שבעתא (*Shibata*),
from the real number of seven (Lit. bl. iv. 451.; conf. § 6. n. 11 a.);
and also דרמוש (Zunz, p. 69., does not explain it; perhaps " Dramma,"
or δρόμων, runner, = רהיט??). This cycle, however, is not adapted to
the first Morning Prayer, but to the Musaf, and occasionally to the
Evening, where, according to the present rite, the 7-prayer is not
recited again aloud by the Cantor (except on the Day of Atonement).
Perhaps, therefore, subsequently to the 11th century some hymns belonging to the Shema (§ 6.) derive their name from the Evening Prayer
time (מעריב, or with masculine or feminine plural מעריבים, מעריבות
[the latter usually called מערבות], *Maarib, -im, -ot*); and an addition
mostly on the subject of the Halacha, or History of the Feast, is called
ביכור (*Bikkur*), i. e. firstlings, having been first composed for the Pentecost; see Zunz, p. 70.

6 Lebrecht, Lit. bl. i. 107. &c.; conf. *Catal.* p. 1802.

7 Conf. n. 12. and § 28. p. 242.; conf. Geig. Zeitschr. vi. 30.
Since the above-mentioned monography of Zunz (n. 4.) contains, in
the principal section (pp. 152—334.), a considerable number of critical remarks, we must refer our readers generally to it for all particulars
on the subject. We will only add two general remarks, which may be
useful for understanding the importance of this class of hymns, the place
of which,.in our sketch, could not well be altered (see n. 4.). According
to Zunz, whose authority we acknowledge even on this point (which is
perhaps still open to question, and has not yet been treated fully), the
Selichot are not a subordinate, but a coordinate class of Synagogue
poetry, in contradistinction to the *Pijjut*, in its narrower sense. He
compares the Pijjut to the revelation of God in the mouth of the Prophets, and their interpreters, the wise men, the authors of the Haggada and Midrash (§ 5.); while the Selicha, like the sacred songs of the
Psalmists, is an expression of Israel's feelings and reflections, suggested
by the present or past fate of his race. With this is connected another
distinction. The Pijjut, being more closely linked with the public service,
is more restricted and confined by its relation to the older basis of prayers;
while the Selicha, embracing the nation as well as the individual, in all
that concerns them, leads the poet to a deeper insight into his own
frailty, and a closer clinging to his Lord and Master, his Redeemer
from persecution and cruelty (conf. Zunz, p. 83.). How constantly
both Christian and Moslem have turned the Jew's devotion in that
direction will be learnt, not without emotion and indignation, by every
one who peruses the section " Sufferings," in the work of Zunz (pp.

8—58.), which, taking the mildest view of crimes committed under the pretext of religion, we must designate as an "index erratorum" of the human mind during a long period of history.   Thus the Selicha was developed on a larger scale, either as a part of public or private devotion, or as a mere literary production; and it has remained in vigour almost down to our own times, and will always continue to be a main source of history.   No less than 250 authors of about 1200 numbers of Selichas of the Middle Ages are known to Zunz (p. 332.).   With respect to single pieces (either separate or inserted in larger compositions), we may point out, without entering upon their technical relation, two distinct tendencies of the poet's mind.   He either dwells objectively rather upon the relation of the past to the present, as in the history of the " Ten Martyrs," the *Gesera* (גזרה, persecution), (Zunz, p. 135.), and the "Temptation of Abraham " (עקידה, *Akeda*, i.e. binding of Isaac), considered as propitiatory, and therefore connected with the intercessory prayer (תחנה, *Tehinna*) (Zunz, p. 147.); or else he takes a more subjective turn, as in the Confession of Sins (וידוי, *Widdui*), and Exhortation (תוכחה, *Tocheha*).

[8] This Arabic word, occurring also in Moses Ibn Ezra (Poetic MS., see *Catal.* p. 1112.), has been rightly explained by Jellinek, Lit. bl. iv. 63., v. 26.; cf. also Freytag, Lex. Arab. s. v.   Notwithstanding this, Dukes (Nahal, p. 28.) derives מרתיה from the Spanish *Mortajo*.   The *Zions*, ציונים, so called from the first word Zion, are a separate class; cf. Zunz, p. 72., and on הושענות, p. 73.

[9] Such, for private use, were composed as early as by SAADJA (p. 166.), omitted by Dukes, p. 111.   Some of them are called שבח, i. e. praise of God, and תושבחות, Arab. تساييح ; cf. *Catal.* p. 2204., and p. 22.; and inf. n. 10 e.   Some of them form a cycle of private devotion, and are divided accordingly under various heads, taken partly from the attitude of the person praying, or from other circumstances, e.g. הזהרה, Admonition; כונה, Intention, Reflection; עמידה, Standing; תושבחות, Praises; השתחויה, Prostration; כריעה, Kneeling; נפילת אפים, Falling upon the face; לחש, Still prayer.   These are marked in a MS. petition of JEHUDA LEVI, partly printed under the name of MOSES IBN EZRA (*Catal.* p. 1814.).   We may remark that the Spanish school seems to attach more importance to the attitude of prayer; and ABRAHAM MAIMONIDES dedicates to this subject much attention, and a large portion of his great work (MS. Bodl.): we suppose that this was in consequence of the influence of Muhammedanism.

[10] For instance, large groups comprising the Shema (§ 6.), &c., as *Jozer*, יוצר; *Ofan*, אופן; *Zulat*, זולת; *Meora*, מאורה; *Ahaba*, אהבה; *Mi-Kamocha*, מי כמוך; *Geulla*, גאולה; *Nishmat*, נשמת; *Kaddish*, קדיש (cf. § 6.); *Barchu*, ברכו; *Shebah*, שבח; and the first three of the 18-prayer mentioned above; *Magen*, מגן; *Mehajje*, מהיה; *Meshallesh*, משלש, or משלוש; and *Elohechem* אלהיכם.   See Dukes, p. 36.; Lit. bl. iv. 451., cf. n. 5.; Zunz, l. c. pp. 61—69.

[10 a] Sachs, p. 222.; Zunz, p. 70.

[10 b] Lit. bl. iv. 89.; Sachs, 247. 254. 277.; Zunz, p. 61.

[10 c] Lit. bl. iv. 489., vi. 19.; Zunz, pp. 66, 67.

[10 d] Lit. bl. v. 483.; Nitronai in Dukes, Rabb. Blumenlese, p. 277.

342 NOTES TO § 19.

¹⁰ᵉ Dukes, pp. 39—111. The subject of the שיר הייחוד, *Song of Unity* (Dukes, p. 153.), its authorship (it was erroneously said to be by BERAHJA NAKDAN), and various hymns of the same name (e. g. one by ISAAC NAKDAN, in a Bodl. MS.), which is also given to a part of Gabirol's great hymn, as well as the connexion of that name with philosophical and Kabbalistic works, called *Books of Unity,* cannot be fully treated here. Cf. *Catal.* p. 2073.

¹⁰ᶠ Zunz, G. V. 377 e.; Dukes, Ehrensäulen, pp. 5. 15. sq. (§ 5. n. 22.).

¹¹ Vide sup. § 6.; Luzz. and Rapop. Ker. Chem. iv. 37.; Annal. i. 301.; Dukes, 47. 141. sq.; Lit. bl. iv. 337. 452. 538. 715., v. 404.; Sachs, p. 176.; Dernburg, Geig. Zeitschr. v. 399. 401. n. 2.; Zunz, S. P. p. 76. sq.

¹² Dukes, pp. 33. 139.; Sachs, p. 175., "for the fast days," is to be limited according to p. 265. For the opposite מיושב, see Ker. Chem. iv. 28.; Nitronai (about 850), Zunz, G. V. 381. (whence Geig. Zeitschr. v. 399.) and Amram (in Dukes, p. 32.) know of Selichot for the Day of Atonement; conf. עמידה (not העמידה!), Hamida de la Magnana in Sachs, p. 308.; comp. p. 262.; Dukes, p. 34.; Zunz, S. P. 78. 137.

¹³ Geig. Zeitschr. v. 403. n., no. i.; conf. Moses Chabib, in Sachs, p. 302. n. 2.; Dukes, Lit. bl. v. 404. n. 26.

¹⁴ Nitronai, in Dukes, Lit. bl. vii. 676. (ix. 179., xi. 335.), appears to know such for Pentecost. Cf. Luzz. Virgo, p. 10.; Zunz, pp. 69. 71. The reference of the 613 precepts to the number of letters in the Decalogue is quoted under the name of NAHSHON, by Nathan ben Jehiel, s. v. תפלה J., and mentioned by Saadja (cf. Dukes, Nahal, p. 3., and the corrections and new notices on Azharot, in *Catal.* p. 2206.). Cf. also § 4. n. 6.

¹⁵ Dukes, pp. 44. 140.; Sachs, 177.; conf. 302.

¹⁶ Zunz, G. V. 420.; conf. 379. 417 e, f.; § 18. n. 31., § 6. n. 12.

¹⁷ Alphabet. lists of 25 in the Spanish ritual, in Zunz, G. V. 419.; see S. P. 218. sq., cf. 332. (and see note 32.). German imitations and descriptions of the characteristics of some of them in Sachs; conf. Humboldt, Kosmos, ii. 119. That Is. Ibn Gaj. is the בן משיע in Dukes, Nahal. p. 12., has been shown by the author (*Catal.* p. 1110.), who, however, had thought to explain it by "Abu Nasar;" but Geiger observed that גיאת is written with Teshdid (غيّات) in a MS., and means the same as מושיע.

¹⁸ Vide sup. 18. n. 18. Jost (Busch's Jahrb. v. 155.) wishes to change this technical expression, as a corruption of speech, to "poets," which, however, destroys the limitation of the special idea.

¹⁹ Notwithstanding the explanation of רהוטה, quoted in § 18. n. 66., we might still adhere to our remark in this note, that Kalir and others were less artificial in those pieces which were composed for the whole congregation; cf. Zunz, p. 119., and our remarks, § 18. n. 21.

²⁰ Zunz, G. V. 391 a.; Del. 137., Ker. Chem. iii. 201.; seldom with Spaniards, vide Dukes, Lit. bl. vi. 19. n. 3. German translation

according to Simon ben Isaac (1040—1050), by Zunz, Geig. Zeitschr. iii. 40. ; cf. § 5. n. 93.

[21] Frankel, Zeitschr. iii. 463.

[22] Zunz, 419 c. ; Delitzsch, p. 43. ; Dukes, z. K. p. 16. sq. ; Sachs, l. c. ; conf. Ker. Chem. iv. 28. ; Zunz, S. P. p. 85.

[23] Landauer (Lit. bl. vi. 180.). It does not occur " several times," as Schor., Lit. bl. iv. 679., supposes (cf. *Catal.* s. v.). Kalir must, therefore, be removed a whole century ; but there is no urgent reason for more than that ; and the general view of the literary development established by Rapoport and Zunz still holds good. The decision which S. Cassel, in Frankel, Zeitschr. iii. p. 191., claims in favour of the " tradition " is probably that of Steinhardt (Annal. ii. 201.; Lit. bl. ii. 386., viii. 246.), a German of the last century, who places Kalir in the time of Saadja. The Midrashim of Palestine know only of the Talmudic authorities of Babylon, and nothing later. The old Pesikta was, however, already known to the R. Achai Gaon (Zunz, G. V. 196.) ; thus the proof of the use of the Pesikta and of the treatise Soferim (Zion, ii. 165.) holds good ; and Cassel, p. 226., must be corrected.

[23a] The expression in the text should be qualified ; we have said above that the existence of an Italian school is rather doubtful ; Luzz. Lit. bl. vi. 683. קדושה קלירית (id. 685.) means probably in Kalir's manner.

[24] With the acrostic הקטן, i. e. *parvus* or *junior*, an appellation which almost at the same period is found for the first time in the Spaniard Chiquitilla, and appears in Hebrew in Gabirol in Spain (cf. Zunz, S. P. 108.). Later it continues to be in use in signatures as an expression of modesty, as it already occurs in the elder Samuel (Jer. Sota, iv. 9., comp. Rap. Ker. Chem. v. 227., vii. 262. 264. ; Resp. Gäon. § 6., with which comp. Megill. 32 a., Lit. bl. vi. 131. 245 n., xi. 335.).

[25] Zunz, S. P. 109. 167. That he was not, however, himself a Babylonian (Luzz. Lit. bl. vi. 680.) appears from the patronymic or surname, and his connexion with the southern French. According to Rapop. (Resp. Gäon, 12 b.), Babel is Rome ; and if Joseph Cohen speaks of Sal. Babli, who died in Spain, he confuses Sol. b. Juda GABIROL, whom Ibn Danan makes a pupil of Nissim (*Catal.* s. v.). The pretended " Dor Rug″ma " (in Fürst, Lit. bl. i. 133.) is nothing but an abbreviation, which he has misunderstood ; בדור רג״מה, i. e. a contemporary of the R. G(erson) M(eor) H(aggola).

[26] Catalogue in Zunz, G. V. 392., Syn. P. p. 166. ; cf. 332., and above, n. 7., on the number, &c.

[27] Alphabetical Catalogue of the Provençal Poets of all kinds in Zunz, zur Gesch. 463. sq.

[27a] Erroneously in Dukes, Mos. b. E., p. 108., anno 1486, the author has established the truth of Zunz's conjecture of his identity with the translator ; see § 21. n. 69. The poem has been published by B. Goldberg, Lond. 1850.

[28] Zunz, G. V. 422 g. ; Geig. Zeitschr. iii. 48. sq. ; comp. Lit. bl. vi. 588. ; Lit. bl. iv. 22. n. 50. v. 403. n. 25. ; *Catal.* p. 788. &c.

[28a] Conf. Luzzatto in Oesterische Wandelingen, p. 50. A *Conspectus succinctus Precum* is prefixed in the *Catal.* (pp. 295—302.) to the editions up to 1732, which occupy more than 200 pages of the *Catal.*

[29] The editor, ELIA HALEVI, is pupil, not teacher, of Elia Misrachi. The 2nd ed. was Const. 1574 (according to the conjecture in *Catal.* p. 398.) ; the author has seen it at Mr. M. Lehren's, at Amsterdam.

[30] Complete description by Zunz, Allg. Zeit. d. Jud. 1838, p. 580. sq. ; conf. Annal. i. 341.

[30a] See Zunz, zur Gesch. 253. and § 28. n. 17.

[31] Luzz. Ker. Chem. iv. 27. On the ritual of *Troyes*, see inf. n. 40 a.

[32] According to Dukes (Lit. bl. v. 452.), an African ; according to Zunz (zur Gesch. 475.), probably a Provençale. DUKES gives a special review of several collections, and of the particular authors, Lit. bl. v. 217. sq., vi. 17. sq., with which his alphabetical list of more than 200 Pajtanim (Lit. bl. ii. 569.) is to be completed. After the completion of this article, LUZZATTO's alphabetical list of 600 Hebrew poets was published ; but the order seems to have been disturbed by the editor of the Lit. bl. ix. 548 – 617. ; some names have been incorrectly taken from acrostics. L. LANDSHUTH has begun a work on the subject. In the author's *Catal.* the special hymns could not in general be enumerated ; cf. also p. 242. The Bodleian library acquired some years ago some very interesting collections of hymns ; one of more than 700 was made by SAADJA [Ibn Danan], who designates some of the authors as "idiots."

[33] § 17. n. 33. ; comp. Zunz, zur Gesch. 164.

[34] The feminine is characteristic ; conf. § 18. n. 31., and § 19. n. 41 a.—Several writings with this title and Siddurim in DUKES, Lit. bl. v. 218., vi. 17.

[35] Rapop. Chanan. n. 35. A compendium written in 1425–6 has been lately purchased by the Bodleian library. A copy in the possesion of Almanzi is described by Luzz. Lit. bl. viii. 289—326.

[36] Geig. Zeitschr. v. 398., Lit. bl. x. 178. There are, however, two of this name ; see Rapop. Nathan, n. 27., one ר"ש.

[37] See p. 161. and the note, and inf. n. 44.

[38] Probably a mistake of Conforte, 18 a (see n. 25.) ; the Solomon in Lit. bl. v. 219. is Rashi, whose Siddur is extracted (?) in his Pardes.

[39] Zion, ii. 103.

[39a] ELHANAN BEN ISAAC, killed in 1184 (?) ; cf. Zunz, z. G. 34., Luzz. in Polak, pp. 45, 46. ; Benjacob to Azulai, ii. f. 84. ; see, however, Zunz, S. P. 249.

[40] See Tosaf. Abod. Zora. 74 b.

[40a] See Schor, Zion, i. 93. sq., Lit. bl. v. 219., sup. § 9. Upon the ritual of Troyes, by MENAHEM BEN JOSEPH BEN JEHUDA, arranged by his pupil JEHUDA BEN ELIESER, see Luzzatto in Oost. Wandel. (Amsterd. 1846.), p. 50.

[41] Zunz, zur Gesch. 476. ; conf. Geig. Zeitschr. ii. 311. ; on Benj. p. 11. ; cf. § 13. n. 21., and the following n. 41 a.

[41a] Probably ASHER BEN JEHIEL is a mistake. Dukes, Lit. bl. v. 219., quotes Zunz on Benj. p. 11., who speaks of Asher ben Meshullam of Lunel. The מנהגים of Asher ben Jehiel in Mai Cod. 484. is probably the ethical work הנהגות ; see *Catal.* p. 748.

[42] *Catal.* p. 2204., Epilogue to Landshuth, on Haggada, p. xxx., n. 8. ; Ker. Chem. ix. 38. From the same work some one has forged

a work of SAMUEL Abu Azaria (cf. § 15. n. 28.) in Cod. Uri. 257.; see Ersch, s. ii. vol. 31. p. 52. n. 56., and *Catal.* p. 1912.

[42a] Munk, Annal. iii. 87. Can אלפאצי ל be an epithet of an anonymous writer? cf. n. 49.

[43] Zunz, Geig. Zeitschr. ii. 305.

[44] Read ISAAC ben Jehuda, &c. (no. 37.). Sachs, p. 263. conf. 219.; Wolf. i. 1180.; Dukes, Lit. bl. viii. 405.

[45] Zunz, G. V. 387 c. and 394 c. names several.

[46] Dukes, Lit. bl. v. 232.

[47] Id., and vi. 17.; Zunz, zur Gesch. 74. 76.

[48] Geig. Zeitschr. iii. 444., nr. 19.; and Simcha, f. 246.

[49] Zunz, G. V. 425., Lit. bl. iv. 718.; conf. Zedner, p. 56. n. 14.; Annal. iii. 93.; conf. the author's note on Ez. Chaj. 379., and vide sup. n. 42 a. Upon the names of prayers, see also Trigland, chap. 10. (Lit. bl. v. 797.). JESHUA in the Maschor Tripolis (Lit. bl. v. 396.), and KALEB in the Greek (ib. 398.), are not Karaites, although these names are common among the latter.

[50] See § 14. n. 31. (cf. Ez. Chajjim. p. 302.). According to Luzz., Lit. bl. ix. 483., they borrowed only from the Greek ritual. Arabic translations are ascribed to SALMON (Geig. Zeitschr. iii. 443. 7.)?

[51] Frankel, Zeitschr. iii. 463.

§ 20.   Page 168.

[Authorities: DUKES, Uebersicht, &c., Annal. i. 67. sq.; the author's Manna, p. 94. sq.; DUKES, Nahal Kedumim, 1853, gives some interesting notices from MSS., but with less accuracy than is desirable. The *Jüdische Dichtungen*, &c., of GEIGER, published by the "Institut zur Förderung der Isr. Lit.," 1856, is indeed only a reprint of the "Blüthen," in Volks Kalender, 1853, p. 15.; and Wiener Vierteljahrschr. 1853, i. p. 35. Some alterations, however (e. g. pp. 13, 14. 20.; cf. Blüthen, pp. 21, 22. 24.), and even the birthplace of JEHUDA LEVI, Toledo, hitherto unknown (and only a recent conjecture of the author), are taken without acknowledgment from the article Moses Ibn Ezra of the author's *Catal.* (pp. 1801. 1807.), where the statements in *Treasures of Oxford* (§ 19. n. 1.), and the conjectures of Geiger built on that basis in the "Blüthen," are shown to be false (cf. inf. n. 24.).]

[1] Dukes (Z. K. 135, 136.) unjustly refers Archivolti's blame especially to Immanuel; see n. 40.

[1a] This figure is traditional with philosophers, poets, and Pajtanim; for instance, Gabirol (in Sachs, 221.; Lit. bl. iv. 382.), Charisi (Introduction and chap. 28. of Tachkem. and commentary on the Mishna; conf. Lebrecht, Lit. bl. ii. 245.), Ibn Aderet and Abbamari (Geig. Zeitschr. v. 109. 160.). The Christians employed it against the Jews (Jost, vi. 62.; cf. also Japhet, sup. § 13. n. 39.). Another stereotyped phrase of the translators is, to divest the matter of its polluted dress, and give it a pure one. Dukes says (Lit. bl. iv. 804.) that the mosaic style was only applied to religious poetry and epigrams; but this observation must be restricted to the actual interweaving of whole passages of the Bible; cf. § 18.

[2] Lebrecht, l. c.

[3] Perhaps Saadja Ibn Danan ben Maimun at Grenada (1455—1485)? See moreover Cod. Vat. Hebr. 375.; 7. 9. 411. (Solomon ben Aaron).

[4] ספרי ניגון (Introduction to the Articles of Faith, in Del. p. 141.), conf. Moreh, 1, 2.; Frankel, Zeitschr. iii. 280. The author has corrected Dukes' translation (Ehrens. p. 47.) in the preface to Schene Hammeorot (Berlin, 1847); cf. also S. Sachs, ha-Techijjah, p. 9.

[5] Dernberg's suggestion (Geig. i. 106 n.). Perhaps Abu'lmaali should also be mentioned here.

[6] Munk, Tanchoum, pp. 10. 101.; conf. Gavison (ob. 1605) in Zunz, zur Gesch. 384.

[7] Lebrecht, Lit. bl. ii. 254.; Zunz, z. G. 428.; Frankel, Zeitschr. iii. 235., where " Modawwes ;" conf. also, Anon. Vat. 397, 5. (Joseph), half Arabic. Upon an ارجوزة, see § 22.

[8] Read, " in Spain and the Maghreb." Charisi (in German by Zedner, p. 66.; Del. 43. sq.; cf. Cod. Vat. 225.; Frank. Zeitschr. iii. 411.), who seems to have taken his classical passage from Moses Ibn Ezra.

[9] See Manna, p. 95.; conf. the Contest between Age and Youth by Joseph Palquera, Vat. 298. (Lit. bl. vi. 148.); of Bread and Wine, of the Birds and wild Beasts, Vat. 303, 3.; and cf. sup. p. 176-7., and inf. § 28.

[9a] It is said that Thodros Halevi, when in prison awaiting judgment, composed in a dream his two verses foretelling his acquittal. (Zunz, zur Gesch. 432.; conf. Lit. bl. vii. 565 o.; comp. Ker. Chem. v. 161.)

[9b] Conf. Manna, no. lxxxiv. p. 107. (cf. Dieterici, Motenebbi, p. 16.). The proverb is given in Mos. Ibn Ezra, Poetic., f. 47 a., as the saying of an Arabic poet.

[Page 170. inf. The authority for the judicial poems is rather doubtful, see § 18. n. 100.]

[10] Frankel, Zeitschr, iii. 279.; conf. Dukes, Rab. Blumenl. p. 43.

[11] The Arabic ארגוזה, i. e. composed in metre رجز (see Casiri, Cod. 826, 2.), not " Archuza," as Reiske, or Schultens on Herbelot, i. 213. corrects it, became ארניזה "irritatio " (Wolf. ii. 1263., ii. p. 7. et 1177.), " theca " (Cat. Opp. 1134 F.), " arca " (Rossi, at Cod. 1169.), ארגיים (Wolf. iv. p. 838.). Wüstenf. makes two separate works of Ardschuza, and Mansuma. Delitzsch (p. 49.) does not know the translator. Deutsch's errors (Cod. 56. in Oesterr. Blätt.) are not entirely removed in the Catal. no. clxvi–vii., even after the author's corrections in private communications.

[11a] Catal. s. v. The connexion between chess and cards has been pointed out lately by Mahn (Etym. Forsch.).

[12] Catal. p. 939. and s. v., where the author will supply the reference to Dukes, Lit. bl. xi. 297.

[12a] Catal. s. v.

[P. 171. inf. Joseph Ibn Chisdai, see the author's article in Ersch, s. v. p. 74., printed in 1853, before the volume of Hammer was published.]

[13] Wolf. iv. p. 1167. sq. (whence Del. p. 70. ; Lit. bl. ii. 769. sq.). ZUNZ, zur Gesch. 390. sq., gives an excellent and elaborate account of them, cf. § 8. n. 15. Concerning a collection by Marini, see Mai, Script. vet. nova Coll. T. V. (Rome, 1831), p. xviii. Within the last two years epitaphs have come into fashion, and collections have been published by different authors but little qualified for such a task. That of Worms contains too much ; but we expect something better from that of the important and ancient burying-place Prague, with a preface by Rapoport.

[14] The statement in the text (following a MS. notice of Michael in Zunz, z. G. 71.) is wrong. SAADJA is the Gaon (ob. 941–2.) who seems to have mentioned the celebrated Rabbins by name, in a rhyming polemic. See *Catal.* p. 2162.

[14a] See the author's treatise in Busch's Jahrb. iv. 227. sq.

[15] Weil, Die poet. Lit. d. Arab. vor Muh. &c. p. 42. The Moallakat are intended by Is. BEN ELEAZAR, who uses the well-known Arabic name מד'הבאת (gilded) (Lit. bl. vii. 711.), which Dukes interprets wrongly. Thaalebi, in Dieterici, p. 73., blames the excessive number in Motenebbi ; conf. the author's notice, Mag. für die Lit. d. Ausl. 1847, p. 128.

[16] Hammer names several ; Wien. Jahrb. xxvii. 293. sq. The Syrian Ebed Jesu (10th century) wrote among other things riddles and proverbs in the Syriac language.

[17] See Dieterici, p. 7. ; conf. p. 12., and § 18. n. 31. The Arabian historian Noweiri devotes a chapter to the passages from the older poets which had become proverbs. See Schultens, Monum. p. 33. Upon particular collections, see Gesenius in the Encyclopedia, i. sect. v. p. 63.

[18] Vide sup. § 5. n. 42. Maimonides quotes (Talmudic) proverbs as being known amongst the Arabs ; see the author's Manna, p. 99. ; conf. Lonzano in Dukes, Sprache der Mischna, 43. Upon Biblical proverbs in later writers, vide sup. § 5. n. 48.

[19] Hence, for instance, in Shemtob Palquera (see n. 22.), the same proverb twice word for word ; conf. Raimond of Beziers in D. Sacy, Not. et Extr. x. 2. p. 56.

[20] Read BEN Sira., see § 5. n. 57.

[21] Testam., ed. Steinschneider, p. 11.

[22] P. 183. (concerning the author, see Rev. Or. i. 345. ; Geig. Zeitschr. v. 98. ; Munk, Lit. bl. vii. 780. n. 3.). Tobia Kohen (Maase Tob. 115 b.), quotes and translates the Turkish proverb, "The apple falls not far from the tree."

[23] Schlesinger (p. 688.) asks whence they are quoted.

[24] Dukes still repeatedly asserts that the quotation refers to a poem of MOSES IBN EZRA ; but the poem belongs to Jehuda Levi (see *Catal.* p. 1807., confirmed by a MS. of Luzz.) ; the Arabic source is given by the author in 1845, and in this note, and again 1851 (note 14. to Jeh. Ibn Tibbon, p. xiii.).

[24a] Igg. B. ch. iv. 5. (conf. Sure, 29. 44. in G. Duran, 19 a.) ; soon afterwards comes הישמעאל.

[25] Busch's Jahrb. iv. p. 230. (where there are other examples belonging to this subject ; conf. Dukes, Mischle (p. xi.), Goldenthal on Ibn Roschd's Rhetor. p. xxiv. ; Dukes, Nahal, p. 76. ; and cf. a passage of

Mos. Ibn Ezra on the subject (*Catal.* p. 2183., cf. § 16.), who defends himself against the over-scrupulosity of his contemporaries amongst the Rabbies. The Persian translator of the Hitopadesa also generally substitutes Persian customs, names, and sayings; see Sacy, Not. et Extr. x. 239.

[26] On the most celebrated writings, see DUKES, Blumenl. p. 54. sq.; Lit. bl. vii. 728. sq. 297. sq.; xi. xii., and on the popular ethical literature, see his Zur Rabb. Spruchk. 1851 (partly from the Lit. bl.).

[27] "Samuel" in Dukes, p. 59., should be corrected. Upon the German translation, see the author's Manna, p. 110. It was the first publication of the celebrated Soncino press, A. D. 1484.

[28] *Catal.* s. v.; cf. § 18. n. 40., about the metre.

[28 a] Should ABRAHAM BEN JEHUDA (Cod. Rossi hebr. 945., hisp. 6.) be the father?

[29] Zunz, zur Gesch. 129.; *Catal.* s. v.

[29 a] On "Alexander-sagas," see the notices given by the author in his Manna, p. 114., and in Zeitschr. der D. M. Gesellsch. ix. 838., where he observes that Spiegel (*Die Alexandersage bei den Orientalen*) has neglected various Jewish authorities, e. g. the work mentioned in the text, and also the Hebrew translation of an Arabic work on the subject by SAMUEL IBN TIBBON; cf. also Dukes, Lit. bl. xi. 828., xii. 111., B. Beer, Zeitschr. &c. ix. 785. The subject deserves and requires a comprehensive monography.

[30] *Catal.* no. 3546.

[31] See Dukes, Annal. i. 416., and the author's Manna, p. 94. sq. Upon additions to fables, moral applications, and the like, conf. Zeitschr. d. Deutsch. Morgenl. Gesellsch. ii. 121, 122.; DERENBOURG (Dernburg), in the introduction to his edition of Lokman, with a French translation (1847), has demonstrated the Christian origin of the fables of this Arabian "Bileam;" and the parallels which he brings forward from Æsop, &c., offer some interesting contributions to the history of the fable.

[32] The author has repeatedly drawn the attention of the learned to a passage in a Hebrew MS. of De Rossi, highly interesting for the history of Arabic translations of Indian poetry and mathematics, which has been neglected or misunderstood (see the notice in Zeitschr. der D. M. Gesellsch. viii. 549.; cf. Notices et Extr. x. 2. p. 15. and 27.; cf. *Catal.* p. 1399.). Hai Gaon (ob. 1037) compares Kalila with R. Meir's fable of the fox (sup. § 5. n. 54 a.); see Dukes, Blumenl. pp. 7. 264.; conf. also Dukes, Annal. i. 416.; the author's Manna, p. 96. That he knew the *Persian* translation, has been shown by the author (Zeitschr. l. c.). Perhaps the polemical tendency of IBN SAHULA (n. 35 a.) is directed against JOHN OF CAPUA.

[33] *Catal.* p. 1399. From the preface of Kalonymos (1316), it appears that the Hebrew version had already, in his time, obtained a certain favour in Provence, like Hariri in Alcharisi's translation. Rödiger's Raisonnement on this subject, in Allg. Lit. Zeit. 1843, p. 151., is contrary to logic and history, since Charisi's age admits of no doubt. Concerning a later version of the M. Send., see § 28. n. 90. The remarks of Landsberger (Lit. bl. ix. 126.) contain nothing new, and p. 70. must be corrected.

[33a] E. g. Joseph Ibn Zaddik, Moses Ibn Ezra, and probably Maimonides (see § 12.) ; also *Catal.* p. 1580.

[34] Delitzsch, p. 49.

[34a] Thus, for instance, the smaller treatise upon Physiognomy in Jourdain, l. c., p. 185., conf. 303., seems, as well as the Diætetics (id. p. 126.), to have arisen from the Secretum Secretorum (see the author's Register to the Catal. Mich. p. 323. n.). In a Bodl. MS. the Physiogn. is ascribed to Alexander M., because the pseudo-Arist. is said to have been dedicated to him.

[35] Dukes, Annal. i. 294.

[35a] Cf. De Castro, i. p. 171. (perhaps Berahja?). *Catal.* p. 1150., and Serapeum, 1854, p. 348.

[36] See the author's remarks, Lit. bl. iv. 59., and in Frankel's Zeitschr. iii. 279. The particular writings belong mostly to the following period ; cf. the notice of Sommerhausen, Lit. bl. xi. 181., which the author will complete elsewhere. Similar subjects were treated also in the Christian literature of that time : the Lamentations of a monk upon fleas (Grässe, ii. 2. p. 5.) does not bear comparison, in an æsthetical and moral point of view, with Charisi's witty treatment of the same subject (translated into German by Krafft, Geig. Zeit. iv. 135. ; cf. 418.).

[37] מחברות, properly dictionaries and the like ; see § 16. n. 38.

[38] *Catal.* s. v.

[39] Charisi, pp. 8 a., 36 a. ; conf. Dukes, Annal. i. 416.

[40] The author's Manna, p. 111. (§ 15. n. 17.). He also (p. 251.), like Dante, sees Greek and Arabian philosophers in hell. No one, to the author's knowledge, has called him a " Jewish Voltaire " (Encyc. Art. Emanuel, sect. 1. vol. xxxiv. p. 15.) · conf. n. 1. Kalonymos pronounces Hariri, as well as Kalila Wedimna, and Mischle Sendebar, to be worthless reading ; see n. 33 a.

[41] Read, " born 1388 " ; see *Catal.* p. 1984. We have forgotten to mention in the text Elia Cohen ben Moses ben Nissim, who translated a work from the Arabic, under the title מגלת עופר, probably in 1276. An imperfect copy of this hitherto unknown work has been discovered by the author in the Bodleian library. Shemtob ben Isaac Ibn Ardulil (1345) was the author of a humorous little work, recently printed, which Dukes formerly (Lit. bl. vi. 149. ; cf. 255.) confused with the anonymous מעשה צופר.

[42] Dukes (Annal. i. 416.) thinks his identity with the grammarian and lexicographer (§ 16.) improbable, but he has neither given his reasons nor published anywhere the specimens which he obtained from the Munich MS. (Mos. b. Ezra, p. 5.).

[43] [Page 177. line 3.] *Catal.* p. 1370. On a passage misunderstood by Dukes (Lit. bl. xii. 374.), see Ersch. ii. vol. xxxi. p. 49., and sup. § 18. n. 30.

[43a] Wolf. i. 1691. Adonia Kalomiti, the copyist at Salonichi (Delitzsch, *Catal.* p. 361. ; cf. Zunz, Add. p. 332.), lived scarcely as early as 1329 (see *Catal.* p. 2162.). Menahem Kalomiti, fl. 1445 (see Wolf. i. 1454.). Isaac Kal. (not Kalomini), 1466 (MS. Uri, 411. f. 30.)

[43b] Biscioni, p. 162. (Carm. Hist. d. Med. p. 135.).

[44] Lit. bl. vii. 565. ; Cod. Vienna, cviii.

⁴⁵ Zunz, zur Gesch. 204.

⁴⁶ Cod. Bislichis, 78. (now in the Bodl.), where the author is called JEHUDA HA-SHAARI, and Vatic.; see Serapeum, 1851, p. 63. The author of Cod. de Ros. 791. taught the rules of poetry to Abba Mari ben Kalonymos.

⁴⁷ *Catal.* p. 1308. sub no. 2.

⁴⁸ See Melo Chofn., p. 104.; Ker. Chem. vii. 78.; conf. Dukes, Beitr. p. 159., and Introd. to Mischle, p. 48. n. 51.

⁴⁹ *Catal.* s. v.

⁵⁰ *Catal.* p. 865. shows that the author is different from David Ibn Jahja, who has also a section on poetry. We forgot to mention SAADJA IBN DANAN's treatise in the introduction to his Hebr.-Arab. Lexicon (MS. Bodl.); see Dukes, Nachal, p. 1.; *Catal.* p. 2155.

⁵¹ Lit. bl. iv. 435., viii. 118.

⁵² See Dukes, Lit. bl. iv. 435., vii. 808. (" Schalom," vii. 403., is wrong), by which Del. p. 4. must be corrected.

⁵³ Vat. 225. (perhaps fragments of the Tachkemoni); see Frankel, Zeitschr. iii. 411. In Dukes, Ehrens. p. 58., and Lit. bl. iv. 435., read שיר for שם. Vat. 236.

⁵⁴ Delitzsch (*sic*), p. 65.

[P. 178. SANTO; see Ticknor, i. 80. Dukes (Lit. bl. xii. 29.) proposes several conjectures (adopted by M. A. Levy, Allg. Zeit. des Jud. 1855, p. 138.), all of which we cannot admît; he also places our Santo wrongly in the 13th cent. The Shemtob mentioned by Zarzah as dead is probably Ibn Ardutil (n. 71.); cf. sup. p. 167. The matter will be treated in the *Catal.* under Schemtob. We will here only add a reference to Perez de Hita, Guerras Civiles de Granada, who names a Hebrew translator, SANTO, of his doubtful Arabic authority. We owe this notice to our learned friend M. Zedner.]

⁵⁵ V. d. Hagen, Minnesänger, ii. no. 119; see Lit. bl. i. 145. sq.

⁵⁶ Zunz, zur Gesch. 166., and *Catal.* p. 1540. sub no. 6. On Jewish literature of that kind in general, cf. Wolf. n. 351.; Gervinus, Nationallit. i. 64. sq. (This reference is wrong, and we are not able to correct it).

⁵⁷ Zunz, zur Gesch. 173., according to Wolfius, iv. p. 201.

§ 21.   Page 179.

¹ According to the Aristotelian system current among the Arabs, the older and general division of mathematics arranges the subject under four (read " four or sometimes seven," p. 179.) heads or disciplinæ, the names of which vary according to the Arabic and Hebr. works introducing them : viz. 1. Mathematics in the stricter sense (מתמאתיקי in Joseph ben Zaddik, p. 2., Arab. الحساب, Hebr. חשבון, or מספר, or מנין); 2. Geometry (גומטריא, in Jehuda ben Barzillai; in Oosterche Wand. p. 71.; Lit. bl. viii. 620.; אגומיט, in Obadja b. David, Comm. cap 18. § 13.); Arab. or Pers. הנדסה (Lit. bl. iii. 182.), or הנדסיה, which is either adopted in Hebrew, or translated by תשבורת (properly Algebra, see p. 179.), or מידה והמשקל (Jehuda ben Barzillai), or מדות, or

שיעורים or ,(.6 .xxxiv .Exod on Eleazar ben Joseph) מדות והערכים
(Jehuda Ibn Tibbon, Rikmah, p. 3.; Lit. bl. viii. 718., and preface
to Bechai); 3. Astronomy (Arab. النجم علم, Hebr. ח', or הכוכבים

ח', or both [Cusari, iii. 29.], or הגלגל, or המזלות, or תכונה) הגלגלים;
4. Music (in Arab. and Hebr. מוסיקא, or מוסיקי [מוזיקא] in pref. Bechai,
and מוצקי in the uncertain Commentary on Jezira, which the author
formerly explained wrongly in § 12. n. 1.; see the correction by S. Sachs,
Ker. Chem. viii. 64., who, however, neglected the present note], or
translated into Hebrew, ח' החבור [i. e. art of composition, or חבור
הנעימות composition of melodies, or ניגון, or היבור הניגון, or הנינונים]
cf. § 18. p. 154.). These four are given by several authors, e. g. the
Comm. on Jezira (10th century); Bechai (where המוסר ח' is a different
reading of رياضه, or the mistake of an interpolater for המדות ח';
cf. אנשי המדות, in Jos. Caspi, Lit. bl. viii. 485. S. Sachs, l. c., gives the
same explanation); Joseph Ibn Zaddik, p. 2.; Maimonides, Logic, chap.
14.; Shemtob ben Isaac, Preface to Alzahrawi, MS.; Nachmanides,
Sermon, p. 20., ed. Leipzig; a dubious Comm. on the Kanon, MS. Bodl.
595.; Warner, 39., and others. In Jehuda ben Salomo Cohen, the seven
disciplinæ are called גימטריא, מוסיקא, תחבולות, הבטות, ח', הכוכבים,
מספר ח' and הגלגל: the latter is divided into theoretical (ידיעה) and practical (מעשה) (Introd. to Midr. Hacochma, MS. Mich. 414.). השיעור ח'
והמדידה, Munich. 255., is the geometry of Euclid. Misrachi (Resp.
56. in Conforte 31 a.) distinguishes תכונה (Astronomy), תשבורת
(Algebra), מספר (Arithmetic). In general, the mathematical sciences
are called לימודיות (Maim. Comm. Erubin, i. 5.), לימודים (Jehuda
ben Solomon Cohen), ספירות is peculiar to Ibn Ezra. To mathematics especially is applied the word בינה (Prov. i. 2., with respect to
1 Chron. xii. 32.) in Jehuda ben Solomon (not Samuel, as in ha-Jona,
p. 26., cf. p. 36.; Serap. 1851, p. 61.) and Emanuel of Rome, who
recognises an allusion to the seven disciplinæ in Prov. ix. 1. (Dukes,
Introd. p. xiii.). With respect to the number of seven, we must remark
that the " seven liberal arts " (§ 18. n. 49.) must not be confounded with
the " seven sciences" mentioned in some Jewish authors (e. g. Abr.
of Granada, quoted in the note to Nachmanides, l. c., and Moses Rieti,
f. 11.). These latter are the four mathematical disciplinæ, and the three
following, Ethics (or Politics), Physics, Metaphysics; while the above-
mentioned Commentary on the Kanon divides Philosophy also into
four, Physics, Mathematics, Politics, and Metaphysics, where we might
expect Ethics instead of Mathematics.

With respect to the general name, S. Sachs (l. c.) has explained the
singular word טרח, which answers to رياضه. Both mathematics and
logic (§ 12. n. 3., against Sachs, p. 64., who wishes to place logic
amongst the philosophical sciences) are properly excluded from philosophy. Logic is the general " organ" (כלי) for thinking, as grammar
is for speaking; mathematics have their own purposes and objects, but
as regards philosophy, they are only preparatory. On עבור, see inf.
n. 22. On גימטריא in its peculiar sense in Talmud (sup. pp. 16. 30.,
p. 52. n. 106.) see the article Gematria of D. Cassel in Ersch, s. i.
vol. lvi. p. 86. (on the Mathematician Elieser Chisma, see inf. n. 88.);

cf. also Zunz, Die relig. Poesie, p. 368. and § 18. n. 30. ; Maimonides, De Novilun. chap. 18. § 13. ; and Obadja ben David, ib., and chap. 12., combine גימ with חשבון.

[2] Zurat haar. Introd., which work itself is called ספר החזיון in Emmanuel (p. 197.). חוזה, for an astronomer, see Zunz, Benj. p. 104., conf. 131. 359., and § 20. n. 18.

[3] Palqu. Mebak. 38 b. (according to which Zunz, Benj. p. 231., is to be corrected) ; conf. also Hammer, Encykl. Uebers. p. 341.

[3a] One seeks in vain in DELAMBRE's Histoire de l'Astronomie for information on the Jews and for critical remarks upon the Arabian period generally ; he did not consult even Herbelot, Casiri, or De Rossi (Dizion. Stor. degli Autori Arabi). His principal authority, Am. Sedillot (vide J. J. Sedillot's Nekrology, in the translation of Abul Hassan, 1834), has not prevented his falling into great mistakes (vide inf.). The astronomy and mathematics of the Jews are with him represented by some works which have been badly edited and translated into Latin, from bad abridgments by Schreckenfuchs (1546), viz. : first, the Astronomy of ABRAHAM BAR CHIJJA ; secondly, the Arithmetic of ELIA MISRACHI (vide inf. n. 70 a.). The Jewish section in IDELER's celebrated Compendium of Chronology is equally open to objection ; see the author's essay in S. Sachs, היונה (printed 1848—1850).

[3b] The principal authority for the history of the Kalendar is ASARJA DE ROSSI, cap. 40. sq., and Appendix, and a special apologetic work printed Lond. 1854 ; see also SLONIMSKI, Kerem Chemed, v. 104. sq., and in היונה (edit. by Sachs) ; also a special compendium, יסוד העבור, 1852, p. 1. sq., and the author's treatise, ib. p. 17. sq., the results of which he has here introduced in brief ; conf. older authorities in Wolf. ii. p. 1302. sq. On IDELER, see n. 3 a. L. M. LEWISOHN has recently published a popular essay under the title Geschichte und System des jüdischen Kalenderwesens, without independent researches, (v. n. 16.) but rich in authorities. The author regrets that he must leave several important questions on the history of the Kalendar without fresh investigation, on account of the extensive astronomical researches which would have been necessary for the purpose ; vide inf. n. 17.

[4] Hamza el Isfahani, ed. Gottwaldt (Petersb. 1844), p. 4. ; cf. Shaharastani, ii. 352., ed. Haarbrücker ; conf. Alfergani in As. de Rossi, cap. 40. sq. 201 b. (ed. Vienna) ; Bailly, Hist. de l'Astr. i. 217. (according to Golius ad Alfrag. and Herbelot) ; Ideler, ii. 495.

[4a] Conf. § 15. n. 28. According to Herbel. (Nassa, iii. 646.), Muhammed forbade it expressly in the Koran (ii. 185.? conf. Sunne, 552. [in Hammer, Fundgr. d. Or.] : "The moon is sometimes twentynine, sometimes thirty days") on account of the superstition connected with it ; cf. Shaharastani, l. c. in n. 4. According to Isaac Israeli (iv. 17.), the reckoning was first determined by inspection. Weil (Muhamm. p. 281.) supposes only the existence of a year with intercalation, but considers the abolition of it before the time of Muhammed as certain. According to Simon Duran (Keshet u-magen, 25 a.), Muhammed forbade the calculation of the new moon. Similarly, an old author quoted by Isa֗֗ ben Baruch (in Abraham bar Chijja, Haibbur. p. 94.) and Ibn Ezra (Ker. Chem. iv. 163. ; conf. As. de Rossi, 213 b. ; Slonimski, Ker. Chem. v. 128.) asserts of the Tekufa of R. Ada (vide

n. 17.), that it was kept secret on account of superstition; while the Egyptian priests opposed intercalation on religious grounds (Ideler, Handb. d. Chronol. i. 95.).   Abr. Krochmal (החלוץ, i. 133.) finds a political reason why the determination of the new moon was made a " secret" (cf. § 5. n. 102.).

[5] Makrisi in Sacy, Christ. Ar. i. 134.; Zion, i. 35.; conf. § 14. n. 10., Annal. i. 137. sq.

[6] See § 14. n. 20.; Ibn Ezra on Gen. viii. 3.; Hedessi, § 184. sq.

[7] Zion, i. 38.; conf. Jost, Busch, v. 159.

[8] Jehuda Halevi (Cus. iv. § 20.) speaks of attacks on the Jewish Easter according to Samuel's solar year; and his renegade opponent, SAMUEL IBN ABBAS, probably treated of the same subject (n. 33.); but Cod. Uri, 257., is a forgery; it contains a fragment of the Liturgy of Solomon ben Nathan (see n. 23.): conf. also the reply of Israeli (1330) to an apostate on this subject (Jesod Olam, ed. Goldb. ii. 36.).   Abraham bar Chijja expressly excuses the strange opinions of Saadja by the polemical tendency against the Karaites.   Maimonides is more candid (see Rap., Erech Millin, p. 91., and *Catal.* p. 2170.).

[9] Rap., Chan. p. 46., Erech Millin, p. 91. (conf. sup. § 5. n. 29.; Geig. Zeitschr. vi. 18.).   On Carmoly's fictions and plagiarisms (Annal. i. 222.), see Rapop., Ker. Chem., vi. 116. sq.; conf. Resp. Gäon. f. 12 b.   Luzzatto, Il Giudaismo, i. 31.

[10] Vide Abrah. ben Chijja, p. 38. (As. de Rossi l. c., and conf. sup. § 5. n. 25.); cf. Aderet Eliahu, f. 19 a. col. 2., ed. 1835, and inf. n. 77.   Herbelot (Resm. iii. 774.) speaks of the Geography of Ptolemy, which was translated from Greek into Hebrew, and afterwards, under Mamun, into Arabic.   The mistake might be occasioned by the double meaning of the word سُرْيَانِي, which signifies Hebrew (Rabbinical) and Syriac; so also Weil (Muhamm. p. 140. n. 209.) thinks that the Jews in Muhammed's time used Syriac; see the author's compilation in Frankel, Zeitschr. iii. 324. n. 20.; conf. Ewald, Beiträge, p. 138.; Munk, Tanhoun, p. 99., and inf. n. 39. § 22. n. 22.   Perhaps the passage in Honein's preface to Musare ha-Philos. is to be explained in the same way.

[11] Slonimski, Ker. Chem. v. 10.   The objection of Luzz. (Lit. bl. xi. 690.) has been removed by his extract from an old MS. (in Ker. Chem. viii. 37. and in Slonimski, Jesod, p. 31.).

[12] Steinschneider, היונה, p. 19. (conf. sup. § 5. n. 32.); Samuel החכם (Ker. Chem. vii. 67.) is certainly not the younger Gaon SAMUEL BEN CHOFNI (Reifmann, פשר דבר, ii. 10.).   Fürst (Lit. bl. viii. 43.) erroneously transfers the quotations in Zunz (G. V. p. 93. n. e.) from Ada to Samuel.   Our observations are not mentioned in the recent essay of Abr. Krochmal (החלוץ, i. 77.) nor in Jellinek, pref. to Donolo, p. v.   Cf. *Catal.* p. 2240.   See also inf. n. 17.

[13] See the author's partial restoration of the text, l. c. p. 20. ELIESER BEN FARUCH, who appears in Makrisi (Ideler, i. 275.) as the founder of the Jewish mode of calculating the Kalendar, is considered by the author (l. c. p. 18.) to be one of the Talmudists, the commencement of whose year (in Tishri) is the foundation of the Kalendar now in use; conf. inf. n. 21 a.   Fürst has appropriated to himself part of our dis-

sertation (Lit. bl. xi. 326.), and afterwards (Lit. bl. xii. 458.) spoken of it as useless.

[14] Vide sup. n. 4.   Ptolemæus (in Israeli, iv. 2. fol. 3 c.) speaks of a cycle of eight years with three leap years.

[15] Vide sup. § 5. n. 109. also respecting the date of the work.   The cycle of 84 years is probably that of Epiphanius and Cyrillus, and the Quartodecimans, of whom Ideler (i. 571., in the passage where he speaks of the Perakim, conf. ii. 202.) asserts that he has found no trace in any Rabbinical writer.   Lewisohn (l. c. p. 25.) sees in the whole passage nothing but " an allegory," which can only be admitted with respect to the day of 1000 years, to which the author never meant to attach any value.   The cycle of 84 years of the fixed stars in Albatani (Delambre, p. 54.) is quite independent.   On the hours of the planets (Ideler, i. 87. 197. sq.) see Steinschn. l. c. p. 21.

[16] The various directions for intercalations of Meton and the Jews (Israeli ascribes the received method to R. CHANANEL; conf. also Ideler, i. 579.; see Achai Gaon in Geiger, Zeitschr. vi. 18.) are, in fact, only *chronological* varieties (see Steinschn. l. c. pp. 29. 33.), and connected with the difference between the Babylonian and Palestine Jews in respect of the commencement of the year.   Neither this short, but important observation, nor the special dissertation of RAPOPORT (Erech Millin, p. 91.; cf. sup. n. 8.), has been noticed by Lewisohn, pp. 32. 40., although he dwells upon the different cycles, and gives the former part of the present note; cf. § 10. n. 25.

[17] Viz. תקופה אליבא דר' אדא, i. e. " according to that " of R. ADA BEN ABIN (not Ben Ahaba, as has been hitherto supposed); see Slonimski, l. c. p. 12.   The 9th vol. of Ker. Chem., p. 27. sq., contains a correspondence between Slon. and PINELES, who attacks the whole system of Slon. by astronomical calculations (sup. n. 3 b.).   We must remark that in such a complicated matter great care ought to be taken not to confuse different questions by using ambiguous expressions. Some recent authors try to claim antiquity for more recent reformations; thus Graetz (Gesch. iii. 552.) and Wiesner (Frankel, Monatschr. iii. 113.) believe that they find the usual " Order of Kalendar" in the Talmud.   But Graetz brings forward only an uncertain general expression, and Wiesner only one practical rule for the day of New Year; see Slonimski, Jesod, p. 34.

[18] See the various authorities and hypotheses in *Catal.* s. v. p. 2131.; cf. n. 20.

[19] בין הגוים; conf. sup. n. 15.

[20] Hedessi, 63. ס, mentions the figures.   (This observation is repeated by Jellinek in the pref. to the Introd., published 1854, under the new title, " Der Mensch als Ebenbild," &c., p. vii.   He, however, omits entirely our dissert. in ha-Jona, and this essay, amongst the authorities, p. iii., as also some others.)   ABU SAHAL (p. 182.) also illustrated the work sent to Chisdai (cf. n. 93.) by figures.

[20a] Ibn Ezra calls Mashallah an Indian sage; cf. *Catal.* p. 1677. Israeli (iv. 7. fol. 11 a.) speaks of Persian sages (עילם ח'), who worked about 790 by royal command; conf. inf. n. 59.

[21] Vide inf. n. 60., and on Abu Sahl, inf. n. 93.

[21a] See Steinschn. p. 18.; conf. the author's Index to Michael's

Catal. p. 317.) on Fürst's incorrect plagiarisms (Lit. bl. xi. 320.);
vide sup. n. 13.

22 On the title עבור, in SAADJA and the later writers (mentioned p.
437.), see *Catal.* p. 2170. Meir Aldabi distinguishes between חכמת
התכונה (see n. 1.) and העבור ח'. Levi ben Abraham (Astr. MS. i.
§ 1, 2.) says that the סוד העבור is founded on המדות והמספר ח' and
ההבטה ח', i. e. Mathem. and Astron. or " Observation."

23 See n. 8. and § 19. n. 42.; Ker. Chem. ix. 37. So also the
Persian Kalendar of the year 1290, in Munk, Not. s. Saadja, p. 67.

24 See, however, the author's remarks on the Leyden MSS. Warner,
25⁴. and 60., out of the pieces of which the one printed is composed.
Cf. also Zunz, z. Gesch. p. 164.

25 On NAHSHON (*sic*) (ob. 898 ?), see *Catal.* p. 2020.

26 Luzz. Lit. bl. vii. 420.

27 Vide e. g. Abraham ben Chijja's forced distinction between the
visible and numerable stars (vide n. 48.) and the countless numbers of
Scripture (Zurat haar. fin.) ; by which one is reminded of the passage
in Pliny (ii. 26.): " Hipparchus ausus sit *rem Deo etiam improbam,*
annuntiare posteris stellas."

28 E. g. the three questions in Ghasali (Munich, 35. n.), which the
author has proved to be the כוונת הכוונות mentioned by Moses Narboni
(*Catal.* p. 1973. ; Cod. Warner, 15.) ; the work of Bathliusi (*Catal.* p.
2001.) ; Ibn Roshd's Subst. Orbis (*Catal.* p. 764. &c.).

29 The astronomer (Casiri, i. 430. and historiographer in Spain,
Ibn Ssaïd (صاعد), whose section on celebrated Jews, however, seems
to be lost (*Catal.* p. 1114.), was⁺in close connexion with the Jews (n.
59 a.) ; he and his companions (according to Isaac Israeli, iv. 7.) confess to have used Jewish authorities, and to have borrowed amongst
other things the cycle of 19 years. Ibn Ssaïd is said to have died 1070,
so that the year 1080 (p. 188. line 1., where read *circa*) could not
be referred to himself. Whether SAHAL BEN BISHR (p. 191.) was in
Spain has become rather doubtful to the author (see *Catal.* s. v.).

30 He had apparently the usual additional name, Abu Ali, which gave
rise to the story of his son ALI (in Obadja, conf. D. Cassel, on Cusari,
p. 120.). We have given his date, 972, according to Zunz, Got. Vortr.
363. (cf. Annal. ii. 225.) ; but the new ed. of Israeli, iv. 14. f. 28.,
gives 952 (hence Slonimski, Jesod, p. 43.). According to Ibn Ezra
(Ibbur MS.) he wrote three works on Ibbur (see *Catal.* p. 2171.).

[Page 183. line 8. ISAAC BEN RAKUFIEL, probably more correctly
JEHUDA ; see *Catal.* l. c. in n. 30. The year 1040 (Annal. ii. 225.) is
probably without any other authority than Carmoly.]

[Page 183. line 14. The word *Samuel* is erroneous. On Isaac ben
Baruch, information is to be found also in Moses Ibn Ezra.]

31 ABRAHAM BEN CHIJJA wrote in 1105–33. ; but we have perhaps
a final redaction after his death, A. 1136; see the author's remarks in
Cod. Warner. 37., and *Catal.* p. 2113.

32 See *Catal.* pp. 687. 1038., and Cod. Scalig. 14.

33 See Nicoll, p. 603. ; see, however, n. 8.

34 ISAAC BEN JUDA (see Wolf. iii. n. 1195 b. ; 1170, according to
Carmoly's Annal. ii. 225.) is rather doubtful.

34a Sedillot (Comptes Rendus, xvii. 167.) divides the Arabian astronomers into — (1.) translators and compilers ; (2.) calculators ; (3.) observers. The same holds good of the Jews.

[35] R. MAIMON., the editor of the Alfergani (As. de Rossi, chap. 40.), is probably neither Maimonides nor his father.

[36] The Latin and Spanish were partly themselves translated by Jews, e. g. by JOHANNES HISPALENSIS, whose works are mentioned in Jourdain in an incomplete manner, and not without mistakes ; see *Catal.* p. 1402., and inf. n. 93.

[37] Wenrich (De Auct. Græc.) introduces him first in the Supplement, p. 306., without reference to a MS. (see Br. Mus. 7473., without the name of the translator in Ewald, Zeitschr. f. d. Kunde des Morgenl. ii. 211.) ; but he is already mentioned by Joseph Ibn Aknin (see Ersch, s. v. p. 51. n. 40.). The Hebrew translation (after another Arabian version, Munich, 36. 4 = 35. 5. in Lilienth.) is mentioned as early as by Del Medigo (in Geig. Mel. Chofn. p. 104.). Carmoly (Itinéraires, p. 346.) calls the translator KALONYMOS, but mutilates the name, and refers to nobody else.

[38] This is the fictitious Jew ISAAC COHEN (Encykl. sect. 2. vol. xxiv. p. 219.), whom De Rossi (Cod. 806. 3.) confounds with a real Jew of the 15th century. Cf. Cod. Bislichis, 69., and Cod. De Rossi, 1170.

[39] This princely Arabian alchymist is obviously the KALID BEN JAZICHI, &c., who under various false names figured as a Jew, and whose Hebrew writings are erroneously said to have been translated into Arabic, and thence into Latin (probably by Robert Retinensis ; see Jourdain, p. 109.). Conf. on " Hebrew," sup. n. 10. ; see *Catal.* p. 813., and cf. *Morienus* Romanus, de Alchemia, printed 1593, &c.

[39a] *Catal.* p. 1567., where the date of this author is first demonstrated from a passage of his work ; cf. inf. n. 68.

[40] His Astrology was translated for Alphonso X. into Spanish by JUDA BEN MOSES (not ben Joseph), and thence into Latin by Ægidius de Tebaldis (conf. § 22. n. 70.) and Petro del Real (Reggio), and, perhaps, afterwards improved by Alvaro (Castro, i. 114.). The Spanish translation, and the Hebrew of ISAAC BEN SAMUEL ABULCHEIR, made from the Latin, are at Oxford. Another Hebrew edition by SOLOMON DOYEN (?) has produced great mistakes ; see *Catal.* p. 1361. — To the Arabian authors belongs also Ali ben Ahmed el-Omrani (ob. 954–55), who is beyond doubt the " Enbrani " in Cod. Lat. Canon. Misc. 396. (in Coxe's *Catal.* p. 734.) ; the year, 1134, and the place, Barcelona, agree better with ABRAHAM BAR CHIJJA than with ABRAHAM JUDÆUS of Tortosa, who is perhaps the same as ABRAHAM of Toledo, sup. p. 184.

[40a] Conf. Abu Bauzel (!) and Abu Malmel (!), Münch. 225.

[41] *Catal.* p. 1181.

[42] In the Escurial there are many Spanish translations made by a Rabbi ZAG, or ÇAG (= Isaac), of Toledo, for Alphonso X. These have occasioned various mistakes and contradictions characteristic of this class of investigations, and discoverable only by a careful collation of the extracts with the MSS. themselves. De Castro has made some unfair deductions from these works. His principal purpose is to prove that the Jews who worked for Alphonso were *baptized* ; see *Catal.* pp. 1156. 1359. 2144. The author does not hesitate to identify R. Isaac with Ibn Sid (see n. 67.). Sachs (Rel. Poes. 196.) regrets that Jourdain

"makes references only from secondhand, without criticism," and yet himself combines even thirdhand authorities (Jourdain and Zunz) from the same origin; see *Catal.* p. 1359.

43 See pref. to Catal. Michael. p. xiii. (*Catal.* p. 1610.; Ker. Chem. ix. 37.), and Catal. of Leyden MSS. Cod. Warner. 20.

44 Not "Abualbari" (Encykl. sect. 2. vol. xxiv. 217., according to Wolf. T. iii., confused with Aboab). See Cod. Warner. 68., in the author's Catal. of the Leyden MSS., and cf. n. 40.

45 Another Hebrew compendium of the same work (הגלגל 'ס), printed together with the translation of Solomon ben Abraham, has not been hitherto recognised as such, and has been falsely ascribed to the same translator. *Catal.* p. 2255.

46 [This reference belongs to JACOB BEN SAMSON, line 12., where read 1123–42; cf. *Catal.* pp. 1838. 2222.; cf. Zunz, zur Gesch. p. 51. (Conforte, f. 17 a., &c.). On ISAAC ALHADIB, see *Catal.* p. 1086., and n. 61 a.]

46a [The passage was inserted at line 22.] See Humboldt, Kosmos, ii. 453. n. 12.

47 Zunz, zur Gesch. 166.

47a See Hadji Chalfa ap. Hammer, Encykl. Uebers. p. 343., and the comparison with the Druzes in De Sacy, Chrest. ii. 384. To the Jewish authors quoted by Sachs, Rel. Poes. p. 230. (cf. § 13. n. 48.), add Jos. Kimchi, Lit. bl. vii. 730., the description in Ibn Sahula, Mashal hakadmoni.

48 Lit. bl. iv. p. 24. n. 59.; conf. Ibn Ezra, Reshit Chochma, init.; on Ex. xxiii. 20. (p. 72. Prag.), Palquera, Mebak. 36 a., conf. Sachs, p. 232., "round numbers." In Joseph Caspi, p. 103., the correct number is placed between brackets. Hadji Chalfa (in Hammer, Encykl. Uebers. p. 479.) reckons 29,000. Conf. sup. n. 27.

49 See Shene Hammeoroth, pref. p. 6.; and, perhaps, hence D. Cassel ad Cusari, iii. 79. p. 279.; cf. Jos. Gikatilla in Ersch, vol. xxxi. p. 78. n. 17.: 5000 is found in Levi ben Gerson ad Gen. i., fol. 11 c.; cf. Milchamot, v. 1. Cf. Saadja Emunot, vii., and in Simon Duran, Magen Abot in fol., f. 9 a.; the quotation of Ptolomæus (הגלגל 'ס in fine) is an addition to Sacrobosco (cf. n. 45.). In determining the distance of the moon, Jehuda ben Solomon Cohen (Treatise on the Letters, MSS.) differs about 1 חלק from Ptolemy.

50 Maim. in As. de Rossi, cap. 28. p. 164.; conf. Chasles, Comptes Rendus, xxiii. 850. The 6000 parasangs of the Talmud are a symbolical number (conf. 8000 in Delambre, p. 198.); cf. Saadja, Emunot, vii.

51 Ibn Ezra on Ps. cxlviii. 9.

52 E. g. in Gabirol (Sachs, p. 231.); the Astronomy of Abraham ben Chijja is full of variations. On the still important question about the motion of the fixed stars (octava sphæra), which much occupied the astronomers, Joseph ben Eleazar finds contradictions in Ibn Ezra (see ad Levit. xxv. 9. &c.); cf. also n. 66.

53 Read *some* antipodes, viz. those on the extremities of the Eastern hemisphere; see Maimonides, Moreh, i. 73.; conf. Palquera, Mebak. 39. The rotation of the earth, however, is adduced as an example of a false conception (Jos. ben Shemtob, Kobez Wikk. fol. 20 a.). A passage of the book Zohar, speaking of rotation, antipodes, &c., has

repeatedly attracted the attention of Jewish authors: see Hurwitz, Deutsche Zugabe zum Sammler, 1809, p. 32.; Zunz, Etwas über die Rabb. Lit. 1818, p. 16.; Jost, Isr. Annal. 1839, p. 70.; Franck, Kabbala, p. 98. (conf. p. 73., where מתנגלא is not exactly translated); and Jost still (Jellinek und die Kabbala, 1852) goes so far as to find here " special geographical notices."

[53a] Gabirol, Keter Malhut, 210.; Jos. Kimchi on Job, x. 22. (Lit. bl. xi. 93.); Maimon., Letter to the Wise Men of Marseilles (or Montpellier).

[54] Jourdain, p. 280.; conf. Shene Hammeor. p. 10. n. 8.; cf. D. Cassel, in Ersch, s. v. Joseph Gikatilla, p. 78. n. 16.

[55] See Annal. ii. 80. 288.; Ker. Chem. vii. 254. The Ephemerides of SOLOMON JORCHUS, in Zach. Corr. Astr. viii. 22. (Nürnberger, Astron. Wörterb. i. 328.), are unknown to the author (conf. ABRAHAM BEN SOLOMON JARCHI ZARPHATI, Wolf. i. 160.; Vat. 297. 13. on Euclid, he was perhaps a mere copyist). On the other hand, we possess similar ones by SABBATAI DONOLO. The existence of this among the Arabs is, in Delambre (p. 6.), only an " on croit! "

[55a] Basnage, p. 259., in Wolf. and Rossi.

[56] Biscioni, 88.; Cod. 28. 3.; perhaps transcriber. Conf. also on the Celidario of Bartholomæus de Jamfredi (?) ibid., Cod. 47. 1., and the instrument נפטור בארוץ (??) Vat. 429. 30.; conf. 379. 7.

[57] כלי פז, Vat. 387. 10. (Wolf. i. 958.).

[58] Irving, in Zunz, Benj. ii. p. 268.; Depping, in Carmoly, Hist. des Médecins, p. 124.; conf. Allg. Zeit. d. Jud. 1847, p. 887. The astrolabe is also called כלי הנחושת in Ibn Ezra and the Mishna Commentary on Erub. iv. 2. JEHUDA BEN BARZILLAI is against the use of it on the Sabbath (Zunz, zur Gesch. 483.).—Also Abraham Zarkali's description of his Tables (צפיחה) is translated into Hebrew (cf. also Geig. Zeitschr. iii. 445.; Munic. 35, 36. &c.); the printed Latin ed. is perhaps extracted from the translation of Abraham (De Castro, i. 143.; cf. Jourdain, in Stahr's translation, p. 147.). See the author's notice in Zeitschr. der d. m. Gesellsch. viii. 379.

[58a] Read 1328–40; the identity is proved by Munk and the author (Catal. p. 1609.; cf. p. 2118.). That the printed verses belong to the instrument is distinctly said in a prefatory remark of the Pocock MS.

[58b] Tables of geographical lengths and breadths (conf. Zunz, Benj. p. 307.) are contained in the astrological work of Ibn Radshal (viii. cap. 37.), according to " Harix' " (?) accounts.

[59] Del Medigo, Mel. Chofn. p. 14., and vide n. 71., viz. either that of Djelali (Mill's Hist. du Mahom. p. 275.), or the Chowaresmi; see n. 60., and conf. sup. n. 20 a.

[59a] Vide sup. n. 29., about the year 1080.

[60] To the Tables themselves, and to their Indian origin, Chasles (Comptes rendus, xiii. 846.; conf. Von Humboldt, Kosmos, ii. 452. n. 10.) alluded lately, so far as they are of importance for the question of the originality of the Indian, Chaldee, and Arabian astronomy. The most interesting older accounts of Ibn Ezra, whose " Super Opere Tabularum " was mentioned as early as by Pico (Wolf. i. p. 85.), have been much mutilated by De Rossi (Cod. 212.). See the quotations in § 20. n. 32., and especially on Canca and JACOB IBN SHEARA (n. 21.) our notices in Zeitschr. der d. Morg. Gesellsch. viii. 550. We must again

regret the want of the Hebrew text of Cod. Rossi. Conf. also Jourdain, p. 104., where Zydj is to be read as an emendation for Zydi, and Taarich Japhari for Erichiapharim.

[61] As an assistant in the composition of the "Six Wings," SOLOMON TALMID appears only in Buxtorf, according to Jacob Romano (see n. 63.); conf. Abraham Talmid (1483), copyist of Cod. Tur. 113. (wrongly in Wolf. iv. p. 919.); conf. Cod. Rossi, 1185., where "Talmid" is probably not the name of the author, and SOLOMON EZOBI (1633), inf. § 30. p. 262.; SOLOMON MIRNACHI (?), Vat. 498. (in Mai). See also the author's index to Catal. Michael. p. 347. — On the commentaries of the celebrated "Six Wings," some researches should still be made; see Index, p. 359. As early as 1380 it was commentated by SAMUEL CHAJJIM BEN JOMTOB MATRON SEFARDI (Cod. Reggio, 42., now in the Bodleiana). On the Greek Commentator, see inf. n. 63.

[61a] See n. 46 a. From the very mutilated extract in Deutsch and Krafft, cxci., we can only gather that he used, beside the tables of Albatani, also those of אלראקם, or אלרקאם (l. Almorakeshi?), which were preferred by many astronomers in Tunis, and also those of אלכמד (l. Alkomad? cf. ابن الجماس in Casiri, i. 393?).

[62] Catal. p. 1457.

[62a] Against the inventions of Carmoly (Frankel, Monatschr. 1854, p. 67.) and the false combinations of De Rossi (Cod. 1181.), repeated by Geiger (Proben, ii. 49.), see Catal. p. 2117., where also a Hebrew retranslation out of Latin is mentioned, now in the Bodl. libr.

[63] Wolf, i. n. 1956., according to Bartol. (Vat. 393. 1. in Assem 14th century! See infra, n. 77.); conf. Wolf. i. pp. 340. 597. SOLOMON RHODIUS (?) MS. Munic. 343. 5.; SOLOMON MIRNACHI (?) n. 61. The poet SOLOMON SHARBIT HASAHAB (Catal. p. 2214.) has nothing upon astronomy in his Keter Malchut (Luzz., Kerem Chemed, iv. 39.). The family name שרביט הזהב (conf. Abraham and Schemarja in Conforte, 48 b.) appears to be translated (Zunz, zur Gesch. 157.), and may correspond to the Greek CHRYSOKOKKA (and not Chrysostephanos, as Zunz, Syn. Poesie, p. 107.), because χρυσόκοκκα is the name not only of the commentator of the "Six Wings" of Immanuel, but also of the translator of the Persian tables in Delambre.

[64] Op. 1666. 9.

[65] The author has tried to investigate the subject as far as he could without the rare Latin work of Ricius, in an essay ("Alfons' x. astronomischer Kongress zu Toledo, and Isaac Ibn Sid der Chasan, Eine Randglosse zur [Humboldt's] Kosmos, ii. 261,") which appeared in the "Magazin für die Literatur des Auslands," unfortunately, in May, 1848 (n. 57. p. 226., and n. 58. p. 230.), when public attention was directed to anything but investigations of that kind. He has shown from clear authorities, in two articles: 1. That no congress of Arabic authors ever existed; 2. That Isaac Ibn Sid was the principal author of the tables (v. Catal. p. 2144.). He intended to treat in a third article the question whether our recension is really a réchauffé of 1256, and was happy enough to find, in 1850, in the Bodleian library, the work of RICIUS (described at large in Catal. pp. 2143–5.); when he found that it requires a more thorough knowledge of astronomy than he

possesses. He will therefore add only one short observation. Ricius (ff. 27. 29.) gives as a reason for the retractation, that in the tables of 1252 *the movement of the fixed stars* was supposed to be 1° in 70 years (which number he attributes to Jewish superstition, f. 24. ; hence Bailly, i. 225., Encykl. s. i. vol. iii. p. 90.), but that by the translation of Abu'lhasin he was convinced of the truth of the system of Albatani (f. 39., in the name of Zacut, but see sup. p. 190.). Asarja de Rossi, however (chap. 40. f. 213 b., where the year 1251 agrees with the Latin ed. of the tables, and hence D. Gans, Zemach David ad A.), asserts that Alfonso did not know "the works" of Albatani, speaking especially of the length of the year.

[66] On the strange mistakes about Jehuda ben Moses (Moischa), of whom de Castro, Jourdain, Jost, and Carmoly, make two different authors, &c., see the extensive note in *Catal.* pp. 1360–2.

[67] See n. 68. On Pedro's behaviour to the Jews, similar to that of his father Alfonso, see the authorities quoted in D. Cassel's note to Jehuda ben Asher, f. 61 b.

[68] Preface, 9 b. (see § 30. n. 11.). Here the confusion pervading the Catalogues can only be unravelled by actual inspection. JACOB BEN ISAAC ALKARSANI is named as translator of a work on the astrolabe, the Arabic author of which is either Ahmed Ibn al-Ssoffar (الصفار) or ben Djaafer (see the author's notice in Zeitschr. der d. m. Gesellsch. viii. 548., and cf. "Abnasafar" in De Castro, i. p. 129.), and probably the same as "Ameth filius Afar," from the Latin of Philipp, Spanish, in Cod. Canon. misc. 340. (p. 693. of Coxe's Catal.), following after Prophaças de Marsilia supra Quadr., &c., by Armengaud in 1299. This Prophaças is JACOB BEN MACHIR, who certainly translated a work on the astrolabe from the Arabic, the Spanish (or Limosin) translation of which is attributed by Deutsch (Catal. p. 186.) to a fictitious GOISU ("guysios des estrellas," see 39 a. *Catal.* p. 1569.) ; so that the authorship of Jacob ben Isaac is rather doubtful. JACOB KARSANI is named as author of tables, or of a commentary on them, in which Peter III. of Arragon (at Barcelona, 1276), among the learned men commissioned by him, is said to mention Magister Peter (Vat. 379. 10.; Rossi, 165., vide sup. § 8. n. 9.), conf. Petro Regio (del Real) sup. n. 40., and *Catal.* p. 1358. JACOB BEN DAVID BEN JOMTOB POEL also reckons according to the era of Peter III. (Vat. 356. 3, 4.), although he wrote in 1361 (see n. 62 a.). Finally, the tables (Almanack) of JACOB BEN MACHIR (1300) have been confused with the translation of Ibn Heitham, &c.; see *Catal.* pp. 1234. 2113.

[69] The identity with the poet (Zunz, zur Gesch. 473., see sup. p. 343. n. 27 a.) is established by comparing the date of his pupil mentioned in the text (Cod. Reggio, 14., now in the Bodleian). Del Medigo (p. 53.) calls the translator KALONYMOS ?

[70] See *Catal.* p. 1658. ; his anonymously printed tables of day and night (different from those of Bianchino) are also in MS. Mich. 525. In the passage given from MS. Mich. 570., the words "which expression," &c., to "above" should be put in brackets, and instead of "*or to* those," read "*and* those of Jac. Poel."

[70 a] According to Delambre, he is later than Ibn Junis (ob. 1008), but is the first (!) who speaks of the extraction of the cube root.

[71] He treated of chronology in his supplement to Aderet Eliahu of Beschitzi.

[72] See n. 45.

[73] Vat. 387. n. 379, 7.

[Page 190. sq.   In general compare the note 72 a. of § 22.]

[74] Hadji Chalfa in Hammer, Encykl. Uebers. p. 475.   If Gesenius (Encykl. sect. 1. vol. v. p. 69.) derives the Arabian astrology from "the Jews" like Alkendi, then the hypothesis falls with its foundation; conf. sup. § 13. n. 7.   In Grässe (ii. 2. 991.) it is said: "Of strictly mathematical studies, astronomy and astrology were, however, principally cultivated, which served their purpose and suited their taste for cheating." Sufficient excuse for this admirable logic is given in the other statements contained in this work on Jewish Literature.   See the observations in Lit. bl. ii. 230.   Jewish authors often derive astrology from heathen-dom, or ascribe it to other nations (see n. 77.).   Ibn Zarzah (f. 20 c.) gives the Arabian name טיאר and "astrology" (אסטרולוגיאה) as used by Christian sages.   On the antiquity of it, see Narboni in Comm. on Averroes de Subst. Orbis, in fine ; on the little value ascribed to it, see Palquera, Mebak. f. 39 b.; cf. also Joseph Nasi, Lit. bl. xi. 768., where בלנס is probably Apollonius.   Even the pseudo-Abraham ben David argues (f. 38.) against the חוזים (n. 1.).   But it would lead us too far to collect the sentences against astrology, and especially its practice; cf. § 22. n. 72 a. sq.

[75] See on the other hand, e. g. Ibn Ezra, Introd. to the Astrol. Vat. 390. ; and on the Doctrine of Freedom of the Jewish philosophers, see Ritter, Gött. gel. Anz., 1847, p. 611.; cf. also S. Sachs, ha-Jona, p. 19. sq. 59. sq.

[76] In his most interesting letter to the learned of Montpellier (or Marseilles) ; see § 22. n. 74.

[77] The wise men of Greece, says Maimonides, never composed such as these, even the Persians recognised the worthlessness of the works produced by Kasdæans, Chaldæans (a distinction common among the Arabians), Egyptians, and Canaanites ; one must not adhere to indi-vidual statements in the Talmud.   Moses ben Samuel Cohen, of Saloniki, who grounds astrology on the oracle of the *Urim we-Tumim* (cf. *Catal.* n. 3392), is probably not so old as stated by Assemani, ad Cod. Vat. 393. 3. (conf. Wolf. i. p. 2093., ii. p. 1259., iv. p. 1039.) ; see sup. n. 63.

[78] Zunz, zur Gesch. 483. ; see, on the other hand, n. 79.

[78 a] See Von Humboldt, Kosmos, ii. 252.   Astrological necromancy, &c., attracted the inquisitive especially to Salamanca (Schmidt, Discipl. Clerical. p. 113., and Sol. Duran, sup. p. 201.), Toledo (Jourdain, pp. 100. 271.), and other seats of Arabian science.

[79] E. g. the care taken of liquids at Quarter Day (תקופות), which even Abrah. ben Chijja (in Asarja de Rossi, add. 2. to cap. 40.) desig-nates as provincial superstitions ; conf. also Brück, p. 43. ; Ker. Chem. iv. 165., vii. 77.   An elucidation of this custom by the baptized Jew Paul William Hirsch (1717) was welcomed as a new antijudaistic argument in the "Unschuldige Nachrichten" (Wolf. iii. p. 908.).   A refutation of this superstition was written by the neophyte Philip Ni-codemus Lebrecht (Wolf. iv. p. 954.).   An interesting article on this

and similar superstitions (which also gave rise to persecutions of the Jews), explaining them in a physical way, is to be found in Lieber-mann's Kalendar, 1855, p. 119.: "Die Wunder des Bluts, von S. Cohn." Another superstition, of looking at the shadow on Hosianna Night, is acknowledged by Elia Levita (Lit. bl. viii. 342.); and Isachar Ibn Shoshan gives the hours (Tikkun, f. 124 a., ed. Ven.).

[80] See Zunz, Annal. ii. 156.; Jehuda ben Solomon Cohen, In-trod. to Astrology; Solomon, transl. of Ali Ibn Radshal; Cod. Vienna, CLXXXVII.

[81] V. sup. § 15. n. 15. A revolution throughout the world was ex-pected in the year 1179 by the Persian, Arabian, Jewish, and Christian astrologers; see Scaliger ad Manilium, p. 9.; conf. Hadji Chalfa in Hammer, Encykl. Uebers. p. 180. On the constellation of the years 1464, 1469, see Zunz, l. c., and *Catal.* p. 1575. Astrological proofs for Muhammed's being a prophet form a chapter in the Annals of Hamza el Isfahani (ed. Gottwaldt, Petersb. 1844).

[82] Zunz, l. c.

[Page 191. lin. 22., for " astronomical " read " astrological."]

[83] Read *Centiloquium* ($\kappa\alpha\rho\pi\grave{o}\varsigma$, فراىس). V. sup. n. 39. sq. Many anonymous astrological works in foreign languages, but in Hebrew cha-racters (e. g. Vat. 245, 246.), have been probably only transcribed by Jews. It must, however, be borne in mind that " Astrologia" in earlier times was used also generally for astronomy. On the other hand the pretended astrological work of Farabi, in Cod. Paris. 382 (according to the Catalogus), is really the preface of SHEMTOB BEN ISAAC (1251) to his translation of the medical work of Zahrawi, where he reckons astrology amongst the subsidiary sciences of medicine. Indeed most astrological notices in Jewish MSS. belong to that category.

[84] See n. 21 a.

[Page 191. lin. 4. from bottom, instead of, "and whose influence," read " the influence of whom " (viz. of Petrus) was, &c. See Renan, pp. 238. 246.]

[85] Vat. in Wolf, i. 1692.

[86] Vat. 477. (Mai).

[87] Wolf. iii. 1502 d.

[88] Vide sup. § 5. n. 1. Thus e. g. RABBA (רבא, 3rd century) men-tions that the Persians called 10 " one " (חד), and thus knew the decimal system of arithmetic (Bechorot 60 a.; v. inf. n. 93.). Abraham Zacut (p. 52.) means by the words בעל מספר ותשבורת, that ELIEZER CHISMA was an able mathematician (Geiger, Zeitschr. vii. 26.; cf. D. Cassel, Encykl. s. v. Gematria; v. sup. n. 1. p. 351. infra); but Wolf., i. n. 315., misunderstands them, and makes Eliezer the author of a work תשבורת.

[89] The title " Mishna," in Emmanuel ben Jacob (MS. Tur. 68.), for the Propositions of Euclid is characteristic.

[90] Zunz, zur Gesch. p. 177. SAMSON OF SENS, the opponent of philosophy (§ 11.), doubts also the validity of geometrical theorems (he quotes חכמי המדות; cf. n. 1.), but is reproved by the recent authors Joseph Karo and Lipman Heller; see Zuckermann on the passage of Erubin, v. 5., in Frankel, Monatschr. iv. (1855, f. 156.).

[91] Zunz, zur Gesch. p. 535., names the authors (adde Cod. Taur. 70. ; cf. W. iii. n. 187 e., Mich. 527. ? MS. Warn. 20. f. 99. ; and cf. *Catal.* pp. 1086. 2004. ; a table of measures and coins in the Bible is printed in the Bible, ed. Ven. 1678 ; *Catal.* n. 594.), and draws from Jewish sources some valuable notices, forming a worthy supplement to Böckh's celebrated metrological work. But his complaints about the neglect of Jewish authorities have not prevented his being himself unnoticed by BERTHEAU in Ersch (see foot note, sup. p. 3.) ; and even Frankel's Notice (Monatschr. iv. 156.) on SAULCY, Recherches sur la Numismatique Jud., does not refer to Zunz.

[92] Terquem, Lit. bl. vi. 474. 494. (where the method of calculation of the doctors of Israel [not the " wise Israelites "] is quoted) ; Luzz. Zion, i. 16. ; conf. Zachot. 8 b., Berlin ed. His division is not that by the difference of 10, in Chasles (Comptes Rend. xvi. p. 172.). Allemano (Shaar haheshek, 12 a.) cites a passage of Ibn Ezra on צורות הודיות, which, however, does not seem to signify Indian ciphers (" figuræ Indorum " in Chasles [l. c. xvii. 143.] ; conf. Sprengel, Gesch. d. Med. ii. 338., and see the following note), but astrological figures. On the formula called " stratagem," which recurs in other literatures, see *Catal.* p. 681. ; dele " besides various other."

[93] On the dubious author, v. sup. § 13. n. 12. Against Saadja, he remarks in his Commentary to Jezira (in Dukes, Kontros, p. 75.), that the calculation of knuckles, intended for common intercourse, does not proceed farther than 10,000, the manner of noting this number being described by him (according to this Rödiger's article in the Jahresber. d. Deutsch. Morgenl. Gesellsch. 1845, 1846, p. 113., is to be supplied. Jellinek, Bet hamidr. iii. p. xxiii.., finds an allusion in the Hechalot, without referring to our essay). On the other hand, he remarks that it is easy to calculate on the table (פנקס) with Indian numbers (מנין בני הודו) larger sums by the combination of ten as unity. The Indians also have only nine signs (אותיות, p. 77., does not mean " letters "). On this subject he refers to his work on חשבון בני הודו (or הנדי ; conf. حساب الهندى, Arithmetic, Cod. Ar., Leyden, 1055 ; hence Landauer's reasoning, Lit. bl. vii. 121., loses ground). Since he thus does not know the existence of the zero (conf. Chasles, l. c. xvi. 1408), his work quoted under the title חסאב אלגובר בחשבון אנשי אלהינד (Zion, i. 47.) must treat of the Arabic " powder writing, Gobar," discovered by Sacy (vide Humboldt, Kosmos, ii. 456.). Our independent conjecture has been confirmed afterwards by Munk (Not. sur Aboulw. p. 51.), who gives the Hebrew translation מספר העפר. In another translation (now in the Bodl.) we read מספר האבק, " number of powder." Munk refers to his communication in Reinaud, Mémoire Géogr. &c. p. 399. ; but the author has not been able to consult this work.—With respect to the question which has of late been so much discussed, about the origin of the decimal notation and the so-called Arabian (Indian) numbers, it must still be remarked, that in the Algorism of JOH. HISPALENSIS, who was a born Jew and a translator from the Arabic (v. sup. n. 36. ; which Chasles, l. c. xvi. 1400., xvii. 147., leaves unnoticed ; conf. Von Humboldt, Kosmos, ii. 262.), the names " arba" (4) and " temenia" (8) (l. c. xvii. p. 148. ; according to which, Themeis, ib. p. 146., is to be

corrected) are to be derived from Arabic or Chaldee; and in the ἀριθμοὶ ἔνδικοι of the monk NEOPHYTOS (Proselyte?) the form for 4 is different (vide Humboldt, p. 456.).

94 Rossi, Wörterb. p. 82., Zunz, Geig. Zeitschr. iv. 189., are to be corrected according to the author's Index, p. 331.

95 MS. Mich. 429.; Uri, 448. 1.   JOSEPH BEN MOSES ZARPHATI, Vat. 397. 2.

96 [Page 192. last line.]   Ibn Ezra on Exod. (shorter recension), p. 71., ed. Prague; Maim. on Erub. i. 5. (where כת נהליה = جاهلية‎, Ignorant); conf. on ii. 5. Klajim. iii. 1.

§ 22.   Page 193.

1 Geschichte der Medicin (1st ed.).

2 Essai Hist. Lit. sur la Médecine des Arabes (Montpellier, 1805).

3 Vide e. g. inf. n. 61.   We cannot think that he understood the Hebrew.

4 P. 259.

5 P. 88.   Conf. Sprengel, ii. 482., on the avarice of the clergy. David Pomis (De Med. Hebr.) does not know of this objection; see in particular pp. 10. 71.

6 Gesch. d. Arab. Aerzte und Naturforscher (Gött. 1840).

7 His notices are repeated by CARMOLY in his *Histoire des Médecins Juifs* (inserted in the Revue Orientale, and also as a separate work, Bruxelles, 1844 [which ed. we quote]; in English by DUNBAR, Baltimore, 1844 [which we have never seen]; German extracts begun in the Kalendar and Jahrbuch für Israel, Vienna, 1854, p. 220., by M. Engel, who praises this work exceedingly for its erudition, "real critical spirit," &c.; but the promised continuation seems to have been wisely suppressed by the editors in the subsequent year), although Carm. quotes only Ibn Abi Oseibia, for instance, p. 36., about the death of JONA IBN GANNAH in 1121, where the Arabic author gives no date at all; and his own statement ("on sait"!), about 1045, has no authority whatever (see *Catal.* p. 1413.).   That Carmoly, in this, as in all his writings, heaps together carelessness, plagiarisms, and inventions, especially as amplifications and exaggerations, has been sufficiently shown by Geiger (nn. 16. 34.) and others.   Moreover, he brings too much non-medical literature into his book.   All those who are themselves not well acquainted with Jewish investigations still need this warning (as we have shown in the example of Engel).   His falsifications, for the purpose of plagiarism, extend even to the *titles* and *years* of his own essays or "notices," which the reader, if he is at all able to get them, will find different from the quotations of Carmoly in his later writings (cf. e. g. l. c., with Revue, i. 178., Lit. bl. ii. 584., and Annal. ii. 225., with Journ. Asiat. 1831, p. 139.).   From Wüstenfeld and Carmoly, J. BRÜG (De Med. Illustr. Jud. qui inter Arab. vixerunt, Halle, 1843) has compiled most uncritically, under the guidance of Fürst (vide *Catal.* p. 1415.).

8 V. inf. examples of mistakes, the extent of which necessitated the

omission of many notices, although the author has been able since to gain some more correct information from MSS. of the Bodleiana. Unfortunately העתק نَقَلَ signifies both to translate and to transcribe.

⁹ See n. 25.

¹⁰ The influence of the laws relating to slaughter and forbidden foods can scarcely (or at any rate only for zoology and zootomy) be taken into account. Thus e. g. Israeli (in Sprengel, ii. 359.) designates pork as good food; Maimonides (Ker. Chem. iii. 13., and the author's remark in the Oesterr. Blätt. 1845, p. 443.) might recommend it to the sultan, if it was not forbidden to a Muhammedan. The contrary is rare, e. g. from the sixteenth century, Ker. Chem. vii. 124., cf. also החלוץ, ii. 31. sq. We must mention here the learned anon. Arabic essay on *Cattle-killing* in the Bodl. Library, already quoted (supra, passim). The Jewish way of cattle-killing has been recently, in a German medical journal (Medic. Jahrbücher, 1855), criticised on modern physiological principles, and a reform proposed. But those who start only with the purpose of getting healthy food forget entirely the other point, viz. the moral influence of the manner of killing upon the man who kills. This point of view ought to have also been brought into account by the recent English censors, who speak of the tormenting of animals.

¹¹ Saadja (iv. 4. f. 32 [second of that number] b., ed. Amst.) and Jehuda Halevi (v. Brecher's and D. Cassel's Introd. to Kusari) quote anatomy (נתוח, חתוך).

¹² Maimonides, himself a physician, does not like the philosophy of the physicians from Galen to Israeli; and indeed apostasy gained the greatest number of recruits from the class of physicians, but their station in life must also be taken into account.

¹³ The general dogmatism did not oppose the use of physicians (see different sentiments on physic, &c., in Dukes, Blumenl. p. 32., and Spruchk. p. 13., cf. Ibn Ezra on Exod. xx. p. 59. short recension). There is no trace of excessive modesty, e. g. against the operation of the stone, as among the Arabians (Amoreux, p. 111.). Sprengel (ii. 285.) asserts that the doctrine of torments in the grave, so pernicious to anatomy, came from the Jews; but the oldest Jewish authority which mentions it is Saadja (933). See also Hammer, Gemälde-saal, i. 40.; Wien. Jahrb. C., p. 113.; conf. also Lit. bl. v. 777. and *Catal.* p. 576. no. 3527. Another impediment, the doctrine of resurrection, is alluded to by Phocylides, according to Bernays, p. vii. On the aversion of the Arabians to anatomy, see also V. Humboldt, Kosmos, ii. 254.

¹⁴ Sprengel (ii. 270.), referring to Benjamin of Tudela, who, however, does not speak of *Jewish* medical schools.

¹⁵ Sprengel (ii. 400.) here also refers to Benjamin (see ii. p. 29. ed. Asher), who, however, speaks only of the medical schools of the Christians and of learned Jews in general. On the other hand Clifton (in Amoreux, p. 255., Carm. p. 29.) names one ELISA, teacher of the Hebrew; cf. Raumer, Gesch. der Hohenstaufen, iii. 482., quoted by S. Cassel, Ersch, s. ii. vol. xxvii. p. 164. n. 27. On the subject of *rhymes* n. 17.

¹⁶ Astruc in Amoreux, p. 259.; Cuvier, Hist. d. Sciences Nat. i.

387., in Humboldt, Kosmos, ii. 450. n. 3.; Steinschneider, Lit. bl. iv. 6.; Die Juden in Oesterreich (Leipzig, 1844), vol. ii. p. 92.; TRUSEN, Darstellung der bibl. Krankh. (Posen, 1843), p. 69., and see inf. n. 39.   On Carmoly's inventions (p. 35.) see Geiger, Zeitschr. v. 463. 467.

16 a It is probably ABU'L FADHL's Pharmacopœia which is made use of in the Raudhat el Atthar of Ibn Hadji (Cod. Arab. Flor. 242.). Maimonides was one of the three men, to meet whom Abdollatif journeyed to Egypt.

17 See § 20. n. 11.; similar to those of Salerno, v. Cod. Paris. Hebr. 424.

18 Some by an anonymous Spaniard on fever, Cod. Leyd. 755., who copied in 1292, and composed according to Avicenna (we owe these specialities to Rev. Prof. Kuenen of Leyden).

19 Cod. Leyd. 763.; cf. inf. n. 31.?

20 Wolf. i. 384.

21 Sprengel, ii. 258. (according to Freind?); Grässe, ii. 1. 548.; Carm. p. 17.; from a mistake of Abulfar. p. 126., where we read " Refert Ebn Jaljal Andolosenus Maserjewaihum Medicum Basorensem lingua Syrum, religione Judæum fuisse, &c., in ling. Arab. &c., transtulisse !"   Ibn Djoldjol is the renowned Muhammedan author.

22 Not from the Hebrew, see the author's corrections of Wüstenfeld and Carmoly in Frankel, Zeitschr. iii. 404. n. 7.   Sprengel (ii. 266.) speaks also of an Arabic translation made from the Hebrew, which the Jews had previously translated from the Greek.   See, however, supra, § 21. n. 10.

23 Catal. pp. 1113—1124.

24 Constantinus is not a Jew (Encykl. ii. vol. xxiv. p. 218.; and his Viaticum is not a work of Israeli but of Ibn ol Gezzar, pupil of Israeli), but he quotes Jewish authorities (see Catal. p. 1123.; inf. n. 34.).

25 Munk, Annal. iii. 84.

26 Carmoly (pp. 59. 67.) makes two persons, different in name and age, out of the same.   On his inventions about IBN AL NAKID see Catal. p. 1933.

27 A correct and probably complete list of genuine and spurious medical works ascribed to Maimonides is first given in Catal. p. 1917. sq., where adde inf. n. 39. and a MS., recently purchased, in Bodl.

28 Conf. Ibn Djoldjol, Encykl. ii. Bd. 15. p. 30.

29 Sacy ad Abdallat. p. 497.   On the mistakes of Carmoly see Th. Cohn, Lit. bl. ii. 649., and on this treatise conf. Wüstenf. § 242.; it is also mentioned by Abraham ben David, Emuna Rama, p. 49.

30 He would appear to be the unknown author of the MS. Escur. 888. 1. (Casiri), where mention is made of a cure of fever by cold water.

31 Escur. 826. 2., " teacher " (Grässe, ii. 1. 553.) is incorrect. Upon anno 975 (!), and other inventions in Carm. p. 32., cf. n. 19.?

31 a Catal. p. 1120. (Wolf. i. n. 1939.?).   ISAAC BEN MISSIM HASAKEN (ante 1342); Vat. 361.

32 Paris, 400. — The work, copied for the physician ABU ISHAK JEHUDA BEN ASTILAG (?), 1387 (Cod. Escur. 868.), is perhaps the Aphorisms of Maimonides?

[33] Carmoly (p. 29.) says that nothing is known of his medical works and makes Sab. a pupil of the school of Salerno, like "Abulhakim," who taught Arabic (Bart. i. 29., Wolf. i. 32.), and FARRAGUTH (p. 82.; see inf. after n. 37.), and others. Jellinek makes him practise 40 years in Modena, not observing that "Modin" in Biscioni must be a typographical error for "Modim," and this a mistake for אורים given by F. Lasinio. On these and other mistakes see *Catal.* s. v. p. 2233.

[34] *Catal.* p. 1123. On Carmoly's plagiarisms and distortions see Geig. Zeitschr. v. 463. 467. To these probably belongs also the misplacement of "JOCHANAN JARCHUNI" into the thirteenth century and to Montpellier (p. 91.; see Ersch. s. ii. vol. 31. p. 83. n. 17.). His recent statements (Lit. bl. xii. 372.) are partly more correct. Our view of the origin of the book (entirely neglected by Jellinek, Donolo, p. vi., cf. Bet hamidrasch, iii. p. xxxii., and sup. § 13. n. 3.) is confirmed by the name ASAF BEN BARACHIA ('Αριψ [sic] υἰὸς 'Ιρακίου in the Greek Viaticum, not explained by Daremberg), whom the Muhammedan legends know as the author of some works; see *Catal.* s. v. Salomo b. David.— The physician and grammarian Koreish (in Ewald, Beitr. p. 121.) understands by רפואות 'ס (as it must be called) medical literature generally; like Maimonides, in a passage (Deot. iv. 21.) which has been repeatedly mistaken for a special quotation (*Catal.* p. 1870.).

[35] See § 5. n. 25.; conf. § 13. n. 3.

[35 a] According to Wüstenfeld; on the other hand, Flügel (Encykl. sect. ii. vol. xxii. p. 225.) admits only one, viz. the younger.

[35 b] In the Encykl. he is twice treated of by Flügel, once as Djezla (sect. ii. vol. xiv. p. 186.), and again as Djozla (sect. ii. vol. xxiv. p. 201.).

[36] In Carmoly the family Ibn Zuhr, as also ISHAK BEN AMRAN (who is divided into three persons! see *Catal.* p. 1115.) and the Syrian JOSHUA IBN NUN (conf. Annal. ii. 96.) appear as Jews.

[37] *Catal.* p. 1308. (Frankel, Zeitschr. iii. 279.).
[Page 197. FARADJ: see author's notice in Zeitschr. der Deutsch Morgenl. Gesellsch. viii. 548., to which we must further add that the Arabic author of the "Tacuinus" is named in some MSS. Ibn Botlan (Wüstenfeld § 133. ed. Argent. 1531), not Ibn Djezla. Faradj also translated from the Arabic (probably of Honein) Galen's "De Medicinis Experimentatis" (unknown in Greek); the authorities (consisting partly in Latin MS. in Oxford) will be given in the Additions to *Catal.* p. 979.]

[38] MS. Uri, 440. Wolfius, iv. p. 861., translates "ad mandatum Friderici;" but באוריות is "in the stables."

[39] He translated (or ordered translations of) some Hebrew works out of Hebrew, for instance (1299) the Astronomy of his colleague PROPHATIUS (sup. p. 187., *Catal.* p. 2113.) and MAIMONIDES on Antidotes to Poison (sup. p. 193.); he is named in the Latin MS. of Christ-Church, no. cxxv. The year 1306 in our text was taken from the Hebrew translator; if our view of the work is correct, it would be Averroes' Commentary on Ibn Sina's poem 1287 (Renan, p. 172.), perhaps itself translated out of the Hebrew? (cf. Renan, p. 196.).

[40] Erroneously "Barnabas" (Vat. 366, 1. [conf. MS. Munic. 288. 1.]

Rossi, Cod. Lat. 59. 1.; conf. 59. 3.!) and "Ranellus" (Biscioni, p. 153.).

[41] So are to be corrected the names of authors on the subject of the plague (Catal. Vien. clviii.; cf. also Zunz, Catal. 1850, p. 12.). In Janus, 1852, vol. ii. p. 401., the Hebrew translation is not mentioned, and generally no notice is taken of the Hebrew authorities.

[42] Carm. p. 108.

[43] Par. 422. 2. (on Epidemics), Sprengel, ii. 538., names two distinct persons; conf. also Grässe, ii. 2. 594. 646. Thus the date could be determined from the Hebrew translations; cf. also Janus, ib. p. 419. (A. D. 1377–1410).

[44] Par. 420.; Rossi, Cod. 1281. Opp. 1646 Q.; the Latin work is in Cod. Lat. clxxi. of New-College in Oxford (Catal. p. 67., where Coxe supposes "Salernitanus" [Jo. Nic. Rogerius]). It is certainly not the Chirurgy of Roger of Parma, whom Sprengel, in the Index, confuses with Roger son of Robert Guiscard. Hence the notice of Carmoly, Itiner. pp. 330. 347., seems one of his inventions. On the Hebrew translator see inf. n. 52.

[45] Hebr. ס' הניזע (MS. of the late Dr. Schönberg at Berlin) concludes with the remark that it is called צירקא אשתנ"ציאה among Christians. The author has found it identical with the Latin ed. 1497. Biscioni (p. 163., conf. Wolf. i. 1381.) confuses it with the Halacha work of Meir of Trinquetaille (vide § 9.). Some doubts and errors in Amoreux (p. 98.) and Sprengel (ii. 463.) must be removed; conf. Grässe, ii. 2. 536. 569.

[46] The title ס' נהרות in Pasini, p. 80. (Zunz, Geig. Zeitschr. iv. 191.), is a mistake; and probably JEHUDA IBN CASTIEL (or CASPIEL) was not a translator, but a copyist.

[47] We have omitted JOSEPH KOLON, because he is not the author of MSS. Opp. 1138, 1139. fol., whose main part is the anon. היושר (see Ersch. s. ii. vol. xxxi. p. 83. n. 16.)

[48] Par. 420. Conf. MENAHEM ZEBI BEN NATHANEL מוזון at Sinigaglia (1474), translator of a compendium of logic.

[49] There were several authors of that name, and not all Jews; older quotations (e. g. in Razi's Antidotarium) refer probably to one of the Syrians of that name (Wüstenf. § 28. sq.).

[50] De Rossi, Cod. 1053. ("ad mag. Gabteir," perhaps Gauthier, according to Zunz), confounds the renowned Liturgist with him; see Catal. p. 1228.

[51] MS. Michael.; see Index Auctorum.

[52] The MS. Catal. of Opp. attributes to him the translation of Roger Brocarde (n. 44.) without sufficient reason; his name occurs only f. 157., before a new tract.

[53] See Oesterreichische Blätter, 1845, p. 288.

[54] Opp. 1139 F.

[54a] Gagnier and Uri, 422., could not read the name which they spell Latik.

[55] Pasini, Cod. 80. 3., where "Cohen" is more than probably a mistake for Natan; in Cod. Opp. 1139 F. the name is corrupted.

[56] Carm. p. 108.

[57] Wolf. 1727. A similar abundance of authorities in MS. Geig.

Zeitschr. iii. 448. n. 49. and some other anonymous MSS.; the authorship of Natan is rather doubtful.

[58] See *Catal.* s. v. Carmoly knows nothing of his medical works.

[59] Rossi, 1168. Carmoly (p. 106.) again knows nothing of the medical works themselves.

[60] MS. Mich. 772. 5.; Vienna, clx.; Wolf. i. 730. (a copyist A. D. 1440, Opp. 938 F.).

[61] Amoreux, p. 200., although stating that the work is Hebrew (p. 52.), would identify him with Abu Daud el Antaki, who wrote in Arabic.

[62] See the author's article Joseph ben Isaac in Ersch, s. ii. vol. xxxi. pp. 82, 83.

[63] MS. Leyd. Leg. Warn. 40.

[64] Wolf. iii. iv. n. 455. (נלב), whence Castro, i. p. 355. Carmoly (p. 121.) adds, "in the year 1450"; cf. Wolf. iii. n. 1883 b. (קלב), i. 439. (נאלאף); קלוף in Opp. 1139 F. f. 72. is Khalaf (خلف) Ibn Abbas, renowned under the name of Zahrawi (sup. p. 197.).

[65] Carm. (p. 131.) confuses the place. See Assem. Cod. 360. 366, 367. and Wolfius, who gives the year 1478.

[66] See the Art. Joseph ben Isaac (l. c. in n. 62.).

[67] Vat. 372, 1.; conf. 368, 1., Wolf. i. 2047. The name אספריאל (Esperial?) appears in later times.

[68] Sup. § 12. n. 3. As "Physics" (the nature of bodies) it belongs to Philosophy (Sprengel, ii. 408.). Humboldt (Kosmos, ii. 248. 282.) considers the Arabians as founders of Physics proper; still this appears especially in the form of alchemy.

[69] Penini, Defence against Aderet.

[70] Jourdain, p. 201. See Humboldt's reference to the study of nature properly so called (Kosmos, ii. p. 31. n. 51.), so much the more strange as he founds his argument on Jourdain's conclusions respecting the interdict of the works of Aristotle (sup. § 11.).

[71] Vide § 17. n. 23. Pills of Elieser "in טוך" are mentioned in MS. Scaliger. 15. f. 32.

[72] Thus e. g. Sam. Ibn Tibbon (in 1200) tells of the rise of a hill in England; cf. *Catal.* p. 1014.

[Page 201. line 12. JACOB BEN REUBEN'S work, as the author has found out since, is a translation of the renowned poem of Marbod, Bishop of Rennes (ob. A. D. 1123); hence the king is not Alexander.]

[72a] With respect to medicine v. Amoreux, p. 26.

[73] See § 13. n. 7. Amoreux (p. 26.) ascribes the use of astrology in medicine to the *Arabians*, while Sprengel (ii. 415.) asserts that he has found nothing of the kind. Some older traces of Arabian magic might be found in Sprengel, pp. 129. 142. Of the sorceries of the Arabians, see Ibn Zarzah (not סראסא) quoted by Allemanno (Schaar hacheshek, 1 b.). Joseph ben Elieser (on Exod. xx.) also appeals to Indian and Arabian images and talismans; and Samuel Ibn Tibbon introduced the Arabic term. techn. ביהון. The history of these superstitious "sciences" must of course begin in the former period, regarding which valuable contributions are given by ELIASBERG (whose work, however, is only known to the author through the notice in

Lit. bl. v. 691., xi. 579), and BRECHER (p. 276. n. 26.), whose epistle in Kochbe Jizchak, as well as the notes of J. L. MISES to Del Medigo, touches upon that subject.   Treatises for our period are not known to the author, neither *has he as yet been able to work out the materials collected,* the subject being alike difficult and interesting in its close connexion with general literature.   We must confine our observations to a short notice on the writers and works belonging to this branch:

a. The parts and branches of magic and witchcraft are given in the encyclopædical work of JEHUDA IBN BOLAT (p. 260.).

b. A *general* dissertation on witchcraft was composed by GEDALJA IBN JAHJA (p. 251.); here belongs also the Responsum on practical Kabbala ascribed to HAI, remarkable for the sober and sound principles contained in it; also Ibn Ezra and others, even the pseudo-prophet ABRAHAM ABULAFIA, condemn those who pretend to do wonders with the name of God (Tetragrammaton).   Comp. MS. Vatic. 245 [2].

c. Individual branches, or superstitions, are illustrated by several authors.   Johanan Allemanno quotes a " chapter" of NACHMANIDES on *Necromancy* (in its narrower sense); cf. n. 77.   An essay of ABRAHAM BEN ISAAC LEVI of Gerona, on the " night women" (נשים הליליות), composed A. D. 1380 (*Catal.* p. 693.), has been discovered by the author in the Bodl.   According to Carmoly (p. 104.), JACOB OF TOLEDO (conf. Zunz, Syn. Poesie, p. 40 A. 1348 ; cf. a correspondent of Arnold de Villanova in De Castro, ii. 743., and an older monk of that name in Jourdain, p. 113.) wrote on the evil eye of the magicians. MEIR BEN ELEAZAR wrote on the evil eye in general (two years before the French exile), from the medical point of view, and knows of no predecessor on the subject (omitted by Uri, 464.).   The astrological medicine of Arnold de Villanova and others was disseminated by translators.

d. Several older titles of tracts treating of the practical Kabbala have been mentioned in § 13. n. 7.; a special branch is formed by the *use* (שימוש) of sacred books for different purposes, as therapeutic, auguristic, &c., for instance, the use of Psalms (שימוש תהלים, see *Catal.* no. 4066., and inf. n. 81.).   Moses de Leon (השם, pref.) mentions also שימושי התורה and שימושי רבה וזוטא (cf. § 13. n 7.)   Analogous use of Koran and Psalms, &c., is to be met with amongst Muhammedans and Christians (see n. 81.)   שימוש of stars, &c., see Zarzah, f. 101 d.

[74] They are also quoted by Abraham Ibn Ezra (on Exodus, ii. 10.); and comp. Zarzah, f. 102.; the authorities in the author's Fremdsprachl. Elem. p. 10. n. 20.; conf. Lit. bl. vii. 233. (the explanation of טוטפות as spectacles !) ; Encykl. ii. vol. xv. p. 32.; Wüstenfeld, § 96.; Sprenger, De Orig. Med. Arab. p. 8. Bötticher (Zeitschr. d. d. m. Gesellsch. vii. 408.) has found in the Arab. MS. parts of Apollonius (see note 77.).   Here, probably, also belongs the work De Agriculturâ, said to be translated from the Chaldee (Syriac?) into Arabic by " Abulhacen," and into Spanish by JEHUDA [BEN MOSES KOHEN], physician to Alfonso XII. (?), if the whole notice is not a mistake (see *Catal.* p. 1361.).

[75] *Catal.* s. v. Salomo b. D. ; cf. note 74. above, and note 77. below.
[76] Uri, 442.[2]·, certainly the same in Casiri, i. 403.
[77] Uri, 434.; cf. Wolf. iv. pp. 841, 842., and *Catal.* pp. 1402, 1403.

To the same class belong the many works on magic, alchemy, &c., under different titles, especially those of *Raziel* (see § 13. n. 3.), *Clavicula,* &c., forged at different periods up to the 18th century, under the name of King SOLOMON! A list of more than thirty titles of such tracts (partly still extant) is given in *Catal.* s. v., where the author thinks he has shown that even the very few of them extant in Hebrew (Raziel is not to be confounded with the printed book of that name), or quoted by Jews (since the 13th century), do not originate in old *Hebrew* works, but spring especially from *Arabic* and *Christian* sources, a very important circumstance for the history of that pseudo-literature. To these sources belong two works, both known to JOHANAN ALLEMANNO, the industrious and zealous collector of everything connected with Solomon's supposed supernatural or metaphysical wisdom. One is the Hebrew translation of a magic work of Abu Aflah al-Saracosti (this is certainly the correct spelling), partly still extant in MS. Munich. 214.; the other is the translation of Apollonius (sup. n. 75.), whom the Arabs call " Belinus," and whom hence some catalogues, &c., confound with Plinius. — To Galen was ascribed an astrological and pneumatical work (conf. § 11. n. 22., and *Catal.* p. 1703.). The *Book of the Moon* (ס׳ הלבנה), on necromancy, quoted by Nachmanides (Rapop., Chananel, n. 15.), is perhaps the magic work of Abu'l Kasim Maslamah al-Medjriti (of Madrid, ob. A. D. 1007; cf. Wüstenfeld, § 122.), of which certainly a Hebrew translation exists in the Cod. Munich. 214., although several other works of that kind treat especially of the twenty-eight *"mansiones"* (מחנות) of the moon; for instance, that extant under the name of Hermes (who is considered the same as Enoch), in the Latin MS. of Christchurch, 145. (p. 45. of Coxe's Catal.), which is certainly of Arabic origin; (probably also Galen's Comm. on Hermes' Lib. Secretorum, in the same codex, and comp. the German MS. of Lipsic, n. 734. p. 193., of Naumann's Catal., Hermetis *Hebræi* Geheimnisse von deren Stunden des Tags, &c.; also the Latin printed book of Hermes "de Judiciis et Signif. Stellarum beibeniarum" [i. e. trepidantium, viz. fixed stars] which is extant in Hebr. translation, see *Catal.* p. 2144.). *All this leads us to suppose the same sources; if we find anonymous quotations* of such works in authors of this period, for instance, the *Book of Talismans* (we read טלסמאות instead of 'טלמסו, in Ibn Zarzah, f. 21.), quoted by David Ibn Bilia, &c. Dukes (Lit. bl. viii. 472.) doubts whether the book פרי of Ptolomæus is still extant; but it is the Arabic ‏ثمرة‎. The title of the *Centiloquium,* and the Comm. ascribed to Ibn Rodhwan in the printed Latin translation, is the same which the Hebrew translator KALONYMOS (1314) ascribes to Abu Djaafer Ahmed ben Jusuf ben Ibrahim. The error of Wenrich (p. 236.) will be corrected in the Catal. of the Leyden MS. on Cod. Scalig. 14.

[78] Cf. Cicero, De Divin. i. 3 —The 9th chapter of the Talmudical tract Berahot is almost an oneirocriticism; on the book Razim, see § 13. n. 3. SAMUEL BEN CHOFNI, in expounding the dream of Jacob, entered at large upon oneirocriticism; which is blamed by Ibn Ezra. The monography אגרת החלום of SHEMTOB PALQUERA, only known by his own

quotation, was probably philosophical, according to the principles which the Arabs and Jews drew from Aristotle's *De Somno et Vigiliâ* (part of the Parva Naturalia, called De Sensu et Sensato). The impostor Botarel gives a formula for dreams, which he asserts to have been proved by Saadja and many other authorities. In the following period monographies were composed on dreams by Moses Almosnino (Spanish) and (A.D. 1557) Gedalja Ibn Jahja (not extant) ; and, before both, there was an interesting one by Solomon Almoli (cir. 1515), who names as his authorities —1. Talmud ; 2. Hai Gaon (see n. 79.) ; 3. the tract "ascribed to" Solomon Isaki (Rashi) ; 4. Joseph הצדיק, which means the Patriarch Joseph (see *Catal.* p. 1542.), Daniel the prophet, and different others, some not Jews. With respect to the works ascribed to patriarchs and prophets, we may suppose the same source as that stated in n. 77. Indeed, A. Bland, in his essay *On Muhammedan Interpretation of Dreams* (in Journ. of the Roy. Asiat. Soc. 1854, vol. xvi. p. i.), points out as authorities, amongst others, Daniel (p. 123.), Joseph (p. 161.), and the Jews Hay ben Akhtab (perhaps hence Hai Gaon ?), Kaab ben Ashraf, and Musa ben Jacub. The author has had no opportunity to inquire about the Latin *Salomonis et Danielis Somnia*, Ven. 1516, which, however, is not of Hebrew origin.

79 *Catal.* p. 1029. ; and see the preceding note.

80 See, however, *Catal.* p. 2218. Cf. לזקק הכסף, in Wolf. ii. p. 1299., with Cod. Urb. 26. ? Ibn Ezra also scorns Alchemy.

81 Vide Emmanuel, Mechabb. p. 197. Wolf. (i. 211.) translated Sabbatai's article incorrectly ; cf. *Catal.* p. 1308. — Midrash Threni (Jalk. on Ez. xxi. 26.) speaks of the *Arabian* method of augury from the liver. Cf. Bamidbar Rabba, cap. 19., טייר, and the parallel in Pesikta ; cf. Kimhi, ad i. Reg. 4. 32. ap. Losius, Biga Dissert. p. 21., and Landau, s. v., who finds here a trace of *Ordeals*. — We have mentioned above, p. 191., some astrologers by profession who were of rank ; some others were renowned as soothsayers, &c. On Moses Cohen see the Resp. attributed to Hai, p. 56. On Abraham קבסי (Wolf. i. 143.), vide Ker. Chem. ii. 40., vi. 191. ; Annal. ii. 248. (a Joshua ben קבסי, Jer. Pesach. cap. 6.).—The use of Holy Scripture for soothsaying (like the Koran, vide Sale, Introd. cap. iii.), is founded on the old custom of asking children for verses of the Bible, vide Lit. bl. viii. 809. ; and cf. n. 73 d.—The augury by arrows belongs to the Arabians ; conf. Opp. 1175 g.

82 Arab. MS. in Hebrew characters, Flor. 537. (in Evod. Assem. and Bisc. in Oct.) ; cf. preface of Biscion. in fol. p. xxxvi., and Abraham Zacut, f. 26 b., ed. Amst.

83 Jeh. Tibbon (transl. of Emunot, v. introd.) has introduced the Arabic word (cf. Zarzah, f. 92. ; Allemanno, f. 2 a.). Ibn Chisdai (translation of the Ethics of Chasali, p. 124.) has the Hebrew. According to Rapop. (Nathan, n. 32. p. 40.), Sherira is the first Gaon who attaches any value to Chiromancy ; the passage quoted belongs to the Responsum of Hai (perhaps also to that of Sherira), which the author has discovered and published in Ha-techija of S. Sachs, p. 42., and is in close connexion with the " divine physiognomy," if we may so speak ; see *Catal.* p. 533. On a cheiromantic tract ascribed to Me-

NAHEM RECANATI (omitted by Uri), see *Catal.* p. 1734.; the source is said to be an Indian author.   Also in Uri, 496. f. 446., there is an anonymous דיני שורות הכף.   As late as JACOB BEN MARDOCHAI (1706), Aristotle is the pretended authority for Chiromancy; and indeed the principles of physiognomy go back as far.   On the physiognomist SABBATAI HAJEWANI (ante 1263), v. *Catal.* p. 2238.   On Maimonides' censure of the physiognomical sayings of Ben Sira, vide Spruchb. f. Jüd. Schulen by Horwitz and Steinschneider, p. 102. n.

[84] Vide § 20. n. 34 a.

CORRECTIONS AND ADDITIONS.

☞ [*Unimportant and easily recognizable errors are left to be corrected by the intelligent reader; the hebrew printing errors are corrected in the Index.*

We have also given here some references to such correcting *notes,* to which no direct reference is given in the text.]

Page 48 lin. penult. History, read Histor*ies.*
— 49 l.5, below *d,* r. p.53.
— 72 footnote after „bloss" adde: *or Hebr.* בלא זאת .
— 74 l. 10: referred to by, r.which is considered to be a compend. of AHRON KOHEN's *Orhot Hayim* (composed about 1340); Ahron was of Majorca, according to a recent essay of Luzzatto. The older Ahron Kohen of *Lunel* is a fiction, see *Catal.* p.1689.
— 86 l.16 „like the last" r. *like Anatoli himself.*
— 89 l.4 „1332" r. 1232.
— 92 l.4 from bottom (see notes p.360) r. PROPHIAT TIBBON ...1306.
— 96 l.5 after collection adde: *at that time at Hannover.*
— 98 l.2 TAISH leg. JAISCH.
— 100 l.13 fr. bot. after ancient, adde: estimation of.
— 104 l.11 fr. bot.: by the author(?). Should it be HILLEL BEN SAMUEL, and the Paris MS. only an extract of דרבן? See the Hebr. passage in Litbl. l. c.
— 107 l.3 fr. bot.: old book Raziel attributed to Salomon(?). See however the inquisitions quoted p.371.
— 110 l.3 ELHANAN, cf. *Catal.* p.2096.
— 111 l. ult. and p.111 l.1–3; the passage has become a little confused; SHEMTOB wrote in 1325 at Safet the most interesting (and perhaps latest) of his works: ISAAC BEN TODROS lived probably about 1305 in Spain, when also ISAAC BEN SAMUEL of ACCO was there (see p.113,115). New researches about these three authors see in *Catal.* s. v. Schemtob Ibn Gaon, who was also to be mentioned as supercommentator on Nachmanides, as well as JOSHUA IBN SHOEIB (p.115). In two MSS., the one anonymous, the other erroneously inscribed JOEL Ibn Shoeib (both recently purchased in Bodl.), we found Ibn (and in one also *Abraham!*) Ezra instead of EZRA (p.109); hence the conjecture in note 29 p.307 gains a solid basis. Naftali Treves mentiones „ben" Ezra between the „Kabbalists" Nachmanides and Shemtob!

Page 114 l.5 fr. bot. The same circumstance occasioned MOSES DE LEON to write his work *ha-Shem*.

— 116 l.12. Our misgiving has, happily, not been quite confirmed, if we have not been mistaken by a private report, that the *French* government has got some old Karaitic MSS. from Sebastopol. We have not heard anything the like from England, although we know of a private letter having been directed from, and to, a Reverend gentleman of that country, to that purpose.

— 119 l. ult SUTA r. SITA.

— 124 l.14 fr. bot. 1405 r. 1415.

— 126 l.6 & 4 fr. bot. see p.317.

— 127 l.10 other authors, adde: *of Pelemics*. The relation of CHAJJIM GALIPAPO however was inserted into his Comm. on tract. Semachot, but has been omitted by the writer of the recently purchased Bodl. MS.

— 128 l.12 fr. bot. before Maimon. adde: ABRAHAM BEN DAVID.

— 130 l.9 v. p.319.

— — l. ult.: MATATJA BEN MOSES [Jizhari?] wrote in rhyming prose against Muhammedism and Christianism (אחיטוב וצלמון).

— 133 l.19: ornamental lettres, r. *ornaments of the letters;* cf. p.323 n.22.

— 135 l.11 fr. bot. 1169 r. 19169.

— 140 l.16 adde BENJAMIN BEN JEHUDA of Rom (about 1300?), whose tract is printed (see *Catal.* p.1840, according to which the query of Fürst, Litbl. 1849 p.431, is to be answered).

— 144 l.2 ELAM r. ELEM.

— — l.16 fr. bot. IRANI r. TRANI.

— 145 l.5 fr. bot. instaed of arrangement r. *part of this essay.*

— 151 l.13 fr. bot. 1260 r. 1612.

— — l. ult. after recur r. *mostly every seventh distichon.*

— 153 l.16 אבן leg. בן .

— — l.17 „prayers with music" r. *melodical prayers.*

— — l.18 he, see p 336: GABIROL.

— 155 lin. penult., instead of: which obtain etc., r. *who have but little favoured the synagogue with their compositions* (the author alluded to HALEVI, MEYERBEER and others, and would by no means say, that the synagogue had any objection to their compositions!).

— 167 l.2 SAMUEL B. SOLOMON belongs to the *Commentators,* see *Catal.* s. v.

— 168 l.7: 1449 r. 1466, see Catal. of the Leyden MSS.

— 171 l.3 Karlin r. בן חרטון (corr. *Catal.* p.1897) wrote a rhytmical paraphrase of the Moreh.

Page 172 l.5 fr. bot IBN SIRA r. BEN S.
— 183, *different emendations v. p.*355.
— 184 l.16 Meriti r. *Medjriti.*
— — l.13 fr. bot. Alph. x., *thither belongs the additional passage p.*185 *lin.*2.
— 185 l.13 r. 1123-42 (v. p.357 n.45) and אלקושי.
— 186 l.9 fr. bot. movement of, adde: the *equinox* or *fixed stars,* or „*octava sphaera*" (cf. p. 357 n.52).
— 189 l.16-19, see p.360 n.70.
— 190 l.7 1465 r. 1461.
— 196 l.18 Izaigh r. *Szaigh* or *Ssaigh.*
— 197 l.4 fr. bot. 1457 r. 1451, cf. p.849 n.41.
— 199 l.12 IS. LAT. BEN JEHUDA etc., r. BEN JAACOB in Provence, probably the same as mentioned p.77 n.12 (A.1372)
— 201 l.12 see p.369.
— 203 end of the § Feischer l. *Fleischer.*
— 208 l.13 fr. bot. *dele*: his teachers; his teacher refered only to BARUCH (also in *Catal.* p.864 David Ibn Jahja is erroneously said teacher of W.).
— 212 l.18 fr. bot. „in a notice of a parody" is a mistake: the parody forms only the mottos of the chapters; and is probably composed by ELIA MAGISTRATOS (=PARNAS?).
— 216 l.19 "key", meaning indeed a mere *Index.*
— 219 l.14 fr. bot. before 1622 r. 1556.
— — l.8 — 1639-1664 r. 1663-1675.
— 222 l.20: 1675 is the year of print, the author *ob.* 1671.
— 232 l. antepenult. commentary, adde: *on the Psalms.*
— 240 l. ult. 1762 r. 1746 (when Solomon died).
— 251 l.12 fr. bot. down to 1587, r. 1553, the year of composition is 1583 (*Catal.* p.2403).
— 262 l. ult. Pereira r. *Peiresc.*

NOTES.

— 274 n.71: end Ta, r. 7a.
— 275 n.25 r. *Jew. authors claim even more against the neglect.*
— 279 n.54 l.7 margin, r. *space* or *time.*
— 281 n.82. Lately B. BEER has published a monography on the Book of Jubilees.
— 286 l.5 adde: LUZZATTO, *Il Giudaismo* I,42.
— 295 n.29 (neglected). Cod. 1704Q. f.130 contains a solemn abjuration of those parts of the Moreh, which might contradict the tradition, dated 29. Tebet 5227.
— 297 n.8 l. penult.: ben Said, r. Ssaid, see p.355 n.29.
— 300 The work of LUZZATTO is not printed in Paris but *Gorice* (Görz).

Page 305 l.5 before: it is, adde: *where* (viz. in the rhyme) at the beginning of the tract we read: „I David ben Jehuda;" Tabjomi seems indeed Jomt. Mühlhausen, who might be the real author or the retractator (*Catal.* p.2415).

— 309 to P.114; see also *Catal.* p.2092.

— 313 n.32 end, adde: *and to whom they have been afterwards acknowledged by* Jost, Culturgeschichte p.112 n.11.

— 315 n.11, adde *Litbl.* X,570.

— 320 l.5 fr. bot.: Tuynboll, r. *Juynboll.*

— 322 n.14, adde: *Litbl.* X,389.

— 330 n.5 the german words ought to have been translated: ANAN's deduction of the circumcision to be made with scissors from Josua V,2.

— 341 n.8 after Dukes etc., adde: *still following the strange mistake of M. Sachs.*

— 346 n.9 „betwen Age and Youth"; r. *between the old and young man,* the author is perhaps SHEMTOB Palquera?

— 349 n.41 end has become itself a little confused. In Litbl. VI,148 two authors are confused, in Litbl. IX,797 perhaps the two works, since MS. Saraval XXXVIII contains also the *printed*; cf. also Litbl. X (sic) 255.

— 350 n.54 l 5: Zarzah as dead, r. *Saba.*

— 358 l.1, adde: *the first* (known to the author), *whose attention it attracted, is Azaria de Rossi* (chap. XI).

— 358 n.55 ABRAHAM etc. seems *not* a mere copist, since the same work is in the library of the *Bet ha-midrash* in London n.3061; the author had only one moment to glance at it (in 1853), and to note, that he quotes the *Arithmetik* (אריחמתיקא) of *Nicomachus* (cf. p.356 n.37).

— 362 n.83, cf. p.371.

— 363 l.8 fr. bot. adde: *nor does he know from what journal it is a „tirage a part".*

— 365 n.13 Shemtob b. Isaac (p.362 n.83, where read 1254-64), in his preface to Alzaharavi, says that he could not help translating things which are against the Jewish laws.

— 370,d, see Jellinek, Beitr. II p. XI and Shemtob Gaon to Nachmanides preface. Cod. *Rossi* 563,[15]; Wolf. anon. n.696.

— 368 n.46: probably, r. certainly JAACOB BEN etc.

☞ The following *Index* is printed in the form of hebrew books from the right to the left.

B) ARABIC.

פרס 142a

INDEX.

1. *The asteriscus denotes the titles of books, and is often substitute of the hebrew word* ספר *„book".*
2. *The article* ה (الـ) *is not regarded in the alphabetical order (of both languages), and often entirely omitted.*
3. *The derivata are in their proper place, not under the root.*
4. *The forms (like* פיעול *etc.) are in most cases spelt plene.*
5. *The Arabic number refers to the pages.*
6. *„Sic" refers to places where there is a printing error corrected, but it is only added, when the erroneous word is not correctly printed in another place.*

A) HEBREW.

HEBREW AND ARABIC
INDEX.